The Men of
Madina
(Volume Two)

Muhammad Ibn Sa'd

translated by
Aisha Bewley

Ta-Ha Publishers
1 Wynne Road
London SW9 0BB

© Shawwal 1420 / Jan 2000 Aisha Bewley

Published by

Ta-Ha Publishers Ltd.
1 Wynne Road
London SW9 0BB
website: http://www.taha.co.uk
e-mail: sales@taha.co.uk

Editing and typesetting by Bookwork, Norwich

Translated by Aisha Bewley
e-mail: ABewley@compuserve.com
website: http://ourworld.compuserve.com/homepages/ABewley

British Library Cataloguing in Publication Data

A catalogue record for this book is available from the British Library.

ISBN 1 897940 91 2 Paperback
ISBN 1 897940 90 4 Hardback

Printed and Bound by Deluxe Printers, London NW10 7NR
website: http://www.de-luxe.com
e-mail: printers@de-luxe.com

Contents

By the Same Author

Books

Subatomic World in the Qur'an (Diwan Press)
A Glossary of Islamic Terms (Ta-Ha Publishers Ltd)
Islam: The Empowering of Women (Ta-Ha Publishers Ltd)
Signs on the Horizons: The Sun, the Moon, the Stars
   (Zahra Publications)
The Islamic Will (Dar al-Taqwa)
   [Co-author with Hajj Abdal-Haqq Bewley and Ahmad Thomson]

Translations into English

Al-Muwatta' of Imam Malik (Madinah Press)
Ash-Shifa' of Qadi 'Iyad (Madinah Press)
The Foundations of Islam – *Al-Qawa'id* of Qadi 'Iyad
   (Madinah Press)
Handbook on Islam, Iman, Ihsan of Shaykh 'Uthman dan Fodio
   (Madinah Press)
Defence against Disaster – *Al-'Awasim min al-Qawasim* of Qadi Abu
   Bakr ibn al-'Arabi with a modern commentary. (Madinah Press)
The Islamic Book of the Dead (Hadith on the Garden and the Fire)
   (Diwan Press)
The Women of Madina – Vol. 8 of the *Tabaqat* of Ibn Sa'd
   (Ta-Ha Publishers Ltd)
The Men of Madina, Vol. 1 – Vol. 7 of the *Tabaqat* of Ibn Sa'd
   (Ta-Ha Publishers Ltd)
The Diwans of the Darqawa (Diwan Press)
The Meaning of Man of Sidi 'Ali al-Jamal (Diwan Press)
The Darqawi Way (the Letters) of Mulay al-'Arabi ad-Darqawi
   (Diwan Press)
Self-Knowledge (Commentaries on Sufic Songs) (Diwan Press)
The Tawasin of Mansur al-Hallaj (Diwan Press)
The Seals of Wisdom – *Fusus al-Hikam* of Ibn al-'Arabi
   (Diwan Press)

Introduction

The *Kitab at-Tabaqat* by Abu 'Abdullah Muhammad ibn Sa'd is one of the earliest collections of biographical details of the early Muslims, extending from the Prophet, may Allah bless him and grant him peace, to Ibn Sa'd's own time (he lived from 148/764 to 230/845 or 236/779). Volumes 1 and 2 of the *Kitab at-Tabaqat* deal with the Sira of the Prophet Muhammad, may Allah bless him and grant him peace. Volumes 3 and 4 contain accounts of the Companions, may Allah be pleased with all of them. Volumes 5, 6 and 7 contain accounts of the *Tabi'un*, the generations after the Companions, and Volume 8 deals exclusively with women.

Of these volumes, the translation of Volume 8 has been published as *The Women of Madina*, while Volume 7 – which deals with the Companions, the *Tabi'un*, and subsequent generations of the people of knowledge in Basra, Baghdad, Khorasan, Syria and Egypt, – has been published as *The Men of Madina – Volume I*. This present translation is of Volume 5 of the *Tabaqat Ibn Sa'd*, and it concentrates on the *Tabi'un* in Madina itself.

It is because of their proximity to the source of Islam that the action (*'amal*) or normative practice of the people of Madina is considered to be legal evidence in itself. The legal basis for this is that their practice was the result of multiple transmission going back to the Prophet, may Allah bless him and grant him peace. It is a well-known and accepted principle that a multiple transmission has greater weight than a transmission which comes from a single individual. The shaykh of Malik ibn Anas, Rabi'a ar-Ra'y, mentioned this and remarked, "A thousand from a thousand is better than one from one."

Thus, for example in his description of the famous qadi of Madina, Muhammad ibn Abi Bakr ibn Muhammad, Ibn Saʻd records that Malik ibn Anas said, "Muhammad ibn Abi Bakr ibn Muhammad was qadi of Madina. Once he gave a judgement which was contrary to a *hadith* and when he returned to his house, his brother ʻAbdullah ibn Abi Bakr, who was a righteous man said to him, 'My brother, you gave such-and-such a judgement.' Muhammad said to him, 'Yes, brother.' ʻAbdullah said to him, 'My brother, where are you in relation to the *hadith* in giving judgement?' Muhammad said, 'Well, where is the action?' meaning the normative practice agreed on in Madina since they considered the practice on which there was agreement to be stronger than the single *hadith*."

In the *Tartib al-Madarik*, Qadi ʻIyad mentions the type of consensus of the people of Madina based on transmission which is considered authoritative:

1. What is transmitted from the Prophet, may Allah bless him and grant him peace, in the form of words – like the *adhan*, the *iqama* and not saying the *basmala* aloud in the prayer. They transmitted these things from his words.

2. His action – like the description of the prayer, the number of its *rakʻats*, its *sajdas* and the like of that.

3. The transmission of his affirmation of what he saw from them when his disapproval was not transmitted from him.

4. The transmission of his leaving things which he saw them doing and judgements which he did not oblige on them although they were well-known among them – like his not collecting *zakat* on vegetables although he knew that they were numerous among them. This type of their consensus in these aspects is a proof which cannot be ignored, and whatever is contrary to it in the form of single tradition or analogy is abandoned since this transmission is verified and known and therefore constitutes definitive knowledge which is not abandoned in favour of what merely seems likely. This is what Abu Yusuf and other opponents of those who debated with Malik and other people of Madina referred to in the question of *waqfs*, the *mudd* and the *saʻ* – until he drew their attention to the

transmission and verified it. It is not permitted for an impartial person with intelligence to debate such evidence, and this which Malik has is from most of our shaykhs, and there is no disagreement about the validity of this method – and that is proof among the intelligent. He was opposed in those questions by other than the people of Madina to whom that transmission had not reached. There is no disagreement in this. As-Sayrafi and other people of ash-Shafiʻi agree with him as al-Ahmadi reported from him. Some of the Shafiʻites disagreed out of sheer obstinacy. (*Madarik*, p. 41)

The occasion referred to in the final point made by Qadi ʻIyad was the discussion which Malik had with Abu Yusuf [one of the founders of the Hanafi school and a student of Abu Hanifa] when he came to Madina to ask him about the *saʻ* and the *mudd*. Malik ordered the people of Madina to bring the containers with which they measured their *saʻs* and they told him how they had been handed down to them by their predecessors. Malik asked, "Do you think, Abu Yusuf, that these people are lying?" He replied, "No, by Allah, they are not lying." He said, "I measured these *saʻs* and I found them to be five and a third *ratls*, according to your *ratls*, people of Iraq." Abu Yusuf said, "I will revert to your statement, Abu ʻAbdullah. If my companion [Abu Hanifa] had seen the same as I have seen, he would have reverted as I have reverted."

Then Abu Yusuf asked him about the *zakat* on vegetables, and he said, "The people of Madina did not take *zakat* on them in the time of the Messenger of Allah, may Allah bless him and grant him peace, nor did Abu Bakr, nor ʻUmar, may Allah be pleased with both of them."

Then he asked Malik about the *habous*, or *waqf*, and he said, "This is the *habous* of so-and-so and this is the *habous* of so-and-so," mentioning their names to make it clear that they were Companions of the Prophet. Abu Yusuf said after each question, "I have reverted, Abu ʻAbdullah. If my companion had seen the same as I have seen, he would have reverted as I have reverted."

This change of position on Abu Yusuf's part was clearly based on the authoritative nature of the normative practice of the Tabiʻun in

Madina which they had inherited from the Prophet, may Allah bless him and grant him peace, and his Companions.

Ibn Taymiyya says about the early generations of Muslims in Madina:

> The people of Madina were the soundest of the people of the cities in both transmission and opinion. Their *hadiths* are the soundest of *hadiths*. The people of knowledge of *hadith* agree that the soundest of *hadiths* are the *hadiths* of the people of Madina, and then the *hadiths* of the people of Basra. As for the *hadiths* of the people of Syria, they are less sound than that. They do not have the connected *isnads* and the precision of expression that those have.
>
> Among the people of Madina, Makka, Basra and Syria, there was not anyone who was known for lying, but there were some who were precise, and some who were not precise. (*Sihhat Usul Madhhab Ahl al-Madina*)

Ibn Taymiyya considers that this excellence lasted until the time of Malik ibn Anas. The reason that Malik preferred Madina was because of its closeness to the Prophet:

> Hammad ibn Waqid as-Saffar asked Malik, "Abu 'Abdullah, which do you prefer? To reside here or in Makka?" He replied, "Here. That is because Allah Almighty chose it for His Prophet, may Allah bless him and grant him peace, from all of the places of the earth." Then he mentioned the *hadith* of Abu Hurayra regarding its excellence.
>
> Ja'far ibn Muhammad said, "Someone remarked to Malik, 'You choose to remain in Madina and you have left the rural and fertile lands.' He said, 'How could I not choose it when there is no road in Madina but that the Messenger of Allah, may Allah bless him and grant him peace, walked on it and Jibril, peace be upon him, came down to him from the Lord of the Worlds in less than an hour?'"
>
> Abu Mus'ab az-Zuhri said, "Malik was asked, 'Why do the people of Madina have soft hearts while the people of Makka

are hard-hearted?' He replied, 'Because the people of Makka drove out their Prophet and the people of Madina gave him refuge.'"

Malik said, "About so many thousand Companions came with the Messenger of Allah, may Allah bless him and grant him peace, from a certain expedition at such-and-such a time. About 10,000 of them died in Madina, and the rest split up in the cities. Which would you prefer to follow and whose words would you prefer to take? Those in whose presence the Prophet, may Allah bless him and grant him peace, died with his Companions I mentioned, or the one who died with one or two of the Companions of the Prophet, may Allah bless him and grant him peace?"

Although Imam Malik was clear about his position – and made it clear to others – he nevertheless understood that it would be impossible and impractical for all Muslims to see and understand the deen in the same way as he did. Thus Ibn Sa'd records that Muhammad ibn 'Umar said that he heard Malik ibn Anas say:

"When al-Mansur went on *hajj*, he summoned me, and I went to him and spoke to him. He asked me and I answered. He said, 'I have decided to command that copies be made of these books of yours which you have written (i.e. the *Muwatta'*), and then I will send a copy of them to every Muslim city and command people to learn what is in them, and not to exceed more than that with anything else and to leave other new knowledge. I think that the basis of knowledge is the transmission of the people of Madina and their knowledge.' I said, 'Amir al-Mu'minin, do not do this. The people already have their positions and they have heard *hadiths* and related transmissions. Each people have taken what came first to them, and they have based their *deen* on it in spite of the disagreement of some people and others. It would be harsh to turn them away from what they believe. Leave people with what they have and with what the people of each city have chosen for themselves.' Al-Mansur said, 'By my life, if you had obeyed me in that, I would have done it.'"

This conversation took place approximately in 150 AH, and it is clear from its content that by this point in time it had become common practice to record *hadiths* in written form, rather than relying simply on oral transmission. Indeed as the reader progresses through *The Men of Madina – Volume II*, this shift in the mode of transmission of knowledge, from the spoken word to the written word, is clear from the comments which Ibn Sa'd makes – which in effect also indirectly record the emerge of the science of verifying *hadiths*, not only by ascertaining the ability and reliability of each person in the chain of transmission, or *isnads*, but also by the meaning of their content when measured against established practice.

Thus we find that as regards the first generation of *Tabi'un*, the best transmitters were regarded as those who had the best memories and who best embodied what they knew. Transmission was direct – by listening and memorising. In the next stage, transmission was also by listening, and then writing down. In the next stage transmission could take place by making a written copy of a written copy and then reading it back to the person who had orally transmitted the collection which was first written down – simply in order to verify that the new copy of the original was accurate. It was then only a matter of time before a written copy would be made of a written copy without verifying it with the living human transmitter who knew it all by heart and embodied it. It is in this context that one can best understand the famous observation of al-Hasan al-Basri – "Islam is going into the books, and the Muslims are going into the graves." An analysis of this process can be found in *Root Islamic Education* by Shaykh Abdalqadir al-Murabit.

Madina's decline as a political force was due to various factors. After 'Ali ibn Abi Talib transferred the centre of the khalifate to Iraq following the assassination of 'Uthman, Madina was no longer the source of authority and hence was outside of the main arenas of power. Madina was geographically too far removed from the wealth and armies of the Muslim state to be able to play a major political role when it was no longer the capital of the Muslims. Those with a penchant for power moved to Iraq or Syria. Those who remained in Madina were those who enjoyed the prosperity and peace of Madina, and those who devoted themselves to knowledge and wanted to be as close as possible to the Prophetic model and its source. Madina became a place to retreat from political conflict and the focus for those devoted to the *Sunna*. Thus Ibn Sa'd records that Muhammad ibn 'Umar said:

> "Malik used to sit in his house, with couches and cushions placed to the right and left in the rest of the room for those of Quraysh, the Ansar and other people who came to him. His assembly was one of gravity and forbearance. Malik was an impressive man in whose assembly there was no wrangling, tumult, nor raising of voices."

Reference to the main political conflicts and deviant ideologies which sorely tested the early generations of Muslims has already been made in the introduction to Volume I of *The Men of Madina*. As regards this volume, some of the salient events mentioned in the course of this volume include:

The Ridda Wars (Wars of Apostasy): 11/632

After the death of the Prophet, may Allah bless him and grant him peace, many Arab tribes rebelled against Abu Bakr, claiming that their pact had been specifically with the Prophet and no one else. These were large tribal groupings, some of whom were not actually Muslim, who wanted to be independent. Several of these groupings were led by false Prophets, like Musaylima among the Banu Hanifa in Yamama, Tulayha of the Banu Asad, al-Aswad in Yemen, and Sajda in Taghlib.

This was a very turbulent time, and the very existence of the Muslim Community in Madina hung in the balance in the face of these rebellions from powerful tribal groupings, not to mention the ongoing threat posed by the Byzantines. Hence the dates for the various battles which took place at this time are confused.

Abu Bakr displayed remarkable steadfastness and resolve throughout the two years of his rule which were crucial to the future of the Muslim Community. He not only brought the tribes which had apostatised back into the fold of Islam, but converted the large tribal groupings who had previously refused to embrace Islam. The Arabian peninsula was finally unified under the banner of Islam. Some of the major battles of this period were:

- **The Battle of Yamama:** In this battle, which took place at 'Aqraba' in 12/633, the Muslim forces led by Khalid ibn al-Walid defeated and killed Musaylima, the false Prophet of the Banu Hanifa. It was a closely fought battle, which at first went against the Muslims but eventually turned in their favour.

  There was a terrible loss of life in this battle. Thirty-nine important Companions of the Prophet were killed. It is estimated that the Muhajirun lost 360 while the Ansar lost 300 along with about 1,200 bedouins who had joined the Muslim forces. The losses in the Banu Hanifa are estimated by at-Tabari to amount to 7,000 on the plain of 'Aqraba', another 7,000 in the 'Garden of Death' around Musaylima, and a similar number in pursuit of the enemy. To put the scale of this loss of life in perspective, at Badr the Muslims lost 14 and the Quraysh 50, and at Uhud the Muslims lost 70 and the Quraysh 23.

- **The Battle of Buzakha:** In this battle, the false Prophet Tulayha of the Asad tribe was defeated by Khalid ibn al-Walid.

- **The Battle of an-Nujayr:** Nujayr was an old fort in Yemen. Fighters from Kinda took refuge there and were utterly defeated by the Muslims after a fierce battle.

The 'Amwas Plague in Syria and Drought in the Hijaz: 18/639

The year 18/639, the fifth year of 'Umar's rule, was known as 'The Year of the Ashes' because of the severe drought and resulting famine. The air of the Hijaz was so full of dry dust that the light was obscured. The situation in Madina was dire. Herds and flocks died and markets were deserted. Eventually Abu 'Ubayda ibn al-Jarrah brought 4,000 camel loads of grain from Syria while other food supplies arrived by sea. After nine months of drought the rain prayer was performed, led by al-'Abbas, and the rains came.

After this a virulent plague broke out in Syria, which especially attacked the Arabs in Hims and Damascus. Abu 'Ubayda, the governor, died, and then Mu'adh ibn Jabal, his successor, died almost immediately. At a later stage Yazid ibn Abi Sufyan also succumbed to it. Over 20,000 people died. In one family of seventy who had emigrated from Madina, for example, only four survived its ravages.

The First Civil War (Fitna): 35/656 - 40/661

The Assassination of 'Uthman: 35/656

The effects of the murder of the third khalif, 'Uthman ibn 'Affan, cannot be underestimated. It left the entire community in a state of shock for days and had reverberations which have continued until this day. It resulted in the First Civil War or *Fitna,* and the division of the Muslims into different distinct parties: those who supported 'Ali, those who supported those who called for revenge for 'Uthman's murder, and those who broke away and disassociated themselves from both groups, and hence from the Muslim Community. This third group were referred to as 'the Haruriyya' at the time and afterwards came to be known as the Kharijites. The murder of 'Uthman also resulted in the transfer of the khalifate from Madina to Iraq.

The Battle of the Camel: 36/656

This battle was the first major incident of the First Civil War. It came about when an army, led by 'A'isha, az-Zubayr ibn al-'Awwam and Talha ibn 'Ubaydullah, set out from the Hijaz to Iraq to demand that 'Ali hand over the murderers of 'Uthman. The murderers, eager to avoid justice, attacked under cover of night, resulting in a situation where each side thought that they had been attacked by the other side. This was the first time that Muslims fought Muslims in a battle. After the battle 'Ali was victorious and az-Zubayr and Talha slain. It is reported that the losses amounted to 10,000, equal numbers on each side, although the actual battle lasted only a few hours.

The Battle of Siffin: 37/657

This was the second major battle fought between Muslims. It was fought between the Syrian forces of Mu'awiya ibn Abi Sufyan and the forces of 'Ali ibn Abi Talib. The confrontation extended over three months, in which most of the fighting took the form of skirmishes. Most of the time was devoted to fruitless negotiations. When the battle proper began, the fighting, which lasted over three days at the end of July, was fierce, and continued well into the night. The battle abruptly stopped when the Syrians raised the Qur'an on their spears to call for further negotiations. Arbitration was agreed on. However, the bloodshed had been terrible. According to one source, 45,000 Syrians and 25,000 Iraqis had been killed.

The Assassination of 'Ali: 40/661

After the Battle of Siffin, many of 'Ali's followers objected to him agreeing to arbitration and consequently broke away from him. Even during the course of the march returning from Siffin, a body of 12,000 men fell out from 'Ali's army and made for a town called Harura'. Hence the earliest term used for the Kharijites is 'the Haruriyya'.

'Ali's initial response to them was to allow them their opinion as long as it did not lead to actual rebellion. According to at-Tabari, after hearing them proclaim their motto, "Judgement belongs to Allah alone," he told them, "Allah is greater! The words are true, but something false is intended by them. We grant you three things. If you remain with us, we will not bar you from the mosques of Allah so that you may mention His Name in them. We will not deny you the spoils as long as you fight with us. We will not fight against you unless you make the first move against us."

However, the Kharijites refused this offer, maintaining that they were obliged to fight innovation (*bid'a*). They promptly began to kill anyone who did not agree with their position. 'Ali eventually met the Kharijites in the Battle of Nahrawan in 38/658 (according to most sources), and crushed them. By the very act of putting down the rising, 'Ali lost yet more support. The Battle of Nahrawan was followed by various risings all over the place against 'Ali. Eventually 'Ali was murdered by a Kharijite assassin in 40/661 as he prostrated in *sajda* during the prayer.

*****

When Mu'awiya became khalif, the Muslim Community enjoyed a period of peace throughout the length of his rule. When he died in 60/679, having delegated his son Yazid to succeed him, we then move into the period of the Second Civil War in which there were four major players: the Umayyads and their supporters, the Kharijites, the various Shi'ite groups, and the Zubayrids. The death of Mu'awiya unleashed the forces he had managed to hold in check during his reign. The first major event in this period was the rebellion of Husayn which resulted in his death at Karbala'.

*****

The Second Civil War (Fitna): 61/680 - 73/692

The Battle of Karbala': 10 Muharram 61/10 October 680

As already mentioned, before Mu'awiya died, he made people swear allegiance to his son, Yazid, based on the precedent of Abu Bakr having delegated the khalifate to 'Umar ibn al-Khattab, but ignoring the precedent set by 'Umar ibn al-Khattab stipulating that he should not be succeeded by his son 'Abdullah ibn 'Umar, even though he would have made a wise ruler. In fact, this precedent continued to be followed by the Umayyads and later by the Abbasids and afterwards, showing – depending on how the matter is viewed – either the intrinsic wisdom of this action or the intrinsic tendency of a ruler to favour a member of his own family as his successor. As Ibn Sa'd records in some detail, the choice of the fifth Rightly-guided Khalif, 'Umar ibn 'Abdu'l-'Aziz, was an exception to this trend and met with considerable opposition from some members of 'the royal family', even though it was self-evident that 'Umar II was by far the best suited to be khalif.

On his deathbed, Mu'awiya warned Yazid to be careful about Husayn and Ibn az-Zubayr. He remarked that the Iraqis would not leave Husayn alone until they provoked him to revolt. He instructed Yazid to deal gently with Husayn ibn 'Ali and warned him that the greatest danger to unity lay with 'Abdullah ibn az-Zubayr.

Indeed, Ibn az-Zubayr and Husayn promptly took themselves off to Makka. The Iraqis, particularly the Kufans, did keep on encouraging Husayn to rebel, and 'Abdullah ibn az-Zubayr also encouraged him to do this. Husayn's cousin, Muslim, was sent to Kufa and he sent back favourable reports about the situation.

However, the plot was uncovered and the agents involved in it were executed. Rejecting the advice of all those who begged him not to go, Husayn set out for Kufa. He was stopped at Karbala', twenty-five miles north of Kufa, by the forces of the Umayyad governor, 'Ubaydullah ibn Ziyad, under the command of 'Amr ibn Sa'd. A battle ensued and Husayn and most of those with him were killed. Yazid professed great distress at the tragedy and sent the survivors back to Madina with every consideration. Wherever the blame lay, however, the harm was already done.

'Abdullah ibn az-Zubayr proclaims himself khalif: 61/680

This is a knotty subject, and since all the reports of the period are quick to attribute the worst possible motives to the people involved, they make it extremely difficult to separate the wheat from the chaff. We are not helped by the fact that these historical accounts are all written well after the events which they purport to describe and thus interpret the events in a manner which will vindicate the position from which the account is written. It is therefore important to note who the authors of such accounts are in order to be able to clearly identify what particular propaganda element is likely to have influenced their perception.

When Mu'awiya announced his decision to make Yazid his successor, it was 'Abdullah ibn az-Zubayr who voiced his opposition to this course of action and encouraged Husayn to revolt, although he did not lend him any real assistance. When the news of the massacre at Karbala' reached him, Ibn az-Zubayr proclaimed himself the Protector of the Sacred House. Before the end of the year he also proclaimed himself Khalif. The inhabitants of Madina also gave allegiance to Ibn az-Zubayr and expelled all the Umayyads from the city. As a result of this action, Yazid then sent an army in order to bring the Madinans to heel and then to move on to deal with Ibn az-Zubayr.

The Battle of al-Harra: 63/26 August 683

The significance of the Battle of al-Harra and the terrible loss of life and the sacking of Madina cannot be minimised. Madina never recovered its political role after this. The number of Ansar who perished in this battle was enormous. Muslim ibn 'Uqba was in charge of the operation, and he allowed his soldiers to kill and loot to such an extent that he was given the nickname 'Musrif' ('the extravagant') in accounts of the event. He was ill at that time, and then died on the way to Makka. The Harra was a field of black volcanic rock to the north-east of Madina.

After this outrage, which had been foretold by the Prophet Muhammad, may Allah bless him and grant him peace, the army proceeded on to Makka. The news of the sudden death of Yazid while Ibn az-Zubayr was under siege in Makka complicated the situation. For a time, it seemed that Ibn az-Zubayr had won since there was some confusion about who should next become khalif after Mu'awiya II, Yazid's son and heir, died almost immediately after assuming office. Eventually, however, the Syrians settled on the leadership of Marwan ibn al-Hakam, and after his death nine months later, his son, 'Abdu'l-Malik, became the new khalif in 65/685.

As far as the Kharijites were concerned, they initially supported Ibn az-Zubayr, but when he failed to denounce his father, they also turned against him, and so Mus'ab ibn az-Zubayr, his brother and governor of Iraq, was forced to direct most of his attention and forces to fighting them rather than the Umayyad forces.

At the same time, things were further muddled by the Shi'ite al-Mukhtar ibn Abi 'Ubayd. Ibn az-Zubayr was not pro-'Alid and treated Muhammad ibn al-Hanafiyya, 'Ali's son by another wife other than Fatima, very badly. At this time, Muhammad ibn al-Hanafiyya had become the focus of opposition to the Umayyads because at that point no 'Alid was old enough to be leader.

The Shi'ite rebellion of al-Mukhtar in Kufa: 66/685

Al-Mukhtar initially passed himself off as a supporter of Ibn az-Zubayr. But when Ibn az-Zubayr did not appoint him governor, he went to Iraq and eventually led a rebellion in Kufa in 66/685 which forced Ibn az-Zubayr's governor, 'Abdullah ibn Muti', to leave Kufa. Al-Mukhtar passed himself off as the *wazir* (helper) of Muhammad ibn al-Hanafiyya, and allegiance was given to him as such.

Al-Mukhtar stated that he was trying to avenge the death of al-Husayn and indeed killed anyone who had been implicated in that. Then he tried to expand his power base. Ibn az-Zubayr was accordingly forced to send the governor of Basra, his brother Mus'ab, to fight al-Mukhtar. Mus'ab defeated him at the Battle of al-Madhar, whereupon al-Mukhtar retreated to Kufa, where he was besieged and then killed in 67/687.

Al-Mukhtar's revolt generated and helped form many Shi'ite ideas – like the idea of an imam living in retirement who was politically represented by a designated *wazir*. This concept was later adopted by the Abbasids when they revolted against the Umayyads. The Shi'ite concept of the *mahdi* took on its political form and significance from this time.

Al-Mukhtar also had a lot of non-Arab clients (*mawali*) among his followers and he seems to have incorporated various elements which were pre-Islamic, perhaps through their influence. For instance, they carried what they called 'the chair of Ali' into battle, like the Ark of the Covenant.

Historically, the Abbasid claim finds its historical justification in this revolt, as they claimed that Muhammad ibn al-Hanafiyya's son, Abu Hashim, was the next imam and that when he died, he transferred his rights to the Abbasid family. Thus al-Mukhtar's revolt had many ramifications in Muslim history, both for the Shi'ites and for the Sunnis.

Muhammad ibn al-Hanafiyya

This was 'Ali's son by a woman of the Banu Hanifa, not by Fatima. He was reluctant to involve himself in politics, but nonetheless found himself used as a figurehead much to his distress. Al-Mukhtar referred to him as 'the *mahdi*', and if you examine the instances when this term is used in the *Tabaqat,* you will notice how the meaning of this term begins to change politically during this time. Thus when Muhammad ibn al-Hanafiyya died, some of those who thought of him as 'the *mahdi*' believed he would return (*raj'a*) from concealment, possibly through transmigration (*tanasukh*) of his soul.

It is clear therefore that the various ideologies which surfaced during this early period of Muslim history after the death of the Prophet Muhammad, may Allah bless him and grant him peace, shaped many of the major events which were to follow. Whoever wishes to understand the differences which exist today will discover their roots buried in this period of the past, painful as it is for any sincere Muslim to examine.

✸✸✸✸✸

The extent and nature of the divisions at the time can be observed in the fact that in 68/688, there were four distinct groups during the *hajj*, each camped apart from one another: that of Ibn az-Zubayr, of Muhammad ibn al-Hanafiyya, of the Kharijite leader Najda, and the Umayyads. It displayed a graphic representation of the situation.

When al-Mukhtar was killed, the Shi'ite element of the power struggle was neutralised, and it was then just a straight fight between the Umayyad leader, 'Abdu'l-Malik ibn Marwan, and 'Abdullah ibn az-Zubayr. The Kharijites were still a problem, but would never have enough support to be able to rule the entire community.

The people of Syria and Egypt gave allegiance to 'Abdu'l-Malik ibn Marwan. Thus Syria and Egypt were under the control of 'Abdu'l-Malik as they had been under his father's control. Iraq and the Hijaz were under the control of Ibn az-Zubayr. The civil war between them lasted seven years. 'Abdu'l-Malik himself led an army to fight the followers of Ibn az-Zubayr in Iraq, and this provides us with a poignant illustration of the consequences of civil war: the leader of the Zubayrid army was his closest childhood friend, Mus'ab ibn az-Zubayr. Eventually the Zubayrids in Iraq were defeated at Dayr al-Jathaliq in 71 or 72/691.

Then 'Abdu'l-Malik sent al-Hajjaj ibn Yusuf ath-Thaqafi to deal with Ibn az-Zubayr in Makka. He laid siege to Makka for six and a half months, until Ibn az-Zubayr was killed on Tuesday, the 17th of Jumada al-Ula, 73/October 692 at the age of 72, thus ending the Zubayrid claim.

Al-Hajjaj was then sent to Iraq to subdue both the Kharijites and the Shi'ites, which he did with such ruthless efficiency that he became notorious for it.

Kharijites

As we have said in the Introduction to Volume I of *The Men of Madina*, the first Kharijites were those who separated from the body of the Muslims in the Great *Fitna* in the wake of the Battle of Siffin, refusing to acknowledge 'Ali after he had agreed to arbitration. They broke away, hence their name, *'al-khawarij'*, and elected their own khalif. One of their characteristics is that they do not acknowledge the *jama'a*, the Muslim community as a whole. In their view, only utterly sincere and devout Muslims who do not commit wrong actions or harbour incorrect beliefs – as defined by the Kharijites – can properly be considered as part of the community.

The worst period of Kharijite activity came in the reign of 'Abdal-Malik, both during and after the Second Civil War. There were the Ibadites around Basra, the Sufrites in Mosul and al-Jazira, the Azraqites around Basra and into Arabia proper, and the Najdites in Yamama.

Najda ibn 'Amir al-Hanfi

The Azraqites or Najdite Kharijites were constantly raiding in the centre of Iraq and came to prominence in 68/687. There was also a certain amount of brigandage in the countryside, like that led by 'Ubaydullah ibn al-Hurr. Najda controlled large areas of Yamama and, as we have seen earlier, he was the leader of one of the groups making the *hajj* in 68/688. He was planning to go to Madina but heard that they would resist him and so he went to Ta'if which gave him allegiance. For a while he stopped food reaching Makka and Madina. Eventually he was overthrown and murdered by another group within the Kharijites.

This offensive might be viewed as a new Ridda, being led as it was by members of the Banu Hanifa. It was not exclusively that, but it was the nomadic tribes who mostly embraced it. In fact, it appears that the tribe of the Banu Hanifa wanted to be autonomous and not be subject to either the Makkan dominance of Ibn az-Zubayr or that of the Syrian Umayyads. Hence they formed an alliance with the Kharijites and together attacked Basra. Thus this indicates another attempt at autonomy, justified as always in the name of a new political ideology claiming to be 'true' Islam.

The Battle of ad-Dujayl: 77/697

Ad-Dujayl refers to a bridge across the Dujayl river at Ahwaz. A battle was fought there in 77/697 in which Shabib the Kharijite was killed. He was a Sufrite Kharijite and a master of guerrilla warfare.

✳✳✳✳✳

As we have seen in the Introduction to Volume I of *The Men of Madina*, the Kharijites continued to be a subversive force for many years, and indeed this particular tendency has never disappeared. Similarly, the Shi'ite phenomenon continued to manifest long after al-Hajjaj had been and gone.

✳✳✳✳✳

The Shi'ite revolt of Muhammad an-Nafs az-Zakiyya and Ibrahim, the grandsons of al-Hasan: 145/764

This revolt was in fact a non-recognition of the Abbasids taking over the khalifate, and it also was a serious claim to power. From the start, the Abbasid khalif al-Mansur felt certain that the two were plotting a rebellion. He did not continue to give them lavish gifts as his predecessor, as-Saffah, had done, and he treated their family harshly. When Muhammad and Ibrahim went into hiding, al-Mansur imprisoned a number of the leading members of the family and interrogated and tortured them to make them reveal their location. He executed several of them.

Eventually they decided to revolt, and Muhammad proclaimed himself khalif in Madina and received the allegiance of the Madinans. His rebellion in Madina lasted two months and seventeen days. Militarily, Madina was impossible to defend. After the city was occupied by Abbasid forces, the army were allowed to steal and not pay the merchants for the goods they took. Eventually, exasperated by the situation in the marketplace, the black slaves in Madina revolted against the governor, Ibn ar-Rabi', and drove him out. It took extensive negotiations to resolve the situation. After the rebellion, al-Mansur ordered a sea embargo against Madina which remained in force until al-Mahdi became khalif in 158/775.

The uprising of Husayn ibn 'Ali ibn al-Hasan: 169/786

Husayn ibn 'Ali rebelled against the Abbasids in Madina while al-Hadi was khalif. He proclaimed himself Amir al-Mu'minin in the mosque of the Prophet, may Allah bless him and grant him peace, but only 300 men followed him. He barricaded himself in the mosque and about a week later, left Madina and made for Makka and was killed on the way at Fakhkh. This seems to have been the end of 'Alid activity in the Hijaz.

✳✳✳✳✳

To conclude, Muhammad ibn Sa'd has made a unique contribution to posterity by recording something of the lives of the early Salaf who lived through these turbulent times. They provide for us a human picture of people trying to deal with difficult choices and difficult situations, and the consequences of those decisions. It can be hoped that their lives may help to throw some light on the problems which we face today. For example, we cannot fail to be moved by the words uttered by 'Abdu'l-Malik ibn Marwan before he fought his oldest friend, Mus'ab ibn az-Zubayr:

"By Allah, the business of this world is extraordinary. I can recall how Mus'ab and I were. One night I missed him in the place where we used to meet and was upset by that. He missed me and had the same reaction. I used to receive a gift and could not eat any of it until some of it was sent to Mus'ab. Now we have taken up swords. But this kingdom is barren; and no son or father desires it without unsheathing the sword."

On the other hand, we have many men of the *deen* like Sa'id ibn al-Musayyab who refused to take part in the fighting. As Ibn Sa'd says:

"In the days of al-Harra, Sa'id ibn al-Musayyab was in the mosque and did not give allegiance and did not leave. He used to pray *Jumu'a* with them and go out to the *'Ids*. The people were fighting and looting while he was in the mosque and only came out at night."

What emerges from this volume of *The Men of Madina* is not only the extraordinary nature of the people of knowledge among the *Salaf* and their vast knowledge – but also a wide ranging picture of what the nature of governance is, however good or bad it may be. This is of great relevance for the Muslims of today who are striving to restore Muslim governance. Ibn Sa'd provides us with a series of descriptions of various khalifs and amirs, ranging from tyrants who had no compunction about murdering innocent members of the People of the House to men of Allah who felt the weight of the responsibility of serving the Community of Muhammad, may Allah bless him and grant him peace, so keenly that they literally died from fear of Allah.

Aisha Bewley
Norwich, 1999

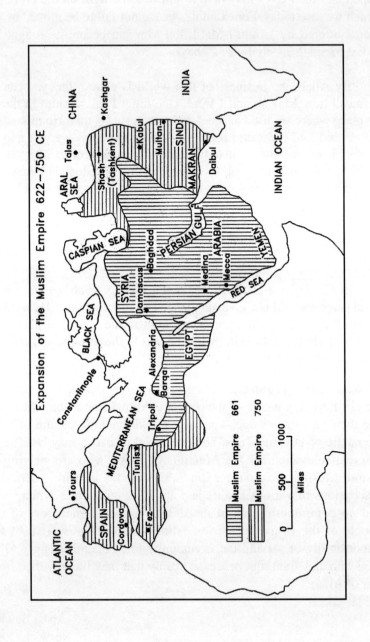

Expansion of the Muslim Empire 622–750 CE

Muslim Empire 661

Muslim Empire 750

0   500   1000

Miles

Chapter One
The First Generation
of the *Tabi'un* of the People of Madina

'Abdu'r-Rahman ibn al-Harith

Of Makzhum. His mother was Fatima bint al-Walid ibn al-Mughira of Makhzum. His *kunya* was Abu Muhammad. He was ten years old when the Prophet صلعم died. His father, al-Harith ibn Hisham, died in the 'Amwas Plague in Syria in 18 AH. Then 'Umar ibn al-Khattab married his widow, Fatima bint al-Walid, and so 'Abdu'r-Rahman grew up in 'Umar's care. He used to say, "I have not seen a step-father better than 'Umar ibn al-Khattab." He transmitted from 'Umar, and he had a house in Madina. 'Abdu'r-Rahman died in Madina while Mu'awiya was khalif. He was noble and generous. He was present at the Battle of the Camel on 'A'isha's side. 'A'isha said, "It would have been better for me to have remained in my house and not to have travelled to Basra than to have had ten children by the Messenger of Allah صلعم, all of whom were like 'Abdu'r-Rahman ibn al-Harith ibn Hisham."

It is reported that 'Abdu'r-Rahman's original name was Ibrahim. He went to 'Umar when he was khalif when 'Umar wanted to change the names of those who had been given the names of the Prophets. He changed his name to 'Abdu'r-Rahman and that remained his name.

'Abdu'r-Rahman's children include: Muhammad, the elder, by whom he receives his *kunya*, Abu Bakr, who was called 'the Monk of Quraysh', 'Uthman, 'Ikrima, Khalid, Muhammad the younger, and Hantama who married 'Abdullah ibn az-Zubayr, Umm Hujayn, Umm Hakim, Sawda, and Ramla: their mother was Fakhita bint 'Utba ibn Suhayl. He also had 'Ayyash, 'Abdullah, Abu Salama, al-Harith, Asma', 'A'isha who was married to Mu'awiya ibn Abi Sufyan, Umm Sa'id, Umm Kulthum and Umm az-Zubayr: their mother was Umm al-Hasan bint az-Zubayr ibn al-'Awwam, whose mother was Asma' bint Abi Bakr. He also had al-Mughira, 'Awf, Zaynab, Rayta – who married 'Abdullah ibn az-Zubayr after her sister, Fatima – and Hafsa: their mother was Su'da bint 'Awf ibn Kharija. He also had al-Walid, Abu Sa'id, Umm Salama who married Sa'id ibn al-'As, and Qurayba: their mother was Umm Hasan bint al-Harith ibn 'Abdullah. He also had Salama, 'Ubaydullah and Hisham by *umm walads*. He also had Zaynab, who is also called Maryam, whose mother was Maryam bint 'Uthman ibn 'Affan.

'Abdu'r-Rahman ibn al-Aswad ibn 'Abdu Yaghuth

His mother was Umayya bint Nawfal. His children were Muhammad and 'Abdu'r-Rahman, whose mother was the daughter of 'Abdullah ibn Wahb; 'Abdullah, whose mother was an *umm walad*; and 'Umar, whose mother was an *umm walad*. 'Abdu'r-Rahman related from Abu Bakr as-Siddiq and 'Umar. He had a house in Madina.

Subayha ibn al-Harith

His mother was Zaynab bint 'Abdullah ibn Sa'ida. Subayha's children were al-Ajashsh, Ma'bad, 'Abdullah the elder, Zabina and Umm 'Amr the elder: their mother was 'Atika bint Ya'mar. He also had 'Abdu'r-Rahman, 'Abdullah the younger, who is Abu'l-Fadl, and Umm 'Amr the younger: their mother was Ama bint 'Amr ibn 'Abdu'l-'Uzza. He also had 'Abdullah, Umm Salih, Umm Jamil, and Umm 'Ubayd, whose mother was Zaynab bint Wahb. He also had Habiba who married Ma'bad ibn 'Urwa of the Banu Kalb. 'Abdu'r-Rahman was the noblest of his children. Subayha had a house in Madina among the people of al-Aqfas.

'Abdu'r-Rahman married a daughter of Rashid ibn Hudhayl and had Muhammad and Musa. It is said that she was Umm 'Ali bint Hilal of Hudhayl. He also had a son Sakhr by Umm Yahya bint Jubayr of Khuza'a.

Subayha at-Taymi said, "Abu Bakr as-Siddiq asked me, 'Subayha! are you going to perform *'umra*?' – 'Yes,' I replied. He said, 'Bring your mount.' So I brought it and we went on *'umra*." Subayha reported the things he did on the journey.

Muhammad ibn 'Umar said that the one who travelled with Abu Bakr was actually his son, 'Abdu'r-Rahman ibn Subayha. It may be that both he and his father went with Abu Bakr and related from him. 'Abdu'r-Rahman was reliable with few *hadiths*.

Niyyar ibn Mukram al-Aslami

One of the four who buried 'Uthman ibn 'Affan and prayed over him and went down into his grave. Niyyar listened to Abu Bakr. He was reliable with few *hadiths*.

'Abdullah ibn 'Amir ibn Rabi'a

His *kunya* was Abu Muhammad. He was born in the time of the Prophet صلى الله عليه وسلم and he was five or six when the Messenger of Allah died.

'Abdullah ibn 'Amir said, "The Messenger of Allah صلى الله عليه وسلم came to our house when I was a little child. I went out to play and my mother said, "Abdullah! Come and I will give you something.' The Messenger of Allah said, 'What do you want to give him?' She replied, 'I want to give him a date.' He said, 'If you had not done so, a lie would have been recorded for you.'"

Muhammad ibn 'Umar said, "I do not think that 'Abdullah ibn 'Amir remembered these words because he was too young." He related from Abu Bakr, 'Umar and 'Uthman, and his father.

Abu'z-Zinad reported that 'Abdullah ibn 'Amir saw Abu Bakr and 'Umar give a slave forty lashes for defamation (*qadhf*).

'Abdullah ibn 'Amir died in Madina in 85 AH while 'Abdu'l-Malik was khalif. He was reliable with few *hadiths*.

Abu Ja'far al-Ansari

Abu Ja'far al-Ansari said, "I saw Abu Bakr as-Siddiq and his head and beard were like hot embers," (meaning dyed with henna).

Aslam, the client of 'Umar ibn al-Khattab

His *kunya* was Abu Zayd.

Aslam said, "'Umar ibn al-Khattab purchased me in 12 AH, the year in which al-Ash'ath ibn Qays was brought as a captive. I saw him in irons speaking to Abu Bakr as-Siddiq. Abu Bakr was telling him, 'You did this and did that!' until I finally heard al-Ash'ath ibn Qays say, 'O khalif of the Messenger of Allah, let me lead your army and marry me to you sister.' Abu Bakr did that. He was gracious to him and married him to his sister, Umm Farwa bint Abi Quhafa, and she bore him Muhammad ibn al-Ash'ath."

Muhammad ibn 'Umar said, "Aslam related that he saw Abu Bakr as-Siddiq take hold of the end of his tongue and say, 'This has had consequences for me.'" Aslam related from 'Umar, 'Uthman and others.

Muhammad ibn 'Umar said that he heard Usama ibn Zayd ibn Aslam say, "We are Ash'arites, but we do not fail to acknowledge the grace of 'Umar ibn al-Khattab."

Sa'id ibn al-Musayyab was asked who Aslam, the client of 'Umar, was. He said, "An Abyssinian from Bajawa."

The *kunya* of Aslam was Abu Zayd. Aslam died in Madina while 'Abdu'l-Malik was khalif.

Hunayy, the client of 'Umar ibn al-Khattab

Hunayy reported that Abu Bakr as-Siddiq did not set aside any land as a reserve (*hima*) except for an-Naqi'. He said, "I saw the Messenger of Allah صلعم turn it into a reserve. It was used for the horses used for military expeditions. When the *zakat* camels were lean they were also released there to graze there as far as ar-Rabadha. There was no reserve for them. He commanded owners of water sources not to exclude those who came to them for water and to graze with them. When 'Umar ibn al-Khattab was khalif, and there were a lot of people and he sent delegations to Syria, Egypt and Iraq, ar-Rabadha was made a reserve and he put me in charge of it."

Malik ad-Dar

He was the client of 'Umar ibn al-Khattab.

Malik ad-Dar related from Abu Bakr as-Siddiq and 'Umar, may Allah have mercy on them. Abu's-Salih as-Samman related from him. His transmission was accepted.

Abu Qurra

He was the client of 'Abdu'r-Rahman ibn al-Harith and was reliable, with few *hadiths*. Ibn Abi Dhi'b said that his master was a man from Mukharraba, not the one who set him free.

Abu Qurra said, "Abu Bakr as-Siddiq divided the booty and he gave me a share as he gave my master a share."

Zubayd ibn as-Salt ibn Ma'dikarib

The four kings, Mikhwas, Mishrah, Jamd and Abda'a, the sons of Ma'dikarib, were the uncles of Zubayd and Kathir, the sons of as-Salt ibn Ma'dikarib. They came to the Prophet صلعم with al-Ash'ath ibn Qays and became Muslim and returned to their land. Then they apostasied and were killed in the Battle of an-Nujayr. They were called 'kings' because each of them had a valley which he ruled. Kathir, Zubayd and 'Abdu'r-Rahman, the sons of as-Salt, emigrated to Madina where they settled, contracting an alliance with the Banu Jumah ibn 'Amr. They were registered with them until the time of the khalif al-Mahdi who removed them from the Banu Jumah and put them among the allies of al-'Abbas ibn 'Abdu'l-Muttalib.

Zubayd ibn as-Salt remarked, "I heard Abu Bakr as-Siddiq say, 'If I were to seize a thief, I would wish for Allah to conceal him.'"

Muhammad ibn 'Umar stated that Zubayd also related from 'Umar and 'Uthman. He had few *hadiths*.

His brother, Kathir ibn as-Salit

Nafi' said that Kathir's name had been Qalil ('a little') and 'Umar renamed him Kathir ('a lot').

Muhammad ibn 'Umar said, "Kathir ibn as-Salt was born in the time of the Prophet صلعم and his *kunya* was Abu 'Abdullah. He related from 'Umar, 'Uthman, Zayd ibn Thabit and others. He was a man of honour and good behaviour. He had a house in Madina which had a large place for prayer and the *qibla* of the place of prayer for the two *'Ids* faced it. It was on the flat of the wadi in the middle of Madina. The sons of Kathir ibn as-Salt include Muhammad ibn 'Abdullah ibn Kathir, who was generous, witty and a *faqih* who was appointed *qadi* of Madina for al-Hasan ibn Zayd, when al-Mansur appointed him governor of Madina. When al-Mahdi became the khalif, 'Abdu's-Samad ibn 'Ali was dismissed and Muhammad ibn 'Abdullah ibn Kathir was appointed in his place.

'Asim ibn 'Umar ibn al-Khattab

His mother was Jamila, the sister of 'Asim ibn Thabit. Nafi' reported that the Prophet صلعم changed the name of 'Asim's mother. She was called 'Asiyya (rebellious) and he said, "No, rather you are Jamila (beautiful)."

'Ubaydullah ibn 'Umar ibn al-Khattab

(Some text missing)[1] ...Jufayna was a servant of Sa'd ibn Abi Waqqas who used to teach writing in Madina. 'Ubaydullah said, "I struck Jufayna with a sword and when he felt the sword, his eyes froze." Then 'Ubaydullah went and killed the daughter of Abu Lu'lu'a [the murderer of 'Umar ibn al-Khattab] although she said she was Muslim. 'Ubaydullah did not want to spare any captives in Madina that day.

The first Muhajirun gathered and thought that what 'Ubaydullah had done in killing these people was dreadful. They overpowered him and prevented him from reaching the captives. He said, "By Allah, I will kill them and some others!" pointing at some of the *Muhajirun*. 'Amr ibn al-'As continued to calm him down until he gave him his sword. Sa'd went for him and each of them seized the other's head by the forelock until they were pulled apart. Then 'Uthman came – that was during the three days of the Counsel before people had given him allegiance – and took hold of the head of 'Ubaydullah and 'Ubaydullah took hold of his head. Then they were pulled apart. The earth was dark for people that day. People were deeply grieved and they were afraid that there would be retribution when 'Ubaydullah killed Jufayna, al-Hurmuzan and Abu Lu'lu'a's daughter.

Abu Wajza reported that his father said, "That day I saw 'Ubaydullah holding 'Uthman by the hair and 'Uthman said, 'May Allah fight you! You have slain a man who prayed, a small girl and another who is under the protection of the Messenger of Allah صلعم.

---

1. This describes what 'Ubaydullah did after his father was murdered.

It is not right to leave you.'" He said, "I marvelled at how 'Uthman could leave him alone when he became khalif, but 'Amr ibn al-'As had intervened and made him change his opinion."

'Imran ibn Mannah said, "Sa'd ibn Abi Waqqas took 'Ubaydullah ibn 'Umar by the forelock when he killed al-Hurmuzan and Abu Lu'lu'a's daughter. Sa'd recited while he was holding his hair:

'There is no lion but you who roared,
    and mischief destroyed the cultivated land for you.'

The poem was by Kilab ibn 'Ilat, the brother of al-Hajjaj ibn 'Ilat. 'Ubaydullah replied:

'You know that I am flesh which you cannot swallow.
    I do not eat all the vermin of the earth.'

'Amr ibn al-'As came and continued to calm 'Ubaydullah until he took his sword from him. He was imprisoned until 'Uthman released him when he became khalif."

Mahmud ibn Labid said, "On that day 'Ubaydullah was like a wild beast attacking the non-Arabs with his sword until he was locked up. I thought that when 'Uthman took power, he would kill him because of what I saw him do to him. He and Sa'd were the harshest of the Companions of the Messenger of Allah against him."

'Ali asked 'Ubaydullah ibn 'Umar, "What was the crime of the daughter of Abu Lu'lu'a when you killed her?" The opinion of 'Ali and the great Companions of the Messenger of Allah was that he should be killed, but 'Amr ibn al-'As spoke to 'Uthman until he spared him. 'Ali used to say, "If I had had authority over 'Ubaydullah, I would have taken retaliation from him."

Az-Zuhri said, "When 'Uthman was appointed, he summoned the Muhajirun and the Ansar and said, 'Give me your advice about killing this one who has rent the *deen* by his actions.' Most of the people said, 'May Allah put al-Hurmuzan and Jufayna far from making 'Ubaydullah follow his father.' They said a lot to that effect. 'Amr ibn al-'As said, 'Amir al-Mu'minin, this business occurred before you had authority over the people, so turn aside from him.' The people disagreed about what 'Amr ibn al-'As said."

Ibn Jurayh said that 'Uthman consulted the Muslims and they agreed on their blood-money and so 'Ubaydullah ibn 'Umar was not killed on account of them. They had become Muslim and 'Umar had allotted them a share in the booty. When allegiance was given to 'Ali, he wanted to kill 'Ubaydullah but he fled from him to Mu'awiya ibn Abi Sufyan and remained with him. He was slain at Siffin.

Muhammad ibn 'Abdullah said, "I heard a Syrian speaking in the gathering of 'Amr ibn Dinar. Later I asked about him and was told that he was Yazid ibn Yazid ibn Jarir. He said, 'Mu'awiya summoned 'Ubaydullah ibn 'Umar and said, "As you see, 'Ali is with the Bakr ibn Wa'il who are protecting him. Will you go with the army?" He said, "Yes."'

"So 'Ubaydullah returned to his tent and donned his weapons and then he reflected and feared that he would be killed with Mu'awiya straightaway. His client said to him, 'May my father be your ransom! Mu'awiya is sending you to your death. If you are victorious, he will be appointed and if you are killed, he will be relieved of you, so do what I say and pretend to be ill.' He retorted, 'Woe to you! I know what you are saying.'

"His wife Bahriyya bint Hani' said to him, 'Why do I see you getting ready?' He replied, 'My commander has ordered me to go with the army.' She said, 'By Allah, it is like the Ark which no one carried without being killed! You will be killed and the one who desires that is Mu'awiya.' He said, 'Be quiet. By Allah, I will slay a lot of your people today.' She said, 'They will not be killed. Mu'awiya has deceived you and deluded you. Your position is burdensome for him. He and 'Amr ibn al-'As have hatched up this business regarding you today. It would be better for you to be with 'Ali or remain in your house. Your brother has done that and he is better off than you.'

"He said, 'Be quiet.' Laughing, he added, 'You will see captives from your people around your tent.' She said, 'By Allah, I can foresee myself riding to my people to request your body for burial. You are deceived. You are going against a people controlled by al-Harun. They look at him like people waiting for death. If he were to command them to abandon food and drink, they would not taste it.'

"He said, 'Cease your rebuking. I will not obey you.'

"So 'Ubaydullah returned to Mu'awiya and joined the army. They were 12,000. 8,000 of the people of Syria joined him, including Dhu'l-Kala' of Himyar. They intended to go against 'Ali. When those with the Banu Rabi'a saw them, they knelt behind their animals and began to shoot arrows. When they reached them, they attacked and there was a fierce battle in which only spikes and swords were used. 'Ubaydullah was killed as was Dhu'l-Kala'. The one who killed 'Ubaydullah was Ziyad ibn Khasafa at-Taymi.

"Mu'awiya asked 'Ubaydullah's wife, 'Could you go to your people and ask for the body of 'Ubaydullah?' So she went to them accompanied by someone to protect her. She arrived and recounted her lineage. They said, 'We know you. Welcome to you. What do you need?' She said, 'This corpse which you have slain: let me take him.' So the young men of Bakr ibn Wa'il tied him on a mule and she went to the army where Mu'awiya met her in a litter. He put him on it and dug his grave, prayed over him and buried him. Then he began to weep, saying, 'The son of the Faruq has been slain obeying your regent, alive and dead, so ask for mercy for him. May Allah have mercy on him and grant him success.'

"While Bahriyya was weeping for him, she heard what Mu'awiya said and said, 'You hastened to make his children orphans and to remove him. Now you fear for him after the fact!' Mu'awiya heard what she said and said to 'Amr ibn al-'As, 'Do you hear what this woman says?' He told him and he said, 'By Allah, you are extraordinary. Do you want people to say nothing? By Allah, they have spoken about those who are better than you and us, so are they likely to say nothing about you? O man, if you do not ignore it, you will find yourself in sorrow.' Mu'awiya said, 'This, by Allah, is my view which I inherited from my father.'"

Nafi' said, "They disagreed about who killed 'Ubaydullah ibn 'Umar. Some say that Rabi'a killed him and some said that a man of Hamdan did. Some said that 'Ammar ibn Yasir killed him and some say that a man of the Banu Hanifa killed him."

Sa'd Abu'l-Hasan, the client of al-Hasan ibn 'Ali, said, "I went out with al-Hasan ibn 'Ali and fifty men of Hamdan in the night at Siffin. He wanted to go to 'Ali. It was a day in which there had been terrible fighting between the two groups. We passed by a blind man of Hamdan who had tied the rein of his horse to the foot of a slain man. Al-Hasan stopped by the man, greeted him and asked, 'Who are you?' He replied, 'A man of Hamdan.' Al-Hasan said to him, 'What are you doing here?' He said, 'I have lost my companions in this place at the beginning of the night and I am waiting for their return.' He asked, 'Who is this slain person?' He said, 'I do not know except that he was fierce against us and put us in great danger. While he was fighting he exclaimed, "I am at-Tayyib son of at-Tayyib!" When he struck he declared, "I am the son of the Faruq." So Allah killed him by my hand.' Al-Hasan dismounted and went over to him and it was 'Ubaydullah ibn 'Umar and his weapons were in the possessions of the man. So 'Ali brought him and handed over his booty to him, which was estimated to be 4,000 dirhams."

Abu Razin said, "I was with my client at Siffin. After a quarter of the night had passed I saw 'Ali going around the people admonishing them. The next morning was Friday and they met and fought a fierce battle. 'Ammar ibn Yasir and 'Ubaydullah ibn 'Umar met. 'Ubaydullah said, 'I am Tayyib son of Tayyib.' 'Ammar ibn Yasir said to him, 'You are a foul son of at-Tayyib.' 'Ammar killed him. It is said that a man of Hadramawt killed him."

It is reported that 'Ubaydullah cut off the ear of 'Ammar on that day. I am certain that 'Ammar lost his ear in the Battle of Yamama.

Muhammad ibn Rabi'a ibn al-Harith

His *kunya* was Abu Hamza and his mother was Humana bint Abi Talib. Muhammad ibn Rabi'a had a son called Hamza, hence his *kunya*. He also had al-Qasim, Humayd and 'Abdullah the elder, who is A'idhullah. His mother was Juwayriyya bint Abi 'Azza, the poet whom the Messenger of Allah صلعم killed on the Day of Uhud. He also had 'Abdullah, Ja'far, al-Harith, 'Uthman, Umm Kulthum, and Umm 'Abdullah: their mother was Amatullah bint 'Adi. He had 'Ali and Muhammad by an *umm walad*; and Umm 'Abdullah and another daughter by an *umm walad*. The Messenger of Allah صلعم died when Muhammad ibn Rabi'a was more than ten but we do not know whether he related anything from the Messenger of Allah. He met 'Umar ibn al-Khattab and related from him.

Muhammad ibn Rabi'a reported that 'Umar ibn al-Khattab saw him when he had long hair. That was at Dhu'l-Hulayfa. Muhammad said, "I was on my camel and it was Dhu'l-Hijja and I was intending to perform *hajj*. He told me to shorten my hair and I did so."

'Abdullah ibn Nawfal

His mother was Durayba bint Sa'id. He was born in the time of the Messenger of Allah صلعم .

Abu Hurayra said, "When Marwan ibn al-Hakam was appointed governor of Madina for Mu'awiya ibn Abi Sufyan for the first time in 42 AH, he appointed 'Abdullah ibn Nawfal *qadi* in Madina." I heard Abu Hurayra say, "This was the first *qadi* I saw in Islam."

Muhammad ibn 'Umar said, "Our companions agree that 'Abdullah ibn Nawfal was the first to be a *qadi* in Madina for Marwan ibn al-Hakam. The people of his house did not want there to be a *qadi* in Madina if he was not one of the Banu Hashim. The people of his house said, 'He died while Mu'awiya was khalif.'" Some say that he lived on for a time after Mu'awiya and died in 84 AH while 'Abdu'l-Malik was khalif.

'Ubaydullah ibn Nawfal

It is reported that 'Ubaydullah ibn Nawfal, Sa'id ibn Nawfal and al-Mughira ibn Nawfal were among the Qur'an reciters of Quraysh. They went early to the *Jumu'a* at sunrise, hoping to coincide with that moment in which prayer is answered. 'Ubaydullah fell sleep and slipped to the ground. It was said, "This is the moment you wanted." He lifted his head and there was a cloud rising in the sky. That was when the sun began to decline.

Al-Mughira ibn Nawfal

His mother was Durayba bint Sa'id. Al-Mughira had Abu Sufyan, whose mother was Amina bint Abi Sufyan. He had 'Abdu'l-Malik and 'Abdu'l-Wahid, whose mother was an *umm walad*; and Sa'id, Lut, Ishaq, Salih, Rabi'a and 'Abdu'r-Rahman by various *umm walads*. He had 'Awn by an *umm walad* and Umama and al-Maghira whose mother was a daughter of Humam.

'Ali ibn al-Husayn said that Ka'b took al-Mughira's hand and said, "Intercede for me on the Day of Rising." He withdrew his hand from his and said, "What am I? I am a man of the Muslims." He took his hand again and clasped it strongly and said, "There is no believer from the family of Muhammad but that he will have intercession on the Day of Rising." Then he said, "Am I mentioned as part of them?" He said, "By the One who has my soul in His hand, Muhammad will begin the intercession on the Day of Rising, and then the next closest and the next closest."

11

Sa'id ibn Nawfal

His mother was Durayba bint Sa'id. His children were Ishaq the elder, Hanzala, al-Walid, Sulayman, al-Ash'ath and Umm Sa'id whose name is Ama: their mother was Umm al-Walid bint Abi Kharasha of Khuza'a. He had Ishaq the younger, Ya'qub, Umm 'Abdullah and Umm Ishaq from *umm walads*. He had Ruqayya, whose mother was Umm Kulthum bint Ja'far. He was a *faqih* and a worshipper.

'Abdullah ibn al-Harith

His mother was Hind bint Abi Sufyan ibn Harb. He was born in the time of the Prophet. His mother, Hind bint Abi Sufyan, brought him to her sister, Umm Habiba bint Abi Sufyan, the wife of the Prophet. The Messenger of Allah صلعم came in and asked, "Who is this, Umm Habiba?" She said, "This is the son of your uncle and my sister: the son of al-Harith ibn Nawfal and Hind bint Abi Sufyan." The Messenger of Allah صلعم spat in his mouth and made supplication for him.

'Abdullah ibn al-Harith's children include 'Abdullah and Muhammad, whose mother was Khalida bint Mu'attib. He had Ishaq and 'Ubaydullah – and they are known as 'the Arjuwan' – and al-Fadl, Umm al-Hakim who bore Muhammad ibn 'Ali, Yahya, Muhammad and al-'Aliyya. He had Zaynab, Umm Sa'id and Umm Ja'far: their mother was Umm 'Abdullah bint al-'Abbas. He had 'Abdu'r-Rahman, whose mother was bint Muhammad ibn Sayfa. He had 'Awn, whose mother was an *umm walad*, Durayba by an *umm walad*, Khalida by an *umm walad*, and Umm 'Amr and Hind by an *umm walad*.

'Ata' ibn Rashid reported that 'Abdullah ibn al-Harith was in charge of Makka in the time of 'Uthman.

'Abdullah ibn al-Harith said, "My father gave me in marriage in the amirate of 'Uthman and he invited some of the Companions of the Messenger of Allah, and Safwan ibn Umayya, a very old man, came. He said, 'The Messenger of Allah صلعم said, "Chew your meat. It is better for your health and more tasty."'"

His *kunya* was Abu Muhammad. He listened to a *khutba* of 'Umar ibn al-Khattab at al-Jabiyya [in Syria]. He listened to 'Uthman ibn 'Affan, Ubayy ibn Ka'b, Hudhayfa ibn al-Yaman, 'Abdullah ibn

'Abbas and to his father, al-Harith ibn Nawfal. He was reliable and had a lot of *hadiths*.

'Abdullah ibn al-Harith moved to Basra with his father and built a house there. He had the title 'Babba'. While Mas'ud ibn 'Amr was governor, 'Ubaydullah ibn Ziyad left Basra and the people disagreed with one another. The tribes and clans summoned one another and agreed to appoint 'Abdullah ibn al-Harith to lead their prayer and be in charge of their booty. They wrote to that effect to 'Abdullah ibn az-Zubayr, "We are pleased with him." So 'Abdullah ibn az-Zubayr confirmed him over Basra. 'Abdullah ibn Nawfal went up the minbar and continued to take the allegiance of the people on behalf of 'Abdullah ibn az-Zubayr until he was exhausted. He continued to take their allegiance while he was asleep with his hand outstretched. Suhaym ibn Wuthayl al-Yarbu'i said:

"I gave allegiance to those awake and I fulfilled my allegiance.
I gave allegiance to him while he was asleep."

He remained the governor of 'Abdullah ibn az-Zubayr over Basra for six months and then he was dismissed and al-Harith ibn 'Abdullah al-Makhzumi was appointed. 'Abdullah ibn Nawfal went to Oman where he died.

Sulayman ibn Abi Hathma

His mother was as-Shifa' bint 'Abdullah. His children include Abu Bakr, 'Ikrima and Muhammad, whose mother was Amatullah bint al-Musayyab. He had a son 'Uthman whose mother was Maymuna bint Qays. Sulayman ibn Abi Hathma was born in the time of the Prophet صلعم. He was an adult in the khalifate of 'Umar, and 'Umar commanded him to be the Imam of the women in prayer. He also listened to 'Umar.

'Urwa reported that Sulayman ibn Abi Hathma used to act as the Imam for the women in the time of 'Umar ibn Ramadan. Sulayman's son, Abu Bakr, also reported that he acted as Imam for the women.

'Umar ibn 'Abdullah al-'Ansi reported that Ubayy ibn Ka'b and Tamim ad-Dari used to stand in the position of the Prophet صلعم leading the men in the prayer, while Sulayman ibn Abi Hathma led the women in the courtyard of the mosque. 'Uthman ibn 'Affan gathered the men and women together behind one reciter, Sulayman ibn Abi Hathma, and commanded the women to hold back until the men had gone and then to leave.

Rabi'a ibn 'Abdullah ibn al-Hudayr

His mother was Sumayya bint Qays. He had 'Abdullah and Umm Jamil by an *umm walad*; and 'Abdu'r-Rahman, 'Uthman, Harun, 'Isa, Musa, Yahya and Salih by various *umm walads*. He was born in the time of the Messenger of Allah صلعم and related from Abu Bakr and 'Umar. He was reliable with few *hadiths*.

Rabi'a said, "I saw 'Umar ibn al-Khattab lead the people in the funeral prayer of Zaynab bint Jahsh."

His brother, al-Munkadir ibn 'Abdullah

His mother was Sumayya bint Qays. His children were 'Ubaydullah and Umm 'Ubaydullah, whose mother was Sa'da bint 'Ubaydullah. They also included the *faqih* Muhammad ibn al-Munkadir, 'Umar, Abu Bakr and Umm Yahya by *umm walads*.

Abu Ma'shar said, "Al-Munkadir ibn 'Abdullah visited 'A'isha and she asked, 'Do you have any children?' He replied, 'No.' She said, 'If I had ten thousand dirhams, I would give them to you.' He said, 'As soon as evening came Mu'awiya sent her some money.' She said, 'How quickly I was tested!' She sent 10,000 dirhams to al-Munkadir and with it he purchased a slavegirl who was the mother of Muhammad, 'Umar and Abu Bakr."

'Abdullah ibn 'Ayyash

Of Makhzum. His mother was Asma' bint Salama and he had al-Harith and Amatullah whose mother was Hind bint Mutarrif. He was born in Abyssinia and we do not know of him relating anything from the Messenger of Allah صلعم at all. He did relate from 'Umar ibn al-Khattab. He had a house in Madina.

Al-Harith ibn 'Abdullah

Of Makhzum. His mother was an *umm walad*. He had 'Abdullah whose mother was Umm 'Abdu'l-Ghaddar bint 'Abdullah. He also had 'Abdu'l-Malik, 'Abdu'l-'Aziz, 'Abdu'r-Rahman, Umm Hakim and Hantama: their mother was Hantama bint 'Abdu'r-Rahman. He had Muhammad, 'Umar, Sa'd, Abu Bakr, Umm Farwa, Qariba, Ubayya and Asma', whose mother was 'A'isha bint Muhammad. He had 'Ayyash by an *umm walad*, 'Umar by an *umm walad*, and Umm Da'ud and Umm al-Harith, whose mother was Umm Aban bint Qays. He had Umm Muhammad and Amatu'r-Rahman, whose mother was Umm Ayyub bint 'Abdullah, and Fatima, whose mother was an *umm walad*. He had 'Abdu'r-Rahman and 'Abdullah the elder, whose mother was 'Atika bint Safwan.

'Abdullah ibn az-Zubayr appointed al-Harith ibn 'Abdullah to govern Basra. He was a man with a disagreeable smell. He passed by a grain measure in Basra and said, "This belongs to a righteous measure,[1]" and so they gave him the title 'al-Qubba''. He was an honest orator. He had some darkness in his complexion because his mother was a Christian Abyssinian. She died and al-Harith ibn 'Abdullah attended her funeral, and some people attended with him, standing on one side. The people of her religion came and took her back and there was a large number present with them. Abu'l-Aswad ad-Du'ali recited about him to 'Abdullah ibn az-Zubayr:

> Amir of the Believers, Abu Bukayr,
> > we come from al-Qubba' of Banu'l-Mughira.
> We praised him and censured him,
> > so he weakened us with what annoys us.
> Perhaps the lad was married and a glutton
> > and the person to whom he proposed had a very bad smell.
> So when we went to him, it was as if we were being circled
> > by two hyenas which had broken into the paddock.

So 'Abdullah ibn az-Zubayr dismissed him. He had been governor of Basra for a year. Mus'ab ibn az-Zubayr was appointed in his place. He went to Basra and then prepared to attack al-Mukhtar ibn Abi 'Ubayd.

Sa'id ibn al-'As ibn Sa'id

His mother was Umm Kulthum bint 'Amr and her mother was Umm Habib bint al-'As.

---

1. *Qubba'*, which also means 'hedgehog'.

Sa'id's children were as follows: 'Uthman the elder, Muhammad, 'Umar, 'Abdullah the elder, al-Hakam the elder, whose mother was Umm al-Banin bint al-Hakam; 'Abdullah, whose mother was Umm Habib, the daughter of Jubayr ibn Mut'im; Yahya and Ayyub the elder, whose mother was al-'Aliyya bint Salama; Aban, Khalid and az-Zubayr, the elder, whose mother was Juwayriyya bint Sufyan; 'Uthman the younger, Da'ud, Sulayman, Mu'awiya and Amina, whose mother was Umm 'Amr, the daughter of 'Uthman ibn 'Affan, whose mother was Ramla bint Shayba; Sulayman the younger, whose mother was Umm Salama bint Habib; Sa'id, whose mother was Maryam, the daughter of 'Uthman ibn 'Affan, whose mother was Na'ila bint al-Furafisa; 'Anbasa by an *umm walad*; 'Utba by an *umm walad*; 'Utba and Maryam by an *umm walad*; Ibrahim, whose mother was a daughter of Salama ibn Qays; Jarir and Umm Sa'id, whose mother was 'A'isha, daughter of Jarir ibn 'Abdullah; Ramla, Umm 'Uthman and Umayma, whose mother was Umayma bint 'Amir, the sister of Abu Araka, who is ar-Ruwwa' bint Jarir; Hafsa, 'A'isha the elder, Umm 'Amr, Umm Yahya, Fatikha, Umm Habib the elder, Umm Habib the younger, Umm Kulthum, Sara, Umm Da'ud, Umm Sulayman, Umm Ibrahim and Humayda from various *umm walads*; and 'A'isha the younger, whose mother was Umm Habib bint Buhayr.

The Messenger of Allah ﷺ died when Sa'id ibn al-'As was about nine years old. His father, al-'As ibn Sa'id, had been killed as an unbeliever at Badr. 'Umar ibn al-Khattab asked Sa'id ibn al-'As, "Why do I see you turning away as if you think I slew your father? I did not kill him. It was 'Ali ibn Abi Talib who killed him. If I had killed him, I would not ask pardon for killing an idolater. I killed my uncle, al-'As ibn Hisham, with my own hand." Sa'id ibn al-'As said, "Amir al-Mu'minin! If you had killed him, you would have been right. He was in the wrong." So 'Umar was happy with him.

Sa'id ibn al-'As went to 'Umar to ask him to increase the size of his house at al-Balat which had been laid out by his uncles with the Messenger of Allah ﷺ. 'Umar said, "Pray with me in the morning before dawn and then tell me what you need." He said, "I did that and when he was about to leave, I said, 'Amir al-Mu'minin, my need which you told me to mention to you.' He got up with me and then he said, 'Go to your house.' When I reached it, he increased it and drew it with his foot. I said, 'Amir al-Mu'minin, give me more. I have a lot of children and family.' He said, 'You have enough. I feel in myself that things will go your way after me from one of your relatives who will fulfil your needs.' After the khalifate of 'Umar ibn al-Khattab, 'Uthman became khalif after the Council and general acceptance. He maintained kinship ties with me, fulfilled my needs and let me share in his responsibility."

They state that Sa'id ibn al-'As remained close to 'Uthman ibn 'Affan because of his kinship. When 'Uthman dismissed al-Walid ibn 'Uqba in Kufa, he appointed Sa'id ibn al-'As. When he arrived in Kufa, he was a young affluent man who had no prominence. He said, "I will not go up on the *minbar* until I am pure." He called for water and performed a *ghusl*. Then he went up the *minbar* and addressed the people of Kufa and said a few brief words and then accused them of schism and dispute. He said, "This Sawad is the garden of some lads of Quraysh." They complained to 'Uthman. He said, "Whenever one of you sees some harshness in his Amir, he wants him to be dismissed."

Sa'id ibn al-'As visited 'Uthman in Madina and he sent gifts and garments to the notable Muhajirun and Ansar and sent some to 'Ali ibn Abi Talib which he accepted. 'Ali said, "The Banu Umayya have much more of the inheritance of Muhammad, peace be upon him, than me. By Allah, if I am over them, I will divest them of that as the butcher strips away the innards."

Then Said ibn al-'As went to Kufa and was very harsh towards its people. He was their governor for a few months less than five years. He once asked in Kufa, "Who of you has seen the new moon?" This was concerning the end of Ramadan. The people said, "We have not seen it." Hashim ibn 'Utba ibn Abi Waqqas said, "I have seen it." Sa'id ibn al-'As said to him, "With that blind eye of yours you saw it but not the people?" Hashim exclaimed, "Are you criticising me for my eye when I lost it in the way of Allah? My eye was pierced at the Battle of Yarmuk!" Then Hashim broke the fast in his house the next morning and the people ate with him. Sa'id ibn al-'As heard about that and he sent for him and beat him and set fire to his house. Umm al-Hakam, the daughter of 'Uqba ibn Abi Waqqas and one of the Muhajirun, and Nafi' ibn Abi Waqqas went from Kufa to Madina and told Sa'd ibn Abi Waqqas what Sa'id had done to Hashim. Sa'd went to 'Uthman and reported that to him. 'Uthman said, "Sa'id is for Hashim. Beat him for his beating. You have the house of Sa'id for the house of Hashim, so burn it as he burned his house." So 'Umar ibn Sa'd ibn Abi Waqqas went and sent a message to Sa'd ibn Abi Waqqas asking him to refrain. He did so.

Al-Ashtar Malik ibn al-Harith, Yazid ibn Mukaffaf, Thabit ibn Qays, Kumayl ibn Ziyad an-Nakha'i, Zayd and Sa'sa'a, the sons of Sawhan, al-Harith ibn 'Abdullah al-A'war, Jundub ibn Zuhayr, Abu Zaynab al-Azdiyan and Asghar ibn Qays al-Harithi travelled from Kufa to 'Uthman to ask him to dismiss Sa'id. Sa'id also travelled to 'Uthman and met them in his presence. 'Uthman refused to dismiss him and told him to return to his post. Al-Ashtar left that very night with a group of his comrades and travelled for ten days to Kufa. He occupied it and went up on the *minbar*. He said, "Sa'id ibn al-'As came to you stating that this Sawad is the Garden of some lads of Quraysh. The Sawad is where you put your heads, plant your spears and the booty of your fathers. Whoever thinks that Allah has a right should go to al-Jar'a."

So the people went out and camped at al-Jar'a, which is between Kufa and Hira. Sa'id ibn al-'As came and stopped at al-'Udhayb. Al-Ashtar summoned Yazid ibn Qays al-Arhabi and 'Abdullah ibn Kinana al-'Abdi, two fighters each of whom had 500 horsemen. He told them: "Go to Sa'id ibn al-'As and alarm him and make him rejoin his companion. If he refuses, then strike off his head and bring it to me." They went to him and said, "Go to your companion." He said, "My camels are thin. I will graze them for some days, go to the city and buy our needs and provision and then go." They said, "No, by Allah, immediately! You will go or we will strike your neck!"

When al-Ashtar saw his army in Kufa, he went up on the *minbar* and praised and lauded Allah. Then he said, "By Allah, people of Kufa! I was only angry for Allah and you. We have made this man join his companion and I have put Abu Musa al-Ash'ari in charge of your prayer and your frontier and Hudhayfa ibn al-Yaman over your booty." Then he went down and said, "Abu Musa, go up." Abu Musa said, "I will not do it. Come and give allegiance to the Amir al-Mu'minun, 'Uthman, and renew the allegiance you owe him." The people did that and he accepted their appointment and renewed the allegiance to 'Uthman. He wrote to 'Uthman to inform him what had happened. 'Uthman agreed with his appointment. 'Utba ibn al-Wa'l at-Taghlibi, the poet of the people of Kufa, said:

"Ibn 'Affan, confirm us, consider,
and put al-Ash'ari in command over us."

'Uthman said, "Yes, for some months and years if I last." What
the people of Kufa did to Sa'id ibn al-'As was the first weakening in
'Uthman's position when the people were encouraged to resist him.
Abu Musa remained governor of Kufa until 'Uthman was murdered.
Sa'id ibn al-'As returned from Kufa and remained in Madina until
the people attacked and besieged 'Uthman. Sa'id stayed with him in
his house and did not leave him.

'Abdullah ibn Sa'ida said, "Sa'id ibn al-'As went to 'Uthman and
asked, 'Amir al-Mu'minin, how long will you restrain our hands?
The people have gnawed away at us. Some of them have shot arrows
at us, some of them have thrown rocks at us, and some of them have
unsheathed their swords. Give us your command.' 'Uthman replied,
'By Allah, I do not want to fight them even if you want to fight them.
I hope that I will be protected from them, but I entrust them to Allah
and to Allah I entrust those who join forces for me. We will return to
our Lord. As for fighting, by Allah, I will not command you to fight.'
Sa'id said, 'By Allah, I will not ask anyone about you ever again!'
He went out and fought at the front of the people."

Mus'ab ibn 'Abdullah said that someone reported to him that he
had seen Sa'id ibn al-'As fighting on that day when a man dealt him
a blow to the head. He passed out.

They said, "When Talha, az-Zubayr and 'A'isha left Makka, making for Basra, Sa'id ibn al-'As, Marwan ibn al-Hakam, 'Abdu'r-
Rahman ibn 'Attab, and al-Mughira ibn Shu'ba went with them.
When they stopped at Marr adh-Dhahran or Dhat 'Irq, Sa'id ibn al-
'As stood up and praised Allah and then said, "Uthman lived praised
in this world and his leaving it was a loss. He died a fortunate martyr
and Allah has multiplied his good actions, removed his evil actions
and raised his degrees with those with *"whom Allah is pleased
among the Prophets, the truthful, the martyrs, and the righteous.
Those are excellent companions."* (4:69) O people, you claim that
you have come out to seek revenge for the blood of 'Uthman. If that
is what you want, the killers of 'Uthman are at the front and back of
these mounts. So either go against them with your swords or return
home. Do not kill for the pleasure of creatures. People will not help
you at all on the Day of Rising.' Marwan ibn al-Hakam said, 'We

will smite them with others. Whoever is killed is defeated. The rest will remain and we will seek them out while they are weak and feeble.' Al-Mughira ibn Shu'ba stood up and praised Allah and said, 'The correct opinion is that of Sa'id ibn al-'As. Any of Hawazin who wants to follow me should do so.'

"So some people followed him. He went to Ta'if where he remained until the battles of the Camel and Siffin were over. Sa'id ibn al-'As returned with some people to Makka where he remained until after the Camel and Siffin. Talha, az-Zubayr, 'A'isha, 'Abdu'r-Rahman ibn 'Attab, Marwan ibn al-Hakam and those of Quraysh and others who followed them went on to Basra where the Battle of the Camel took place."

When Mu'awiya became khalif, he appointed Marwan ibn al-Hakam over Madina and then dismissed him. Then he appointed Sa'id ibn al-'As over it and then dismissed him. Then he again appointed Marwan ibn al-Hakam and then dismissed him, and again appointed Sa'id ibn al-'As over it. Al-Hasan ibn 'Ali died while he was governor in 50 AH and Sa'id ibn al-'As prayed over him.

Marwan ibn al-Hakam ibn Abi'l-'As

His mother was Umm 'Uthman, who is Amina bint 'Alqama, and her mother was as-Sa'ba bint Abi Talha. Marwan ibn al-Hakam had thirteen sons and several daughters: 'Abdu'l-Malik, from whom he took his *kunya*, Mu'awiya, and Umm 'Amr, whose mother was 'A'isha bint Mu'awiya; 'Abdu'l-'Aziz and Umm 'Uthman, whose mother was Layla bint Zabban; Bishr and 'Abdu'r-Rahman, whose mother was Qutayya bint Bishr; Aban, 'Ubaydullah, 'Abdullah, Ayyub, 'Uthman, Da'ud, and Ramla, whose mother was Umm Aban, the daughter of 'Uthman ibn 'Affan, whose mother was Ramla bint Shayba; 'Amr and Umm 'Amr, whose mother was Zaynab bint Abi Salama; and Muhammad, whose mother was Zaynab, an *umm walad*.

Marwan was eight years old when the Messenger of Allah ﷺ died. He remained in Madina with his father, al-Hakam ibn al-'As, until his father died during 'Uthman's khalifate. Marwan then stayed with his cousin, 'Uthman ibn 'Affan, and acted as his scribe. 'Uthman commanded some property for him and that was interpreted as being the result of kinship. People resented the fact that 'Uthman had brought Marwan close to him and followed him. They thought that many of 'Uthman's orders originated from Marwan and not 'Uthman. They disliked what 'Uthman had done for Marwan and thought that Marwan had turned him against his companions and the people. 'Uthman was a shy, noble man. He accepted part of what people reported and rejected part of it. Marwan argued with the Companions of the Messenger of Allah صلى الله عليه وسلم in his presence and he rebuked him for that and chided him.

When 'Uthman was under siege, Marwan fought fiercely for him. 'A'isha wanted to go on *hajj* while 'Uthman was besieged and Marwan, Zayd ibn Thabit, and 'Abdu'r-Rahman ibn 'Attab went to her and said "Umm al-Mu'minin, would you stay? The Amir al-Mu'minin is under siege as you see and your position is part of what Allah might use to defend him." She replied, "I have undertaken the obligation and cannot stay." They repeated the words to her and she repeated the same answer to them. Marwan stood up, saying:

"A brand burned the land for me when she ignited its stump."

'A'isha said, "O you who burden me with poems, I wish, by Allah, that both you and your companion whose affair concerns you were a millstone in the sea." She left for Makka.

'Isa ibn Talha said, "Marwan fought fiercely on the Day of the House. On that day his ankle was wounded so badly that it was thought that he must die from the wound."

Abu Hafsa, the *mawla* of Marwan, said, "Marwan ibn al-Hakam went out that day reciting *rajaz* poetry and said, 'Who will do battle?' 'Urwa ibn Shayyam ibn al-Bayya' al-Laythi went out to him and Marwan was dealt a blow on the neck by his sword and he fell on his face. Then 'Ubayd ibn Rifa'a az-Zuraqi went to him with a knife to cut off his head. Marwan's foster mother, Fatima ath-Thaqafiyya, the grandmother of Ibrahim ibn al-'Arabi, stood in front of him and said, 'If you wanted to kill him, you have done so. What will you do with his flesh if you carve it up?' 'Ubaydullah ibn Rifa'a was shamed by her and left him alone."

It was reported by one of those who was present with Ibn al-Bayya' on that day that Marwan ibn al-Hakam issued a challenge. The ends of his outer garment were tucked in his belt. He was wearing armour under the garment. Marwan was dealt a blow which cut his neck and he fell on his face. They wanted to rush on him and it was said, "You are carving up flesh." So he was left alone.

Ibrahim ibn 'Ubaydullah said, "My father told me about the fight at the house, mentioning Marwan ibn al-Hakam, saying, 'Slaves of Allah, by Allah, I struck his ankle and I thought he was dead, but the woman disturbed me. She said, "What will you do with his flesh if you cut it up?" So I left him alone.'"

Nafi' said, "On the day of the House, I struck Marwan a blow with which I cut his ears. A man came wanting to finish him off and his mother said to him, 'Glory be to Allah! Will you mutilate a dead corpse!' So he left him alone."

People claim that when 'Uthman was killed and Talha, az-Zubayr and 'A'isha set out for Basra to avenge the blood of 'Uthman, Marwan ibn al-Hakam went along as well and fought fiercely in that battle. When he had a clear view of the people, he saw Talha ibn 'Ubaydullah and exclaimed, "By Allah, 'Uthman's blood is at the door of this one! He was the strongest of people in opposition to him. I will not seek for tracks after I have found the source!" So he shot an arrow at him and killed him.[1]

Marwan fought until he was carried off gravely wounded. He was carried to the house of a woman of the 'Anaza and they treated him and cared for him. The family of Marwan remained grateful for that. The people of the Camel were defeated and Marwan concealed himself until he was given a safe conduct from 'Ali ibn Abi Talib. Marwan said, "I will not be happy until I go to him and give him my allegiance." So he went to him and gave him his allegiance.

Then Marwan went to Madina and remained there until Mu'awiya ibn Abi Sufyan became khalif. He appointed Marwan over Madina in 42 AH and then dismissed him and appointed Sa'id ibn al-'As. Then he dismissed him and again appointed Marwan. Then he dismissed him and again appointed Sa'id. In turn, he dismissed him and appointed al-Walid ibn 'Utba ibn Abi Sufyan, who remained in charge of Madina until Mu'awiya's death. Marwan at that time was away from Madina. Then after al-Walid ibn 'Utba, Yazid appointed 'Uthman ibn Muhammad ibn Abi Sufyan over Madina.

When the people of Madina rebelled in the time of the Battle of al-Harra, they expelled 'Uthman ibn Muhammad and the Banu

---

1. This not considered a proper source since the relater is not mentioned.

Umayya, including Marwan, from Madina. They took oaths from them that they would not return to them with the army which was coming against them under Muslim ibn 'Uqba al-Murri. When they reached Muslim ibn 'Uqba, they greeted him and he began to question them about Madina and its people. Marwan began to tell him about it and incite him against them. Muslim asked him, "What do you think? Will you go to the Amir al-Mu'minin or return with me?" They replied, "We will go to the Amir al-Mu'minin." Marwan said, "I will return with you." He returned with him and advised and helped him until he defeated the people of Madina and they were killed and Madina was looted for three days.

Muslim ibn 'Uqba wrote this to Yazid, mentioning Marwan's assistance, advice and his remaining with him. Marwan went to Yazid in Syria and Yazid thanked him and favoured him. Marwan remained in Syria until Yazid died and allegiance was given to Mu'awiya II, Yazid's son, after him.

The people of all regions gave him their allegiance except for Ibn az-Zubayr and the people of Makka. Mu'awiya II was khalif for three months, or forty days. He was ill and remained in his house and did not go out to the people. He commanded ad-Dahhak ibn Qays al-Fihri to lead the people in the prayer in Damascus. When Mu'awiya II became very ill, he was told, "You should delegate the business to a man and designate a khalif." He replied, "By Allah, it did not benefit me when I was alive so that I take it on when I am dead. If it is good, the family of Abu Sufyan have had a lot of it. The Banu Umayya will not have its sweetness while I take its bitterness. By Allah, Allah will not ever ask me about that! When I die, have al-Walid ibn al-'Uqba pray over me and let ad-Dahhak ibn Qays lead the people in prayer until the people choose for themselves and someone becomes khalif."

When he died, al-Walid ibn 'Uqba prayed over him and ad-Dahhak ibn Qays saw to the business of the people. When Mu'awiya II was buried, Marwan ibn al-Hakam stood at his grave and said, "Do you know whom you have buried?" They replied, "Mu'awiya ibn Yazid." He said, "This is Abu Layla. Aznam al-Fazari said:

'I see seditions whose cauldrons boil.
     After Abu Layla the kingdom belongs to he who overcomes.'"

The people in Syria disagreed and the first to oppose the generals of the armies and call people to Ibn az-Zubayr were an-Nu'man ibn Bashir in Hims and Zufar ibn al-Harith in Qinnisrin. Then ad-Dahhak ibn Qays in Damascus invited people secretly and then openly to give allegiance to Ibn az-Zubayr. The people did that and gave him allegiance on his behalf. Ibn az-Zubayr heard about this and wrote to ad-Dahhak ibn Qays appointing him over Syria. Ad-Dahhak wrote to the amirs of the armies whom he had called to Ibn az-Zubayr and they came to him. When Marwan saw that, he set out for Ibn Az-Zubayr in Makka to give him allegiance and seek security from him for the Banu Umayya. 'Amr ibn Sa'id ibn al-'As went with him.

When they were at Adhra'at, 'Ubaydullah ibn Ziyad, who was coming from Iraq, met them. He asked Marwan, "Where are you going?" He told him. He said, "Glory be to Allah! Are you pleased to do this? You give allegiance to Abu Khubayb when you are a chief among the Banu 'Abd Manaf! By Allah, you are more entitled to it than he is." Marwan asked him, "What should be done?" He replied, "Go back and summon the people to you and I will take care of Quraysh and its clients for you. None of them will oppose you." 'Amr ibn Sa'id said, "'Ubaydullah speaks the truth. You are the shaykh and chief of Quraysh. People only look to this lad, Khalid ibn Yazid ibn Mu'awiya. Marry his mother and he will be in your care. Summon people to you and I will take care of Yamana for you. They will not oppose you. They will obey provided that allegiance is given to me after you." Marwan agreed.

So Marwan and 'Amr ibn Sa'id and those with them went back, and 'Ubaydullah ibn Ziyad went to Damascus on Friday. He entered the mosque and prayed and then went out and stopped at the Bab al-Faradis. He used to ride to ad-Dahhak ibn Qays every day to greet him and then he would return home. One day he said to him, "Abu Unays, it is extraordinary that you, a shaykh of Quraysh, call people to Ibn az-Zubayr and leave yourself while people would be more pleased with you. Call people to yourself." So he called people to himself for three days and people said to him, "You took our allegiance and pact for a man and then you call for him to be removed without anything happening!" When he saw that, he resumed calling people to Ibn az-Zubayr but that had undermined his position with people and their hearts changed towards him.

'Ubaydullah ibn Ziyad, coming back to him, said, "Whoever wants what you want should not remain in the cities and fortresses. They should go out and collect cavalry. Leave Damascus and call the armies to you." So ad-Dahhak ibn Qays went out and camped at al-Marj while 'Ubaydullah and Marwan remained in Damascus, the Banu Umayya at Tadmur, and Khalid and 'Abdullah, the sons of Mu'awiya at al-Jabiyya with their uncle, Hassan ibn Malik.

Then 'Ubaydullah wrote to Marwan: "Call on the people to give you allegiance. Write to Hassan ibn Malik to come to you. He will not refuse to give you allegiance. Then go to ad-Dahhak ibn Qays. He is related to you by marriage." Marwan called the Banu Umayya and their clients and they gave him allegiance. He married Khalid's mother. He wrote to Hassan ibn Malik calling on him to give him allegiance and come to him. He refused and Marwan was at a loss. He sent word to 'Ubaydullah who wrote back to him, "Go out against him with the Umayyads you have with you."

So Marwan went out against him with all the Umayyads who were with him. He called on him to give allegiance at al-Jabiyya. Hassan said, "By Allah, if you give allegiance to Marwan, he will envy your whip-strap, sandal-strap and the shade of the tree. Marwan and his family are from a house of Qays." He meant that Marwan was part of a tribe. "If you give him allegiance, you will be his slaves. Therefore obey me and give allegiance to Khalid ibn Yazid." Rawh ibn Zinba' said, "Give allegiance to the adult and allow the child to grow up." Hassan ibn Malik told Khalid, "Nephew, I want you but the people reject you because of your youth. They prefer Marwan to you and to Ibn az-Zubayr." He replied, "You are powerless." He said, "Not so."

So Hassan and the people of Jordan gave allegiance to Marwan provided that Marwan would not give allegiance to anyone except Khalid ibn Yazid. Khalid was given command of Hims and 'Amr ibn Sa'id was put in charge of Damascus. The allegiance to Marwan took place at al-Jabiyya on Monday, the 15th of Dhu'l-Qa'da 64 AH. 'Ubaydullah ibn Ziyad took allegiance for Marwan ibn al-Hakam from the people of Damascus and informed Marwan of that. Marwan said, "If Allah desires the khalifate for me, no one will deny it to me after that." Hassan ibn Malik said, "You have spoken the truth."

Marwan left al-Jabiyya with 6,000 men and camped at Marj Rahit. Then he was joined by 7,000 of his people from the people of

Damascus and other armies. So he had 13,000, mostly infantry. There were not more than 80 ex-slaves in Marwan's army, forty of them belonging to 'Abbad ibn Ziyad and forty to other people. 'Ubaydullah ibn Ziyad was on Marwan's right flank and 'Amr ibn Sa'id was on his left. Ad-Dahhak ibn Qays wrote to the generals of the armies and they came to him at Marj. He had 30,000 men. They were there for twenty days, meeting every day and fighting until ad-Dahhak ibn Qays was killed. Many of the Banu Qays were killed with him.

When ad-Dahhak was slain and the people defeated, Marwan and those with him returned to Damascus and he sent his governors over the armies and all the people of Syria gave him allegiance. Marwan encouraged Khalid ibn Yazid to forego the command and then it seemed to him that he should delegate his sons 'Abdu'l-Malik and 'Abdu''l-'Aziz for the khalifate after him. He wanted to belittle Khalid ibn Yazid, disparage him and make people overlook him.

When Khalid ibn Yazid visited him, he used to have him sit with him on his seat. One day when he came to him, he went to sit in the place where he normally sat. Marwan scolded him, "Move away, son of the moist anus! By Allah, you are brainless."

Khalid left in anger, went to his mother and said, "You have disgraced me, disparaged me, lowered me and abased my affair." She asked, "How is that?" He replied, "You married this man who has done such-and-such!" Then he told her what he had said. She said to him, "Do not let anyone hear you say this and do not tell Marwan that you told me anything about it. Come to me as you normally come and conceal this matter until you see its consequence. I will spare you from him and give you victory over him." Khalid was silent and went home.

Marwan came and went in to Umm Khalid, his wife. He asked her, "What did Khalid say to you about what I said to him today? What has he told you about me?" She replied, "He did not report anything or say anything to me." He said "Didn't he complain to you and tell you how I disparaged him and what I said to him?" She replied, "Amir al-Mu'minin, you are too majestic in Khalid's eye and he has too much respect for you to relate something about you or to resent something that you said. You are like a father to him." Marwan was contrite and thought that the matter was as she had told him and that she was speaking the truth.

After this, when it was near the middle of the day, he went to sleep in her quarters and she and her slavegirls jumped up and locked the doors. Then she took a pillow and covered his face with it and she and her slavegirls smothered him until he died. Then she got up and tore her garment and commanded her slavegirls and servants to tear theirs. They shouted about him and shrieked, "The Amir al-Mu'minin has died!" This was at the time of the new moon of Ramadan in 65 AH. Marwan was 64 and his rule over Syria and Egypt lasted not more than eight or six months.

The people of Syria then gave allegiance to 'Abdu'l-Malik ibn Marwan. Syria and Egypt were under the control of 'Abdu'l-Malik as they had been under his father's. Iraq and the Hijaz were under the control of Ibn az-Zubayr. The civil war between them lasted seven years. Then Ibn az-Zubayr was killed in Makka on Tuesday, the 17th of Jumada al-Ula, 73 AH, at the age of 72. Command was in 'Abdu'l-Malik's control after that.

Marwan related from 'Umar, 'Uthman, Zayd ibn Thabit, and Busra bint Safwan. Marwan reported from Sahl ibn Sa'd as-Sa'idi. When Marwan was governor of Madina, he used to gather the Companions of the Messenger of Allah to consult them and act according to their consensus. He collected the *sa'* measures and tested them until he selected the fairest of them and he commanded that it be used for measures. It was called 'the *sa'* of Marwan', but it was not the *sa'* of Marwan. It was the *sa'* of the Messenger of Allah صلعم , but Marwan tested them until he set up the measure based on the fairest.

'Abdullah ibn 'Amir ibn Kurayz

Of Qusayy. His *kunya* was Abu 'Abdu'r-Rahman. His mother was Dujaja bint Asma' ibn as-Salt. He had twelve sons and six daughters: 'Abdu'r-Rahman, by an *umm walad*, who was killed in the Battle of the Camel, 'Abdullah, who died before his father, 'Abdu'l-Malik and Zaynab, whose mother was Kayyasa bint al-Harith, whose mother was the daughter of Arta' ibn 'Abd Shurahbil, whose mother was Arwa bint 'Abdu'l-Muttalib; 'Abdu'l-Hakim and 'Abdu'l-Hamid, whose mother was Umm Habib bint Sufyan; 'Abdu'l-Majid, by an *umm walad*; 'Abdu'r-Rahman the younger, who is Abu's-Sanabil; 'Abdu's-Salam, whose mother was an *umm walad*; 'Abdu'r-Rahman, who is Abu'n-Nadr, by an *umm walad*; 'Abdu'l-Karim, 'Abdu'l-Jabbar and Amatu'l-Hamid, whose mother was Hind bint Suhayl, whose mother was al-Hanfa' bint Abi Jahl, whose mother was Arwa bint Usayd; Umm Kulthum, whose mother was Amatu'llah bint al-Warith; Amatu'l-Ghaffar, whose mother was Umm Aban bint Maklaba; 'Abdu'l-A'la and Amatu'l-Wahid, by an *umm walad*; and Umm 'Abdu'l-Malik, whose mother was one of the Banu 'Uqayl.

They say that 'Abdullah ibn 'Amir was born in Makka four years after the *hijra* in the year of the Fulfilled *'Umra* in 7 AH. The Messenger of Allah صلعم came to Makka on *'umra* and Ibn 'Amir was carried to him. He was three then. He rubbed his palate, and he licked his lips and yawned. The Messenger of Allah spat in his mouth and said, "This is the son of as-Salamiyya?" They said, "Yes." He said, "This is our son and he most resembles us among you. He is given water." 'Abdullah was noble, and generous, and had a lot of wealth and children. His son 'Abdu'r-Rahman was born when he was 13.

They say that when 'Uthman was appointed khalif, he confirmed Abu Musa al-Ash'ari over Basra for four years as 'Umar had commanded him to keep al-Ash'ari for four years. Then 'Uthman dismissed him and appointed his nephew, 'Abdullah ibn 'Amir, over Basra when he was 25. He wrote to Abu Musa, "I have dismissed you for lack of strength, not treachery. I preserve the measure of your appointment by the Messenger of Allah, Abu Bakr and 'Umar. I acknowledge your excellence. You are one of the first Muhajirun. But I want to maintain ties of kinship of 'Abdullah ibn 'Amir and I have commanded him to give you 30,000 dirhams."

Abu Musa said, "By Allah, 'Uthman dismissed me from Basra when I had no dinar or dirham until the stipends of my family came to me from Madina. I did not leave Basra with a dinar or dirham of their property." He did not take anything from Ibn 'Amir. Ibn 'Amir went to him and said, "Abu Musa, none of your cousins acknowledges your excellence more than me. You are the amir of the land if you stay, and will be provisioned if you travel." He replied, "May Allah repay you well, cousin." Then he went to Kufa.

Ibn 'Amir was a generous and courageous man who maintained his ties with his people and kin, loved them and was merciful. Sometimes he would go on an expedition and a load would fall off in the army and he would get down and fix it.

Ibn 'Amir sent 'Abdu'r-Rahman ibn Samura to Sijistan and he conquered it by treaty provided that weasels and hedgehogs would not be killed there. That was because of the vipers there which these two animals used to eat. Then he went to the land of ad-Dawar and conquered it. Then Ibn 'Amir attacked the land of al-Bariz and the fortresses of Persia. The people of al-Bayda' from Istakhr had overcome it and Ibn 'Amir went there and conquered it a second time. He conquered Jur al-Kariyan and al-Finsajan, which are part of Darabjirad. Then he went to Khorasan as he was told that Yazdagird ibn Shahriyar ibn Kisra was there with Persian cavalry. They had carried the treasures to Kisra when the people of Nihawand were defeated. He wrote about that to 'Uthman and 'Uthman wrote back to him, telling him to go against them if he wished.

He said, "He prepared, assigned delegations, and then appointed Abu'l-Aswad ad-Du'ali over the prayer in Basra and Rashid al-Judaydi of Azd over the *kharaj*. Then he went by way of Istakhr and then proceeded between Khorasan and Kirman until he came out at at-Tabasayn and he defeated them. Qays ibn al-Haytham was in the vanguard with some of the lads of the Arabs. Then he went towards Marw and sent Hatim ibn an-Nu'man al-Bahili and Nafi' ibn Khalid al-Bahili there and each of them conquered half of the city. They conquered its provinces by force and the city by treaty. Yazdagird had been killed before that. He had gone out hunting and passed by a millstone carver who hit him with an axe and scattered his brains.

"Then Ibn 'Amir made for Marw ar-Ruz and sent 'Abdullah ibn Sawwar al-'Abdi there and he conquered it. He sent Yazid al-Khurashi to Zam, Bakhwar, and Juwayn and he conquered them all. He sent 'Abdullah ibn Khazim to Sarakhs and its *marzban* made peace with him. Ibn 'Amir conquered Abrashahr as well as Taws, Takharistan, Naysapur, Pushanj, Badaghis, Abivard, Balkh, at-Talaqan and al-Firiyab. Then he sent Sabira ibn Shiman al-Azdi to Herat and he conquered its provinces but could not overcome the city. Then he sent 'Imran ibn al-Fudayl al-Burjumi to Amul and he conquered it. Then Ibn 'Amir appointed al-Ahnad ibn Qays over Khorasan and he camped in Marw with 4,000 men."

Then Ibn 'Amir went into *ihram* for the *hajj* from Khorasan and 'Uthman wrote to him to admonish him. He said, "You are exposing yourself to affliction." When he came to 'Uthman, he said to him,

"Give to your people of Quraysh." He did that and he sent 3,000 dirhams and some clothes to 'Ali ibn Abi Talib. When they reached him, he said, "Praise be to Allah! We see other than us consuming the inheritance of Muhammad." 'Uthman heard about that and said to Ibn 'Amir, "May Allah make your opinion ugly! Did you send 3,000 dirhams to 'Ali?" He said "I disliked being excessive without knowing your view." He said, "Be excessive." He sent him 20,000 dirhams and what followed it.

'Ali went to the mosque and reached his circle where they were discussing the gifts of Ibn 'Amir to his clan of Quraysh. 'Ali said, "He is the master of the lads of Quraysh who is not opposed." The Ansar spoke and said, "'The freed'[1] reject anything except aggression." 'Uthman heard about this and summoned Ibn 'Amir and said, "Abu 'Abdu'r-Rahman! Protect your honour from the Abode of the Ansar. They are free with their tongues, as you know." He said, "I will dispense gifts and clothes among them which they will praise." 'Uthman said, "Get to work." He went and soon the people were saying, "Ibn 'Amir said this. Ibn 'Amir did that." Ibn 'Amir said, "If the earning is wholesome, the spending purifies."

Basra could not hold him and so he wrote to 'Uthman requesting permission to go on expeditions which he gave him. He wrote to Ibn Samura to advance, and so he advanced and conquered Bust and the land next to it. Then he went to Kabul and Zabulistan, and conquered them both and sent the booty to Ibn 'Amir. Ibn 'Amir continued to take Khorasan piece by piece until he had conquered Herat, Pushang, Sarakhs, Abrashhar, at-Taliqan, al-Fariyab and Balkh. This was the Khorasan which existed in the time of Ibn 'Amir and 'Uthman.

Ibn 'Amir remained in charge of Basra. He sent 'Amir ibn 'Abd Qays al-'Anbari from Basra to Syria at the command of 'Uthman ibn 'Affan. He had made a market for people in Basra. He purchased houses and demolished them and made a market. He was the first to wear rough silk in Basra. He wore a dark *jubbah* and people said, "The Amir wears a bear-skin." Then he wore a red *jubbah* and they said, "The Amir wears a red shirt." He was the first to make water basins at 'Arafa and make the spring flow to them and give the people water. It still flows today.

When 'Uthman was criticised for his choice of governors, one of

---

1. Those who became Muslim at the conquest of Makka.

the preconditions which they made was that Ibn 'Amir be confirmed in Basra because of his love for them and his giving to this tribe of Quraysh. When the people were involved in the affair of 'Uthman, Ibn 'Amir summoned Mujashi' ibn Mas'ud and had him form an army to support 'Uthman. They set out until they were close to the Hijaz. Some of his people went ahead and met a man and asked, "What news?" He replied, "The enemy of Allah, Na'thal, [i.e. 'Uthman] has been killed. This is a lock of his hair." Zufar ibn al-Harith, who was at that time a lad with Mujashi' ibn Mas'ud, attacked the man and killed him. He was the first to be killed in revenge for 'Uthman. Then Mujashi' returned to Basra.

When Ibn 'Amir saw what had happened, he took what was in the treasury and appointed 'Abdullah ibn 'Amir al-Hadrami over Basra and set out for Makka. He met Talha, az-Zubayr and 'A'isha who were making for Syria. He said, "No, go to Basra. I have influence there and it is a land of wealth and there are many men. By Allah, if you wish, I will not leave it until some people smite others." Talha said, "No, I will do it. I fear the highlands of Tamim." So they agreed to go to Basra.

When Ibn 'Amir arrived there, the Battle of the Camel took place soon after and the people were defeated. 'Abdullah ibn 'Amir went to az-Zubayr beforehand and took his hand and said, "Abu 'Abdullah, I beseech by Allah for the community of Muhammad. There will never be any community of Muhammad after today." Az-Zubayr said, "Leave the two armies alone to contend. There are incentives when there is great fear." Ibn 'Amir went to Syria to Damascus. His son 'Abdu'r-Rahman was killed in the Battle of the Camel.

When Ibn 'Amir left Basra, 'Ali sent 'Uthman ibn Hunayf al-Ansari to them, and they remained there until Talha, az-Zubayr and 'A'isha came there. 'Abdullah ibn 'Amir remained with Mu'awiya in Syria and nothing is heard of him having been at Siffin. However, when al-Hasan ibn 'Ali gave allegiance to Mu'awiya, he appointed Busr ibn Abi Arta'a over Basra and then dismissed him and Ibn 'Amir said, "I have trusts there with the people. If you do not appoint me over Basra, they will be lost." So he appointed him over Basra for three years. Ibn 'Amir died a year before Mu'awiya. Mu'awiya said, "May Allah have mercy on Abu 'Abdu'r-Rahman about whom we boast and extol!"

'Ubadyullah ibn 'Adi the elder

Of Qusayy. His mother was Umm Qattal bint Usayd. His children were al-Mukhtar, whose mother was an *umm walid*; Hamida, whose mother was Maymuna bint Sufyan, and another daughter whose mother was from Fahm. 'Ubaydullah ibn 'Adi related from 'Umar and 'Uthman. He had a house in Madina near the house of 'Ali ibn Talib. He died in Madina while al-Walid ibn 'Abdu'l-Malik was khalif. He had few *hadiths*.

'Abdu'r-Rahman ibn Zayd ibn al-Khattab

His mother was Lubaba bint Abi Lubaba, one of the Ansar. His children were 'Umar, whose mother was Umm 'Ammar bint Sufyan; 'Abdullah and another boy, whose mother was Fatima bint 'Umar ibn al-Khattab, whose mother was Umm Hakim bint al-Harith; 'Abdu'l-'Aziz, 'Abdu'l-Hamid – the governor of Kufa for 'Umar ibn 'Abdu'l-'Aziz, Umm Jamil, and Umm 'Abdullah, whose mother was Maymuna bint Bishr; Usayd, Abu Bakr, Muhammad and Ibrahim, whose mother was Sawda bint 'Abdullah ibn 'Umar; and 'Abdu'l-Malik, Umm 'Amr, Umm Hamid, Hafsa and Umm Zayd, by various *umm walads*. The Messenger of Allah صلعم died when 'Abdu'r-Rahman ibn Zayd was six years old. He listened to 'Umar ibn al-Khattab.

Salim Abu'n-Nasr or Nafi' reported that 'Abdu'r-Rahman ibn Zayd said, "I and 'Asim ibn 'Umar ibn al-Khattab were travelling by sea while we were in *ihram*. I covered my head while he left his uncovered. 'Umar was looking from the shore."

'Abdu'r-Rahman ibn Abi Layla said that 'Umar ibn al-Khattab looked at Abu 'Abdu'l-Hamid whose name was Muhammad when a man said to him, "May Allah do such-and-such and such-and-such to you, Muhammad!" He heard him abusing him and said, "Come here, Ibn Zayd. I will not see the Messenger of Allah (or he said, 'Muhammad') abused on account of you. By Allah, you will not be called Muhammad as long as I am alive!" He renamed him 'Abdu'r-Rahman.

It is reported from Ibn 'Umar that he perfumed 'Abdu'r-Rahman, shrouded him and carried him. Then he went into the mosque and prayed without doing *wudu'*.

Muhammad ibn 'Umar said that 'Abdu'r-Rahman died in the time of 'Abdullah ibn az-Zubayr.

The grandson of 'Abdu'r-Rahman said, "'Abdu'r-Rahman ibn Zayd was the governor of Yazid ibn Mu'awiya over Makka and remained as such for seven months. Then he went out on a horse with a blaze and white shanks, wearing a cloak with a falcon on his wrist. I said, 'There is no good in this.' I went up to him and spoke to him and criticised him. Then he returned to Makka and favoured 'Abdullah ibn az-Zubayr. Yazid heard about this and dismissed him and appointed al-Harith ibn 'Abdullah instead.

'Abdu'r-Rahman ibn Sa'id ibn Zayd

His mother was Umama bint ad-Dujayj of Ghassan. His children were Zayd, Sa'id and Fatima, whose mother was an *umm walad*; and 'Amr, whose mother was from the Banu Khatma. It is said that his mother was Umm Thabit and it is said that she was Umm Anas bint Thabit.

Abu Bakr ibn 'Uthman said, "'Abdullah ibn Sa'id visited 'Umar ibn al-Khattab. His name was Musa and he re-named him 'Abdu'r-Rahman. That name remained. That was when 'Umar wanted to change the names of those with the names of the Prophets.

Nafi' said, "Ibn 'Umar was invited to prepare 'Abdu'r-Rahman ibn Sa'id for burial when he was burning incense for *Jumu'a*. When he went to him, we went with him. He commanded me to help wash him. This I did while Ibn 'Umar poured the water and a man washed the front of his head and his face and put water in his nostrils and in his mouth. Then he washed his neck, chest and private parts. He put a cloth over his private parts at the beginning when he stripped him. He washed him down to his feet and then turned him over. We washed his back as we had washed his front. Then he sat him across his knees and a man held his shoulders while he pressed on his stomach as a man poured water over him. Then he wetted his head. This washing was with water. Then he washed him a second time with lote and water, and then washed him a third time with water and camphor which he poured over him. So he was washed three times. Then he dried him with something and then stuffed cotton in his nostrils, mouth, ears, and anus. Then he was brought five shrouds. He dressed him in a shirt without buttons and then put *hanut* perfume on his front, head and face down to his feet. What was left was put on his feet. Then he wrapped his head and face in a turban. Then he was wrapped in the three remaining cloths which were put like that and like that and they were not knotted."

Then Nafi' said, "That is how 'Umar ibn al-Khattab, 'Abdu'r-Rahman ibn Sa'id and Waqid ibn 'Abdullah were washed." 'Abdu'r-Rahman was reliable with few *hadiths*.

Muhammad ibn Talha ibn 'Ubaydullah

His mother was Hamna bint Jahsh, whose mother was Umayma bint 'Abdu'l-Muttalib. His children were Ibrahim al-A'raj – a stern noble whom 'Abdullah ibn az-Zubayr appointed over the *kharaj* of Iraq, Sulayman – by whom he had his *kunya*, Da'ud, and Umm al-Qasim, whose mother was Khawla bint Mandhur. Their half-brother by the same mother was Hasan ibn Hasan ibn 'Ali.

Ibrahim ibn Muhammad said, "When Hamna bint Jahsh gave birth to Muhammad ibn Talha, she brought him to the Messenger of Allah and she said, 'Name him, Messenger of Allah.' He said, 'His name is Muhammad and his *kunya* is Abu Sulayman. I will not give him both my name and my *kunya*.'"

One of the sons of Talha reported that the wet-nurse of Muhammad ibn Talha said, "When Muhammad ibn Talha was born, we brought him to the Messenger of Allah, peace be upon him, and he said, 'What have you named him?' We replied, 'Muhammad.' He said, 'This is my name, and his *kunya* is Abu'l-Qasim.'"

'Abdu'r-Rahman ibn Abi Layla said, "'Umar ibn al-Khattab looked at Abu 'Abdu'l-Hamid whose name was Muhammad, and a man said to him, 'May Allah do such and such to you,' and began to curse him. Then 'Umar said, 'Ibn Zayd, come here to me. I will not see the name Muhammad abused because of you. By Allah, you will not be called Muhammad as long as I live!' He renamed him 'Abdu'r-Rahman. Then he sent for the sons of Talha, of whom there were seven at that time, and the oldest of them and their master was Muhammad ibn Talha. He wanted to change his name. Muhammad ibn Talha said, 'Amir al-Mu'minin, I beseech you by Allah – By Allah, Muhammad صلعم named me Muhammad.' 'Umar said, 'Get up. There is no way to do anything. Muhammad, may Allah bless him and grant him peace, named him.'"

'Uthman al-'Umari said that the Messenger of Allah, may Allah bless him and grant him peace, said, "It will not harm any of you to have one, two or three Muhammads in his house."

Muhammad ibn 'Umar said: "Muhammad ibn Talha was called as-Sajjad (the prostrater) because of his worship and his excellence. He listened to 'Umar ibn al-Khattab and 'Umar told him to descend in the grave of his aunt, Zaynab bint Jahsh, the wife of the Messenger of Allah صلعم . He was present with his father at the Camel, and was killed on that day. He was reliable with few *hadiths*."

When they reached Basra, they seized control of the Treasury and Talha and az-Zubayr sealed it completely. The prayer time came and Talha and az-Zubayr guarded it until the time of the prayer was almost past. Then they arranged for 'Abdullah ibn az-Zubayr to pray first and then Muhammad ibn Talha would pray. Ibn az-Zubayr went forward to lead and Muhammad ibn Talha went behind him, and Muhammad ibn Talha went forward to lead it and then 'Abdullah ibn az-Zubayr went back behind. Then they drew lots and the lot of Muhammad ibn Talha came out. He recited, *"An inquirer asked about an impending punishment."* (70:1) They said, "Muhammad ibn Talha fought fiercely on the Day of the Camel."

When the situation was grave and the Camel hamstrung and all of those who held its rein had been killed, Muhammad ibn Talha advanced and grabbed the rein of the camel which 'A'isha was on. He said to her, "What do you think, mother?" She replied, "I think that you are the best of the sons of Adam." He continued to hold fast. 'Abdullah ibn Muka'bir, a man of the Banu 'Abdullah ibn Ghatafan, the allies of Banu Asad, went forward and attacked him with a spear. Muhammad said to him, "I remind you of *Ha Mim.*" But he stabbed him and killed him. It is said that the one who killed him was called Ibn Mukays al-Azdi. One of them said that it was Mu'awiya ibn Shaddad al-'Abasi. One of them said it was 'Isa ibn al-Muqta'irr an-Nasri. Muhammad was called as-Sajjad and was one of the people longest in prayer. The one who killed him said:

The dishevelled one who stands with the *ayats* of his Lord
 – of little harm in the eye of the Muslim who sees –
I killed him with the spear through the pocket of his shirt,
 and he fell flat on his hands and mouth.

He reminded me of *Ha Mim*
    when the spear was already on its way.
    Is there not pressing before advancing
For nothing other than the fact that he does not follow 'Ali?
    Whoever does not follow the truth has regrets.

They said, "The people on the Day of the Camel were distressed by the 13,000 dead. In the night 'Ali passed by the dead with torches and he passed by the body of Muhammad ibn Talha and he turned his head to al-Hasan ibn 'Ali and said, 'Hasan, as-Sajjad, by the Lord of the Ka'ba, is slain as you see.' Then he said, 'His father brought him down in this manner.' He said, 'If it had not been for his father and his dutifulness to him, he would not have come out in this manner because of his scrupulousness and virtue.' Al-Hasan said to him, 'That does not absolve you from this.' 'Ali said, 'What is the matter with me and you, Hasan?' Before that he said, 'Hasan, your father wishes that he had died twenty years before this day.'"

Ibrahim ibn 'Abdu'r-Rahman ibn 'Awf

His mother was Umm Kulthum bint 'Uqba. Her mother was Arwa bint Kurayz and her mother was Umm Hakim, who is al-Bayda' bint 'Abdu'l-Muttalib. Ibrahim's children were Qurayr, Umm al-Qasim and Shufayya, who is ash-Shifa', and their mother was Umm al-Qasim bint Sa'd ibn Abi Waqqas; 'Umar, al-Miswar, Sa'd, Salih, Zakariyya and Umm 'Amra, whose mother was Umm Kulthum bint Sa'd ibn Abi Waqqas; 'Atiq and Hafsa, whose mother was the daughter of Muti' ibn al-Aswad; Ishaq, whose mother was Umm Musa bint 'Abdullah; 'Uthman, whose mother was 'Ulya' bint Ma'ruf; Hud and Shufayya the younger, whose mother was an *umm walad*; az-Zubayr and Umm 'Abbad, whose mother was an *umm walad*; Umm 'Amr the younger by an *umm walad*; and al-Walid by an *umm walad*. Ibrahim's *kunya* was Abu Ishaq.

Ibrahim said, "'Umar ibn al-Khattab set fire to the house of Ruwayshid ath-Thaqafi which was a drinking shop. 'Umar had forbidden it. It blazed like a coal."

Muhammad ibn 'Umar said, "We do not know of any of the children of 'Abdu'r-Rahman who related from 'Umar by direct sight and hearing except Ibrahim. He also related from his father, 'Uthman,

'Ali, Sa'd ibn Abi Waqqas, 'Amr ibn al-'As and Umm Bakra. Ibrahim died in 76 AH at the age of 75."

Malik ibn Aws

They say that he rode horses in the *Jahiliyya* and that he was old, but he became Muslim late and we have not heard that he saw the Prophet, peace be upon him, or related anything from him. He related from 'Umar and 'Uthman. He died in Madina in 72 AH.

'Abdu'r-Rahman ibn 'Abdu'l-Qari

He was from al-Qara. They called it al-Qara because Ya'mar ash-Shuddakh ibn 'Awf al-Laythi wanted to divide them among the sub-tribes of Kinana and a man of them said :

> "Let us abide (*qara*) and do not drive us away
> so that we shy away as the ostrich shies."

Because of this they were called 'al-Qara'. They were shooters. Al-Qara were among the Ahabish. The Ahabish were al-Harith ibn 'Abd Manat, al-Mustaliq whose name was Jahima, al-Haya whose name was 'Amir, the sons of Sa'd from Khuza'a and 'Asl, who is the son of Ibn ad-Daysh ibn Muhallim. They call them Ahabish because they gathered together. They were all allies of Quraysh via Banu Bakr. It is said that they made an alliance with a chief called Hubshi ten miles from Makka and that it was because of this that they were called al-Ahabish. Al-Qara made a private alliance with Banu Zuhra ibn Kila which was sound in the *Jahiliyya*. They married with the Banu Zuhra whenever they wished. Most of their mothers were from the Banu Zuhra. 'Abdu'r-Rahman related from 'Umar and 'Urwa ibn az-Zubayr related from him. 'Abdu'r-Rahman died in Madina in 80 AH while 'Abdu'l-Malik was khalif. Aban ibn 'Uthman was governor of Madina then. He was 78 when he died.

Ibrahim ibn Abi Qariz

Abu Qariz's name was Khalid ibn al-Harith. Abu Qariz, who was a handsome poet, came to Makka and Quraysh said, "Our ally, our confederate, our brother and helper and comrade." All of them invited him to settle with them and marry with them. He said, "Grant me a delay for three days." He went out to Hira' and worshipped on top of it for three days and then he came down and decided to form an alliance with the first man of Quraysh he met. The first he met was 'Abd 'Awf ibn 'Abd, the grandfather of 'Abdu'r-Rahman ibn 'Awf. He took his hand and they went and entered the mosque and stood at the House and became allies. 'Abd 'Awf had a strong alliance with him. Ibrahim ibn Qariz listened to 'Umar ibn al-Khattab. He said, "I heard 'Umar say, 'The people of Kufa give me a headache. They are not pleased with any amir nor is any amir pleased with them.'"

'Abdullah ibn 'Utba ibn Mas'ud

His *kunya* was Abu 'Abdu'r-Rahman. Az-Zuhri reported that 'Umar ibn al-Khattab put 'Abdullah ibn 'Utba in charge of the market and commanded him to collect what was due from pulses.

Muhammad ibn 'Umar said, "'Abdullah ibn 'Utba reported from 'Umar ibn al-Khattab and then he moved to Kufa and settled there and died there while 'Abdu'l-Malik was khalif and Bishr ibn Marwan was governor of Iraq. He was reliable and respected, and had many *hadiths* and *fatwa*. He was a *faqih*.

Nawfal ibn Iyas al-Hudhali

Nawfal said, "In the time of Umar we used to stand in different groups in the mosque for the *tarawih* prayer in Ramadan – here and there. People gravitated to the one with the best voice. 'Umar said, 'Do I not see you make the Qur'an into songs! By Allah, if I am able, I will change this.' Three days later he commanded Ubayy ibn Ka'b to lead them in the *tarawih* prayer and he stood at the end of the rows and said, 'If this is an innovation, then it is an excellent innovation!'"

Al-Harith ibn 'Umar al-Hudhali

He was born in the time of the Prophet صلعم and related *hadiths* from 'Umar which include his letter to Abu Musa al-Ash'ari about the prayer. He also related from 'Abdullah ibn Mas'ud and others. Al-Harith died in 70 AH.

'Abdullah ibn Sa'ida al-Hudhali

His *kunya* was Abu Muhammad. He related from 'Umar.

Ibn Sa'ida said, "I saw 'Umar ibn al-Khattab striking the merchants with his whip when they agreed on the price of food in the market, until they went out into the roads of Aslam, saying, 'Do not cut off our passers-by from us!'" He is related from.

'Alqama ibn Waqqas

He related from 'Umar. He is reliable with few *hadiths*. He had a house in Madina among the Banu Layth and has descendants there. His grandson, Muhammad ibn 'Amr, related from Abu Salama. 'Alqama died in Madina while 'Abdu'l-Malik was khalif.

'Abdullah ibn Shaddad ibn Usama

His mother was Salma bint 'Umaysh, the sister of Asma' bint 'Umaysh al-Khath'amiyya. His great grandfather was called 'Amr al-Hadi ('the Guide') because he lit fires at night for guests and to show the way for travellers. 'Abdullah ibn Shaddad related from 'Umar and 'Ali. He was reliable with few *hadiths*. He was a supporter of 'Ali.

Ibn 'Awn reported that 'Abdullah ibn Shaddad was the brother of Hamza's daughter by the same mother. 'Abdullah said, "Do you know what relation the daughter of Hamza is to me? She is my sister by the mother."

Muhammad ibn 'Umar said, "'Abdullah ibn Shaddad went to Kufa a lot and settled there, and he rebelled with Ibn al-Ash'ath. He was killed in the Battle of ad-Dujayl.

Ja'wana ibn Sha'ub

He was one of the children of al-Aswad ibn 'Abdu Shams. Sha'ub was a woman of Khuza'a, and she is Umm al-Aswad. Al-Aswad was an ally of Abu Sufyan ibn Harb. He was at Uhud with him. He is the one who rescued him in the Battle of Uhud when he killed Hanzala al-Ghasil. Ja'wana listened to 'Umar.

Malih ibn 'Awf as-Sulami

Malih said, "''Umar ibn al-Khattab heard that Sa'd ibn Abi
Waqqas had put a dividing door made of wood across the entrance to
his house and had had a reed hut erected inside his fortress. He sent
Muhammad ibn Maslama there and told me to go with him. I was a
guide in the land. We left with the order to burn down that door and
the hut, and he ordered him to have Sa'd stand before the people of
Kufa in their mosques. This was because 'Umar had heard from
some of the people of Kufa that Sa'd had shown favouritism when
selling some of the *khums*. We went to Sa'd's house, and Muhammad
burned down the door and the hut and put Sa'd in the mosques and
began to ask them about Sa'd as instructed by the Amir al-Mu'minin
– and he did not find anyone who told him other than good."

Sunayn Abu Jamila

A man of the Banu Sulaym who had *hadiths*. He listened to
'Umar. Az-Zuhri related from Sunayn Abi Jamila as-Saliti. His
dwelling was at al-'Umaq.

Az-Zuhri said that he heard him say, "I was found abandoned in
the time of 'Umar and my overseer mentioned me to him and he sent
for me and called me and said to me, 'He is free and his *wala'* is
yours and we have his suckling.'"

Malik ibn Abi 'Amir

From Dhu Asbah. One of his ancestors was Mu'rib who was
given his name because of his eloquence in Arabic. Malik ibn Anas,
the *faqih* of the people of Malik, was descended from Malik ibn Abi
'Amr.

It is reported from ar-Rabi' ibn Malik, the uncle of Malik ibn
Anas, the *mufti*, that his father said, "While we were on the road to
Makka on *hajj* or *'umra* under a tree, 'Abdu'r-Rahman ibn 'Uthman
said to me, 'O Malik.' I replied, 'What do you want?' He said, 'Will
you have what others do not invite you do?' I asked, 'For how long?'
He said, 'Our blood will be your blood and our destruction is your
destruction.' Malik agreed to that and from that day they were
included in the Banu Taym for that reason."

Malik ibn 'Amir said, "I saw 'Umar at the *Jamra* when a stone hit him and made him bleed. A man called to a man, 'O khalif!' A man from Khath'am said, 'By Allah, he left. Your khalif was bleeding.' A man called, 'O Khalif!' It was from the direction from where 'Umar was hit." Malik ibn Abi 'Amir related from 'Umar, 'Uthman, Talha ibn 'Ubaydullah and Abu Hurayra. He was reliable and had righteous *hadiths*.

'Abdullah ibn 'Amr ibn al-Hadrami

He was one of the allies of the Banyu Umayya. He listened to 'Umar and related from him. It is reported from as-Sa'ib ibn Yazid that 'Abdullah ibn 'Amir brought a slave of his who had stolen to 'Umar. He was reliable with few *hadiths*.

'Abdu'r-Rahman ibn Hatib ibn Abi Balta'a

His *kunya* was Abu Yahya. He was born in the time of the Prophet صلعم and reported from 'Umar. He died in Madina in 68 AH. He was reliable with few *hadiths*.

Muhammad ibn al-Ash'ath

His mother was Farwa bint Abi Quhafa.

It is reported from Ibrahim that Muhammad ibn al-Ash'ath's *kunya* was Abu'l-Qasim. He used to visit 'A'isha and they called him Abu'l-Qasim. He related from 'Umar and 'Uthman that he asked them what to do about a Jewish aunt of his who had died.

'Abdullah ibn Hanzala al-Ghasil

His mother was Jamila bint 'Abdullah. His children were 'Abdu'r-Rahman and Hanzala, whose mother was Asma' bint Abi Sayfa; 'Asim and al-Hakam, whose mother was Fatima bint al-Hakam of Banu Sa'ida; Anas and Fatima, whose mother was Salma bint Anas; Sulayman, 'Umar and Amatu'llah, whose mother was Umm Kulthum bint Wahwah; Suwayd, Ma'mar, 'Abdullah, al-Hurr, Muhammad, Umm Salama, Umm Habib, Umm al-Qasim, Qurayba, and Umm 'Abdullah, whose mother was Umm Suwayd bint Khalifa.

When Hanzala wanted to go out to Uhud, he had had intercourse with his wife, Jamila bint 'Abdullah before that and she became pregnant with 'Abdullah in Shawwal, at the beginning of the 32nd month of the *Hijra*. Hanzala was martyred that day and the angels washed him. His children are called the Banu Ghasil al-Mala'ika [the tribe of the one washed by the angels]. Jamila gave birth nine days after that. The Messenger of Allah صلعم died when he was seven. Some say that he saw the Messenger of Allah, Abu Bakr and 'Umar. He related from 'Umar.

'Abdullah ibn Hanzala said, "'Umar led us in the *Maghrib* prayer and he did not recite anything in the first *rak'at*. In the second, he recited the *Fatiha* of the Qur'an and a *sura*. Then he continued and recited the *Fatiha* and a *sura*, and then he prayed until he finished. Then he did two prostrations of forgetfulness and then the *salam*."

'Abdullah ibn Zayd and others reported, "When the people of Madina rebelled in the time of al-Harra, they expelled the Banu Umayya from Madina and refused to recognise Yazid ibn Mu'awiya and his khalifate. They agreed on 'Abdullah ibn Hanzala and supported him and he took their allegiance to fight to the death. He said, 'People, fear Allah alone who has no partner! By Allah, we did not rebel against Yazid until we feared that we would be stoned with stones from heaven. A man marries mothers, daughters and sisters at the same time, and drinks wine and abandons the prayer. By Allah, if there was no one else with me, I would suffer for Allah.' So the people urged each other on that day to give allegiance from every quarter.

"At that time, 'Abdullah ibn Hanzala only spent the nights in the mosque. He did not do more than drink gruel on which he broke his fast in the mosque in the evening. He fasted all the time. He was not seen raising his head towards heaven out of his humility.

"When the people of Syria approached from Wadi al-Qura, 'Abdullah ibn Hanzala led the people in the *Dhuhr* prayer. Then he mounted the *minbar* and praised and glorified Allah and then he said, 'O people! You came out in indignation to protect your *deen*, so suffer for Allah so that His forgiveness will be obliged for you and His pleasure alight on you. One of the people at as-Suwayda' has informed me that the people have camped at Dhu Khushub and that Marwan ibn al-Hakam is with them. By Allah, if Allah wills, He will destroy him for breaking the pact and agreement which he made [not to return] at the *minbar* of the Messenger of Allah صلعم.'"

The people shouted and began to decry Marwan, saying: "A viper, the son of a viper!" Ibn Hanzala began to calm them, saying, "Verbal abuse is nothing, but be true in the encounter. By Allah, no people are true but that they obtain victory by the power of Allah." Then he raised his hands towards heaven and faced *qibla* and said, "O Allah, we place our reliance in You. We believe in You. We put our trust in You and seek refuge in you." Then he came down.

In the morning the people of Madina fought a fierce battle until they were overwhelmed by the Syrians and Madina was entered from all sides. On that day 'Abdullah ibn Hanzala wore two shirts of chain-mail and encouraged his companions to fight. They began to fight. People were killed and only the banner of 'Abdullah ibn Hanzala was seen holding firm with a group of his companions. *Dhuhr* came and he told a client of his, "Guard my back for me so that I can pray." He prayed *Dhuhr* with four long *rak'ats*. When he had finished the prayer, his client said to him, "By Allah, Abu 'Abdu'r-Rahman, no one is left. Why should we stand?" His banner was upright with five around it. He said, "Woe to you! We came out to fight to the death."

When he finished the prayer he had many wounds. He girded on his sword and removed the armour and put on two armlets of brocade. Then he encouraged the people to fight. The people of Madina were like scattered ostriches and the Syrians were killing them on every side. When the people were routed, he cast off the armour and his weapons. He began to fight them bare-handed until they killed him. A man dealt him a blow with the sword which cut through his shoulder as far as his lung. He fell down dead.

Musrif went around on his horse among the dead with Marwan ibn al-Hakam. He passed by 'Abdullah ibn Hanzala and his right index finger was extended. Marwan said, "By Allah, if you raise him dead, it will remain as it was when he was alive."

When 'Abdullah was killed, the people could not continue and they fled in every direction. There were two men of the people who were involved in slaying 'Abdullah ibn Hanzala, as they both attacked and struck him together. One of them took his head to Musrif, saying, "The head of the leader of the people." Musrif made a gesture of prostration while he was on his animal. He asked, "Who are you?" The reply came, "A man of the Banu Fazara." He asked, "What is your name?" – "Malik," he replied. He asked, "You killed him and cut off his head?" – "Yes," He replied.

Another man of Sakun from the people of Hims called Sa'd ibn al-Jawn came. He said, "May Allah put the Amir right. We put our spears in him and we ran him through with them and then we struck him with our swords until they were blunt." The Fazari said, "Liar!" The Sakuni said, "Ask him to swear to it by divorce and freedom." He refused to swear. Then the Sakuni swore to what he had said. Musrif said, "The Amir al-Mu'minin will decide between you. So he sent them with the post and they went to Yazid about the slaying of the people of al-Harra and the killing of Ibn Hanzala. He gave them immense stipends and put them in the highest rank of the *diwan*. Then he returned them to al-Husayn ibn Numayr and they were killed while beseiging Ibn az-Zubayr. The Battle of al-Harra took place in Dhu'l-Hijja, 63 AH.

'Abdullah ibn Sufyan said that he heard his father say, "I saw 'Abdullah ibn Hanzala after he had been killed in a dream in the best form with his banner with him. I said, 'Abu 'Abdu'r-Rahman, haven't you been killed?' He replied, 'Yes, and I met my Lord and He brought me into the Garden and I roam wherever I wish among its fruits.' I said, 'What has happened to your companions?' He replied, 'They are with me around my standard which you see which will not be undone until the Last Hour.' He said, 'I woke up and thought that it was the best dream that I had had.'"

Muhammad ibn 'Amr ibn Hazm

One of an-Najjar. His *kunya* was Abu 'Abdu'l-Malik. His mother was 'Amra bint 'Abdullah ibn al-Harith. His children were 'Uthman, Abu Bakr the *faqih*, and Umm Kulthum, whose mother was Kabsha bint 'Abdu'r-Rahman; and 'Abdu'l-Malik, 'Abdullah, 'Abdu'r-Rahman and Umm 'Amra, whose mother was Thubayta bint an-Nu'man. The Messenger of Allah صلعم appointed 'Amr ibn Hazm over Najran al-Yaman and a son was born there in the time of the Messenger of Allah صلعم in 10 AH whom he named Muhammad with the *kunya* Abu Sulayman. He wrote that to the Messenger of Allah صلعم . The Messenger of Allah wrote back to him, "Name him Muhammad and make his *kunya* Abu 'Abdu'l-Malik." So he did that.

Abu Bakr, his son, said that 'Umar ibn al-Khattab gathered all the boys with the names of Prophets and brought them to his house in order to change their names. Their fathers came and brought clear evidence that the Messenger of Allah صلعم had named most of them and so he left them. Abu Bakr said, "My father was one of them."

Muhammad ibn 'Umar said, "Muhammad ibn 'Amr related from 'Umar and listened to him. He was reliable with few *hadiths*."

Muhammad ibn 'Amr said that he purchased a square of rough silk for 700 dirhams and wore it.

It is reported that in the Battle of al-Harra Muhammad ibn 'Amr was the fiercest against the Syrians. He would attack a group of them and scatter them. He was a horseman. One of the Syrians said, "This one has burned us and we fear that he will get away on his horse, so attack him all at once. He will not evade all of you. We see that he is a man with insight and courage." So they attacked and surrounded him with their spears and he fell dead. One of the Syrians held on to him so that they fell together. When Muhammad ibn 'Amr was killed and the people defeated on every front, the Syrians entered Madina and their horses ran through it pillaging and killing.

His grandson said, "Muhammad ibn 'Amr prayed on the Day of al-Harra while his wound was spurting blood. He was only killed after being surrounded with spears."

Al-Qasim said, "I saw Muhammad ibn 'Amr with a helmet. When he wanted to pray, he placed it by his side and did the full prayer."

Ibrahim ibn Yahya said, "Muhammad ibn 'Amr said on that day, raising his voice: 'Company of the Ansar! Be true against them in your blows! They are people who fight for the desire of this world and you are people who fight for the Next World!' Then he began to attack the squadron and scatter them until he was killed."

Abu Sufyan, the client of Abu Ahmad ibn Jahsh, reported, "The deviant Musrif ibn 'Uqba went around the dead on his horse with Marwan. He passed by Muhammad ibn 'Amr who was lying on his face with his brow on the earth. He said, 'By Allah, if you are on your face after death, you must have lain on it for a long time when you were alive.' Musrif said, 'By Allah, I think that these are only the people of the Garden. Do not let any of the people of Syria hear this from you or they will withhold obedience.' Marwan replied, 'They altered and changed.'"

'Umara ibn Khuzayma

One of the Ansar. His mother was Safiyya bint 'Amir. His children were Ishaq, whose mother was 'Ubadya bint 'Abdullah; Muhammad and Safiyya, whose mother was Wadi'a bint 'Abdullah ibn Mas'ud; Mani'a and Hammada, whose mother was an *umm walad*. He listened from 'Amr ibn al-'As and his father, Khuzayma ibn Thabit, 'the possessor of two testimonies'. 'Umara's *kunya* was Abu Muhammad. He died in Madina at the beginning of the khalifate of al-Walid I at the age of 74. He was reliable with few *hadiths*.

Yahya ibn Khallad

His children were Malik, 'Ali, 'A'isha and 'Uthayma, whose mother was Umm Thabit bint Qays; Umm Kulthum and Hamida, whose mother was Umm Yahya bint 'Amir; and Ramla, whose mothers is not named.

Ishaq ibn 'Abdullah reported that Yahya ibn Khallad said, "When Yahya ibn Khallad was born, he was brought to the Prophet صلعم and he rubbed his palate and said, 'I will give him a name with which I will not name anyone after him: Yahya ibn Zakariyya.' So he named him Yahya." Muhammad ibn 'Umar said, "Yahya related from 'Umar."

'Amr ibn Sulaym

His mother was an-Nawwar bint 'Abdullah. His children were 'Amr and an-Nu'man, whose mother was Habiba bint an-Nu'man of Ansar; and Sa'd and Ayyub, whose mother was Umm al-Banin Abi 'Ubada. He related from 'Umar ibn al-Khattab and also from Abu Qatada and Abu Humayd of the Ansar. He was reliable, with few *hadiths*.

Hanzala ibn Qays

His mother was Umm Sa'd bint Qays. His children were Muhammad and Umm Jamil, whose mother was Umm 'Isa bint 'Abdullah; 'Amr, whose mother was Umm 'Uthman bint 'Amr; 'Amr the younger, whose mother was an *umm walad*; 'Abdullah, whose mother was Umm Musa bint al-Harith; and 'Ubaydullah and Sa'd, whose mother is not named.

Az-Zuhri said, "I did not see any man of the Ansar with more resolve or generosity than Hanzala ibn Qays az-Zuraqi."

Muhammad ibn 'Umar said that Hanzala ibn Qays related from 'Umar, 'Uthman and Rafi' ibn Khadija, and az-Zuhri related from him. He was reliable with few *hadiths*.

Mas'ud ibn al-Hakam

His mother was Habiba bint Shariq. His children were Ibrahim, 'Isa, Abu Bakr, Sulayman, Musa, Isma'il, Da'ud, Ya'qub, 'Imran, Ayyub the elder, and Umm Ibrahim, whose mother was Maymuna bint Abi 'Ubada; and Ayyub the younger and Sara, whose mother was Umm 'Amr bint al-Muthanna.

Muhammad ibn 'Umar said, "Mas'ud ibn al-Hakam was born in the time of the Prophet صلعم . His *kunya* was Abu Harun. He was noble, honourable, and reliable. He related from 'Umar, 'Uthman and 'Ali. Muhammad ibn al-Munkadir and Abu'z-Zinad related from him.

'Abdullah ibn Abi Talha

His name was Zayd ibn Sahl of an-Najjar. His mother was Umm Sulaym bint Milhan of an-Najjar. She was the mother of Anas ibn Malik. His children were Al-Qasim, by an *umm walad*; 'Umayr, Zayd, Isma'il, Ya'qub, Ishaq, 'Abda and Umm Aban, whose mother was Thubayta bint Rifa'a; Muhammad, whose mother was an *umm walad*; 'Abdullah and Kulthum, by an *umm walad*; Ibrahim, Ruqayya and Umm 'Amr, whose mother was 'A'isha bint Jabir; and 'Umar, Ma'mar and 'Umara, whose mother was Umm Kulthum bint 'Amr ibn Hazm. Umm Sulaym was pregnant with 'Abdullah on the Day of Hunayn which she attended. 'Abdullah remained in Madina in the house of Abu Talha.

Anas ibn Malik said, "Abu Talha's son was ill. Abu Talha went out and the child died. When he returned, he asked, 'How is the boy?' Umm Sulaym replied, 'He is quieter than he was.' She brought him supper and he ate and then he had intercourse with her. When he finished she said, 'They have buried the boy.' Abu Talha went to the Messenger of Allah صلعم in morning and told him. He said, 'Did did you have sex in the night?' – 'Yes,' he replied. He said, 'O Allah, bless them.' She gave birth to a boy and Abu Talha said, 'Keep him until we take him to the Messenger of Allah.' He was taken to the Prophet, peace be upon him, with some dates, and the Prophet صلعم took him and said, 'Is there anything with him.' They replied, 'Yes, dates.' The Prophet صلعم took one of them and chewed it and then took it from his mouth and put it in the child's and rubbed his palate and named him 'Abdullah."

Anas said, "Umm Sulaym's son by Abu Talha was ill and Abu Talha went to the mosque and the boy died. Umm Sulaym said, 'Do not tell Abu Talha about his son's death.' He returned from the mosque and she prepared him his dinner as usual. He asked 'How is the boy?' She replied, 'Better than he was.' She brought him his dinner and he and his companions who were with him ate. Then she did what a woman does and he had intercourse with her. At the end of the night, she said, 'Abu Talha, what do you think about the family of a person who borrow something and enjoy it, and then when they are asked for it back, they find it hard to do?' He replied, 'They have no right to keep it.' She said, 'Your son was a loan from Allah and He has taken him back to Him.' He said, 'Surely we return to Allah!' and praised Allah.

"In the morning he went to the Messenger of Allah صلعم and when he saw him, he said, 'May Allah bless the two of you in your night.' She became pregnant with 'Abdullah ibn Abi Talha. It was night when she gave birth to him. She disliked rubbing his palate until the Messenger of Allah had done so. So she sent him with me. I took excellent dates and went to the Messenger of Allah صلعم while he was tending to some camels of his. I said, 'Umm Sulaym gave birth in the night and disliked to rub his palate until you have done so.' He asked, 'Do you have anything with you?' I said, 'Excellent dates.' He took one of them and chewed it and then squeezed it together with his spit and gave it to him and the child sucked it. He said, 'The Ansar love dates.' I said, 'Name him, Messenger of Allah.' He said, 'He is 'Abdullah.'" He was reliable with few *hadiths*.

Muhammad ibn Ubayy ibn Ka'b

Of an-Najjar. His mother was Umm at-Tufayl bint at-Tufayl of Daws. His children were Al-Qasim, Ubayy, Mu'adh, 'Umar, Muhammad and Ziyad, whose mother was 'A'isha bint Mu'adh. His *kunya* was Abu Mu'adh. He was born in the time of the Messenger of Allah صلعم. He related from 'Umar, and Busr ibn Sa'id related from him. He was reliable with few *hadiths*. Muhammad was killed in the Battle of al-Harra in Dhu'l-Hijja 63 AH while Yazid was khalif.

At-Tufayl ibn Ubayy ibn Ka'b

Of an-Najjar. His mother was Umm at-Tufayl bint at-Tufayl of Daws. His children were Ubayy, Muhammad, 'Abdu'l-'Aziz, 'Uthman and Umm 'Amr, whose mother was Umm al-Qasim bint Muhammad. At-Tufayl was nicknamed Abu Batn. He was a friend of 'Abdullah ibn 'Umar. He related from 'Umar, his father and Ibn 'Umar. He was reliable with sound *hadiths*.

Ar-Rabi' ibn Ubayy ibn Ka'b

Their brother. He is also related from. He related from his father that the Prophet صلعم asked Ka'b ibn Malik, "Have you married?" "Yes," he repled.

Mahmud ibn Labid ibn 'Uqba

His mother was Umm Manzur bint Mahmud of Aws. His children were Hudayr and Umm Manzur, whose mother was an *umm walad*; 'Umara and Umm Kulthum, whose mother was an *umm walad*; Shayba, whose mother was the daughter of 'Amr ibn Damra; and Umm Labid, whose mother was an *umm walad*. Mahmud was born in the time of the Prophet صلعم. It was concerning his father that there came the allowance to feed people as expiation in the case of the one who is unable to fast. Mahmud listened to 'Umar. He died in 76 AH in Madina. He was reliable with few *hadiths*.

Suwayd ibn 'Uwaym

Of Aws. His children were Husayn and Mulayka, whose mother was Umm al-Hasan bint Rifa'a; Mu'awiya, Bashir and Umm al-Hasan, whose mother was an *umm walad*; and Zaynab, whose mother was an *umm walad*. As-Sa'ib's *kunya* was Abu 'Abdu'r-Rahman. He was born in the time of the Prophet صلعم. He related from 'Umar. He had few *hadiths* and was reliable. He died in the khalifate of al-Walid I.

'Abdu'r-Rahman ibn 'Uwaym

His mother is not named. He was born in the time of the Prophet صلعم. He related from 'Umar and died in Madina at the end of the khalifate of 'Abdu'l-Malik. He was reliable with few *hadiths*.

Ayyub ibn Bashir ibn Sa'd

One of the Ansar of Aws. His *kunya* was Abu Sulayman. He was born in the time of the Prophet صلعم and related from 'Umar. Az-Zuhri related from him. He was reliable but did not have a lot of *hadiths*. He was present at al-Harra and sustained several wounds. He died two years later at the age of 75.

Tha'laba ibn Abi Malik al-Qurazi

Abu Malik's name was 'Abdullah ibn Sam. Tha'laba's *kunya* was Abu Yahya. Abu Malik came from the Yemen and said, "We of Kinda are following the religion of the Jews." He formed a marriage alliance with the Ibn Sa'ya of Banu Qurayza and made an alliance with them. He related from 'Umar and 'Uthman. His *kunya* was Abu Ja'far. He said that his *kunya* is related from Dawud ibn Sunan.

Da'ud ibn Sinan said, "I saw that Tha'laba ibn Abi Malik dyed his head and beard with henna."

Muhammad ibn 'Umar said, "Tha'laba was the Imam of the Banu Qurayza until he died. He was old and had many *hadiths*."

Al-Walid ibn 'Ubada ibn as-Samit

His mother was Jamila bint Abi Sa'sa'a ('Amr ibn Zayd) of an-Najjar. His children were Khalid, whose mother was from Tayy'; Muhammad whose mother was Habba bint an-Nu'man; 'Ubada, al-Harith, Mus'ab, 'Abdullah and Maslama, whose mother was Bazi'a bint Abi Haritha; Salih whose mother was from Banu Sa'd; Hisham whose mother was an *umm walad*; Yahya, whose mother was an *umm walad*; and Umm 'Isa and Hukayma, whose mother was an *umm walad*. He was born while the Prophet صلعم was alive and died while 'Abdu'l-Malik was khalif. He was reliable with many *hadiths*.

Sa'id ibn Sa'd ibn 'Ubada

Of al-Khazraj. His mother was Ghuzziyya bint Sa'd. His children were Shurahbil, Khalid, Isma'il, Zakariyya, Muhammad, 'Abdu'r-Rahman, Hafsa, and 'A'isha, whose mother was Buthayna bint Abi'd-Darda'; Yusuf, whose mother was Umm Yusuf bint Hammam of Banu Nasr of Hawazi; Yahya, 'Uthman, Ghuzziyya, 'Abdu'l-'Aziz, Umm Aban, and Umm al-Banin, by various *umm walads*.

Sa'id ibn Sa'd met the Prophet صلعم . In some of his transmission he listened to him He was reliable with few *hadiths*.

'Abbad ibn Tamim

Of an-Najjar. His mother was an *umm walad*. He had brothers by the father and by his mother. Ma'mar and Thabit, the sons of Tamim, were killed at al-Harra in Dhu'l-Hijja, 63 AH.

'Abbad ibn Tamim al-Mazini said, "I was five at the Battle of the Ditch and I remembered some things and retained them. We were with the women in the fortresses, and the people of the fortresses only slept in turns out of fear that the Banu Qurayza would attack them."

Muhammad ibn 'Umar said that az-Zuhri related from 'Abbad ibn Tamim.

Muhammad ibn Thabit

Of Khazraj. His mother was Jamila bint 'Abdullah. His maternal half-brother was 'Abdullah ibn Hanzala. Muhammad's son, 'Abdullah, was killed in the Battle of al-Harra, as were Sulayman and Yahya. Their mother was Umm 'Abdullah bint Hafs. He also had Isma'il and 'A'isha, whose mother was Umm Kathir bint an-Nu'man; Ishaq, Ibrahim, Yusuf, and Qurayba, whose mother was Amatullah bint as-Sa'ib; and 'Isa and Humayda, whose mother was Umm 'Awn bint 'Abdu'r-Rahman.

Sa'd ibn al-Harith ibn as-Simma

Of an-Najjar. His mother was Umm al-Hakam, whose mother was Khawla bint 'Uqba of Aws. His children were as-Salt and Umm al-Fadl, whose mother was Jamal bint Qays of Quraysh; and 'Umar, whose mother was Umm Sa'id bint Sahl. Sa'd was killed at Siffin on the side of 'Ali ibn Abi Talib.

Abu Umama ibn Sahl

Of Aws. His mother was Habiba bint Abi Umama of an-Najjar. Habiba was one of the women who gave allegiance. Abu Umama's name was As'ad after the name of his maternal grandfather and he had his *kunya*. His grandfather As'ad was a chief of the Banu'n-

Najjar. Abu Umama's children were Muhammad, Sahl, 'Uthman, Ibrahim, Yusuf, Yahya, Ayyub, Da'ud, Habiba and Umama, whose mother was Umm'Abdullah bint 'Atik of Aws; and Salih, whose mother was an *umm walad*.

Muhammad ibn 'Umar said, "It was mentioned to us that the Messenger of Allah صلعم was the one who named As'ad and gave him the *kunya* Abu Umama because of his maternal grandfather. It has not reached us that he related anything from 'Umar. He related from 'Uthman, Zayd ibn Thabit, Mu'awiya, and his father, Sahl ibn Hunayf. He was reliable with many *hadiths*.

'Abdu'r-Rahman ibn Abi 'Amra

Abu 'Amra's name was Bashir ibn 'Amr of an-Najjar. His mother was Hind bint al-Muqawwim of Quraysh, whose mother was Qilaba bint 'Amr, whose mother was Barra bint 'Adi. His children were 'Abdullah, Hamza, 'Alqama, and Habbana, whose mother was Umm Sa'd bint Shayban. Abu 'Amra was a Companion. He was with 'Ali and was killed at Siffin. He related from 'Uthman, Zayd ibn Khalid al-Juhani and Abu Hurayra. He was reliable with many *hadiths*.

'Abdu'r-Rahman ibn Yazid

Of Aws. His mother was Jamila bint Thabit. His half-brother was 'Asim ibn 'Umar ibn al-Khattab. His children were 'Isa – who was killed at al-Harra, Ishaq, Jamila, Umm 'Abdullah, Umm Ayyub, and Umm 'Asim, whose mother was Hasana bint Bukayr; Jamila, whose mother was an *umm walad*; 'Abdu'l-Karim and 'Abdu'r-Rahman, whose mother was Umama bint 'Abdullah. He was born in the time of the Prophet صلعم and was early. He related from 'Umar and was appointed *qadi* of Madina for 'Umar ibn 'Abdu'l-'Aziz. He died in Madina in 93 AH while al-Walid I was khalif. His *kunya* was Abu Muhammad. He was reliable with few *hadiths*.

Mujammi' ibn Yazid

His mother was Habiba bint al-Junayd of Banu 'Abs. His children were Isma'il, Ishaq, Ya'qub, Su'da, Umm Ishaq and Umm an-Nu'man, whose mother was Salima bint 'Abdullah.

Abu Sa'id al-Maqburi

His name was Kaysan. He was a client of the Banu Junda'. His house was near the graveyard and so he was called 'al-Maqburi'.

His son reported that he said, "I was the slave of a man of the Banu Junda' and he gave me a *kitaba* for 40,000 dirhams and a sheep for every *Adha*. The money was ready and I brought it to him, but he refused to accept it except in instalments. So I went to 'Umar ibn al-Khattab and mentioned that to him He said, 'Yarfa'! Take the money and place it in the treasury. Come to us in the evening and we will write your freedom. Then if your master wishes to take it, he can. If he wishes, he can leave it.' I took the money to the treasury. When my master heard, he went and took the money. Then I went to 'Umar with the *zakat* of my property after that. He said, 'Have you taken any money since you were freed?' I said, 'No.' He said, 'Take it back until you take something from us and then come to us afterwards.'"

Abu Sa'id al-Maqburi said, "I went to 'Umar with 200 dirhams and said, 'Take the *zakat* of my property.' He said, 'You are freed, Kaysan?' I said, 'Yes.' He said, 'Go and give it as *sadaqa*.'"

Muhammad ibn 'Umar said, "Abu Sa'id related from 'Umar. He was reliable with many *hadiths*. He died in 100 AH while 'Umar ibn 'Abdu'l-'Aziz was khalif. Others said that he died in Madina while al-Walid I was khalif.

Abu 'Ubayd

Az-Zuhri once said that he was the client of 'Abdu'r-Rahman ibn Azhar, but another time elsewhere he said that he was the client of 'Abdu'r-Rahman ibn 'Awd. Others said that. Az-Zuhri said that he was one of the early ones and one of the people of *fiqh*. He said, "I was present at the *'Id* with 'Umar." He related from 'Uthman, 'Ali and Abu Hurayra. His name was Sa'd. He died in Madina in 98 AH. He was reliable and had *hadiths*.

Aflah

The client of Abu Ayyub al-Ansari. His *kunya* was Abu Kathir.

Muhammad ibn Sirin said that Abu Ayyub gave Aflah a *kitaba* for 40,000 dirhams. People began to congratulate him and say, "Congratulations on your freedom, Abu Kathir." When Abu Ayyub returned to his family he regretted the *kitaba* and sent to him and said, "I would like to have the *kitaba* returned to me and for to you to be as you were." His son and family said, "Will your return a slave when Allah has freed you?" Aflah said, "By Allah, he does not ask me for anything but that I give it to him." So he took his *kitaba* and tore it up and then remained his slave as long as Allah willed. Then Abu Ayyub sent to him, "You are free and whatever property you have is yours."

Muhammad ibn 'Umar said, "Aflah was one of the captives of 'Ayn at-Tamr taken by Khalid ibn al-Walid in the khalifate of Abu Bakr. He sent them to Madina. I heard someone mention that Aflah's *kunya* was Abu 'Abdu'r-Rahman. He listened to 'Umar and had a house in Madina. He was killed at al-Harra in Dhu'l-Hijja, 63 AH while Yazid was khalif. He was reliable with few *hadiths*.

'Ubayd

The client of 'Ubayd ibn al-Mu'alla, the brother of Abu Sa'id az-Zuraqi. His *kunya* was Abu 'Abdullah. He was one of the captives of 'Ayn at-Tamr taken by Khalid ibn al-Walid in Abu Bakr's khalifate and sent to Madina. They say it is 'Ubayd ibn Murra. He was the grandfather of Nafis ibn Muhammad at-Tajir, the owner of the castle of Nafis in the area of Harra and Aqam. He died at al-Harra in Dhu'l-Hijja, 63 AH. He was reliable with few *hadiths*.

Shammas

The client of al-'Abbas ibn 'Abdu'l-Muttalib. He memorised *Surat Yusuf* from the mouth of 'Umar ibn al-Khattab when he recited it in the prayer. His son, 'Uthman, related from him.

As-Sa'ib ibn Khabbab

The client of Fatima bint 'Uqba. His *kunya* was Abu 'Abdu'r-Rahman. Some said it was Abu Muslim. He was reliable with few *hadiths*. He related from 'Umar and Zayd ibn Thabit.

Muhammad ibn 'Umar said that he died in Madina in 97 AH at the age of 72. Malik ibn Anas said that as-Sa'ib ibn Khabbab died before Ibn 'Umar.

'Ubayd ibn Umm Kilab

He listened to 'Umar ibn al-Khattab. He is 'Ubayd ibn Salama al-Laythi. He is the one who left Madina because of the murder of 'Uthman and met 'A'isha at Sarif and told her that he had been murdered and that people had given allegiance to 'Ali ibn Abi Talib, so she returned to Makka. 'Ubayd was a supporter of 'Ali.

Al-Hurmuzan

He was a Persian. When the fighting at Jalula ended, Yazdagird left Hulwan for Isfahan and then went to Istakhr and sent al-Hurmuzan to Tustar. He fortified himself in the citadel with his cavalry and collected many of the people of Tustar. It was in the furthest part of the city next to the mountains and water surrounded it. Supplies reached them from Isfahan and they remained like that for as long as Allah wished. Abu Musa laid siege to them for two years, or eighteen months.

Then the people of the citadel submitted to the authority of 'Umar and Abu Musa sent al-Hurmuzan to him with twelve Persian captives wearing brocade, gold torques and gold bracelets. They were brought to Madina in their finery. People began to admire them. They were brought to 'Umar's house, but they did not find him there and began to look for him. Al-Hurmuzan said in Persian, "Your king has gone missing." They were told, "He is in the mosque."

They entered and found him sleeping using his cloak as a pillow. Al-Hurmuzan exclaimed, "This is your king!" They replied, "This is the khalif." He asked, "Doesn't he have a chamberlain or a guard?" They replied, "Allah is his guard until his time comes." Al-Hurmuzan said, "This is indeed a comfortable king."

'Umar looked at al-Hurmuzan and said, "I seek refuge with Allah from the Fire." Then he said, "Praise be to Allah Who has humbled this man and his followers by Islam." 'Umar said to the delegation, "Speak, but beware of divisive speech and being long-winded." Anas ibn Malik said, "Praise be to Allah Who carried out His promise and exalted His *deen* and disappointed those who opposed it and bequeathed their land and homes to us and gave us their property and children as booty to us and has given us power over them. We will kill whom we wish and let live whomever we wish."

'Umar wept and then said to al-Hurmuzan, "What is your property?" He replied, "My inheritance from my fathers is with me. What I had from the property of the kingdom and the treasuries was taken by your agent." He said, "Hurmuzan, what do you think of what Allah has done to you?" He did not reply. 'Umar asked, "Why don't you speak?" He replied, "Shall I speak the words of a living man or the words of a dead man?" He asked, "Are you not alive?" Al-Hurmuzan asked for water and 'Umar said, "We will not combine thirst with execution for you."

He called for water and water was brought in a wooden cup and he took it with his hand. 'Umar said, "Drink. Don't be afraid. I will not have you killed until you have drunk it." So he threw the vessel to the ground and said, "Company of Arabs! You were and are without a religion. We enslaved you, annihilated you, and killed you, and you were the worst of nations in our eyes for a time and in the lowest position. Then Allah was with you – and none has any power against Allah."

'Umar commanded that he be killed. He said, "Have you not granted me safe conduct?" – "How?" he asked. He said, "You said to me: 'Speak and do not be afraid.' You said, 'Drink and do not be afraid. I will not have you killed until you have drunk it.'" Az-Zubayr ibn al-'Awwam, Anas ibn Malik. and Abu Sa'id al-Khudri said, "He has spoken the truth." 'Umar said, "May Allah fight him! He secured his safe-conduct without my realising it!"

He commanded that the jewellery and brocade al-Hurmuzan was wearing be taken from him. He said to Suraqa ibn Malik, who was a lean dark man with thin blackened arms, "Wear the bracelets of al-Hurmuzan." He put them on and put on his robe. 'Umar said, "Praise be to Allah who has stripped Chosroes and his people of their jewels and robes and put them on Suraqa ibn Malik!"

'Umar invited al-Hurmuzan and his people to accept Islam and they refused. 'Ali said, "Amir al-Mu'minin, separate them from their brothers." So 'Umar had al-Hurmuzan, Jufayna and some others moved by sea. He said, "O Allah, wreck them." He wanted to send them to Syria and they were shipwrecked but not drowned. So they returned and became Muslim. 'Umar allotted them two thousand dirhams each and renamed al-Hurmuzan 'Urfuta.

Al-Miswar ibn Makhrama and Ibrahim ibn 'Abdu'r-Rahman said, "I saw al-Hurmuzan in ar-Rawha' proceeding slowly on *hajj* with 'Umar. He was wearing a shawl."

*****

Other Tabi'un include **Abu Sahl as-Sa'idi**, of whom Makhul reported that he prayed behind Abu Bakr and described his recitation; **an-Nadr ibn Sufyan al-Hudhali,** who related from 'Umar and is related from; **Himas al-Layth,** one of the Banu Kinana who had a house in Madina and related from 'Umar and had few *hadiths*: **'Abdullah ibn Abi Ahmad ibn Jahsh**, an ally of Banu 'Abd Shams; **Suwayd ibn 'Uwaym**, whose mother was Umama bint Bukayr of Khazra and was killed in the Battle of al-Harra; **Ibn Marsa**, a client of Quraysh who related from 'Umar; and **Abu Sa'id**, a client of Abu Usayd who related from 'Umar.

*****

Those who related from 'Uthman, 'Ali, 'Abdu'r-Rahman ibn 'Awf, Talha, az-Zubayr, Sa'd, Ubayy ibn Ka'b, Sahl ibn Hunayf, Hudhayfa ibn al-Yaman, Zayd ibn Thabit and others

Muhammad ibn al-Hanafiyya

He is Muhammad the elder, son of 'Ali ibn Abi Talib. His mother was the Hanafiyya woman, Khawla bint Ja'far. It is also said that his mother was one of the captives of Yamama in 'Ali's share.

Al-Hasan ibn Salih said, "I heard 'Abdullah ibn al-Hasan say that Abu Bakr gave 'Ali the mother of Muhammad ibn al-Hanafiyya."

Asma' bint Abi Bakr said, "I saw the mother of Muhammad ibn al-Hanafiyya who was a dark Sindi woman. She was a slave of the Banu Hanifa and not one of them."

Mundhir ath-Thawri said that he he heard Muhammad ibn al-Hanafiyya say: "It was an allowance to 'Ali. He said, "Messenger of Allah, if I have a son after you, I will give him your name and your *kunya*." He said, "Yes."

Mundhir ath-Thawri said, "There was a quarrel between 'Ali and Talha and Talha said to him, 'No, like your boldness against the Messenger of Allah صلعم in giving both his name and *kunya* when the Messenger of Allah forbade that any of his community after him should have them both.' 'Ali said, 'Bold is the one who is bold against Allah and His Messenger. Call so-and-so and so-and-so for me,' and he named some men of Quraysh. They came and he said, 'To what will you testify?' They said, 'We testify that the Messenger of Allah صلعم said, "You will have a boy after me and I give him my name and my *kunya*, and it is not lawful for any of my community after him.""

Abu Bakr ibn Hafs and Ibrahim said that Muhammad said, "My *kunya* is Abu'l-Qasim."

Muhammad ibn Isra'il said that Muhammad's *kunya* was Abu'l-Qasim. He had a lot of knowledge and was scrupulous. His children were 'Abdullah, who is Abu Hashim, Hamza, 'Ali, and Ja'far the elder, whose mother was an *umm walad*; al-Hasan, who was one of the cultured and intelligent Banu Hashim and the first to speak about *irja'* (Murji'ism)[1] and whose mother was Jamal bint Qays; Ibrahim, whose mother was Musri'a bint 'Abbad; al-Qasim, 'Abdu'r-Rahman, and Umm Abiha, whose mother was Umm 'Abdu'r-Rahman Barra bint 'Abdu'r-Rahman; Ja'far the younger, 'Awn, and 'Abdullah the younger, whose mother was Umm Ja'far bint Muhammad; and 'Abdullah and Ruqayya, whose mother was an *umm walad*.

Mundhir ath-Thawri said, "I heard Muhammad ibn al-Hanafiyya say while discussing the Battle of the Camel, 'When he was forming the rows, 'Ali gave me the standard but saw some reluctance on my part when the men drew near to one another, so he took it from me and fought with it. On that day I attacked a man of the people of Basra. When I overcame him, he said, 'I am on the *deen* of Abi Talib.' When I realised what he meant, I refrained from finishing him off. When they were defeated, 'Ali said, 'Do not finish off anyone who is wounded or pursue anyone running away.' The weapons and mounts of those who had been killed were divided up. We took from them what they brought us of mounts and weapons."

'Abdullah ibn Muhammad said that he heard Muhammad ibn al-Hanafiyya say, "My father wanted to attack Mu'awiya and the Syrians and he began to tie his banner. Then he swore he would not undo it until he went. People refused to do likewise and their banners were dispersed and they were cowardly – and so he untied it and expiated his oath. He did this four times. I saw his state and it did not make me happy. I asked al-Miswar ibn Makhrama that day, 'Won't you speak to him about where to go with the people? By Allah, I think they are useless.' Al-Miswar said, 'Abu'l-Qasim, he has travelled for something which has already been decided. I spoke to him and I think he will refuse to do anything except go.'"

Muhammad ibn al-Hanafiyya said, "When he saw what he saw of them, he said, 'O Allah, I am fed up with them and they are fed up me. I hate them and they hate me, so replace them with better than them for me, and replace me with worse than me for them."

---

1. See Introduction to Vol. I, p. xvi.

Muhammad ibn Ka'b al-Qurazi said, "In the Battle of Siffin 'Ammar ibn Yasir was in charge of the infantry and Muhammad ibn al-Hanafiyya carried his banner."

'Abdullah ibn Zurayr al-Ghafiqi, who was present at Siffin with 'Ali said, "I remember when we met the people of Syria and fought until I thought that none would survive. I heard someone shouting, 'O company of Muslims! Allah! Allah! Who will care for the women and children? Who will be against the Byzantines! Who will stand against the Turks! Who will stand against Daylam! Allah! Allah! The rest!' I heard a commotion behind me and turned and there was 'Ali running with the banner, hurrying to set it up. His son Muhammad joined him and I heard him say, 'Son, hold your banner. I am going to attack the people.' I saw him striking with his sword until he parted them and then returned back through them."

Mundhir ath-Thawri said "I was with Muhammad ibn al-Hanafiyya and heard him say, 'I do not testify that anyone is saved or one of the people of the Garden after the Messenger of Allah صلعم, not even my father who sired me.' The people looked at him and he said, 'Who was like 'Ali and had his precedence?'"

Abu Ya'la said that Muhammad ibn al-Hanafiyya said, while he was at ash-Shi'b, "If my father 'Ali had encountered this situation, this is where he would have made a stand."

Mundhir Abi Ya'la reported that Muhammad ibn al-Hanafiyya said, "We, the people of two houses of Quraysh, are relied on instead of Allah: we and the Banu Umayya." Muhammad al-Azdi said something similar.

Abu Hamza said, "We used to greet Muhammad ibn 'Ali, 'Peace be upon you, Mahdi.' He replied, 'Yes, I am a mahdi. I guide to right guidance and good. My name is the name of the Prophet of Allah and my *kunya* is the *kunya* of the Prophet of Allah. When one of you greets me, he should say, "Peace be upon you, Muhammad," or, "Peace be upon you, Abu'l-Qasim."'"

Al-Minhal ibn 'Amr said, "A man came to Ibn al-Hanafiyya and greeted him and he returned the greeting. The man said, 'How are you?' He removed his hand and said, "'How are you?" It is time for you to recognise how we are. In this community we resemble the tribe of Israel among the people of Pharaoh. He was slaughtering their sons and letting their women live. These people slaughter our sons and marry our women without our permission. The Arabs claimed that they have excellence over non-Arabs and the non-Arabs asked, "Why is that?" They replied, "Muhammad was an Arab." They replied, "You have spoken the truth." Quraysh claimed that it has precedence over the Arabs and the Arabs asked, "Why?" They replied, "Muhammad was a Qurayshi." If the people had recognised the truth, we would have been granted excellence over people.'"

Al-Aswad ibn Qays said, "In Khorasan I met a man of 'Azza whose name I do not know. He said, 'Shall I show you a letter of Ibn al-Hanafiyya?' – 'Certainly,' I replied. He said, 'I went to him while he was speaking in a group and I said, "Peace be upon you, O Mahdi." "And peace be upon you," he returned. I said, "I need something from you." He asked, "Secret or public?" – "Secret," I replied. He said, "Sit." I sat with him and he spoke to the people for a time and then he got up and I got up with him.

"'When he entered his house, I went in with him. "Tell me your need," he said. I praised Allah and testified that there is no god but Allah alone and that Muhammad is the slave of Allah and His Messenger. Then I said, "By Allah, you are the closest of Quraysh to us by kinship and we love you by your kinship. You are the closest of Quraysh to our Prophet. That is why we love you by your kinship to our Prophet. We suffered disgrace for your sake until heads were severed for it and testimonies invalidated and we were hounded through the lands. We have suffered to the point that I would have gone off to some desert where I could worship Allah until I meet Him – were it not that the business of the family of Muhammad would have been hidden from me. It has reached the point where I want to rebel against our amirs. If they would come out and fight, we would stand fast. ('Umar said he meant the Kharijites.) We have heard things about you so I wanted to speak directly to you rather than ask anyone about you. You are the most trustworthy of people in my opinion and I prefer to follow you. I will follow your opinion and whatever you think best. I say this and I ask the forgiveness of Allah for you and for me."

"'Muhammad ibn 'Ali praised Allah and testified that there is no god but Allah and Muhammad is His slave and Messenger. Then he said, "Beware of these tales. They are a fault in you. You must have the Book of Allah Almighty. It is the guidance of the first of you and by it the last of you will be guided. By my life, if you have been suffering, those better than you have been suffering too. As for your statement about wanting to to go to some desert where you could worship Allah until you meet Him and to avoid the affairs of people – were it not that the affairs of the family of Muhammad would be hidden from you – do not do it. That is the innovation of monasticism. By my life, the family of Muhammad are more evident than the rising of this sun. As for your words about wanting to rebel with some people who have the same ideas as you about their amirs – so that if they would come out and fight, you would stand fast – do not do it. Do not divide the Community. Guard yourself against those people by *taqiya*. ('Umar said that he meant the Umayyads.) Do not fight them."

"'I asked, "What is this *taqiya*?" He said, "You present a face to them when they are there and by that Allah will defend your blood and your *deen* for you. You will obtain from the property of Allah what you are more entitled to than they are."

"'I said, "What if fighting engulfs me and there is no way to avoid it?" He replied "You give allegiance with one of your hands while the other is for Allah. Allah will make people enter the Garden by what they keep secret and will make people enter the Fire by what they keep secret. I remind you by Allah not to convey from me what you did not hear from me or to attribute to me what I did not say. This is what I say and I ask the forgiveness of Allah for you and for me.""'"

Abu't-Tufayl reported that Muhammad ibn al-Hanafiyya said to him, "Cling to this place and be like one of the pigeons of the Haram until our command comes. If our command comes, there will be no hiding it as the sun is not hidden when it rises. What will inform you if the people tell you that it comes from the east and Allah brings it from the west? What will inform you if the people tell you that it comes from the west and then Allah brings it from the east? What will inform you? Perhaps it will be brought to us as clearly as the bride is brought."

Al-Mundhir ath-Thawri said that Ibn al-Hanafiyya said, "If anyone loves us, Allah will help him, even if he is in ad-Daylam."

Al-Mundhir reported that Ibn al-Hanafiyya said, "I wished that I could ransom our party, even if it was by some of my blood." Then he placed his right hand on his left and then said, "What they say are lies and they broadcast evil to such an extent that one of them would even deceive his mother who gave birth to him until she was killed."

Al-Harith al-Azdi reported that Ibn al-Hanafiyya said, "May Allah have mercy on a man who is self-sufficient, restrains his hand, holds his tongue and sits in his house, has what is enough for him, and is with those he loves. The agents of the Umayyads are quicker in seeking them than the swords of the Muslims. Otherwise the people of truth will have a state which Allah will bring about when He wishes. Whoever among you and us achieves that will be with us in the highest station, and whoever dies will have what is better and more lasting with Allah."

Abu Ya'la reported that Ibn al-Hanafiyya said, "If someone loves a man for Allah for justice which appears from him – while in the knowledge of Allah he is one of the people of the Fire, Allah will reward him for his love for him just as if he had loved a man of the Garden. If someone hates a man for Allah by injustice which has appeared from him – while in the knowledge of Allah he is one of the people of the Garden, Allah will reward him for his hatred of him just as if he had been the most hated man of the people of the Fire."

Umm Bakr bint al-Miswar said, "Al-Mukhtar ibn Abi 'Ubayd was with 'Abdullah ibn az-Zubayr in his first siege. He was the strongest of people with him and regarded himself as belonging to his party. Ibn az-Zubayr admired him and regarded him as his supporter and did not listen to any words against him. Al-Mukhtar used to keep the company of Muhammad ibn al-Hanafiyya, but Muhammad did not have a good opinion of him, nor did he accept much of what he brought. Al-Mukhtar said, 'I am going to Iraq.' Muhammad said to him, 'Go, and 'Abdullah ibn Kamil al-Hamdani will go with you.' He said to 'Abdullah, 'Keep an eye on him. He is not very trustworthy.' Al-Mukhtar went to Ibn az-Zubayr and said, 'My being in Iraq is better for you than my being here.' So 'Abdullah ibn az-Zubayr gave him and Ibn Kamil permission to go. Ibn az-Zubayr did not doubt his good intentions, but he was intent on being disloyal to Ibn az-Zubayr. They left and met at al-'Udhayb. Al-Mukhtar said, 'Tell me about the people?' He replied, 'I left the people rolling about like an unmanned ship.' Al-Mukhtar said, 'I am the mariner who will put it right.'"

'Urwa said, "When al-Mukhtar reached Iraq, he went straight to 'Abdullah ibn Muti', Ibn az-Zubayr's governor of Kufa at this time. He made a display of loyalty to Ibn az-Zubayr but criticised him in private. He called on people to follow Ibn al-Hanafiyya and encouraged them to oppose Ibn Muti' and set up a faction with a large amount of horsemen. When Ibn Muti' saw this, he fled to 'Abdullah ibn az-Zubayr."

Ishaq ibn Yahya and others said, "When al-Mukhtar came to Kufa, he was the strongest of people against Ibn az-Zubayr and criticised him. He began to tell people that Ibn az-Zubayr used to seek support for Abu'l-Qasim, meaning Ibn al-Hanafiyya, and then wronged him. He mentioned Ibn al-Hanafiyya, his situation and scrupulousness and that he had sent him to Kufa to summon people to himself and that he had written a letter that he was not to pass on to anyone else. He read that letter to those he trusted and began to call on people to give allegiance to Muhammad ibn al-Hanafiyya and they did so secretly. Some of those who gave allegiance had doubts about him and said, 'We gave this man our pledges since he claims that he is the messenger of Ibn al-Hanafiyya. Ibn al-Hanafiyya is in Makka not far from us nor concealed. We should send some of us to him to ask about what this man has brought. If he is telling the truth, we will help him and assist him in his business.'

"They sent some people who met Ibn al-Hanafiyya in Makka and told them about what al-Mukhtar was doing and what he was calling them to. He said, 'You see that we await our reward with Allah. I do not want the power of this world by killing a believer without a lawful reason. I wish that Allah will help us with what He wishes of His creation. Beware of liars. Look to yourselves and your *deen*.'

"So they left on that note. Al-Mukhtar composed a letter in the name of Muhammad ibn al-Hanafiyya to Ibrahim ibn al-Ashtar and he came and asked permission to enter. Al-Mukhtar was said to be the trustee of the family of Muhammad and his messenger. So he gave him permission, welcomed him, and had him sit with him on his bed. He spoke to al-Mukhtar and he was eloquent. He praised Allah and said the prayer on the Prophet صلعم . Then he said, 'The people of the House have honoured you by letting you help the family of Muhammad. Those of them whom you have helped have been pursued, and they have been deprived and denied their right and have been reduced to what you see. Al-Mahdi wrote you a letter and these witnessed it.' Yazid ibn Anas al-Asadi, Ahmar ibn Shumayt al-Bajali, 'Abdullah ibn Kamil ash-Shakiri and Abu 'Amra Kaysan, the client of Bajila, said, 'We testify that this is his letter which we saw when he gave it to him.'

"Ibrahim took and read it and said, 'I am the first to respond. He has commanded us to obey you and support you. Say what you think and call on me as you like.' Then Ibrahim rode to see him every day and that had an effect on the hearts of people. The news reached Ibn az-Zubayr and he treated Muhammad ibn al-Hanafiyya with hostility. The power of al-Mukhtar began to strengthen every day and his followers increased. He began to pursue the killers of al-Husayn and those who had participated in that and he killed them. Then he sent Ibrahim ibn al-Ashtar with 20,000 men to 'Ubaydullah ibn Ziyad. He killed him and sent his head to al-Mukhtar. Al-Mukhtar put it in a bag and then sent it to Muhammad ibn al-Hanafiyya, 'Ali ibn al-Husayn and the rest of the Banu Hashim .

"When 'Ali ibn Husayn saw 'Ubaydullah's head, he asked for mercy on al-Husayn and said, "Ubaydullah ibn Ziyad was brought al-Husayn's head while he was having lunch. We have been brought 'Ubaydullah's head while we are having lunch. There is no one left among the Banu Hashim but that he is praising al-Mukhtar, praying for him and speaking well of him.' Ibn al-Hanafiyya disliked the business of al-Mukhtar and what he heard about him. He did not like most of what he brought. Ibn 'Abbas said, 'He has secured our revenge, realised our enmity, preferred us and given to us.' When al-Mukhtar's power increased, he wrote to Muhammad ibn 'Ali al-Mahdi: 'From al-Mukhtar ibn Abi 'Ubayd, the seeker of revenge for the family of Muhammad صلعم . Allah, the Most Blessed and Exalted, does not take revenge on a people in order to excuse them. Allah has destroyed the iniquitous and the followers of iniquity. As for those who remain, I hope that Allah will join the last of them with the first of them.'"

Various people reported: "When the death of Mu'awiya ibn Abi Sufyan was announced in Madina, al-Husayn ibn 'Ali, Muhammad ibn al-Hanafiyya and Ibn az-Zubayr were there while Ibn 'Abbas was in Makka. Al-Husayn and Ibn az-Zubayr went to Makka while Ibn al-Hanafiyya remained in Madina until he heard of the approach of the army of Musrif and the Battle of Harra; so he went to Makka and stayed with Ibn 'Abbas. When the death of Yazid ibn Mu'awiya was announced, Ibn az-Zubayr chose himself as leader and summoned people to him. He called on Ibn 'Abbas and Muhammad ibn al-Hanafiyya to give allegiance to him, but they refused to do so and said, 'Only when all lands agree on you.' That was their stance.

Sometimes he was harsh to them, sometimes he was gentle towards them, and sometimes he was openly hostile towards them. Then he was harsh towards them and words were exchanged between them. The matter continued to worsen until they feared for themselves and their women and children. He was a bad neighbour to them, and blockaded them and injured them. He went to Muhammad ibn al-Hanafiyya and abused and criticised him, and commanded him and the Banu Hashim to stay in their ravine in Makka. He put guards on them and told them, 'By Allah, either you will give homage or I will burn you with fire,' and so they feared for themselves."

Abu 'Amir Sulaym said, "I saw Muhammad ibn al-Hanafiyya confined at Zamzam while people were prevented from going to him. I said, 'By Allah, I will visit him!' I went in and said, 'What is your opinion of this man?' He said, 'He summoned me to give homage and I said, "I am one of the Muslims. When they agree on you, then I am like them." He was not content with that from me. Go to Ibn 'Abbas and greet him for me. Tell him that his cousin asks for his opinion.'"

Sulaym continued, "I went to Ibn 'Abbas who had gone blind. He asked, 'Who are you?' – 'An Ansari,' I replied. He said, 'Many an Ansari is harsher to us than our enemies.' I said, 'Fear not. I am one of those who are totally for you.' He said. 'Go ahead.' So I told him what Ibn al-Hanafiyya had said and he told me, 'Tell him not to obey him. There is no delight except in what he said and do not do more than that.' I went back to Ibn al-Hanafiyya and told him what Ibn 'Abbas had said. Ibn al-Hanafiyya wanted to go to Kufa and and tell that to al-Mukhtar, but it was difficult for him to go. He said, 'The Mahdi has a sign which will be seen in your land – a man will strike him with a sword in the market, and it will not harm him nor deceive him.'

"Ibn al-Hanafiyya listened to this and got up and was told, 'You should contact your party in Kufa and inform them about your situation.' So he sent 'Amir ibn Wathila to their party in Kufa. He came to them and said, 'We do not trust Ibn az-Zubayr in respect of our people.' He told them about the fear they were in, and al-Mukhtar sent a delegation to Makka and with them were 4,000 men. He put Abu 'Abdullah al-Jadali in charge of them and told him, 'Go. If you find the Banu Hashim alive, you and those with you should support them and do what they command you to do. If you find that Ibn az-Zubayr has killed them, then go against the people of Makka until you reach Ibn az-Zubayr and then do not spare any of the family of az-Zubayr at all.' He said, 'Police of Allah! Allah has honoured you with this journey, and by it you will have the equivalent of ten *hajjs* and ten *'umras.'* So the people went with their weapons until they over-looked Makka. Someone seeking help came saying: 'Make haste! I do not think you will reach them in time!' People said, 'The strongest should go ahead,' and so they sent 800 under 'Atiyya ibn Sa'd ibn Junada al-'Awfi to enter Makka and they uttered a *takbir* which Ibn az-Zubayr heard. He fled to the Dar an-Nidwa. It is said that he clung to the curtain of the Ka'ba and said, 'I am the refugee of Allah.'"

'Atiyya said, "Then we went to Ibn 'Abbas, Ibn al-Hanafiyya and their companions in their houses. Firewood had been piled around them so that they had been surrounded with it to the tops of the walls. If fire had been set to it, none of them would have been identifiable until the Final Hour. So we cleared the doorways and 'Ali ibn 'Abdullah ibn 'Abbas made haste. He was a man then. He hurried in clearing away the wood in his desire to leave until he made his thighs bleed. The followers of Ibn az-Zubayr advanced and we formed two separate lines — us and them — in the mosque on that day. We only left off the prayer until morning. Abu 'Abdullah al-Jadali advanced with some people and we said to Ibn 'Abbas and Ibn al-Hanafiyya, 'Let us relieve the people of Ibn az-Zubayr!' They both said, 'This is a land which Allah has made inviolate. It was not made lawful to attack for anyone except the Prophet صلعم for one hour. It was not lawful for anyone before him and will not be for anyone after him. Defend us and give us protection.'"

"They were steadfast, even though there was a caller calling from the mountain, 'No expedition after that of its Prophet has looted what this has looted. Expeditions loot gold and silver, but we will loot blood.' So they brought them out and camped at Mina where they remained for as long as Allah wished, and then they left for Ta'if for a stay. 'Abdullah ibn 'Abbas died in Ta'if in 68 AH and Muhammad ibn al-Hanafiyya said the prayer over him. We remained with Ibn al-Hanafiyya. When the time of the *hajj* came, Ibn az-Zubayr made *hajj* from Makka. He stopped in 'Arafa with his followers. Muhammad ibn al-Hanafiyya came from Ta'if with his companions and stopped at 'Arafa. Najda ibn 'Amir al-Hanafi came that year with his

Kharijite followers and camped to one side. The Umayyads made *hajj* under their banner and stopped at 'Arafa with them."

'Awn said, "There were four banners at 'Arafa that year: Muhammad ibn al-Hanafiyya with his followers under a banner at Habl al-Musha; Ibn az-Zubayr who made *hajj* with his people with a banner and who stopped at the present station of the imam – while Ibn al-Hanafiyya stopped opposite Ibn az-Zubayr; Najda al-Haruri who stopped behind them with his people and a banner; and then the Umayyads with their banner who stopped to the left of them. The first banner to be unfurled was that of Muhammad ibn al-Hanafiyya, then that of Najda, then the banner of the Umayyads, and then the banner of Ibn az-Zubayr – and most people followed him."

Nafi' said, "Ibn az-Zubayr did not press on that evening until Ibn 'Umar pressed on. When Ibn az-Zubayr was slow, Ibn al-Hanafiyya, Najda and the Umayyads overtook him. Ibn 'Umar said, 'Is Ibn az-Zubayr waiting for the business of the *Jahiliyya*?' Then he pressed on and Ibn az-Zubayr pressed on behind him."

Makhrama ibn Sulayman said, "I heard Ibn al-Hanafiyya say, 'I pressed on from 'Arafa when the sun set. That year I heard that Ibn az-Zubayr said, 'Muhammad has hastened as Muhammad صلعم hastened. Who will remove confusion from ibn az-Zubayr?'"

Muhammad ibn Jubayr said, "Ibn az-Zubayr went on *hajj* that year and Ibn al-Hanafiyya went on *hajj* with the Khashabiyya of whom there were 4,000 who camped in the right ravine of Mina. I feared there would be a *fitna* and went to all of them. I went to Muhammad ibn 'Ali in the ravine and said, 'Abu'l-Qasim, fear Allah. We are in the Mash'ar Haram and a sacred land. People have come to Allah and His House. Do not spoil their *hajj* for them.' He replied, 'By Allah, I do not desire that, and I will not come between anyone and His House. Nothing will come from me against any *hajji* – but I am a man who defends himself against Ibn az-Zubayr and what he desires of me. I do not seek this command, unless no two would differ about me. Rather go to Ibn az-Zubayr and speak to him – and you must speak to Najda as well.'

"So I went to Ibn az-Zubayr and spoke to him in similar manner as I had done to Ibn al-Hanafiyya. He said, 'I am a man on whom people have agreed, and people have given me allegiance. These others are people of dispute.' I said, 'It is good for you to forbear.' He replied, 'I will do so.' Then I went to Najda al-Haruri and found him with his followers and I found 'Ikrima, the slave of Ibn 'Abbas, with him. I said, 'Ask your companion for permission for me to enter.' He went in and shortly gave me permission. I entered and spoke with feeling to him as I had to the other two men. He said, 'I will not start any fighting, but if someone starts a fight with me, we will fight him.' I said, 'I think that the other two men do not want to fight you.' Then I went to the ravine of the Umayyads and spoke to them as I had done to the others. They said, 'We are with our banner and will not fight anyone else unless they fight us.' I did not see any of those banners more tranquil and safe than that of the companions of Ibn al-Hanafiyya.

"On that evening, I stood beside Muhammad ibn al-Hanafiyya. When the sun set, he turned to me and said, 'Abu Sa'id, press on.' So he pressed on and I went with him. He was the first to press on."

Abu 'Awn said, "I saw the companions of Ibn al-Hanafiyya saying the *talbiya* at 'Arafa and I glanced at Ibn az-Zubayr and his companions and they were saying the *talbiya* until the sun set and then he stopped. That was also what the Umayyads did. Najda said the *talbiya* until he stoned the *Jamrat al-'Aqaba*."

Abu'l-'Uryan al-Mujasha'i said, "Al-Mukhtar sent us with 2,000 horsemen to Muhammad ibn al-Hanafiyya. Ibn al-'Abbas said about al-Mukhtar, 'He has secured our revenge, paid our debts off and spent on us.' Muhammad ibn al-Hanafiyya did not speak either good or evil of him." He said that Muhammad heard that they were saying, "They have something (i.e. knowledge)." He said, "He stood among us and stated, 'By Allah, we only inherited from the Messenger of Allah صلى الله عليه وسلم what is between these two book-covers [i.e. the Qur'an].' Then he said, 'O Allah, and this page at the end of my sword.' I asked, 'What is the page?' He replied, 'Whoever innovates or gives refuge to an innovator ...'"

Al-Walid ar-Rammah said, "We heard that Muhammad ibn 'Ali left Makka and camped in the ravine of 'Ali. We left Kufa to come to him. We were met by Ibn 'Abbas who was with him in the ravine. He said to us, 'Keep your weapons and say the *talbiya* for 'umra. Then enter the House and perform *tawaf* and run between Safa and Marwa.'"

Wardan said, "I was in the group who were with Muhammad ibn 'Ali. Ibn az-Zubayr had prevented him from entering Makka until he gave him allegiance, which he refused to do. We joined him and he wanted to go to Syria, but 'Abdu'l-Malik would not let him enter it until he had given him allegiance, which he refused to do. We went with him. If he had commanded us to fight, we would have fought with him. We gathered one day and he divided something small between us. Then he praised Allah and said, 'Go to your mounts and fear Allah. You must have what you know to be correct and leave what you dislike. You must attend to yourselves and leave the affair of the common. Remain constant in our business as the heaven and earth are constant. When our command comes, it is as clear as the sun.'"

They said that al-Mukhtar ibn Abi 'Ubayd was killed in 68 AH. At the beginning of 69 AH, 'Abdullah ibn az-Zubayr sent 'Urwa ibn az-Zubayr to Muhammad ibn al-Hanafiyya to tell him that he would leave him alone forever if he gave homage. Otherwise he would return him to prison. He said, "Allah has slain the liar whom you used to summon your supporters and collect the people of Iraq against me. Give allegiance to me. It is war between you and me if you refuse." Ibn al-Hanafiyya said to 'Urwa, "How swift your brother is to cut off kinship and to make light of rights! How heedless he is of Allah hastening the punishment! Your brother does not doubt eternity. He used to praise al-Mukhtar and his gift from me. By Allah, I did not send al-Mukhtar as an agent or helper. If he was a liar, then he kept him close to him for a long time in spite of his lies. If he was other than that then Allah knows best. I do not have any dispute. If there was any dispute, I would not have stayed near him and I would have gone forth to the one who called me. I refused to do that. But here, by Allah, your brother has a contemporary who seeks the like of what your brother seeks, and they both fight for this world: 'Abdu'l-Malik ibn Marwan. By Allah, it seems that you surround your brother with his armies. I think that the vicinity of 'Abdu'l-Malik is better for me than that of your brother. He used to write to me offering what he accepted and calling me to it."

'Urwa asked, "What keeps you from doing that?" He replied, "I did an *istakhara* prayer to Allah. I prefer that to your companion." He said, "I mentioned that to him. Some of the companions of Ibn al-Hanafiyya said, 'By Allah, if you were to command us, we would strike his neck.' Ibn al-Hanafiyya said, 'For what would you strike his neck? He brought a letter from his brother and visited us. There were words between us and him, and we returned him to his brother.

What you have suggested is treachery and there is no good in treachery. If I were to do what you say, there would be fighting in Makka. You know my opinion that if all people except one were to gather against me, I would not fight him.'" So 'Urwa went and told Ibn az-Zubayr what Muhammad ibn al-Hanafiyya had said to him. He said, "By Allah, I do not think that you should concern yourself with him. Let him go. 'Abdu'l-Malik is before him and he will not let him settle in Syria until he gives him allegiance – and Ibn al-Hanafiyya will never give him allegiance until all the people agree on him. If he goes to him he will deal with him for you – and if he imprisons or kills him, you will not be responsible for that." So he appeased Ibn az-Zubayr about him.

Abu't-Tufayl said, "A letter from 'Abdu'l-Malik ibn Marwan was brought to the ravine by messenger and Muhammad ibn al-Hanafiyya read the letter. If 'Abdu'l-Malik had written to one of his own brothers or children, he could not have been more gracious. He said, 'I have heard that Ibn az-Zubayr has constricted you, cut off your kin and made light of your rights unless you give him allegiance. You have attended to yourself and your *deen* and you know best where to do what you do. Syria is here. Settle in it wherever you like. We will honour you, maintain your kinship and acknowledge your due.' Ibn al-Hanafiyya said to his companions, 'We will go there.' He went and they went with him. Kuthayyir was with him and recited:

'You are the Imam of the Truth. We do not doubt that you are
    the one with whom we are pleased and for whom we hope.
You are the son of the best of mankind after the Prophet.
    O son of 'Ali and one who is like 'Ali, travel
until you alight in the land of Kalb and Baliyy.'"

Abu't-Tufayl said, "We went to Ayla and camped and were well received and we reciprocated better still. They loved Abu'l-Qasim very deeply and esteemed him and his companions, and we commanded the correct and forbade the bad – no one was wronged near us nor in our presence. News of this reached 'Abdu'l-Malik and that was hard for him and he discussed it with Qabisa ibn Dhu'ayb and Rawh ibn Zinba' who were close to him. They said, 'We do not think that we should leave him near you. You should make him travel to give allegiance to you or return him to Hijaz.' So 'Abdu'l-Malik wrote to him, 'You have come to our land and camped in part of it.

71

There is a war between me and Ibn az-Zubayr as you know and you have renown and position. I do not think that you should stay within my region without giving me allegiance. If you give me allegiance, then take the hundred ships which come to you from Qilzum. They are yours along with what is in them, You will have 200,000 dirhams: 50,000 immediately and 150,000 later as a duty for you, your children, relatives, clients and those with you. If you refuse, then leave my land for a place in which I have no authority.'

"Muhammad ibn al-Hanafiyya wrote back to him: 'In the Name of Allah, the Merciful, the Compassionate, I praise Allah to you. There is no god but Him.You knew my view on this matter before I came. I do not declare anyone unsuited to it. By Allah, if all of this community were to agree on me except for the people of az-Zurqa', I would never fight them or disassociate with them to make them agree. I camped at Makka fleeing from what was in Madina, and I was a good neighbour to Ibn az-Zubayr while he was a bad one to me. He wanted me to give him allegiance and I have refused to do so until the people agree on either you or him. Then I will support whomever the people support and be like one of them. Then you wrote to me to invite me to your region and I accepted. I camped within your borders. By Allah, I have no dispute with you and my companions are with me. We said, "A land with reasonable prices," and approached your region. Then you wrote what you wrote. We are leaving you, Allah willing.'"

Abu Hamza said, "I was with Muhammad ibn 'Ali and we went from Ta'if to Ayla forty days after the death of Ibn 'Abbas. 'Abdu'l-Malik had written to Muhammad to come to his land with his companions until the people agreed on a leader. When Muhammad came to Syria, 'Abdu'l-Malik informed him, 'Either you give me homage or you leave my land.' There were 7,000 people with him on that day. Muhammad ibn 'Ali requested of him, 'You must guarantee my companions' security.' He did that. Then Muhammad stood up and praised Allah and then said, 'Allah is in charge of all matters and He is their Judge. Whatever Allah wills will be and what He does not will will not be. All that is coming is near at hand. You hasten the matter before it has happened. By the One who has my soul in His hand, among your family are those who fight with the family of Muhammad over something concealed from the people of *shirk* regarding the business of the family of Muhammad – and so the business of the family of Muhammad is delayed. By the one who has the soul of Muhammad in His hand, it will come back to you as it began. Praise be to Allah who has spared your blood and preserved your *deen*! Whoever of you wants to come to his land safe and protected should do so.' So 900 men remained with him. He went into *ihram* for the *'umra* and garlanded the camels and we made for the House. When we wanted to enter the Haram, Ibn az-Zubayr's cavalry stopped us. Muhammad sent to him, 'I left and did not want to fight you. Let us enter and complete our rites. Then we will leave you.' He refused. We had sacrificial camels with us which were garlanded. We returned to Madina and remained there until al-Hajjaj came and killed Ibn az-Zubayr and then went to Basra and Kufa. When he left, we went and completed our rites. I saw the fleas falling off Muhammad ibn 'Ali. When we had finished our rites, we returned to Madina and he died three months later."

Muslim at-Ta'i said, "'Abdu'l-Malik ibn Marwan wrote: 'From 'Abdu'l-Malik, the Amir al-Mu'minin, to Muhammad ibn 'Ali.' When he saw the introduction to the letter he said, 'We belong to Allah and to Him we are returning. The freed ones and the cursed ones of the Messenger of Allah, may Allah bless him and grant him peace, are on the minbars of the people. By the One who has my soul in His hand, things will not remain stable.'"

Abu't-Tufayl said, "We turned around to go back and he gave permission to the clients and those with them of the people of Kufa and Basra to return from Madyan. We went to Makka and camped with him in the ravine in Mina. Only two or three nights had passed before Ibn az-Zubayr told him to leave this camp and not to remain so close to him. Ibn al-Hanafiyya said, 'Be steadfast. There is no steadfastness except by Allah. Whoever is not steadfast in that in which he can find no steadfastness until Allah appoints a way out from it for him is not great. By Allah, I do not desire the sword. If I wanted it Ibn az-Zubayr would not injure me, even If I were alone and he had a group with him. But, by Allah, I do not want this and I think that Ibn az-Zubayr will not confine himself to being a bad neighbour and so I will withdraw from it.' Then he went to Ta'if and had not been there long before al-Hajjaj came to fight Ibn az-Zubayr at the beginning of Dhu'l-Qa'da in 72 AH. He beseiged Ibn az-Zubayr and killed him on Wednesday 17 Jumada al-Akhira. Ibn al-Hanafiyya went on *hajj* that year from Ta'if and then returned to his ravine and camped there."

'Ali ibn Muhammad said, "When Muhammad ibn 'Ali went to the ravine in 72 AH before Ibn az-Zubayr had been killed and al-Hajjaj was besieging him, he sent a message to him that he should give allegiance to 'Abdu'l-Malik. Ibn al-Hanafiyya replied, 'You know what my position was in Makka and about my going to Ta'if and Syria. All of that prevents me from giving allegiance either to Ibn az-Zubayr or to 'Abdu'l-Malik until the people agree on one of them. I am a man who has no dispute. When I see the people disagreeing, I withdraw until they agree. I sought refuge in the most sacred of the lands of Allah in which even the birds are secure but Ibn az-Zubayr was bad to me. So I went to Syria, but 'Abdu'l-Malik disliked having me near and so I went to the Haram. If Ibn az-Zubayr is killed and the people agree on 'Abdu'l-Malik, then I will give you my allegiance.' Al-Hajjaj refused to be satisfied until he gave allegiance to 'Abdu'l-Malik and Ibn al-Hanafiyya refused to do that. Al-Hajjaj refused to let him remain on that basis, but Muhammad continued to stall him until Ibn az-Zubayr was killed."

Sahl ibn 'Ubayd said, "When 'Abdu'l-Malik sent al-Hajjaj to Makka and Madina, he told him, 'You have no authority over Muhammad ibn al-Hanafiyya.' When al-Hajjaj arrived, al-Hajjaj sent to him to threaten him and then said, 'I hope that Allah will give me power over you for a day and then I will act.' He replied, 'You lie, enemy of yourself! Are you not aware that in every day Allah has 360 instants or breaths. I hope that Allah will provide me with some of His instants or breaths and will not give you power over me.' Al-Hajjaj wrote about this to 'Abdu'l-Malik and 'Abdu'l-Malik wrote the same to the emperor of Byzantium who wrote back to him, 'By Allah, this is not part of your treasure nor of the treasure of the people of your house, but it is part of the treasure of the people of a house of prophethood.'"

Al-Hasan ibn Muhammad said, "My father did not give homage to al-Hajjaj. When Ibn az-Zubayr was killed, al-Hajjaj sent for him. He came and al-Hajjaj said, 'Allah has killed the enemy of Allah.' Ibn al-Hanafiyya said, 'When the people give allegiance, I will give allegiance.' He said, 'By Allah, I will kill you!' He replied, 'Do you not know that Allah has 360 instants in every day and in every instant there are 360 more instants. Perhaps He will restrain you in one of His instants.'

"Al-Hajjaj wrote about this to 'Abdu'l-Malik. When his letter came, he liked it and wrote the same to the emperor of Byzantium who had written to him threatening that massive troops were gathered against him. 'Abdu'l-Malik used the same words when writing to the Byzantine emperor. 'Abdu'l-Malik wrote to al-Hajjaj, 'We know that Muhammad does not oppose. He will come to you and give you allegiance, so be gentle towards him.' When the people agreed on 'Abdu'l-Malik and Ibn 'Umar had given allegiance, Ibn 'Umar said to Ibn al-Hanafiyya, 'Nothing remains, so give allegiance.' So Ibn al-Hanafiyya wrote to 'Abdu'l-Malik, 'In the Name of Allah, the Merciful, the Compassionate. To the slave of Allah 'Abdu'l-Malik, the Amir al-Mu'minin, from Muhammad ibn 'Ali. When I saw that the community disagreed, I withdrew from them. When the matter went to you and people gave allegiance to you, I am like a man among them who enters into that into which they enter. I give you allegiance and I give allegiance to al-Hajjaj for you. I have sent my allegiance to you. I have seen that the people have agreed on you. We request you to grant us safe conduct and to give us your pledge of fidelity. There is no good in treachery. If you refuse, the land of Allah is wide.'

"When 'Abdu'l-Malik read the letter, Qabisa ibn Dhu'ayb and Rawh ibn Zinba' said, 'You have no reason to oppose him. If he wanted a split, he would be able to make one. He has submitted and given allegiance so we think that you should write him a pledge and a document of safe conduct – and one for his companions.' So he did that. 'Abdu'l-Malik wrote to him, 'You are praised with us. You are dearer and closer to us in kinship than Ibn az-Zubayr. You have a contract, pledge and guarantee that neither you nor any of your companions will be disturbed. Return to your land and go wherever you please. I will not stop helping you as long as I live.' He wrote to al-Hajjaj commanding him to be good to him. Ibn al-Hanafiyya returned to Madina."

'Abdullah ibn 'Ubaydullah said, "When Muhammad ibn 'Ali returned to Madina and built his house in al-Baqi', he wrote to 'Abdu'l-Malik asking leave to visit him and 'Abdu'l-Malik wrote back to him granting him permission. So he came to him in 78 AH which is the year in which Jabir ibn 'Abdullah died. He came to 'Abdu'l-Malik in Damascus and he granted him permission to visit, allocated a house close to him for him and ensured that he and those with him were given adequate hospitality. He used to visit 'Abdu'l-Malik whenever he wished. Sometimes he sat and sometimes he left. When this had gone on for a month or thereabouts, he spoke to 'Abdu'l-Malik privately and mentioned his kinship to him and mentioned a debt that he owed. 'Abdu'l-Malik promised to pay his debt and told him to present his needs. So Muhammad presented his debt and needs and the requirements of his children, in-laws and clients. 'Abdu'l-Malik granted him all of this but was reluctant to allot something to the clients. Muhammad insisted and so he alloted them a small amount. He spoke to him again and he increased that. There was no request which he did not grant. He asked him for permission to leave and he gave it."

Ibn al-Hanafiyya said, "I went to 'Abdu'l-Malik and he fulfilled my needs and then I bade him farewell. When I was about to leave him, he called out to me, 'Abu'l-Qasim! Abu'l-Qasim!' I came back and he said to me, 'Do you not know that Allah knows the day that you did what you did to the shaykh to wrong him?'" He was referring to when Ibn al-Hanafiyya had seized Marwan ibn al-Hakam on the day of the House and pushed him by his cloak. 'Abdu'l-Malik said, "I was watching him and on that day I still had long hair."

Zayd ibn 'Abdu'r-Rahman said, "I went with Aban ibn 'Uthman to 'Abdu'l-Malik when Ibn al-Hanafiyya was with him. 'Abdu'l-Malik called for the sword of the Messenger of Allah صلعم, and it was brought. He called for a polisher. He looked at it and said, 'I have never seen iron better than it.' 'Abdu'l-Malik said, 'No, by Allah, people have not seen the like of its owner. Muhammad, give me this sword!' Muhammad said, 'Let whichever one of us you think is more entitled take it.' 'Abdu'l-Malik said, 'You have kinship and so each of us has kinship and a right to it.' So Muhammad gave it to 'Abdu'l-Malik and said, 'Amir al-Mu'minin, this man (meaning al-Hajjaj who was with him) has harmed me and made light of my right, including 500 dirhams sent to me in it.' 'Abdu'l-Malik said, 'You have no authority over him!' When Muhammad turned away, 'Abdu'l-Malik said to al-Hajjaj, 'Go after him and soothe his anger.' He caught up to him and said, 'The Amir al-Mu'minin has sent me to soothe your anger. Nothing which vexes you is welcomed.' Muhammad replied, 'Woe to you, Hajjaj. Fear Allah and beware of Allah. There is no morning which comes to people but that Allah has

360 instants in it for every slave of His. If He seizes, He seizes by power – and if He overlooks, He overlooks by forbearance. So beware of Allah.' Al-Hajjaj told him, 'I will give you anything you ask me.' Muhammad asked him, 'You will do it?' – 'Yes,' al-Hajjaj replied. He said, 'I ask you for permanent separation.' Al-Hajjaj mentioned this to 'Abdu'l-Malik. 'Abdu'l-Malik sent a message to Ra's al-Jalut and told him what Muhammad had said, saying, 'A man from among us said something which I have only heard coming from him.' He told him what Muhammad had said. Ra's al-Jalut replied, 'This could only have come from a house of prophethood.'"

Ibrahim reported that al-Hajjaj wanted to put his foot on the Maqam and Ibn al-Hanafiyya rebuked him and forbade him to do so.

Salim ibn Abi'l-Ja'd said, "I heard that Muhammad ibn al-Hanafiyya entered the Ka'ba and prayed two *rak'ats* in each corner, eight in total."

Muhammad ibn al-Hanafiyya said, "This world will not come to an end until the people quarrel about their Lord."

Sufyan at-Tammar said, "I saw Muhammad ibn al-Hanafiyya dye his hair with henna and black dye on the Day of *Tarwiyya* while he was in *ihram*." Thawr said the same.

Sufyan at-Tammar said, "I noticed that Ibn al-Hanafiyya had more hair on his body on his right side."

Sulayman ash-Shaybani said, "I saw Muhammad ibn al-Hanafiyya wearing a yellow rough silk shawl at 'Arafa." Abu Ishaq ash-Shaybani said the same.

Rishdin said, "I saw Muhammad ibn al-Hanafiyya wearing a black turban with its end hanging down a handspan or less."

Abu Idris said, "Muhammad ibn al-Hanafiyya asked me, 'What prevents you from wearing rough silk/wool? There is no harm it.' I replied, 'There is silk in it.'"

Abu Idris said, "I saw that Ibn al-Hanafiyya used henna and black dye and I asked him 'Did 'Ali use to dye?' He said, 'No.' I asked, 'So why do you use it?' He replied, 'It makes me look younger for the women.'"

Salih ibn Maysam said, "I saw the trace of henna on the hand of Muhammad ibn al-'Ali, Ibn al-Hanafiyya, and asked him, 'What is this?' He said, 'I was putting henna on my mother.'"

It is reported from Abu Ya'la that Muhammad ibn al-Hanafiyya used to henna his mother and comb her hair.

'Abdu'l-Wahib ibn Ayman said, "I saw Muhammad ibn al-Hanafiyya dying with henna and I saw him with kohl around his eyes. I saw him wearing a black turban."

'Abdu'l-Wahib ibn Ayman said, "My father sent me to Muhammad ibn al-Hanafiyya. I visited him and he had kohl around his eyes and his beard was dyed red. I went back to my father and said, 'You sent me to an effeminate shaykh!' He said, 'Son of an uncircumcised woman, that is Muhammad ibn 'Ali!'"

Mundhir ath-Thawri reported that Ibn al-Hanafiyya used to drink *nabidh* made in an earthenware jug.

Al-Mundhir said, "We were with Ibn al-Hanafiyya and he wanted to do *wudu'*. He was wearing leather socks. He removed them and wiped over his feet."

Abu 'Umar reported that Ibn al-Hanafiyya used to perform *ghusl* on the two *'ids* and on Fridays and at ash-Shi'b. He said that he used to have a *ghusl* after cupping.

Rishdin ibn Kurayb said, "I saw Ibn al-Hanafiyya wearing a ring on his left hand."

'Abdullah ibn Muhammad said, "I heard Ibn al-Hanafiyya say in 81 AH, 'I am 65 and I have now lived longer than my father who died when he was 63.' Ibn al-Hanafiyya died that same year, in 81 AH."

Zayd ibn as-Sa'ib said, "I asked Abu Hashim 'Abdullah, the son of Muhammad ibn al-Hanafiyya, 'Where was your father buried?' He replied, 'In Baqi'.' I asked, 'What year?' He replied, 'At the beginning of 81 AH when he was not yet 65.'"

Abu Hashim 'Abdullah ibn Muhammad ibn al-Hanafiyya said, while indicating part of Baqi', "It was the year of the flood. There was a tremendous flood in Makka. When we placed him in al-Baqi', Aban ibn 'Uthman ibn 'Affan led the prayer over him. At that time he was governor of Madina for 'Abdu'l-Malik. He said, 'My brother, what do you think?' I said, 'Aban will not pray over him unless he has asked that of us.' Aban said, 'You are more entitled to conduct your father's funeral. Choose whomever you wish to pray over him.' We said, 'Go forward and pray,' and he went forward and led the prayer over him."

'Umaymir al-Aslami said, "Abu Hashim said on that day, 'We know that the Imam is more entitled to lead the prayer. Were it not for that, we would have chosen you.'"

'Umar ibn 'Ali ibn Abi Talib, the elder

His mother was as-Sahba', the sister of Umm Habib bint Rabi'a. She was a captive taken by Khalid ibn al-Walid when he attacked the Taghlib tribe at 'Ayn at-Tamr. His children were Muhammad, Umm Musa, and Umm Habib, whose mother was Asma' bint 'Aqil ibn Abi Talib. 'Umar related *hadiths*, and there were a number of his children who were related from and will be mentioned later.

'Ubaydullah ibn 'Ali ibn Abi Talib

His mother was Layla bint Mas'ud of Tamim. 'Ubaydullah ibn 'Ali went from the Hijaz to al-Mukhtar in Kufa and asked him for something but he did not give to him. He said, "Do you have a letter from the Mahdi?"– "No." He imprisoned him for some days and then let him go. He said, "Leave us." He went to Mus'ab ibn az-Zubayr in Basra, fleeing from al-Mukhtar, and stayed with his maternal uncle, Nu'aym ibn Mas'ud at-Tamimi. Mus'ab ordered 100,000 dirhams be given to him. Then Mus'ab commanded people to prepare for their enemy and set a time to go. Then he formed an army, set out from his military camp and appointed 'Ubaydullah ibn 'Umar over it. When Mus'ab left, 'Ubaydullah ibn 'Ali stayed behind with his uncles while his uncle Nu'aym ibn Mas'ud went with Mus'ab.

When Mus'ab reached Basra, the Banu Sa'd went to 'Ubaydullah ibn 'Ali and said, "We are your maternal uncles and are a part of you. Move to us. We want to honour you." He moved and stayed among them. They offered him allegiance as khalif which he disliked. He said, "People, do not be hasty. Do not do this." They refused. Mus'ab heard about this and he wrote to 'Ubaydullah ibn 'Umar and informed him that he had neglected 'Ubaydullah ibn 'Ali who was accepting the people's allegiance to him. Then Mus'ab summoned his uncle Nu'aym ibn Mas'ud and said, "I honoured you and was good to you in our relations. What moved you to do what you did regarding your nephew? You left him behind in Basra conspiring with people and deceiving them." He swore by Allah that he had not done so and did not know anything at all about it. Mus'ab believed him and said, "I have written to 'Ubaydullah ibn 'Umar censuring him for his negligence in this business." Nu'aym ibn Mas'ud said, "Do not provoke anyone against him. I will take care of him for you and send him to you."

Nu'aym went to Basra, and the Banu Hanzala and Banu 'Amr ibn Tamim gathered. He took them to the Banu Sa'd and said, "By Allah, you have not done well in this matter. You only desire the destruction of all Tamim! Give me my nephew." They reproached one another and then handed him over and he took him to Mus'ab. He said, "Cousin, what moved you to do what you did?" 'Ubaydullah swore by Allah that he did not desire any of that and had no knowledge of it until they had done it. He said that he had disliked it and had refused it. Mus'ab accepted what he said. Then Mus'ab commanded that the master of his vanguard, 'Abbad al-Habati, should advance against the troops of al-Mukhtar. He went with 'Ubaydullah ibn 'Ali and camped at al-Madhar. The army of al-Mukhtar came and camped opposite them and the people of Mus'ab attacked them at night, but the army was killed and only a few escaped. 'Ubaydullah ibn 'Ali was killed that night.

Sa'id ibn al-Musayyab ibn Hazn

His mother was Umm Sa'id bint Hakim ibn Umayya as-Sulamiyya. His children were Muhammad, Sa'id, Ilyas, Umm 'Uthman, Umm 'Amr and Fatikha, whose mother was Umm Habib bint Abi Karim; and Maryam by an *umm walad*.

Sa'id reported that when his grandfather Hazn came to the Prophet صلعم, he asked, "What is your name?"– "Hazn," he replied. He said, "Rather you are Sahl." He said, "Messenger of Allah, my parents gave me that name and I am known by it among people." The Prophet صلعم was silent. Sa'id ibn al-Musayyab said, "The people of our house continued to be known as as the Hazniyya."

'Ali ibn Zayd said, "Sa'id ibn al-Musayyab was born four years after 'Umar was given allegiance and he died at the age of 84."

His son said that Sa'id was born two years before 'Umar's death and that he died when he was 72.

Muhammad ibn 'Umar said, "I think that people agree that Sa'id ibn al-Musayyab was born two years before the end of 'Umar's khalifate. It is related that he listened to Umar, but I do not see any of the people of knowledge thinking that this is correct, even if they report it."

Sa'id ibn al-Musayyab said, "I was born when there were two

years remaining of the khalifate of 'Umar ibn al-Khattab." 'Umar was khalif for ten years and four months.

Sa'id ibn al-Musayyab said, "I heard a sentence from 'Umar which no one alive except me heard. When 'Umar saw the Ka'ba, he said, 'O Allah, You are Peace and peace is from You.'"

Sa'id ibn al-Musayyab said, "I heard 'Umar say on the minbar, 'I do not find anyone who has had intercourse without having had a *ghusl* afterwards, whether or not he has ejaculated, but that I punish him.'"

Bukayr ibn al-Ashajj said that Sa'id ibn al-Musayyab was asked, "Did you meet Umar ibn al-Khattab?" He said, "No."

Malik reported that he heard that Sa'id ibn al-Musayyab said, "I used to travel for days and nights in quest of a single *hadith*."

Sa'id ibn al-Musayyab said, "There is not anyone left with more knowledge of every decision which the Messenger of Allah صلى الله عليه وسلم made, every decision of Abu Bakr and every decision of 'Umar than me." My father said, "I think that he also said, 'And every decision that 'Uthman made.'"

When someone asked az-Zuhri about the ones from whom Sa'id ibn al-Musayyab took his knowledge, he said, "Zayd ibn Thabit. He also sat with Sa'd ibn Abi Waqqas, Ibn 'Abbas and Ibn 'Umar, and visited the wives of the Prophet, 'A'isha and Umm Salama. He listened to 'Uthman ibn 'Affan, 'Ali, Suhayb and Muhammad ibn Maslama, and many of his transmitters go back to Abu Hurayra whose daughter he married. He listened to the companions of 'Umar and 'Uthman. He said, 'No one has better knowledge of the decisions of 'Umar and 'Uthman than me.'"

Yahya ibn Sa'id said, "Ibn al-Musayyab was said to be the principal transmitter from 'Umar." Layth said, "Because he had the best memory of the people regarding his rulings and judgements."

Qudama ibn Musa al-Jumahi said, "Sa'id ibn al-Musayyab gave *fatwas* while the Companions of the Messenger of Allah صلى الله عليه وسلم were still alive."

Muhammad ibn Yahya ibn Hayyan said, "Sa'id ibn al-Musayyab was the the most eminent of those in Madina in his time, superior to them in *fatwa*. He was called 'the *faqih* of the *fuqaha'*.'"

Makhul said, "Sa'id ibn al-Musayyab was the scholar of the scholars."

Ibn Abi'l-Huwayrith said that he saw Muhammad ibn Jubayr asking Sa'id ibn al-Musayyab for a *fatwa*.

Abu 'Ali ibn Husayn was heard to say, "Sa'id ibn al-Musayyab had the most knowledge of people of the traditions before him and had the greatest understanding in reaching an opinion."

Maymun ibn Mihran said, "I came to Madina and asked who was the person with the most *fiqh* there and I was sent to Sa'id ibn al-Musayyab, and so I asked him."

Shihab ibn 'Abbad al-'Asari said, "I went on *hajj* and we went to Madina and asked who was the most knowledgeable of the people of Madina. They said, 'Sa'id ibn al-Musayyab.'"

Malik ibn Anas said, "'Umar ibn 'Abdu'l-'Aziz did not give a decision until he had asked Sa'id ibn al-Musayyab. He sent a man to him to ask him something but instead he summoned him. He came and entered. 'Umar said, 'The messenger made a mistake. We sent him to ask you in your assembly.'"

Malik ibn Anas said, "'Umar ibn 'Abdu'l-'Aziz used to say, 'There is no scholar in Madina who does not bring me what he knows without bringing what is with Sa'id ibn al-Musayyab.'"

'Imran ibn 'Abdullah al-Khuza'i said, "Sa'id ibn al-Musayyab asked for me and I was assigned to him. He said, 'My father sat with me while Mu'awiya was khalif and asked me about this and this, and I told him such and such.'"

'Imran said, "By Allah, I do not see anything reaching his ear at all without his heart retaining it," meaning Sa'id ibn al-Musayyab.

'Abdullah ibn Ja'far and others said, "'Abdullah ibn az-Zubayr appointed Jabir ibn al-Aswad 'Awf az-Zuhri over Madina and he called people to give allegiance to Ibn az-Zubayr. Said ibn al-Musayyab said, 'No, not until the people agree.' He gave him sixty lashes. Ibn az-Zubayr heard about that and wrote to Jabir censuring him. He said, 'We have no quarrel with Sa'id. Leave him alone.'"

'Abdu'l-Wahid ibn Abi 'Awn said, "Jabir ibn al-Aswad, the governor of Madina had married a fifth wife before the *'idda* of the fourth was finished. When he had Said ibn al-Musayyab beaten, Sa'id shouted at him when the whipper was taking him away, 'By Allah, you have not stayed with the Book of Allah. Allah says *'Marry what seems good to you, two, three and four.'* You have married a fifth before the end of the *'idda* of the fourth. It is only a few nights more, so do what you think best.' What you dislike will come to you. It was not long before Ibn az-Zubayr was killed."

'Umar ibn Habib said, "I was sitting with Sa'id ibn al-Musayyab one day when things were difficult for me and I was burdened by a debt. I sat with Ibn al-Musayyab, not knowing where to go. A man came to him and said, 'Abu Muhammad, I had a dream.' – 'What was it?' he asked. He said, 'I dreamt that I took 'Abdu'l-Malik and laid him on the ground and then stretched him out and put four pegs into his back.' He said, 'You did not dream that.' He said, 'Yes I did.' He said, 'I will not tell you its meaning unless you tell me the truth.' He said, 'Ibn az-Zubayr had the dream and sent me to you.' He said, 'If his dream is true, 'Abdu'l-Malik will kill him and four will emerge from the loins of 'Abdu'l-Malik who will be khalifs.'" He said, "I visited 'Abdu'l-Malik ibn Marwan in Syria and told him what Sa'id ibn al-Musayyab had said. That cheered him up and he asked about Sa'id and how he was and I told him. He ordered that my debts be paid and I received good from him."

Isma'il ibn Abi Halim said, "I dreamt of a man looking like 'Abdu'l-Malik ibn Marwan urinating in the *qibla* of the mosque of the Prophet four times. I mentioned it to Sa'id ibn al-Musayyab who said, 'If your dream was true, then there will be four khalifs from his loins.'"

Muhammad ibn 'Umar said, "Sa'id ibn al-Musayyab was one of the best people at interpreting dreams. He took that from Asma' bint Abi Bakr and Asma' took it from her father Abu Bakr."

Sharik ibn Abi Namir said, "I said to Ibn al-Musayyab, 'I dreamt that my teeth fell into my hands and then I threw them away.' Ibn al-Musayyab said, 'If your dream was true, then you have thrown your teeth from the people of your house.'"

Muslim al-Khayyat said, "A man said to Ibn al-Musayyab, 'I dreamt that I urinated in my hand.' He said, 'Fear Allah. You are married to a relative.' He investigated this and discovered she was a woman with whom he had relationship established by suckling. Another man came and said, 'Abu Muhammad, I dreamt that I was urinating on the root of a fig tree.' He said, 'Look into the identity of the one to whom you are married. You are married to a relative.' He found that she was a woman whom it was not lawful for him to marry."

Muslim al-Khayyat reported that Ibn al-Musayyab said that a man said to him, "I dreamt that a dove landed on the minaret of the mosque." He said, "Al-Hajjaj will marry the daughter of 'Abdullah ibn Ja'far ibn Abi Talib."

Muslim al-Khayyat said, "A man came to Ibn al-Musayyab and said, 'I dreamt that a billy goat came running from Thaniyya.' He responded, 'Sacrifice! Sacrifice!' He said, 'I have sacrificed.' He said, 'The son of Umm Sila',' and the news of his death came soon afterwards." Muhammad ibn 'Umar said, "The son of Umm Sila' was one of the clients of the people of Madina who strove with people."

A man of Qara said, "A man of Fahm told Ibn al-Musayyab that he had dreamt he was plunging into the Fire. He said, 'If your dream is true, then you will not die until you travel on the sea and then you will be killed.' He went to sea and nearly lost his life. Then he was killed at Qudayd by the sword."

Al-Husayn ibn 'Ubaydullah said, "I wanted children but did not have any. I told Ibn al-Musayyab, 'I dreamt that an egg was thrown into my lap.' Ibn al-Musayyab said, 'The chicken is foreign, so look for a non-Arab captive.' I then had a child by her when I had no children."

'Uthaym ibn Nastas said, "I heard Sa'id ibn al-Musayyab tell a man who had told him his dream, 'You have had a good dream.'"

Sharik ibn Abi Namir reported that Ibn al-Musayyab said, "Dried dates in a dream indicate provision in every case and fresh dates in their time indicates provision."

Muslim al-Khayyat reported that Ibn al-Musayyab said, "The fetter in a dream represents firmness in the *deen*." A man said to him, 'O Abu Muhammad, I dreamt that I was sitting in the shadow and I went into the sunlight.' Ibn al-Musayyab said, 'By Allah, if your dream is true, you will leave Islam.' He said, 'Abu Muhammad, I dreamt that I was brought out until I was in the sunlight and then I was cast aside.' He said, 'You will be forced into disbelief.' He went out in the time of 'Abdu'l-Malik ibn Marwan and was captured and forced to disbelieve and then he came to Madina and reported that.

It is related from 'Abdullah ibn Ja'far and from other companions of ours that 'Abdu'l-'Aziz ibn Marwan died in Egypt in Jumada 84 AH, so 'Abdu'l-Malik made a pledge of allegiance to his sons al-Walid and Sulayman and wrote to the lands to accept this. His governor over Madina at that time was Hisham ibn Isma'il al-Makhzumi. He summoned the people to give allegiance to them and the people did so. He summoned Sa'id ibn al-Musayyab to give them allegiance and he refused, saying, "Not until I have investigated him." So Hisham gave him sixty lashes and paraded him in hair breeches as far as the top of ath-Thaniya. When he had him brought back, he asked, "Where are you taking me?" He replied, "To jail." He said, "By Allah, were it not that I think I might incur crucifixion, I would not ever wear these breeches." So they imprisoned him and he wrote to 'Abdu'l-Malik to inform him of his opposition and what he had ordered. 'Abdu'l-Malik wrote back censuring him for what he had done to him and stating, "By Allah, I am in greater need of maintaining ties with Sa'id than beating him. We know that Sa'id is not involved in any schism or opposition."

Al-Miswar ibn Rifa'a said, "Qabisa ibn Dhu'ayb went to 'Abdu'l-Malik ibn Marwan with Hisham's letter which mentioned that he had flogged Sa'id and paraded him. Qabisa said. 'Amir al-Mu'minin, Hisham has acted to your detriment by this. He beat Ibn al-Musayyab and paraded him. By Allah, Sa'id would never be duplicitous nor stubborn. Even if Sa'id did not give allegiance, he is not one from whom schism or danger is feared for Islam and its people. He is one of the people of the Community and *Sunna*.' Qabisa added, 'Write to him, Amir al-Mu'minin, about this.' 'Abdu'l-Malik said, 'You write to him for me telling him my opinion and how I disagree with what Hisham did.' So Qabisa wrote to Sa'id. When he read the letter, Sa'id said, 'Allah is between me and the one who wronged me.'"

'Abdullah ibn Yazid al-Hudhali said, "I visited Sa'id ibn al-Musayyab in prison. When a sheep was slaughtered for him, he put its skin on his back. After that they put moist herbs on it. When he looked at his arms, he said, 'O Allah, help me against Hisham.'"

Muhammad said, "Abu Bakr ibn 'Abdu'r-Rahman visited Sa'id ibn al-Musayyab in prison and he began to speak to Sa'id and said to him, 'Your mother is upset about you.' He said, 'Abu Bakr, fear Allah and prefer Him to other than Him.' So Abu Bakr began to repeat, 'Your mother is upset about you and you are not being reasonable.' Sa'id said, 'You, by Allah, are blind in eyes and heart.' Abu Bakr left and Hisham sent for him and said, 'Has Sa'id ibn al-Musayyab relented since we beat him?' Abu Bakr said, 'By Allah, he has a stronger voice since you did what you did. Leave the man alone.' Then the letter of 'Abdu'l-Malik reached Hisham censuring him for beating Sai'd ibn al-Musayyab. He said, 'What harm would it have done you if you had left Sa'id alone?' Hisham repented for what he had done to Sa'id and let him go."

Muhammad ibn 'Umar said that Abu Umayya Aslam, the client of Banu Makhzum, told him: "Sa'id ibn al-Musayyab's daughter prepared a lot of food when he was imprisoned and sent it to him. When the food arrived, Sa'id called me and said, 'Go to my daughter and tell her not to ever send the like of this again. This is just the excuse which Hisham needs to remove my property so that I will need what they have. I do not know why I am imprisoned. Look to the food which I eat in my house and send it me.' So she sent him that and he used to fast all the time."

'Imran ibn 'Abdullah al-Khuza'i said, "I think that the the life of Sa'id ibn al-Musayyab is less significant to him in the Essence of Allah than the life of a fly."

More than one person reported that 'Abdu'l-Malik ibn Marwan had Sa'id ibn al-Musayyab flogged and made him stand at al-Harra clothed in hair breeches. Sa'id said, "By Allah, if I knew that they would not do anything more than beat me, I would not wear the breeches for you. I feared that they would kill me and so I said, 'Breeches are more concealing than anything else.'"

Sufyan related that a man of the family of 'Umar said, "Sa'id ibn al-Musayyab was told, 'Curse the Umayyads.' He replied, 'O Allah, exalt Your *deen*, give victory to Your friends and disgrace Your enemies for the well-being of the community of Muhammad صلعم.'"

'Ali ibn Zayd said, "I said to Sa'id ibn al-Musayyab, 'Your people claim that what keeps you from the *hajj* is that you vowed to Allah that when you saw the Ka'ba you would ask Allah to curse Ibn Marwan.' He said, 'I did not do so and I have never prayed a prayer without invoking Allah against them. I performed *hajj* and *'umra* for some years. One *hajj* and *'umra* were written for me. I see that some people borrow money and make *hajj* and *'umra* and then die without settling the debt. I prefer the *jumu'a* prayer to *hajj* or voluntary *'umra*.'"

'Ali said that he told al-Hasan that and he said, "He did not say anything. If it has been as he said, then the Companions of the Messenger of Allah صلعم would not have made *hajj* or *'umra*."

Abu Yunus al-Qazzi said, "I entered the mosque of Madina and Sa'id was sitting alone. I said, 'What is up with him?' I was told, 'It is forbidden for anyone to sit with him.'"

'Imran said, "Sa'id ibn al-Musayyab had some 30,000 dirhams of his stipend in the treasury. He refused to take it, saying, 'I have no need of it until Allah judges between men and the Banu Marwan.'"

'Ali ibn Zayd reported that Sa'id ibn al-Musayyab was asked, "Why does al-Hajjaj not send for you or punish you?" He replied, "By Allah, I do not know – unless it is that one day I entered the mosque with my father and he was praying a prayer and began not to fully do his *ruku'* or prostration. I took a handful of pebbles and threw them at him." He claimed that al-Hajjaj said, "After that I continued to do the prayer well."

'Imran ibn 'Abdullah al-Khuza'i said, "'Abdu'l-Malik ibn Marwan went on *hajj*. When he came to Madina, he stopped at the door of the mosque and sent a man to Sa'id ibn al-Musayyab to call him but not to provoke him. The messenger came to him and said, 'The Amir al-Mu'minin is standing at the door wanting to speak to you.' He said, 'The Amir al-Mu'minin has no need of me and I have no need of him. His need for me is what has not been accomplished.' The messenger returned to him and told him. He said, 'Go back to him and say that I want to speak to him, but do not provoke him.' So he returned to him and said, 'Respond to the Amir al-Mu'minin.' Sa'id repeated what he had said to him the first time. The messenger said to him, 'If it were not that he had already given me instructions about how to treat you, I would have taken him your head! The Amir al-Mu'minin asks to speak to you and you say the like of this!' He replied, 'If he wants to do something good to me, then you can have it. If it is other than that, I will not move until he does what he decides.' He went and told him and 'Abdu'l-Malik said, 'May Allah have mercy on Abu Muhammad! He refuses everything but steadfastness.'"

'Amr ibn 'Asim said, "When al-Walid ibn 'Abdu'l-Malik became khalif, he came to Madina and entered the mosque. He saw a shaykh around whom people had gathered and asked, 'Who is this?' – 'Sa'id ibn al-Musayyab,' was the reply. When he had sat down, he sent for him and the messenger went to him: 'Respond to the Amir al-Mu'minin.' He said, 'Perhaps you make a mistake with my name or else he sent you to someone else.' So the messenger returned and told him. He grew angry and went for him. The people turned to him and said, 'Amir al-Mu'minin, the *faqih* of the people of Madina, the shaykh of Quraysh and the friend of your father. No king has attacked him before you came to him.' They kept on at him until he turned away from him."

Maymun ibn Mihran said, "'Abdu'l-Malik came to Madina and could not sleep in his midday nap and woke up. He told his attendant, 'Look in the mosque to see if there are any of the people of Madina with whom we can talk.' He went and Sa'id ibn al-Musayyab was there in a circle of his. He stood and looked at him and then beckoned to him and pointed to him with his finger and then turned away, but Sa'id did not move or follow him. He said, 'I think he is clever.' He came close to him, beckoned and pointed at him. He said, 'Didn't you see me pointing at you?' He replied, 'What do you need?' He said, 'The Amir al-Mu'minun has woken up and said, "Look in the mosque for someone with whom I can talk." So respond to the Amir al-Mu'minin.' He asked, 'Did he send you to me?' – 'No,' he replied. 'He said, "Go and look for one of the people of Madina." I did not see anyone more suitable than you.' Sa'id said, 'Go and tell him I am not one of those with whom he chats.' The attendant went off saying, 'I think this shaykh is mad.' He went to 'Abdu'l-Malik and told him, 'I only found a shaykh in the mosque and I pointed to him but he did not get up. I said, "The Amir al-Mu'minin said to look to see whether there was anyone in the mosque with whom he could converse." He said, "I am not one of those who chat with the Amir al-Mu'minin." He told me, "Tell him."' He said, 'That is Sa'id ibn al-Musayyab. Leave him be.'"

Abu Bakr ibn 'Abdullah said, "When Sa'id ibn al-Musayyab was asked about these people, he said, 'I say about them what my Lord says to me, *"Our Lord, forgive us and our brothers ..."* (59:10) to the end of the *ayat.*'"

'Uthman ibn Hakim said, "I heard Sa'id ibn al-Musayyab say, 'I have not heard of any harm happening to my family for the last thirty years.'"

'Abdu'r-Rahman ibn Harmala reported that Sa'id ibn al-Musayyab said. "I have not met people coming from the prayer for the last forty years."

'Imran ibn 'Abdullah reported that Sa'id ibn al-Musayyab said, "I have not missed the group prayer for forty years nor seen the backs of their necks."

'Imran said, "Sa'id used to go to the market a lot."

Ibn Shihab reported about Sa'id ibn al-Musayyab: "I said to him, 'Why don't you go to the desert?' and I described the desert to him, its life and its darkness (*'atam*). Sa'id said, 'What about being present at the evening prayer (*'atama*)?'"

'Imran ibn 'Abdullah reported that Sa'id ibn al-Musayyab said, "I have remained in a house of Madina although sometimes I go to visit a daughter of mine."

Bishr ibn 'Asim said, "I asked Sa'id, 'My uncle, will you not come out and eat garlic with your people?' He replied, 'I seek refuge with Allah, nephew, that I should leave twenty-five prayers for five prayers! I heard Ka'b say, "Shaytan is with the one who is alone and he is further away from two."'"

Ibn Harmala reported from Sa'id ibn al-Musayyab that he complained about his eyes and they told him, "If you would go out, Abu Muhammad, to 'Aqiq and look at the greenery, you would find that a relief." He said, "Then how can I be present at *'Isha'* and *Subh*?"

Abu Hazim said, "I heard Sa'id ibn al-Musayyab say, 'In the days of al-Harra there was none of Allah's creatures in the mosque but me. The people of Syria entered in a group saying, "Look at this mad old man." No time of the prayer came but that I heard an *adhan* coming from the grave and then I came and repeated the *iqama* and prayed and there was no one in the mosque but me.'"

Muhammad, Sa'id's son, said, "In the days of al-Harra, Sa'id ibn al-Musayyab was in the mosque and did not give allegiance and did not leave. He used to pray *jumu'a* with them and go out to the *'Ids*. The people were fighting and looting while he was in the mosque and only came out at night.

Ibn Harmala said, "I asked Burd, the client of Ibn al-Musayyab, 'What was the prayer of Ibn al-Musayyab in his house like? As for his prayer in the mosque, we know it.' He said, 'By Allah, I do not know. He prayed a lot and recited *Sad*.'"

'Ata' reported that when Sa'id ibn al-Musayyab entered the mosque on Fridays, he did not speak until the prayer was finished and the Imam had left. Then he prayed some *rak'ats* and then turned to his companions and was asked questions.

Yazid ibn Hazim said, "Sa'id ibn al-Musayyab used to fast all the time, and when the sun set, he would be brought a drink from his house to the mosque and drink it."

'Asim ibn al-'Abbas al-Asadi said, "Sa'id ibn al-Musayyab warned people to fear Allah."

'Asim ibn al-'Abbas said, "I heard Ibn al-Musayyab recite the Qur'an in the night on his camel and he did a lot."

'Asim said, "I heard Sa'id ibn al-Musayyab saying, 'In the Name of Allah, the Merciful, the Compassionate' aloud."

'Asim said, "Sa'id ibn al-Musayyab liked to listen to poetry but did not recite it."

'Asim said, "I saw Sa'id ibn al-Musayyab walking barefoot in the day, and I saw him wearing breeches."

'Asim said, "I saw that Sa'id ibn al-Musayyab did not let his nails grow long, and I saw Sa'id trim his moustache until it was almost shaved, and I saw him shake hands with all he met. I saw that Sa'id disliked laughing a lot and I saw that Sa'id always did wudu' after he had urinated. When he did *wudu'*, he put his fingers between each other."

Da'ud ibn Abi Hind reported that Sa'id ibn al-Musayyab used to not like to name children with the names of the Prophets.

'Ali ibn Zayd said, "Sa'id ibn al-Musayyab used to pray voluntary prayers on his mount."

'Imran said, "I could not count the number of times I saw Sa'id ibn al-Musayyab wearing Harawi shirts. He used to wear these rich white cloaks. He used to fraternise with people in the two *'Ids*: *Fitr* and *Nahr*."

'Imran ibn 'Abdullah al-Khuza'i said, "Sa'id ibn al-Musayyab did not argue with anyone. Even if a man wanted his cloak, he would throw it to him."

Qatada said, "I asked Sa'id ibn al-Musayyab about praying on carpets and he said, 'It is something new.'"

Ghunayma, the slavegirl of Sa'id, said, "Sa'id did not allow his daughter to play with ivory dolls. He let her play with drums."

Qatada said, "Sa'id ibn al-Musayyab was invited and he accepted. Then he was invited and he accepted. Then he was invited a third time and he threw some pebbles at the messenger."

Muhammad ibn Hilal reported that Sa'id ibn al-Musayyab said, "There is no commerce I prefer to dealing with linen since there are no oaths taken regarding it."

'Abdu'r-Rahman ibn Harmala reported that he said to Sa'id ibn al-Musayyab, "I found a man drunk. Do you think that I should report him to the Sultan?" Sa'id replied, "If you can conceal him with your garment, then do so."

'Imran ibn 'Abdullah al-Khuza'i said, "In Ramadan drinks were brought to the mosque of the Prophet but no one dared to bring a drink to Sa'id ibn al-Musayyab so that he could drink. When drink was brought from his house, he drank it. If nothing was brought from his house, he did not drink anything until after he had left."

Sufyan reported that one of the Madinans asked Sa'id ibn al-Musayyab about clipping dirhams. He said, "It is part of causing corruption on the earth."

Az-Zuhri reported that Sa'id ibn al-Musayyab used to pray with his legs wrapped up, and when he wanted to prostrate, he unwrapped his garment, prostrated, and then stood up again and wrapped his garment.

Burd, the client of Ibn al-Musayyab said to Sa'id ibn al-Musayyab, "I have not seen anyone do better than what they did." Sa'id asked, "What did they do?" He replied, "One of them prayed *Dhuhr* and remained praying until *'Asr.*" Sa'id said, "Woe to you, Burd! By Allah, that is not worship. Do you know what worship is? Worship is to reflect on the command of Allah and to refrain from the things which Allah has forbidden."

Al-Hakam ibn Abi Ishaq said, "I was sitting with Sa'id ibn al-Musayyab and he said to a client of his, 'Fear Allah and do not falsely attribute things to me as the client of Ibn 'Abbas did with Ibn 'Abbas.' I said to his client, 'That is because I do not know whether Abu Muhammad prefers Ibn az-Zubayr or the people of Syria.' Sa'id heard us and said, 'O Iraqi! which of them do you love best?' The reply was, 'I prefer Ibn az-Zubayr to the people of Syria.' He said, 'And should I not seize you now and say, "This is a Zubayri?"' I said, 'You asked me and I told you, so tell me which of them you prefer?' He replied. 'I do not like either of them.'"

Yahya ibn Sa'id said, "Sa'id ibn al-Musayyab often used to say, 'O Allah, grant safety! Grant safety!'"

'Ali ibn Zayd reported that Sa'id ibn al-Musayyab said, "I have reached the age of 80 and there is nothing I fear more than women." He had gone blind.

'Imran ibn 'Abdullah said that Sa'id ibn al-Musayyab said, "I do not fear anything for myself as much as I fear women." They said, "O Abu Muhammad, the like of you does not desire women nor do they desire you." He said, "That is not what I am saying to you." He was an old blind man.

'Abdullah ibn Yazid al-Hudhali reported that Sa'id ibn al-Musayyab used to fast all the time and would break his fast during the days of *tashriq* in Madina.

Sa'id's son reported that he said, "A small number of dependents is one of the two eases."

'Ali ibn Zayd said, "Sa'id ibn al-Musayyab said to me, 'Tell your guide to stand and look at the face and body of that man.' I said, 'Go and look,' and the man had a black face. He came back and said, 'I saw the face of a black man and the body of a white man.' He said, 'This man cursed that group: Talha, az-Zubayr and 'Ali. I forbade him to do it, but he refused and so I invoked against him. I said, "If you are a liar, then Allah will blacken your face." So his face became black.'"

Yahya ibn Sa'id said, "Ibn al-Musayyab was asked about an *ayat* in the Book of Allah and he replied, 'I do not say anything about the Qur'an.'"

Ibn Harmala said, "Sa'id ibn al-Musayyab met a Qurayshi man with a lamp on a rainy night and greeted him: 'How are you, Abu Muhammad?' He replied, 'I praise Allah.' When the man reached his house, he entered and said, 'We will send a lamp with you.' He said, 'I have no need of your light. I prefer the light of Allah to your light.'"

Ibn Harmala reported that Sa'id ibn al-Musayyab said, "Do not say 'little copy of the Qur'an' or 'little mosque'. Esteem what Allah has esteemed. All that Allah has esteemed is good and great."

Ibn Harmala said, "I went out to ad-Dabh and found a drunkard there. I looked after him and brought him into my house. I met Sa'id ibn al-Musayyab and I said, 'If a man is found drunk, should I take him to the ruler so that the *hadd* can be carried out on him?' He said to me, 'If you are able to shield him with your garment, do so.' I returned to my house and the man had come around. When he saw me, I recognised shame in him and I asked, 'Are you ashamed? If you had been taken yesterday, you would have received the *hadd* and you would have been like a corpse among people whose testimony is not allowed!' He said, 'By Allah, I will never do it again!'" Ibn Harmala said, "I saw that his state was good after that."

Yasar ibn'Abdu'r-Rahman said that Sa'id ibn al-Musayyab married a daughter of his to his nephew for a dowry of two dirhams.

'Imran ibn 'Abdullah al-Khuza'i said, "Sa'id ibn al-Musayyab married a daughter of his to a young man of Quraysh. In the evening he told her, 'Put on your wedding garment and follow me.' So she put on her garment and then he told her, 'Pray two *rak'ats*.' She prayed two *rak'ats* and he prayed two *rak'ats*. Then he sent for her husband and put her hand in his, and said, 'Go with her.' He took her to his house. When his mother saw her, she asked, 'Who is this?' He replied, 'My wife, the daughter of Sa'id ibn al-Musayyab. He has given her in marriage to me.' She said, 'My face is unlawful to yours if you go to her before I have prepared what is prepared for women of Quraysh.' So he gave her to his mother and she was good to her and then the marriage was consummated."

'Ubayd ibn Nastas said, "I saw Sa'id ibn al-Musayyab wearing a black turban whose end hung down behind him, and I saw him wearing a waist-wrapper, shawl and leather socks."

Muhammad ibn Hilal said that he saw Sa'id ibn al-Musayyab wearing a turban consisting of a fine hat with a white turban round it which had a red end which hung behind him a span.

'Uthaym said, "I saw Sa'id ibn al-Musayyab wearing a black turban on the *Fitr* and *Adha* and he had on a red burnoose." Others stated the same.

'Abdullah ibn Yazid al-Hudhali said, "I saw that sometimes Sa'id had his waistwrapper untied in the prayer and sometimes tied."

Khalid ibn Ilyas said, "I saw Sa'id ibn al-Musayyab wearing a shirt which came down to the middle of his calves, and its sleeves went over the ends of his fingers, and then there was a cloak over the shirt measuring five cubits and a span."

Isma'il ibn 'Imran said, "Sa'id ibn al-Musayyab wore a shawl whose tassels were brocaded." He said, "We found it more lasting."

Muhammad ibn Hilal said, "I did not see Sa'id ibn al-Musayyab wearing a garment which was not white."

Sa'id ibn Muslim said, "I used to see Sa'id ibn al-Musayyab wearing trousers. I saw that he had thick hair which he parted."

'Uthaym ibn Nastas said, "I saw Sa'id ibn al-Musayyab at *'Isha'* wearing trousers and a cloak."

Muhammad ibn Hilal said that he saw that Sa'id ibn al-Musayyab had no prostration mark between his eyes.

Muhammad ibn Hilal said, "I saw that Sa'id ibn al-Musayyab did not trim his moustache too much, taking a fair amount from it."

Muhammad ibn 'Amr said, "Sa'id ibn al-Musayyab did not use hair dye." But Muhammad ibn Hilal said, "I saw Sa'id ibn al-Musayyab dye his beard yellow."

Abu'l-Ghusn reported that he saw Sa'id ibn al-Musayyab with a white head and beard.

Rabi'a ibn 'Uthman said, "I saw that Sa'id ibn al-Musayyab did not alter his hair colour."

Hisham ibn Ziyad Abu'l-Miqdam said, "I saw that Sa'id ibn al-Musayyab used to pray in his sandals."

Yahya ibn Sa'id said, "Whenever 'Abdullah ibn 'Umar was asked about something which was not clear to him he would say, 'Ask Sa'id ibn al-Musayyab. He used to sit with the righteous.'"

Yahya ibn Sa'id said, "I met people who were in awe of books. Even if we were to write for one day, we would write down a lot of the knowledge of Sa'id and his opinion."

Yahya ibn Sa'id said, "When Sa'id ibn al-Musayyab passed by the school, he said of the boys, 'These are the people who will come after us.'"

'Abdu'r-Rahman ibn Harmala said, "I saw Sa'id ibn al-Musayyab when he was ill praying lying down indicating with his head to his chest, and not raising anything to his head. Sa'id said, 'When the sick person cannot sit, he indicates and does not raise anything to his head.'"

'Abdu'r-Rahman ibn Harmala said, "I visited Sa'id ibn al-Musayyab when he was very ill and he was praying *Dhuhr.* He was lying down on that day, indicating, and I heard him recite *ash-Shams.*"

'Abdu'r-Rahman ibn Harmala said, "I was with Sa'id ibn al-Musayyab at a funeral and a man said, 'Ask forgiveness for him.' He said, 'Whatever their *rajaz* poet says. I have forbidden my people to recite *rajaz* for me or to say, "Sa'id ibn al-Musayyab has died." Those who have already gone to my Lord are enough for me. I have forbidden them to remember me with incense. If I am good, there is nothing more fragrant with Allah than goodness.'"

Yahya ibn Sa'id reported that Sa'id ibn al-Musayyab said, "I have given three orders to my people when I die: no *rajaz* poet nor fire should follow me, and I should be taken quickly. If there is good for me with my Lord, it will be better than what is with you."

Abu Hazim said, "Sa'id ibn al-Musayyab said in his final illness, 'When I die, do not put a tent over my grave, do not carry me on a red cloth, do not follow me with fire, and do not injure anyone on my account. It is enough for me that you convey me to my Lord. None of your *rajaz* poets should follow me.'"

'Abdu'r-Rahman ibn al-Harith al-Makhzumi said, "Sa'id ibn al-Musayyab fell ill and his pain was intense. Nafi' ibn Jubayr visited him and he fainted. Nafi' ibn Jubayr said, 'Turn his bed towards *qibla*.' They did so. He recovered and asked, 'Who told you to turn my bed towards *qibla*? Did Nafi' ibn Jubyar command that?' Nafi' said, 'Yes.' Sa'id said to him, 'If I were not already on the *qibla* and the religion, turning my bed would not benefit me.'"

Nafi' ibn Jubayr said, "I visited Sa'id ibn al-Musayyab while he was lying on his bed and I said to his son Muhammad, 'Turn his bed towards the *qibla*.' He said, 'No, do not do it. I was born on it and I will die on it and I will be resurrected on it, Allah willing.'"

Al-Mughira ibn 'Abdu'r-Rahman said that he visited Sa'id ibn al-Musayyab with his father and he fainted and so he turned his face towards *qibla*. When he came around he asked, "Who did this to me? Am I not a Muslim who turns my face to Allah wherever I am?"

Zur'a ibn 'Abdu'r-Rahman said, "I saw Sa'id ibn al-Musayyab on the day he died and he said, 'Zur'a, I testify to you that my son Muhammad should not injure anyone on my account. It is enough that four men carry me to my Lord. No shouter should follow me saying what is not true about me.'"

Yahya ibn Sa'id said, "When Sa'id ibn al-Musayyab was dying, he left some dinars and said, 'O Allah, You know that I have not left these except to preserve my lineage and *deen* by them.'"

'Abdu'l-Hakam ibn 'Abdullah said, "I saw Sa'id ibn al-Musayyab on the day he died and I saw his grave being sprinkled with water."

'Abdu'l-Hakam ibn 'Abdullah said, "Sa'id ibn al-Musayyab died in Madina in 94 AH at the age of 75 when al-Walid ibn 'Abdu'l-Malik was khalif. The year in which Sa'id died is called 'the Year of the *Fuqaha'* because of the great number of *fuqaha'* who died during it."

They said, "Sa'id ibn al-Musayyab was comprehensive, reliable with a lot of *hadith*, a firm *faqih*, a trustworthy *mufti*, scrupulous, respected and venerated."

'Abdullah ibn Muti' ibn al-Aswad

His mother was Umm Hisham bint Abi'l-Khiyar 'Abd Yall ibn 'Abd Manaf. His children were Ishaq and Ya'qub, whose mother was Rayta bint 'Abdullah; Muhammad and 'Imran, whose mother was Umm 'Abdu'l-Malik bint 'Abdullah ibn Khalid; Ibrahim and Burayha, whose mother was an *umm walad*; Isma'il and Zakariyya, whose mother was an *umm walad*; Fatima, whose mother was Umm Hakim bint 'Abdullah; and Umm Salama and Umm Hisham, whose mother was a daughter of Kharash ibn Umayya.

'Abdullah was born in the time of the Messenger of Allah صلعم. He had property and a well between as-Suqya and al-Abwa' which was known as the Well of Ibn Muti' to which people came.

Umayya ibn 'Abdullah reported that 'Abdullah ibn Muti' wanted to flee from Madina during the civil war with Yazid. 'Abdullah ibn 'Umar heard of this and went to him and said, "Where are you going, cousin?" He replied, "I will never give him allegiance." He entreated, "Cousin, do not do it. I testify that I heard the Messenger of Allah صلعم say, 'Whoever dies without allegiance, dies the death of the *Jahiliyya*.'"

Abu 'Awn said, "When Husayn ibn 'Ali left Madina for Makka, he passed by Ibn Muti' who was digging his well. He asked Husayn, 'Where are you going, may my mother and father be your ransom?' – 'Makka,' he replied and he mentioned that his party there had written to him. Ibn Muti' said to him, 'May my mother and father be your ransom, give us the pleasure of your company and do not go to them!' Husayn refused and Ibn Muti' said to him, 'This well of mine is leaking and today sometimes there is no water in the bucket. Would you supplicate to Allah to bless us in it?' He said, 'Get some of its water.' He brought him some of its water in a bucket and he drank from it and then he spat in it and put it back in the well and it became sweet and abundant."

Ibrahim ibn 'Abdu'r-Rahman reported, "When Yazid agreed to send the armies to Madina which eventually resulted in the Battle of al-Harra, 'Abdullah ibn Ja'far ibn Abi Talib spoke to him about them and made him relent towards them. He said, 'You fight with them yourself.' He said, 'I will send the first army and command them to bypass Madina on the way to Ibn az-Zubayr. He has declared war on us. They will not attack the people of Madina. If they affirm obedience, he will leave them and pass on to Ibn az-Zubayr. If they refuse, he will fight them.' 'Abdullah ibn Ja'far said, 'I think this is an immense relief.' He wrote to three of Quraysh: 'Abdullah ibn Muti', Ibrahim ibn Nu'aym an-Nahham, and 'Abdu'r-Rahman ibn 'Abdullah ibn Abi Rabi'a. The people of Madina entrusted their affair to these three. He told them what had been agreed and said, 'Accept what has happened and ensure peace and security for yourselves. Do not oppose the armies. Let them pass.' They refused to do this and said, 'They will never enter Makka thanks to us.'"

Sa'id ibn Abi Hind said, "They entrusted their command to 'Abdullah ibn Muti', and he was the one who took charge in this matter."

Ibrahim ibn 'Abdu'r-Rahman reported, "Quraysh argued about appointing an amir among themselves. At that time those who had no equal in age and honour were: Ibn Muti', Ibrahim ibn Nu'aym, Muhammad ibn Abi Jahm and 'Abdu'r-Rahman ibn 'Abdullah."

Ishaq ibn Yahya reported, "I was informed by someone who saw 'Abdullah ibn Muti' on the *minbar* when the vanguard of the people could be seen at Makhid and the army at Dhu Khushub. He spoke from the *minbar* and said, 'O people! You must have fear of Allah and strive in His command. Beware of losing heart, of conflict and disagreement. Submit to death. By Allah, there is no flight or escape. By Allah, it is better for a man to be slain advancing and expecting a reward than to be killed running away. Do not think that the people will endure. Expend yourselves against them. They dislike death as much as you dislike it.'"

'Isa ibn Talha said, "I asked 'Abdullah ibn Muti', 'How were you saved at the Battle of al-Harra when you saw what I saw of the victory of the Syrians?' 'Abdullah said, 'As you say, if we had stood fast for a month, not one of us would have been killed. When what happened happened to us and we were penetrated and the people retreated, I recalled the words of al-Harith ibn Hisham:

"I know that if I fight alone, I will be killed
– and my martyrdom will not harm my enemy."

'So I concealed myself and then joined Ibn az-Zubayr later. I had great admiration for Ibn az-Zubayr since they did not reach him for three months, and they found him hard to defeat, and had to set up catapults against him. No one fought to defend Ibn az-Zubayr except a small group and some other Kharijites. There were two thousand men with us at the Battle of al-Harra, all of them armed, and yet we were not able to resist for a single day.'"

'Isa ibn Talha said, "'Abdu'l-Malik ibn Marwan mentioned 'Abdullah ibn Muti' and said, 'He was saved from Muslim ibn 'Uqba at the Battle of al-Harra and then joined Ibn az-Zubayr in Makka and survived. He went to Iraq and often opposed us on every side, but I think that he should be pardoned along with others among his people. I fought them for my self.'"

'Amir ibn 'Abdullah ibn az-Zubyar said, "'Abdullah ibn Muti' was with 'Abdullah ibn az-Zubayr throughout. When the people of Makka gave allegiance to 'Abdullah ibn az-Zubayr, he was the swiftest of people to give his allegiance along with 'Abdullah ibn Safwan, al-Harith ibn 'Abdullah, and 'Ubayd ibn 'Umayr. All of the people who were present gave him their allegiance and he appointed al-Mundhir ibn az-Zubayr over Madina, 'Abdullah ibn Muti' over Kufa and 'Abdullah ibn Abi Rabi'a over Basra."

'Urwa said, "Al-Mukhtar ibn Abi 'Ubayd pressed 'Abdullah ibn az-Zubayr to allow him to go to Iraq and he gave him permission. Ibn az-Zubayr wrote to Ibn Muti', his governor of Kufa, to make known al-Mukhtar's position with him. When al-Mukhtar reached Kufa he went to Ibn Muti' and showed him the instructions of Ibn az-Zubayr – but he criticised him secretly, called people to Ibn al-Hanafiyya, encouraged people against Ibn Muti' and set up his own following. He amassed a large cavalry until the number of his calvary was equal to that of the police of Ibn Muti', and then he attacked them and Ibn Muti' fled."

Ya'qub ibn 'Utba reported that his father said, "Ibn Muti' was informed that al-Mukhtar was turning the people of Kufa against him. So he sent Iyas ibn al-Mudarib al-'Ijli, the chief of the police, to arrest him. Iyas seized him and took him to the castle, but the Shi'a and their clients rescued him from their hands. Iyas was killed and his men defeated. Ibn Muti' put Rashid ibn Iyas in charge of the police and al-Mukhtar sent a group of al-Khashabiyya against him.

They killed him and sent his head to al-Mukhtar. When 'Abdullah ibn Muti' saw what had happened, he requested safe conduct for himself and his property so that he could join Ibn az-Zubayr. Al-Mukhtar granted him that and he went to Ibn az-Zubayr."

Umm Bakr al-Miswar said, "Ibn Muti' fled without obtaining a safe conduct, but al-Mukhtar did not pursue him. He said, 'I obey Ibn az-Zubayr. Why did Ibn Muti' leave?'"

Muslim reported, "Ibn Muti' told 'Umar ibn Sa'd ibn Abi Waqqas, 'You preferred Hamadhan and Rayy to killing your cousin.' 'Umar said, 'They were matters decided by heaven. I excused myself to my cousin before the battle, but he refused to do other than what he did.' When Ibn Muti' fled from al-Mukhtar, al-Mukhtar took his men to the house of 'Umar ibn Sa'd and killed him and his son in the worst possible manner."

'Abdullah ibn Farwa said, "When Ibn Muti' left Kufa, al-Mukhtar sent a letter to 'Abdullah ibn az-Zubayr in which he attacked Ibn Muti'. He said, 'I came to Kufa in obedience to you and I saw that 'Abdullah ibn Muti' was flattering the Umayyads and I could not confirm him in that since I have my responsibilities to you. He left Kufa and I and those with me obey you.' Ibn Muti' came to Ibn az-Zubayr and told him a different story and said that al-Mukhtar was calling people to Ibn al-Hanafiyya. Ibn az-Zubayr did not accept his statement and wrote to al-Mukhtar, 'Much has been said to me about you regarding something of which I think you are innocent, but the heart cannot help being affected by what people say. If you return, I will restore you to better than what you think. We accept you and believe you.' Then he confirmed him as governor over the people in Kufa."

After that, 'Abdullah ibn Muti' stayed in Makka with 'Abdullah ibn az-Zubayr until he died, shortly before Ibn az-Zubayr was killed.

'Abdu'r-Rahman ibn Muti'

His mother was Umm Kulthum bint Mu'awiya ibn 'Urwa. His children were Hisham, Muhammad the elder, Muti', 'Abdu'l-Malik and Muhammad the younger, whose mother was Umm Salama bint Mas'ud ibn al-Aswad. His *kunya* was Abu 'Abdullah.

Their brother, Sulayman ibn Muti'

His mother was Umm Hisham Amina bint Abi'l-Khiyar 'Abd Yalil. He had a son Muhammad, whose mother was one of the Banu Nadr. He was killed in the Battle of the Camel.

'Abdu'r-Rahman ibn Sa'id ibn Yarbu'

His mother was Umm 'Ubayd Arwa bint 'Arki. His children were 'Uthman, Abu Bakr, Sa'id, and 'Umar, whose mother was ar-Rabi'a bint Yazid ibn 'Abdullah; 'Abbas, Khalid and Yahya, whose mother was Umm al-Hakam bint Bal'a'; 'Ikrima, whose mother was Umm al-Fadl bint 'Ikrima; Muhammad, by an *umm walad*; and Umm Hakim, whose mother was 'Atika bint Sa'd. His *kunya* was Abu Muhammad. He died in 109 AH at the age of 80. He was reliable in *hadith*.

'Amr ibn 'Uthman ibn 'Affan

His mother was Umm 'Amr bint Jundub. His children were 'Uthman and Khalid, whose mother was Ramla bint Mu'awiya ibn Abi Sufyan; 'Abdullah the elder, who is al-Mutraf, whose mother was Hafsa bint 'Abdullah ibn 'Umar; 'Uthman the younger, whose mother was 'Umara ibn al-Harith; 'Umar, al-Mughira, Abu Bakr, 'Abdullah the younger and al-Walid, by *umm walads*; and 'A'isha and Umm Sa'id, by an *umm walad*. 'Amr related from his father and Usama ibn Zayd. He was reliable and has *hadiths*.

Sa'id al-Maqburi said, "I saw the sons of the Companions of the Messenger of Allah صلعم using black dye, including 'Amr ibn 'Uthman ibn 'Affan.

'Umar ibn 'Uthman ibn 'Affan

His mother was Umm 'Amr bint Jundub. His children were Zayd and 'Asim, by an *umm walad*. He related from Usama ibn Zayd, and az-Zuhri related from him. He had a house in Madina. He had few *hadiths*.

Aban ibn 'Uthman ibn 'Affan

His mother was Umm 'Amr bint Jundub. His children were Sa'id – by whom he has his *kunya* – whose mother was the daughter of

'Abdullah ibn 'Amir ibn Kurayz; 'Umar, 'Abdu'r-Rahman and Umm Sa'id, whose mother was Umm Sa'id bint 'Abdu'r-Rahman ibn al-Harith; and 'Umar the younger, Marwan and Umm Sa'id the younger, by an *umm walad*.

Muhammad ibn 'Umar reported from one of his companions, "Yahya ibn al-Hakam was governor of Madina for 'Abdu'l-Malik. He was somewhat stupid and went to see 'Abdu'l-Malik without obtaining his permission. 'Abdu'l-Malik asked, 'What brought you to me without my permission? Who did you leave in charge of Madina?' 'Aban ibn 'Uthman,' he replied. He said, 'You must not return there.' So 'Abdu'l-Malik confirmed Aban over Madina and wrote to him to that effect. Aban dismissed 'Abdullah ibn Qays as *qadi* and appointed Nawfal ibn Musahiq *qadi* of Madina. Aban was governor of Madina for seven years. He made *hajj* with the people twice. While he was governor, Jabir ibn 'Abdullah and Muhammad ibn al-Hanafiyya died and he prayed over them in Madina. Then 'Abdu'l-Malik dismissed Aban and appointed Hisham ibn Isma'il over Madina."

Kharija ibn al-Harith said, "Aban had a lot of white splotches. He used to dye the places on his hands, but did not dye them on his face."

Muhammad ibn 'Umar said, "He was very hard of hearing."

Bilal ibn Abi Muslim said, "I saw that Aban ibn 'Uthman had a slight prostration mark between his eyes."

Da'ud ibn Sinan, the client of 'Umar ibn Tamim al-Hakami, said, "I saw that Aban ibn 'Uthman dyed his beard yellow with henna."

Al-Hajjaj ibn Furafisa reported that a man said, "I visited Aban ibn 'Uthman and he said, 'Whoever says in the morning: "There is no god but Allah alone, the Immense. Glory be to Allah the Immense and by His praise. There is no strength nor power except by Allah," will be safe from every affliction that day.' At that time Aban was suffering from semi-paralysis. He said, 'The *hadith* is as I have reported it. The day this happened I did not say it.'"

Muhammad ibn 'Umar said, "Aban was afflicted by semi-paralysis in the year before he died. It is said that it happened to him in Madina because of his severity. He died in Madina while Yazid II was khalif. Aban related from his father. He was reliable and had *hadiths*."

Sa'id ibn 'Uthman ibn 'Affan

His mother was Fatima bint al-Walid ibn 'Abd Shams of Makhzum, whose mother was Asma' bint Abi Jahl, whose mother was Arwa bint Abi'l-'Is, whose mother was Ruqayya bint al-Harith, whose mother was Ruqayya bint Asad, whose mother was Khalida bint Hisham ibn 'Abd Manaf. He had a son Muhammad, whose mother was Ramla bint Abi Sufyan. He had few *hadiths*.

Humayd ibn 'Abdu'r-Rahman ibn 'Awf

His mother was Umm Kulthum bint 'Uqba ibn Abi Mu'ayt, whose mother was Arwa bint Kurayz, whose mother was Umm Hakim al-Bayda' bint 'Abdu'l-Muttalib, whose mother was Fatima bint 'Amr whose mother was Sakhra bint 'Abd, whose mother was Takhmir bint 'Abd, whose mother was Salma bint 'Amira. His *kunya* was Abu 'Abdu'r-Rahman. His children were Ibrahim, al-Mughira, Habbaba the elder, Umm Kulthum, and Umm Hakim, whose mother was Juwayyria bint Abi 'Amr ath-Thaqafiyya; 'Abdullah, whose mother was Qurayba bint Muhammad; 'Abdullah the younger, Bilal, 'Awna, Hukayma the younger and Burayha, by an *umm walad*; 'Abdu'l-Malik, by an *umm walad*; and 'Abdu'r-Rahman, by an *umm walad*.

Humayd said, "I saw 'Umar and 'Uthman praying *Maghrib* in Ramadan when they saw the darkness of night and then they broke the fast afterwards."

Muhammad ibn 'Umar said, "We consider the *hadiths* of Malik to be firmer. Humayd did not see 'Umar nor listen to him, as his age and death indicate. But he listened to 'Uthman, because he was his maternal uncle. He used to visit him as a child and as an adult. He related from Sa'id ibn Zayd, Mu'awiya ibn Abi Sufyan, Abu Hurayra, and an-Nu'man ibn Bashir. He was reliable, a scholar with a lot of *hadiths*. He died in Madina in 95 AH when he was 73."

Muhammad ibn Sa'd said, "I heard someone say that he died in 105 AH. This is a mistake. It could not have been like that, either with regard to his age or his transmission. 95 AH is more likely and more likely to be correct. Allah knows best."

Abu Salama ibn 'Abdu'r-Rahman ibn 'Awf

His mother was Tumadir bint al-Asbagh, the first Kalbite woman to marry a Qurayshi. His children were Salama, by whom he takes his *kunya*; Tumadir, whose mother was an *umm walad*; Hasan, Husayn, Abu Bakr, 'Abdu'l-Jabbar, 'Abdu'l-'Aziz, Na'ila and Salima, whose mother was Umm Hasan bint Sa'd; 'Abdu'l-Malik and Umm Kulthum the younger, whose mother was an *umm walad*; Umm Kulthum the elder, who married Bishr ibn Marwan and whose mother was Umm Uthman bint 'Abdullah; Umm 'Abdullah, Tumadir the younger and Asma', whose mother was Burayha bint 'Abdu'r-Rahman; and 'Umar, whose mother is not named.

When Sa'id ibn al-As was appointed over Madina by Mu'awiya for the first time, he made Abu Salama *qadi* of Madina. When Sa'id was dismissed and Marwan appointed over Madina for the second time, he dismissed Abu Salama and appointed his brother Mus'a ibn 'Abdu'r-Rahman as *qadi* and chief of police.

Muhammad ibn 'Abdullah said, "Abu Salama ibn 'Abdu'r-Rahman came to us in Basra during the amirate of Bishr ibn Marwan. He was a man with a fresh face like a Heraclean dinar."

Ash-Sha'bi said, "Abu Salama ibn 'Abdu'r-Rahman came to us in Kufa, and walked between me and Abu Burda and we asked him, 'Who has the most *fiqh* among those you left behind in your land?' He said, 'The man who is between you two.'"

Muhammad ibn Hilal reported that he saw Salama ibn 'Abdu'r-Rahman dyeing with henna. Ibn Abi Uways said, "his head and beard." Sa'd ibn Ibrahim said that he saw Abu Salama ibn 'Abdu'r-Rahman using black dye. He used woad.

Muhammad ibn 'Amr reported that Abu Salama saw him wearing a yellow silk/wool cloak.

Az-Zuhri reported that Abu Salama ibn 'Abdu'r-Rahman heard Hassan ibn Thabit ask Abu Hurayra: "Did you hear the Messenger of Allah say, 'Hassan, respond to the Messenger of Allah صلعم. O Allah, support him with the Spirit of Purity.'?" Abu Hurayra said, "Yes."

Muhammad ibn 'Umar said, "Abu Salama related from his father, Zayd ibn Thabit, Abu Qatada, Jabir ibn 'Abdullah, Abu Hurayra, Ibn 'Umar, 'Abdullah ibn 'Amr, Ibn 'Abbas, 'A'isha and Umm Salama.

He was reliable, a *faqih* with a lot of *hadith*. He died in Madina in 94 AH at the age of 72 while al-Walid I was khalif. This is more reliable than the statement that he died in 104 AH."

Mus'ab ibn 'Abdu'r-Rahman ibn 'Awf

His *kunya* was Abu Zurara. His mother was Umm Hurayth, one of the captives of Bahra'. His children were Zurara – the source of his *kunya* – and 'Abdu'r-Rahman, whose mother was Layla bint al-Aswad; Mus'ab, whose mother was an *umm walad*; Umm al-Fadl, whose mother was Umm Sa'id bint al-Makhariq; and Fatima and Umm 'Awn, whose mother was Umm Kulthum bint 'Ubaydullah.

They said, "When Marwan ibn al-Hakam was appointed over Madina during the khalifate of Mu'awiya for the second time, he put Mus'ab in charge of its police and appointed him *qadi* of Madina. He was severe on suspects. The governors of Madina were the ones who chose the *qadis* and appointed them."

'Amr ibn Dinar said, "Mus'ab ibn 'Abdu'r-Rahman joined 'Abdullah ibn az-Zubayr and remained with him. When 'Amr ibn az-Zubayr came to Makka, wanting to fight 'Abdullah ibn az-Zubayr, 'Abdullah ibn az-Zubayr sent Mus'ab ibn 'Abdu'r-Rahman to him with some people. His companions ran away from him and captives were taken. He fled and entered the house of Ibn 'Alqama and shut it against him and Mus'ab ibn 'Abdu'r-Rahman and his men surrounded him."

Abu 'Awn said, "We fought al-Husayn ibn Numayr. Mus'ab sent out al-Miswar with an armed party from Madina against him. We were fighting and al-Miswar was wearing his armour. Mus'ab ibn 'Abdu'r-Rahman was charging them ferociously. They attacked us and breached our line. Al-Miswar said to Mus'ab ibn 'Abdu'r-Rahman, 'Cousin, do you not see what they have inflicted on us?' He asked, 'What should be done, Abu 'Abdu'r-Rahman?' He said, 'We will ambush them. I hope that Allah will give us victory over them. Select some men from among those who are firm.' Mus'ab and some of his companions concealed themselves and ambushed them. Only one of their men escaped by running away. The news reached al-Miswar and he was happy about that."

Abu 'Awn said, "I was sitting with al-Miswar and I heard Ibn Safwan say, 'O Abu 'Abdu'r-Rahman, we are delighted with what

Mus'ab did to those people who injured us!' Al-Miswar said, 'They deserved it! O Allah, make Mus'ab last for us! He is the most harmful to our enemies.' Al-Miswar said, 'That was the case.'"

'Abbad said, "I can see myself in one of the battles we had with al-Husayn ibn Numayr when he sent a squadron against us which included 'Abdullah ibn Mas'ada al-Fazari. They inflicted great injury on us. I saw my father furious against them. He said, 'What kind of war is this? This is women's work!' He shouted to Mus'ab, 'Abu Zurara! Attack with us!' Mus'ab attacked like an enraged camel and my father attacked too. I followed them and some of us with resolve stood firm. I saw the swords grow sluggish for a time and it was as if the men were wandering with their arms moving like cucumbers – until we reached 'Abdullah ibn Mas'ada. Mus'ab dealt him a blow and his sword cut through his armour to his thigh. My father's son struck him on the arm on the other side and inflicted another wound. We did not see him come out to meet us after that. He stayed wounded in their camp until they retreated."

Abu 'Awn said, "We used to recognise those killed by Mus'ab ibn 'Abdu'r-Rahman among those killed by others by his reach. I saw the place where Ibn Mas'ada al-Fazari made his stand when he was fighting on that day. When they retreated, the dead of the Syrians were counted and I found fourteen whom Mus'ab ibn 'Abdu'r-Rahman had killed, seven of whom we could tell by his reach, and his reach was his leap.

'Abdullah ibn 'Urwa said, "Ibn az-Zubayr and his people killed many of the companions of al-Husayn ibn Numayr, but for a while a man would be killed by someone in concealment and so no one would see who had killed him." Then he said, "Mus'ab ibn 'Abdu'r-Rahman sallied forth one day when Ibn az-Zubayr was the ruler. He killed five people with his own hand and then returned, and his sword was bent. He recited:

'We took it out white and brought it back red,
    and it was bent after being straight.'

My father said, 'One blow from Mus'ab and someone is orphaned.'"

Abu 'Awn said, "When some stones struck the cheek and left temple of al-Miswar, he passed out and we carried him off. The news reached Ibn az-Zubayr and he came running over to us and was one of those who carried him. We met Mus'ab ibn 'Abdu'r-Rahman and 'Ubayd ibn 'Umayr. Then he died and they buried him. Mus'ab ibn 'Abdu'r-Rahman died a short time after that. That was after al-Husayn ibn Numayr was in Makka. When al-Miswar ibn Makhrama and Mus'ab died, Ibn az-Zubayr made supplication for them and the people gave him allegiance as khalif. Before that he had thought that the matter was based on consultation with them. His motto before the deaths of al-Miswar and Mus'ab had been, 'No judgement except for Allah.'"

Mus'ab died in Makka in 64 AH. He was reliable with few *hadiths*.

Talha ibn 'Abdullah ibn 'Awf

His mother was Fatima bint Muti' ibn al-Aswad. His children were Muhammad – by whom he takes his *kunya*, 'Atika and Tayba, whose mother was Hisn bint Abi Uthayla; 'Imran whose mother was Umm Ibrahim bint al-Miswar ibn Makhrama, whose mother was Juwayriya bint 'Abdu'r-Rahman ibn 'Awf; Umm 'Abdullah, whose mother was Amatu'r-Rahman bint al-Miswar; Ibrahim, Umm Ibrahim, Umm Abiha and Rubayha, whose mother was Hind bint 'Abdu'r-Rahman; 'Abdullah, whose mother was Fakhita bint Kulayb; 'Umar, whose mother was an *umm walad*; and a woman whom he married to Marwan ibn Muhammad before he was khalif and she died while married to him.

Talha ibn 'Abdullah was appointed over Madina. Sa'id ibn al-Musayyab said about him, "His like has never been appointed over us before." He was generous and magnanimous. Al-Farazdaq came to Madina and praised him and praised others of Quraysh. He started with him and so he gave him a thousand dinars. Then he came to others and they began to ask, "How much did Talha give him?" – "A thousand dinars," it was said Then he went to another and they began to ask, "How much did Talha give him?" – "A thousand dinars," it was said. They did not want to give less than that and expose themselves to the tongue of al-Farazdaq, but they began to be reluctant to give what Talha had given him. People were saying, "Is Talha making things difficult for people?"

When Talha had money, he opened his door and his companions and people visited him, and he fed them. When he had nothing, he locked his door and no one came to him. Some of his family said to him, "There is nothing in the world worse than your companions. They come to you when you have something, but when you have nothing, they do not come to you." He said, "There are no better companions in the world than them. If they came to us in times of hardship, we would want to burden ourselves on their behalf. When they hang back until something comes to us, that is correctness and charity on their part."

Talha listened to his uncle, 'Abdu'r-Rahman ibn 'Awf, Abu Hurayra and Ibn 'Abbas. He was reliable with a lot of *hadiths*. He died in Madina in 97 AH when he was 72.

Musa ibn Talha ibn 'Ubaydullah

His mother was Khawla bint al-Qa'qa' ibn Ma'bad of Tamim. His children included 'Isa and Muhammad, who was in charge of the people of Kufa in the time when they went to Abu Fudayk al-Khariji. 'Ubaydullah ibn Shibl al-Bajali said to him:

"Ibn Musa may excel. But, O Ibn Musa, both your hands together are not equal to one hand of his."

He was referring 'Umar ibn Musa ibn 'Ubaydullah.

His children also included Ibrahim and 'A'isha, who married 'Abdu'l-Malik ibn Marwan and bore him Bakkar and then she married 'Ali ibn 'Abdullah ibn 'Abbas; Qurayba, whose mother was Umm Hakim bint 'Abdu'r-Rahman ibn Abi Bakr; and 'Imran, whose mother was an *umm walad* called Jayda'. A poet said about him:

"O Junah, if I owe you a debt
    then 'Imran ibn Musa will settle it."

Khalid ibn Sumayr said, "The liar al-Mukhtar ibn Abi 'Ubayd came to Kufa and the notables of the people of Kufa fled from him and came to us here in Basra. Musa ibn Talha was one of them." He said, "People saw him in his time as 'the Mahdi'. People visited him and I was one of those who visited him. He was a silent shaykh of few words and great sorrow and grief. One day he said, 'By Allah, I would prefer to know that *fitna* will end than to having such-and-such. It poses a far greater danger.' A man of the people said, 'Abu Muhammad, what do you fear which is worse than *fitna*?' He said, 'I fear slaughter (*haraj*).' He asked, 'What is slaughter?' He said, 'It is what the Companions of the Messenger of Allah صلعم reported: killing before the Final Hour in which people will not decide on an Imam until the Final Hour is almost upon them while things are like that. By Allah, if we have come to this, I wish that I could be on the top of a mountain not hearing any voice nor answering any of your callers until the caller of my Lord comes for me.' He was silent and then he said, 'May Allah have mercy on 'Abdullah ibn 'Umar (or Abu 'Abdu'r-Rahman – he either used his name or his *kunya*). By Allah, I think that he remained true to the contract of the Messenger of Allah صلعم which he made with him and he was not subverted nor did he change. By Allah, Quraysh did not provoke him in its first civil war.' I said to myself, 'This man faults his father in his murder.'"[1]

They said, "Musa ibn Talha moved to Kufa, settled there and died there in 103 AH. As-Safr ibn 'Abdullah al-Muzani prayed over him. He was in charge of Kufa for 'Umar ibn Hubayra." Muhammad ibn Sa'd and al-Fadl ibn Dukayn said that he died in 104 AH.

'Amr ibn 'Uthman said, "I saw Musa dyeing his hair black." 'Umar ibn Abi Za'ida said the same.

Ishaq ibn Yahya said, "I saw the sleeves of 'Isa and Musa extended four fingers or a span beyond their fingertips."

'Isa ibn 'Abdu'r-Rahman said, "I saw Musa ibn Talha wearing a silk/wool burnouse."

Abu'z-Zubayr al-Asadi said that Musa ibn Talha reinforced his teeth with gold.

Muhammad ibn 'Umar said, "I think that his *kunya* was Abu 'Isa. He was reliable with many *hadiths*."

'Isa ibn Talha

His mother was Su'da bint 'Awf of Murra. His children were Yahya, whose mother was 'A'isha bint Jarir ibn 'Abdullah; Muhammad, whose mother was Umm Habib bint Asma' ibn Kharija'; and 'Isa, whose mother was Umm 'Isa bint 'Iyad ibn Nawfal. He died in the khalifate of 'Umar ibn 'Abdu'l-'Aziz. He was reliable with a lot of *hadiths*.

---

1. Referring to his father, Talha ibn 'Ubaydullah, who was killed at the Battle of the Camel.

Yahya ibn Talha

His mother was Su'da bint 'Awf. His children were Talha, whose mother was Umm Aban or Umm Unas, the daughter of Abu Musa al-Ash'ari, whose brother by his mother was 'Abdullah ibn Ishaq; Ishaq, whose mother was al-Hasna' bint Zabbar; and Salama, 'Isa, Salim and Bilal, who was praised by al-Hazin al-Kinani in the following verse:

> "Bilal ibn Yahya is a clear new moon,
>   and the new moon is not hidden from anyone."

His children also included Muhja', Yahya, Maslama and Umm Muhammad, by *umm walads*; Umm Hakim, Su'da, who married Sulayman ibn 'Abdu'l-Malik, and Fatima whose mother was Sawda bint 'Abdu'r-Rahman ibn al-Harith al-Makhzumiyya.

Ya'qub ibn Talha ibn 'Ubaydullah

His mother was Umm Aban bint 'Utba ibn Rabi'a. His children were Yusuf, whose mother was Umm Humayd bint 'Abdu'r-Rahman, whose mother was Umm Kulthum bint Abi Bakr; Talha, whose mother was Umma al-Hullas bint 'Abdullah; and Isma'il, Ishaq and Abu Bakr, whose mother was Ja'da bint al-Ash'ath al-Kindiyya. He was generous. He was killed in the Battle of al-Harra in Dhu'l-Hijja 63 AH. News of his death and the calamity at al-Harra was brought to Kufa by al-Karawwas ibn Zayd at-Ta'i. 'Abdullah ibn az-Zubayr al-Asadi said on that:

> "By my life, al-Karawwas full of anger,
>   bearing painful news for the Muslims.
> A tale has reached me about Lu'ayy ibn Talib,
>   and my tears have not ceased for the entire night.
> He reports that only widows are left,
>   and blood flows down every hill.
> Lords of Quraysh met and were made to drink
>   a red wine infused with liquid poison.
> How many old grieved women have been left prostrate,
>   their heads split open, their hands outstretched.
> The notion of glorious deeds inspires before it ends,
>   shortly before the clash between the noble and the powerful.

No one with a *sunna* remains beneath the sun – and the one
   who follows whims, the infant, disregards the great.
The houses of a young man like Ya'qub ibn Talha
   are destitute from Rome and Baqi'.
By Allah, this is not a life which is enjoyable and wholesome
   nor is it a swift and easy death."

Zakariyya ibn Talha ibn 'Ubaydullah

His mother was Umm Kulthum bint Abi Bakr as-Siddiq, whose mother was Habiba bint Kharija. His children were Yahya and 'Ubadyullah, whose mother was al-'Aytal bint Khalid; Umm Isma'il and Umm Yahya, whose mother was Umm Ishaq bint Jabala; and Umm Harun, whose mother was an *umm walad*.

Ishaq ibn Talha ibn 'Ubaydullah

His mother was Umm Aban bint 'Utba ibn Rabi'a. His children were 'Abdullah, Abu Bakr and 'Ubaydullah, whose mother was Umm Unas bint Abi Musa al-Ash'ari; Mus'ab, by an *umm walad*; Ya'qub by an *umm walad*; and Hafsa and Umm Ishaq, whose mother was an *umm walad*.

'Imran ibn Talha ibn 'Ubaydullah

His mother was Hamna bint Jahsh. His children were 'Abdullah, Ishaq, Muhammad and Humayd, whose mother was the daughter of Awfa ibn al-Harith.

Muhammad ibn Sa'd ibn Abi Waqqas

His mother was Mariya bint Qays ibn Ma'dikarib. His children were Isma'il, Ibrahim, 'Abdullah, Umm 'Abdullah and 'A'isha, by *umm walads*. He listened to 'Uthman and was reliable with *hadiths* but he does not have a lot of them. He rebelled with 'Abdu'r-Rahman ibn Muhammad ibn al-Ash'ath and was present at the Battle of Dayr al-Jamajim. He was brought to al-Hajjaj ibn Yusuf who executed him. It is reported that his *kunya* was Abu'l-Qasim.

'Amir ibn Sa'd ibn Abi Waqqas

His mother was Umm 'Amir whose name was Makita bint 'Amr. His children were Da'ud, Ya'qub, 'Abdullah, Umm Ishaq, Hafsa, Humayda, Umm Hisham, and Umm 'Ali, whose mother was Umm 'Ubaydullah bint 'Abdullah ibn Mawhab of the Ash'arites. 'Abdullah ibn Mawhab was an ally of Banu Zuhra.

Muhammad ibn 'Umar said that he died in 104 AH. Another said that he died in Madina while al-Walid I was khalif. He was reliable with a lot of *hadiths*.

'Umar ibn Sa'd ibn Abi Waqqas

His mother was Mariya bint Qays ibn Ma'dikarib. His children were Hafs and Hafsa, whose mother was Umm Hafs Maryam bint 'Amir; 'Abdullah the elder, whose mother was an *umm walad* called Salma; 'Abdu'r-Rahman the younger and Umm 'Amr, whose mother was Umm Yahya bint 'Abdullah; Hamza, 'Abdu'r-Rahman, Muhammad, Mughira and Hamza the younger, whose mother was an *umm walad*; Muhammad the younger, al-Mughira and 'Abdullah, by *umm walads*; 'Abdullah the younger, whose mother was from Kinda; Umm Yahya, Umm Alama, Umm Kulthum, Humayda, Hafsa the younger, Umm 'Amr the younger, and Umm 'Abdullah, by *umm walads*.

In Kufa 'Ubaydullah ibn Ziyad appointed 'Umar over Rayy and Hamadhan. When al-Husayn ibn 'Ali came to Iraq, 'Ubaydullah commanded 'Umar ibn Sa'd to go against him with 4,000 soldiers. He said, "Either he will come to me and put his hand in my hand, or else fight him." He refused. He said, "If you do not do it, I will dismiss you from your post and destroy your house." So he agreed to go. He fought Husayn until he was killed. When al-Mukhtar ibn Abi 'Ubayd overcame Kufa, he killed 'Umar ibn Sa'd and his son Hafs.

Mus'ab ibn Sa'd ibn Abi Waqqas

His mother was Khawla bint 'Amr ibn Aws. His children were Zurara, Ya'qub and 'Uqba, whose mother was Umm Hasan bint Farqad; Salama and Umm Hasan, whose mother was Sukayna bint al-Hulays. He was reliable with a lot of *hadiths*. Muhammad ibn 'Umar said that he died in 103 AH.

Ibrahim ibn Sa'd ibn Abi Waqqas

His mother was Zabra'. His sons claim that she was the daughter of al-Harith ibn Ya'mar. She was captured in Siba'. Ibrahim related from 'Ali. He was reliable with many *hadiths*.

Isma'il ibn Sa'd ibn Abi Waqqas

His mother was Umm 'Amir, whose name was Makita bint 'Amr. His children were Yahya, whose mother was a daughter of Sulayman ibn Azhar; Ibrahim, Abu Bakr, Muhammad, Ishaq, Ya'qub, Musa and 'Imran, by various umm *walads*; Umm Yahya, whose mother was an *umm walad*; and Umm Ayyub, whose mother was an *umm walad*.

Ibrahim ibn Nu'aym an-Nahham

His mother was Zaynab bint Hanzala. Zaynab was married to Usama ibn Zayd and he divorced her when he was 14. The Messenger of Allah صلعم began to say, "Who will I direct to a pure girl and I will be his in-law?" The Messenger of Allah began to look at Nu'aym. Nu'aym said, "It seemed that he meant me. So I said, 'Yes.'" So Nu'aym married her and she bore him Ibrahim.

Ibrahim's children were Muhammad, whose mother was the daughter of al-'Abbas ibn Sa'id; Zayd, 'Abdullah, 'Ubaydullah and Abu Bakr, by umm *walads*; and a daughter, whose mother was Ruqayya bint 'Umar ibn al-Khattab, whose mother was Umm Kulthum bint 'Ali ibn Abi Talib, whose mother was Fatima.

Ibrahim was one of the leaders in the Battle of al-Harra and he was killed that day. While he was with Musrif ibn 'Uqba, Marwan ibn al-Hakam passed by his body and saw that his hand was over his private parts. He said, "By Allah, he guards it in death as he guarded it in life." Musrif said to him, "By Allah, I think that these are only people of the Garden. Do not let the people of Syria hear you saying this – or they will cease to obey you." Marwan said to them, "They changed and altered."

Muhammad ibn Abi'l-Jahm ibn Hudhayfa

His mother was Khawla bint al-Qa'qa'. His children were 'Ubaydullah, Hudhayfa, Sulayma, Umm Khalid, Umm al-Jahm, Maryam and 'Abdu'r-Rahman, by various umm *walads*. Muhammad ibn Abi'l-Jahm was one of the leaders in the Battle of al-Harra. He was killed on that day in 63 AH.

'Abdu'r-Rahman ibn 'Abdullah ibn Abi Rabi'a

His mother was Layla bint 'Utarid. His children were 'Amr, whose mother was Umm Bashir bint Abi Mas'ud, who is 'Uqba ibn 'Amr, and his half-brother was Zayd ibn Hasan ibn 'Ali; 'Uthman, Ibrahim, Musa, Umm Humayd and Umm 'Uthman, whose mother was Umm Kulthum bint Abi Bakr as-Siddiq, whose mother was Habiba bint Kharija ibn Zayd; Abu Bakr and Muhammad, whose mother was Fatima bint al-Walid, and her mother was Asma' bint Abi Jahl; and 'Abdullah and Umm Jamil, by an *umm walad*.

'Abdu'r-Rahman ibn 'Abdullah was one of the leaders at the Battle of al-Harra and survived and died later.

'Abdu'r-Rahman ibn Huwaytib ibn 'Abdu'l-'Uzza

His mother was Unaysa bint Hafs. His children were 'Abdullah and 'Ubaydullah, whose mother was Umm 'Utba bint 'Abdullah; and Muhammad and 'Atika, whose mother was Umm Habib bint Sa'id. He was killed in the Battle of al-Harra in 63 AH.

Abu Sufyan ibn Huwaytib ibn 'Abdu'l-'Uzza

His mother was Amina bint Abi Sufyan ibn Harb, whose mother was Sufayya' bint Abi'l-'As. He had a son, 'Abdu'r-Rahman, whose mother was Amatu'r-Rahman bint 'Amr.

'Ata' ibn Yasar

The client of Maymuna bint al-Harith, the wife of the Messenger of Allah صلعم .

'Uthaym ibn Nastas said, "A bedouin proposed to the daughter of 'Ata' and 'Ata' said to him, 'We do not deny your lineage or your rank , but we marry those like us and you should marry those of your tribe.'"

'Uthaym mentioned that Sa'id ibn al-Musayyab said, "Excellent is what 'Ata' wishes."

'Ata' ibn Yasar reported that he used to oil and comb his hair with a staff in his hand. 'Ata' ibn Yasar listened to Ubayy ibn Ka'b,

'Abdullah ibn Mas'ud, Khawwat ibn Jubayr, Abu Ayyub al-Ansari, Abu Waqid al-Laythi, Abu Rafi', 'Abdullah ibn Sallam, Zayd ibn Khalid al-Juhani, Abu Hurayra, Abu Sa'id al-Khudri, Ibn 'Umar, 'A'isha, Maymuna, Abu Malik al-Ashja'i, 'Abdullah ibn 'Abbas, Ka'b al-Ahbar, and 'Abdullah as-Sunabihi. He was reliable with a lot of *hadiths*.

Zayd ibn Aslam said, "'Ata' died in 94 AH at the age of 84. His *kunya* was Abu Muhammad."

His brother, Sulayman ibn Yasar

The client of Maymuna bint al-Harith, the wife of the Prophet صلعم. It is said that Sulayman himself was her *mukatib*.

Sulayman ibn Yasar said, "I asked permission to visit 'A'isha and she recognised my voice and asked, 'Is it Sulayman?' I said, 'It is Sulayman.' She inquired, 'Have you paid off what you contracted or decided?' I replied, 'Yes, almost, only a small amount remains.' She said, 'Enter, you are owned as long as you still owe anything.'"

Al-Hasan ibn Muhammad said, "Sulayman ibn Yasar had better understanding than Sa'id ibn al-Musayyab."

'Abdullah ibn Yazid al-Hudhali said, "I saw that Sulayman ibn Yasar trimmed his moustache until it was as if he had shaved it."

Muhammad ibn 'Umar said, "I do not think that there any is disagreement among our companions that Sulayman's *kunya* was Abu Turab. He used to camp among the Banu Hudayla. He was put in charge of the market by 'Umar ibn 'Abdu'l-'Aziz who was governor of Madina at that time for Walid I. Sulayman related from Zayd ibn Thabit, Abu Waqid al-Laythi, Abu Hurayra, Ibn 'Umar, 'Umar, 'Ubaydullah and 'Abdullah, the sons of al-'Abbas, 'A'isha, Umm Salama, Maymuna, and 'Urwa ibn az-Zubayr. He was reliable, noble and elevated, a *faqih* with a lot of *hadiths*. Sulayman ibn Yasar died in 107 AH at the age of 73."

Someone other than Muhammad ibn 'Umar said, "Sulayman died in 103 AH while Yazid II was khalif."

Qabisa ibn Dhu'ayb

Of Khuza'a. His *kunya* was Abu Ishaq. He listened to 'Uthman ibn 'Affan and he had a house in Madina among the Tammarites in the Alley of the Painters. He moved to Syria and was the favourite of

'Abdu'l-Malik. He was in charge of the seal of 'Abdu'l-Malik. The post came to him and he would read the letters when they arrived and then bring them to 'Abdu'l-Malik and tell him what was in them. Qabisa died in 86 AH while 'Abdu'l-Malik was still khalif. His father was a companion. He was reliable and trusted and had a lot of *hadiths*.

Abu Ghatafan ibn Tarif al-Murri

One of the Banu 'Usaym. Abu Ghatafan clung to 'Uthman and wrote for him, and he also wrote for Marwan. He had few *hadiths*. He had a house in Madina at ath-Thaniya, near the house of 'Umar ibn 'Abdu'l-'Aziz. Abu Bakr ibn Muhammad reported that Abu Ghatafan ibn Tarif was a scribe for Marwan.

Abu Murra, the client of 'Aqil ibn Abi Talib

Muhammad ibn 'Umar said, "He was a client of Umm Hani' bint Abi Talib. He clung to 'Aqil. He was an old shaykh who related from 'Uthman ibn 'Affan, Abu Hurayra and Abu Waqid al-Laythi. He was reliable with many *hadiths*.

Ja'far ibn 'Abdullah ibn Buhayna

Buhayna was Umm 'Abdullah, who was the daughter of al-Aratt, who is al-Harith ibn al-Mutallib. He was an ally of al-Muttalib. Ja'far was killed in the Battle of al-Harra in Dhu'l-Hijja in 63 AH.

*****

This generation also includes: **'Amr ibn Sa'd ibn Abi Waqqas**, whose mother was Salma bint Khasfa ibn Thaqf and who was killed at the Battle of al-Harra in 63 AH; **'Umayr ibn Sa'd ibn Abi Waqqas**, whose mother was Salma bint Khasfa ibn Thaqf and who was killed at the Battle of al-Harra; **'Abdu'r-Rahman ibn Abi Waqqas**, whose mother was Umm Hilal bint Rabi'; **'Abdullah ibn Yasar**, the client of Maymuna bint al-Harith, who is also related from and has few *hadiths*; **'Abdu'l-Malik ibn Yasar**, who died in 110 AH and who is related from and has few *hadiths*; **al-Furafisa ibn**

'**Umayr**, an ally of Quraysh who related from 'Uthman ibn 'Affan;
'**Abdullah ibn 'Utba ibn Ghazwan**, who was killed in the Battle of
al-Harra; and **al-Walid ibn Abi'l-Walid**, the client of 'Uthman
ibn'Affan who listened to 'Uthman ibn 'Affan.

Chapter Two
The Second Generation
of the *Tabi'un* of the People of Madina
Those who related from Usama ibn Zayd,
'Abdullah ibn'Umar, Jabir ibn'Abdullah, Abu
Sa'id al-Khudri, Rafi' ibn Khadij, 'Abdullah ibn
'Amr, Abu Hurayra, Salama ibn al-Akwa',
'Abdullah ibn 'Abbas, 'A'isha, Umm Salama,
Maymuna and others

'Urwa ibn az-Zubayr

His mother was Asma' bint Abi Bakr. His children were
'Abdullah, 'Umar, al-Aswad, Umm Kulthum, 'A'isha and Umm
'Umar, whose mother was Fakhita bint al-Aswad; Yahya,
Muhammad 'Uthman, Abu Bakr, 'A'isha, and Khadija, whose mother
was Umm Yahya bint al-Hakam; Hisham and Safiyya, by an *umm
walad*; 'Ubaydullah, whose mother was Asma' bint Salama; Mus'ab
and Umm Yahya, whose mother was an *umm walad* whose name was
Wasila; and Asma', whose mother was Sawda bint 'Abdullah ibn
'Umar, whose mother was Safiyya bint Abi 'Ubayd.

Hisham reported that his father said, "Abu Bakr ibn 'Abdu'r-
Rahman and I were rejected as too young to fight on the Day of the
Camel."

Muhammad ibn 'Umar said, "'Urwa related from his father, Zayd
ibn Thabit, Usama ibn Zayd, 'Abdullah ibn al-Arqam, Abu Ayyub,
an-Nu'man ibn Bashir, Abu Hurayra, Mu'awiya, 'Abdullah ibn
'Umar, 'Abdullah ibn 'Abbas, 'Abdullah ibn az-Zubayr, al-Miswar
ibn Makhrama, 'A'isha, Marwan ibn al-Hakam, Zaynab bint Abi
Salama, 'Abdu'r-Rahman ibn 'Abdu'l-Qari, Bashir ibn Abi Mas'ud
al-Ansari, Zubayd ibn as-Salt, Yahya ibn 'Abdu'r-Rahman, and

Jumhan the client of the Aslamis. He was reliable with a lot of *hadith*, a noble *faqih*, trustworthy and reliable."

Hisham ibn 'Urwa said, "On the day of the Battle of al-Harra, my father burned some books of *fiqh* which he had. He used to say after that, 'I would rather still have them than have the like of my family and property twice over.'"

Muhammad ibn Hilal said, "I saw that 'Urwa ibn az-Zuayr did not cut his moustache a lot. He trimmed a fair amount from it."

Hisham said that this father said to him, "My sons, ask me – I have lived so long that I almost forget. I am asked about the *hadith*, so begin the *hadith* for today."

Hisham ibn 'Urwa said that his father used to perform a *ghusl* every day.

Ishaq ibn Yahya said, "I saw 'Urwa wearing a saffron cloak."

Hisham ibn 'Urwa reported that his father used to dye a cloak with saffron for a dinar. He said, "The last garment he wore was one dyed with saffron for a dinar."

Hisham ibn 'Urwa reported that his father used to pray in a long shirt with a cloak wrapped over the shirt. He said that he saw his father wearing a silk/wool garment.

Hisham said, "When it was hot, 'Urwa used to wear a silk brocade gown lined with silk."

Muhammad ibn 'Amr reported that he saw 'Urwa wearing a cloak of silk/wool. 'Isa ibn Hafs said that he saw 'Urwa wearing a jubbah of silk/wool.

Muhammad ibn 'Amr said, "'Urwa used to dye his hair close to black. I do not know whether there was woad in it or not."

Hisham ibn 'Urwa said that his father used to fast all the time, except for the *'Ids*, and that he died fasting.

Hisham ibn 'Urwa said, "We were travelling with 'Urwa and some of us were fasting and some not. He did not command us to fast nor to stop fasting."

Abu'l-Miqdam Hisham ibn Ziyad said, "I saw 'Urwa praying in his sandals."

Ibn Shihab said, "'Urwa used to relate to me and then 'Amra confirmed the *hadith* of 'Urwa. When I had studied them thoroughly, I concluded, "Urwa was an inexhaustible sea.'"

It is reported from Hisham ibn 'Urwa that 'Urwa used to dislike writing, "Peace be upon you. Following on from that …" unless added to it was: "I praise Allah to you. There is no god but Him."

'Abdullah ibn Hasan said, "'Ali ibn Husayn ibn 'Ali ibn Abi Talib sat every night with 'Urwa ibn az-Zubayr at the end of the mosque of the Messenger of Allah صلعم after *'Isha'*. I used to sit with them. On one occasion they discussed the injustice of some of the Umayyads and the proper way of dealing with them when they could not change that. Then they mentioned what they feared about Allah punishing them. 'Urwa said to 'Ali, "Ali, when someone withdraws from the people of injustice, and when Allah knows that he is angry about what they are doing, and if he is on the same slope as them when the punishment of Allah smites them, I hope that he will be safe from what befalls them.' Then 'Urwa went out and settled at al-Suwayqa."

Hisham ibn 'Urwa said, "My father told me, 'Do not sprinkle *hanut* on me.'"

'Abdu'l-Halim ibn 'Abdullah said, "'Urwa ibn az-Zubayr died in his property at Majah in the vicinity of al-Fur' and was buried there on a Friday in 74 AH."

Muhammad ibn 'Umar said, "This was called the 'Year of the *Fuqaha'*' because of the large number of them who died that year. 'Urwa's *kunya* was Abu 'Abdullah. He had a house in Madina."

Al-Mundhir ibn az-Zubayr

His mother was Asma' bint Abi Bakr.

Al-Qasim reported in a *hadith* that al-Mundhir's *kunya* was Abu 'Uthman. His children were Muhammad, whose mother was 'Atika bint Sa'id; Ibrahim and Qurayza, whose mother was Hafsa bint 'Abdu'r-Rahman ibn Abi Bakr; 'Ubaydullah, whose mother was the daughter of Hassan ibn Nahshal of the Banu Salama; 'Amr, Abu 'Ubayda, Mu'awiya, 'Asim and Fatima, the wife of Hisham ibn 'Urwa, whose mother was an *umm walad*; and 'Umar, 'Awn and 'Abdullah, by *umm walads*.

Mus'ab ibn az-Zubayr

His mother was ar-Rabab bint Unayf. His children were 'Ukasha, 'Isa the elder – who was killed with his father – and Sukayna, whose mother was Fatima bint 'Abdullah; 'Abdullah and Muhammad, whose mother was 'A'isha bint Talha, whose mother was Umm

Kulthum bint Abi Bakr as-Siddiq; Hamza, 'Asim and 'Umar, by an
umm walad; Ja'far, by an *umm walad*. Mus'ab, by an *umm walad*;
Sa'd, by an *umm walad*; al-Mundhir, by an *umm walad*; 'Isa the
younger, by an *umm walad*; ar-Rabab, whose mother was Sukayna
bint al-Husayn ibn 'Ali; and Sukayna, whose mother was an *umm
walad*.

It is reported that his *kunya* was Abu 'Abdullah although he did
not have a son called 'Abdullah.

Muhammad ibn 'Umar said, "'Abdullah ibn az-Zubayr appointed
his brother Mus'ab over Iraq and he went to Basra and settled there.
Then he set out with a large army to confront al-Mukhtar ibn Abi
'Ubayd in Kufa. He fought and killed him, and sent his head to his
brother. He divided his governorship between al-Kuwar and as-
Sawad."

Isma'il ibn Abi Khalid stated, "I did not see any amir on the minbar more handsome than Mus'ab ibn az-Zubayr."

Mus'ab ibn Thabit said, "I asked 'Amir ibn 'Abdullah ibn az-
Zubayr, 'When was Mus'ab ibn az-Zubayr killed?' He replied, 'He
was killed on Thursday, 15 Jumada al-Ula 72 AH. The one who
killed him was 'Abdu'l-Malik ibn Marwan.'"

Ja'far ibn az-Zubayr ibn al-'Awwam

His mother was Zaynab, who is Umm Ja'far bint Marthad. His
children were Muhammad, Umm Hasan and Hammada, by an *umm
walad*; Thabit and Yahya, whose mother was Bassama bint 'Umara;
Salih, Hind and Umm Salama, by an *umm walad*; Shu'ayb, Adam,
'Amr and Nuh, by an *umm walad*; Umm Salih, 'A'isha and Umm
Hamza, whose mother was an *umm walad*; Ya'qub, Fatima, and
Umm 'Ubayda, whose mother was an *umm walad*; Umm 'Abdullah,
Umm az-Zubayr and Sawda, whose mother was an *umm walad*;
Maryam, whose mother was an *umm walad*; Umm 'Urwa, whose
mother was an *umm walad*; and A'isha, whose mother was an *umm
walad*."

Muhammad ibn Hilal said, "I saw that Ja'far ibn az-Zubayr did
not trim his moustache a lot. He removed a reasonable amount from
it."

Mus'ab ibn 'Abdullah said, "Ja'far grew old and lived until the
end of the khalifate of Sulayman."

Khalid ibn az-Zubayr ibn al-'Awwam

His mother was Umm Khalid Ama bint Khalid. His children were Muhammad the elder and Ramla, whose mother was an *umm walad*; Muhammad the younger, Musa, Ibrahim and Zaynab, whose mother was Hafsa bint 'Abdu'r-Rahman ibn Azhar ibn 'Awf; Sulayman and Umm Sulayman, whose mother was Umm Muhammad bint 'Abdullah; Nabih and Humayna, by an *umm walad*; Khalid and Hind, whose mother was an *umm walad*; and Umm 'Amr, by an *umm walad*.

'Amr ibn az-Zubayr ibn al-'Awwam

His mother was Umm Walid Amat bint Khalid. His children were Muhammad and 'Amr, whose mother was Umm Yazid bint 'Adi; 'Amr and Habib, whose mother was an *umm walad*; and Umm 'Amr, whose mother was one of the Banu Ghifar.

Yazid I wrote to 'Amr ibn Sa'd when he was his governor in Madina to send an army against 'Abdullah ibn az-Zubayr. 'Amr ibn Sa'd asked, "Who is the most hostile of people towards 'Abdullah ibn az-Zubayr?" He was told, "His brother, 'Amr ibn az-Zubayr." So he appointed him over his police in Madina and he proceeded to flog many of Quraysh and the Ansar, remarking, "These people are the party of 'Abdullah ibn az-Zubayr." Then 'Amr ibn Sa'id was told to move against 'Abdullah ibn az-Zubayr with an army of the people of Syria and to fight him. 'Amr went to Makka and camped at Dhu Tuwa. 'Abdullah ibn az-Zubayr sent Mus'ab ibn 'Abdu'r-Rahman to meet him with a group, one of whom was 'Abdullah ibn Safwan. They met – and Unays ibn 'Amr al-Aslami, the commander of the army of 'Amr ibn az-Zubayr, was killed. He and his companions were defeated and scattered. 'Ubayda ibn az-Zubayr came up to 'Amr ibn az-Zubayr and stated, "I will grant you protection from 'Abdullah." He was taken to him as a prisoner with blood flowing onto his feet. 'Abdullah ibn az-Zubayr asked, "What is this blood?" 'Amr replied:

"It is not from the heels that our wounded bleed,
but the blood runs over the front of our feet."

'Abdullah said, "You are wounded, O enemy of Allah who would violate the Haram of Allah!" Then he commanded that retaliation be inflicted on him for all those whom he had flogged or wronged. Mus'ab stated, "'Amr gave me a hundred lashes although he was not a governor and I had not done anything wrong, nor done something objectionable, nor denied obedience." He commanded that 'Amr be made to stand and a whip was handed to Mus'ab. 'Abdullah told him "Beat." He flogged him with a 100 lashes.

After that he recovered and then 'Abdullah commanded that he be brought out from prison to sit in the courtyard of the house where he was. He said, "Abu Yaksum! I see you are alive!" He commanded him to be taken back to prison but he died before he reached it. 'Abdullah commanded that he be thrown into the ravine of Jayf, which is the place where 'Abdullah ibn az-Zubayr's body was later crucified.

'Ubayda ibn az-Zubayr ibn al-'Awwam

His mother was Zaynab, who was Umm Ja'far bint Marthad. His children were al-Mundhir, by an *umm walad*; and Zaynab, by Umm 'Abdullah bint Musahiq.

Al-Qasim ibn Muhammad ibn Abi Bakr as-Siddiq

His mother was an *umm walad* called Sawda. His children were 'Abdu'r-Rahman, Umm Farwa (the mother of Ja'far as-Sadiq), Umm Hakim and 'Abda, whose mother was Qurayba bint 'Abdu'r-Rahman ibn Abi Bakr.

Al-Qasim said, "'A'isha used to shave our heads in the evening of 'Arafa. She shaved us and sent us to the mosque and then sacrificed with us on the following day."

Muhammad ibn 'Umar said, "Al-Qasim related from 'A'isha, Abu Hurayra, Ibn 'Abbas, Aslam the client of 'Umar, 'Abdullah ibn 'Umar, and Salih ibn Jubayr al-Ansari."

Ibn 'Awn said, "Al-Qasim related *hadith* literally."

'Ubaydullah said, "Al-Qasim did not commentate on the Qur'an."

Abu'z-Zinad said, "Al-Qasim only gave an answer concerning the outward and apparent."

Ibn 'Awn reported that al-Qasim said about something, "This is what I think, but I do not say that it is the truth."

Ibn 'Awn said, "Al-Qasim ibn Muhammad was asked about something and he said, "I was not compelled to be part of this consultation and I am not involved in it at all."

Al-Ansari said, "It seems that he thought that when the governor consulted him about any area of knowledge, then he should exercise *ijtihad*."

Al-Qasim said, "It is better for a man to remain silent after learning what Allah has obliged on him than for him to talk about what he does not know."

'Imran ibn 'Abdullah said, "Al-Qasim said to a group of people who discussed *Qadar*, 'Refrain from what Allah has refrained from.'"

'Ikrima ibn 'Ammar said, "I heard al-Qasim and Salim cursing the Qadariyya."

'Abdullah ibn al-'Ala' said, "I asked al-Qasim to read some *hadiths* to me and he said, 'There were many *hadiths* in the time of 'Umar ibn al-Khattab and people began to bring them. When they brought them, 'Umar commanded that they be burned. He said, "A secondary text, like that of the People of the Book."' On that day al-Qasim prevented me from writing down *hadiths*."

Yahya ibn Sa'id reported that al-Qasim ibn Muhammad used to relate *hadith* after '*Isha*' with his companions."

Muhammad ibn 'Umar said, "Al-Qasim and Salim ibn 'Abdullah had a single gathering in the mosque of the Messenger of Allah صلعم After that 'Abdu'r-Rahman ibn al-Qasim and 'Ubaydullah ibn 'Umar sat in it. Then after them Malik ibn Anas sat in it. It faced the grille of 'Umar between the grave and the minbar."

'Abdullah ibn Maslama reported: "I heard Malik ibn Anas say that 'Umar ibn 'Abdu'l-'Aziz had said, 'Would that al-Qasim could have it!' meaning the khalifate."

Sulayman ibn Qatta said, "'Umar ibn Ubaydullah sent me with 1,000 dinars for 'Abdullah ibn 'Umar and al-Qasim. I went to Ibn 'Umar who was washing in a bathing place and he put out his hand and I put the money in his hand. He said, 'He maintains ties of kinship. It has come to us when we have a need.' Then I went to al-Qasim ibn Muhammad but he refused to accept them. His wife said, 'Al-Qasim ibn Muhammad is the son of his uncle and I am the daughter of his uncle, so give them to me.'" He gave them to her.

Ayyub said, "I saw al-Qasim ibn Muhammad with a green silk/wool hat and a fine cloak which had a coloured border dyed with some saffron."

Sufyan mentioned al-Qasim ibn Muhammad and his excellence, and then said, "His son 'Abdu'r-Rahman ibn al-Qasim has excellence."

Suyfan said that 'Abdu'r-Rahman heard them when they were talking about some *sadaqa* in his father's care and he said, "By Allah, you are talking about a man who never took a single date of it." Al-Qasim said, "My son, as far as you know."

Al-Qasim ibn Muhammad said, "The disagreement of the companions of the Messenger of Allah is a mercy for people."

'Abdu'r-Rahman ibn Abi'l-Mawwal said, "I saw al-Qasim ibn Muhammad come to the mosque at the beginning of the day and pray two *rak'ats* and then he sat among people who asked him questions."

Rabi'a ibn Abi 'Abdu'r-Rahman said, "Al-Qasim ibn Muhammad was very weak. He rode from his camp to the mosque of Mina and alighted at the mosque and walked from the mosque to the *jamras* and stoned them on foot. Then he walked back to the mosque and then went on from the mosque mounted."

Aflah stated that the signet-ring of al-Qasim was engraved with his name. He said, "The bezel of al-Qasim ibn Muhammad had 'al-Qasim ibn Muhammad' engraved on it. The ring was silver and its bezel was silver." Hanzala and Sufyan ibn Hanzala also reported that. He wore it on the little finger of his left hand.

Muhammad ibn Hilal said, "I saw that al-Qasim did not trim his moustache a lot. He took a fair amount from it."

Mukhtar ibn Sad al-Ahwal said, "I noticed that al-Qasim's nails were white with no yellow from henna on them."

Aflah ibn Humayd said, "I saw that the sleeves of the shirt and jubbah of al-Qasim ibn Muhammad extended four fingers or a handspan beyond his fingertips."

Khalid ibn Ilyas said, "I saw al-Qasim ibn Muhammad wearing a silk/wool jubbah, a silk/wool cloak and a turban of silk/wool." Others, like Musa ibn 'Ubayda, Musa ibn Abu Bakr al-Ansari, Abu Mash'ar and others, remarked that he wore silk/wool.

'Isa ibn Hafs said, "I saw al-Qasim ibn Muhammad. We visited him when he was ill and he was wearing a red cloak from under which half of his thigh showed."

Abu Zabr 'Abdullah ibn al-'Ala' said, "I visited al-Qasim ibn Muhammad while he was in a red tent and under him was a red carpet and red cushions. I said, 'Abu 'Abdu'r-Rahman, this is part of what I wanted to ask you about.' He said, 'There is nothing wrong in what is commonly used of them.'"

Khalid ibn Abi Bakr said, "I saw al-Qasim wearing a white hat."

Sa'id ibn Muslim said, "When he wed, I saw al-Qasim ibn Muhammad wearing a cloak with saffron dye."

'Abdu'r-Rahman ibn al-Qasim reported that his father used to wear rose-coloured garments when he was in *ihram* dyed with light saffron.

Khalid ibn Abi Bakr said, "I saw al-Qasim ibn Muhammad wearing a white turban whose end hung down behind him more than a span."

Muhammad ibn Hilal said, "I did not see al-Qasim ibn Muhammad dye his hair."

Abu'l-Ghusn reported to us that he saw al-Qasim dye his head and beard with henna. Fitr said, "I saw al-Qasim dye his beard yellow." Da'ud ibn Sinan said, "I saw al-Qasim ibn Muhammad dye his head and beard with henna."

Muhammad ibn 'Amr said, "Al-Qasim ibn Muhammad used to use almost the same dye as me on his head and beard. Muhammad dyed his beard yellow with henna and his hair a very deep red."

Fitr said, "I saw al-Qasim ibn Muhammad with a fine shirt on and he had dyed his beard yellow with oil."

Aflah ibn Humayd said, "When al-Qasim ibn Muhammad dictated his will, he said, 'Write.' So the scribe wrote, 'This is the will of al-Qasim ibn Muhammad, who testifies that there is no god but Allah.' Al-Qasim said, 'We would be in a terrible state if we had not testified to this before today.'"

Sulayman ibn 'Abdu'r-Rahman said, "Before al-Qasim ibn Muhammad died at Qudayd he said, 'Shroud me in my garments in which I used to pray: my shirt, my waist-wrapper and my cloak.' His son said, 'My father, do you not want two garments?' He said, 'My son, that is how Abu Bakr was shrouded, in three garments. The living are more entitled to the new than the dead.'"

Khalid ibn Abi Bakr reported that al-Qasim commanded that he should not be praised at his graveside.

'Umar ibn Husayn said, "I think that Yazid said, 'I was present when al-Qasim died at Qudayd. He was buried at al-Mushallal about three miles away. His son put the bier on his shoulder and walked to al-Mushallal.'"

Muhammad ibn 'Umar said, "Al-Qasim died in 108 AH. He had gone blind at the age of 70 or 72. He was reliable. He was elevated, noble, a *faqih* and imam with a lot of *hadith* and scrupulousness. His *kunya* was Abu Muhammad."

'Abdullah ibn 'Abdu'r-Rahman ibn Abi Bakr

His mother was Qurayba bint Abi Umayya of Makhzum. Her maternal aunt was Umm Salama, the wife of the Prophet صلعم and his paternal aunt was 'A'isha bint Abi Bakr, the wife of the Prophet. His children were Abu Bakr, Talha, 'Imran, 'Abdu'r-Rahman, Nafisa, who married al-Walid I, and Umm Farwa. Their mother was 'A'isha bint Talha, whose mother was Umm Kulthum bint Abi Bakr. He had another daughter, Umm Abiha, whose mother was Maryam bint 'Abdullah.

'Abdullah ibn Muhammad ibn 'Abdu'r-Rahman ibn Abi Bakr as-Siddiq

He is known as Ibn Abi 'Atiq. His mother was Rumaytha bint al-Harith ibn Hudhayfa. His children were Muhammad, Abu Bakr, 'Uthman, 'Abdu'r-Rahman, 'Umar, 'Atika, 'A'isha and Zaynab, whose mother was Umm Abiha bint 'Abdullah; 'A'isha, who is said to be Umm Kulthum, whose mother was an *umm walad*; and Amina, whose mother was Umm Ishaq bint Talha, whose maternal sister was Fatima bint Husayn ibn'Ali.

Salim ibn 'Abdullah ibn 'Umar ibn al-Khattab

His mother was an *umm walad*. His *kunya* was Abu 'Umayr. His children were 'Umar and Abu Bakr, whose mother was Umm al-Hakam bint Yazid; 'Abdullah, 'Asim, Ja'far, Hafsa and Fatima, whose mother was an *umm walad*; and 'Abdu'l-'Aziz and 'Abda, whose mother was an *umm walad*. Muhammad ibn Hilal said that his *kunya* was Abu 'Umar.

Ibn Abi Fudayk said that Muhammad ibn Hilal met him and asked him questions.

Sa'id ibn al-Musayyab said, "The child of 'Umar who most resembled him was 'Abdullah and the most like 'Abdullah among his children was Salim."

'Ata' ibn as-Sa'ib said, "Al-Hajjaj sent a sword to Salim ibn 'Abdullah and commanded him to kill a man. Salim said to the man, 'Are you a Muslim?' – 'Yes,' he replied. 'Do what you have been commanded.' He asked, 'Have you prayed *Subh* today?' – 'Yes,' he replied. He went to al-Hajjaj and pointed at him with the sword and said that the man had said that he was a Muslim and that he had prayed the *Subh* prayer, and therefore he was in the protection of Allah. He mentioned that the Messenger of Allah صلى الله عليه وسلم said, 'Whoever prays the *Subh* prayer is in the protection of Allah.' Al-Hajjaj said, 'We are not killing him for doing the *Subh* prayer. He is one of those who helped to kill 'Uthman.' Salim said, 'Here is someone else who is more entitled to take revenge for 'Uthman than me.' 'Abdullah ibn 'Umar heard about this and asked, 'What did Salim do?' They told him what he had done and Ibn 'Umar said, 'Cheat, cheat.'"

Hanzala said, "The signet-ring of Salim ibn 'Abdullah was silver and worn on his left hand on the little finger and was engraved with 'Salim ibn 'Abdullah'."

Khalid ibn Abi Bakr said, "I saw Salim ibn 'Abdullah wearing a ring on his left hand." He said that he wore it in *ihram*.

Muhammad ibn Hilal said, "I saw that Salim ibn 'Abdullah did not trim his moustache a lot. He took a fair amount from it."

Muhammad ibn Hilal said, "I saw that Salim dyed his beard."

Abu'l-Ghusn said, "I saw Salim with a white head and beard."

Khalid ibn Abi Bakr said, "I saw Salim wearing a white hat and I saw him with a white turban whose end hung down behind him more than a span."

Da'ud ibn Sinan, the client of 'Umar ibn Tamim said, "I saw Salim with a shirt which hung down to the middle of his thigh."

'Abdu'r-Rahman ibn Abi'l-Mawwal said, "I saw Salim ibn 'Abdullah wearing cotton, a shirt and a cloak."

'Attaf ibn Khalid said, "I saw Salim ibn 'Abdullah wearing a small wrapper which had no hem, and he had a large belly."

Kathir ibn Zayd said, "I saw Salim ibn 'Abdullah praying in one shirt with the buttons undone." Others said the same.

Usama ibn Zayd said, "I did not see Salim ibn 'Abdullah button up his shirt in either summer or winter."

Khalid ibn Abi Bakr said, "I saw Salim ibn 'Abdullah with his back to the sun a lot while he was in *ihram*."

Muhammad ibn Hilal said, "I saw Salim ibn 'Abdullah on the road to Makka in *ihram* during the *hajj* saying the *talbiya*. His back was uncovered and the top piece of cloth was thrown across his thighs, and I saw that his skin was peeling from the sun."

Musa ibn 'Uqba said, "We met with Salim ibn 'Abdullah while we were coming from *'umra,* and he did not meet a group saying the *'la ilaha illa' llah'* but that he and his people said the *takbir*."

Sulayman ibn Abi ar-Rabi' said, "I went in to Salim ibn 'Abdullah and saw him doing the prayer sitting. He began his standing cross-legged and when he wanted to sit, he knelt."

Khalid ibn Abi Bakr said, "I saw Salim trim the straps of his sandals until they were level with his sandals. Sometimes he made his straps from palm leaves."

Khalid ibn Abi Bakr said, "When we were children, Salim used to enter the house and find us playing and he would flick us with the end of his cloak."

Khalid ibn Abi Bakr said, "I saw that Salim ibn 'Abdullah used to give his *zakat al-Fitr* in dates. Salim used to dislike wailing."

Khalid ibn Abi Bakr said, "I saw the daughter of Salim when she was young playing in front of him"

'Abdu'r-Rahman ibn al-Mujabbar said, "We were orphans in the care of Salim ibn 'Abdullah and he used to pick up our clothes and hide them somewhere."

'Ikrima ibn 'Ammar said, "I heard Salim cursing the Qadariyya who used to lie about *Qadar* until they believed in His good and evil.

'Ikrima ibn 'Ammar said, "I saw that Salim did not permit a story-teller of a group or its others testify."

Musa al-Mu'allim said, "I saw Salim ibn 'Abdullah eating dates in handfuls."

'Attaf ibn Khalid said, "I was standing with Salim ibn 'Abdullah when he was brought a boy with two other boys. He was the most difficult of them. Salim removed a thread from his button and cut it and then he rolled it between two fingers and then spat on it two or three times and then stretched it out and it was whole with nothing wrong with it. Salim said, 'If I turned away from any of his business, I would harden him.'"

Khalid ibn al-Qasim al-Bayadi said, "I saw the sleeve-ends of Salim ibn 'Abdullah around his fingers."

'Ubaydullah ibn 'Umar said, "Salim did not do Qur'anic commentary."

Muhammad ibn Umar said, "Salim related from Abu Ayyub al-Ansari, Abu Hurayra and his father. 'Abdullah ibn Muhammad ibn Abi Bakr listened mostly to his father from 'A'isha from the Prophet صلعم on the building of the Ka'ba: 'Your people have shortened the foundations of Ibrahim.' He was reliable with a lot of *hadith*, knowledge of men and scrupulous."

'Ubaydullah ibn 'Umar said, "Hisham ibn 'Abdu'l-Malik saw Salim ibn 'Abdullah on the day of 'Arafa wearing two threadbare garments. He asked, 'Abu 'Umar, what is your food?' – 'Bread and oil,' he replied. Hisham said, 'How can you survive on bread and oil?' He said, 'I leaven it and when I want it, I eat it.' He said, 'Your fragrance, Salim, on that day extended as far as Madina.'"

'Abdu'l-Halim ibn 'Abdullah said, "Salim ibn 'Abdullah died in 106 AH at the end of Dhu'l-Hijja while Hisham was in Madina. He had made *hajj* with the people that year and then came to Madina and happened to be there when Salim died. He prayed over him."

Aflah and Khalid ibn al-Qasim said, "Hisham ibn 'Abdi'l-Malik prayed over Salim ibn 'Abdullah at Baqi' because of the great number of people who were present. When Hisham saw the great number in Baqi', he told Ibrahim ibn Hisham al-Makhzumi, 'Organise an expedition of 4,000 for the people.' So it was called 'the Year of the Four Thousand'. When summer arrived, the people left Madina for the coasts during the hot months."

Abu Salama ibn 'Ubaydullah said, "On the day Salim died, I saw his son Ja'far remove his cloak and walk in a shirt. Al-Qasim ibn Muhammad sent for me to tell him to wear his cloak. Al-Qasim was blind on that day, but he was informed of it."

'Abdullah ibn 'Abdullah ibn 'Umar ibn al-Khattab

His mother was Safiyya bint Abi 'Ubayd ibn Mas'ud of Thaqif, whose mother was 'Atika bint Usayd, whose mother was Zaynab bint Abi 'Amr. His children were 'Umar, whose mother was Umm Salama bint al-Mukhtar who was governor of Madina; 'Abdu'r-Rahman, Ibrahim, and Umm 'Abdu'r-Rahman, whose mother was

Umm 'Abdullah bint 'Abdu'r-Rahman; and Riyah, whose mother was Habbaba bint 'Abdullah. He was the executor of his father's will, who was 'Abdullah ibn 'Umar.

Nafi' said, "'Abdullah ibn 'Abdullah used to wear silk/wool, and Ibn 'Umar put his hand on him to lean on him and he did not object to it."

Muhammad ibn 'Umar said, "'Abdullah died at the beginning of the khalifate of Hisham ibn 'Abdu'l-Malik in Madina. He was reliable with few *hadiths*.

'Ubaydullah ibn 'Abdullah ibn 'Umar ibn al-Khattab

His mother was an *umm walad*, Umm Salim ibn 'Abdullah. His children were Abu Bakr, 'Abdullah, 'Umar, Muhammad, and Umm 'Umar, whose mother was 'A'isha bint 'Abdu'r-Rahman ibn Abi Bakr; al-Qasim, Abu 'Ubayda, 'Uthman, Abu Salama, Zayd, 'Abdu'r-Rahman, the twins Hamza and Ja'far, Qurayba, and Asma', whose mother was Umm 'Abdullah bint al-Qasim ibn Muhammad ibn Abi Bakr; and Isma'il, by an *umm walad*.

Khalid ibn Abi Bakr said, "I saw 'Ubaydullah ibn 'Abdullah wearing a white hat with a turban around it whose end hung behind him more than a span."

'Isa ibn Hafs said, "I saw 'Ubaydullah ibn 'Abdullah wearing two red garments in which he went home after *'Asr* and in which he attended *'Isha'*."

Muhammad ibn 'Umar said, "According to what they say, 'Ubaydullah ibn 'Abdullah was older than 'Abdullah ibn 'Abdullah. Az-Zuhri related from him."

Khalid ibn Abi Bakr said, "I saw Salim attend 'Ubaydullah ibn 'Abdullah. 'Ubadyullah's grave had a tent over it and water was sprinkled on his grave. He was reliable with few *hadiths*."

Hamza ibn 'Abdullah ibn 'Umar ibn al-Khattab

His mother was an *umm walad* called Umm Salim ibn 'Abdullah. His *kunya* was Abu 'Umara. Az-Zuhr related from him. He was reliable with few *hadiths*. His children were 'Umar, Umm al-Mughira and 'Abda, whose mother was Umm Hakim bint al-Mughira; and 'Uthman, Mu'awiya, Umm 'Amr, Umm Kulthum, Ibrahim, Umm Salama, 'A'isha and Layla, by various *umm walads*.

Zayd ibn 'Abdullah ibn 'Umar ibn al-Khattab

His mother was an *umm walad*. His children were Muhammad, Umm Humayd, Umm Zayd, and Fatima, whose mother was Umm Hakim bint 'Ubaydullah; 'Abdullah, Ibrahim, 'Umar, Fatima and Hafsa, whose mother was Hukayma, an *umm walad*; and Sawda, whose mother was a Yamani *umm walad*. He was the oldest of the children of 'Abdullah ibn 'Umar, and left him while he was still alive. He went to Kufa and settled there where he died, and he has offspring in Kufa and Yemen.

Waqid ibn 'Abdullah ibn 'Umar ibn al-Khattab

His mother was Safiyya bint Abi "Ubayd. He had a son 'Abdullah, whose mother was Amatullah bint 'Abdullah.

Ibn Abi Dhi'b said, "I heard az-Zuhri say that Waqid died in Suqya in *ihram* and Ibn 'Umar shrouded him in five garments, including a long shirt and turban."

The father of 'Abdullah ibn Nafi' said, "Waqid ibn 'Abdullah died at Suqya and Ibn Umar prayed over him and buried him. Then he called the bedouins and began to run races between them. I remarked, 'You buried Waqid a moment ago and now you are racing the bedouins?' He said, 'Woe to you, Nafi', when you see that Allah has completed a matter, then leave it to Him.'"

Muhammad ibn Jubayr ibn Mut'im

His mother was Qutayla bint 'Amr of Kinana. His children were Sa'id – by whom he has his *kunya*, Umm Sa'id, Umm Sulayman, Umm Habib, Umm 'Uthman and Humayda, whose mother was Fakhita bint 'Adi the younger; Sahla, whose mother was Umm Sa'id bint 'Iyad; 'Umar, Ayyub, Aban and Abu Sulayman, whose mother was Umm Ayyub bint Sa'd ibn Abi Waqqas; Jubayr and Muhammad, whose mother was Kabsha bint Shurahbil; and 'Abdu'r-Rahman, 'Abdullah and 'Ubayda, by *umm walads*.

'Abdu'r-Rahman ibn Abi'z-Zinad said, "Muhammad ibn Jubayr and his brother Nafi' lived in their father's house in Madina. Muhammad died while Sulayman was khalif."

Abu Malik al-Himyari said, "I saw Nafi' ibn Jubayr on the day his brother Muhammad ibn Jubayr died with his cloak thrown off his back while he walking." Muhammad was reliable with few *hadiths*.

Nafi' ibn Jubayr ibn Mut'im

His mother was Umm Qital bint Nafi'. His children were Muhammad, 'Amr and Abu Bakr, whose mother was Umm Sa'id bint 'Iyad; and 'Ali, whose mother was Maymuna bint 'Ubayda. His *kunya* was Abu Muhammad.

Al-Walid ibn 'Abdullah and 'Ubaydullah ibn 'Abdu'r-Rahman said, "I saw Nafi' ibn Jubayr dye his hair black."

Abu'l-Ghusn Thabit ibn Qays said, "I saw Nafi' ibn Jubayr bind his teeth with gold rings."

Abu'l-Ghusn said that he saw that Nafi' ibn Jubayr only wore white. He also said that he saw Nafi' ibn Jubayr wearing an unlined hat and a white turban.

Musa ibn 'Ubayda said, "I saw Nafi' ibn Jubayr wearing silk/ wool." Nafi' ibn Jubayr was told that people said that it was from pride. He retorted, "By Allah, I ride donkeys, wear a cloak and milk sheep. The Messenger of Allah said, 'There is no pride in doing any of that.'"

'Imran ibn Musa said that Nafi' ibn Jubayr used to walk in the *hajj* leading his mount behind him.

It was said that Nafi' ibn Jubayr sat in the circle of al-'Ala' ibn 'Abdu'r-Rahman al-Huraqi while he was reading to people. When he finished, he asked, "Do you know why I have sat for you?" They replied, "You have sat so that you can be heard." – "No," he said, "Rather I have sat in order to humble myself before Allah by sitting with you." Someone else reported that the time for the prayer came and he sent a man forward to lead them. After the prayer, he asked, "Do you know why I advanced you?" He replied, "You advanced me to lead you in the prayer." – "No," was the reply. "Rather I advanced you to humble myself before Allah by praying behind you."

'Abdu'r-Rahman ibn Abi'z-Zinad said, "Nafi' ibn Jubayr died in Madina in 99 AH at the end of Sulayman's khalifate. Nafi' related from Abu Hurayra. He was reliable with a lot of *hadith* from his brother."

Abu Bakr ibn 'Abdu'r-Rahman ibn al-Harith

His mother was Fakhita bint 'Inba. His children were 'Abdu'r-Rahman, 'Abdullah, Abdu'l-Malik, Hisham, Suhayl, al-Harith and

Maryam, whose mother was Sara bint Hisham; Abu Salama, 'Umar and Umm 'Amr Rubayha, whose mother was Qariba bint 'Abdullah, whose mother was Zaynab bint Abi Salama, whose mother was Umm Salama bint Abi Umayya, the wife of the Prophet; and Fatima, whose mother was Rumaytha bint al-Walid.

Muhammad ibn 'Umar said, "Abu Bakr was born in the khalifate of 'Umar ibn al-Khattab. He was called 'the monk of Quraysh' due to the great amount that he prayed and his virtuousness. He went blind and has no name other than his *kunya*, Abu Bakr. He was too young to fight in the Battle of the Camel and he and 'Urwa ibn az-Zubayr were sent back. Abu Bakr related from Abu Mas'ud al-Ansari, 'A'isha and Umm Salama. He was reliable, a *faqih* with a lot of *hadith*, knowledgeable, intelligent, noble and generous.

Hisham ibn 'Urwa said, "I saw Abu Bakr ibn 'Abdu'r-Rahman wearing a silk/wool garment."

Muhammad ibn Hilal said that he saw that Abu Bakr ibn 'Abdu'r-Rahman did not over trim his moustache.

'Uthman ibn Muhammad said that 'Urwa entrusted Abu Bakr ibn 'Abdu'r-Rahman with some property from the Banu Mus'ab. He said, "Some or all of that property suffered a loss while in his possession. 'Urwa told him, 'You are not responsible. You are a trustee.' Abu Bakr said, 'I know that I am not responsible, but you will not say to Quraysh that I am not worthy of my trust.' So he sold some property of his to cover it."

'Abdu'l-Hakam ibn Abi Farwa said, "Abu Bakr ibn 'Abdu'r-Rahman entered his bathing place and died there suddenly."

'Abdullah ibn Ja'far said, "Abu Bakr ibn 'Abdu'r-Rahman prayed *'Asr* and then went to his bath-house and fell over. He began to say, 'By Allah, I didn't feel anything at the beginning of the day.' He died before sunset. That was in 94 AH in Madina."

Muhammad ibn 'Umar said, "That was called 'the Year of the *Fuqaha'*' because of the great number of them who died in it."

Muhammad ibn 'Umar said, "'Abdu'l-Malik ibn Marwan was generous to Abu Bakr and respected him and told al-Walid and Sulayman to honour him. 'Abdu'l-Malik said, 'I considered what I should do to the people of Madina because of their bad treatment of me. Then I remembered Abu Bakr ibn 'Abdu'r-Rahman and I felt embarassed before him and so I left that matter alone.'"

'Ikrima ibn 'Abdu'r-Rahman ibn al-Harith

His mother was Fakhita bint 'Inba. His children were 'Abdullah the elder, whose mother was 'Atika bint 'Abdullah; Muhammad, whose mother was Umm Salama bint 'Abdullah; 'Abdullah the younger and al-Harith, whose mother was the daughter of 'Abdullah ibn 'Amr; 'Uthman, whose mother was Umm 'Abdu'r-Rahman bint 'Abdu'r-Rahman; and Umm Sa'id, by an *umm walad*. His *kunya* was Abu 'Abdullah. He died in Madina in the khalifate of Yazid II. He was reliable with few *hadiths*.

Muhammad ibn 'Abdu'r-Rahman ibn al-Harith

His mother was Fakhita bint 'Inba. His children were al-Qasim and Fakhita, whose mother was Umm 'Ali bint Yasar; and Khalid, Abu Bakr, Salama, Hisham, Hantama and Umm Hakim, whose mother was Umm Salama bint 'Abdullah. Az-Zuhri related from Muhammad ibn 'Abdu'r-Rahman. He was reliable with few *hadiths*.

Al-Mughira ibn 'Abdu'r-Rahman ibn al-Harith

His mother was Su'da bint 'Awf. His *kunya* was Abu Hashim. His children were al-Harith, Mu'awiya, and Su'da, whose mother was Umm al-Banin bint Habib; 'Uyayna and Umm al-Banin, whose mother was al-Fari'a bint Sa'id; Ibrahim and al-Yasa', by an *umm walad*; Yahya and Salma, by an *umm walad*; 'Abdu'r-Rahman, Hisham and Abu Bakr, whose mother was Umm Yazid bint al-Ash'ath; 'Uthman, Sadaqa and Rubayha, whose mother was al-Bahim bint Sadaqa; Muhammad, whose mother was Umm Khalid bint Khalid; Umm al-Banin, whose mother was Umm al-Banin bint 'Abdullah; Rayta, whose mother was Qurayba bint Muhammad; Hafsa and 'Atika, whose mother was Umm al-Banin; and Amina, whose mother was an *umm walad*.

Muhammad ibn 'Umar said, "Al-Mughira ibn 'Abdu'r-Rahman went to Syria more than once on expeditions. He was in the army of Maslama which laid siege to the Byzantines until 'Umar ibn 'Abdu'l-'Aziz recalled them. He lost an eye. Then he returned to Madina and died there. He left instructions that he be buried at Uhud with the martyrs. His family did not do that – they buried him at Baqi'. He is related from. He was reliable with few *hadiths* except for those about the expeditions of the Prophet صلعم . He learned them from Aban ibn 'Uthman and he often used to read them to him and commanded us to learn them."

Abu Sa'id ibn 'Abdu'r-Rahman ibn al-Harith

His mother was Umm Rasan bint al-Harith. His children were Muhammad, whose mother was Maymuna bint 'Ubaydullah ibn 'Abbas; and al-Walid, whose mother was Umama bint 'Abdullah. He was killed in the Battle of al-Harra in Dhu'l-Hijja 63 AH while Yazid I was khalif.

This generation also included **Hamza ibn az-Zubayr ibn al-'Awwam,** whose mother was ar-Rabab bint Unayf and who had a son 'Umara; **'Abdullah ibn Muhammad ibn Abi Bakr as-Siddiq**, whose mother was an *umm walad* called Sawda, and who was killed in the Battle of al-Harra; and **Bilal ibn 'Abdullah ibn 'Umar ibn al-Khattab**, whose mother was an *umm walad* and who had a son 'Abdu'r-Rahman, whose mother was Umm Sa'id bint Abi Nu'aym.

✻✻✻✻✻

The Rest of the Second Generation
of the *Tabi'un*

'Ali ibn al-Husayn ibn 'Ali ibn Abi Talib

His mother was an *umm walad* named Ghazzala. After Husayn, she was married to Zayd, the client of al-Husayn ibn 'Ali and bore him 'Abdullah ibn Zayd, the half-brother of 'Ali ibn Husayn. This 'Ali ibn Husayn is 'Ali ibn al-Husayn the younger. As for 'Ali the elder, he was killed with his father at Karbala'. 'Ali's children were al-Hasan, al-Husayn the elder, Muhammad Abu Ja'far the *faqih*, and 'Abdullah, whose mother was Umm 'Abdullah bint al-Hasan ibn 'Ali; 'Umar, Zayd – who was killed and crucified in Kufa by Yusuf ibn 'Umar ath-Thaqafi while Hisham was khalif, 'Ali and Khadija, whose mother was an *umm walad*; Husayn the younger, and Umm 'Ali who is 'Ulayya, whose mother was an *umm walad*; Kulthum and Mulayka, from an *umm walad*; and al-Qasim, Umm al-Hasan who is Hasana, Umm al-Husayn and Fatima, by an *umm walad*. 'Ali was thirteen when he was with his father at Karbala'. He was ill and asleep on his bed. When al-Husayn was killed, Shamir ibn Dhi'l-Jawshan said, "Kill this one." One of his men said, "Glory be to Allah! Kill a young lad who is ill and has not fought!" 'Umar ibn Sa'd came and said, "Do not attack the women nor this invalid."

'Ali ibn al-Husayn said: "One of them took me and was very hospitable and attentive to me. He began to weep whenever he went out and came in until I began to say to myself, 'There is no better and faithful man than this.' Then the herald of Ibn Ziyad said, 'Whoever finds 'Ali ibn Husayn should bring him. We are offering 300 dirhams for him.' He came in, by Allah, weeping, and began to bind my hands to my neck, saying, 'I am afraid.' He took me to them and took the 300 dirhams while I was looking at him. I was brought to Ibn Ziyad. He asked, 'What is your name?' "'Ali ibn Husayn,' I replied. He said, 'Did not Allah kill 'Ali?' I replied, 'I had a brother called 'Ali older than me whom the people killed.' He said, 'Allah killed him.' I said, 'Allah takes the souls when they die.'"

He ordered that he be killed but Zaynab bint 'Ali shouted, "Ibn Ziyad! You have had enough of our blood! I ask you by Allah, if you kill him, kill me with him." So he left him alone. When the belongings of al-Husayn and the survivors were brought to Yazid, a Syrian stood up and said, "Their captives are lawful for us!" 'Ali ibn Husayn said, "You lie and are censured. What is that unless you have left our religion and invented another religion?" Yazid was silent for a while and then told the Syrian, "Sit down." He said to 'Ali ibn Husayn, "I would like you to remain with us so that we can honour you and acknowledge your due. But if you prefer, I will return you to your land and still maintain our ties with you." He said, "Return me to my land," and so he returned him to his land and maintained ties of kinship with him.

Abu Ja'far mentioned that the *kunya* of 'Ali ibn al-Husayn was Abu'l-Husayn. Some say that it was Abu Muhammad.

Al-'Ayraz ibn Hurayth said, "I was with Ibn 'Abbas when 'Ali ibn Husayn came to him and he said, 'Welcome to the beloved son of the beloved.'"

Nadr ibn Aws said, "I went to 'Ali ibn Husayn and he asked, 'Who are you?' I replied, 'I am from Tayy.' He said, 'May Allah give you life and give life to the people of whom you are a part. Your tribe is an excellent one.' I inquired, 'Who are you?' He replied, 'I am 'Ali ibn al-Husayn.' I said, 'Wasn't he killed with his father?' He replied, 'If he had been killed, lad, you would not be seeing me.'"

Al-Maqburi said, "Al-Mukhtar sent 100,000 dinars to 'Ali ibn Husayn which he disliked to accept but feared to return lest they were unlawfully acquired. So he kept them with him. When al-Mukhtar was killed, 'Ali wrote to 'Abdu'l-Malik, 'Al-Mukhtar sent me 100,000 dirhams and I did not want to accept them or return them. They are still with me, so send someone to take them.' 'Abdu'l-Malik wrote to him, 'Nephew, take them. I am happy for you to have them.' So he accepted them."

'Isa ibn Dinar the *mu'adhdhin* said, "I asked Abu Ja'far about al-Mukhtar and he said, "'Ali ibn Husayn stood at the door of the Ka'ba and cursed al-Mukhtar. A man remarked to him, "May Allah make me your ransom, you curse him when he was slain for you?" He replied, "He was a liar who spoke lies against Allah and His Messenger.""

Abu Ja'far said, "We pray behind them [i.e. the followers of al-Mukhtar] and it is not *taqiya*. I testify that 'Ali ibn Husayn used to pray behind them and that was not out of *taqiya*."

'Ali ibn al-Husayn said, "Someone who abandons commanding the correct and forbidding the objectionable is like a person who casts the Book of Allah behind his back – unless he is acting out of *taqiya*." He was asked, "What is *taqiya*?" He replied, "It is from someone who is in fear of a stubborn tyrant whom he fears will transgress."

Yahya ibn Sa'id said, "I heard 'Ali ibn Husayn, the best Hashimite I ever met, say, 'O people, love us with the love of Islam – but do not let your love for us go so far that it becomes a dishonour for us.'"

He also reported that 'Ali ibn Husayn said, "Love us with the love of Islam. By Allah, you will continue to talk about us until you make the people hate us."

'Ubaydullah ibn 'Abdu'r-Rahman said, "A group came to 'Ali ibn al-Husayn and praised him. He said, 'How much you lie! How reckless you are towards Allah! We are among the righteous of our people. It is enough for us to be among the righteous of our people.'"

Yazid ibn 'Iyad said, "Az-Zuhri shed blood by accident and went out, left his people and set up a tent. He stated, 'No roof of a house shall shade me.' 'Ali ibn Husayn passed by him and said, 'O Ibn Shihab, your despair is worse than your wrong action. Fear Allah and ask His forgiveness. Send the man's people the blood money and return to your family.' Az-Zuhri used to say, "Ali ibn Husayn gave me the greatest favour of anyone.'"

'Uthman ibn 'Uthman said, "'Ali ibn Husayn married a daughter of his client and he also freed a slavegirl of his and married her. 'Abdu'l-Malik ibn Marwan wrote to him to censure him for that and 'Ali wrote back to him, 'You have a good model in the Messenger of Allah. The Messenger of Allah صلعم freed Safiyya bint Huyayy and married her. He freed Zayd ibn Haritha and married him to his cousin Zaynab bint Jahsh.'"

'Abdullah ibn 'Ali said, "When al-Husayn was killed, Marwan told my father, 'Your father asked me for 4,000 dinars and I did not have them with me. I have them today. If you want you can have them.' My father took them. None of the Marwanids spoke to him about that until Hisham asked my father, 'What was done with our due to you.' He replied, 'Ample and thanked.' He said, 'It is yours.'"

Shu'ayb ibn Abi Hamza said, "When az-Zuhri mentioned 'Ali ibn Husayn, he said, 'He was the most sought after of the people of his house, the best of them in obedience, and the most beloved of them to Marwan ibn al-Hakam and 'Abdu'l-Malik ibn Marwan."

Yahya ibn Shibl asked Abu Ja'far about the Battle of al-Harra, "Did any of the people of your house take part in it?" He replied, "None of the family of Abu Talib took part in it, nor did any of the Banu 'Abdu'l-Muttalib. They kept to their houses. When Musrif came and killed the people and went to al-'Aqiq, he asked whether Abu 'Ali ibn Husayn was present and was told that he was. He asked, 'Why don't I see him?' My father heard of this and came to him with Abu Hashim 'Abdullah and al-Hasan, the sons of Muhammad ibn 'Ali al-Hanafiyya. When Musrif saw my father, he greeted him and made room for him on his seat. Then he asked him, 'How are you?' He replied, 'I praise Allah to you.' Musrif said, 'The Amir al-Mu'minin ordered me to be good to you.' My father said, 'May Allah reward the Amir al-Mu'minin.' Then he asked me about Abu Hashim and al-Hasan, the sons of Muhammad, and I said, 'They are my cousins.' He welcomed them and then they left."

Malik ibn Anas said, "''Ali ibn Husayn went to 'Ubaydullah ibn 'Abdullah to ask him about something. His companions were with him and he was praying. He waited until he had finished the prayer and then 'Ubaydullah turned to him. His companions said, 'May Allah restore you. This man has come to you, and he is the grandson of the Messenger of Allah صلى الله عليه وسلم, to ask you about something. You should have attended to him and fulfilled his need and then completed what you were doing.' 'Ubaydullah told them 'Bring him in! The one who seeks this matter must follow me!'"

A shaykh called Mustaqim said, "We were with 'Ali ibn Husayn when a beggar came to us. He got up to give him something and said, 'Sadaqa falls into the hand of Allah before it falls into the hand of the asker.' He made a gesture with his hands."

Mas'ud ibn Malik said, "''Ali ibn Husayn asked me, 'What did Sa'id ibn Jubayr do?' I replied, 'He was righteous.' He said, 'He passed by us and we asked him about shares of inheritance and other things, by which Allah helped us. With us he was not as those people accuse him,' and he pointed towards Iraq."

'Ali ibn Husayn said, "By Allah, 'Uthman was not killed rightly."

'Abdullah ibn Abi Sulayman said, "When 'Ali ibn al-Husayn walked, his hand did not go beyond his thigh and he did not swing his arm. When he rose for the prayer, he began to tremble. He was asked, 'What is up with you?' He replied, 'Do you not know Who I am standing before and with Whom I converse?'"

'Ali ibn Muhammad reported that 'Ali ibn Husayn used to forbid fighting. The people of Khurasan met him and complained to him of the injustice of their governors, but he told them to be patient and refrain. He said, "I tell you what 'Isa said: *'If You punish them, they are Your slaves. If you forgive them, You are the Almighty, the All-Wise.'* (5:118)"

Hisham ibn 'Urwa said, "'Ali ibn Husayn went out on his mount to Makka and returned before he had reached it. He used to sit with Aslam, the client of 'Umar. A man of Quraysh said to him, 'You leave Quraysh and sit with a slave of the Banu 'Adi?' 'Ali replied, 'A man sits where he finds benefit.'"

Yazid ibn Hazim said, "I saw 'Ali ibn Husayn and Sulayman ibn Yasar sitting between the grave and the *minbar* speaking until mid-morning, reminding one another. When they wanted to leave, 'Abdullah ibn Abi Salam recited a *sura* to them. When he finished, they made supplication."

Musa ibn Abi Habib at-Ta'ifi said, "I saw that 'Ali ibn Husayn dyed his hair with henna and *katm*. I saw that the sandals of 'Ali ibn Husayn were round at the end with no tongue."

Habib ibn Thabit said, "'Ali ibn Husayn had a yellow silk/wool garment which he wore on Fridays."

'Uthman ibn Hakim said, "I saw 'Ali ibn Husayn wearing a silk/wool garment and a silk/wool jubbah."

Nasr ibn Aws at-Ta'i said, "I visited 'Ali ibn Husayn and he was wearing an old red shawl and he had thick shoulder-length hair which was parted." Yazid ibn Hazim said, "I saw 'Ali ibn Husayn wearing a thick Kurdish shawl and two thick Yamani khuffs."

'Umar ibn 'Ali ibn 'Ali said that 'Ali ibn Husayn bought a silk/wool garment for fifty dinars and wore it in the winter and then sold it and gave away its price as *sadaqa*. He had two Ashmuni Egyptian garments for the summer which cost a dinar, and he wore any sort of clothes. He said, *"Who has forbidden the fine clothing of Allah which He has produced for His slaves?"* (7:32) He wore a turban and made *nabidh* in a skin during the *'Ids* without dregs. He used to use oil or perfume after his *ghusl* when he intended to go into *ihram*.

Muhammad ibn Hilal said, "I saw 'Ali ibn al-Husayn wearing a turban whose end he let hang down behind his back. It was white."

Thabit ath-Thumaii said, "I heard Abu Ja'far say, "Ali ibn Husayn went to the toilet while I was standing near the door. I set out some *wudu'* water for him. He came out and said, 'My son!' I said, 'At your service!' He said, 'I saw something in the toilet which made me think.' I asked, 'What is that?' He said, 'I saw the flies landing on the faeces and then flying off and landing on people's clothes and so I wanted to have a garment just for going to the toilet.' Then he said, 'I have no need of anything since this is easier for people.'"

Abu Ja'far reported that his father 'Ali ibn Husayn gave away his property for Allah twice and said, "Allah loves the believer who sins and repents."

Muhammad ibn 'Aqil said, "On the night of 'Arafa and morning of Jam' 'Ali ibn Husayn joined prayers when he was on the *hajj*. 'Ali ibn Husayn used to join *Dhuhr* and *'Asr*, and *Maghrib* and *'Isha'* on a journey. He said, 'The Messenger of Allah صلعم used to do that when he was neither in a hurry nor in fear.'"

Abu Ja'far reported that 'Ali ibn Husayn used to walk to the *jamras* and he had a camp in Mina. The people of Syria annoyed him and so he moved to Qurayn ath-Tha'alab or close to it. He used to ride from there. When he came to his camp, he walked to the *jamras*.

Nasr ibn Aws said. "'Ali ibn Husayn filled his hand with dates and gave to both old and young."

Al-Husayn ibn 'Ali said, "My father, 'Ali ibn al-Husayn visited us while I and Ja'far were playing in a garden. My father asked Muhammad ibn 'Ali, 'How old is Ja'far?' – 'Seven,' he replied. He said, 'Tell him to do the prayer.'"

Suhayl ibn Shu'ayb an-Nuhaymi, who lived among them, said, "I visited 'Ali ibn Husayn and asked, 'How are you this morning?' He replied, 'I have not yet seen a shaykh among the people of Egypt like you who does not know how we are. If you do not perceive or know, I will tell you. Among our people we are in a similar position to that of the tribe of Israel among the people of Pharaoh when they were slaughtering their sons and letting their women live. Our shaykh curries favour with our enemies while he is cursed and abused on their minbars. The Quraysh now consider that they are superior to other Arabs because Muhammad صلعم was one of them. The Arabs now affirm that for them, while the Arabs consider that they are better than the non-Arabs because Muhammad صلعم was one of them and so they only have superiority by him. The non-Arabs affirm them in that. If the Arabs truly are superior to the non-Arabs, and if Quraysh are truly superior to the Arabs because Muhammad صلعم was one them, then we, the people of the House, are superior among Quraysh because Muhammad صلعم was one of us. So they claim our right and do not acknowledge any right for us. So that is how we are, if you really do not know how we are." He said, "I think that he wanted those in the house to hear."

Salim, the client of Ja'far said, "Hisham ibn Isma'il used to abuse 'Ali ibn Husayn and the people of his house. He attacked 'Ali from the *minbar*. When al-Walid became khalif, he dismissed Hisham and ordered that he be made to stand before the people. He was saying, 'No, by Allah, there is no person more important to me than 'Ali ibn Husayn. I used to say, "A righteous man whose word is heard."' He was made to stand before the people. 'Ali ibn Husayn forbade his children to attend. On the following day 'Ali ibn Husayn went by on an errand but did not acknowledge him. Hisham ibn Isma'il called out to him, *'Allah knows best where to place His Message.'* (6:124)"

'Abdullah ibn 'Ali ibn Husayn said, "When Hisham ibn Isma'il was dismissed, 'Ali forbade us to harm him. He gathered us and said, 'This man has been dismissed and commanded to stand before the people. None of you should interfere with him.' I said, 'O father, why? By Allah, he has behaved badly towards us and we only seek just retribution today.' He said, 'My son, his punishment is up to Allah. By Allah, none of the house of Husayn will say a single thing to him until this business is finished.'"

Abu Ja'far reported that 'Ali ibn Husayn ordered that when he died they should not cause annoyance to anyone, that he should be prepared for burial swiftly and shrouded in cotton with no musk put in the *hanut*. He told an *umm walad* of 'Ali ibn Husayn to wash 'Ali's private parts when he died.

'Abdul-Hakim ibn 'Abdullah said, "'Ali ibn Husayn died in Madina and was buried in Baqi' in 94 AH. That was called 'the Year of the *Fuqaha"* because of the great number of them who died that year." Al-Fadl ibn Dukayn said that he died in 92 AH. Ja'far ibn Muhammad said, "'Ali ibn Husayn died when he was 58."

Muhammad ibn 'Umar said, "This will show you that 'Ali ibn Husayn was with his father when he was 23 or 24 and that therefore the statement is incorrect that [at the Battle of Karbala'] he was young and not at all grown up – but on that day he was ill and did not fight. How could he not have been grown up when he had a son at the time, Abu Ja'far Muhammad ibn 'Ali? Abu Ja'far met Jabir ibn 'Abdullah and they related from him. Jabir died in 78 AH."

Abu Mash'ar al-Maqburi said, "When 'Ali ibn Husayn's body was set down to be prayed over, the people and the people of the mosque attended. Sa'id ibn al-Musayyab remained alone in the mosque. Khashram said to Sa'id ibn al-Musayyab, 'Abu Muhammad, why don't you attend this righteous man of a righteous house?' Sa'id said, 'I prefer praying two *rak'ats* in the mosque to attending this righteous man of a righteous house.'"

'Uthaym ibn Nastas said, "I saw Sulayman ibn Yasar go out to him, pray over him, and follow him. He said, 'I prefer attending the funeral to doing voluntary prayers.'"

Shayba ibn Na'ama said, "'Ali ibn Husayn made do with little. When he died, they found that he had been feeding a hundred people of a house in Madina secretly." They said that 'Ali ibn Husayn was reliable and trustworthy. He had a lot of *hadiths*. He was noble, elevated and scrupulous."

'Abdu'l-Malik ibn al-Mughira ibn Nawfal

His mother was an *umm walad*. His children were Khadija, 'Abdu'r-Rahman, Nawfal, Ishaq, Yazid, Durayba and Habbaba, whose mother was Umm 'Abdullah bint Sa'id. His *kunya* was Abu Muhammad. He had few *hadiths* and died while 'Umar ibn 'Abdu'l-'Aziz was khalif.

Abu Bakr ibn Sulayman ibn Abi Hathma

His mother was Amatullah bint al-Musayyab of Makhzum. His children were Muhammad, 'Abdullah and some daughters whose mother was an *umm walad*; al-Harith, whose mother was an *umm walad*; and Umm Kulthum, whose mother was the daughter of Shafi' ibn Anas. He listened to Sa'd ibn Abi Waqqas and az-Zuhri related from him.

'Abdu'l-Malik ibn Marwan

His mother was 'A'isha bint Mu'awiya ibn al-Mughira. His children were al-Walid – who became khalif, Sulayman – who became khalif, Marwan the elder, Da'ud and 'A'isha, whose mother was Umm al-Walid, the daughter of al-'Abbas ibn Jaz'; Yazid – who became khalif, Marwan and Mu'awiya, whose mother was 'Atika bint Yazid ibn Mu'awiya; Hisham – who became khalif, whose mother was Umm Hisham bint Hisham ibn Isma'il; Abu Bakr Bakkar whose mother was 'A'isha bint Musa ibn Talha; al-Hakam whose mother was Umm Ayyub bint 'Amr, whose mother was Umm al-Hakam bint Dhu'ayb; 'Abdullah, Maslama, al-Mundhir, 'Anbasa, Muhammad, Sa'id al-Khayr and al-Hajjaj, by *umm walads*; and Fatima who married 'Umar ibn 'Abdu'l-'Aziz and whose mother was Umm al-Mughira bint al-Mughira. His *kunya* was Abu'l-Walid. He was born in 26 AH while 'Uthman was khalif and was present at the siege of 'Uthman's house with his father, aged ten. He preserved their business and *hadith*.

The Muslims spent the winter in Greek territory in 42 AH. It was the first winter expedition there, and Mu'awiya appointed 'Abdu'l-Malik over the people of Madina when he was sixteen. 'Abdu'l-Malik also went on a naval expedition with some people.

Muhammad ibn Isma'il al-Madani said, "I heard an old man report in the house of Kathir ibn as-Salt, that one day Mu'awiya ibn Abi Sufyan was sitting with 'Amr ibn al-'As when 'Abdu'l-Malik ibn Marwan passed by them. Mu'awiya said, 'How much *adab* this youth has! What excellent manliness!' 'Amr ibn al-'As said, 'Amir al-Mu'minin, this youth has embodied four qualities and abandoned three. When he speaks, he speaks well; when he listens, he listens well; when he meets someone, he is welcoming; and he has good speech and great forbearance when opposed. He abandons unnecessary words; he does not keep company with blameworthy people; and he does not joke like someone whose intellect or manliness is not reliable.'"

Al-Maqburi reported that 'Abdu'l-Malik ibn Marwan remained in Madina while his father was alive and governor, until the Battle of al-

Harra. When the people of Madina expelled Yazid's governor from Madina, who was 'Uthman ibn Muhammad ibn Abi Sufyan, and expelled the Umayyads, 'Abdu'l-Malik was expelled with his father. Muslim ibn 'Uqba met them on the road. Yazid had sent him with an army against the people of Madina. Marwan and 'Abdu'l-Malik returned with him. 'Abdu'l-Malik stopped at Dhu Khushub and told a messenger to wait at Makhis, which is between Madina and Dhu Khushub, twelve miles from Madina, and to bring him news of the battle. He feared that the people of Madina would be victorious. While 'Abdu'l-Malik was waiting in the fortress of Marwan at Dhu Khushub, his messenger came to him swinging his garment. 'Abdu'l-Malik said, "This one brings good news." The messenger who had been at Makhis brought him the news that the people of Madina had been killed and that the people of Syria had entered it. 'Abdu'l-Malik prostrated and entered after Madina was safe.

Muhammad ibn 'Umar said, "When the people of Madina expelled the Banu Umayya, they extracted pledges from them that they would not reveal any weakness of theirs nor help their enemies against them. When Muslim ibn 'Uqba met them at Wadi al-Qura, Marwan told his son 'Abdu'l-Malik, 'Go into him before me. Perhaps he will be bolder towards you than me.' So 'Abdu'l-Malik went in and Muslim said to him, 'Come, what information do you have? Tell me about the people and what you think.' He said, 'Yes,' and informed him about the people of Madina, how they could be reached, where they could be breached and where to camp. Then Marwan entered and he asked, 'What information do you have?' He said, 'Didn't 'Abdu'l-Malik come to you?' – 'Yes,' he replied. He said, 'When you meet 'Abdu'l-Malik, you meet me.' He said, 'Yes.' Then Muslim remarked, 'What a man 'Abdu'l-Malik is! Rarely among the men of Quraysh have I spoken to a man like him!'"

A man of Hamdan of the people of Jordan said, "We were with Muslim ibn 'Uqba when he approached Madina. We entered a garden at Dhu'l-Marwa where there was a handsome youth praying. We walked around in the garden for a while until he had finished his prayer. He asked me, 'Slave of Allah, are you are part of this army?' – 'Yes,' I replied. He asked, 'Are you heading for Ibn az-Zubayr?' – 'Yes,' I replied. He said, 'Even if I had what is on the face of the entire earth I would not like to go against him. There is no one on the face of the earth today better than him.' That was 'Abdu'l-Malik ibn

Marwan. He was tested by him until he killed him in the Masjid al-Haram."

They say that 'Abdu'l-Malik sat with the *fuqaha'* and scholars and studied with them. He had few *hadiths*.

Muhammad ibn 'Umar said, "Marwan was given allegiance as the khalif in al-Jabiyya on Wednesday, 27 Dhu'l-Qa'da 64 AH. He met ad-Dahhak ibn Qays al-Fihri at Marj Rahit and killed him and then after that allegiance was given to his son 'Abdu'l-Malik and 'Abdu'l-'Aziz, Marwan's sons."

Abu'l-Huwayrith said, "Marwan ibn al-Hakam died in Damascus at the new moon of Ramadan in 65 AH. 'Abdu'l-Malik was khalif from that day."

Ibrahim said, "Mus'ab ibn az-Zubayr prepared to set out against 'Abdu'l-Malik and camped at Bajumayra, a village on the bank of the Euphrates nine miles below Anbar. 'Abdu'l-Malik learned of this, rallied his troops, and headed for Iraq to fight Mus'ab. He remarked to Rawh ibn Zinba', 'By Allah, the business of this world is extraordinary. I can recall how Mus'ab and I were. One night I missed him in the place where we used to meet and was upset by that. He missed me and had the same reaction. I used to receive a gift and could not eat any of it until some of it was sent to Mus'ab. Now we have taken up swords. But this kingdom is barren; and no son or father desires it without unsheathing the sword.' 'Abdu'l-Malik said this because Khalid ibn Yazid and 'Amr ibn Sa'id were sitting with him. He meant to warn them. He knew that 'Amr ibn Sa'id had the greatest following among the people of Syria and that Marwan had first included Khalid ibn Yazid in the agreement about his successor, but then Marwan settled on 'Abdu'l-Malik to succeed him, and 'Abdu'l-Aziz after 'Abdu'l-Malik, leaving Khalid in despair. He was with 'Abdu'l-Malik out of avarice and fear."

'Abdullah ibn Abi Farwa said, "When 'Abdu'l-Malik went from Damascus to Iraq to fight Mus'ab, one night near Butnan Habib Khalid ibn Yazid and 'Amr ibn Sa'id discussed 'Abdu'l-Malik and their accompanying him in spite of his lack of sincerity and false promises to them. 'Amr said, 'I will return and encourage Khalid to make a move.' 'Amr returned to Damascus. Its walls were secure at that time. He stirred up the Syrians. 'Abdu'l-Malik missed him and asked, 'Where is Abu Umayya?' He was told, 'He has gone back.' 'Abdu'l-Malik returned with his people to Damascus and remained there for sixteen days until 'Amr opened the city to him and gave him allegiance. 'Abdu'l-Malik pardoned him but then decided to kill him. One day he sent an invitation to him and it occurred to 'Amr that the letter was a ploy. He rode to him together with those with him, wearing armour, and went in to 'Abdu'l-Malik and they spoke for a time. He had told Yahya ibn al-Hakam that when he went out for the prayer he should strike 'Amr's neck. Then 'Abdu'l-Malik came to him and said, 'Abu Umayya, who are these ghouls and fornicators whom you have dragged out against us?' Then 'Abdu'l-Malik reminded him of what he had done. 'Abdu'l-Malik went to the prayer and returned but Yahya had not moved against him. 'Abdu'l-Malik abused him for that. Then he and those with him went up to 'Amr ibn Sa'id and killed him."

Ibrahim said, "'Abdu'l-Malik set out that year but did not attack Mus'ab. Mus'ab went to Kufa. When he advanced, Mus'ab left Kufa and came to Bajumayra and camped there. 'Abdu'l-Malik heard about this and prepared to go out against him."

Raja' ibn Haywa said, "When 'Abdu'l-Malik mustered his forces to go against Mus'ab, he made his preparations and set out with a large army of Syrians. 'Abdu'l-Malik and Mus'ab met at Maskin. Then they went out to fight and the people formed in ranks. Rabi'a and other tribes deserted Mus'ab, who observed, "A man ends up dead in any case. By Allah, it is better to die nobly than to beg from someone who is going to cheat you. I will never ask for their help nor for the help of anyone!' Then he told his son 'Isa, 'Advance and fight!' His son fought until he was killed. Ibrahim ibn al-Ashtar advanced and fought fiercely but several people attacked him and he was killed. Then they attacked Mus'ab who was on his chair and he fought them fiercely from his chair until he was slain. 'Ubaydullah ibn Ziyad cut off his head and took it to 'Abdu'l-Malik who gave him a 1,000 dinars. He refused to accept them. Then 'Abdu'l-Malik called on the people to give allegiance to him which they did. Then he returned to Syria."

Abu 'Awn and others reported: "After 'Abdu'l-Malik ibn Marwan had killed Mus'ab, he sent al-Hajjaj ibn Yusuf with two thousand Syrian troops against 'Abdullah ibn az-Zubayr in Makka. He wrote to Tariq ibn 'Amr commanding him to join al-Hajjaj. Tariq went with his men, who were 5,000, and joined al-Hajjaj. They besieged Ibn az-Zubayr, fought him and set up catapults. Al-Hajjaj made *hajj* with his people in 72 AH while Ibn az-Zubayr was under siege. Then al-Hajjaj and Tariq went and camped at the Well of Maymun and did not perform *tawaf* of the House, or approach women, or put on perfume until Ibn az-Zubayr had been killed. Then they performed *tawaf*, and slaughtered camels. Ibn az-Zubayr was besieged on the first night of Dhu'l-Qa'da in 72 AH for six months and 17 days. He was killed on Tuesday, 17 Jumada al-Ula 73 AH. His head was sent to 'Abdu'l-Malik in Syria."

Abu 'Awn said, "The people agreed on 'Abdu'l-Malik ibn Marwan in 73 AH and Ibn 'Umar wrote to inform him of his allegiance. Abu Sa'id al-Khudri and Salama ibn al-Akwa' also wrote to him stating their allegiance."

Abu'z-Zinad said that 'Abdu'l-Malik ibn Marwan minted dinars and dirhams in 75 AH. He was the first to initiate their minting and embossing.

Abu Hilal said, "In contrast to the *mithqal* of the *Jahiliyya*, the *mithqal* of 'Abdu'l-Malik ibn Marwan was minted as 22 *qirats* less one grain for the Syrians. Ten dirhams were the weight of seven *mithqals*."

Ibn Ka'b ibn Malik said, "There was agreement with 'Abdul-Malik on these weights."

Abu'z-Ziyad said, "The *hajj* in 75 AH was led by 'Abdu'l-Malik. When he passed by Madina, he stayed some days in his father's house. Then he went as far as Dhu'l-Hulayfa and the people went out with him. Aban ibn 'Uthman told him, 'Go into *ihram* at al-Bayda',' so he went into *ihram* at al-Bayda'."

Abu 'Ubayd said, "I heard Qabisa ibn Dhu'ayb say, 'I told 'Abdu'l-Malik to go into *ihram* at al-Bayda'.'"

Nafi' said, "I saw 'Abdu'l-Malik ibn Marwan saying the *talbiya* after he had gone into *ihram* until he had performed *tawaf* of the House and then he stopped the *talbiya*. Then he resumed saying it until he went to the place of Standing. I mentioned that to Ibn 'Umar and he said, 'I saw all of that. We do the *takbir*.'"

'Abdu'l-Majid ibn Suhayl reported that 'Abdu'l-Malik ibn Marwan gave a *khutba* during his *hajj* on four days: before *Tarwiya*, on the day of 'Arafa, on the following day – the Day of Sacrifice, and on the first day of Nafr: four days in all."

'Abdullah ibn 'Amr al-'Amiri said, "I heard 'Abdu'l-Malik ibn Marwan say to Qabisa ibn Dhu'ayb, "Did you hear of making a supplication at a specific time in the Farewell (*tawaf*)?' – 'No,' he replied. 'Abdu'l-Malik said, 'Nor I.'"

Al-Harith ibn 'Abdullah said, "I performed *tawaf* of the House with 'Abdu'l-Malik ibn Marwan. On the seventh circuit, he approached the House seeking refuge and I tugged at him. He asked, 'What is it, Hari?' I said, 'Amir al-Mu'minin, do you know who was the first to do this? Was it one of the old men of your community?' 'Abdu'l-Malik went on and did not seek refuge."

Musa ibn Maysara said, "'Abdu'l-Malik ibn Marwan did *Tawaf al-Qadum*. When he had prayed two *rak'ats*, al-Harith ibn 'Abdullah said, 'Return to the Black Stone before you go to Safa.' 'Abdu'l-Malik turned to Qabisa. Qabisa said, 'I did not see any of the people of knowledge return to it.' 'Abdu'l-Malik said, 'I did *tawaf* with my father and I did not see him return to it.' 'Abdu'l-Malik said, 'Hari, learn from me as I learned from you, when I wanted to cling to the House and you prevented me.' He said, 'Act, Amir al-Mu'minin. It will not be the first knowledge I have learned from your knowledge.'"

'Awf ibn al-Harith said, "I saw Jabir ibn 'Abdullah go to 'Abdu'l-Malik. 'Abdu'l-Malik greeted him. Jabir said, 'Amir al-Mu'minin! Madina is as you see and it is a good place which the Messenger of Allah صلعم named. Its people are besieged. The Amir al-Mu'minin should maintain their ties of kinship and recognise their rights.' 'Abdu'l-Malik disliked this and turned away from him. Jabir began to press him until Qabisa made a gesture to his son, who was his guide, to make him be quiet. Jabir was blind. His son made a movement to silence him. Jabir exclaimed, 'Bother you! What are you doing to me!' – 'Be quiet,' he replied. Jabir was quiet. When he left, Qabisa took his hand and said, 'Abu 'Abdullah, these people have become kings.' Jabir said to him, 'Allah has inflicted an excellent affliction. You and your companion will have no excuse which will be heard.' He said, 'Heard and not heard. What is acceptable to him will be heard. The Amir al-Mu'minin commanded 5,000 dirhams be given to help you.' Jabir took them."

Abu'z-Zinad said, "'Abdu'l-Malik ibn Marwan led the *hajj* in 75 AH and passed by Madina and spoke to its people from the minbar. Then another *khatib* stood up to speak on his behalf while he remained seated on the minbar. Part of what he spoke about on that day was what had befallen the people of Madina. He mentioned their opposition to obedience, their bad opinion of 'Abdu'l-Malik and the people of his house, and what the people of al-Harra had done. Then he said, 'I have not found any example for you, O people of Madina, except the city which Allah mentions in the Qur'an. Allah says, *"Allah makes an example of a city which was safe and at peace, its provision coming to it plentifully from every side. Then it showed ingratitude for Allah's blessings so Allah made it wear the robes of hunger and fear for what it did."* (16:112)' Ibn 'Abd knelt and said to the *khatib*, 'You lie. We are not like that. Read the *ayat* after it: *"A Messenger from among them came to them but they denied him. So the punishment seized them and they were wrongdoers."* (16:113) – We believe in Allah and His Messenger!' When he said that, the guards leapt on Ibn 'Abd and hung on to him until we thought that they would fight him. 'Abdu'l-Malik told them to release him. When the *khatib* had finished and 'Abdu'l-Malik entered his house, Ibn 'Abd asked to enter. He did not reward anyone more than he did him, nor clothe anyone more than he clothed him."

'Abdu'r-Rahman ibn Muhammad ibn 'Abd said, "When 'Abdu'l-Malik said what he said and my father answered him and the police grabbed my father and brought him to 'Abdu'l-Malik, some of the Syrians were harsh towards him. When the Syrians had left, he told him, 'Ibn 'Abd, I saw what you did and I forgive that, but beware of doing it with a governor: I fear that he will not put up with what I put up with from you. The dearest of people to me from this area are Quraysh. Our ally is one of us and you are one of us. How much are you in debt?' He replied, '500 dinars.' He commanded 500 dinars for him and gave him a 100 dinars on top and gave him a garment of green silk/wool. We have a piece of it."

Tha'laba ibn Abi Malik al-Qurazi said, "I saw 'Abdu'l-Malik ibn Marwan praying *Maghrib* and *'Isha'* in the Ravine. He caught up with me before Jam'. I continued with him and he asked, 'Have you prayed yet?' I replied, 'No, by my life.' He asked, 'What prevented you from praying?' I replied, 'I am still in time.' He said, 'No, by my life, you are not in time!' Then he said, 'Perhaps you are one of those who attack the Amir al-Mu'minin 'Uthman, may Allah have mercy on him? I testify to you that my father reported that he saw him pray *Maghrib* and *'Isha'* in the Ravine.' I replied, 'Is someone like you, Amir al-Mu'minin, saying this when you are the ruler! Why would I attack him or anyone else? I clung to him, but I saw that 'Umar, may

Allah have mercy on him, did not pray until he reached Jam'. There is no *sunna* which I prefer more than the *sunna* of 'Umar.' He said, 'May Allah have mercy on 'Umar. 'Uthman had more knowledge about 'Umar. If 'Umar had done this, 'Uthman would have followed him. There was no one who followed the actions of 'Umar more than 'Uthman. 'Uthman did not differ from 'Umar in any of his conduct except in his leniency. 'Uthman was gentle to them until he was overcome. If he had been as severe with them as Ibn al-Khattab was with them, then they would not have done to him what they did! And how can the people today be compared with the people among whom 'Umar was! Tha'laba! I think that the proper conduct for the ruler is to mix with people. If this stops, a man will become jealous of people in their houses, the roads will be beset by robbers, people will wrong one another and there will be seditions. There must be a ruler in every age to act in accordance with what will put it right.'"

Ibn Ka'b said, "I heard 'Abdu'l-Malik ibn Marwan say, 'O people of Madina, the most entitled of people to cling to the original practice are you. Tales have come to us from the east which we do not recognise. In them we only recognise the recitation of the Qur'an. Cling to the copy of the Qur'an which you have which your wronged ruler collected, may Allah have mercy on him, and you must apply the shares (*fara'id*) which your wronged leader had you agree on. In that he consulted Zayd ibn Thabit. He was an excellent leader for Islam.'"

They said, "'Abdu'l-Malik wanted to depose his brother 'Abdu'l-'Aziz ibn Marwan, and to assign the khalifate to his sons al-Walid and Sulayman after him. Qabisa ibn Dhu'ayb told him not to do so and said to him, 'Do not do it. By so doing you will create resentment against you. Perhaps he will die and you will be relieved of him.' So 'Abdu'l-Malik refrained from that but he still had the urge to depose him. One night Rawh ibn Zinba' visited him and spent the night with 'Abdu'l-Malik. He was the most pleasant of people with 'Abdu'l-Malik. He said, 'Amir al-Mu'minin, if you depose him, no one will give a hoot.' He asked, 'Do you really think that, Abu Zur'a?' He said, 'Yes, by Allah. I am the first of people to agree with your doing that.' Nasih added, 'If Allah wills.'

"Nasih said, 'We agreed on that and 'Abdu'l-Malik ibn Marwan went to sleep with Rawh ibn Zinba' beside him. Qabisa ibn Dhu'ayb came to them, knocking at the door. 'Abdu'l-Malik had told his attendant, "Do not keep Qabisa from me whatever time he comes, night or day, when I am alone or if there is one person with me. If I am with the people, he should enter the assembly and announce his presence." Qabisa was also in charge of the seal of the khalif. Letters reached him before 'Abdu'l-Malik and he would read them and then bring them unrolled to 'Abdu'l-Malik to read. This was out of esteem for Qabisa.'

"He entered and said, 'May Allah reward you, Amir al-Mu'minin, for your brother.' – 'Has he died?' He asked. 'Yes,' he replied. 'Abdu'l-Malik said, 'We belong to Allah and to Him we return!' Then he turned to Rawh and said, 'Abu Zura'a, Allah has spared us what we intended. That was in opposition to you, Abu Ishaq.' Qabisa asked, 'What was it?' He told him. Qabisa said, 'Amir al-Mu'mimin, it is always best to bide one's time. Haste should only be used in its proper place.' 'Abdu'l-Malik said, 'Sometimes there is much good in haste. Do you think that in the case of 'Amr ibn Sa'id haste was better than slowness?' 'Abdu'l-Malik put his son 'Abdullah in charge of Egypt and contracted allegiance to his sons al-Walid and Sulayman as khalifs after him. He wrote to all the territories and the people gave them allegiance. 'Abdu'l-'Aziz died in Jumada al-Ula 85 AH."

Muhammad ibn 'Umar reported that the men of Madina said, "'Abdu'l-Malik memorised from 'Uthman and listened to Abu Hurayra, Abu Sa'id al-Khudri, Jabir ibn 'Abdullah and other companions of the Messenger of Allah. He was a devout worshipper before becoming khalif."

Nafi' said, "I saw 'Abdu'l-Malik ibn Marwan and there was no youth in Madina who strived harder in seeking knowledge than him." I think that he also said, "Nor stronger in *ijtihad*."

Qabisa ibn Dhu'ayb said, "We used to hear the call of 'Abdu'l-Malik ibn Marwan from beyond his rooms, 'O people of blessings! Do not think any of them insignificant when you have good health.'"

Ibn Jurayj said, "I heard Ibn Shihab asking about binding teeth with gold and he replied, 'There is no harm in it. 'Abdu'l-Malik ibn Marwan bound his teeth with gold.'" 'Amr ibn Qays said the same as did az-Zuhri.

Abu Mash'ar Najih said, "'Abdu'l-Malik ibn Marwan died in Damascus on a Thursday, in the middle of Shawwal 86 AH at the age of 60. He ruled for 21 years and one and a half months, from the day he was given allegiance to the day he died. For nine of them he fought 'Abdullah ibn az-Zubayr. The khalifate in Syria was surrendered to him first, and then in Iraq after the death of Mus'ab. After the death of 'Abdullah ibn az-Zubayr the people agreed on him for 13 years and four months less seven days. It is related to us that he died when he was 58, but the first figure is sounder, and it is calculated from his birthday as well.

'Abdul-'Aziz ibn Marwan ibn al-Hakam

His mother was Layla bint Zabban of Kalb. His *kunya* was Abu'l-Asbagh. His children were 'Umar – who became khalif, 'Asim, Abu Bakr and Muhammad, whose mother was Umm 'Asim bint 'Asim ibn al-Khattab; Suhayl and Umm al-Hakam, whose mother was Umm 'Abdullah ibn 'Abdullah ash-Sahmiyya; Zabban and Juzayya, by an *umm walad*; and Umm al-Banin whose mother was Layla bint Suhayl. He related from Abu Hurayra and was reliable but had few *hadiths*.

Marwan ibn al-Hakam had assigned the khalifate to 'Abdu'l-Malik ibn Marwan and after him to 'Abdu'l-'Aziz ibn Marwan. He appointed him over Egypt, and 'Abdu'l-Malik confirmed his governorship. However, his presence was onerous for 'Abdu'l-Malik and he wanted to depose him so that allegiance could be given to his sons al-Walid and Sulayman as khalifs after him. Qabisa ibn Dhu'ayb prevented him from doing that. Qabisa was in charge of the seal and was honoured and respected by him and so he refrained from doing that. Then 'Abdu'l-'Aziz died in Egypt in Jumada al-Ula 85 AH. The news reached 'Abdu'l-Malik in the night. In the morning he summoned the people to give allegiance to al-Walid and Sulayman as khalifs after him. It was to go to Sulayman after al-Walid.

Muhammad ibn Marwan ibn al-Hakam

His mother was an *umm walad* called Zaynab. His children were Marwan – who later became khalif and was the last of the Umayyad khalifs and was killed by the Abbasids when they were victorious, whose mother was an *umm walad*; Yazid, whose mother was Ramla bint Yazid; 'Abdu'r-Rahman, whose mother was Umm Jamil bint 'Abdu'r-Rahman; Mansur, by an *umm walad*; 'Abdu'l-'Aziz, by an *umm walad*; and 'Abda and Ramla, by *umm walads*. Az-Zuhri related from Muhammad ibn Marwan.

'Amr ibn Sa'id ibn al-'As

His mother was Umm al-Banin bint al-Hakam ibn Abi'l-'As. His children were Umayya, Sa'id, Isma'il, Muhammad and Umm Kulthum, whose mother was Umm Habib bint Hurayth; 'Abdu'l-Malik, 'Abdu'l-'Aziz and Ramla, whose mother was Sawda bint az-Zubayr ibn al-'Awwam; Musa and 'Imran, whose mother was 'A'isha bint Muti'; 'Abdullah and 'Abdu'r-Rahman, by an *umm walad*; Umm Musa, whose mother was Na'ila bint Furays of Kalb; and Umm 'Imran, whose mother was an *umm walad*.

They said, "'Amr ibn Sa'id was one of the men of Quraysh. Yazid ibn Mu'awiya appointed him over Madina. Al-Husayn was killed while he was governor of Madina. He was sent the head of al-Husayn and shrouded it and buried it in Baqi' beside the grave of his mother, Fatima, the daughter of the Messenger of Allah صلعم . Yazid wrote to him commanding him to send an army against 'Abdullah ibn az-Zubayr under the command of 'Amr ibn az-Zubayr. 'Amr ibn Sa'id made *hajj* with the people one year. He was the most beloved of people to the Syrians. They listened to him and obeyed him. When 'Abdu'l-Malik became khalif, he was worried about him, because 'Amr had deceived him and fortified himself in Damascus. Then 'Amr ibn Sa'id conquered it for him and gave him allegiance as khalif. 'Abdu'l-Malik continued to keep an eye on him and did not trust him until one day he sent for him to come alone. Then he censured him for things he had overlooked previously. Then he attacked and killed him. 'Amr's *kunya* was Abu Umayya. He related from 'Umar.

Yahya ibn Sa'id ibn al-'As

His mother was al-'Aliyya bint Salama. His children were Sa'id, Isma'il, Rubayha – who is Umm Rabah, Fakhita, Ruqayya and Umm 'Umar, whose mother was Umm 'Isa bint 'Ubaydullah ibn 'Umar ibn al-Khattab; 'Amr and 'Uthman, whose mother was Zaynab bint 'Abdu'r-Rahman ibn al-Hakam; 'Umar, whose mother was Umm 'Amr bint 'Umar al-Bahiliya; Aban, 'Anbasa, Husayn, Muhammad and Hisham, by *umm walads*; Amina, whose mother was Umm Salama bint al-Hulays; Ramla, 'Ulayya, and Fakhita the younger, whose mother was an *umm walad*; and Umm 'Uthman, whose mother was an *umm walad*. He had few *hadiths*.

'Anbasa ibn Sa'id ibn al-'As

His mother was an *umm walad*. His children were 'Abdullah, by an *umm walad*; 'Abdu'r-Rahman, by an *umm walad*; Khalid, whose mother was Umm an-Nu'man bint Muhammad ibn al-Ash'ath; 'Abdu'l-Malik, whose mother was Arwa bint 'Abdullah; 'Uthman, by an *umm walad*; Sa'id, Umm 'Anbasa and Umm Kulthum, whose mother was Umm 'Umar bint 'Umar; al-Hajjaj, Muhammad, Sulayman, Ziyad, Marwan, Amina, Umm 'Uthman, Umm Aban and Umm Khalid, by various *umm walads*; and Umm al-Walid, whose mother was ar-Raddah bint 'Umayr. He related from Abu Hurayra.

'Abdullah ibn Qays ibn Makhrama

His mother was Durra bint 'Uqba. His children were Muhammad, Musa and Ruqayya, whose mother was Umm Said bint Kabatha; al-Muttalib and Hakim, whose mother was Umm Iyas bint Yazid; 'Abdu'r-Rahman, al-Hakam, 'Abdullah and Umm al-Fadl, whose mother was 'Abdullah ibn 'Abdu'r-Rahman; and 'Abdu'l-Malik and Umm Salama, whose mother was an *umm walad*.

His brother, Muhammad ibn Qays

His mother was Durra bint 'Uqba. His children were Yahya the elder, 'Amr the elder, Umm al-Qasim, Jamal, as-Sa'ba the elder and Umm 'Abdullah, whose mother was Umm Jamil bint al-Musayyab; al-Hasan, al-Husayn, al-Hukaym, as-Sa'ba the younger, Qays the elder, Qays the younger, Muhammad the younger, Jamal the younger, Hafsa, Umm al-Hasan and Fatima, whose mother was Umm al-Hasan bint al-Hukaym; 'Amr the younger, by an *umm walad*; and Yahya the younger, by an *umm walad*.

'Abdullah ibn 'Abdu'r-Rahman ibn Azhar

His mother was Umm Salama bint Khaffaja. His children were Ja'far, 'Abdu'r-Rahman, Umm 'Amr and Hafsa, whose mother was Umm Jamil bint 'Abdullah. Az-Zuhri related from 'Abdullah.

Mu'adh ibn 'Abdu'r-Rahman ibn 'Uthman

His mother was an *umm walad*. His children were 'Abdu'r-Rahman, whose mother was Zuyayna, who is Umm 'Amr bint 'Utayba; Uways, whose mother was Maryam bint 'Uqba; and Asma' whose mother was al-Minqariyya.

Nawfal ibn Musahiq ibn 'Abdullah

His mother was Maryam bint Muti'. His children were Sa'd, whose mother was Umm 'Abdullah bint Abi Sabra; Ma'qil, whose mother was Da'iba bint Sabra; and 'Abdu'l-Malik and Sulayman, by *umm walads*. He had a few *hadiths*.

'Uthman ibn Ishaq ibn 'Abdullah

His mother was Umayma bint 'Abdullah ibn Mas'ud. His children were 'Abdu'r-Rahman and another boy, whose mother was Umm Habib bint Murr. Az-Zuhri related from him.

Shu'ayb ibn Muhammad ibn 'Abdullah

His mother was an *umm walad*. His children were 'Umar and 'Amr, whose mother was Habiba bint Murra; 'Abdullah, Shu'ayb and 'A'idha who married Husayn ibn 'Abdullah, whose mother was 'Amr bint 'Ubaydullah ibn al-'Abbas. Shu'ayb related from his grandfather 'Abdullah ibn 'Amr, and his son 'Amr ibn Shu'ayb related from him.

'Uthman ibn 'Abdullah ibn 'Abdullah

His mother was Zaynab bint 'Umar ibn al-Khattab. She was the youngest of 'Umar's children. His children were 'Amr, by whom he has his *kunya*, 'Abdullah, 'Umar, Abu Bakr, az-Zubayr and 'Abdu'r-Rahman, whose mother was 'Abda bint az-Zubayr ibn al-Musayyab; Hafsa by an *umm walad*; and Fatima, by an *umm walad*. 'Uthman related from Jabir ibn 'Abdullah.

Hisham ibn Isma'il ibn Hisham

His mother was Ama bint al-Muttalib. His children were al-Walid and Umm Hisham (the mother of Hisham ibn 'Abdu'l-Malik), whose mother was Maryam bint Laja'; Ibrahim and Muhammad, by an *umm walad*; and Khalid and Habib, by an *umm walad*. Hisham was one of the people of knowledge and transmission. He was governor of Madina for 'Abdu'l-Malik ibn Marwan until 'Abdu'l-Malik died. He is the one who beat Sa'id ibn al-Musayyab after he had called on him to give allegiance to al-Walid ibn 'Abdu'l-Malik when he was designated the next khalif. Sa'id refused and said, "I look to see what the people do." So he beat him, paraded him and imprisoned him. 'Abdu'l-Malik heard about that, disliked it and was not pleased with what he had done. He said, "What does he have to do with Sa'id? There is no opposition from Sa'id."

'Abdullah ibn Khabbab ibn al-Aratt

Of Tamim. He was captured in the *Jahiliyya* and went to Umm Anmar bint Siba' al-Khuza'iyya who set him free.

Ayyub ibn Humayd reported that a man of 'Abd al-Qays who had been with the Kharijites and then left them said that they entered a town and 'Abdullah ibn Khabbab was afraid of them. They said, "Do not be alarmed." He said, "By Allah, you alarm me." They said, "Do not be alarmed." He said, "By Allah, you alarm me." They asked, "You are 'Abdullah son of Khabbab, the Companion of the Messenger of Allah?" – "Yes," he replied. They asked, "Did you hear any *hadith* of the Messenger of Allah صلعم from your father which he reported?" – "Yes," he replied, "I heard my father report that the Prophet صلعم mentioned that during sedition the one who sits is better than the one who stands, the one who stands is better than one who walks, and the one who walks is better than the one who runs." They said, "If you know that, then be 'Abdullah the slain."

Ayyub, said, "They took him to the river bank and cut off his head and his blood flowed freely, and they split open the mother of his son. For that reason it is lawful for me to fight them."

Ja'far ibn 'Amr ibn Umayya of Kinana

'Abdu'r-Rahman ibn Abi'z-Zinad said, "Ja'far ibn 'Amr was the brother by suckling of 'Abdu'l-Malik. He came to 'Abdu'l-Malik while he was khalif and sat in the mosque of Damascus while the people of Syria were presented to their *diwan*. The Yemenis around him were saying, 'Obedience! Obedience.' Ja'far stated, 'There is no obedience due except to Allah.' They leapt on him and said, 'Do you doubt that obedience means obedience to the Amir al-Mu'minin?' And they tied him to a pillar and he only got free with great effort. 'Abdu'l-Malik heard about the incident and sent for him. When he was brought to him, he said, 'What do you think about what you did? By Allah, if they had killed you, I could have done nothing for you. What possessed you to involve yourself in something which does not concern you? You saw people supporting my rule and obedience to it and you began to weaken it. Take care! Take care!'"

Muhammad ibn 'Umar said, "Ja'far died while al-Walid I was khalif. He related from his father and az-Zuhri related from him. He was reliable and had *hadiths*.

Iyas ibn Salama ibn al-Akwa'

Of Khuza'a. His *kunya* was Abu Salama. He died in Madina in 110 AH at the age of 77. Ya'la ibn al-Harith reported that Iyas's *kunya* was Abu Bakr. He was reliable with many *hadiths*.

'Ata' ibn Yazid al-Laythi

Of Kinana. He died in 107 AH when he was 82. He related from Abu Ayyub, Tamim ad-Dari, Abu Hurayra, Abu Sa'id al-Khudri, and 'Ubadyullah ibn 'Adi ibn al-Khiyar. Az-Zuhri related from him. He had a lot of *hadiths*.

'Umara ibn Ukayma al-Laythi

One of Kinana. His *kunya* was Abu'l-Walid. He died in 101 AH at the age of 79. He related from Abu Hurayra and az-Zuhri related one *hadith* from him. Some did not accept him as authoritative and say that he is unknown.

Humayd ibn Malik ibn al-Khutham ad-Di'li

Of Kinana. He was early on. He related from Sa'd and Abu Hurayra. Bukayr ibn 'Abdullah and az-Zuhri related from him. He had few *hadiths*.

'Ubaydullah ibn 'Abdullah ibn 'Utba

His *kunya* was Abu 'Abdullah. Abu'z-Zinad said, "'Ubaydullah used to quote poetry and he was asked about that. He replied, "Don't you see that when someone with tuberculosis does not cough it up he will die?"

Muhammad ibn 'Umar said, "'Ubaydullah was a scholar who had gone blind. He related from Abu Hurayra, Ibn 'Abbas, 'A'isha, Abu Talha, Sahl ibn Hunayf, Zayd ibn Khalid, and Abu Sa'id al-Khudri. He was a reliable *faqih* with a lot of *hadith* and knowledge, and a poet."

Muhammad ibn Hilal said, "I noticed that 'Ubaydullah ibn 'Abdullah did not trim his moustache a lot. He trimmed a reasonable amount from it. He died in Madina in 98 AH." Someone else said in 99 AH.

Yahya ibn 'Abdu'r-Rahman ibn Hatib

He was born while 'Uthman was khalif. His *kunya* was Abu Muhammad. He listened to Ibn 'Umar and Abu Sa'id al-Khudri. He was reliable with a lot of *hadith*. He died in Madina in 104 AH.

'Awf ibn at-Tufayl ibn al-Harith

Of Azd. At-Tufayl was the brother of 'Abdu'r-Rahman and 'Abdu'r-Rahman, the children of Abu Bakr as-Siddiq by their mother, Umm Ruman. Al-Harith came from as-Sura and made an alliance with Abu Bakr. He was accompanied by his wife, Umm Ruman. Then he died and Abu Bakr married her.

Safwan ibn 'Iyad

The nephew of Usama ibn Zayd. He was the husband of the daughter of Usama. He related from Usama and az-Zuhri related from him.

'Irak ibn Malik al-Ghifari

Of Kinana. He lived in Madina among the Banu Ghifar and died in Madina while Yazid was khalif. He related from Abu Hurayra, and az-Zuhri related from him as did his son Khuthaym ibn 'Irak. He was abstinent and unyielding. He was put in charge of the police in

Madina by Ziyad ibn 'Abdullah al-Harithi. Ziyad was in charge of Madina and Makka while as-Saffah was khalif and in the beginning of the khalifate of al-Mansur.

Abu'l-Ghusn said, "I saw that 'Irak ibn Malik did not trim his moustache so that it was almost shaved. He removed a fair amount from it."

Abu'l-Ghusn said, "I saw 'Irak ibn Malik fasting all the time."

❊❊❊❊❊

Others in this generation also include **Muhammad ibn 'Abdu'r-Rahman ibn Ma'iz**, from whom az-Zuhri related; **Muhammad ibn 'Ammar ibn Yasir**, who is related from; **Hamza ibn Suhayb ibn Sinan** of Quraysh, who related from his father; **'Umara ibn Suhayb**, who was killed at the Battle of al-Harra in 63 AH; **az-Zibriqan ibn 'Amr**, who is related from; **Tariq ibn Abi Mukhashin al-Aslami**, who lived in Madina and related from az-Zuhri; **Abu 'Uthman ibn Sanna al-Khuza'i**, from whom az-Zuhri related; **'Abdullah ibn 'Abdu'r-Rahman ibn Hatib,** who was killed at the Battle of al-Harra; **Hanzala ibn 'Ali ibn al-Asqa' al-Aslami**, who related from Abu Hurayra and from whom az-Zuhri related; **'Iyad ibn Khalifa al-Khuza'i**, from whom az-Zuhri related; **'Abdu'r-Rahman ibn Malik ibn Ju'shum**, of Kinana, from whom az-Zuhri related *hadiths*; **'Abida ibn Sufyan al-Hadrami**, who related from Abu Hurayra and had few *hadiths;* **as-Sa'ib ibn Malik al-Kinani**, from whom az-Zuhri related; and **Nahar ibn 'Abdullah al-Qaysi**, who listened to Abu Sa'id al-Khudri.

This generation also includes: **'Uthman ibn Sulayman ibn Abi Hathma**, whose mother was Maymuna bint Qays of Kinana and who related from 'Uthman; **'Iyad ibn 'Abdullah ibn Sa'd**, whose mother was an *umm walad* and whose children were Wahb, 'Abdullah and Salim, whose mother was Umm Hasan bint 'Amr, and Sa'd; **Muhammad ibn Usama ibn Zayd**, who died in Madina while al-Walid I was khalif and from whom Yazid ibn 'Abdullah reported; his brother, **al-Hasan ibn Usama**, who is reliable with few *hadiths*; **Muhammad ibn Hamza al-Aslami**, who related from Usama ibn Zayd al-Laythi and from his father; **'Abdu'r-Rahman ibn Jarhad**, who related from his father, and who had a son called Zur'a, and from whom Abu'z-Zinad related; **Sinan ibn Abi Sinan ad-Di'li**, who died in 105 AH at the age of 82 and from whom az-Zuhri related; **ar-Rabi' ibn Sabra al-Juhani**, who related from his father who was a Companion and from whom az-Zuhri related; **'Ubayd ibn as-Sabbaq ath-Thaqafi**, who related from Sahl ibn Hunayf and Ibn 'Abbas; **Malih ibn 'Abdullah as-Sa'di**, who related from Abu Hurayra and from whom Muhammad ibn 'Amr al-Laythi related; **Muharrar ibn Abi'l-Hurayra ibn 'Amir**, who died in Madina while 'Umar II was khalif; and **'Amr ibn Abi Sufyan ibn Usayd**, of Thaqif, a companion of Abu Hurayra, from whom az-Zuhri related.

The Ansar of the Second Generation

'Abbad ibn Abi Na'ila

His mother was Umm Sahl bint Rumi. His children were Yunus, Umm Salama, Umm 'Amr, Umm Musa, Salama and Qurayba, whose mother was Umm al-Harith bint al-Hubab; Umm al-'Ala' and Umm 'Amr, whose mother was Safiyya bint Ma'bad. He was killed along with his son Salama at the Battle of al-Harra in Dhu'l-Hijja 63 AH while Yazid was khalif.

Zayd ibn Muhammad ibn Maslama

Of Aws. His mother was an *umm walad*. His children were Qays and Umm Zayd, whose mother was one of the Banu Muharib. He was killed at al-Harra.

Al-Husayn ibn 'Abdu'r-Rahman said, "The first houses of Madina to be looted when the fighting of the Battle of al-Harra was still unfinished were those of the Banu 'Abd al-Ashhal. They did not leave any utensils in their houses, nor any jewellery on a woman, nor any garments or rugs, nor any chicken or pigeon which they did not slaughter. They tied the chickens and pigeons behind them. We were driven from house to house. We remained like that for three days while Musrif was at al-'Aqiq, and then things continued like that until the beginning of Muharram. When they entered the house of Muhammad ibn Maslama, the women started shouting and Zayd ibn Muhammad and some people came running to the noise and found ten men looting. They fought at the door, in the house and in the room until the Syrians were slain and what they had taken was recovered. Whatever of their possessions came from a free person they threw into a waterless well and piled dirt over it. Then some more looters came and they fought in that place until Zayd ibn Muhammad was killed at his door along with Salama ibn 'Abbad and Ja'far ibn Yazid. They were all found where they had fallen. Zayd ibn Muhammad had fourteen sword wounds, four of them on his face."

'Abdullah ibn Rafi' ibn Khadij

Of Aws. His mother was Lubna bint Qurra ibn 'Alqama. His children were Na'isa and 'A'isha, whose mother was Umm al-Ash'ath; and Umm Ja'far, whose mother was Umm al-Ash'ath bint Rifa'a. He related from his father and he was reliable with few *hadiths*.

'Ubaydullah ibn Rafi'

His mother was Asma' bint Ziyad. His children were al-Fadl, by whom he had his *kunya*, 'Awna, Umm al-Fadl, Burayha and Umm Rafi', whose mother was an *umm walad*. 'Ubaydullah related from his father and had few *hadiths*. He died in Madina in 111 AH while Hisham was khalif at the age of 85.

Sahl ibn Rafi'

His mother was Asma' bint Ziyad. His children were al-Mundhir, 'Imran, Sulayman, Muhammad, 'A'isha, Umm 'Isa and Umm Humayda, whose mother was al-Mundhir bint Rifa'a.

Rifa'a ibn Rafi'

His mother was Asma' bint Ziyad. His children were 'Abaya and Imru'l-Qays, by an *umm walad*; Zumayl, by an *umm walad*; Yanfa', by an *umm walad*; Sahl, 'A'isha and Maymuna, whose mother was Hind bint Tha'laba; and 'Abda, Asma' and Bakra, by an *umm walad*. His *kunya* was Abu Khadij. He died in Madina while 'Umar ibn 'Abdu'l-'Aziz was khalif.

Haram ibn Sa'd

Of Aws. Az-Zuhri related from him. He was reliable, with few *hadiths*. His *kunya* was Abu Sa'id. He died in Madina in 113 AH when he was 70.

Namla ibn Abi Namla

Abu Namla was 'Amr ibn Mu'adh. His mother was Kabsha bint Hatib. He had children whose line came to an end. He related from his father and az-Zuhri related from him.

Salih ibn Khawwat ibn Jubayr

His mother was one of the Banu Tha'laba. His children were Khawwat, Abu Hanna and Umm Musa, whose mother was Umm Hasan bint Abi Hanna ibn Ghaziya; and Hadba, whose mother was one of the Banu Unayf. He related from his father, but had few *hadiths*.

Habib ibn Khawwat

His mother was one of the Banu Tha'laba. He had a son, Da'ud, whose mother was an *umm walad*. Habib was killed in the Battle of al-Harra in 63 AH.

'Ubaydullah ibn Mujammi'

His mother was Salma bint Thabit. His children were 'Imran, Dahdaha and Maryam, whose mother was Lubna bint 'Abdullah. 'Ubaydullah was killed at the Battle of al-Harra.

Yazid ibn Thabit ibn Wadi'a

His mother was one of the Banu Unayf. He had two sons, 'Abdullah and Isma'il. Az-Zuhri related from Yazid ibn Thabit.

Muhammad ibn Jabr

Of Bali, allies of Aws. He was killed at the Battle of al-Harra. His father was martyred at Badr on the side of the Messenger of Allah.

Abu'l-Baddah ibn 'Asim

Of Bali, allies of Aws. Muhammad ibn 'Umar said, "Abu'l-Baddah was his nickname. His *kunya* was Abu 'Amr. He died in 117 AH at the age of 84 while Hisham was khalif. He was reliable with few *hadiths*."

Kharija ibn Zayd ibn Thabit

Of an-Najjar. His mother was Umm Sa'd Jamila bint Sa'd ibn ar-Rabi'. His children were Zayd, 'Amr, 'Abdullah, Muhammad, Habiba, Humayda, Umm Yahya and Umm Sulayman, whose mother was Umm 'Amr bint Hazm. Ibrahim ibn Yahya reported that his *kunya* was Abu Zayd.

Zayd ibn as-Sa'ib reported that Kharija wore a ring on his left hand. He said, "I saw the mark of prostration between Kharija's eyes. It was not large and none of it was on his nose."

Zayd ibn as-Sa'ib said, "I saw that Kharija ibn Zayd sometimes let his cloak hang down when he undressed. When he had a shirt on, I did not see that. He had a beautiful body." He also said, "I saw Kharija ibn Zayd wearing a silk/wool garment and I saw him wear a red cloak. I saw him wearing a white turban. Kharija related from his father Zayd. He was reliable with few *hadiths*."

Kharija said, "I dreamt that I built 70 steps. When I finished them, I collapsed. I have now completed 70 years." He died that year.

Abu'z-Zinad said, "Kharija ibn Zayd died in 100 AH while 'Umar II was khalif. He died in Madina and Abu Bakr ibn Muhammad, the governor of Madina at that time, prayed over him. I saw a cloak left on his seat."

Zayd ibn as-Sa'ib said, "I saw water being sprinkled on the grave of Kharija ibn Zayd."

Sa'd ibn Zayd ibn Thabit

Of an-Najjar. His mother was Umm Sa'd bint Sa'd. His children were Qays, Sa'id, who is Sa'dan, and 'Abdu'r-Rahman, whose mother was an *umm walad*; Musa, Bishr and Maryam, whose mother was an *umm walad*; Da'ud and Habiba, by an *umm walad*; and Sulayman and Sa'd, by an *umm walad*. He related from Sa'd ibn Zayd. He was killed in the Battle of al-Harra in 63 AH.

Sulayman ibn Zayd ibn Thabit

Of an-Najjar. His mother was Umm Sa'd bint Sa'd. His children were Sa'id, Humayd, Muhammad and 'Abdullah, whose mother was Umm Humayd bint 'Abdullah. He was killed at the Battle of al-Harra.

Yahya ibn Zayd ibn Thabit

His mother was Umm Sa'd bint Sa'd. His children were Zakariyya and Ibrahim, whose mother was Bassama bint 'Umara. He was killed at the Battle of al-Harra.

165

Isma'il ibn Zayd ibn Thabit

His mother was Umm Sa'd bint Sa'd. His *kunya* was Abu Mus'ab. His children were Mus'ab, whose mother was Umama bint Julayha; and Sa'd, whose mother was Maymuna bint Bilal. He was the youngest child of Zayd ibn Thabit. He did not see his father or meet him. He related from others and had few *hadiths*.

Salit ibn Zayd ibn Thabit

His mother was an *umm walad*. His children were Yasar, whose mother was Zaynab; and Habiba and Khulayda, whose mother was Na'ila bint 'Amr. He was killed in the Battle of al-Harra.

'Abdu'r-Rahman ibn Zayd ibn Thabit

His mother was an *umm walad*. His children were Sa'id, Umm Kulthum and Umm Aban, whose mother was 'Amra bint 'Abdu'l-'Ala. He was killed in the Battle of al-Harra.

Zayd ibn Zayd ibn Thabit

He was killed at al-Harra. Seven of the sons of Zayd ibn Thabit were killed in the Battle of al-Harra.

'Abdu'r-Rahman ibn Hassan ibn Thabit

His mother was Sirin the Copt, the sister of Mariya, the mother of Ibrahim, the son of the Messenger of Allah. The Messenger of Allah صلعم gave her to Hassan ibn Thabit, and she had 'Abdu'r-Rahman by him. So he was the maternal cousin of Ibrahim the son of the Prophet. He was a poet and related from his father and others. His children were al-Walid, Isma'il and Umm Firas, whose mother was Umm Shayba bint as-Saib; and Sa'id who was a poet who is related from and whose mother was an *umm walad*; and Hassan and al-Furay'a. His *kunya* was Abu Sa'id. He was a poet with few *hadiths*.

Muhammad ibn Nubayt ibn Jabir

Of Najjar. His mother was al-Furay'a bint Abi Umama. His children were 'Uthman Abu Umama, 'Abdullah and Umm Kulthum, whose mother was Umm 'Abdullah bint 'Umara. He was killed at the Battle of al-Harra and left no descendants.

'Abdu'l-Malik ibn Nubayt ibn Jabir

Of Najjar. His mother was al-Furay'a bint Abi Umama. His children were 'Amr, Abu Umama, Muhammad and Nubayt, whose mother was Umm Kulthum bint Yahya. He was killed at al-Harra.

'Abdu'r-Rahman ibn Abi Sa'id al-Khudri

His mother was Umm 'Abdullah bint 'Abdullah ibn al-Harith.

Muhammad ibn 'Umar said that his *kunya* was Abu Muhammad. 'Abdullah ibn Muhammad said that it was Abu Ja'far. His children were 'Abdullah and Sa'id, who is Rubayh, whose mother was Umm Ayyub bint 'Umayr. He had a lot of *hadith* but was not firm. They thought his transmission weak and did not use it as proof. He related from his father. Muhammad ibn 'Umar said that he died in Madina in 112 AH at the age of 77.

Hamza ibn Abi Sa'id al-Khudri

His mother was Umm 'Abdullah bint 'Abdullah ibn al-Harith. His children were Mas'ud, whose mother was Khawla bint ar-Rabi'; and Malik and Umm Yahya, whose mother was al-Fari'a bint Khalid. He related from his father.

Sa'id ibn Abi Sa'id al-Khudri

His mother was Umm 'Abdullah bint 'Abdullah ibn al-Harith. His children were Hamza and Hind – who is related from and who related from her father – and their mother was Fa'ma bint Bashir; and al-Walid, whose mother was Umm Hasan ibn Muhammad.

Bashir ibn Abi Mas'ud

His children were Umm Tha'lab and Umm Salama, whose mother was one of the Banu Sulaym. 'Urwa ibn az-Zubayr related from him.

Yazid ibn an-Nu'man ibn Bashir

His mother was Na'ila bint Bashir of Kalb. His children were 'Abdu'l-'Aziz, Sadaqa and Nu'aym, whose mother was an *umm walad*; 'Abdu'l-Wahid and 'Abdu'r-Razzaq, whose mother was an *umm walad*; Shabib whose mother was an *umm walad*; 'Abdu'l-Malik and 'Abdu'l-Karim, whose mother was an *umm walad*; Isma'il, whose mother was an *umm walad*; Jabir and Sa'id, whose mother was an *umm walad*; Umm al-Banin and Humayda, whose mother was an *umm walad*; Khulayda, whose mother was an *umm walad*; Sufyan, whose mother was an *umm walad*; and Ubayya by an *umm walad*.

'Abdu'r-Rahman ibn 'Abdullah ibn Khubayb

Of Khazraj. His mother was 'Awna bint Abi Mas'ud. He had a son Khubayb from whom 'Ubaydullah ibn 'Amr, Shu'ba, Malik ibn Anas and others related. 'Abdu'r-Rahman was killed at al-Harra in 63 AH while Yazid was khalif.

Khallad ibn as-Sa'ib ibn Khallad

Of Khazraj. His mother was Unaysa bint Tha'laba. His children were Ibrahim, whose mother was an *umm walad*; Khadima, whose mother was Jamila bint Tamim; and Umm Sa'd and Umm Sahl, whose mother was an *umm walad*. He was reliable with few *hadiths*. His father was a Companion of the Prophet صلعم .

Al-'Abbas ibn Sahl ibn Sa'd

His mother was 'A'isha bint Khuzayma. His children were Ubayy, 'Abdu's-Salam, Umm al-Harith, Amina and Umm Salama, whose mother was Jamal bint Ja'da; and 'Abdu'l-Muhayman and 'Anbasa, whose mother was an *umm walad*. He was born while 'Umar was khalif. 'Uthman was murdered when al-'Abbas ibn Sahl was fifteen. He related from 'Uthman. After that he was loyal to 'Abdullah ibn az-Zubayr. He related from Abu Humayd as-Sa'idi. He was reliable but did not have a lot of *hadiths*.

Al-'Abbas said, "I was fifteen in the reign of 'Uthman when the people were putting their hands in their garments to protect them from the cold and the heat."

Muhammad ibn 'Umar and others said that he died in Madina while al-Walid I was khalif.

Hamza ibn Abi Usayd

His mother was Salama bint Wa'lan. His *kunya* was Abu Malik. He had a son called Yahya.

His client, Abu Usayd, said, "I saw Hamza ibn Usayd as-Sa'idi wearing a garment with a plaited border."

Ibn al-Ghasil said, "Hamza ibn Abi Usayd died in Madina while Walid I was khalif. He had few *hadiths*. His son Yahya related from him."

Al-Mundhir ibn Abi Usayd as-Sa'idi

His mother was Salama bint Wahb of Khazraj. His children were az-Zubayr, Suwayd and al-Hawsa' – who is Umm al-Hasan, whose mother was Mariya bint 'Abdullah; Bishr and Khulayda, whose mother was an *umm walad*; Khalid and Hafsa, whose mother was Umm Ja'far bint 'Amr; Sa'id, by whom he has his *kunya*, 'A'isha, Sawda and Fatima, whose mother was 'Amra bint Abi Humayd.

'Abdullah ibn Ka'b ibn Malik

Of Khazraj. His mother was 'Umayra bint Jubayr. His children were 'Abdu'r-Rahman, Ma'mar, Ma'qil, Nu'man, Kharija, 'Amra and 'A'isha, whose mother was Khalida bint 'Abdullah. He was blind. His son 'Abdullah was his guide. He listened to 'Uthman. He was reliable with *hadiths*.

'Ubaydullah ibn Ka'b

His mother was 'Umayra bint Jubayr. His children were Umm Abiha, whose mother was Mulayka bint 'Abdullah; Umm 'Uthman and Umm Bishr, whose mother was Sahla bint an-Nu'man; and 'Amira, whose mother was an *umm walad*. His *kunya* was Abu Fadala. He was reliable with few *hadiths*.

Ma'bad ibn Ka'b

His mother was 'Umayra bint Jubayr. His children were Ka'b and Umm Kulthum, whose mother was Hafsa bint an-Nu'man. He related from Abu Qatada.

'Abdu'r-Rahman ibn Ka'b

His mother was an *umm walad*. His children were Bashir, Ka'b, Muhammad and Humayd, whose mother was Umm al-Banin bint Abi Qatada; and Umm al-Fadl, whose mother was Umm Sa'id bint 'Abdullah. His *kunya* was Abu'l-Khattab. He was reliable with a lot of *hadiths* from his brother. He died while Sulayman was khalif.

'Abdullah ibn Abi Qatada

Of Khazraj. His mother was Sulafa bint al-Bara'. His children were Qatada, Busra and Umm al-Banin, whose mother was Umm Kathir bint 'Abdu'r-Rahman; and Yahya and Zabiyya, whose mother was an *umm walad*. His *kunya* was Abu Yahya. He related from his father. He died in Madina while al-Walid I was khalif. He was reliable with few *hadiths*. His brother, 'Abdu'r-Rahman ibn Abi Qatada, was killed at the Battle of al-Harra.

Thabit ibn Abi Qatada

His mother was an *umm walad*. His children were 'Abdu'r-Rahman, Mus'ab, Abu Qatada, Kabsha, 'Abda and Umm al-Banin, whose mother was an *umm walad*. His *kunya* was Abu Mus'ab. He related from his father and died in Madina while al-Walid I was khalif. He had few *hadiths*.

Yazid ibn Abi'l-Yasar

Of Khazraj. His children were Sa'd and 'Abdullah, whose mother was Kabsha bint Thabit; Yazid and Umm Sa'id, whose mother was an *umm walad*; and Umm Aban, whose mother was Fatima bint Abi Salma. He was killed in the Battle of al-Harra in 63 AH.

'Abdu'r-Rahman ibn Jabir ibn 'Abdullah

His mother was Suhayma bint Mas'ud. His children were 'Uqba, whose mother was Umm al-Banin bint Salama; and Umm Khalid, whose mother was Ayyub bint Yazid. He related from his father. There is some weakness in his transmission, and in that of his brother. They were not used as evidence.

His brother, Muhammad ibn Jabir ibn 'Abdullah

His mother was Umm al-Harith bint Muhammad. He had a son, Kulayb, whose mother was Umm Salama bint ar-Rabi'. He related from his father.

'Ubayd ibn Rifa'a ibn Rafi'

His mother was an *umm walad*. His children were Zayd, Sa'id and Rifa'a, whose mother was Hind bint Rafi'; Isma'il, Umm Musa, Humayda, Burayha, Umm al-Banin the elder, Zayda and Umm 'Amr, whose mother was Sumayka bint Ka'b; 'Abdu'r-Rahman and Umm 'Abdu'r-Rahman, whose mother was an *umm walad*; Ishaq, whose mother was Umm Safwan bint Abi 'Uthman; and Amatullah, 'A'isha, Umm al-Banin the younger and 'Ubayd, by various *umm walads*.

Mu'adh ibn Rifa'a ibn Rafi'

His mother was Umm 'Abdullah Salma bint Mu'awwidh. His children were al-Harith, Sa'd, Muhammad and Musa, whose mother was 'Amra bint an-Nu'man.

An-Nu'man ibn Abi 'Ayyash

His mother was an *umm walad*. His children were Talha, whose mother was Umm 'Ubada bint Qays; and Muhammad and Yahya, whose mother was Habiba bint Ka'b.

Mu'awiya ibn Abi 'Ayyash

His mother was an *umm walad*. His children were Muhammad, Ramla Ja'da and Umm Ishaq, whose mother was an *umm walad*.

Sulayman ibn Abi 'Ayyash

His mother was an *umm walad*. His children were 'Isa, Hasan, Umm al-Walid and Zayd, whose mother was Umm Kulthum bint Muhammad. He was killed in the Battle of al-Harra.

Bashir ibn Abi 'Ayyash

His mother was an *umm walad*. His children were Yahya, Zakariyya, Umm Iyas, Umm al-Qasim and Hikma, whose mother was from Kalb Quda'a; and Umm al-Harith, whose mother was one of the Banu Salima. Bashir was killed in the Battle of al-Harra.

Farwa ibn Abi 'Ubada

His mother was Umm Khalid bint 'Amr. His children were 'Uthman – who was killed at al-Harra along with his father, Salama, Da'ud and Umm Jamil, whose mother was Umm Kulthum bint Qays; and 'Abdu'r-Rahman, whose mother was Kabsha bint 'Abdu'r-Rahman. Farwa was killed at the Battle of al-Harra. His father, Sa'd ibn 'Uthman, was one of the people present at the Battle of Badr.

'Uqba ibn Abi 'Ubada

His mother was an *umm walad*. His children were Sa'd, Isma'il, 'Abdullah and 'A'isha, whose mother was Jamila bint Abi 'Ayyash. He was killed in the Battle of al-Harra.

Thabit ibn Qays ibn Sa'd

His mother was Kabsha bint Yazid. His children were 'Abdu'r-Rahman, Muhammad, Umm Sa'id, Hafsa, Umm Hasan and Umm Mas'ud, whose mother was Kabsha bint Abi 'Ayyash.

'Umar ibn Khalda az-Zuraqi

He listened to Abu Hurayra and was made governor of Madina by 'Abdu'l-Malik. Rabi'a ibn Abi 'Abdu'r-Rahman reported that he saw Ibn Khalda giving judgement in the mosque.

Ibn Abi Dhi'b said, "I was with 'Umar ibn Khalda when he was giving judgement in Madina. He said to a man who was presented to him, 'Go, you foul person, and imprison yourself.' The man went without any guard accompanying him. We children followed him to the prison and he jailed himself."

Muhammad ibn 'Umar said, "'Umar ibn Khalda was reliable with few *hadiths*. He was an imposing man who was unyielding, scrupulous and abstinent. He did not take any recompense for giving judgement. When he was dismissed, it was said to him, 'Abu Hafs, what do you think of what you were doing?' He replied, 'We had brothers and we cut them off, and we had land from which we had a livelihood and we sold it and spent its price.'"

Muhammad ibn 'Umar said, "Two men had an arguement in Madina at the beginning of that time and one of them said to his companion, 'You are more bankrupt than the qadi!' Today the qadis have become governors, tyrants and kings, with revenue, estates, commerce and property."

Ishaq ibn Ka'b ibn 'Ujra

Hisham ibn Muhammad al-Kalbi and 'Abdullah ibn Muhammad al-Ansari said, "He was from Bali Quda'a, the ally of the Banu Qawqal of Khazraj. He was killed in the Battle of al-Harra in 63 AH.

Abu 'Ufayr Muhammad ibn Sahl ibn Abi Hathma

Of Aws. His mother was Tuhya bint al-Bara' ibn 'Azib. His children were 'Ufayr, Ja'far, al-Bara', Dubayya, Amira (who is Talla) and Budayya, whose mother was 'Afra' bint Dihya; and 'Isa, whose mother was an *umm walad*. He related from his father.

'Umar ibn al-Hakam ibn Abi'l-Hakim

He is one of the Banu 'Amr ibn 'Amir, one of the Fitiyun, the allies of Aws of the Ansar. They were summoned for the debts of the Banu Umayya ibn Zayd and the Banu Umayya asked Aws for help. His *kunya* was Abu Hafs. He was reliable with sound *hadiths*. He died in 117 AH at the age of 80 while Hisham was khalif.

*****

Others in this group include **'Amr ibn Khawwat**, who was killed in the Battle of al-Harra; **'Abdu'l-Malik ibn Jabr**, who related from Jabir ibn 'Abdullah; **'Abbad ibn 'Asim**, who was killed in the Battle of al-Harra; **'Abdullah ibn Zayd ibn Thabit**, whose mother was an *umm walad* and who was killed al-Harra; **'Umara ibn 'Uqba ibn Kudaym**, whose mother was an *umm walad* and who was killed in the Battle of al-Harra; **Mas'ud ibn 'Ubada**, whose mother was an *umm walad* and who was killed at the Battle of al-Harra; **'Umar ibn Thabit al-Khazraji**, from whom az-Zuhri related; **Muhammad ibn Ka'b**, who was killed at the Battle of al-Harra; **'Abdu'r-Rahman**

ibn Rafi', whose mother was Asma' bint Ziyad and who had two children, Hurayr and Sukayna, whose mother was Umm al-Hasan bint Usayd; **'Ubayd ibn Rafi'**, whose children were Rafi', 'Ayyash and Rifa'a, whose mother was Humayda bint Abi 'Abs; **'Amr, Muhammad and Zayd ibn Thabit ibn Qays**, whose mother was Umm Habib bint Qays, and who were all killed in the Battle of al-Harra; **Yahya ibn Mujammi'**, whose mother was Salma bint Thabit and who died at al-Harra; **al-Hajjaj ibn 'Amr**, of Najjar, whose mother was Umm al-Hajjaj bint Qays ibn Rafi'; **Muhammad ibn an-Nu'man ibn Bashir**, of Khazraj, whose children were an-Nu'man, Rawaha, 'Abdu'l-Karim and 'Abdu'l-Hamid, by various *umm walads*; and **Muhammad ibn 'Abdullah ibn Zayd**, whose mother was Su'da bint Kulayb and who had a son called Bashir.

Some of the Clients
of the Second Generation

Busr ibn Sa'id

The client of the Hadramis, or of Ibn al-Hadrami. He lived among the Hadramis of the Banu Hudayla. Busr related from Sa'd ibn Abi Waqqas, 'Abdullah ibn Unays, Zayd ibn Thabit, Abu Hurayra, Abu Sa'id al-Khudri and 'Ubaydullah al-Khawlani. 'Ubaydullah was in the care of Maymuna bint al-Harith. Busr was one of the devout worshippers and one of the people of *zuhd* in this world. He was reliable with many *hadiths*. He was scrupulous. He came to Basra and then wanted to return to Madina, and al-Farazdaq, the poet, accompanied him. The people of Madina only became aware of this when the two looked down at them from a *mahmil*. The people of Madina were astonished by that. Al-Farazdaq use to say, "I have not seen a companion better than Busr ibn Sa'id." He used to reply, "And I did not see a companion better than al-Farazdaq."

Muhammad ibn 'Umar said, "Busr died in Madina in 100 AH while 'Umar II was khalif, at the age of 78."

Malik ibn Anas said, "Busr died and did not leave a shroud. 'Abdullah ibn 'Abdu'l-Malik ibn Marwan died and left eight bushels of gold. 'Umar II heard about their deaths and said, 'By Allah, their record is the same because I would prefer that 'Abdullah ibn 'Abdu'l-Malik was still alive.' Maslama ibn 'Abdu'l-Malik said to him, 'Amir al-Mu'minin, this sacrifice is for the people of your house.' He replied, 'By Allah, we do not remember the people of excellence except by their excellence."

'Ubaydullah ibn Abi Rafi'

The client of the Prophet صلعم . He related from 'Ali ibn Abi Talib and wrote for him. He was reliable with a lot of *hadiths*.

Muhammad ibn 'Abdu'r-Rahman ibn Thawban

The client of the family of al-Akhnas ibn Shariq ath-Thaqafi. Some of them came from Yemen. His *kunya* was Abu 'Abdullah. He related from Zayd ibn Thabit, Abu Hurayra, Abu Sa'id al-Khudri, Ibn 'Abbas, Ibn 'Umar, Muhammad ibn Iyas and from his mother, from 'A'isha. He was reliable with a lot of *hadiths*.

Humran ibn Aban

The client of 'Uthman ibn 'Affan. He related from 'Uthman and moved to Basra where he settled. His son claimed that they were from an-Namir ibn Qasit. He had a lot of *hadith* but I did not see them use his *hadith* as evidence.

'Abdu'r-Rahman ibn Hurmuz al-A'raj

His *kunya* was Abu Da'ud, the client of Muhammad ibn Rabi'a ibn al-Harith ibn 'Abdu'l-Muttalib. He related from 'Abdullah ibn Buhayna, Abu Hurayra and 'Abdu'r-Rahman ibn 'Abdu'l-Qari'.

'Uthman ibn 'Ubaydullah said, "I saw someone who read to al-A'raj his *hadith* from Abu Hurayra from the Messenger of Allah صلعم. He asked, 'Is it your *hadith*, Abu Da'ud?' – 'Yes,' he replied. He asked, 'Can I say, "'Abdu'r-Rahman related to me ..." when I read to you?' – 'Yes,' he replied, 'Say: "'Abdu'r-Rahman ibn Hurmuz related to me ..."'"

Abu'z-Zinad and 'Abdullah ibn al-Fadl said, "'Abdu'r-Rahman ibn Hurmuz went over to Alexandria and stayed there until he died in 117 AH. He was reliable with a lot of *hadiths*.

Yazid ibn Hurmuz

The client of the family of Abu Dhubab ibn Daws. His *kunya* was Abu 'Abdullah. He was in charge of the clients in the Battle of al-Harra and died after it. His son 'Abdullah was one of the important *fuqaha'* of Madina. Yazid was reliable with few *hadiths*.

Sa'id ibn Yasar Abu'l-Hubab

The client of al-Hasan ibn 'Ali ibn Abi Talib. He related from Abu Hurayra and Ibn 'Umar. He died in Madina in 117 AH. It is also said that Sa'id was the client of Shamsa who was a Christian woman in Madina who became Muslim through al-Hasan ibn 'Ali. Sa'id was reliable with many *hadiths*.

Salman Abu 'Abdullah al-Agharr

The client of Juhayna. He was a story-teller who reported from Abu Sa'id al-Khudri and Abu Hurayra.

Muhammad ibn 'Umar said, "I heard his sons say that he met 'Umar ibn al-Khattab but that is not affirmed by anyone except him. He was reliable with few *hadiths*."

Sa'id ibn Marjana

His *kunya* was Abu 'Uthman. He had excellence and transmission from himself. He was devoted to 'Ali ibn Husayn ibn 'Ali. He died in Madina in 97 AH at the age of 77. He was reliable and had *hadiths*.

'Ubayd ibn Hunayn

The client of the family of Zayd ibn al-Khattab. His *kunya* was Abu 'Abdullah. He was the uncle of Abu Fulayh ibn Sulayman. It is said that he was one of those captured at 'Ayn at-Tamir whom Khalid ibn al-Walid sent to Madina when Abu Bakr was khalif. 'Ubayd ibn Hunayn related from Zayd ibn Thabit, Abu Hurayra, and Ibn 'Abbas. He was reliable, with a lot of *hadiths*.

'Ubayd ibn Hunayn said, "When 'Uthman was murdered, I said to Zayd ibn Thabit, 'Recite *Surat al-A'raf* (7) to me.' He said, 'I do not know it by heart. You read it to me.' So I read it to him and he did not correct me, even an *alif* or a *waw*.'"

Muhammad ibn 'Umar said, "'Ubayd ibn Hunayn died in Madina in 105 AH at the age of 95."

'Abdullah ibn Hunayn

The client of al-'Abbas ibn 'Abdu'l-Muttalib. He has descendants in Madina. His son Ibrahim ibn 'Abdullah was a transmitter of knowledge, and az-Zuhri and others took from him. His descendants still say that they are the clients of al-'Abbas ibn 'Abdu'l-Muttalib even today. It is said that Hunayn was the client of Mithqab. Mithqab was the client of Mishal, Mishal was the client of Shammas, and Shammas was the client of 'Abbas.

Usama ibn Zayd al-Laythi said, "I visited 'Abdullah ibn Hunayn in the nights when Yazid ibn 'Abdu'l-Malik was appointed, and he died soon after that." He had few *hadiths*.

'Umayr

The client of Umm al-Fadl bint al-Harith al-Hilaliyya, the mother of the sons of al-'Abbas. His *kunya* was Abu 'Abdullah. He related from Umm al-Fadl and Ibn 'Abbas. In some transmissions 'Umayr is referred to as the client of Ibn 'Abbas, but he is the client of his mother. He died in Madina in 104 AH.

'Ikrima

The client of 'Abdullah ibn 'Abbas. His *kunya* was Abu 'Abdullah.

Muhammad ibn Rashid said, "Ibn 'Abbas died and his slave 'Ikrima was bought by Khalid ibn Yazid for 4,000 dinars. 'Ikrima heard of this and he came to 'Ali ibn 'Abdullah and said, 'You sold me for 4,000 dinars?' – 'Yes,' he replied. He said, 'That is not good for you! You sold your father's knowledge for 4,000 dinars!' 'Ali went to Khalid and asked him to revoke the sale, which he did, and then he freed him."

Mujahid transmitted that Ibn 'Abbas used to give his slaves Arab names: 'Ikrima, Sumay' and Kurayb. He told them, "Marry. When a slave fornicates, Allah removes the light of belief from him – which He may later return to him or keep."

Az-Zubayr ibn al-Khirrit reported that 'Ikrima said, "Ibn 'Abbas used to put a fetter on my foot, and he taught me the Qur'an and he taught me the *Sunna*."

Da'ud reported that 'Ikrima said, "Ibn Abbas recited the *ayat*, *'Why do you rebuke a people whom Allah is going to destroy or severely punish?'* (7:164), and then he said, 'I do not know whether the people will be saved or destroyed.' I continued to study and examine it until I knew that they were saved. He clothed me in a robe."

Sallam ibn Miskin said, "'Ikrima was the person with the greatest knowledge of *tafsir*."

'Abdu'l-Malik ibn Bashir reported that 'Ikrima said, "Ibn 'Abbas remarked to me while we were going from Mina to 'Arafat, 'This is one of your days.' I began to be friendly and Ibn 'Abbas was open to me."

Ayyub reported that 'Ikrima said, "I went to the market and heard a man say something which opened fifty doors of knowledge to me."

'Amr ibn Dinar said, "Kabir ibn Zayd gave me some questions to ask 'Ikrima about. He said, 'There is 'Ikrima, the client of Ibn 'Abbas. He is a sea of knowledge, so ask him.'"

Ayyub said, "I was told that Sa'id ibn Jubayr said, 'If 'Ikrima had withheld his *hadiths* from them, people would have ridden on their camels to him.'"

Abu Ishaq heard Sa'id ibn Jubayr say, "You relate *hadiths* from 'Ikrima which, if I had been with him, he would not have related." Abu Ishaq went and told 'Ikrima and he reported all those *hadiths* to him. He said, "The people were silent, and Sa'id did not speak. Then 'Ikrima rose to his feet and said, 'Abu 'Abdullah, how many do you have?' He indicated thirty. He said, 'He has got the *hadiths*.'"

'Ikrima said, "Do you see those who deny me behind my back? Why do they do not deny me to my face? If they deny me to my face, then, by Allah, they deny me."

A man said to Ayyub, "Abu Bakr, 'Ikrima is suspect." He was silent and then he stated, "I do not suspect him."

Habib said, "'Ikrima and Sa'id passed by 'Ata'. He related some *hadiths* to them and when he got up, I asked them, 'Did you object to anything that he reported?' – 'No,' they replied."

Ayyub was heard to say, "I wanted to visit 'Ikrima. I was in the Basra market when suddenly there he was on a donkey. I was told, 'This is 'Ikrima.' People gathered round him. I went close to him but was unable to ask him anything. I forgot my questions and just stood there beside his donkey. People began to ask him and I remembered what he said."

'Abdu'r-Razzaq mentioned that his father said, "When 'Ikrima joined the army, Tawus put him on a fine camel of his. He was told, 'You gave him a camel and he would have been content with less.' He said, 'I bought the knowledge of this slave with this camel.'"

'Amr ibn Muslim said, "'Ikrima came to Tawus and he mounted him on a fine camel worth 60 dinars and said, 'Shall we not purchase the knowledge of this slave for sixty dinars?'"

Ayyub said, "'Ikrima came to us and people gathered around him until I had to climb on top of the roof of the house."

Ayyub said, "We were told by someone who went before Sa'id ibn al-Musayyab and 'Ikrima about a man who made a vow to do something sinful. Sa'id said, 'He should fulfil it.' 'Ikrima said, 'He should not fulfil it.' So a man went to Sa'id and told him what

'Ikrima had said. Sa'id said, 'Ibn 'Abbas's slave will not leave off until a rope is put around his neck and he is paraded about.' So the man went to 'Ikrima and told him. 'Ikrima said to him, 'You are a bad man.' – 'Why?' he asked. He said, 'As you have conveyed to me, so convey to him. Say to him: "Is the vow made to Allah or to shaytan?" By Allah, if he claims it is to Allah, he is lying. If he claims it is to shaytan, then he should do expiation for it.'"

Ayyub said, "A friend told us, 'We were sitting with Sa'id, 'Ikrima, Tawus (and he also may have said 'Ata') and a group of people. 'Ikrima was speaking at the time. It was as if there were birds on their heads. When he had finished, someone indicated 'thirty' with his hand and someone inclined his head. None of them contradicted him in anything until he mentioned the fish [in the story of Musa]. He said, 'They were keeping it in a small amount of water.' Then Sa'id ibn Jubayr said, 'I testify that I heard Ibn 'Abbas say, "They carried it in a basket."'"

Khalid ibn Safwan said, "I said to al-Hasan, 'Are you not aware that the client of Ibn 'Abbas claims that the Messenger of Allah صلعم forbade *nabidh* made in a jar?' He said, 'By Allah, the client of Ibn 'Abbas has spoken the truth. The Messenger of Allah صلعم forbade the *nabidh* of the jar.'"

Al-Mughira ibn Muslim said, "When 'Ikrima came to Khorasan, Abu Miljaz said, 'Ask him what *'jalajal al-hajj'* is.' He asked 'Ikrima about this and he said, 'I am here in this land. The *'jalajal al-hajj'* is the *ifada*.' This was communicated to Abu Miljaz and he said, 'He has spoken the truth.'"

Musa ibn Yasar said, "I saw 'Ikrima coming from Samarqand on a donkey with a sack or saddlebag under him in which there was silk. The governor of Samarqand had given it to him. He had a slave with him." He said, "I heard that 'Ikrima was asked when he was in Samarqand, 'What brings you to this land?' – 'Need,' he replied."

'Imran ibn Hudayr said, "A man and I went to see 'Ikrima and we saw that he was wearing a tattered turban. My companion said to him, 'What is this turban? We have some turbans.' 'Ikrima replied, 'We do not take anything from people. We only take from amirs.' I remarked, 'A person has knowledge of himself.' He was silent. Only al-Hasan spoke. He said, 'Son of Adam, you are more entitled to do what you do.' He said, 'Al-Hasan has spoken the truth.'"

Khalid al-Hadhdha' said, "Everything that Muhammad said which I reported from Ibn 'Abbas I heard through 'Ikrima. I met him in the days when al-Mukhtar was in Kufa."

Ayyub said, "Khalid al-Hadhdha' asked 'Ikrima some questions. Then Khalid was silent and 'Ikrima said, 'What are you naturally disposed towards?' meaning, 'What you have is almost used up.'"

Sa'id ibn Muslim said, "I saw that 'Ikrima used henna."

Simak said, "I saw a gold ring on 'Ikrima's hand."

'Isam ibn Qudama said, "'Ikrima came to us wearing a white jubbah with no shirt, wrapper or cloak."

Sulayman ibn Harb and 'Arim ibn al-Fadl reported that Ayyub said, "A man asked 'Ikrima, 'How are you this morning, Abu 'Abdullah?'" 'Arim said, "This morning I am in a bad condition, scabby and unhappy." Sulayman said, "This morning I am in a bad condition." Then he mentioned that he had scabies and was grumpy on account of it.

Ya'la ibn Hakim said, "'Ikrima was asked, 'How are you this morning?' He replied, 'In evil.' He was asked, 'Abu 'Abdullah, why do you say that?' He said, 'Allah says it: *"We will test you with both good and evil as a trial."*' (21:35)."

'Ikrima's son reported that 'Ikrima died in 105 AH at the age of 80.

Khalid ibn al-Qasim al-Bayadi said, "Both 'Ikrima and Kuthayyir the poet died on the same day in 105 AH, and I saw the prayer being performed for both of them in the same place after *Dhuhr* in the place where funerals were held. People were saying, 'Today the person with the most *fiqh* and the person with the most poetry have died.'"

Someone else said that people were surprised at their meeting in death given the differences between their viewpoints. 'Ikrima was suspected of being a Kharijite because he denied the Vision [of Allah on the Last Day], while Kuthayyar was a Shi'ite who believed in the return (of the Mahdi). 'Ikrima related from Ibn 'Abbas, Abu Hurayra, al-Husayn ibn 'Ali and 'A'isha.

Abu Nu'aym ibn Dukayn said, "'Ikrima died in 107 AH." Someone else else said in 106 AH.

Musab ibn 'Abdullah said, "'Ikrima held the opinion of the Kharijites so one of the governors of Madina searched for him and so he hid with Da'ud ibn al-Husayn until he died. They said that 'Ikrima had a lot of *hadith* and knowledge like one of the oceans. His *hadiths* are not used as evidence and people say things about him."

Kurayb ibn Abi Muslim

Abu Rishdin. He was the client of 'Abdullah ibn al-'Abbas.

Musa ibn 'Uqba said, "Kurayb deposited a camel load – or the equivalent of a camel load – of the books of Ibn 'Abbas with us. When 'Ali ibn 'Abdullah ibn 'Abbas wanted a book, he wrote to him, 'Send me page such-and-such of so-and-so.' So he copied it and sent it with one of them."

Abu Ishaq reported that he saw al-Kurayb and his companions wearing long shawls with brocaded buttons.

Musa ibn 'Uqba said, "Kurayb died in Madina in 98 AH at the end of Sulayman's khalifate. He was reliable with excellent *hadiths*."

Abu Ma'bad

He was Naqid, the client of 'Abdullah ibn al-'Abbas. Muhammad ibn 'Umar said, "Abu Ma'bad died in Madina in 104 AH at the end of the khalifate of Yazid II. He was reliable with good *hadiths*."

Shu'ba

The client of 'Abdullah ibn al-'Abbas. His *kunya* was Abu 'Abdullah. Ibn Abi Dhi'b and a number of the people of Madina and others related from him, but Malik ibn Anas did not relate from him.

Yahya ibn Sa'id al-Qattan said, "I asked Malik ibn Anas, 'What do you say about Shu'ba, the client of Ibn 'Abbas?' He replied, 'He did not resemble the reciters. He has many *hadiths* but they are not used for evidence.'" Ibn Abi Dhi'b and others related from him.

Muhammad ibn 'Umar said, "Shuba, the client of Ibn 'Abbas, died in the middle of Hisham's khalifate."

Dufayf

The client of 'Abdullah ibn al-'Abbas. He died in 109 AH while Hisham was khalif. Humayd al-A'raj and others related from him. He has few *hadiths*.

Abu 'Ubaydullah

The client of 'Abdullah ibn 'Abbas. Abu Mus'ab at-Tahhan reported that Abu 'Ubaydullah, the client of Ibn 'Abbas reported that Ibn 'Abbas forbade cracking knuckles during the prayer.

Miqsam

The client of 'Abdullah ibn al-Harith. He is said to be the client of Ibn 'Abbas since he devoted himself to him, clung to him, related from him, and his *wala'* went to the Banu Hashim. His *kunya* was Abu'l-Qasim. He related from Umm Salama.

Dhakwan

Abu 'Amr, the client of 'A'isha, the wife of the Prophet صلعم .

'Urwa reported that Dhakwan, 'the slave of Qur'an', used to lead the Quraysh in the prayer, followed by 'Abdu'r-Rahman ibn Abi Bakr, because he had the most recitation of the Qur'an.

'Abdullah ibn Abi Mulayka said, "'A'isha was between Hira' and Thabir when the leading men of Quraysh came to her. When it was time for the prayer, 'Abdu'r-Rahman ibn Abi Bakr led them. If he was not present, then Dhakwan led them."

Muhammad ibn 'Umar and others said, "'A'isha gave him a *tadbir*. She said, 'When you have paid me, then you are free.' He had few *hadiths*. He died during one of the nights of al-Harra. Some said that he may actually have been killed in the battle of al-Harra.

Abu Yunus

The client of 'A'isha, the wife of the Prophet صلعم . He related from 'A'isha, and al-Qa'qa' ibn Hakim and others related from him.

Nabhan

The client of Umm Salama, the wife of the Prophet صلعم . She gave him a *kitaba* which he fulfilled and was freed. Az-Zuhri related two *hadiths* from him. His *kunya* was Abu Yahya.

Thabit

The client of Umm Salama, the wife of the Prophet صلعم. Musa ibn 'Ubayda ar-Rabadhi said, "Thabit, the client of Umm Salama, died in Madina while 'Umar II was khalif." He had few *hadiths*.

Nisah ibn Sarjis

The client of Umm Salama, the wife of the Prophet صلعم by a *kitaba*.

Nisah said, "Umm Salama gave me a *kitaba* by instalments and I paid them. I asked her to reduce it and to end it for me with a gift of gold or silver and she did so. I paid it off early and she reduced it for me."

Muhammad ibn 'Umar said, "We do not know of anyone who reports from Nisah except his son Shayba ibn Nisah. Shayba was the Imam of the people of Madina in recitation in his time along with Abu Ja'far ibn al-Qa'qa', the client of Ibn 'Ayyash."

'Abdullah ibn Rafi'

The client of Umm Salama, the wife of the Prophet صلعم, by emancipation. He listened to Umm Salama and lived until 'Abdullah ibn Abi Yahya, Musa ibn 'Ubayda, Qudama ibn Musa and Jariya ibn 'Imran related from him. He was reliable with a lot of *hadiths*.

Qays

The client of Umm Salama, the wife of the Prophet صلعم. His *kunya* was Abu Qudama. He related from Umm Salama that she was cupped while fasting.

Abu Maymuna

The client of Umm Salama, the wife of the Prophet صلعم. His *kunya* was Abu Qudama. He related from Umm Salama, and Salim ibn Yasar, the client of the Dawsites, related from him. He was the reciter of the people of Madina in his time. Nafi' ibn Abi Nu'aym recited with him.

Kathir ibn Aflah

The client of Abu Ayyub al-Ansari. Muhammad said, "I met Kathir ibn Aflah in a dream. He had already been struck down in the Battle of al-Harra and I knew that he was dead. I was asleep and had this dream. I did not want to call him by his *kunya*. He was in the house of al-Hudhayl ibn Hafsa bint Sirin. They had the same *kunya*. I was afraid that I might disturb al-Hudayl. I called him by his name and he answered me. I said, 'Haven't you been killed?' – 'Yes,' he replied. I asked, 'What did you do?' – 'Good,' he replied. I asked, 'Are you martyrs?' – 'No,' he replied, 'When Muslims fight each other and people are killed in the fighting, they are not martyrs. They are lamented.'"

His brother, 'Abdu'r-Rahman ibn Aflah

The client of Abu Ayyub al-Ansari and the brother by suckling of Kharija ibn Zayd ibn Thabit al-Ansari. He listened to 'Abdullah ibn 'Umar.

'Amr ibn Rafi'

It is related from Hafsa that he wrote out a copy of the Qur'an for her. He was the client of 'Umar ibn al-Khattab. He is the one about whom it was said:

"Serve the people until you are served
– then you are a lofty and sounder partner."

He has descendants ascribed to Lakhm. One of his children was 'Asim al-Mubarassam the poet.

Nafi'

The client of az-Zubayr ibn al-'Awwam. Mus'ab ibn Thabit related from him. He had few *hadiths*.

Abu Habiba

The client of az-Zubayr ibn al-'Awwam and the grandfather of Musa ibn 'Uqba – the client of az-Zubayr, and Umm Musa ibn 'Uqba.

Al-Jarrah

The client of Umm Habiba bint Abi Sufyan, the wife of the Prophet صلعم. He related from Umm Habiba and Salim ibn 'Abdullah, and Nafi' related from him.

Salim ibn Sarj

He is known as Abu'n-Nu'man Salim ibn al-Kharrabudh. He related from Umm Subayha al-Juhayniyya. Usama ibn Zayd al-Laythi related from him.

Salim Sabalan

The client of Banu Nasr ibn Mu'awiya of Hawazin. He originally came from Egypt. He used to transport the wives of the Prophet صلعم, and he related from 'A'isha.

Abu Salih as-Samman

He is az-Zayyat. His name is Dhakwan, the client of Ghatafan. It is said that he was the client of Juwayriya, a woman of Qays. He is Abu Suhayl ibn Abi Salih al-Madani. Among the people of Madina who relate from him are 'Abdullah ibn Dinar, al-Qa'qa' ibn Hakim, Zayd ibn Aslam, Sumayya, the client of Abi Bakr ibn 'Abdu'r-Rahman, and among the people of Kufa, al-Hakam, 'Asim ibn Abi'n-Nujud, and Sulayman al-A'mash. Abu Salih was reliable with a lot of *hadiths*. He went to Kufa to work and settled among the Banu Asad and then went to the Banu Kahil.

Abu Salih said, "There is no one who reports from Abu Hurayra but that I know whether he is lying or telling the truth."

'Asim said, "Abu Salih had a large beard. He used to rinse it with water." They say that he died in Madina in 101 AH.

Abu Salih Badham

The client of Umm Hani' bint Abi Talib. Simak, Muhammad ibn as-Sa'ib and Isma'il ibn Abi Khalid related from him.

Muslim ibn Yasar

His *kunya* was Abu 'Uthman. He was a client of the Ansar. Yahya ibn Sa'id al-Ansari and other people related from him. The people of Makka also related from him.

Bushayr ibn Yasar

The client of the Banu Haritha ibn al-Harith of the Ansar and then Aws. He was a great *faqih* shaykh. He met most of the Companions of the Messenger of Allah صلعم and especially the Companions of the Messenger of Allah from among the people of the Banu Haritha: Rafi' ibn Khadij, Suwayd ibn an-Nu'man and Sahl ibn Abi Hathma. The *hadith* of *qasama* is related from him from the Prophet صلعم Yahya ibn Sa'id al-Ansari related from him. He had few *hadiths*.

Nafi'

The client of Abu Qatada al-Ansari. He is Abu Muhammad from whom Salih ibn Kaysan related. He had few *hadiths*.

Wuhayb

The client of Zayd ibn Thabit al-Ansar by emancipation. He was a scribe of Zayd ibn Thabit. He is related from.

Harmala

The the client of Zayd ibn Thabit.

Abu'z-Zinad said, "He was the client of Usama ibn Zayd ibn Harith al-Kalbi. He clung to Zayd ibn Thabit. It was said that he was the client of Zayd. Az-Zuhri related from him. He had few *hadiths*.

Humayd ibn Nafi'

The client of Safwan ibn Khalif al-Ansari. He related from Abu Ayyub and went on *hajj* with him. He related from Ibn 'Umar. He is the father of Aflah ibn Humayd from whom ath-Thawri and men of the people of Madina and others related.

Shu'ba said, "I asked 'Asim al-Ahwal about women in mourning. He said that Hafsa bint Sirin said that Humayd ibn Nafi' gave a *kitaba* to Humayd al-Himyari. He also mentioned the *hadith* of Zaynab bint Abi Salama." Shu'ba said, "I told 'Asim, 'I listened to Humayd ibn Nafi'.' – 'You?' he asked. I said, 'Yes, that was when he was alive.'" Shu'ba said, "'Asim reported that he had died a hundred years ago."

Rafi' ibn Ishaq

The client of the father of ash-Shifa'.

It is also said that he was the client of Abu Talha. He listened to Abu Ayyub, and Ishaq ibn 'Abdullah related from him.

Ziyad ibn Abi Ziyad

The client of 'Abdullah ibn 'Ayyash al-Makhzumi.

Malik ibn Anas said, "Ziyad, the client of Ibn 'Ayyash was a reclusive man devoted to worship who continually invoked Allah alone. He had some incorrect pronunciation. He wore wool and did not eat meat. He had a few dirhams on which he lived."

Someone other than Isma'il said, "He was a friend of 'Umar II. He came to him while he was the khalif and admonished him, and 'Umar brought him near and made him a friend. They spoke together a lot. Ziyad had descendants in Damascus. Isma'il ibn Abi Khalid and others related from him."

Ishaq

The client of Za'ida. He listened to Sa'd ibn Abi Waqqas and Abu Hurayra. Abu Salih as-Samman, Abu Suhayl and Bukayr ibn 'Abdullah related from him.

'Ajlan

The client of Fatima bint 'Utba. He is Abu Muhammad ibn 'Ajlan. He related from Abu Hurayra. His son Muhammad ibn 'Ajlan and Bukayr ibn 'Abdullah related from him.

Jumhan

The client of the Aslamites. He listened to Abu Hurayra and 'Urwa ibn az-Zubayr, and Musa ibn 'Ubayda ar-Rabadhi related from him.

Al-Bahi

His name was 'Abdullah ibn Yasar, the client of az-Zubayr ibn al-'Awwam. His *kunya* was Abu Muhammad. He settled in Kufa and the Kufans related from him.

One of his children told me his name and *kunya*. He is called Muhammad ibn Yahya ibn Muhammad ibn 'Abdullah al-Bahi.

Abu's-Sa'ib

The client of Hisham ibn Zuhra. He listened to Abu Hurayra, and al-'Ala' ibn 'Abdu'r-Rahman related from him.

Abu Sufyan

The client of 'Abdullah ibn Ahmad ibn Jahsh. He related from Abu Sa'id al-Khudri. He was reliable with few *hadiths*.

Ibn Abi Habiba said, "He was a client of the Banu'l-Ashhal. He was devoted to Ibn Abi Ahmad ibn Jahsh and ascribed to his *wala'*."

Abu Sufyan said, "I used to stay with the Banu 'Abdu'l-Ashhal in the month of Ramadan and Muhammad ibn Maslama and Salama ibn Salama listened to my recitation. They stood listening. On that day I was a slave. They said, 'There is no harm in this imam.'"

Da'ud ibn al-Husayn reported that Abu Sufyan used to lead the Banu 'Abdu'l-Ashhal in their mosque in Ramadan when he was a *mukatib* and people who had been at Badr and al-'Aqaba were there.

It is reported from Da'ud ibn al-Husayn that Abu Sufyan, the client of Ibn Abi Ahmad, used to lead the Banu'l-Ashhal in the prayer in the month of Ramadan while Companions of the Messenger of Allah صلعم were among them when he was a *mukatib*. He was reliable with few *hadiths*.

Thabit al-Ahnaf ibn 'Iyad

The client of 'Abdu'r-Rahman ibn Zayd ibn al-Khattab.

Thabit al-A'raj, the client of 'Abdu'r-Rahman ibn Zayd, said, "I married Zaynab, the mother of 'Abdu'r-Rahman ibn Zayd while 'Abdullah ibn 'Abdu'r-Rahman was away. When he came, he summoned me – and he had prepared ropes and whips for me. He said, 'Why did you marry the mother of the child of my father without my knowledge or permission?' I said, 'I was married to her by someone who understood the marriage contract. I married her openly and not secretly.' He commanded that I be tied up and said, 'I will continue to beat you until you die unless you divorce her.' So I divorced her three times and there were witnesses to it. Then I went and asked for the *fatwa* of 'Abdullah ibn 'Umar about that. He said, 'You are not divorced.' Then I rode to Ibn az-Zubayr who was the ruler of Makka at that time. I asked him about it and he told me that I was not divorced and he told me to join her. So I joined her and had a marriage feast. Ibn 'Umar was among those invited." Fulayh, who also related this, said, "I saw her with him and I have seen her child by him."

Ziyad ibn Sa'd said, "I asked Thabit al-A'raj, 'Where did you listen to Abu Hurayra?' He said, 'The clients used to send me on Friday to take a place, and Abu Hurayra would come and relate to the people before the prayer.'"

Muhammad ibn 'Umar said, "The governor of Madina when 'Abdullah ibn 'Abdu'r-Rahman forced Thabit al-Ahnaf to divorce his wife was Jabir ibn al-Aswad, a governor appointed by 'Abdullah ibn az-Zubayr. Malik ibn Anas heard this from Thabit al-Ahnaf."

'Abdu'r-Rahman ibn Ya'qub

He is Abu'l-'Ala' ibn 'Abdu'r-Rahman, the client of al-Huraqa. He related from Abu Hurayra.

Nu'aym ibn 'Abdullah al-Mujammar

The client of 'Umar ibn al-Khattab by emancipation. He listened to Abu Hurayra and Muhammad ibn 'Abdullah ibn Zayd ibn 'Abdu Rabbih al-Ansari, and to 'Ali ibn Yahya az-Zuraqi. He was reliable, with *hadiths*.

Shurahbil ibn Sa'd

The client of the Ansar. His *kunya* was Abu Sa'd. He was an old shaykh who related from Zayd ibn Thabit, Abu Hurayra, Abu Sa'id al-Khudri and a group of the Companions of the Messenger of Allah صلعم. He lived until he became confused. He had *hadiths* which are not considered authoritative.

Da'ud ibn Farahij

The client of Quraysh. Muhammad ibn 'Umar said, "I think that he is the client of the Banu Makhzum. He listened to Abu Hurayra and Abu Sa'id al-Khudri and he died early on and has *hadiths*."

Shu'ba said that Da'ud ibn Farahij said, "My client Sufyan related to me."

Al-Hakam ibn Mina

The client of the family of Abu 'Amir ar-Rahib. His father mentioned that Abu 'Amir gave him to Abu Sufyan ibn Harb and that Abu Harb sold him to al-'Abbas ibn 'Abdu'l-Muttalib who freed him. He still has descendants who have the *wala'* of al-'Abbas. Mina was at Tabuk with the Messenger of Allah صلعم .

❋❋❋❋❋

Also included in this generation are: **'Abdullah ibn 'Ubaydullah ibn Abi Thawr**, the client of Banu Nawfal; **Abu 'Ubayd**, the client of 'Abdullah ibn 'Abbas; **Muhammad ibn Aflah**, the client of Abu Ayyub al-Ansari, who is related from; **Salim ibn Shawwal**, the client of Umm Habiba bint Abi Sufyan; **Salim al-Barrad**; **Salim Abu 'Abdullah**, the client of Shaddad known as Salim ad-Daws who related from Sa'd; **Salim ibn Salama**; **Abu Salih Sumay'**, who related from 'Abdullah ibn 'Abbas: **Abu Salih**, the client of 'Uthman ibn 'Affan, who is related from; **Abu Salih al-Ghifari**; **Abu Salih Maysara**; **Abu Salih**, the client of Duba'a; **Abu Salih**, the client of as-Saffah, and his name is 'Ubayd, from whom Busr ibn Said related; **Abu Salih**, the client of the Sa'dis; **'Ajlan**, the client of al-Mushma'il who related from Abu Hurayra; **Abu'l-Walid**, the client of 'Amr ibn Khidash who related from Abu Hurayra; **Abu'l-Hasan al-Barrad**, the client of Banu Nawfal from whom az-Zuhri related; **'Ubaydullah ibn Dara**, the client of the family of 'Uthman ibn 'Affan from whom az-Zuhri related; **'Ata'**, Abu Mansur, the client of Ibn Siba' from whom az-Zuhri related; **Ziyad ibn Mina**, the client of Ashja' from whom 'Abdu'-Hamid ibn Ja'far related; **Abu 'Abdullah**

al-Qarraz, who listened to Sa'd ibn Abi Waqqas and Abu Hurayra and was reliable with few *hadiths*; **Abu Lubaba**, the client of 'A'isha, the wife of the Messenger of Allahﷺ, whose name was Marwan; **Na'im ibn Ujayl**, the client of Umm Salama, the wife of the Prophetﷺ, who related from 'Abdullah ibn 'Amr; **Salim Abu'l-Ghayth**, the client of 'Abdullah ibn Muti' al-'Adawi who related from Abu Hurayra and was reliable with good *hadiths*.

Chapter Three
The Third Generation
of the *Tabi'un* of the People of Madina

'Ali ibn 'Abdullah ibn 'Abbas

His mother was Zur'a bint Mishrah ibn Ma'dikarib. His *kunya* was Abu Muhammad. He was born the night that 'Ali ibn Abi Talib was murdered, in Ramadan 40 AH, and was named after him and given his *kunya*, Abu'l-Hasan. 'Abdu'l-Malik ibn Marwan said to him, 'By Allah, I will not tolerate your having both the name and the *kunya*. Change one of them." So he changed his *kunya* to Abu Muhammad. His children were Muhammad, whose mother was al-'Aliyya bint 'Ubaydullah ibn al-'Abbas; Da'ud and 'Isa, by an *umm walad*; Sulayman and Salih, by an *umm walad*; Ahmad, Bishr, Mubashshir, Isma'il and 'Abdu's-Samad, by an *umm walad*; 'Abdullah the elder, by Umm Abiha bint 'Abdullah bint Ja'far; 'Ubadyullah, whose mother was one of the Banu'l-Harish; 'Abdu'l-Malik, 'Uthman 'Abdu'r-Rahman, 'Abdullah the younger, as-Saffah, Yahya, Ishaq, Ya'qub, 'Abdu'l-'Aziz, Isma'il the younger and 'Abdullah the middle, who is al-Ahnaf, by various *umm walads*; Fatima, Umm 'Isa the elder, Umm 'Isa the younger, Amina, Lubaba, Burayha the elder, Burayha the younger, Maymuna, Umm 'Ali and al-'Aliyya, by various *umm walads*; and Umm Habib, whose mother was Umm Abiha bint 'Abdullah.

Umm 'Isa the younger was married to 'Abdullah ibn al-Husayn ibn 'Abdullah but had no children. He died and left her a widow. Amina was married to Yahya ibn Ja'far ibn Tammam and had no children. Lubaba was married to 'Ubaydullah ibn Qutham ibn al-'Abbas and had Muhammad and Burayha. Muhammad had no children and Burayha married Ja'far ibn Abi Ja'far al-Mansur, the Amir al-Mu'minin, who is Ja'far the younger, who is called Ibn al-Kurdiyya. The rest of his daughters did not marry. Fatima was the oldest, the best of them and the most generous. His sisters and nephews, Abu'l-'Abbas, Abu Ja'far al-Mansur and others honoured her, esteemed her and exalted her because of her resolve, intelligence and opinion.

'Ali ibn 'Abdullah was the youngest of his father's children and he was the most handsome and comely Qurayshi on the face of the earth and the most frequent in prayer. He was called as-Sajjad because of the abundance of his prayer and his virtue.

Abu'l-Mughira said, "We looked for *khuffs* for 'Ali ibn 'Abdullah. We did not find them until we made them for him. We did not find any sandals for him until we made them for him. When he was angry, it showed in him for three days. He would pray a thousand *rak'ats* in twenty-four hours."

'Ubaydullah ibn Muhammad al-Qurayshi said, "'Ali ibn 'Abdullah left instructions for his son Sulayman in his will. He was asked 'Do you instruct Sulayman and leave out Muhammad?' He said, 'I do not want to demean him with instructions.'"

Muhammad said, "I heard the shaykhs say, 'By Allah, the khalifate has gone to them, and there is no one on the earth with more recitation of the Qur'an, nor better worshippers, nor more devoted people than those at al-Hamima.'"

'Attaf ibn Khalif al-Wabisi said, "I saw 'Ali ibn 'Abdullah using black dye. 'Abdullah ibn Tawus related from him. He was reliable with few *hadiths*."

Muhammad ibn 'Umar said, "'Ali ibn 'Abdullah died in 118 AH." Abu Ma'shar and others said that he died in Syria in 117 AH.

Al-'Abbas ibn 'Abdullah ibn 'Abbas

His mother was Zur'a bint Mishrah ibn Ma'dikarib. She was the mother of his brother 'Ali ibn 'Abdullah. He was the oldest of the children of Ibn 'Abbas and his *kunya* is by him. Al-'Abbas ibn 'Abdullah is related from. His children were 'Abdullah, whose mother was Maryam bint 'Abbad; 'Awn, whose mother was Habiba bint az-Zubayr ibn al-'Awwam; Muhammad and Qurayba, whose mother was Ja'da bint al-Ash'ath. Then she was married to al-'Abbas ibn 'Abdullah and the line of al-'Abbas ibn 'Abdullah died out. There was importance and the khalifate among them.

'Abdullah ibn 'Ubaydullah ibn 'Abbas

His mother was an *umm walad*. His children were al-Hasan and al-Husayn, whose mother was Asma' bint 'Abdullah. He related from 'Abdullah ibn 'Abbas. He listened to him and his son Husayn, and others related from him. He was reliable and had *hadiths*. His line died out.

His brother, al-'Abbas ibn 'Ubaydullah ibn 'Abbas

His mother was another *umm walad*. He was not a brother of 'Abdullah by his mother. His children were al-'Abbas, who had no children, Sulayman, Da'ud, Qutham the elder, Qutham the younger (the governor of Yamana for Abu Ja'far), Umm Ja'far, Maymuna, whose *kunya* is Umm Muhammad, 'Abda, al-'Aliya and Umm Ja'far, by various *umm walads*. He is also related from.

Ja'far ibn Tammam ibn al-'Abbas

His mother was al-'Aliyya bint Nuhayk. His children were Yahya, Ahmad and 'Ulayya, by an *umm walad*; Umm Habib, whose mother was ar-Ra'un; and Umm Ja'far, whose mother was Umm 'Uthman bint Abi Bakr. *Hadiths* are related from him.

'Abdullah ibn Ma'bad ibn 'Abbas

His mother was Umm Jamil bint as-Sa'ib. His children were Ma'bad, 'Abbas the elder, 'Abdullah and Umm Abiha, whose mother was Umm Muhammad bint 'Ubaydullah ibn al-'Abbas; Muhammad whose mother was Jamra bint 'Abdullah; and Ibrahim, 'Abbas the middle, 'Abbas the younger, who was governor of Makka, 'Abdullah and Lubaba, by various *umm walads*. He is related from and is reliable.

'Abdullah ibn 'Abdullah ibn al-Harith

His mother was Khalida bint Mu'attib. His children were Sulayman and 'Isa, whose mother was an *umm walad*; 'Atika, whose mother was an *umm walad*; and Hammada, by an *umm walad*. Az-Zuhri related from 'Abdullah ibn 'Abdullah. He was reliable with few *hadiths*.

Ishaq ibn 'Abdullah ibn al-Harith

His mother was Umm 'Abdullah bint al-'Abbas. His children were 'Abdullah, 'Abdu'r-Rahman, Tallab and Ya'qub, whose mother was Umm 'Abdullah bint 'Abdu'r-Rahman; and Hind and Umm 'Umar, whose mother was an *umm walad*.

As-Salt ibn 'Abdullah ibn Nawfal

His mother was an *umm walad*. His children were Yahya, whose mother was Umama bint al-Mughira; Humayd, whose mother was Zaynab bint 'Abdullah; and Fatima, whose mother was an *umm walad*. As-Salt was a *faqih* devoted to worship.

Muhammad ibn 'Abdullah ibn Nawfal

His mother was Hind, who is Umm Khalid bint Khalid. His children were al-Qasim and Mu'awiya, whose mother was Durayba bint al-Harith; Ja'far and Qusayma, whose mother was Hamida bint Abi Sufyan. Az-Zuhri related from Muhammad ibn 'Abdullah.

Zayd ibn Hasan ibn 'Ali ibn Abi Talib

His mother was Umm Bashir bint Abi Mas'ud. His children were Muhammad, whose mother was an *umm walad*; Hasan, governor of Madina for al-Mansur, whose mother was an *umm walad*; Nafisa, who married al-Walid I and died while married to him, and whose mother was Lubaba bint 'Abdullah ibn al-'Abbas.

'Abdu'r-Rahman ibn Abi'l-Mawwal said, "I saw Zayd ibn Hasan riding and he went to the Dhuhr market and stopped there. I saw the people looking at him and admiring his great stature. They said, 'His grandfather was the Messenger of Allahصلعم.'"

Muhammad ibn 'Umar said, "Zayd related from Jabir ibn 'Abdullah."

'Abdullah ibn 'Ubaydullah said, "I buried my father on the day that Zayd ibn Hasan died. He died at Batha' ibn Azhar some miles from Madina and was carried to Madina. When we reached the top of ath-Thaniyya, between the two minarets, we could see the body of Zayd ibn Hasan wrapped up on a camel. 'Abdullah ibn Hasan was walking in front of him. He had his cloak bound around his waist and there was nothing on his back. My father told me, 'My son, I will dismount and hold the stirrup. By Allah, if I ride while 'Abdullah is walking, I will never be at ease with him.' I rode the donkey and my father dismounted and walked. He continued to walk until Zayd was brought to his house among the Banu Hudhayla and then he was washed and taken out on a bed to Baqi'."

Hasan ibn Hasan ibn 'Ali

His mother was Khawla bint Manzur. His children were Muhammad, whose mother was Ramala bint Sa'id ibn Zayd; 'Abdullah who died in al-Mansur's prison in Kufa, Hasan who died in al-Mansur's prison, Ibrahim who also died in prison with his brother, Zaynab who married al-Walid I and was then divorced, and Umm Kulthum, whose mother was Fatima bint Husayn ibn 'Ali, whose mother was Umm Ishaq bint Talha; Ja'far, Da'ud, Fatima, Umm al-Qasim who is Qusayma, and Mulayka, whose mother was an *umm walad* called Habiba Farisiyya who belonged to the family of Abu Abs; and Umm Kulthum, by an *umm walad*.

Al-Fudyal ibn Marzuq said, "I heard al-Hasan ibn al-Hasan say to a man who was excessive towards them, 'Woe to you! Love us for Allah. If we obey Allah, love us. If we disobey Allah, then hate us.' A man said to him, 'You are the relatives of the Messenger of Allah and the People of his House.' He replied, 'Woe to you! If Allah had defended anyone by their kinship with the Messenger of Allah rather than by their obedience to Allah, then that would have given an advantage to those who are nearer to him by their mother and father. By Allah, I fear that the punishment will be doubled for the disobedient among them, and I hope that the one who does good among us will have his reward twice over. Woe to you! Fear Allah and say the truth about us. That is more eloquent if that is what you desire, and we will be content with that from you.' Then he said, 'Our fathers brought us up badly if what you are saying is part of the *deen* of Allah and yet they did not tell us about it nor make us desire it.'"

A Rafidite said to him, "Did not the Messenger of Allah, peace be upon him, say to 'Ali, 'If I am the master of someone, 'Ali is his master?'" He replied, "By Allah, if he meant by that amirate and rulership, he would have been more explicit to you in expressing that, just as he was explicit to you about the prayer, *zakat*, and *hajj* to the House. He would have said to you, 'O people! This is your protector after me.' The Messenger of Allahﷺ gave the best good counsel to people. If the business had been as you say it is, and Allah and His Messenger had chosen 'Ali for this matter after the Prophet ﷺ, then he would have been the person with the gravest error and wrong action since this would mean either that he ignored what the Messenger of Allahﷺ commanded him to do, or he would have made excuses to the people for having done so."

Abu Ja'far Muhammad ibn 'Ali ibn Husayn

His mother was Umm 'Abdullah bint Hasan. His children were Ja'far and 'Abdullah, whose mother was Umm Farwa bint al-Qasim; Ibrahim, whose mother was Umm Hakim ibn Usayd; 'Ali and Zaynab, whose mother was an *umm walad*; and Umm Salama, whose mother was an *umm walad*.

Jabir said, "Muhammad ibn 'Ali said to me, 'Jabir, do not argue. Arguing causes the Qur'an to be denied.'"

Layth reported that Abu Ja'far said, "Do not sit with the people of disputes. They are those who delve into the *ayats* of the Qur'an."

Zuhayr reported that Jabir said, "I asked Muhammad ibn 'Ali, 'Does any of you, the People of the House, claim that any of the sins amount to *shirk*?' He replied, 'No.' I asked, 'Is there any of you, the People of the House, who confirms the Return [of the Imam]?' – 'No,' he replied. I said, 'Is there any of you, the People of the House, who curses Abu Bakr and 'Umar?' – 'No,' he replied, 'I love them, pray for them and ask forgiveness for them.'"

Abu'd-Dahhak reported that Abu Ja'far said, "O Allah, I declare to you that I am free of al-Mughira ibn Sa'id and Bayan."[1]

Sufyan ath-Thawri said that Ja'far ibn Muhammad reported that his father used to delouse his mother's head.

Yusuf ibn al-Muhajir al-Haddad said, "I saw Abu Ja'far riding on a mule with a servant walking beside him."

Mu'awiya ibn 'Abdu'l-Karim said, "I saw Muhammad ibn Abi Ja'far wearing a silk/wool jubbah and a silk/wool wrapper."

Jabir reported that Abu Ja'far said, "We, the family of Muhammad, wear silk/wool, saffron-dyed clothes, Egyptian cloth and Yemeni cloth." Jabir said the same.

---

1. Kufan Shi'ites who claimed that Muhammad ibn al-Hanafiyya was a Prophet. They rebelled in 119/737 and were executed.

Isma'il ibn 'Abdu'l-Malik said, "I saw Abu Ja'far wearing a bordered garment, and I drew it to his attention. He said, 'There is no harm in two fingers of silk on the border of a garment.'"

Mawhab said, "I saw Abu Ja'far wearing a red wrapper."

'Abdu'l-A'la said that he saw Muhammad ibn 'Ali letting the end of his turban hang down behind him.

Muhammad ibn Ishaq said, "I saw Abu Ja'far praying in a garment which he had knotted behind him."

Hakim ibn Hakim said, "I saw Abu Ja'far reclining on a folded shawl in the mosque." Muhammad ibn 'Umar said, "That continued to be the custom of the nobles and manly people among us who clung to the mosque and reclined on their shawls or cloaks folded up."

'Abdu'l-A'la said, "I asked Muhammad ibn 'Ali about using indigo (or black dye). He said, 'It is the dye used by us, the People of the House.'"

Thubayr said that Abu Ja'far asked, "Abu'l-Jahm, with what do you dye your hair?" – "Henna and *katm*," he replied. He said, "This is our dye, the People of the House."

Harun ibn 'Abdullah said, "I saw that Muhammad ibn 'Ali had the mark of prostration on his forehead and nose, but it was not large."

Abu Ja'far said, "Beware of laughing," or he said, "a lot of laughter." – "It spits out knowledge."

Muhammad ibn 'Ali said, "My name was engraved on my ring. When I had intercourse, I used to put it in my mouth."

Abu Mus'ab reported that he saw Muhammad ibn 'Ali wearing a mantle. He said, "Salim, the client of 'Abdullah ibn 'Ali, told me that Muhammad had left a will that he be shrouded in it."

'Urwa ibn 'Abdullah said, "I asked Ja'far about what his father was shrouded in. He said, 'He commanded me that it be in his shirt, and his waistwrapper cut open, and in his cloak which he used to wear, and that I buy a Yamani mantle. The Prophet صلى الله عليه وسلم was shrouded in three garments, one of which was a Yamani mantle.'"

Sa'id ibn Muslim ibn Banak said, "I saw a mantle of silk on the bier of Muhammad ibn 'Ali."

Ja'far ibn Muhammad said that he heard Muhammad ibn 'Ali discussing some of the *sadaqa* of the Prophet صلى الله عليه وسلم with Fatima bint

Husayn. He said, "I had 85 dirhams when he died," – and when Muhammad ibn 'Ali died, he still had them.

Muhammad ibn 'Umar said, "As for what has been transmitted to us, he died in 117 AH at the age of 73. Someone else said that he died in 118 AH. Abu Nu'aym al-Fadl ibn Dukayn said, 'He died in Madina in 114 AH.' He was reliable with a lot of knowledge and *hadiths*. He is not related from as being authoritative."

'Abdullah ibn 'Ali ibn Husayn ibn 'Ali

His mother was Umm 'Abdullah bint al-Hasan ibn 'Ali. She is Umm Ja'far. His children were Muhammad al-Arqat, who is al-Ahdab, Ishaq al-Abyad, Umm Kulthum, who is Kulthum as-Samma', and Umm 'Ali, who is 'Ulayya, by an *umm walad*; and al-Qadim and al-'Aliya, by an *umm walad*.

'Umar ibn 'Ali ibn Husayn ibn 'Ali

His mother was an *umm walad*. His children were 'Ali, Ibrahim and Khadija, whose mother was an *umm walad*; Ja'far, who is al-Buthayr, whose mother was Umm Ishaq bint Muhammad; and Muhammad, Musa, who is Kardam, Khadija, Habba, Muhabba, and 'Abda, whose mother was Umm Musa bint 'Umar ibn 'Ali.

Fudayl ibn Marzuq said, "I asked 'Umar ibn 'Ali and Husayn ibn 'Ali about my uncle Ja'far. I asked, 'Is there a man among you, the People of the House, whom it is obligatory to obey, and whom you acknowledge as such – so that anyone who does not accept that dies the death of the *Jahiliyya*?' They replied, 'No, by Allah, we do not say this. Whoever says this among us is a liar.' I said to 'Umar ibn 'Ali, 'May Allah have mercy on you. This is a position which you claim was bequeathed to 'Ali by the Prophet صلعم, then it was for al-Hasan when 'Ali left it to him, then for al-Husayn when al-Hasan left it to him, and then it went to 'Ali ibn al-Husayn when al-Husayn left it to him, and then to Muhammad ibn 'Ali when 'Ali left it to him.' He replied, 'By Allah, when my father died he did not leave two wills. May Allah fight them! By Allah, those people are feeding off us. This is the doing of Kunays al-Kharu', and who is Kunays al-Kharu'?' I replied, 'Al-Mu'alla ibn Khunays.' He said, 'Yes, it is al-Mu'alla ibn Khunays. By Allah, I have reflected long on my bed and I am astonished by those people whose intellects have been confused by Allah so that al-Mu'alla ibn Khunays has been able to mislead them.'"

Zayd ibn 'Ali ibn Husayn ibn 'Ali

His mother was an *umm walad*. His children were Yahya, by Rayta bint Abi Hasim 'Abdullah – who was killed in Khorasan by Salm ibn Ahwaz on the orders of Nasr ibn Sayyar, 'Isa, Husayn al-Makfuf, and Muhammad, by an *umm walad*.

'Abdullah ibn Ja'far said, "Zayd ibn 'Ali visited Hisham ibn 'Abdu'l-Malik and informed him of a large debt of his and some needs, but Hisham did not take care of any of his needs, frowned at him and spoke harshly to him."

Salim, Hisham's client and attendant, reported that Zayd ibn 'Ali left Hisham twisting his moustache. He said, "No one loves life but that he is abased." Then he made for Kufa. Yusuf ibn 'Umar ath-Thaqafi was Hisham's governor over Iraq. He sent someone to fight Zayd, and they fought and those who were with Zayd split from him. Then he was killed and crucified.

Salim said, "I later informed Hisham about what Zayd had said when he left him. He said, 'May your mother be bereft! Why did you not tell me that before today! 500,000 would have been enough for him. That would have been easier for us then than what has happened to him now.'"

Sahbal ibn Muhammad said, "I did not see any of the khalifs who disliked the shedding of blood more intensely nor felt more intensely about it than Hisham ibn 'Abdu'l-Malik. He felt terrible about the killing of Zayd ibn 'Ali and Yahya ibn Zayd. He said, 'I wish that I could have ransomed them!'"

Abu'z-Zinad said, "There is not one among them who hated the shedding of blood more than Hisham. It was hard for him when Zayd ibn 'Ali rebelled. That remained the case until his head was brought and his body crucified in Kufa. Yusuf ibn 'Umar did that while Hisham was khalif."

Muhammad ibn 'Umar said, "When the son of al-'Abbas sent 'Abdullah ibn 'Ali to Hisham's grave and commanded that his body be exhumed and crucified, he said, 'This is what was done to Zayd ibn 'Ali." Zayd was killed on Tuesday 2 Safar 120 AH, or 122 AH. He was 42 when he was killed. Zayd listened to his father and

'Abdu'r-Rahman ibn al-Harith related from him. Bassam as-Sayrafi, 'Abdu'r-Rahman ibn Abi'z-Ziyad and others related from him.

Husayn the younger ibn 'Ali ibn Husayn

His mother was an *umm walad*. His children were 'Abdullah, 'Ubaydullah al-A'raj, 'Ali and Hushayma, whose mother was Umm Khalid bint Hamza; Muhammad, by an *umm walad*; Hasan al-Ahwal and Jariya, whose mother was an *umm walad*; Umayna, whose mother was a woman of the Ansar from Banu Haritha; and Ibrahim and Fatima, by an *umm walad*. Husayn was the youngest of his father's children. Muhammad ibn 'Umar met him and related from him. We have included him in their generation since he was their brother, but he was not the same as them in age and as regards those whom he met.

'Abdullah ibn Muhammad ibn al-Hanafiyya

His *kunya* was Abu Hashim. His mother was an *umm walad*. His children were Hashim, by whom he has his *kunya*, and Muhammad the younger, whose mother was the daughter of Khalid ibn 'Alqama; Muhammad al-Akbar and Lubaba, whose mother was Fatima bint Muhammad; 'Ali and an unnamed son, whose mother was Umm 'Uthman bint Abi Judayr; Talib, 'Awn, and 'Abdullah, by *umm walads*; Rayta, who was the mother of Yahya ibn Zayd who was killed in Khorasan, and whose mother was Rayta, who is Umm al-Harith bint al-Harith; and Umm Salama, by an *umm walad*.

Abu Hashim had knowledge and transmission. He was reliable with few *hadiths*. The Shi'a used to meet him. He was in Syria with the Banu Hashim. He died and left a bequest to Muhammad ibn 'Ali. He said, "You have this command and then it is among your children," and he directed the Shi'a to him. He gave him his books and transmission. He died in Humayma while Sulayman was khalif.

Al-Hasan ibn Muhammad ibn al-Hanafiyya

His mother was Jamal bint Qays ibn Makhrama. His *kunya* was Abu Muhammad. He was one of the elegant Hashimites and people of intelligence among them. He used to be preferred above his brother, Abu Hashim, as regards both virtue and looks. He was the first to speak of *irja'*.

Zadhan and Maysara visited al-Hasan ibn Muhammad and criticised him for the book which he had written on *irja'*. He said to Zadhan, "Abu 'Umar, I wish that I had died without writing it."

Muhammad ibn 'Umar said, "Al-Hasan ibn Muhammad died while 'Umar II was khalif, leaving no descendants."

Muhammad ibn 'Umar ibn 'Ali ibn Abi Talib

His mother was Asma' bint 'Aqil ibn Abi Talib. His children were 'Umar, 'Abdullah, and 'Ubaydullah, all of whom relate *hadith,* and whose mother was Khadija bint 'Ali ibn Husayn; and Ja'far, whose mother was Umm Hashim bint Ja'far.

Mu'awiya ibn 'Abdullah ibn Ja'far

His mother was an *umm walad*. His children were al-Kharij, born in Kufa at the end of the time of Marwan ibn Muhammad, Ja'far and Muhammad, whose mother was Umm 'Awn ibn al-'Abbas; Sulayman, by an *umm walad*; al-Hasan, Yazid, Salih, Hammada and Ubayya, whose mother was Fatima bint Hasan ibn Hasan; and 'Ali whom 'Amir ibn Dubara killed, and whose mother was an *umm walad*. Yazid ibn 'Abdullah related from Mu'awiya.

Isma'il ibn 'Abdullah ibn Ja'far

His mother was an *umm walad*. His children were 'Abdullah, Abu Bakr and Muhammad, whose mother was an *umm walad*; Umm Kulthum and Ja'far, by an *umm walad*; and Zayd by an *umm walad*. Isma'il related from his father and 'Abdullah ibn Mus'ab related from him.

'Umar ibn 'Abdu'l-'Aziz

His mother was Umm 'Asim bint 'Asim ibn 'Umar ibn al-Khattab. His *kunya* was Abu Hafs. His children were 'Abdullah, Bakr and Umm 'Ammar, whose mother was Lamis bint 'Ali; Ibrahim, whose mother was Umm 'Uthman bint Shu'ayb; Ishaq, Ya'qub and Musa, whose mother was Fatima bint 'Abdu'l-Malik; and 'Abdu'l-Malik, al-Walid, 'Asim, Yazid, 'Abdullah, 'Abdu'l-'Aziz, Zabban, Ama and Umm 'Abdullah, whose mother was an *umm walad*.

He was born in 63 AH, the same year that Maymuna, the wife of the Prophet صلى الله عليه وسلم died.

Khasif said, "I dreamt that I saw a man sitting with one man on his right and another man on his left when 'Umar ibn 'Abdu'l-'Aziz arrived. He wanted to sit between him and the one on his right, but he clung to his companion. So he turned and wanted to sit between him and the one on his left, but he clung to his companion. Then the one in the middle pulled him and made him sit on his lap. I asked, 'Who was this?' They said, 'This one was the Messenger of Allah and this one was Abu Bakr and this one was 'Umar.'"

Nafi' reported that Ibn 'Umar said, "I often heard Ibn 'Umar say, 'I hope that there will be one of the children of 'Umar with a mark on his face who will fill the earth with justice.'"

Ibn 'Umar said, "We used to say that this matter would not come to an end before this community was ruled by one of the descendants of 'Umar with a mole on his face who would behave as 'Umar used to behave.' We used to say that it was Bilal ibn 'Abdullah ibn 'Umar. He had a mole on his face. This was until 'Umar ibn 'Abdu'l-'Aziz came, whose mother was Umm 'Asim bint 'Asim ibn 'Umar."

Ibn Shawdab said, "When 'Abdu'l-'Aziz wanted to marry Umm 'Umar ibn 'Abdu'l-'Aziz, he told his administrator, 'Collect 400 dinars for me out of my best property. I want to marry into a house of righteousness.' So he married Umm 'Umar ibn 'Abdu'l-'Aziz."

Abu'z-Zinad said, "'Umar ibn 'Abdu'l-'Aziz was appointed over Madina in Rabi' al-Awwal in 87 AH at the age of 25. Al-Walid I appointed him when he became khalif. 'Umar appointed Abu Bakr ibn Muhammad ibn 'Amr as qadi."

Hafs ibn 'Umar al-Ansari said, "When 'Umar ibn 'Abdu'l-'Aziz wanted to go on *hajj* from Madina while he was governor in the khalifate of al-Walid I, Anas ibn Malik, who was in Madina at that time, came to him. He said, 'Abu Hamza, will you tell us about the *khutbas* of the Prophet صلى الله عليه وسلم?' He replied, 'The Messenger of Allah صلى الله عليه وسلم gave a *khutba* at Makka a day before Tarwiya, one at 'Arafa, one at Mina on the morning of the Day of Sacrifice and one on the Day of Nafr.'"

Anas ibn Malik said, "I did not pray behind anyone whose prayer more resembled that of the Messenger of Allah صلى الله عليه وسلم than this youth," meaning 'Umar ibn 'Abdu'l-'Aziz.

Ad-Dahhak said, "I used to pray behind him. He made the first two *rak'ats* of *Dhuhr* long and the other two short. He made *'Asr* short and recited the short *Mufassal suras* in *Maghrib*. In *'Isha'* he recited the middle *Mufassal suras*. In *Subh* he recited the long *Mufassal suras*."

Ad-Dahhak said, "I saw 'Umar ibn 'Abdu'l-'Aziz at a loss for words while on the minbar. Then he resumed and said, 'I ask forgiveness of Allah. I ask forgiveness of Allah!'"

'Abdu'l-Hatim ibn 'Abdullah said, "I saw 'Umar ibn 'Abdu'l-'Aziz walking to the *'Id*."

Abu Isra'il mentioned 'Umar ibn 'Abdu'l-'Aziz and said that 'Ali ibn Badhima said, "When I saw him at Madina he was the best dressed of people and had the best scent and was one of the proudest of people in his gait. Then I later saw him walking like a monk. Whoever tells you that gait is innate is not believed after 'Umar."

Usama ibn Zayd said, "'Umar ibn 'Abdu'l-'Aziz said to his qadi Abu Bakr ibn Muhammad, 'I do not find anything more pleasing than a right in harmony with desire.'"

Yahya reported that 'Umar used to fast on Mondays and Thursdays.

A man asked Sa'id ibn al-Musayyab, "Abu Muhammad, who is the Mahdi?" Sa'id said to him, "Have you been inside the house of Marwan?" – "No," he replied. He said, "Enter the house of Marwan and you will see the Mahdi." 'Umar ibn 'Abdu'l-'Aziz used to let the people come to him, and the man entered Marwan's house and saw the Amir al-Mu'minin among the people. Then he went back to Sa'id ibn al-Musayyab and said, "Abu Muhammad, I entered the house of Marwan and did not see anyone that I would say is the Mahdi." Sa'id said to him, "Did you see 'Umar ibn 'Abdu'l-'Aziz sitting on his seat?" – "Yes," he replied. He said, "He is the Mahdi."

Muhammad ibn 'Ali said, "The Prophet was from us and the Mahdi is from the 'Abd Shams. We only know it to be 'Umar ibn 'Abdu'l-'Aziz." This was while 'Umar was khalif.

Fatima bint 'Ali ibn Abi Talib mentioned 'Umar II and asked for mercy on him a lot. She said, "I visited him when he was the amir of Madina and he dismissed every eunuch and guard so that there was no one in the room but me and him. Then he said, 'Daughter of 'Ali, by Allah, there is no house on the face of the earth dearer to me than your house, and you are dearer to me than my own family.'"

Abu'z-Zinad said "When 'Umar II came to Madina as its governor, his attendant invited its people. So they came and greeted him. After he had prayed *Dhuhr*, he summoned ten of the *fuqaha'* of the city: 'Urwa ibn az-Zubayr, 'Ubaydullah ibn 'Abdullah, Abu Bakr ibn 'Abdu'r-Rahman, Abu Bakr ibn Sulayman, Sulayman ibn Yasar, al-Qasim ibn Muhammad, Salim ibn 'Abdullah, 'Abdullah ibn 'Abdullah ibn 'Umar, 'Abdullah ibn 'Amir and Kharija ibn Thabit. He praised Allah as befits Him and then he said, 'I have invited you for something for which you will be rewarded and in which you will help the Truth prevail. I do not want to decide any matter except after hearing your opinion or the opinion of those of you who are present. If you see anyone transgressing or hear that an agent of mine is being unjust, then by Allah I forbid anyone to inform anyone other than me of it.' Then they asked Allah to bless him and dispersed."

Hajjaj as-Sawwaf said, "When he was governor of Madina, 'Umar ibn 'Abdu'l-'Aziz told me to buy a garment for him. I bought him a garment the cloth of which cost 400 dirhams. He cut it down into a shirt and then touched it to his face and said, 'How coarse and rough!' When he was khalif, he commanded that a garment be bought for him and they bought it for 14 dirhams. He touched it with his hand and said, 'Glory be to Allah! How soft and fine!'"

Ta'ma ibn Ghaylan and Ibn Muhammad ibn Khalid said, "'Umar used to be one of the most fragrant and best dressed people. When he became khalif, he was one of those who dressed in the coarsest clothes and ate the most frugal meals. He preferred leftovers."

Muhammad ibn 'Ammar said, "We used to announce the prayer to 'Umar in his house and we would say, 'Peace be upon you, O amir, and the mercy of Allah and His blessings. Come to prayer. Come to success. The prayer, may Allah have mercy on you.' The *fuqaha'* did not object to that."

He also said, "'Umar ibn 'Abdu'l-'Aziz, the governor of Madina, said, 'When you have given the call for *Dhuhr* or *'Isha'*, pray two *raka'ts* and then sit for the amount of time which you reckon it will take for a man from the furthest part of Madina who could hear it, to go to the lavatory, do *wudu'*, put his garment on, walk easily to the mosque, pray four *rak'ats*, and then sit down. Then give the *iqama*.'"

'Abdu'l-Hakim ibn 'Abdullah said, "'Umar ibn 'Abdu'l-'Aziz used to lead us in the prayer in Madina and he did not say 'In the

Name of Allah, the Merciful, the Compassionate' (after the opening *takbir*) aloud."

'Imran ibn Abi Anas reported that 'Umar used to say one *salam* towards *qibla* (to end the prayer): '*As-Salamu 'alaykum.*'

Raja' ibn Hawya said, "On Friday, Sulayman ibn 'Abdu'l-Malik put on a green garment of silk/wool and looked at himself in a mirror. He said, 'By Allah, I am the young king.' He went out and led the people in the *Jumu'a* prayer. As soon as he returned he became ill. When he was very ill, he wrote a letter appointing his son Ayyub who was a young lad as his successor. I said, 'What are you doing, Amir al-Mu'minin? He is one of those who will be protected by the khalif from his grave if he appoints a righteous man.' Sulayman said, 'It is a letter for which I will do an *istikhara*. I will think about it and not decide straightaway.'

"He waited one or two days and then he feared for himself and he summoned me. He said, 'What do you think of Da'ud ibn Sulayman?' I said, 'He is away at Constantinople and you do not know for sure whether he is dead or alive.' He said, 'Raja', who do you think?' I said, 'What is your opinion, Amir al-Mu'minin?' wanting to see what he would say. He asked, 'What do you think of 'Umar ibn 'Abdu'l-'Aziz?' I said, 'By Allah, I know him to be virtuous and an excellent Muslim.' He said, 'He is that. By Allah, if I appoint him and do not appoint any of the children of 'Abdu'l-Malik, there will be civil war. They will never let him rule them unless I stipulate one of them after him.' Yazid ibn 'Abdu'l-Malik was absent at that time. He said, 'So I will appoint Yazid ibn 'Abdu'l-Malik after him. That will calm them and please them.' I said, 'As you think.'

"He wrote with his hand, 'In the Name of Allah, the Merciful, the Compassionate. This is the letter of the slave of Allah, Sulayman, the Amir al-Mu'minin, appointing 'Umar ibn 'Abdu'l-'Aziz. Hear and obey him. Fear Allah and do not disagree so that people are emboldened against you.' He sealed the letter and sent for Ka'b ibn Hamiz, the chief of police, to command the people of his house to gather. Ka'b sent for them and they gathered."

Then after they had gathered Sulayman said to Raja', "Take this letter of mine to them and inform them that it has been written by me and command them to give allegiance to the one I have appointed." Raja' did this and when Raja' told them what they had to do, they said, "We will hear and obey whoever is named in it." They said, "We will enter and submit to the Amir al-Mu'minin." He said, "Yes." So they entered and Sulayman said to them, "This is the letter," pointing to it as they looked at it in the hand of Raja' ibn Hawya. "This is my document. Hear and obey and give allegiance to the one whom I have named in this letter." They gave their allegiance to him to do so, man after man. Then he took the sealed letter out of Raja's hand.

Raja' said, "When they had gone, 'Umar came to me and said, 'Abu'l-Miqdam, Sulayman is someone I respect and love, and he has already been honest and kind to me. I ask you by Allah and by my respect and love, will you confirm for me what he has written so that I can ask him to dismiss me now before the situation is such that I can no longer do what I can still do now.' Raja' said, 'No, by Allah, we will not tell you a single letter.' 'Umar left angrily."

Raja' said, "I met Hisham ibn 'Abdu'l-Malik and he said, 'Raja', I have a long-standing respect and love for you and I am grateful – tell me whether this business is for me. If it is for me, I will know. If it is for someone else, I will speak out. Someone like me should not be restricted, nor should this matter be kept from me. Tell me and, by Allah, I will remember your name forever.'"

Raja' said, "I refused and said, 'No, by Allah, I will not tell you a single letter of what has been confided in me.' Hisham bade us farewell and left, striking one hand against the other and saying, 'Who will have it if not me? Am I to be put aside from the sons of 'Abdu'l-Malik? By Allah, if so, then I am the accursed of the sons of 'Abdu'l-Malik.'"

Raja' said, "I went to Sulayman and found him dying. When the death throes began, I turned him towards *qibla*. He began to say while he was sobbing, 'It is not time for that yet, Raja'.' I did that twice. The third time, he said, 'It is now, Raja'. I want to testify that there is no god but Allah and I testify that Muhammad is His slave and Messenger.' I turned him and he died. When I had closed his eyes, I covered him with a green cloth and locked the door. His wife sent someone to me to see how he was. I said, 'He is asleep and covered up.' The messenger looked at him covered up, returned and informed her. She believed him and thought he was asleep.

"I put someone I trusted at the door and told him not to move until I came back to him and not to admit anyone to the khalif. I sent for

Ka'b ibn Hamiz al-'Anbasi and he collected the household of the Amir al-Mu'minin together. They met in the Dabiq mosque. I said, 'Give allegiance.' They said, 'We have already given allegiance. Should we do so again! We gave allegiance to what the Amir al-Mu'minin commanded and to the person he named in his sealed letter.' They gave allegiance a second time, man by man.

"When they had given their allegiance after the death of Sulayman, I thought that I had settled the matter. I said, 'Go to your companion. He has died.' They said, 'We belong to Allah and to Him we return.' Then I read the letter out to them, and when it mentioned 'Umar ibn 'Abdu'l-'Aziz, Hisham shouted out, 'We will never give allegiance to him!' I said, 'By Allah, I will strike your neck. Rise and give allegiance.' He got up, dragging his feet.

"I took 'Umar's arm and sat him on the minbar. He was saying, 'We belong to Allah and to Him we return,' as he sat down heavily on it. Hisham was saying, 'We belong to Allah and to Him we return,' for his error. When Hisham reached 'Umar, he said, 'We belong to Allah and to Him We return. How did this command go to you instead of the sons of 'Abdu'l-Malik?' 'Umar said, 'Indeed we belong to Allah and to Him we return. It has come to me although I do not want it.' Then Sulayman was washed and shrouded and 'Umar prayed over him.

"When his burial was finished, the mounts of the khalif were brought: work horses, steeds, mules, and every managed animal. He asked, 'What is this?' They said, 'The mounts of the khalif.' 'Umar said, 'My animal is more suitable for me.' So he rode his mule, and I had those animals taken away. Then it was said, 'Stay in the residence of the khalif.' He said, 'The family of Abu Ayyub is there. I have enough room in my dwelling until they have moved out.' So he stayed in his house until they had vacated it."

Raja' said, "On the evening of that day he said, 'Raja', summon a scribe for me.' I called him. I found that everything about 'Umar delighted me. He had done what he did with the mounts and with Sulayman's house. I thought, 'What will he do now with the scribes? Will he make copies or what?' When the scribe had sat down, he dictated a letter to him from his mouth to the hand of the scribe without making a rough copy. He dictated in the best, most eloquent and most succinct manner. Then he commanded the scribe to send copies of it to every land.

"'Abdu'l-'Aziz ibn al-Walid, who was absent, heard about Sulayman's death. He did not know that people had given allegiance to 'Umar on Sulayman's instructions. Those who were with him gave allegiance to him and then he came to Damascus, wanting to take it, only to hear that they had given allegiance to 'Umar after Sulayman in accordance with Sulayman's directive. He went to 'Umar. 'Umar said to him, 'I hear that you have taken allegiance from those who are with you and wanted to enter Damascus.' He replied, 'That was the case. That was before I had heard that the khalif had stipulated anyone. I feared that property might be looted.' 'Umar said, 'By Allah, if you had been given allegiance and taken command, I would not have challenged you for it and I would have stayed in my house.' 'Abdu'l-'Aziz said, 'I do not want anyone but you to be in command.' He gave his allegiance to 'Umar."

Raja' ibn Hawya said, "When Sulayman ibn 'Abdu'l-Malik was very ill, 'Umar saw me going in and out of the house frequently. He called me and said to me, 'Raja', I remind you by Allah and Islam to remember me when you are with the Amir al-Mu'minin and not to suggest me to him if he asks your advice. By Allah, I am not strong enough for this business. I ask you by Allah to direct the Amir al-Mu'minin away from me.' I chided him and said, 'You are eager for the khalifate and so you want me to suggest you.' He was embarrassed. I went in and Sulayman said to me, 'Raja', to whom do you think I should entrust this command?' I said, 'Amir al-Mu'minin, fear Allah. You are going to Allah Who will ask you about this business and what you did in it.' He asked, 'What is your view?' I replied, "Umar ibn 'Abdu'l-'Aziz.' He asked, 'What can I do with the position of Amir al-Mu'minin which 'Abdu'l-Malik gave to al-Walid and then to me, while any of the sons of 'Atika remain?' I said, 'Make it for them after him.'

"He said, 'You are right! Bring me some paper.' I brought it to him and he wrote the pledge for 'Umar and then for Yazid after him and sealed it. Then I summoned the men and they came in and he told them, 'I have recorded my decision on this paper. I give it to Raja'. I commend my command which is in the paper to him. Bear witness and seal the document.' They sealed it and left and Sulayman died soon after.

"I kept the women from crying out and went out to the people. They asked, 'Raja', how is the Amir al-Mu'minin?' I replied, 'He has not been more at peace since he became ill than he is at this moment.' They said, 'Praise be to Allah.' I said, 'Are you aware that this is the decision of the Amir al-Mu'minin to which you testified?' – 'Yes,' they replied. I asked, 'Are you pleased with it?' Hisham said, 'If it contains one of the children of 'Abdu'l-Malik. Otherwise, no.' I said, 'And if it contains one of the children of 'Abdu'l-Malik?' He said, 'Then yes.' So I went in and waited for a while and then told the women, 'Shout!' I went out and read the letter while the people were gathered together and 'Umar was in a corner of the verandah."

Some shaykhs of Thaqif said, "'Umar was given the pledge as khalif after Sulayman's death while 'Umar was in a corner at Dabiq. A man of Thaqif called Salim, one of the maternal uncles of 'Umar, took his arm and made him stand. 'Umar said, 'By Allah, I do not want this and this world will not catch me by it.'"

Bishr said, "When 'Umar ibn 'Abdu'l-'Aziz was appointed, he addressed the people, and a carpet was laid out for him. He came down and ignored the rug and sat in a corner. It was said, 'You should move to Sulayman's room.' He recited:

'Were it not for the meeting and prohibition out of fear of ruin,
    I would disobey. Every chider loves the child.
He did what he did in what is past
    and now we will not see the youth of bygone days again.'"

Sayyar ibn al-Hakim said, "The first thing of which 'Umar disapproved was that when Sulayman was buried, he was brought the mount which Sulayman used to ride. He did not mount it but rode his own animal. He entered the castle and Sulayman's rugs on which he used to sit had been spread out for him but he did not sit on them. Then he went to the mosque, went up on the minbar and praised Allah and then said, 'There is no Prophet after your Prophet and there is no Book after the Book which was revealed to him. What Allah has made lawful is lawful until the Day of Rising and what Allah has made unlawful is unlawful until the Day of Rising. I am not a qadi but an executor. I am not an innovator, but a follower. No one should be obeyed in disobedience to Allah. I am not the best of you, but a man from among you, although Allah has given me the heaviest burden of you.' Then he said what he wanted."

'Ubaydullah said, "When 'Umar left Sulayman's grave, the

mounts of Sulayman were shown to him. He thought that they were too much and called for his grey mule. It was brought to him and he rode it. He went home and the rugs of Sulayman had been put in his house. He said, 'You have been too hasty.' Then he moved an Armenian cushion and put it between him and the earth. He said, 'By Allah, were I not involved in the needs of the Muslims, I would not have sat down for you.'"

Al-Mundhir ibn 'Ubayd said, "'Umar II was apppointed after the *Jumu'a* prayer and by *'Asr* I could not recognise him."

Abu'z-Zinad said, "Sulayman had appointed Abu Bakr ibn Muhammad ibn Hazm over Madina. When Sulayman died, and 'Umar was made khalif, he put him in charge of Madina and made Abu Tuwala the *qadi*. He put 'Abdu'l-Hamid ibn 'Abdu'r-Rahman in charge of Kufa and made Abu'z-Zinad his scribe. He remained in charge of its army and collecting the *kharaj* until his death. He appointed 'Amir ash-Sha'bi as its *qadi*. He appointed 'Adi ibn Arta'a over Basra and made al-Hasan ibn Abi'l-Hasan its *qadi*, but he asked to be dismissed and so he dismissed him. He appointed 'Urwa ibn Muhammad as-Sa'di over Yemen and 'Adi ibn 'Adi al-Kindi over Jazira. He appointed Isma'il ibn 'Ubaydullah over North Africa until he died there. He appointed Muhammad ibn Suwayd al-Fihri over Damascus. He appointed al-Harraj ibn 'Abdullah al-Hakami over Khorasan."

Sulayman ibn Musa said, "'Umar continued to remedy injustices from the day he was khalif until the day he died."

'Abdu'l-Majid ibn Suhayl said, "I saw that 'Umar began with the people of his house and remedied whatever they had acquired unjustly. Then he did that with other people next. 'Umar ibn al-Walid said, 'We brought a man from the family of 'Umar ibn al-Khattab and apppointed him over you. So this is what he has done with you.'"

Abu Bakr ibn Sabra said, "When 'Umar started to remedy the injustices, he said, 'I must begin with myself,' and he examined the land and goods which were in his possession, to the extent that he even considered his signet-ring. He said, 'This is part of what al-Walid gave me which came to him from the Maghrib.' So he removed it."

Ishaq ibn 'Abdullah said, "'Umar continued to remedy injustices from the time of Mu'awiya up until he was made khalif. He retrieved rights from the possession of the heirs of Mu'awiya and Yazid."

Ayyub as-Sakhtiyati relates that 'Umar remedied injustices in respect of property, returned what was in the treasury, and commanded that *zakat* be paid for the years that it had not been collected from its people. Then he followed that with another letter, "I looked and there was a bad debt on which *zakat* had only been paid for one year."

Abu'-Zinad said, "'Umar II wrote to us in Iraq telling us to restore whatever its people were entitled to, and we returned them until we had spent everything that was in the treasury of Iraq and 'Umar sent money to us from Syria."

Ja'far said, "No letter came to Abu Bakr ibn Muhammad from 'Umar but that it referred to remedying injustices, reviving the *Sunna*, suppressing innovations, or alloting or determining a gift or benefit, until he left this world."

Abu Bakr ibn Muhammad ibn 'Amr said, "'Umar wrote to me to administer the diwans and to examine every injustice which had been committed by those before regarding rights of Muslims or what had been agreed and to put things right. If the people who had suffered an injustice had died, then the remedy was to be granted to their heirs."

Musa ibn 'Ubadya said, "I heard the letter of 'Umar II to Abu Bakr ibn Muhammad: 'Beware of staying in your house. Go out to the people. Involve them in your meetings and when your appear. Do not let any of the people be favoured by you more than others and do not say, 'Those are part of the people of the house of the Amir al-Mu'minin.' The people of the house of the Amir al-Mu'minin and others are equal with me today. I am responsible for taking the people of the house of the Amir al-Mu'minin into account, because they are in a position to overpower the one who contends with them. When anything is unclear to you, write to me about it.'"

'Umar II said, "If there is any innovation which Allah ends at my hands, or any *sunna* which Allah revives at my hands, even in return for a piece of my flesh, then that will be easier for me for the sake of Allah."

Hammad ibn Sulayman reported that 'Umar II stood up in the Damascus Mosque and then called out in his loudest voice, "We are not to be obeyed if it involves disobedience to Allah!"

Sayyar said, "'Umar used to say to people, 'Stay in your lands – I will remember you in your cities and ignore you if you come to me, except for someone who has been wronged by a governor. He needs no permission from me and should come to me.'"

'Abdullah ibn Waqid said, "In the final speech which 'Umar II gave, he praised Allah. Then he said, 'O people, stay in your lands. I will remember you in your lands. I will ignore you if you come to me. I have appointed over you men whom I do not say are the best of you, but they are better than the worst of you. If anyone is wronged by a governor, that is without my permission. By Allah, if I were to deny this wealth to myself and my family and then be stingy with it to you, then I would be a miser. By Allah, were it not for reviving a *sunna* or pursuing a right, I would not want to live another minute.'"

Isma'il ibn Abi Hakim said, "A letter came to 'Umar from one of the Banu Marwan which angered him. He was furious and then said, 'Allah is able to wreak slaughter among the Marwanids. By Allah, if it is to be so, then that slaughter will be at my hands.' When they heard that, they refrained. They knew his firmness and that when he undertook something he would carry it through."

Abu 'Amr al-Bahili said, "The Marwanids came to 'Umar and said, 'You have fallen short in doing for us what those before you did.' They censured him. He said, 'If you do the like of this again, I will go to Madina and make it my counsel. I acknowledge its master, little al-'Amash, that is, al-Qasim ibn Muhammad ibn Abi Bakr as-Saddiq.'"

Afalah ibn Humayd said, "I heard al-Qasim ibn Muhammad say, 'Today all those who did not speak will speak, and we hope that Sulayman will appoint 'Umar ibn 'Abdu'l-'Aziz. 'Umar said when he was dying, "If I had something in the business, I would have let it pass to al-Qasim ibn Muhammad." Al-Qasim heard of this and asked for mercy on him and said, "Al-Qasim is too weak to be worthy of it. How could he undertake the business of the Community of Muhammad!"'"

Isma'il ibn Umayya said, "'Umar II said, 'If I had something to say in this matter, I would only let it go to al-Qasim ibn Muhammad, or the master of al-A'was, Isma'il ibn 'Amr ibn Sa'id.'"

Muhammad ibn 'Umar said, "Isma'il ibn 'Amir was a solitary worshipper who had withdrawn. He lived in al-A'was."

Salim ibn 'Abdullah said, "We used to hope that Sulayman would appoint 'Umar ibn 'Abdu'l-'Aziz." 'Amr ibn 'Uthman said, "I heard Kharija ibn Zayd ibn Thabit say that."

'Ali ibn Muhammad said, "I heard that when 'Umar II was

214

appointed, he looked at the slaves, clothes, perfume and superfluous things he had and sold everything with which he could do without. That went for 23,000 dinars, which he spent in the Way (of Allah)."

'Abdu'r-Rahman ibn 'Abdu'l-'Aziz reported that 'Umar's son said that he heard from 'Umar's servant that he did not eat his fill of food from the day that he was appointed until he died.

Muhammad ibn Qays said, "When 'Umar was appointed, he abolished all taxes on land and stopped the *jizya* being collected from everyone who was a Muslim."

Isma'il ibn Abi Hakim reported that when 'Umar II was appointed, he opened up all the government pastures except for an-Naqi'.

Yahya ibn Wadih said, "'Umar II ordered inns to be set up along the road to Khorasan."

'Amr ibn 'Uthman said, "I attended two distributions made by 'Umar II to all people equally."

Rabi'a ibn 'Ata', the client of Ibn Siba' al-Khuza'i, said, "I sat with Sulayman ibn Yasar and mentioned to him the letter of Abu Bakr ibn Hazm which came from 'Umar II telling him not to allot a stipend to a merchant. He said, "Umar was correct. The merchant is distracted by his trade from what is beneficial to people.'"

Muhammad ibn Hilal reported that 'Umar II allotted men two thousand each, which was the highest stipend.

'Abdu'l-Hamid reported, "'Umar II paid three stipends to the people of Madina in the space of two years and five months less ten days. May Allah have mercy on him."

Sa'id ibn Muslim said, "I heard 'Umar II say when he was khalif, 'It is not lawful for you to take for your dead and present them to us. Record for us every live person and we will allot for him."

Thabit ibn Qays said, "I heard the letter of 'Umar II read to us, 'Present every living person and we will allot. Present your dead. It is your property which we return to you.'"

Muhammad ibn 'Umar reported that his father told him, "My wet-nurse took me to Abu Bakr ibn Hazm and he put a dinar in my hand since I was alive. I was born in 100 AH. Then the next year, we were given another dinar, and so it was two dinars. That is who I was named after."

The uncle of Muhammad ibn 'Umar, al-Haytham ibn Waqid, said, "I was born in 97 AH and 'Umar was made khalif when I was three. I received three dinars from the division."

Muhammad ibn Hilal said, "'Umar II considered people equal as regards the food of the neighbour. The largest share to be distributed of the food of the neighbour was four and a half *ardibs* for every person."

Ibrahim ibn Yahya said, "I used to have 20 *ardibs* in the food of the neighbour. When 'Umar was appointed, I was confirmed and given the same share as was allotted to the people of my house who were allotted it."

Ja'far said, "I saw that Abu Bakr ibn 'Amr ibn Hazm acted at night as he did in the day since 'Umar encouraged him to do so."

Muhammad ibn Qays said, "I saw that when 'Umar II had prayed *'Isha'*, he called for a candle from the property of Allah so that he could write about the business of the Muslims and the complaints which were being presented to him from every land. In the morning, he sat to remedy injustices and to command that *zakat* be distributed among its people. I saw that someone to whom he gave *zakat* one year had zakatable camels the following year."

Muhajir ibn Yazid said, "'Umar II sent us out to distribute the *zakat* among those entitled to it. We collected it from those to whom we have given the previous year. I saw that when he was writing to his family, or for a need he had concerning himself, he would request a candle from his own property and then go inside and use a different candle. I saw that he washed his own clothes and did not come out to us or speak to us because he did not have any others to wear. I saw that a lintel of his house was ruined and he spoke about repairing it. Then he said, 'Muzaham, will you let us leave it alone and leave this world without having introduced anything new?' He forbade wine in every land."

'Abdullah ibn al-'Ala' said, "I said to 'Umar, 'Amir al-Mu'minin, I have been starved for years. I was with the rebels and I was deprived of my stipend.' So he returned my stipend to me and commanded that I be given what was outstanding from past years."

Khulayd ibn Da'laj said, "When 'Umar II became khalif, he sent to al-Hasan and Ibn Sirin and said to them, 'I will return to you what was kept from you out of your stipends.' Ibn Sirin said, 'If you do that for all the people of Basra, then do it. Otherwise, no.' 'Umar wrote that there was not enough money. Al-Hasan accepted his offer."

Ibrahim ibn Yahya reported that 'Umar II wrote to give Kharija ibn Zayd his debts, and Kharija went to Abu Bakr ibn Hazm and said, 'I do not want to oblige the Amir al-Mu'minin to do this. I have peers. The Amir al-Mu'minin is their uncle by what he has done. I do not want him to single me out for this.' 'Umar wrote, 'There is not enough money to do that. If there was, I would do it.'"

Abu Bakr ibn Hazm said, "We used to bring out the diwan of the people who were imprisoned and they would receive their stipends in accordance with the letter of 'Umar. He wrote to me, 'If anyone has been gone only recently, then give it to the people of his diwan, and if anyone has been gone for a long time, then set aside his stipend until he comes, or there is news of his death, or he has an agent who has evidence that he is alive, in which case, give it to his agent.'"

'Isa ibn Abi 'Ata' said, "I saw 'Umar pay a creditor 75 dinars from the share allotted for creditors."

Ya'qub ibn 'Umar said, "'Asim ibn 'Umar and Bashir ibn Muhammad came to 'Umar II while he was khalif. They went to him in Khanasira and told him of a debt which they owed. He gave each of them 400 dinars to pay it off. He made out a cheque stating that it was to be given from the *zakat* of Kalb and so it was withdrawn from the treasury."

Muhammad ibn 'Umar said, "The cheque presented to him was to pay off his debt and whatever was left over was put in the treasury as discharged because this is the manner in which debts are paid."

'Abdu'r-Rahman ibn Jabir said, "Al-Qasim ibn Mukhaymara came to 'Umar II and asked him to settle his debt. 'Umar asked, 'How much is your debt?' He replied, '90 dinars.' He said, 'I will settle it for you from the share allotted for creditors.' He said, 'Amir al-Mu'minin, enable me to be free of commerce.' He asked, 'With what?' He said, 'With a share.' He said, 'I have allotted you 60 dinars and commanded a house and servant for you.' Al-Qasim said, 'Praise be to Allah who has enabled me to dispense with having to trade. I will lock my door with no further worry.'"

Abu 'Ufayr Muhammad ibn Sahl said, "'Umar II settled my debt for me when he was khalif. It was 150 dinars, paid from the *zakat* of the Banu Kilab. He wrote it."

Talha ibn 'Abdullah said one day that 'Umar II continued to hold to his opinion and indicated that the one in command among the people of his family should take care of the people of his household out of the *khums*. They used to not do that. When he became khalif, he investigated it and distributed it among its five categories, preferring the people in need within the five categories wherever they were. If their needs were the same, he would expand their allocations in proportion to the amount of the fifth.

Al-Muhajir ibn Yazid reported that he saw 'Umar II being brought the fifth as regards captives: "Sometimes I saw him line them up in a single row. I asked Umar II about water placed by the roadside as *sadaqa*, and if one could drink from it. He replied, 'Yes, there is no harm in that. I remember when I was governor of Madina and the mosque had water which was *sadaqa*, and I did not see any of the people of *fiqh* refrain from drinking that water.'"

'Isa ibn Abi Ata', a man of the people of Syria, was in charge of the diwan of Madina for 'Umar II. He sometimes gave wealth to make people friendly to Islam. A man reported that 'Umar II gave a patrician a 1,000 dinars to make him friendly to Islam."

'Asim ibn Kulayb and Abu'l-Juwayriya al-Jarmi said that 'Umar II ransomed a man from the enemy and returned him for 100,000 dirhams.

'Amr ibn al-Muhajir reported that 'Umar II did not oblige hospitality from the people of cities.

'Amr ibn 'Uthman said that 'Umar II wrote, "The Imam should not take more than a third of the booty."

'Amr ibn Maymun reported that 'Umar II wrote, "Include mules with horses."

Nafi' said, "When he was khalif, 'Umar II wrote to his governors in all his territories not to give a share to fourteen year olds in the fighting, but to give a share to fifteen year olds in the fighting."

Bishr ibn Humayd said, "When the stipend was being paid, I heard 'Umar II write to his governors that it was not to be accepted by a man who already had 100 dinars, an Arab horse, armour, a sword, a spear, and arrows."

Rabi'a ibn 'Ata' reported that 'Umar II said, "The apostate should be asked to repent for three days. If he does not repent, his neck is severed."

Abu'z-Zinad reported that 'Umar II said, "The Sultan has discretion in His words, *'The reprisal against those who wage war on Allah and His Messenger...'* (5:33)"

'Uthman ibn Sulayman said, "I heard 'Umar II say, 'There are two matters concerning which the people and the governor have no discretion – they are for Allah and the ruler to decide: murder which arises from villainy and causing corruption in the earth, and treacherous murder."

Bukayr reported that 'Umar II said, "A woman may not marry a captive as long as he remains a captive."

Sulayman ibn Habib reported that 'Umar II said, "A prisoner is allowed to do what he wants with his property."

Al-Muhajir reported that 'Umar II said, "When a man is fighting on the back of his horse in war, he may do what he wants with his property."

Al-Mundhir ibn 'Ubayd reported that 'Umar II said, "The *dhimmi* is not allowed to grant safe conduct."

Suhayl al-A'sha said, "'Umar's letter was read to us in Byzantine territory commanding our governor to set up catapults against the fortress. Salim ibn 'Abdullah was beside me listening to the letter and he did not object to it."

Salih ibn Muhammad said that he heard that 'Umar II did not see anything wrong in smoking out the enemy from their fortresses.

'Amr ibn al-Muhajir reported that 'Umar II said that two men who had been captured in Byzantine territory were brought to him as spies: a Muslim and a *dhimmi*. He killed the *dhimmi* and punished the Muslim.

Ma'qil ibn 'Abdullah reported that 'Umar forbade hamstringing an animal while it was standing.

'Abdullah ibn Abi Bakr ibn Hazm reported that while he was khalif 'Umar wrote to him not to take the *khums* from the mines, but to take *zakat* from them."

Al-Qasim ibn Muhammad said, "'Umar did well when he took *zakat* from the mines. That is how it was at the beginning."

Mubashshir ibn 'Ubayd reported that 'Umar II allowed pearl diving.

Layth ibn Abi Sulaym reported that 'Umar wrote that there was a fifth tax on amber. Isma'il ibn Abi Hakim said, "I heard 'Umar II say at the end of his life, 'There is nothing payable on amber."

Humayd reported that 'Umar II said, "The messenger, courier and agent sent from the army have their shares along with the Muslim fighters."

Salih reported that 'Umar II used to command those who had too much to sell their booty.

'Amr ibn Sharahil said, "'Umar II wrote, 'There is no harm in eating animals slaughtered by Samaritans.'"

Salih ibn 'Umar said, "I heard 'Umar say, 'Two horses both have shares [of the booty] but any more than that do not.'"

Sulayman ibn al-Hajjaj at-Ta'ifi reported that 'Umar used to have horses presented to him to examine while he was khalif.

Rabi'a said that 'Umar II wrote, "When the summer expedition begins, do not let anyone follow after them unless they are reinforcing them with increased strength in the form of men, horses and equipment."

Rabi'a ibn 'Ata' said, "'Umar sent some money to the coast of Aden to ransom a man, a woman, a slave and a *dhimmi*." He said that 'Umar gave back ten Greeks in return for a Muslim.

'Abdullah ibn 'Amr reported that 'Umar was brought a captive taken by Maslama ibn 'Abdu'l-Malik whose family offered to ransom him for a 100 *mithqals* and 'Umar returned him to them for that.

Rabi'a ibn 'Ata' said, "I heard that when he was khalif, 'Umar II disliked killing captives: they were either enslaved or set free."

Bukayr reported that 'Umar II said, "Whoever steals in the land of the enemy and then returns from it has his hand cut off."

Yazid ibn Abi Sumayya said, "I saw that 'Umar II carried out the *hadd* of 80 lashes on a man who had slandered a man in enemy territory on their return."

Khazim ibn Husayn said, "I saw 'Umar II in Khanasira when a man was brought before him against whom there was testimony that he had drunk wine in enemy territory and he was flogged with 80 lashes."

Abu Sakhr said, "Someone who stole from the booty before it was divided up was brought to 'Umar II. He asked him whether he was someone who had been deprived of any of the booty. He said no, and so he cut off his hand."

Al-Mundhir ibn 'Ubayd said, "I saw 'Umar at Dabiq. When he did the full prayer, the people joined their prayers. When he prayed (the shortened prayer of) two *rak'ats*, he did not join prayers unless he came to a city where they joined them."

Bishr ibn Humayd reported that 'Umar II said, "The complete *ribat* is 40 days."

Salih said, "I heard 'Umar say at Dabiq, "We are in *ribat*."

'Abdullah ibn 'Ubayda said, "I heard 'Umar II say, 'People only perish in small groups.' He used to write: 'Only go against a small group with strength and numbers. Then either they will all return or they will perish.'"

Safwan ibn 'Amr said, "The letter of the khalif 'Umar II to his representative said not to attack any Greek fortress or any group of them until they had first been invited to Islam. If they accepted they were to be left alone. If they refused, then they were to pay the *jizya*. If they refused this, then they were to be all treated the same."

'Abdu'l-'Aziz said, "My father's sword was inlaid with silver. He removed the silver and decorated it with iron."

'Umar ibn al-Harith reported that 'Umar used to say the *takbir* aloud in the opening of the prayer.

'Isa ibn Abi 'Ata' reported that 'Umar said, "Anyone who seeks security with me in any language is safe."

Al-Mundhir ibn 'Ubayd said, "'Umar II wrote to me about the *dhimmis* raiding with the Muslims and giving security to the enemy. He wrote, 'He is not allowed to grant safe conduct. The Messenger of Allahصلعم said, "The least of the Muslims can give protection." This one is not a Muslim.'"

Ishaq ibn Yahya said that he heard the khalif 'Umar II declare that he was not responsible for isolated outrages committed by the army. He said, "'Umar ibn al-Khattab declared that he was not responsible for isolated outrages committed by the army."

'Ayyash ibn Sulayman reported that 'Umar II said that the *waqf* of a *dhimmi* who leaves a place of worship as a *waqf* from his property for the Christians or Jews is allowed.

Husayn reported that 'Umar II wrote that if someone became a Muslim while his *jizya* was being weighed, then it was not to be taken from him.

'Amr ibn al-Muhajir reported that 'Umar II said that if a *dhimmi* became Muslim a day before his *jizya* was due, then it was not taken from him.

Musa ibn 'Ubayda said, "'Umar II wrote that the prisons should be investigated and the hardened criminals among them identified. He commanded that they should be given provision for the summer and the winter." He said, "I saw that they were provisioned monthly by us, and had a garment for the winter and one for the summer."

Yahya ibn Sa'id, the client of al-Mahri, said, "'Umar wrote to the army generals: 'Look into those who are in prison on whom sentence has been passed. Do not imprison a person until after sentence has been passed. If his case is unclear, then write to me about it. Verify who the hardened criminals are. Incarceration is a punishment for them. Do not be excessive in imposing penalties. Care for those who are sick and who have no family or wealth. When you imprison people for a debt, do not put them together with criminals in the same room or prison. Set up a separate prison for women. Be careful to choose those whom you trust and who do not take bribes. Someone who takes bribes does what he is told.'"

'Abdullah ibn Abi Bakr reported that 'Umar wrote to Abu Bakr ibn Hazm to review the people in prison every Saturday and to see who the hardened criminals were.

Al-Hajjaj said, "'Umar II wrote to 'Abdu'l-Hamid to keep hardened criminals in prison, to clothe them with one garment in the winter and two garments in the summer, and so on, about their interests."

Abu Bakr ibn 'Amr ibn Hazm said, "'Umar wrote to me to imprison hardened criminals and murderers in fetters. I wrote back to him to ask how could they pray in chains. 'Umar wrote back, 'If Allah wished, He could have tested them with worse than irons. They can still pray however it is feasible for them since they have an excuse.' Abu Bakr sent some men to him in chains, including Qays ibn Makshuh al-Muradi and others."

Usama ibn Zayd said, "'Umar's letter came and was read to us: 'Do not enter the bath-house without wearing a wrapper. If someone does so, I think that both the owner of the bath-house and the one who goes in like that should be punished.' I also saw the letter of 'Umar which read: 'Make your animals for slaughter face *qibla*.' So I turned to Nafi' ibn Jubayr who was beside me and said, 'Who does not know this!'"

Abu'z-Zinad said, "The Kharijites rebelled in Iraq while 'Umar was khalif. I was in Iraq then with 'Abdu'l-Hamid ibn 'Abdu'r-Rahman, the governor of Iraq. When the news reached 'Umar, he wrote to 'Abdu'l-Hamid ordering him to call on them to act in accordance with the Book of Allah and the *Sunna* of His Prophet صلعم. When his call was unsuccessful, he wrote to him to fight them, saying: 'Allah, Who is praised, has not given them any *Salaf* as evidence against us.' So 'Abdu'l-Hamid sent an army against them and the Kharijites defeated them. When 'Umar heard that, he sent Maslama ibn 'Abdu'l-Malik against them with an army of Syrians and wrote to 'Abdu'l-Hamid saying, 'I have heard what your army did was bad and so I have sent you Maslama ibn 'Abdu'l-Malik.' Maslama met them and Allah soon gave him victory over them."

'Awn ibn 'Abdullah said, "During his khalifate 'Umar II sent me against the Kharijites who had rebelled. I asked them, 'What do you hold against him?' They said, 'We do not hold anything against him except that he does not curse those before him of the people from his house. This is dissimulation.' So 'Umar refrained from fighting them until they had stolen property and attacked people as highway robbers. He wrote to 'Abdu'l-Hamid: 'When they take property and cause fear on the roads, then fight them for they are filth.'"

Khazim ibn Husayn said, "I heard the letter of 'Umar II to his governor about the Kharijites: 'If Allah gives you victory over them, then return what you have taken of their property to their families.'"

Al-Mundhir ibn 'Ubayd said, "I heard 'Umar's letter to 'Abdu'l-Hamid ibn 'Abdu'r-Rahman: 'Imprison any Kharijite captive you take until he brings out good.'" He said, "'Umar died while a number of them were in prison."

Kathir ibn Zayd said, "I came to Khanasir while 'Umar II was khalif and I saw him paying the *mu'adhdhins* from the treasury."

Al-Mundhir ibn 'Ubayd said, "I heard 'Umar say to his *mu'adhdhin*, 'Say the *iqama* rapidly and do not repeat in it.'"

Abu 'Ubayd, the client of Sulayman, said, "I saw the *mu'adhdhin* stand at 'Umar's door in Khanasira and say, 'Peace be upon you, Amir al-Mu'minin, and the mercy and blessing of Allah. Come to the prayer. Come to the prayer. The prayer, may Allah have mercy on you.' I did not see him wait for the second call to prayer. Sometimes we sat with him in the mosque and when the *mu'adhdhin* said, 'The prayer is established,' he said, 'Rise.'" He said, "When he was khalif, I saw 'Umar II sitting in a circle which was facing *qibla*. The *mu'adhdhin* gave the *adhan* and they rose from their circle and waited until the *iqama* was given and stood for the *iqama*. I saw that at *Maghrib*."

Muslim ibn Ziyad, the client of Umm Habiba, the wife of the Prophetﷺ, said, "'Umar II had thirteen *mu'adhdhins* fearing that they would be cut short before he came out."

Muslim said, "I did not ever see any of them give the *adhan* more than once. Sometimes he came out during the first *adhan* and sometimes during the second or sometimes the third."

'Amr ibn al-Muhajir said, "I saw Salim ibn 'Abdullah and Abi Qilaba with 'Umar II, and his *adhan* was twice and his *iqama* was once, and they did not object."

Usama ibn Zayd reported that 'Umar II used to wash in his house wearing a waist-wrapper."

Yazid ibn Abi Malik said, "I saw 'Umar II doing *wudu'* from a copper vessel."

Al-Mundhir ibn 'Ubayd said, "I saw that after 'Umar II had done *wudu'*, he wiped his face with a handkerchief."

'Amr ibn 'Ata' reported that 'Umar II used to do *wudu'* after touching his penis. He also reported that 'Umar did *wudu'* after eating something which had been cooked, even sugar.

Az-Zuhri reported that 'Umar used to do *wudu'* with warm water. If he drank from it, he did not do *wudu'* with it.

A female client of 'Umar said, "I noticed that 'Umar covered his head when he went to the lavatory."

Ishaq ibn Yahya said, "I saw 'Umar II pray over his brother Suhayl ibn 'Abdu'l-'Aziz. I saw him raise his hands opposite his shoulders in each *takbir*. Then he said the *salam* to his right lightly. I saw him walk in front of the bier. I saw him on that day with the bier carried between poles. I prayed behind him in Khanasira and I heard him raise his voice in the first *takbir* and then he recited so that the first row could hear in a slow recitation: '*Praise belongs to Allah, the Lord of the worlds, the Merciful, the Compassionate, Master of the Day of Rising...*' (1:2-4) He did not say the *basmala*."

Ishaq said, "When he finished, I asked him, 'Do you say it silently, Amir al-Mu'minin?' He replied, 'If I said it silently, I would not say it aloud!'"

'Amr ibn 'Uthman said, "I saw 'Umar II giving the *khutba* in a loud voice in the *Jumu'a* so that most of the people of the mosque could hear his admonition, but he was not shouting."

Sa'id ibn 'Abdu'l-'Aziz said, "'Umar wrote to his governor of Damascus, 'Uthman ibn Sa'd, 'When you lead them in the prayer, make sure they can hear your recitation. When you give a *khutba*, make sure they can understand your admonition.'"

'Amr ibn al-Muhajir said, "'I saw 'Umar II giving two *khutbas* on Fridays. He sat and was silent between them. He gave the first one seated with a staff in his hand which he had placed on his thighs. They claim that it was the staff of the Messenger of Allah صلى الله عليه وسلم. When he finished the first *khutba* he was silent, then he stood and gave the second one leaning on it. When he was tired, he did not lean on it but carried it. When he began the prayer, he placed it beside him."

Muhammad ibn al-Muhajir reported that when 'Umar sat in the *tashahhud* in the *Jumu'a* prayer, he put the staff on his thighs until he said the *salam*. He also said that after 'Umar had given the *salam* for *Jumu'a*, he carried the staff to his house without leaning on it. When he brought it out from his house, he carried it. When he gave the *khutba*, he leaned on it. When he finished the *khutba* and began the prayer, he put it beside him.

Al-Mundhir ibn 'Ubayd reported that 'Umar prayed on a rug.

Bishr ibn Humayd said, "When he was khalif, I heard 'Umar say, "The whiteness of dawn is after its redness."

Ishaq ibn Yahya said, "When 'Umar was in Khanasira, I saw him leave after *'Asr* on the afternoon of 'Arafa and enter his house. He did not sit in the mosque until he went there for *Maghrib*. On the *'Id al-Adha*, I saw him come out when the sun rose and he gave a short *khutba*. I saw him give a longer one than that on the *'Id al-Fitr*. I saw that he walked to the *'Id*."

Ja'far ibn Burqan reported that when he was khalif, 'Umar II wrote: "Do not ride to *Jumu'a* and the *'Id*-prayer."

'Abdullah ibn al-'Ala' reported that 'Umar II used to say the *takbirs* from after the *Dhuhr* prayer on the day of 'Arafa until after *'Asr* on the last of the days of *tashriq*. 'Abdullah ibn al-'Ala' also reported that he heard 'Umar II say, "Allah is greater, and praise be to Allah" three times after every prayer.

'Ata' al-Khurasani reported that 'Umar II used to eat something before going out to the *'Id*-prayer.

'Amr ibn 'Uthman said, "I saw Umar at Khanasira walking to the place for the *'Id*-prayer. Then he went up on the minbar and said seven *takbirs* in a row and then gave a short *khutba*, and then five *takbirs*, and then a shorter *khutba* than the first. I saw him bring a ram to the place of prayer and sacrifice it with his own hand, and then he ordered that it be shared out and he did not take any of it to his house."

'Amr ibn 'Uthman said, "I heard 'Umar II saying seven *takbirs* out loud in the first *rak'at* so that the people at the back could hear it. Then he recited. He said five *takbirs* in the second *rak'at*. He recited *Qaf* (50) in the first and *al-Qamar* (54) in the second. He used to make supplication between every two *takbirs* praising Allah, proclaiming His greatness, and doing the prayer on the Prophet صلعم."

He also said, "I saw 'Umar say the *salam* when he ascended the minbar on the *'Id*."

Isma'il ibn Abi Hakim said, "When 'Umar was khalif, I saw him call for dates from the *zakat* of the Messenger of Allah صلعم for us on the Day of *Fitr*. He said, 'Eat before you go to the *'Id*.' I asked 'Umar, 'Is there something reported on this?' – 'Yes,' he said, 'Ibrahim ibn 'Abdullah informed me from Abu Sa'id al-Khudri that the Messenger of Allah صلعم used to not go out on the day of the *'Id* until he had eaten.' He commanded that no one go out until they had eaten."

'Amr ibn 'Uthman said. "While he was khalif, I heard 'Umar at Khanasira addressing the people a day before the Day of *Fitr*, which was a Friday. He mentioned the *zakat al-fitr* and encouraged it, saying, 'Every person owes a *sa'* of dates or two *mudds* of Syrian wheat.' He said, 'There is no prayer for the one who has not paid the *zakat al-fitr*.' Then he divided it on the Day of *Fitr*. He would accept two *mudds* each of Syrian flour and *sawiq* (mush)."

Yazid ibn Malik said, "While he was khalif, 'Umar II was the quickest of people to break the fast. He used to recommend delaying *sahur*. When he was unsure about dawn, he refrained from eating and drinking."

Yahya ibn Sa'id reported that when 'Umar II saw the people swearing the *qasama* oath without understanding, he made them swear to accept the blood money and avoided killing in retribution.

Ayyub reported that someone was murdered in Basra and Sulayman ibn 'Abdu'l-Malik wrote to ask fifty men to take an oath. If they took an oath, they were recorded. They had not all taken the oath when Sulayman died and 'Umar became khalif. 'Umar was written to and he replied, "If two just witnesses should testify to his killing then register it. Otherwise, do not charge anyone by the *qasama*."

'Uthman al-Batti said, "While he was khalif, 'Umar's letter came ordering us to discipline the one who made an oath in the *qasama* by inflicting about ten lashes."

Abu Bakr ibn Muhammad said, "'Umar II wrote to me when he was khalif to renew the posts of the Haram."

'Abdu'r-Rahman ibn Yazid said, "'Umar II wrote to Abu Bakr ibn Hazm and appointed him over the *hajj*. He was appointed a day before *Tarwiya* and led the people in the *Dhuhr* prayer. The end of his office was when the sun declined on the last of the days of Mina."

Muhammad ibn 'Umar remarked, "That is the established practice with us."

'Abdu'l-'Aziz ibn Rawwad said, "'Umar's letter came to Makka in 100 AH forbidding the renting out of houses in Makka [during the *hajj*]. He did not build any structure at Mina."

Muhammad said, "I saw 'Umar II at Khanasira commanding wine-skins to be slit and wine jars to be broken."

Hisham ibn al-Ghaz and Sa'id ibn 'Abdu'l-'Aziz said, "When he was khalif, 'Umar wrote telling us not to let the *dhimmis* bring wine into Muslim cities. They did not bring any in."

'Abdu'l-Majid ibn Suhayl said, "I came to Khanasira when 'Umar was khalif, and there were some people in a house of the people of wine and foolishness. I told the chief of police of 'Umar, 'They are meeting to drink. It is a tavern.' He said, 'I mentioned this to 'Umar II and he said, 'Leave those who are concealed privately in houses alone.'"

'Ubada ibn Nusayy said, "I saw 'Umar beat a man with the *hadd* for wine and he removed his garments and gave him 80 lashes. Some cut and some did not. He then said, 'If you do it a second time, I will beat you again and then put you in prison until you reform.' He said, 'Amir al-Mu'minin, I repent to Allah. I will never repeat this.' So 'Umar left him alone."

Muhammad ibn Qays said, "When he was khalif, 'Umar wrote to the governor of Egypt not to increase any punishment beyond 30 lashes unless it was a *hadd*."

Sakhr al-Mudliji said that a man who had committed bestiality was brought to 'Umar II. He did not inflict the *hadd* on him, and flogged him less than the *hadd*."

Az-Zubayr ibn Musa reported that 'Umar II said about pre-emption, "When the borders are fixed and the roads laid out, there is no pre-emption."

Az-Zuhri said, "When he was khalif, 'Umar wrote to 'Abdu'l-Hamid, 'Do not judge by the neighbourhood.'"

Khalid al-Hadhdhal reported that 'Umar II decided that *dhimmis* were entitled to exercise pre-emption."

Abu Bakr reported that he sent the khalif 'Umar II a letter together with statements and descriptions of disputes which he sealed. The petitioner produced it without any witness to it, and 'Umar allowed it.

Isma'il ibn Hakim said, "'Umar II rarely failed to read some of the Qur'an in the morning, but did not take too long."

Juwayriyya ibn Asma' said, "'Umar said, 'Muzahim, buy me a holder for my Qur'an.' He brought him a holder which he liked. He asked, 'Where did you get it?' He replied, 'Amir al-Mu'minin, I went to one of the treasuries and found this wood and fashioned a holder from it.' He said, 'Go and evaluate it in the market.' He went and its value was estimated to be half a dinar. He returned and told 'Umar. He said, 'Do you think that if I put a dinar in the treasury I will have compensated adequately for it?' He replied, 'They estimated its value at half a dinar.' He said, 'Put two dinars in the treasury.'"

Juwariyya ibn Asma' reported that 'Umar II dismissed a scribe of his who wrote "*Bismi*" and did not properly form the letter *sin*.

Al-Mughira ibn Hakim said, "Fatima bint 'Abdu'l-Malik, 'Umar's wife, said to me, 'Mughira, I think that there is no one among the people who prays and fasts more than 'Umar. If there is a man with stronger fear of his Lord than 'Umar, I have not seen him. After he has prayed *'Isha'*, he puts himself in his mosque, and supplicates and weeps until he falls asleep. Then he awakens and makes supplication and weeps until he falls asleep. He is like that until morning.'"

Ibn 'Ulatha said, "'Umar II had companions who kept company with him to help him with their opinions and he would listen to them. Then one day they were waiting for him and he took a long time to come for *Subh*. They said to one another, 'Do you fear that he has changed?' Muzahim heard this and told the person who used to awaken him what he had heard his companions say. He gave them permission to come in. When they entered, he said, 'Last night I ate chickpeas and lentils and they gave me wind.' One of the people said, 'Amir al-Mu'minin, Allah says in His Book, *"Eat of the good things We have provided for you."* (20:81)' 'Umar said, 'How far you take this out of context! He is indicating good earning and not just good food.'"

Muhammad ibn Abi Sadra said, "I visited 'Umar II in the night and he was binding his belly. I asked, 'What is wrong, Amir al-Mu'minin?' He said, 'I ate some lentils and they are giving me pain.' Then he said, 'My stomach! My stomach! It is contaminated with wrong actions.'"

Ibn Abi Sadra said, "'Umar used to command people to face the *qibla* when the *mu'adhdhan* began the *iqama*."

Maymun ibn Mihran said, "'Umar II was the teacher of the scholars."

'Abdu'l-'Aziz ibn 'Umar said, "'Umar II conversed after *'Isha'* before praying the *witr*. After he had prayed the *witr*, he did not talk to anyone."

Riyah ibn 'Ubayda said, "Some musk was brought from the treasury and when it was put before 'Umar, he held his nose fearing to smell its fragrance. One of his companions said to him, 'Amir al-Mu'minin, what harm would there be if you smelt its scent?' 'Umar replied, 'Is anything but the scent desired from this?'"

Malik ibn Anas reported that 'Umar II said, "I am not a qadi but an implementer. I am not better than anyone, but I bear the greatest burden of all of you. I will be held to account for it." He said, "I am not an innovater but a follower."

Usama ibn Zayd said, "'Umar said to his qadi, Abu Bakr ibn Muhammad ibn Hazm, 'I do not find anything more pleasing than a right which is in harmony with desire.'"

Nu'aym ibn 'Abdullah reported that 'Umar II said, "I leave many words fearing boasting."

Abu Hilal said, "'Umar II wrote concerning prisons, 'No one should be chained in a manner which prevents him from performing the prayer in full.'"

Abu Sa'id, the client of Thaqif, said, "The first letter which 'Abdu'l-Hamid read from 'Umar II stated: 'What remains for a man to do after the whispering of Shaytan and the injustice of the sultan? When this letter of mine comes to you, accord everyone with a right his right. Peace.'"

'Amr ibn Qays reported that 'Umar II put him in charge of the summer expedition and told him, "'Amr, do not be the person who goes out first and gets killed so that your fellows are routed. Do not be the last of them and handicap them and avoid them. Be in the middle of them where they can see you and hear you. Pay the ransom of what Muslims you can, as well as their slaves and *dhimmis*."

Khalid al-Hadhdha' said, "'Umar II did not spread the cushions of the common for the elite, nor did he use the saddles of the common for the elite. He did not eat from the food of the elite. He was told, 'When you withhold your hand, the people withhold their hands.' So he commanded that three or four dirhams be cast in the food and began to eat with them."

Yahya ibn Sa'id said, "''Abdu'l-Hamid ibn 'Abdu'r-Rahman wrote to 'Umar, 'A man has been handed over to me who has been insulting you. I wanted to strike off his head, so I have imprisoned him and have written to you to consider this and to ascertain your opinion.' He wrote back to him, 'If you had killed him, I would have taken blood money from you. No one is killed for cursing anyone except for cursing the Prophet صلعم. Insult him if you wish, or let him go.'"

Muzaham ibn Zufar said, "I went to 'Umar in a delegation of the people of Kufa and he asked us about our land, our amir and our qadi. Then he said, 'If a qadi lacks one of five qualities, he has a defect. He should be understanding, forbearing, abstinent, firm and knowledgeable – and he should ask about what he does not know.'"

Yahya ibn Sa'id reported that 'Umar II said, "No one should be a qadi unless he has five qualities: abstinence, forbearance, knowledge of the way things were before him, consultation with those with sound opinion, and lack of concern for people's blame."

Yahya ibn Fulan said, "Muhammad ibn Ka'b al-Qurazi came to see 'Umar ibn 'Abdu'l-'Aziz. 'Umar had once had a good body. He began to look at him intensely without blinking. He said, 'Ibn Ka'b, why are you staring at me as you have never done before?' He replied, 'Amir al-Mu'minin, you used to have a good body, but I see now that you are sallow and thin and have lost your hair.' He said, 'Ibn Ka'b, what would it be like if you were to see me after I have been in my grave for three (days) when my eyes are sunken, putrefaction flows from my nostrils and my mouth is full of pus and worms? I would appear even more unpleasant.'"

Muhammad ibn Ka'b said, "Slave of Allah, if you yourself desire success in this matter, then treat the slaves of Allah in one of three ways when they are with you. As for the one who is older than you, make him like a father to you. As for the one who is the same age as you, make him like a brother to you. As for the one who is younger than you, make him as a son to you. Which of these would you want to treat badly or see something he dislikes coming from you?" 'Umar said, "None of them, O slave of Allah."

Yahya ibn Sa'id said, "'Umar said, 'Whoever makes his *deen* a target for disputes shifts a lot."

Maymun ibn Mihran said, "I was conversing with 'Umar II one night and he was admonishing. He became aware of a man wiping away his tears and fell silent. I said, 'Amir al-Mu'minin, repeat what you said. Perhaps Allah will benefit through you the one who conveys it and the one who hears it.' He replied, 'Maymun, words are a test, and action is better for a man than speech.'"

Maymun ibn Mihran said, "I was speaking with 'Umar one night and I said, 'Amir al-Mu'minin, why do you continue as I see? You are involved in the needs and business of people during the day, and you are with us now. And Allah knows best how long you are in worship.' He did not answer me at first. Then he said, 'Maymun, I find that meeting men stimulates their minds.'"

Sallam reported that 'Umar ascended the minbar and said, "O people! Fear Allah. *Taqwa* of Allah dispenses with everything except it, and there is no substitute for *tawqa* of Allah. O people, fear Allah and obey those who obey Allah and do not obey those who disobey Allah."

Sufyan ibn Sa'id reported from a man of Makka that 'Umar said, "Anyone who acts without knowledge corrupts things more than he puts them right. Anyone who does not consider his words a part of his actions makes a lot of mistakes. One is rarely content. The believer relies on being steadfast."

Yahya ibn Sa'id reported that 'Umar said, "Today I have no passion in affairs except in the places where Allah has decreed it."

'Anbasa ibn Sa'id said to 'Umar, "The khalifs before you used to give us stipends. I see that you and your family refrain from this source of wealth. We have families, so give us permission to return to our estates." He replied, "The dearest of you to me is the one who does that." As he turned to go, 'Umar called to him and said, "'Anbasa, remember death a lot! You are not constricted in your affair and in your livelihood. So remember death – unless that expands you – and do not be self-satisfied about yourself or envious of others. Remember death – otherwise you will feel constricted."

Muhammad ibn az-Zubayr al-Hanzali said, "I visited 'Umar when he was having bread and oil for supper. He said, 'Come near and eat.' I said, 'Evil is the food of the sedentary.' So he recited:

> 'When someone of Tamim is dying
> and you would like him to live,
> Then bring provision of bread, meat, and dates,
> or something wrapped up in a cloth.'"

Muhammad at-Taymi and others report that when 'Umar was appointed, he denied his relatives what they used to receive and took away from them the land grants which had been in their possession. They complained about this to his aunt, Umm 'Umar. She went to him and said, "Your relatives are complaining about you and claiming that you have taken away the blessings bestowed by others." He said, "I have not denied them any right or anything that is theirs, nor have I taken from them any right or anything which is theirs." She said, "I see them talking together and I fear that one day they will attack you in a group." He said, "Any day I fear is less than the Day of Rising. Allah will not protect me from its evil." He called for a dinar, a basket and an incense burner and he put the dinar on a live charcoal and began to blow on the dinar until it was red-hot. Then he picked it up with something and put it in the basket and it sizzled and made a smell. He said, "O aunt, can you protect your nephew from the like of this?" She got up and went to his relatives and said, "Go to 'Umar. If he removes what is doubtful, you become agitated. Be patient with him."

'Umar II was asked, "Why have you changed everything, even your walk?" He said, "By Allah, I only saw it as a kind of madness." When he walked, he lifted his hands.

Mujasha' said, "'Umar II was going out to the mosque one day and he lifted his hand and then he stopped and wept. They said, 'What has made you weep, Amir al-Mu'minin?' He replied, 'I lifted my hand and then I feared that Allah will chain it up in the Next World.'"

Ja'far ibn Burqan said, "A man came to 'Umar II and asked him about some of the sects and he said, 'Cling to the *deen* of the child and the bedouin as it is described in the Book, and disregard other than that.'"

Sufyan reported that a man said, "A man criticised 'Umar II and he was asked, 'What will protect you from him?' He replied, 'Whoever fears God is bridled.'"

Abu Mijlaz reported that 'Umar II forbade people to come to him on the festivals of Nayruz and Mihrajan.[1]

Rabi'a ash-Sha'wadhi reported, "I was bringing some mail to 'Umar and I was waylaid in part of Syria. Then I rode to him in Khanasira and he said, 'What happened to the wing of the Muslims?' – 'What is the wing of the Muslims?' I asked. 'The post,' he replied. I said, 'It was waylaid,' naming the place. He asked, 'How did you reach us then?' I said, 'On a beast which I commandeered from among the animals of the Nabateans.' He said, 'You commandeered by my authority?' He ordered that I be given forty lashes, may Allah have mercy on him."

Abu'l-'Ala', a vendor of clothes stands, said, "'Umar's letter was read to me in the mosque of Kufa while I was listening: 'Anyone who is liable for a trust but cannot fulfil it should be given some of Allah's property. Anyone who marries a woman and cannot give her the dowry should be given some of the property of Allah. *Nabidh* is lawful, but drink it from skins.' All the people drank it."

Al-Awza'i and Sa'id ibn 'Abdu'l-'Aziz reported that 'Umar II wrote to the master of the mint in Damascus, "If some of the poor Muslims bring you a sub-standard dinar, exchange it for them by weight."

Ibn Thawban reported that 'Umar collected the *zakat* correctly and distributed it correctly and he gave to the agents according to the amount of work they did in it, at the same rate as he paid those who did similar work. He said, "Praise be to Allah who did not make me die until I had established one of the obligations."

Al-Awza'i said, "'Umar ibn al-Muhajir reported that 'Umar II used to say, 'Every warner is a *qibla*.'"

Abu Bakr ibn Abi Maryam reported that 'Umar treated the Arabs and their clients equally in providing food, clothing, support and stipends, although he made the share of the freed client 25 dinars.

'Amr ibn Muhajir said, "I heard 'Umar say, 'If I were allowed to discipline people for something and beat them for it, then I would beat them to make them stand at the beginning of the *mu'adhdhin's*

---

1. Magian festivals held at the spring and autumn equinoxes.

iqama, so that each man would be level with the ones on his right and his left.'"

Al-Awza'i said, "'Umar wrote to the generals of his armies, 'Only ride an animal on your expeditions as far as the weakest animal in the army can go.'"

Sa'id ibn 'Abdu'l-'Aziz reported that 'Umar II was consulted about being straightforward with governors. He said, "They will meet Allah with their treachery. I prefer to meet with their blood."

Maymun said, "'Umar II wrote to his governor, 'Allow the people who have land to sell the *kharaj* land in their possession.' They were already selling the booty of the Muslims and the stipulated *jizya*."

Maymun said, "A governor went to 'Umar and he said, 'How much *zakat* have you collected?' He told him how much. He asked, 'How much was collected before you?' and he named a larger amount. 'Umar asked, 'Where was that from?' He replied, 'Amir al-Mu'minin, a dinar used to be taken for horses, a dinar for servants, and five dirhams for oxen. You have discarded all of that.' He said 'No, by Allah, I did not cast that aside, but Allah did.'"

Abu'l-Malih said, "'Umar II wrote telling us to revive the *Sunna* and kill off innovations. He said, 'It is necessary that your opinion of me is that I have no need of your property, either by my hands or by your hands. It is proper that anyone who commits acts of disobedience against Allah be punished by Him.'"

Furat ibn Muslim said, "'Umar wanted some apples and sent word to his house but nothing could be found with which to buy them. He rode on and we went with him. He passed by some houses and some servants of the Dayranis came out to meet him with some plates with apples on them. He paused at one plate, took an apple from it, smelt it, and then returned it. He said, 'Go back to your houses. I do not know if you have sent anything to any of my friends as well.' I hurried on my mule, caught up with him, and said, 'Amir al-Mu'minin, you desired apples and did not find any and then they are offered to you and you refuse them!' He said, 'I have no need of them.' I asked, 'Did not the Messenger of Allah صلعم, Abu Bakr and 'Umar accept gifts?' He replied, 'It was a gift for them but it became a bribe for the rulers after them.'"

Furat ibn Muslim said, "I used to present my books of account to 'Umar II every Friday. I would present them to him and he once tore out part of a page from them, about the size of a span or four fingers, and then wrote on it what he needed. I said, 'The Amir al-Mu'minin has forgotten.' The following day he sent for me to bring the books and I brought them and he asked me to look at them. I said, 'You looked at them yesterday.' Later he said, 'Take them until I send for you again.' When I opened my books, I found in them a piece of paper the size of the paper which he had taken from me."

Ma'mar reported that 'Umar wrote, "Treat those who are in your prisons and in your land well so that they are not constricted and make sure that they are given proper food and condiments."

'Ubaydullah ibn 'Amr said, "'Umar II wrote, 'Do not single me out in any supplication. Pray for the believers, men and women, in general. If I am one of them, I will be included among them.'"

Abu'l-Malih said, "'Umar II wrote, 'As far as I am concerned, establishing the *hudud* is as important as establishing the prayer and the *zakat*.'"

Ja'far ibn Burqan said, "'Umar II wrote, 'I think that if agents are placed on bridges and at fords to take *zakat* directly, then these agents will transgress badly, beyond what they are commanded. I think that I should appoint a man in every city to collect *zakat* from its people and let the people travel freely across their bridges and fords.'"

Yazid ibn al-Asamm said, "While I was sitting with Sulayman ibn 'Abdu'l-Malik, a man called Ayyub arrived. He had been stationed on the bridge of Manbaj to bring the money taken on the bridge. 'Umar said, 'Here is an affluent man bringing bad money.' When 'Umar came to power, the people were allowed to cross bridges and fords freely."

Wuhayb ibn al-Ward said, "We heard that 'Umar II set up a feeding place for the poor, the wretched and travellers. He told his family, 'Beware of taking anything from this food house. It is for the poor, the wretched and travellers.' He came there one day and found a female client of his with a piece of paper in which was a handful of curd. He asked, 'What is this?' She said, 'As you know, your wife is pregnant and she has a craving for a bit of curd. When a woman is pregnant and has a craving which is not satisfied, it is feared that she may suffer a miscarriage. So I have taken this from this house.' 'Umar grabbed her hand and took her to his wife shouting, 'If only the food which belongs to the poor and the wretched can retain what is in your belly, then may Allah not keep it!' He went to his wife and she said to him, 'What is the matter with you?' He said. 'This one claims that only the food which belongs to the poor and the wretched will retain what is in your belly. If that is the only thing which will keep it there, then may Allah not keep it!' His wife replied, 'Take it back, bother you! By Allah, I will not have it!' She returned it."

Suhayl ibn Abi Salih reported that 'Umar II said, "No one is killed for cursing anyone except for cursing a Prophet."

Malik ibn Anas reported that he heard that 'Umar II said, "In the case of someone whose business is other than this business, part of what concerns me – which Allah has prescribed – is to oblige an agent in it to act in accordance with what I know so that if he does fall short it is by my falling short. Whatever good I establish is by the help and direction of Allah and I hope for its blessing from Him. Whatever is other than that, I ask Allah for forgiveness for my immense wrong action."

Abu Sinan said, "When 'Umar II came to Jerusalem, he stayed in the house where I was. Then he said, 'Abu Sinan, do not let any of the people of the house heat a pot until after I have left.' When he went to bed, he recited in a sorrowful voice, *'Your Lord is Allah, Who created the heavens and the earth ...'* (7:54) to the end of the *ayat*, and then he recited, *'Do the people of the cities feel secure against Our violent force coming down on them in the night while they are asleep?'* (7:97) to the words *'while they are playing games?'* (7:98) He continued with similar *ayats*."

Muhammad ibn Abi 'Uyayna al-Muhallabi said, "I heard the letter of 'Umar II to Yazid ibn al-Muhallab: 'Peace be upon you. I praise Allah to you. There is no god but Him. Following on from that, Sulayman ibn 'Abdu'l-Malik was one of the servants of Allah and Allah took him in the best of times and states. May Allah have mercy on him. He made me succeed him, and those near you gave allegiance to me and to Yazid ibn 'Abdu'l-Malik after me. If what I am concerned with had been for the sake of taking wives and reliance on wealth, Allah could have taken me to the best of what He takes His creation, but I fear a severe reckoning and a detailed questioning unless Allah helps me. Peace be upon you and the mercy of Allah.'"

'Umar ibn Bahram as-Sarraf said, "'Umar's letter was read to us: 'In the Name of Allah, the Merciful, the Compassionate, from the slave of Allah, 'Umar, Amir al-Mu'minin, to 'Adi ibn Arta'a and those Muslims and believers who are near him. Peace be upon you. I praise Allah to you. There is no god but Him. Following on from that, look after the people of the *dhimma* and be kind to them. When a man from among them is old and has no one, spend on him. If he has a close friend, then tell his friend to spend on him and pay him compensation for his inconvenience. It is as when you have a slave who grows old: you must spend on him until he dies or is freed.' He added, 'I have heard that you take *'ushr* from wine and it remains in the treasury of Allah. Beware of putting anything which is not wholesome in with the property of Allah. Peace be upon you.'"

Al-Awza'i reported from a man that 'Umar II wrote to one of his governors, "Beware of mutilating the head and beard."

'Abdu'r-Rahman at-Tawil said, "'Umar II wrote to Maymun ibn Mihram, 'You wrote to me, Maymun, concerning the severity of judgement and taxation. As regards that I have only obliged you in respect of what concerns you. Collect tax by right and judge by the right you discern. If something is unclear to you, then present it to me. If it had always been the case that whenever something was difficult for people they left it, then neither the *deen* nor this man would have become established.'" He said, "I was in charge of the diwan of Damascus and they allotted a share to a man who was critically ill. I said, 'One must be charitable to the chronically ill, but he does not receive the wage of a healthy man.' They complained about me to 'Umar II, saying, 'He troubles us, is hard on us and constricts us.' 'Umar wrote to me, 'When my letter reaches you, do not be hard on people or constrict them. I do not like that.'"

'Abdu'r-Rahman ibn Hasan reported that 'Umar II wrote concerning mines, "I looked into them and ascertained that they have a private benefit and a general harm, so prevent people from working in them." He also wrote, "As regards government owned grazing land, no one should be denied access to places where it rains. So allow people to use government owned pastures."

'Abdu'r-Rahman ibn Hasan reported that 'Umar II wrote, "Do not dress a slavegirl in a veil. They should not resemble free women."

Ayyub ibn Musa said, "'Umar II wrote to 'Urwa, his governor over Yemen: 'I write to you to command you to settle injustices done to Muslims and to consult me without being concerned by the distance between you and me. If there is a sheep wrongly taken from a Muslim, then have it returned, brown or black. Seek to redress injustices done to Muslims without first consulting me.'"

Sufyan said, "They said to 'Abdu'l-Malik ibn 'Umar, 'Your father is being hard on his people and does this and that.' He replied, 'My father said, *"Say: If I disobey my Lord I fear the punishment of an immense day."* (6:15)' Then he visited his father and told him about it and he asked, 'What did you say? Did you not say that your father says, *"Say: If I disobey my Lord I fear the punishment of an immense day"*?' He said, 'I did.'"

A man reported that a man said to 'Umar II, "May Allah make you last!" He replied, "That will come to an end. Ask for righteousness for me."

'Umar ibn Sa'id said, "Once when a *mu'adhdhin* of 'Umar gave the *adhan*, he made his voice quaver. He heard a slavegirl of his say, 'The pigeon has given the *adhan*.' He sent to him, 'Give the *adhan* smoothly and do not sing it. Otherwise stay in your house.'"

Muhammad ibn an-Nadr said, "We mentioned the disagreement of the Companions of Muhammad صلعم in the presence of 'Umar II. He said, 'A matter in which Allah did not include your hands in what your tongues say about it!'"

Qatada said, "'Umar II took *zakat al-fitr* from people who had debts – half a dirham."

Isma'il ibn Abi Hakim reported that 'Umar II said, "Allah does not punish the common people for the actions of the elite, but when acts of disobedience become commonplace, the punishment alights on everyone."

'Abu'l-'Aziz ibn Abi Hazm reported that Usama said, "When 'Umar II prayed *Jumu'a*, he posted guards and commanded them to stand at the doors of the mosque. They were not to allow a man with combed hair who did not part it to pass without trimming it."

Humayda, 'Umar's nurse, reported that when 'Umar II forbade his daughters to sleep on their backs, he said, "Shaytan continues to look at one of you when she is laying on her back, desiring her."

'Adi ibn Arta'a wrote to 'Umar, "The people of Basra have received so much good that I fear that they may become proud." So 'Umar wrote to him, "Allah is pleased for the people of the Garden to say 'Praise be to Allah' when He admits them to the Garden. Command those near you to praise Allah."

Mughira said, "'Umar II had people who looked into the affairs of people. The sign between him and them when he wanted to stand was to say, 'If you wish.'"

'Abdu'r-Rahman said, "'Umar II wrote to 'Adi ibn Arta'a, 'Remove from people guard duty and taxes. By my life, it is not tax, but the diminution which Allah has mentioned: *"Do not diminish people's goods, and do not cause corruption in the land after it has been put right."* (7:85) Whoever pays the *zakat* of his property, accept it from him. If he does not bring it, Allah is his reckoner.'"

'Abdu'r-Rahman said, "'Umar II wrote to one of his governors, 'If you can establish justice, generosity and putting things right, as opposed to those before you who established injustice, transgression and doing wrong, then do so. There is no power nor strength except by Allah.'"

'Abdu'r-Rahman reported that a man said to 'Umar II, "Peace be upon you, Amir al-Mu'minin." He said, "Direct your *salam* to everyone present."

'Abdu'r-Rahman reported that Hayyan ibn Shurayh, 'Umar's governor over Egypt, wrote to him: "The people of the *dhimma* are hastening to Islam and depleting the *jizya*." 'Umar wrote back to him, "Allah sent Muhammad as a summoner and not as a tax-collector. If a *kitabi* comes to you, and is one of the people of *dhimma* who are hastening to Islam and depleting the *jizya*, then close your register and accept it."

Nafi' ibn Malik said, "'Umar II recited, *'You and those you worship: you will entice no one to them except for him who is to roast in the Blazing Fire.'* (37:161-163) He said to me, 'Abu Suhayl, this *ayat* does not leave any argument in favour of the Qadariyya. What is your opinion about them?' I replied, 'That they be asked to repent. If they do not, then strike off their heads.' He said, 'That is the correct view. That is the correct view.'"

Ibrahim ibn Maysara said, "I did not see Umar II beat anyone while he was khalif except for one man who attacked Mu'awiya. He gave him three strokes."

'Abdu'r-Rahman said, "I was present with 'Umar II when some Qurayshis brought a dispute to him and they began to back up one another. 'Umar said to them, 'Beware of backing each other up, even if it means that I will judge in your favour.' Then other witnesses came to testify. The one against whom testimony was being made began to give fierce looks at the witness. 'Umar said, 'Ibn Suraqa! People are on the point of not testifying truthfully between themselves. I see him looking fiercely at the witness. When a man intimidates a truthful witness, give him 30 lashes and make an example of him before the people."'

Ibn Shihab reported that he visited 'Umar II and spoke to him often. 'Umar once said, "You have not said anything to us but that we have remembered it, but you mention and then forget."

Muhammad ibn Qays said that 'Umar II wrote to his governor in Egypt, "Do not exceed 30 lashes when giving punishment, except for one of the *hudud* of Allah."

Muhammad ibn Qays reported that 'Umar commanded that his *wudu'* water should not be heated. He washed with it in the common kitchen.

Ja'far ibn Burqan said, "'Umar II wrote, 'Anyone who can walk to the *'Id* should do so.'"

Talha ibn Yahya said, "'Umar II would not say the funeral *takbir* until the *hanut* had been removed from the corpse."

Isma'il ibn Rafi' said, "We went to 'Umar II while he was in a church after he had been made khalif."

'Abdu'l-Hamid ibn Lahiq said, "A man recited poetry in the presence of 'Umar when a group was with him. One of the people remarked, 'Ungrammatical.' 'Umar said, 'As for your job, what do you know about bad grammar?'"

Al-Khiyar said, "I was in an assembly when 'Umar II joined us, before he became khalif. He sat down without greeting anyone. Then he realised, stood up, greeted us and then sat down."

Raja' ibn Hawya said, "'Umar II told Makhul, 'Beware of saying what those people say about *Qadar*,' meaning Ghaylan ad-Dimishqi and his people."

Al-Jarrah ibn 'Abdullah al-Hakami said that he was with 'Umar II when he was judging between a group of Quraysh who had a dispute. The one who lost said, "May Allah put you right! I have more evidence which is not here." 'Umar said, "I will not delay judgement after I have seen that the right belongs to your companions. If you bring me proof, and a right which is truer than theirs, then I will be the first to reverse the judgement."

'Abdu'r-Rahman said that while he was khalif, 'Umar II wrote to his governor over Khorasan, al-Jarrah ibn 'Abdullah al-Hakami, commanding him to invite the people of the *jizya* to Islam. He said, "If they become Muslim, their Islam is to be accepted and they are to be relieved of paying *jizya*. They have what the Muslims have and owe what the Muslims owe." One of the nobles of the people of Khorasan said to him, "By Allah, they will be quick to accept Islam if it means being relieved of the *jizya*, so test them by insisting on circumcision." He replied, "Am I to turn them away from Islam by insisting on circumcision? If they become Muslim and are good Muslims, then they will quickly move to purity." About 4,000 became Muslims through him.

Malik ibn Dinar said, "When 'Umar II was appointed over people, the shepherds at the top of the mountains said, 'Who is this righteous slave in charge of people?' They were asked, 'How do you know this?' They said, 'When there is a just khalif over the people, then the wolves stay away from our sheep.'"

Musa ibn A'yan, a shepherd of Muhammad ibn Abi 'Uyayna, said, "We grazed sheep in Kirman while 'Umar II was khalif. The sheep, wolves and wild animals all grazed in one place. One night a wolf attacked our sheep and we said, 'I think that the righteous man must have died.'" Hammad ibn Zayd said that he was told that they enquired about this and found that he had died that very night.

Yunus ibn Abi Shabib said, "I saw 'Umar II doing *tawaf* of the House before he was khalif and the top of his waist-wrapper was hidden under his belly. Then I saw him after that he was khalif, and if I had wished I could have counted his ribs without touching him."

Yunus ibn Abi Shabib said, "I saw 'Umar on one of the *'Ids*. The nobles came and surrounded the minbar, leaving a gap between them and other people. When 'Umar came, he mounted the minbar and greeted them. When he saw the gap, he indicated that the people should move forward until they mixed with them."

Abu Hashim, the companion of ar-Ramman, reported that a man came to 'Umar II and said, "I dreamt that the Banu Hashim complained to the Prophetﷺ about a need of theirs and he asked them, 'Where is 'Umar ibn 'Abdu'l-'Aziz?'"

Ja'far ibn Muhammad al-Ansari said, "Fadak[1] was special for the Messenger of Allahﷺand it belonged to Ibn as-Sabti. His daughter asked him to give her Fadak and the Messenger of Allahﷺrefused that and no one desired it. Then the Messenger of Allah ﷺ died when things were like that. Abu Bakr was appointed and acted with it

---

1. A small, rich oasis which had been the property of the Jews of Banu Murra and Banu Sa'd ibn Bakr who surrendered it to the Prophet.

as the Messenger of Allah had done. Then Abu Bakr died and 'Umar was appointed and he behaved with it as the Messenger of Allah had done. Then 'Uthman was like that. When the Community agreed on Mu'awiya in 40 AH, Mu'awiya appointed Marwan ibn al-Hakam over Madina. He wrote to Mu'awiya asking for Fadak and he gave it to him. Marwan could sell its fruit for 10,000 dinars every year. Then Marwan was divested of Madina: Mu'awiya was angry wth him, and he took Fadak from him and placed it in the care of his agent in Madina. Al-Walid ibn 'Utba asked Mu'awiya for it and he refused to give it to him. Sa'id ibn al-'As asked for it and Mu'awiya refused to give it to him. When Mu'awiya appointed Marwan over Madina again, he restored it to him without any request on the part of Marwan, and he also gave him the past revenue. It remained in Marwan's possession, and then he divided it between his sons, 'Abdu'l-Malik and 'Abdu'l-Aziz. 'Abdu'l-'Aziz gave his half to 'Umar II. When 'Abdu'l-Malik died, 'Umar II asked al-Walid for his share in it and he gave it to him, and he asked Sulayman for his share in it and he gave it to him, and so on with the rest of 'Abdu'l-Malik's sons, until 'Umar had all of it."

Ja'far said, "When 'Umar II became khalif, he and his family were supported by a yearly revenue of 10,000 dinars, more or less. When he became khalif, he asked about Fadak and investigated it and was told about how it had been in the time of the Messenger of Allah, Abu Bakr, 'Umar and 'Uthman, until Mu'awiya. Then 'Umar wrote a letter to Abu Bakr ibn Muhammad which said: 'In the Name of Allah, the Merciful, the Compassionate, from the slave of Allah, 'Umar, the Amir al-Muminin, to Abu Bakr ibn Muhammad. Peace be upon you. I praise Allah to you. There is no god but Him. I have looked into Fadak, and it is not proper for me to retain it. I think that I should restore it as it was in the time of the Messenger of Allah, Abu Bakr 'Umar and 'Uthman, and leave what happened after them. When this letter reaches you, take Fadak and appoint a man over it to manage it properly. Peace be upon you.'"

Abu Bakr ibn Muhammad ibn Hazm said, "''Umar II wrote to me when he was khalif to ask me about al-Kutayba and whether it was the fifth of the Messenger of Allahصلعم from Khaybar, or whether it was part of the private property of the Messenger of Allah." Abu Bakr questioned 'Amra bint 'Abdu'r-Rahman, who said that al-Kutayba had been part of the fifth under the treaty with the Banu

Abi'l-Huqayq. She said that there was some confusion about some of the shares." Abu Bakr wrote informing 'Umar of that.

Bishr ibn Humayd al-Muzani said, "'Umar II called me and said to me, 'Take this 4,000 dinars – or it was 5,000 dinars – and give them to Abu Bakr ibn Hazm.' He told him to add 5,000 or 6,000 more dinars to it until it was 10,000 dinars and that these other thousands should be taken from al-Kutayba. Then it was to be divided among the Banu Hashim, equally between male and female, old and young. Abu Bakr did so. Zayd ibn Hasan was angered by that. He criticised 'Umar in what he had said to Abu Bakr. He complained, 'He puts me on a par with children!' Abu Bakr said, 'This statement which you have made should not reach the Amir al-Mu'minin so that it angers him, because he has a good opinion of you.' Zayd said, 'I ask you by Allah to write informing him of it.' Abu Bakr wrote to 'Umar telling him that Zayd ibn Hasan had said something harsh about him, and told him what he had said. He added, 'Amir al-Mu'minin, he has kinship.' So 'Umar was not upset and left him alone. Fatima bint Husayn wrote to him to thank him for what he had done and she swore by Allah, 'Amir al-Mu'minin, you have served those who had no servant and clothed those who were naked.' 'Umar was happy at that."

Yahya ibn Abi Ya'la said, "When the money came to Abu Bakr ibn Hazm, he divided it up and everyone received fifty dinars." He said, "Fatima bint Husayn called me and said, 'Write.' So I wrote: 'In the Name of Allah, the Merciful, the Compassionate, to the slave of Allah, 'Umar, the Amir al-Mu'minin, from Fatima bint Husayn. Peace be upon you. I praise Allah to you. There is no god but Him. Following on from that, may Allah make the Amir al-Mu'minin thrive, help him in what he has undertaken, and protect His *deen* by him. The Amir al-Mu'minin wrote to Abu Bakr ibn Hazm to divide the income of al-Kutayba among us and to handle it in the same way as the rightly-guided Rashidun rulers used to act with it. We heard about this and received a share. May Allah reward the Amir al-Mu'minin and repay his governor with the best of what any governors are repaid. We had experienced some alienation and we needed to be dealt with properly. I swear by Allah, Amir al-Mu'minin, that those among the family of the Messenger of Allah ﷺ who had no servant now have a servant, those who had no clothes are now clothed, and those who could find no maintenance now have maintenance.' She sent it with a messenger to him. The messenger told me, 'I went to him and read out her letter, and he praised and thanked Allah and commanded 10 dinars for me and sent 500 to Fatima, saying, "Help me by letting me know what befalls you." He wrote a letter to her in which he mentioned her excellence and the excellence of the people of her house and mentioned the duty which Allah had obliged towards them. I brought that money to her.'"

Ja'far ibn Muhammad reported that 'Umar II divided the shares of the relatives of the Banu 'Abdu'l-Muttalib among them. He did not give any to the wives of the Banu 'Abdu'l-Muttalib who were not actually part of the Banu 'Abdu'l-Muttalib, but he gave shares to the women of the Banu 'Abdu'l-Muttalib who had married outside the Banu 'Abdu'l-Muttalib.

'Abdu'l-Malik an-Nawfali said, "When the property of the *khums* was given to us by 'Umar II, and when what came from him and al-Kutayba was divided between us, he was generous to the Banu Hashim, to the men and the women. He was written to about the Banu'l-Muttalib, and he wrote back that they were part of the Banu Hashim, and so they received shares as well."

'Abdul'l-Malik ibn al-Mughira said, "A group of the Banu Hashim met and wrote a letter which they sent with a messenger to 'Umar II complaining of what he had done to them regarding maintaining their kinship and saying that they had been harshly treated since Mu'awiya. 'Umar wrote back: 'My opinion in the past was such-and-such, and I spoke to al-Walid I and to Sulayman about it and they both rejected me. When I was appointed to command, I carried out what I thought was most correct, Allah willing.'"

Hakim ibn Muhammad of the Banu'l-Muttalib said, "When 'Umar's letter came to distribute the shares to the Banu Hashim, Abu Bakr ibn Hazm wanted to exclude us. The Banu 'Abdu'l-Muttalib said, 'We will not receive one dirham until they also receive it,' and so Abu Bakr hesitated a few days and then wrote to 'Umar. His reply came to us about 20 days later: 'By my life, I have not made a distinction between them. It is based only on the Banu 'Abdu'l-Muttalib and the old ancient alliance,' and so he treated them like the Banu 'Abdu'l-Muttalib."

Ibn'Aqil said, "The first thing that 'Umar II allotted to us was the wealth sent to us, the People of the House. He gave our women the same as what he gave our men, and he gave a child the same as what he gave a woman. We, the People of the House, received 3,000 dinars. He wrote to us, 'As long as I live, I will give you all your rights.'"

Isma'il ibn Abi'l-Muhajir said, "'Umar II wrote to 'Adi ibn Arta'a: 'I have heard that your governors in Persia estimate the value of fruits for their people, and that they have been assessing them at a price lower than the price for which they are actually sold, and that they haved accepted silver based on their estimated value. Also, some Kurdish groups have been taking the *'ushr* at the the roadside. If I learned that you had ordered any of that, or had been pleased with it after learning about it, then I would confront you with what you dislike. I have sent Bishr ibn Safwan, 'Abdullah ibn 'Ajlan, and Khalid ibn Salim to look into this. If they find it is true, then they will return the fruit to the people and then accept payment based on the price at which the people of the land buy it. They will not fail to investigate all that I have heard. Do not hinder them.'"

A man of the Ansar went to 'Umar and said, "Amir al-Mu'minin, I am so-and-so, son of so-and-so. My grandfather was killed at Badr and his father at Uhud." He began to recount the deeds of his ancestors. 'Umar looked at 'Anbasa ibn Sa'id who was beside him. He remarked, "By Allah, these feats are not your feats – the Battles of Maskin and Dayr al-Jamajim:

'These are noble qualities, not wooden cups of white milk
and water which becomes urine afterwards.'"

Bishr ibn 'Abdullah said, "'Umar II wrote to Humayd ibn Salama: 'Put right what is between you and Allah, and know that I have made you a partner in an immense trust. If you neglect one of the rights of Allah thinking it inconsequential, 'Umar cannot help you at all against Allah.'"

Khalid ibn Yazid said, "'Umar II wrote to a governor about wailing and amusements: 'I have heard that some foolish women go out whenever someone dies, showing their hair and wailing like the people of the *Jahiliyya*. Women have no allowance to remove their scarves, since they are commanded to pull their scarves over their chests. So they are behaving horribly in wailing like this. These foreigners have amusements which Shaytan has made appear attractive to them, so restrain those Muslims who are near you from that. By my life, I will deal with them if they ignore what they read of the Book of Allah about that. Curb such vanities and amusements – singing and the like. If they do not stop, then punish whoever persists in that but without being excessive.'"

Khulayd ibn 'Ajlan said, "Fatima bint 'Abdu'l-Malik had a jewel. 'Umar asked her, 'Where did you get this from?' She replied, 'The Amir al-Mu'minin gave it to me.' He said, 'Either return it to the treasury or give me permission to divorce you. I do not want it and you and I to be in the same room.' She said, 'No, I would still choose you over many more jewels if I possessed them.' So she put it in the treasury. When Yazid II became khalif, he said to her, 'If you want, I will return it to you or its price.' She said, 'I do not want it. If I was happy without it while he was alive, why should I take it back now that he is dead? I have no need of it.' So Yazid II divided it among his family and children."

Lut ibn Yahya al-Ghamidi said, "The Umayyad governors before 'Umar II used to curse 'Ali. When 'Umar was appointed, he stopped that. Kuthayyar 'Azza al-Khuza'i said:

'You were appointed – and you did not curse 'Ali, nor fear people,
    nor follow the statement of a wrongdoer.
You spoke the clear truth –
    and you clarified the signs of guidance with words.
You confirmed what is known by your acting on it –
    and so every Muslim is pleased with you.'"

Idris ibn Qadim said, "'Umar II said to Maymun ibn Mihran, 'Maymun, how can I have helpers in this matter whom I can trust and feel sure about?' He replied, 'Amir al-Mu'minin, do not preoccupy your heart with this. You are a market, and people bring to each market what sells in it. When people know that only what is sound finds a market with you, then only the sound will come to you.'"

Yazid ibn Bishr said, "'When Umar II was asked about 'Ali and 'Uthman and the Battles of the Camel and Siffin and what happened between them, he said, 'That was bloodshed from which Allah kept my hands and I have no desire for my tongue to plunge into it.'"

Yazid ibn Bishr said, "In the course of their summer expedition the Muslims captured a young Greek lad and his family sent word to ransom him. 'Umar consulted people about him and they disagreed about him. He said, 'What bother is it to you if we let a child be ransomed? Perhaps Allah will give us power over him again when he is an adult.' So they ransomed him for a lot of money – and then he was captured again at the end of the khalifate of Hisham and killed."

Muhammad ibn az-Zubayr al-Hanzali said, "'Umar II saw a man writing on the earth, 'In the Name of Allah, the Merciful, the Compassionate'. He forbade him and said, 'Do not do it again.'"

Yazid ibn 'Iyad said, "'Umar II wrote to Sulayman ibn Abi Karima, 'The most entitled of people to exalt Allah and fear Him is the one who has been tested in the same way as He has tested me. No one will have a stronger reckoning. I do not think it insignificant for me to disobey Allah in anything. I am not capable of what I am doing and I fear that the position in which I am will destroy me unless Allah has mercy on me. I have heard that you want to go out in the Way of Allah. My brother, when you set out to realise your aim, I want you to ask Allah to provide me with martyrdom. My situation is severe and my predicament is immense, so ask Allah Who has tested me as He has to have mercy on me and pardon me.'"

Yazid ibn Bishr said, "Those close to 'Umar II included Maymun ibn Mihran, Raja' ibn Hawya and Riyah ibn 'Ubayda al-Kindi. There were also people less than them with him: 'Amr ibn Qays, 'Awn ibn 'Abdullah ibn 'Utba, and Muhammad ibn az-Zubayr al-Hanzali."

Maslama ibn Muharib and others said, "Bilal ibn Abi Burda and his brother 'Abdullah went to 'Umar II and they argued in his presence about the *adhan* in their mosque. 'Umar suspected them and had a man go to them and ask them, 'If I were to suggest to the Amir al-Mu'minin that he should appoint you over Iraq, what would you give me?' The man went to Bilal first and asked him that and he said, 'I will give you 100,000.' Then he went to his brother and he said something similar to him. The man told 'Umar and he said to them, 'Go back to your city.' He wrote to 'Abdu'l-Hamid ibn 'Abdu'r-Rahman, 'Do not appoint Bilal, Bilal the evil, or any of the children of Abu Musa over anything.'"

'Awana ibn al-Hakam al-Kalbi said, "Sulayman ibn 'Abdu'l-Malik died in Dabiq and 'Umar was appointed khalif. 'Umar spoke to the people, saying, 'By Allah, I did not want this or desire it. Fear Allah and pay what is due from yourselves and remedy injustices. By Allah, I have no anger towards any of the people of the *qibla* except whoever is excessive until Allah makes him temperate.' He wrote to

Maslama, who was in Greek territory, commanding him to return and to give his men permission to return."

'Abdullah ibn 'Umar ath-Tha'labi and al-Muthanna ibn 'Abdullah said, "''Umar II told Salim to write to him about the behaviour of 'Umar. Salim wrote back to him, "'Umar was in a different time than yours and with different men than your men. If you act in your time and with your men as 'Umar did in his time with his men, then you will be like 'Umar and better.'"

'Abdu'r-Rahman ibn Yazid said, "Some people brought some horses to Sulayman ibn 'Abdu'l-Malik but he died before he could race them. 'Umar did not like to disappoint people. The horses which had been gathered were raced. Then he gave them all away, down to the last horse so that no one would be disappointed. Then he did not race horses again before he died."

Maslama ibn Muharib said, "''Umar wrote to 'Adi, 'The people in charge of your tribes have a responsibility. Investigate those in charge of the army, and confirm those whom you are satisfied can be trusted by us and by his own people. If you are not satisfied with someone, replace him with someone better than him. Ensure a high degree of trustworthiness and scrupulousness.'"

Al-Hasan ibn Abi'l-'Amarrata said, "I saw 'Umar II before he was khalif and I used to recognise good health in his face. When he was made khalif, I saw death in his face."

Malik ibn Anas said, "When 'Umar II left Madina, he said, 'Muzaham, do you fear that we will be among those who are spat out by Madina.'"

Sahl ibn Sadaqa, the client of 'Umar II, said, "One of the elite of the family of 'Umar told me that when 'Umar became khalif, they heard the sound of loud weeping in his house. People asked what that weeping was and were told that 'Umar had given his slavegirls a choice. He said, 'Something has happened to me which will distract me from you. So whoever of you wants me to free her, I will do so, and whomever I keep will have nothing of me.' So they wept out of despair at this."

Abu 'Ubayda ibn 'Uqba al-Qurashi said that he visited Fatima bint 'Abdu'l-Malik and said to her, "Will you tell me about 'Umar II?" She said, "I am not aware that he washed for *janaba* or a wet dream from the time Allah made him khalif until he died."

Hisham reported that Fatima bint 'Abdu'l-Malik sent a message to one of the *fuqaha'* and said, "I fear that the Amir al-Mu'minin will not be able to do what he does." He asked, "What is that?" She said, "He has had no way to his family since he took office." The man met 'Umar and said, "Amir al-Mu'minin, I have heard of something of which I fear you are incapable?" He asked, "What is that?" He said, "Your family are entitled to a right from you." 'Umar said, "How can a man go to that when the business of the Community of Muhammad is on his neck – about which Allah will ask him on the Day of Rising?"

A shaykh said, "When 'Umar II was appointed at Dabiq, he went out one night with a guard. He entered the mosque and in the darkness he stumbled over a man who was asleep. He lifted his head and said, 'Are you mad?' He said, 'No.' The guard made for him, but 'Umar said, 'Leave him alone. He asked whether I was mad and I said no.'"

Sufyan said, "A man said to "Umar II, 'If you could devote some free time …' 'Umar said, 'Where is leisure? Leisure has gone – and there is no leisure except with Allah.'"

As-Sari ibn Yahya said that 'Umar II praised Allah and then he was lost for words. Then he said, "O people, put your Next world in order and then this world will be in order for you. Put your secrets in order and then your public aspect will be in order. By Allah, a slave has no father between him and Adam who has not died. He is deeply rooted in death."

Riyah ibn Zayd said that 'Umar II wrote to 'Urwa, "You write in return to me. Implement the rights which I write to you about. Death has no known time."

Mazyad ibn Hawshab, the brother of al-'Awwam, said, "I did not see anyone more fearful than al-Hasan and 'Umar II – as if the Fire had only been created for them."

Arta' ibn al-Mundhir said, "Some people who were with 'Umar II told him to be cautious about his food, and they asked him to have a guard when he did his prayers, so that no one could assassinate him. They also asked him to stay away from the plague. They told him that the khalifs before him used to do that. So 'Umar said to them, 'Where are they now?' When they persisted in that, he said, 'O Allah, if You know that I fear a day other than the Day of Rising, then do not make me safe from what I fear.'"

Khusayf ibn Mujahid said, "We came to 'Umar II thinking that he needed us but we did not leave until we realised that we needed him." He added, "I did not see any man at all better than 'Umar."

Muhammad ibn 'Ajlan said that the governors before 'Umar II used to arrange to burn incense in the Mosque of the Messenger of Allahصلعم for *Jumu'a* and to perfume it in the month of Ramadan, paying for this from the *'ushr* and *zakat*. When 'Umar II was appointed, he wrote to stop that and to remove the traces of that perfume from the mosque.

Ishaq ibn 'Ubayd said that 'Umar's *wudu'* water was heated for him in the common kitchen without his knowledge. When he learned about it, he asked, "For how long have you been heating it?" – "About a month," was the reply. He put some wood in the common kitchen to compensate for that.

Al-Walid reported that when 'Umar II talked at night about public business, he paid for lighting the lamp from the Muslim treasury. When he talked at night about his own affairs, he paid for lighting it from his own property. He said, "One night the lamp flickered and he went over to it to put it right. He was told, 'Amir al-Mu'minin, we will take care of it for you.' He replied, 'I am still 'Umar when I stand and 'Umar when I sit.'"

Ibrahim as-Sakri said, "There was a quarrel between the clients of Sulayman ibn 'Abdu'l-Malik and the clients of 'Umar. Sulayman mentioned it to 'Umar. While he was speaking to him, Sulayman said to 'Umar, 'You lied.' He replied, 'I have not lied ever since I knew that lies are a source of shame for whoever tells them.'"

Hafs ibn 'Umar said, "'Umar II kept a slave of his who gathered firewood and camel dung for him. The slave said to him, 'Everyone is well off except for me and you.' He said, 'Go. You are free.'"

Ishaq ibn Yahya said, "I went to 'Umar II while he was khalif and I found that he had put the *khums* in one part in the treasury, and the *zakat* in one part, and the booty in another part."

'Amr ibn Maymun said, "I continued with 'Umar to be thrifty in the administration of the affairs of the community until I even said to him, 'Amir al-Mu'minin, what about these registers from the Muslim treasury which have been written with a large pen and elongated script?' So he wrote to all regions that they should not write on their registers with large pens or use elongated script. His own letters were about a span or thereabouts."

Hafs ibn 'Umar said, "'Umar wrote to Abu Bakr ibn Hazm: 'You wrote to say that the parchments which you have are all used up and that we have allocated you less than what used to be allocated to those before you. Use fine-nibbed pens, put the lines close together and collate your needs. I dislike spending the wealth of the Muslims in a manner which is not beneficial for them.'"

'Abdullah ibn Dinar said, "'Umar did not live off the Muslim treasury at all and he did not incur any loss to it prior to his death."

Ar-Rabi' ibn Sabra said, "One day 'Umar said, 'By Allah, I wish that I could be just for at least one day and that then Allah would take my soul.' His son 'Abdu'l-Malik said, 'By Allah, Amir al-Mu'minin, I wish that you could be just for the period between two milkings and that then Allah would take your soul.' He said, 'Allah: there is no god but Him.' His son said, 'Allah: there is no god but Him. Would that out graves were filled with me and you!' 'Umar said, 'May Allah repay you well.'"

Juwayriyya ibn Asma' reported that 'Umar II said, "My soul yearns, and it has not been given anything but that it yearns for what is better than it. When it was given the best thing in this world, it yearned for what is better than that." The narrator stated, "The Garden is better than the khalifate."

Maymun said, "I stayed with 'Umar for six months and I never saw him change his cloak. He used to have a *ghusl* every Friday. It had some saffron in it."

An *umm walad* of 'Umar said, "'Umar asked me for some oil and I brought it together with a comb made of elephant bone and he returned it. He said, 'This is carrion.' I asked, 'What makes it carrion?' He replied, 'Bother you! Who sacrifices elephants?'"

Isma'il ibn Abi Hakim said, "'Umar II sent for me and Muzaham for the *Subh* prayer before he had prayed in the morning. Muzaham came without oiling his hair or making it tidy. He said, 'You have come without oiling! Is one of you unable to get a comb and comb his beard?'"

Isma'il ibn 'Ayyash said, "I said to 'Umar ibn al-Muhajir, the chief of the guards of 'Umar II, 'What does 'Umar wear at home?' He replied, 'A black lined jubbah.'"

Ya'la ibn Hakim said, "The cloaks of 'Umar II measured six cubits and a span by seven spans."

Maslama ibn 'Abdu'l-Malik visited 'Umar and said to his sister Fatima, 'Umar's wife, "I see that the Amir al-Mu'minin is awake today and I notice that his shirt is shabby. Have him wear another shirt so that he can see people." She was silent and he repeated, "Have the Amir al-Mu'minin wear another shirt." She replied, "By Allah, he does not have another."

Raja' ibn Hawya said, "'Umar II used to be one of the most perfumed of people, the best dressed and the proudest in gait. After he became khalif, they estimated that his clothes amounted to 12 dirhams worth of Egyptian cloth: sleeves, turbans, shirts, gowns, tunics, leather socks and cloak."

Sa'id ibn Suwayd said that 'Umar II prayed *Jumu'a* with them wearing a shirt with a patched pocket in front and behind. When he finished he sat and we sat with him. A man of the people said to him, "Amir al-Mu'minin, Allah has given to you. You should dress and act accordingly." He bowed his head for a while and we knew that he had annoyed him. Then he raised his head and said, "The best moderation is shown when one is angry and the best forgiveness is shown when one is powerful."

Azhar said, "I saw 'Umar in Khanasira addressing the people in a torn shirt."

'Amr ibn Muhajir said, "I saw that the shirts and jubbahs of 'Umar II reached down to between his ankles and his shoelaces."

Al-Walid ibn Abi's-Sa'ib ad-Dimishqi mentioned that 'Umar II had a dust-coloured silk/wool jubbah and a yellow jubbah, and a dust-coloured silk/wool wrapper and a yellow silk/wool wrapper. When he wore the dust-coloured jubbah, he wore the yellow wrapper, and when he wore the yellow jubbah, he wore the dust-coloured wrapper. Then he stopped doing that.

Ar-Rabi' ibn Subayh said that someone saw 'Umar II praying in a shawl-like jubbah without a waist-wrapper.

Muhammad ibn Hilal said, "I saw that 'Umar II did not trim his moustache a lot. He trimmed a moderate amount from it."

Abu'l-Ghusn said, "I used to smell musk on 'Umar II."

Abu'l-Ghusn and Muhammad ibn Hilal said that they saw that 'Umar had no mark of prostration between his eyes.

Abu'l-Ghusn said that he did not see 'Umar ever wear a sword while he was on the minbar.

Ayyub said, "It was said to 'Umar II, 'Amir al-Mu'minin, if you go to Madina, and Allah makes you die there, you could be buried in the fourth burial place next to the graves of the Messenger of Allah صلعم, Abu Bakr and 'Umar.' He replied, 'By Allah, I would rather have Allah punish me with every punishment except the Fire which I cannot endure to Allah knowing that in my heart I was thinking that I was worthy of that.'"

Muhammad ibn al-Miqdam asked Fatima bint 'Abdu'l-Malik, the wife of 'Umar, "What did you see of the beginning of the illness from which 'Umar died?" She said, "Its beginning, or most of it, was dread."

'Abu'l-Hamid ibn Suhayl said, "I saw the doctor leaving 'Umar and we asked, 'How is his urine today?' He said. 'There is nothing harming his urine except concern for the business of the people.'"

Ibn Lahi'a said, "We found in one of the books that fear of Allah killed him."

Muhammad ibn Qays said, "I was present with the Amir al-Mu'minin 'Umar at the beginning of his illness at the time of the new moon of Rajab 101 AH. He was ill for twenty days. He sent for a *dhimmi*. We were at Dayr Sim'an, and he bargained with him for his grave site. The *dhimmi* said, 'Amir al-Mu'minin, it is good that your grave will be in my land. Let me give it to you.' 'Umar refused until he bought it from him for two dinars. Then he called for the two dinars which he gave to him."

Ibrahim ibn Maysara reported that 'Umar II purchased his grave site before he died for ten dinars.

One of the shaykhs of the people of Makka said, "Fatima bint 'Abdu'l-Malik and his brother Maslama were with 'Umar II. One of them said to his companion, 'We will not trouble him.' They left while he was not facing towards *qibla*. They said, 'We returned soon afterwards and he was facing *qibla*.' He said, 'Then someone we did not see spoke, saying, *"That Abode of the Next World: We grant it to those who do not seek to exalt themselves in the earth or to cause corruption in it. The successful outcome is for the godfearing."* (28:83)'"

Maslama ibn 'Abdu'l-Malik visited 'Umar II when he was in his final illness and asked him, "Who do you appoint as executor for your family?" He replied, "When I forget Allah, remind me." Then he returned and asked, "Who do you appoint as executor for your family?" He said, *"My Protector is Allah who sent down the Book. He takes care of the righteous."* (7:196)

Sulayman ibn Musa said, "When 'Umar was dying he wrote to Yazid ibn 'Abdu'l-Malik, 'Beware of being caught by a downfall in might. The error cannot be undone, and it is not possible to go back. Those after you will not praise you and those before you will not excuse you. Peace.'"

Salim ibn Bashir reported that when 'Umar was dying, he wrote to Yazid II, 'Peace be upon you. Following on from that, I see that the command will go to you. By Allah, by Allah, it for the community of the Prophet Muhammad صلعم. Leave this world for the one who does not praise you, for then you will reach those who will not excuse you. Peace be upon you.'"

Abu Bakr ibn Muhammad said, "'Umar II ordered that he be shrouded in five garments, which included a shirt and a turban. Khalid ibn Abi Bakr said the same." Khalid ibn Abi Bakr said the same and added, "That was how Ibn 'Umar used to shroud those of his family who died."

'Abdu'r-Rahman ibn Muhammad said, "When 'Umar was dying, he called for a hair of the Prophet صلعم and some of his nails and said, 'When I die, put the hair and nails in my shroud.' They did that."

Sufyan ibn 'Abdu'l-'Aziz said, "'Umar said to a female client of his, 'When you prepare the *hanut* do not put any musk in it.'"

Sufyan ibn 'Asim said, "When 'Umar was dying, he ordered that he be turned to face *qibla* on his right side."

Al-Mughira ibn Hakim said, "Fatima bint 'Abdu'l-Malik said to me, 'In his final illness, I heard 'Umar saying, "O Allah, my death will make things easier for them, even if it is for an hour of the day." On the day he died, I left him and sat in another room with a door between me and him. He was in his tent. I heard him say, *"That Abode of the Next World: We grant it to those who do not seek to exalt themselves in the earth or to cause corruption in it. The successful outcome is for the godfearing."* (28:83) Then he was calm and I did not hear any movement from him. I told the servant who served him, "See whether the Amir al-Mu'minin is sleeping." When he went in to it, he shouted. I jumped up and entered and he was dead, facing *qibla* with one hand over his mouth and the other over his eyes.'"

Raja' ibn Hawya said, "'Umar said to me when he was ill, 'Be one of those who wash me, shroud me and put me in my grave.

When you place me in my grave, untie the knot and look at my face. I have buried three khalifs. In the case of each of them, when I put him in the grave, I untied the knot and then looked at his face. His face showed distress and was not facing the *qibla*.'" Raja' continued, "I was among those who washed 'Umar, shrouded him and put him in his grave. When I undid the knot, I looked at his face, and his face was as smooth as parchment, facing *qibla*."

'Amr ibn 'Uthman said, "'Umar II died on the 20th of Rajab 101 AH at the age of 39 and some months. He was khalif for two years and five months. He died at Dayr Sim'an."

Al-Haytham ibn Waqid said, "I was born in 87 AH. 'Umar became khalif at Dabiq on Friday, 20th Safar, 99 AH. I received three dinars from his distribution. He died in Khanasira on Wednesday, 25th Rajab, 101 AH. He was ill for 20 days. He was khalif for two years, five months and four days. He died at the age of 39 and some months and was buried at Dayr Sim'an." Abu'z-Zinad said the same.

Sa'id ibn 'Amir said, "'Umar II was 39 and six months the day he died." Abu Bakr ibn 'Ayyash also said that.

Sufyan ibn 'Uyayna asked his son, "How old was he?" He said, "He had not reached more than 40. He ruled for two years and a bit."

Mu'awiya ibn Salih said, "When 'Umar II was dying, he left a will which said, 'Dig my grave for me, and do not make it deep. The best of the earth is above and the worst is below.'"

Wuhayb ibn al-Ward said, "We heard that when 'Umar II died, the *fuqaha'* came to his wife to console her and they said to her, 'We have come to give you our condolences regarding 'Umar. The loss to the Community is felt by everyone. May Allah have mercy on you, tell us how 'Umar was in his house. The wife knows her man best.'

"She said, 'By Allah, 'Umar was not the most prolific of you in prayer and fasting, but by Allah, I have never seen a slave with greater fear of Allah than 'Umar. By Allah, if he was where a man would normally be happy with his wife, with a blanket between him and me, some aspect of Allah's command would occur to his heart and he would tremble as a bird which has just fallen into the water shakes itself, and then he would sob and weep until I said, "By Allah, get rid of what is between your sides." So he would remove the blanket from me while I would be saying, "Would that there was the distance between the two easts between us and this command. By Allah we have not seen any happiness since we entered it!"'"

Ja'far ibn Sulayman said, "Malik ibn Dinar sometimes mentioned 'Umar II and wept. He said, 'None of us was worthy of him.'"

Abu Bakr ibn'Ayyash mentioned 'Umar and said, "Dayr Sim'an acquired a man who feared his Lord."

They said, "'Umar ibn 'Abdu'l-'Aziz was reliable and trustworthy. He had *fiqh*, knowledge and scrupulousness. He related many *hadiths*. He was a just Imam. May Allah have mercy on him and be pleased with him."

'Abdullah ibn 'Amr ibn 'Uthman ibn 'Affan

His mother was Hafs bint 'Abdullah ibn 'Umar ibn al-Khattab, whose mother was Safiyya bint Abi 'Ubayd, whose mother was 'Atika bint Usayd, whose mother was Zaynab bint Abi 'Amr.

His children were Khalid, 'Abdullah, and 'A'isha whom Sulayman ibn 'Abdu'l-Malik married, and their mother was Asma' bint 'Abdu'r-Rahman, whose mother was Umm al-Hasan bint az-Zubayr ibn al-'Awwam, whose mother was Asma' bint Abi Bakr. He also had 'Abdu'l-'Aziz, Umayya, Umm 'Abdullah, whom al-Walid ibn 'Abdu'l-Malik married, and Umm 'Uthman, whose mother was Umm 'Abdu'l-'Aziz bint 'Abdullah; 'Amr, Umm Sa'id who married Yazid ibn 'Abdu'l-Malik, Muhammad ad-Dibaj, al-Qasim and Ruqayya, whose mother was Fatima bint Husayn, whose mother was Umm Ishaq bint Talha; Muhammad the elder, who is al-Hazuq, whose mother was an *umm walad*; Umm 'Abdu'l-'Aziz who married al-Walid ibn Yazid, and whose mother was al-Jalal bint Bukhayt.

'Abdullah ibn 'Amr is the one called al-Mutraf because of his beauty. He died in Egypt in 96 AH.

Ibrahim ibn Muhammad ibn Talha ibn 'Ubaydullah

His mother was Khawla bint Manzur. He was the brother of Hasan ibn Hasan by the mother. He was lame, and a fierce *sharif*. He was called 'the Lion of Quraysh' and 'the Lion of the Hijaz'. He had a noble soul. He was swift to speak the truth with the governors and khalifs. He had few *hadiths*.

His children were 'Imran, whose mother was Zaynab bint 'Amr; Ya'qub, Salih, Sulayman, Yunus, Da'ud, al-Yasa', Shu'ayb, Harun, Umm Kulthum and Umm Aban, whose mother was Umm Ya'qub bint Isma'il, whose mother was Lubaba bint al-'Abbas. He also had

'Isa, Isma'il, Musa, Yusuf, Nuh and Ishaq, by *umm walads*. He had Isma'il the elder, Umm Abihi, who married 'Umar ibn 'Abdu'l-'Aziz, and Umm Kulthum, whose mother was Umm 'Uthman bint 'Abdu'r-Rahman, whose mother was Umm Kulthum bint Abi Bakr.

He related from Abu Hurayra, Ibn 'Umar and Ibn 'Abbas.

'Abdu'r-Rahman ibn Abi'z-Zinad said, "Hisham the khalif went on *hajj* that year as did Ibrahim ibn Muhammad. He met him at Makka – Ibrahim ibn Muhammad waited for Hisham at the Stone when Hisham was doing *tawaf* of the House. As he passed by Ibrahim, Ibrahim shouted out to him, 'I call on you by Allah to right my wrong!' He asked, 'What is your wrong?' He said, 'My house has been seized.' He asked, 'What was your standing as regards the Amir al-Mu'minin, 'Abdu'l-Malik?' He replied, 'He wronged me, by Allah.' He said, 'Where were you in relation to al-Walid?' He replied, 'He wronged me, by Allah.' He asked, 'And where were you in relation to Sulayman?' He replied, 'By Allah, he wronged me.' He asked, 'Where were you in relation to 'Umar II?' He said, 'May Allah have mercy on him. He restored it to me. Then when Yazid took office, he seized it. Today it is wrongfully in the hands of your agents.' He said, 'By Allah, if there is something for which you should be beaten, I will cause you pain.' He said, 'By Allah, my beating is for the whip and the sword.' Hisham went and left him. Then he summoned al-Abrash al-Kalbi who was his personal friend. He said, 'Abrash, what do you think of this language? This is the language of Quraysh, not the language of Kalb. Quraysh still have something in them. What is in them is like this.'"

'Abdullah ibn Abi Ubayda said, "A letter came from Hisham to Ibrahim ibn Hisham al-Makhzumi, the governor of Madina, to reduce the share of the family of Suhayb ibn Sinan to the equivalent of the clients. They went to Ibrahim ibn Muhammad, the guardian and head of the Banu Taym. He said, 'I will not fail to do something about this.' They thanked him. Ibrahim ibn Hisham used to go to Quba every Saturday, so Ibrahim ibn Muhammad sat at the door of the house of Talha ibn 'Abdullah at al-Balat. When Ibrahim ibn Hisham came along, Ibrahim ibn Muhammad went to him and took hold of his animal's mane. He said, 'May Allah put the amir right! The allies of the sons of Suhayb! Suhayb has the position in Islam that he has.' He replied, 'What shall I do? The letter of the Amir al-Mu'minin concerning them has been received. By Allah, if you had received it, you would not find any way to avoid carrying it out.' He said, 'By Allah, if you desire to do good, then do it. The Amir al-Mu'minin will not reject your position. You are a parent, so do what is correct in that respect.' He replied, 'What do I have which belongs to you except what I have mentioned to you?' Ibrahim ibn Muhammad said, 'I will say one thing to you. By Allah, not one of the Banu Taym will receive a single dirham until the family of Suhayb also receives.' Ibrahim ibn Hisham granted what he wanted then. Ibrahim ibn Muhammad left. Ibrahim ibn Hisham came up to Abu 'Ubayd ibn Muhammad, who was with him. He said, 'Quraysh will continue to have might as long as this one lives. When he dies, then Quraysh will be abased.'"

'Abdu'r-Rahman ibn Abi'z-Zinad said, "A stipend was commanded for the people of Madina while Hisham was khalif. It could not be paid in full from the booty, and so Hisham ordered that the remainder be paid out of the *zakat* of Yamana. It was sent to them and Ibrahim ibn Muhammad heard about it. He said, 'By Allah, we will not accept our stipend from the *zakat* and impurities of people. We will only accept it from the booty.' When the camels arrived with that money, Ibrahim and the people of Madina came out and began to turn away the camels, striking their faces with their sleeves and saying, 'By Allah, we will not let them in with a single dirham of *zakat*!' So the camels were sent back."

Hisham heard about this and he commanded that the *zakat* be taken back and that the rest of their stipend be brought to them from the booty.

Ibn Abi Dhi'b said, "I was with Ibrahim ibn Muhammad when he died at Mina or in the night of Jam' and he was buried at the bottom of al-'Aqaba in his *ihram*. I saw that his face and head were uncovered. I asked why and they said, 'He commanded that.' While I was looking on, 'Abdullah ibn 'Waqid came and fumigated his face and head, as had been done with his father. Al-Muttalib ibn 'Abdullah came and uncovered his face and head as had been done with 'Abdullah ibn al-Walid al-Makhzumi. He was buried like that."

Az-Zuhri said that 'Abdullah ibn al-Walid al-Makhzumi died while he was in *ihram*. 'Uthman ibn 'Affan was asked about him and he commanded that his head not be fumigated.

Muhammad ibn Ibrahim ibn al-Harith

His mother was Hafsa bint Abi Yahya 'Umayr. He was one of the foremost clients of the Banu Taym. There were many of them in Madina. Then they were ascribed to him.

He had a son Musa, who was a *faqih* and *muhaddith*, and also Ibrahim and Ishaq. Their mother was Umm 'Isa bint 'Imran. Muhammad ibn 'Umar said that his *kunya* was Abu 'Abdullah. His grandfather was al-Harith ibn Khalid, one of the first Muhajirun. He died in 120 AH in Madina at the end of the khalifate of Hisham. He was reliable, with a lot of *hadiths*.

Muhammad ibn Talha ibn Yazid

His mother was Fakhita bint Mas'ud. His children were Ja'far, Ibrahim and Fakhita, whose mother was al-Fadila bint al-Fudayl; 'Ulayya and Salama, whose mother was Kuluka bint 'Awn. He died in Madina while Hisham was khalif. He had few *hadiths*.

Abu 'Ubayda ibn 'Abdullah ibn Zam'a

His mother was Zaynab bint Abi Salama al-Makhzumiyya, whose mother was Umm Salama bint Abi Umayya, the wife of the Prophet صلعم. His children were 'Abdullah, who is Wukayh, Zaynab, Hind, who married 'Abdullah ibn Husayn ibn Hasan (and bore him Muhammad, Ibrahim and Musa), Ibrahim, Musa and Amatu'l-Wahhab, whose mother was Qurayba bint Yazid; and 'Abdu'r-Rahman and 'Ubaydullah, whose mother was Umm al-Qasim bint 'Umar. He had few *hadiths*.

His brother, Wahb ibn 'Abdullah

His mother was Zaynab bint Abi Salama al-Makhzumiyya. His children were 'Abdu'r-Rahman, by an *umm walad*, and Kulthum, whose mother was Khabiyya bint Yazid. He was killed at the Battle of al-Harra in Dhu'l-Hijja 63 AH while Yazid was khalif.

Their brother Yazid ibn 'Abdullah

His mother was Zaynab bint Abi Salama al-Makhzumiyya. He had a son Yazid, by an *umm walad*.

When Muslim ibn 'Uqba entered Madina and looted it and killed people, he called on people to give allegiance. The Banu Umayya were the first to give allegiance. Then he called the Banu Asad ibn'Abdu'l-'Uzza, against whom he bore animosity, to his castle. He said, "Give allegiance to the slave of Allah, Yazid, the Amir al-Mu'minin, and to those appointed after him, over your properties and lives to decide as he wishes about them." One of them reported that he said to Yazid ibn 'Abdullah, "Give allegiance on the basis that you are the slave of the staff." Yazid replied, "O amir, we are a group of the Muslims. We are due what the Muslims are due and we owe what the Muslims owe. I give allegiance to the son of my uncle, my khalif and my Imam, on the basis of the allegiance which Muslims owe." He said, "Praise be to Allah who has let me drink your blood. By Allah, I will never accept it from you." So he went up to him and struck off his head.

Ja'far ibn Kharija said, "Musarrif left Madina for Makka and was followed by an *umm walad* of Yazid ibn 'Abdullah at a distance of two or three days behind the army. Musarrif died and was buried at Thaniyya al-Mushallal. News of this reached her and she went to where he was, dug him up and then crucified him at Thaniyya al-Mushallal.

'Abdullah ibn Wahb

His mother was Zaynab bint Shayba, whose mother was Fakhita bint Harb. His son Yazid's mother was Tamima bint al-Harith.

'Abbad ibn 'Abdullah ibn az-Zubayr

His mother was the daughter of Manzur ibn Zabban. His children were Muhammad and Salih, whose mother was Umm Shayba bint 'Abdullah; and Yahya, whose mother was 'A'isha bint 'Abdu'r-Rahman, whose mother was Umm al-Hasan bint az-Zubayr. He was reliable with a lot of *hadiths*.

Khubayb ibn 'Abdullah ibn az-Zubayr

His mother was the daughter of Manzur ibn Zabban. He was a scholar. Al-Walid I heard *hadiths* from him which he disliked, so he wrote to his governor of Madina to give him a hundred lashes, which he did. Then he poured a waterskin of cold water on him and he spent the night like that. He lived for some days and then died.

Hamza ibn 'Abdullah ibn az-Zubayr

His mother was the daughter of Manzur ibn Zabban. His children were 'Umara, by whom he has his *kunya*, and 'Abbad, whose mother was Hind bint Qutba; Abu Bakr and Yahya, whose mother was Umm al-Qasim, whose mother was Umm Kulthum bint 'Abdullah, whose mother was Zaynab bint 'Ali, whose mother was Fatima, the Prophet's daughterصلعم; Sulayman and Umm Salama, whose mother was Umm al-Khattab bint Shayba; and 'Abdu'l-Wahid, Hashim, 'Amir, Ibrahim, 'Abdu'l-Hamid, Amatu'l-Jabbar, Amatu'l-Malik, Umm Habib and Saliha, by *umm walads*.

Ibn az-Zubayr appointed his son Hamza over Basra and then dismissed him.

Hamza is related from, and his sons, 'Abbad and Hashim, are related from. Hashim was one of the devout worshippers.

Thabit ibn 'Abdullah ibn az-Zubayr

His mother was the daughter of Manzur ibn Zabban. His children were Nafi', Mus'ab, Khubayb and Bukayra, by various *umm walads*; Sa'd, by an *umm walad*; Asma', whose mother was Sufyan bint 'Abdullah; and Hukayma and Ruqayqa, whose mother was 'A'isha bint Muhammad ibn 'Abdu'r-Rahman ibn Abi Bakr.

Abu Bakr ibn 'Abdullah ibn az-Zubayr

His mother was Rayta bint 'Abdu'r-Rahman. He had a son 'Abdu'r-Rahman, whose mother was Amatu'r-Rahman bint al-Ja'd. He is also related from.

'Amir ibn 'Abdullah ibn az-Zubayr

His mother was Hantama bint 'Abdu'r-Rahman. His children were 'Atiq, 'Abdullah, al-Harith, 'A'isha, Umm 'Uthman the elder and Umm 'Uthman the younger, whose mother was Qurayba bint al-Mundhir.

His *kunya* was Abu'l-Harith. He was a man of worship. He died just before Hisham or shortly afterwards. Hisham died in 124 AH.

Malik ibn Anas said, "'Amir ibn 'Abdullah had a *ghusl* every day after the sun rose, as did 'Abdullah ibn Abi Bakr, out of desire for purity."

Malik said, "I saw 'Amir ibn 'Abdullah fast continuously – on the seventeenth and then in the evening he did not taste anything until the following night: altogether two days and a night." He said, "I saw that 'Amir angled his hands in the supplication."

Sufyan said, "They say that 'Amir ibn 'Abdullah purchased himself from Allah by paying six blood wits." He said that he saw 'Amir ibn 'Abdullah standing for a long time at the *jamras*.

He was reliable and trustworthy but has few *hadiths*.

Muhammad ibn Ja'far ibn az-Zubayr

His mother was an *umm walad*. His children were Ibrahim and Zaynab, whose mother was an *umm walad*.

Muhammad ibn Ishaq reported from Muhammad ibn Ja'far, as did Ibn Jurayj and al-Walid ibn Kathir. He was a scholar and has *hadiths*.

Nubayh ibn Wahb ibn 'Uthman

His mother was Su'da bint Zayd ibn Mulays. Zayd was one of the idolaters captured on the Day of Badr. Nubayh's children were Wahb, 'Abdullah, 'Abdu'r-Rahman, 'Umar, Umm Salama and Umm Jamil, whose mother was Umm Jamil bint Shayba.

Nafi', the client of 'Umar, related from Nubayh, although he was not older than him. Nubayh died in the civil war of al-Walid I. He was reliable, with few *hadiths*. His *hadiths* were *hasan*.

'Abdu'r-Rahman ibn al-Miswar ibn Makhrama

His mother was Amatu'llah bint Shurahbil. His children were 'Abdullah and Maymuna, whose mother was the daughter of Ziyad ibn 'Abdullah; Abu Bakr, who was a poet, Shurahbil, Rabi'a and Ja'far, by *umm walads*. His *kunya* was Abu'l-Miswar. He died in Madina in 90 AH while al-Walid I was khalif. He had few *hadiths*.

Salama ibn 'Umar ibn Abi Salama

His mother was Mulayka bint Rifa'a. His children were 'Abdullah, 'Umar and Asma', who married 'Urwa ibn az-Zubayr, and their mother was Hafsa bint 'Ubaydullah, whose mother was Asma' bint Zayd ibn al-Khattab.

Al-Muttalib ibn 'Abdullah ibn al-Muttalib

His mother was Umm Aban bint al-Hakam. His children were al-Hakam, whose mother was as-Sayyida bint Jabir; Sulayman, 'Abdu'l-'Aziz, the *qadi* of Madina for al-Mansur, al-Fadl, al-Harith and Umm 'Abdu'l-Malik, whose mother was Umm al-Fadl bint Kulayb; 'Ali, whose mother was Fatikha bint 'Abdullah; and Qurayba, whose mother was Umm al-Qasim bint Wahb.

He had a lot of *hadiths*, but his *hadiths* are not used as evidence because he has many *mursal hadiths* from those whom he did not meet. A lot of people in the *isnad* are falsely inserted.

Al-Muhajir ibn 'Abdullah ibn Abi Umayya

Yahya ibn Abi Kathir related from him from Abu Bakr ibn 'Abdu'r-Rahman that the Messenger of Allah صلعم said, "It is not lawful for a Muslim man who believes in Allah and the Last Day to inflict more than ten lashes except for a *hadd*."

Hafs ibn 'Asim ibn 'Umar ibn al-Khattab

His mother was Sayyida bint 'Umayra. His children were 'Umar, Rabah, who is 'Isa, Umm Jamil and Umm 'Asim, whose mother was Maymuna bint Da'ud. 'Isa ibn Hafs said, "I saw my father wear silk/wool."

His brother, 'Ubaydullah ibn 'Asim ibn 'Umar

His mother was 'A'isha bint Muti'. His children were 'Abdullah, whose mother was an *umm walad*; and 'Asim and Ubayya, whose mother was Umm Salama bint 'Abdullah.

'Abdu'l-Hamid ibn 'Abdu'r-Rahman ibn Zayd ibn al-Khattab

His mother was Maymuna bint Bishr. His chidren were Ibrahim, whose mother was a daughter of Yazid ibn al-Asamm; Muhammad, 'Umar, Zayd, 'Abdu'r-Rahman the elder and 'Abdu'l-Kabir – who was appointed over the summer expedition, by *umm walads*; and 'Abdu'r-Rahman the younger, whose mother was a daughter of al-Harith ibn 'Abdullah.

'Umar II appointed him over Iraq and sent Abu'z-Zinad with him as a scribe in charge of the *kharaj*.

Nufayl ibn Hisham ibn Zayd ibn Sa'id

His mother was Umm Habib bint ibn Qariz. He had a son, Hisham, whose mother was a daughter of al-Aswad ibn Sa'id.

'Amr ibn Shu'ayb ibn Muhammad ibn 'Abdullah

His mother was Habiba bint Murra. His children were 'Abdullah, whose mother was Ramla bint 'Abdullah; Ibrahim, whose mother was Umm 'Asim; and 'Abdu'r-Rahman, by an *umm walad*.

Da'ud ibn Qays said that his *kunya* was Abu Ibrahim.

Malik ibn Anas said, "I saw 'Amr ibn Shu'ayb praying a lot between *Dhuhr* and *'Asr*."

Habib al-Mu'allim said, "'Amir ibn Shu'ayb told me that his father confirmed 20,000 dirhams for his mother when he died."

His brother, 'Umar ibn Shu'ayb

His mother was Habiba bint Murra. He has no descendants and was related from.

'Abdu'l-Malik ibn Qudama al-Jumahi said that 'Umar ibn Shu'ayb reported in Syria from his father that his grandfather said that his mother was a daughter of Munabbih ibn al-Hajjaj, a woman who gave herself to the Messenger of Allah صلعم and was kind to him. He came to her one day and said, "How are you, Umm 'Abdullah?"

Muhammad ibn 'Amr ibn 'Ata'

His mother was Umm Kulthum bint 'Abdullah. His *kunya* was Abu 'Abdullah. He had good conduct and manliness. They used to say in Madina that the khalifate should go to him because of his bearing, manliness, intelligence and perfection. He met Ibn 'Abbas and other Companions of the Messenger of Allah صلعم.

He died while al-Walid II was khalif. He was reliable with *hadiths*.

Abu Bakr ibn Muhammad ibn 'Amr ibn Hazm

His mother was Kabsha bint 'Abdu'r-Rahman and his aunt was 'Amra bint 'Abdu'r-Rahman who related from 'A'isha. His children were Muhammad, 'Abdullah and 'Abdu'r-Rahman, whose mother was Fatima bint 'Umara; and Amatu'r-Rahman, by an *umm walad*. Abu Bakr was his actual name.

Yahya ibn Sa'id reported that Abu Bakr ibn Muhammad was *qadi* of Madina.

Sa'id ibn Muslim said, "I saw Abu Bakr ibn Muhammad giving judgement in the mosque in the time of Umar II – that is, while 'Umar was governor of Madina for al-Walid II."

Rabi'a ibn 'Abdu'r-Rahman reported that he saw Abu Bakr ibn Muhammad giving judgement in the mosque with two guards by him, leaning against a pillar at the grave.

Muhammad ibn 'Umar said, "When 'Umar II became khalif, he appointed Abu Bakr over Madina and he appointed his nephew, Abu Tuwala ibn 'Abdullah, *qadi* of Madina." Abu Bakr used to lead the people in prayer and take charge of their business.

Abu'l-Ghusn said, "I did not see Abu Bakr ibn Muhammad wear a sword on the *minbar* at all." He also said, "I saw Abu Bakr ibn Muhammad wearing a white turban on the *'Id* and on the *Jumu'a*. I saw him remove his sandals when he went up on the *minbar* of the Prophet صلعم."

Abu'l-Ghusn also said that he saw Abu Bakr ibn Muhammad using henna and brown dye. He wore a gold and red ruby ring on his right hand. He also saw a blue sapphire ring on his right hand.

Muhammad ibn 'Umar said, "Abu Bakr ibn Muhammad died in Madina at the age of 84 in 120 AH while Hisham was khalif. He was reliable with a lot of *hadiths*."

'Asim ibn 'Umar ibn Qatada ibn an-Nu'man

His mother was Umm al-Harith bint Sinan. His *kunya* was Abu 'Umar and he had no children.

He had transmission of knowledge, knowledge of *sira*, and knowledge of the expeditions of the Messenger of Allah صلعم Muhammad ibn Ishaq and other people of knowledge related from him. He was a reliable scholar, with a lot of *hadiths*.

'Asim ibn 'Umar went to 'Umar II when he was khalif about a debt he owed and 'Umar paid it for him and he commanded maintenance for him after that. He told him to sit in the Damascus Mosque and he reported the expeditions of the Messenger of Allahصلعم and the virtues of his Companions. He said, "The Banu Marwan used to dislike that and forbid it." He sat and related that to people. Then he returned to Madina and remained there until he died in 120 AH while Hisham was khalif.

His brother, Ya'qub ibn 'Umar ibn Qatada

His mother was Umm al-Harith bint Sinan. His children were Amatu'r-Rahman, whom Rubayh ibn 'Abdu'r-Rahman married. His line has died out. He related from Ya'qub and has a few *hadiths*.

'Abdu'r-Rahman ibn 'Abdullah ibn Ka'b ibn Malik

His mother was Khalida bint 'Abdullah. His children were Muhammad and Ubayya, whose mother was Khalida bint 'Ubaydullah; 'Abdullah and 'Abdu'r-Rahman, whose mother was Umm Kuj bint Thabit; and Rawh ibn 'Abdu'r-Rahman, whose mother was an *umm walad*.

His *kunya* was Abu'l-Khattab by his uncle's *kunya*. Az-Zuhri related from 'Abdu'r-Rahman ibn 'Abdullah. He had few *hadiths*. He died while Hisham was khalif.

Waqid ibn 'Amr ibn Sa'd ibn Mu'adh

His mother was an *umm walad*. His children were Muhammad, Sa'd, Abu Bakr and Umm Abiha, whose mother was Umm Kulthum bint Salama. He was reliable and had *hadiths*.

Sa'id ibn 'Abdu'r-Rahman ibn Hassan ibn Thabit

His mother was an *umm walad*. His children were al-Far'a and Fatima whose mother was an *umm walad*; and 'Abda whose mother was an *umm walad*. He was a poet with few *hadiths*.

Muhammad ibn Yahya ibn Hibban

His mother was Umm al-'Ala' bint 'Abbad. His children were Sukayna and Fatima, whose mother was Umm al-Harith bint Wasi';

and Burayka, whose mother was Muwaysa bint Salih. His *kunya* was Abu 'Abdullah. He died in Madina in 121 AH at the age of 74 while Hisham was khalif.

Muhammad ibn 'Umar said, "Muhammad ibn Yahya had a circle in the mosque of the Messenger of Allahﷺ. He used to give *fatwa*. He was reliable with a lot of *hadiths*." He related from his uncle Wasi' ibn Hibban, Ibn Muhayrayz and 'Abdu'r-Rahman al-A'raj.

'Abdullah ibn 'Abdu'r-Rahman ibn al-Harith

His mother was Umm al-Harith bint Qays. His children were 'Abdu'r-Rahman, Muhammad, Qays and Thubayta, whose mother was Na'ila bint al-Harith. He related from Abu Sa'id al-Khudri. Malik ibn Anas met him and related from him. Malik also related from his sons, Muhammad and 'Abdu'r-Rahman.

Muhammad ibn Ka'b ibn Hibban al-Qurazi

One of the allies of Aws. His *kunya* was Abu Hamza.

Muhammad ibn Abi Humayd al-Ansari reported that Muhammad ibn Ka'b al-Qurazi's *kunya* was Abu Hamza. Muhammad ibn Abi Humayd met him and listened to him.

'Abdullah ibn Mu'attib or Mughith ibn Abi Burda reported that his grandfather heard the Messenger of Allahﷺ say, "A man will emerge from among the soothsayers who will study the Qur'an in a manner which none after him will study it."

'Abdullah ibn Habib ibn Abi Thabit said, "I saw Muhammad ibn Ka'b al-Qurazi telling a story. A man began to weep and so he stopped his story and asked, 'Who is weeping?' The reply was, 'One of the Banu so-and-so.' He seemed to dislike it."

I heard someone other than Abu Ma'shar say that while Muhammad ibn Ka'b was telling a story the mosque collapsed on him and his companions and killed them.

Al-Fadl ibn Dukayn said, "Muhammad ibn Ka'b died in 108 AH. Muhammad ibn 'Umar and other people of knowledge disagreed and said, 'Ibn Ka'b died in 117 or 118 AH.' Allah knows best."

He was reliable in knowledge with a lot of *hadiths* and scrupulousness, may Allah have mercy on him.

Isma'il ibn 'Abdu'r-Rahman

He listened to Ibn 'Umar, and 'Abdullah ibn Abi Nujayh and Sa'id ibn Khalid al-Qarizi related from him. He was reliable and had *hadiths*.

Muslim ibn Jundub al-Hudhali

His *kunya* was Abu 'Abdullah. He listened to 'Abdullah ibn 'Umar and the companions of 'Umar, Aslam, the client of 'Umar and others. He died in Madina while Hisham was khalif.

Malik ibn Anas reported that 'Umar II paid Muslim ibn Jundub a salary of two dinars. Before that he used to give judgement without a salary.

Sa'id ibn al-Musayyab heard that Muslim ibn Jundub said, "The greatest part of the *hajj* is the Day of Sacrifice." He said that he was a bedouin who thought blood important. Muhammad ibn 'Umar said that Zayd ibn Aslam related from Muslim ibn Jundub.

Nafi'

The client of 'Abdullah ibn 'Umar ibn al-Khattab. His *kunya* was Abu 'Abdullah. He was one of the people of Abrashbar. 'Abdullah captured him in one of his raids. Various people said that there was a letter which Nafi' heard from 'Abdullah ibn 'Umar which was written on a page, and they used to read it to him and say, "O 'Abdullah, can we read to you and say, 'Nafi' related to us.'?" He said, "Yes."

Muhammad ibn 'Umar said, "I heard Nafi' ibn Nu'aym say, 'When someone tells you that Nafi' read to him, do not believe it. His pronunciation was too incorrect for that.'"

'Ubaydullah said, "Nafi' did not do *tafsir*."

Isma'il said, "We tried to help Nafi' stop using his poor grammar, but he refused."

Sufyan said, "Which *hadith* is more reliable than that of Nafi'?"

'Ubaydullah ibn 'Umar said that 'Umar II sent Nafi' to Egypt to teach them *sunnas*.

Nafi' related from Ibn 'Umar, Abu Hurayra, Rubayya' bint Mu'awwidh, Safiyya bint Abi 'Ubayd and Aslam, the client of 'Umar. He was reliable, with a lot of *hadiths*. Nafi' died in Madina in 117 AH while Hisham was khalif.

Sa'id ibn Abi Sa'id al-Maqburi

The client of the Banu Layth ibn Bakr. He related from Sa'd ibn Abi Waqqas, Jubayr ibn Mut'im, Abu Shurayh al-Ka'bi, Abu Hurayra, Abu Sa'id al-Khudri, Ibn 'Umar, 'Abdu'r-Rahman ibn Abi Sa'id al-Khudri, Sa'id ibn Dinar, 'Urwa ibn az-Zubayr, Abu Salama ibn 'Abdu'r-Rahman, 'Abdullah ibn Rafi', the client of Umm Salama, 'Ubayd ibn Jurayj, 'Abdullah ibn Abi Qatada, 'Abdu'r-Rahman ibn Mihran, al-Qa'qa' ibn Hakim, his father, and from his brother, 'Abbad ibn Abi Sa'id.

He was reliable, with a lot of *hadiths*, but he grew old until he became muddled four years before he died. He died in Madina in 123 AH while Hisham was khalif.

Salih ibn Abi Salih

His *kunya* was Abu 'Abdullah. He was the client of at-Tawa'ma, the daughter of Umayya bint Khalaf. She had a twin sister which is why she had the name 'twin'. She freed Abu Salih, whose name was Nabhan.

He related from Abu Hurayra. He was early. He died in Madina in 124 AH. He has a few *hadiths*. I saw that they respected his *hadiths*.

Abu 'Amr ibn Himas

The client of Banu Layth ibn Bakr. Muhammad ibn Talha said, "Abu 'Amr ibn Himas was one of the Banu Layth, with few *hadiths*. He was a worshipper and *mujtahid* who prayed at night. He often looked at women. He asked Allah to remove his sight. He lost his sight but could not endure blindness, so he asked Allah to restore his sight to him. While he was praying in the mosque he lifted his head and saw a candle. He called his slave and asked, 'What is this?' – 'A candle,' he replied. He said, 'And this?' He told him – and so on, until he had identified all the candles in the mosque. Then he prostrated out of thankfulness to Allah for restoring his sight."

After that whenever he saw a woman, he lowered his head. He used to fast constantly. When he had prayed *Maghrib*, he went to his house and broke the fast. He became exhausted and sleep would overcome him so that he often missed the *'Isha'* prayer.

Sa'id ibn Abi Hind

The client of Samura ibn Jundub al-Fazari. They claim to be among the Banu'l-Abjur, because of the alliance of Samura with them. He died in Madina at the beginning of Hisham's khalifate. He has sound *hadiths*.

Abu Ja'far al-Qari'

He is Yazid ibn al-Qa'qa', the client of 'Abdullah ibn 'Ayyash al-Makhzumi by emancipation. He related from Abu Hurayra, Ibn 'Umar and others. He was the Imam of the people of Madina in recitation and he is called 'the reciter' because of that. He was reliable with few *hadiths*. He died while Marwan II was khalif.

Ibrahim ibn 'Abdullah ibn Hunayn

The client of al-'Abbas ibn 'Abdu'l-Muttalib. Az-Zuhri related from him. He was reliable with few *hadiths*.

'Abdullah ibn Abi Salama

The client of the family of al-Munkadir of the Banu Taym ibn Murra. The name of Abu Salama was Dinar. 'Abdullah ibn Abi Salama was a scribe of Abu Bakr ibn Muhammad ibn 'Amr ibn Hazm. He was governor for 'Umar II over Madina. He was reliable, and had *hadiths*.

His brother, Ya'qub ibn Abi Salam

His *kunya* was Abu Yusuf. He is al-Majishun. He and his son were called that and they were all known as al-Majishun.

There were men of *fiqh* and transmission of *hadith* and knowledge among them. Ya'qub has a few *hadiths*.

Muslim ibn Abi Hurra

The client of one of the people of Madina. He related directly from Umm Salama, the wife of the Prophet صلعم, and Rabi'a ibn Abi 'Abdu'r-Rahman related from him. He had few *hadiths*.

Ishaq ibn Yasar

The client of Qays ibn Makhrama. He is Abu Muhammad ibn Ishaq, the author of *al-Maghazi*. He related from Ishaq ibn Yasar and mentioned that Yasar was someone who was captured at 'Ayn at-Tamar and was one of those whom Khalid ibn al-Walid sent to Abu Bakr as-Siddiq in Madina.

Al-Walid ibn Rabah

The client of the Dawsites. He related from Abu Hurayra, and Kathir ibn Zayd and others related from him.

'Abdullah ibn Nistas

He related from Jabir ibn 'Abdullah. Hashim ibn Hashim related from him.

This generation also includes **Hashim ibn 'Abdullah ibn az-Zubayr,** whose mother was Umm Hashim Rakhla bint Manzur and who belonged to his father's cavalry; **Shu'ayb ibn Shu'ayb ibn Muhammad**, whose mother was an *umm walad* and who is related from; **'Ali ibn 'Abdu'r-Rahman al-Mu'awi**, one of the Banu Mu'awiya ibn Malik, and az-Zuhri related from him; **'Abdullah ibn Khirash al-Kalbi**, who related from Abu Hurayra and Ka'b. Bukayr ibn Mismar, Musa ibn 'Ubayda ar-Rabadhi and others related from him; **Yazid ibn Talha ibn Yazid**, whose mother was Fakhita bint Mas'ud and who died in Madina at the beginning of Hashim's khalifate and has a few *hadiths;* **'Abdullah ibn Dinar al-Aslami**, who had a few *hadiths*; **Abu Salama al-Hadrami**; **Qariz ibn Shayba**, of the Banu Layth, who died in Madina while Sulayman was khalif and had a few *hadiths*; his brother **'Umar ibn Shayba**, who had a few *hadiths*; **Mu'awiya ibn 'Abdullah ibn Badr al-Juhani**, who died early on at an advanced age and who met some Companions of the Messenger of Allah; his brother, **Ba'ja ibn 'Abdullah**, who had a few *hadiths*; **Mu'adh ibn 'Abdullah ibn Khubayb al-Juhani**, who met Ibn 'Abbad and related from him and had a few *hadiths*; **Muhammad ibn 'Abdu'r-Rahman**, who is related from and had a few *hadiths*; **'Ubaydullah ibn Miqsam**, who related from Ibn 'Umar and Jabir ibn 'Abdullah; **'Umar ibn al-Hakam**, Abu'l-Walid, the client of 'Amr ibn Khirash, who related from Abu Hurayra; **Abu Wahb**, the client of Abu Hurayra, who had a few *hadiths*, and Abu Ma'shar related from him; **Musa ibn Yasar**, who is related from and who related from Abu Hurayra; and **'Abdu'r-Rahman ibn Yasar**, who is related from.

This is the end of the chapter on the third generation.

Chapter Four
The Fourth Generation
of the *Tabi'un* of the People of Madina

Az-Zuhri

Muhammad ibn 'Ubaydullah ibn 'Abdullah ibn Shihab. His mother was 'A'isha bint 'Abdullah and his *kunya* was Abu Bakr.

'Abdu'r-Rahman ibn 'Abdu'l'Aziz said, "I heard az-Zuhri say, 'I grew up and as a boy I had no money allotted to me from the *diwan*. I used to learn genealogy from 'Abdullah ibn Tha'laba al-'Adawi. He knew the genealogy of my people and was their ally. A man came to him and asked him a question about divorce. He did not know the answer to it and directed him to Sa'id ibn al-Musayyab. I asked myself, 'Why am I not with this shaykh who understands what this is!' So I went with the asker to Sa'id ibn al-Musayyab who answered his question. So I sat with Sa'id and left 'Abdullah ibn Tha'laba. Then I sat with 'Urwa ibn az-Zubayr, 'Ubaydullah ibn 'Abdullah ibn 'Utba and Abu Bakr ibn 'Abdu'r-Rahman ibn al-Harith until I had learned *fiqh*.

"'Then I travelled to Syria and went to the Damascus mosque before dawn and made for a large circle sitting opposite the *maqsura* and sat down in it. The people asked me for my lineage and I replied, "A man of Quraysh from the inhabitants of Madina." They asked, "Do you know the judgement about *umm walads*?" I told them what 'Umar ibn al-Khattab had said about *umm walads*. The people said to me, "This is the assembly of Qabisa ibn Dhu'ayb, and he will come to you. 'Abdu'l-Malik asked him about this and then he asked us but none of us had any knowledge of it."

"'Qabisa came and they told him the news. He asked for my lineage and I told him. He asked me about Sa'id ibn al-Musayyab and his companions and I told him. He said, "I will take you to the Amir al-Mu'minin." He prayed *Subh* and then went and I followed him. He went in to 'Abdu'l-Malik ibn Marwan and I sat at the door for a time

273

until the sun rose. Then he came out and said, "Where is this Qurayshi Madinan?" – "Here I am," I said. I rose and went with him to the Amir al-Mu'minin. I found that he had a Qur'an in front of him which he had closed and commanded it be removed. Only Qabisa was sitting with him. I greeted him as the khalif. He asked, "Who are you?" I replied, "Muhammad ibn Muslim ibn 'Ubaydullah ibn 'Abdullah ibn Shihab ibn 'Abdullah ibn al-Harith ibn Zuhra." He said, "Oh, a people who yield to seditions." He continued, "Muslim ibn 'Abdullah was with az-Zubayr." Then he asked, "What do you have concerning *umm walads*?" I told him, "Sa'id ibn al-Musayyab reported it to me." He said, "How is Sa'id? What is his situation?" I told him. Then I said, "Abu Bakr ibn 'Abdu'r-Rahman ibn al-Harith ibn Hisham reported to me," and he asked after him. I said, "'Urwa ibn az-Zubayr reported to me," and he asked after him. I said, "'Ubaydullah ibn 'Abdullah ibn 'Utba reported to me," and he asked about him. Then I told him the *hadith* about the *umm walads* from 'Umar ibn al-Khattab.

"'He turned to Qabisa ibn Dhu'ayb and said, "This should be written down and sent to all regions."

"'I said to myself, "I will not find him freer than he is now, and I may not be admitted after this." So I said, "'If the Amir al-Mu'minin sees fit to allot me a share for the people of my house, I am a man who is cut off, with no allocation from the *diwan*." He said, "Oh, from now on! Proceed with your business." I went out, by Allah, delighted. By Allah, at that time I was destitute and had very little. I sat outside until Qabisa came out and began to tell me off. He said, "What made you do what you did without my command or consulting me?" I replied, "I thought, by Allah, that I would never see him again after this." He asked, "Why did you suppose that? You will return to him. Stay with me," – or "Come home with me."

"'I walked behind his animal while the people were conversing with him and he entered his house. Very soon after a servant brought me a paper which read: "100 dinars, a mule for you to ride, a servant to serve you and ten garments are commanded." I asked the messenger, "From whom do I ask this?" He said, "Do you not see on this paper the name of the person to whom you are commanded to go?" I looked at the bottom of the paper and it said to go to a certain person and collect everything from him. I asked who he was and was told, "He is so-and-so and he is his steward." So I took the paper to him and he said, "Yes," and commanded everything be given to me immediately. So I left and he had enriched me.

"'I went to him the following day on the saddled mule and I rode beside him. He said, "Meet me at the door of the Amir al-Mu'minin so that I can connect you to him." I attended at the agreed time and he took me in to him. He said, "Do not speak to him about anything unless he asks you something first. I will take care of things for you." I greeted him and he indicated that I should sit down. When I had sat down, 'Abdu'l-Malik began to ask me about the lineages of Quraysh, which he knew better than I did. I began to wish that he would stop that since he knew about it better than I did. Then he told me, "I have allotted you a share for the people of your house." Then he turned to Qabisa and commanded him to record that in the *diwan*. Then he said, "Where do you want your share to be registered: Here with the Amir al-Mu'minin, or will you take it in your land?" I replied, "Amir al-Mu'minin, I am with you. When you and the people of your houses receive from the *diwan*, I will receive it there too." So he commanded that my choice be noted down and that a copy of this be sent to Madina. When the *diwan* for the people of Madina was sent out, 'Abdu'l-Malik ibn Marwan and the people of his house received their share from the *diwan* in Syria.' Az-Zuhri said, 'I did the like of that. Sometimes I took it in Madina and was not impeded.'

"He continued: 'Then Qabisa came out later and said, "The Amir al-Mu'minin commands that you be included among his companions and that you be given the salary of the companions and that your share be increased. Stay at the door of the Amir al-Mu'minin." There was a man in charge of the presentation of companions who was harsh and coarse with a severe demeanour. I failed to come for one or two days and he scowled at me and so I did not fail to come again, but in the beginning I did not like to say anything about it to Qabisa. I used to visit 'Abdu'l-Malik often.

"'Part of what 'Abdu'l-Malik asked me was, "Whom have you met?" I named some people to him but told him only those of Quraysh. He asked, "Where are you with the Ansar? You will find knowledge among them too. Where are you in relation to their master Kharija ibn Zayd ibn Thabit? Where are you with 'Abdu'r-Rahman ibn Yazid ibn Jariya?" He named several men. I went to Madina and asked them questions and listened to those Ansar and I found a lot of knowledge with them.

""'Abdu'l-Malik died and I remained with al-Walid ibn 'Abdul-Malik until he died and then with Sulayman, 'Umar, and Yazid ibn 'Abdu'l-Malik.' Yazid asked az-Zuhri and Sulayman ibn Habib al-Muhajir to act as qadis together.

"He said, 'Then I stayed with Hisham.' Hisham went on *hajj* in 106 AH and az-Zuhri went with him. Hisham appointed him to teach his son and instruct him in *fiqh* and *hadith*. He went on *hajj* with him. He did not leave them until he died in Madina."

Ma'mar said, "The first of what was known of az-Zuhri was when he was in the assembly of 'Abdu'l-Malik and 'Abdu'l-Malik asked them, 'Who among you knows what the stones of Jerusalem did on the day al-Husayn was killed?' None of them had any knowledge of this. Then az-Zuhri said, 'I have heard that on that day not one of these stones was turned over but that there was fresh blood under it.' He was known from that day."

Az-Zuhri reported that a man asked 'Umar ibn al-Khattab, "Shall I not be in a house of someone who does not fear the criticism of any critic for Allah?" He said, "If you are put in charge of any of the affairs of the Muslims, do not fear the criticism of any critic for Allah about anything. Otherwise, leave your command and turn to yourself and command the correct and forbid the bad."

Az-Zuhri reported that Hisham put his son Abu Shakir, whose name was Maslama, in charge of the *hajj* in 112 AH. He commanded az-Zuhri to go with him to Makka. He took out 16,000 dinars for az-Zuhri from the diwan of the treasury. When Abu Shakir came to Madina, az-Zuhri encouraged him to do good for the people of Madina. He stayed in Madina for a month, divided the *khums* among the people and did good things. Az-Zuhri commanded him to assume *ihram* from the mosque of Dhu'l-Hulayfa. Muhammad ibn Hisham, however, commanded him to go into *ihram* from al-Bayda' and he did that.

Then Hisham put his son Yazid in charge of the *hajj* in 123 AH and commanded az-Zuhri to go on *hajj* with him that year.

Malik reported that az-Zuhri said, "I sat with Sa'id ibn al-Musayyab for ten years – which seemed like a single day."

Ma'mar reported that that az-Zuhri said, "I spoke in the night with 'Umar II and related to him, and he said, 'I listened to everything you said during the night, but some I remember and some I forget.'"

Abu'z-Zinad said, "I used to go around with Ibn Shihab who had tablets and pages. We used to laugh at him. Az-Zuhri said, 'Were it not that *hadiths* come to us from the east which we do not accept, I would not have written a single *hadith* which I heard in a book.'"

Az-Zuhri said, "I did not ever have to have a *hadith* repeated to me, nor was I ever unsure about a *hadith,* except for one. I asked my companions and it was as I had remembered it."

Sa'd said, "I did not see anyone after the Messenger of Allahصلعم amass what Ibn Shihab amassed."

Sufyan ibn 'Uyayna said, "Abu Bakr al-Hudhali, who sat with al-Hasan and Ibn Sirin, said, 'Memorise this *hadith* for me: a *hadith* which az-Zuhri reported.' Abu Bakr said, 'I did not see the like of this man anywhere, that is, az-Zuhri.'"

Malik ibn Anas said, "I did not meet any *muhaddith faqih* in Madina except one." Mutarrif ibn 'Abdullah asked, "Who?" He said, "Ibn Shihab az-Zuhri."

Salih ibn Kaysan said, "While I and az-Zuhri were both seeking knowledge, we met and said, 'We will record the *sunan.*' So we wrote down what came from the Prophetصلعم. Then az-Zuhri said, 'We will record what comes from his Companions. It is *sunna.*' I said, 'No, it is not *sunna.* We will not write it.' So he wrote but I did not write. He was successful and I lost.' Sa'd said, 'My father said, "Ibn Shihab did not precede us in acquiring any knowledge but that we used to come to him, and he would get ready, wrap his garment round his chest and ask what we wanted."'"

Az-Zuhri said, "We used to dislike transmitting the chapter on knowledge until those rulers forced us to it. We thought that we should not deny it to any of the Muslims."

Ma'mar said, "Az-Zuhri was asked, 'They claim that you do not relate from the clients.' He replied, 'I relate from them, but when I find the sons of the Muhajirun and the Ansar, I rely on them. I do not do that with any others.'"

Ma'mar said, "We used to think that we had gathered a lot from az-Zuhri until al-Walid II was killed. Then the notebooks were carried out on animals from his treasury, (i.e. containing knowledge from az-Zuhri)."

He said that az-Zuhri said, "I used to go to the door of 'Urwa ibn az-Zubayr and sit there and then leave, even though I could have entered if I wished. This was out of my respect for him."

He said that when az-Zuhri was among his companions he was like al-Hakam ibn 'Utayba among his. 'Urwa and Salim related that about him. He said, "I came to az-Zuhri at Rusafa and no one asked him about *hadith*." He added, "He used to teach me."

He said, "'Umar II and I went on *hajj*. Sa'id ibn Jubayr came to me at night and he was afraid. He came to me in my house and said, 'Do you fear your companion will do something to me?' I replied, 'No, be calm.'"

He said that az-Zuhri said, "We transmit a *hadith* which measures a span, but it comes back measuring a cubit (i.e. from Iraq)." He made a gesture with his hand and said, "When a *hadith* comes from there, take care."

He said, "I did not see the like of az-Zuhri in his presence at all. I did not see the like of Hammad in his presence at all."

Ma'mar said, "I heard Ibrahim ibn al-Walid, a man of the Banu Umayyad, question az-Zuhri, and he reviewed a book of knowledge with him. Then he said, 'Can I relate this from you, Abu Bakr,?' 'Yes,' he replied, 'From whom can you relate it except for me?'"

He said, "I saw Ayyub reviewing knowledge with him and he gave him an *ijaza*. Mansur ibn al-Mu'tamir did not see any harm in reviewing."

'Ubaydullah ibn 'Umar said, "I saw Ibn Shihab when one of his books was brought to him and it was said to him, 'Abu Bakr, this is your book and your *hadith*. Can we relate it from you?' – 'Yes,' he said. He did not first read through it nor was it read out to him."

Muhammad ibn 'Abdullah said, "I heard my uncle say countless times, 'It is the same to me if I read to a *muhaddith*, or he reports words to me and then says of me in them, "he related to us ..."'"

'Abdu'r-Rahman ibn 'Abdu'l-'Aziz said, "'Ubaydullah ibn 'Umar and Malik ibn Anas went to visit az-Zuhri and they saw that az-Zuhri's eyes became moist when he saw them and he bowed his head. He had a black cloth on his face. They asked, 'How are you, Abu Bakr?' He replied. 'By Allah, my eye is afflicted.' 'Ubaydullah said, 'We have come to review some of your *hadiths* with you.' He said, 'I am ill.' 'Ubaydullah said, 'O Allah, forgiveness! By Allah, we did not do this to you when we used to go to Salim ibn 'Abdullah.' Then 'Ubadyullah said, 'Read, Malik.' I saw Malik read to him.

"Then az-Zuhri said, 'That is enough for you, may Allah excuse you.' Then 'Ubaydullah repeated, 'Read.'" 'Abdu'r-Rahman said, "I saw Malik read to az-Zuhri."

'Amr ibn Dinar said, "I have not see anyone with more insight into *hadith* than az-Zuhri."

Sufyan said, "Az-Zuhri sat 'Ali ibn Zayd with him on his bed. Az-Zuhri was wearing two garments which he had washed and they smelled of soap. He said, 'Will you not order them to be fumigated?' Az-Zuhri came at *Maghrib* and entered the mosque. I do not know whether he looked around or not. He sat in a corner, while 'Amr sat down next to one of the columns. A man said to him, 'This is 'Amr,' so he sat down with him. 'Amr said to himself, 'What kept you from going anywhere except where I was sitting?' Then they talked for a time and asked each other questions. When az-Zuhri related, he used to say, 'So-and-so related to me, and he was one of the vessels of knowledge.'"

He said, "'Abdu'r-Rahman ibn Mahdi reported that Wuhayb heard Ayyub say, 'I have not seen anyone with more knowledge than az-Zuhri.' Sakhr ibn Juwayriyya said, 'Not even al-Hasan?' He repeated, 'I have not see anyone with more knowledge than az-Zuhri.'"

Burd ibn Makhul said, "I did not see anyone with more knowledge of a past *sunna* than az-Zuhri."

Malik ibn Anas said, "We used to sit with az-Zuhri and with Muhammad ibn al-Munkadir. Az-Zuhri said, 'Ibn 'Umar said such-and-such.' After that, we sat with him and we asked him, 'Those *hadiths* which you related from Ibn 'Umar – from whom did you report them?' He said, 'His son Salim.'"

Salama ibn al-'Ayyar listened to az-Zuhri who said, "What are these *hadiths* which have no halter or rein (i.e. no reliable *isnad*)?"

Mu'awiya ibn Salih said that Abu Jabala lent Ibn Shihab az-Zuhri 30 dinars in his house and then he paid them back along with ten dinars more. He said to him, "Do you not fear that something will be held against us for this?" Az-Zuhri laughed and said, "This is your right which we have repaid to you, and this is a gift which we have given you."

One of az-Zuhri's uncles said, "Az-Zuhri employed fifteen women for a night, and he paid each servant 30 dinars."

Makhrama ibn Bukayr said, "I met Ibn Shihab on the road while I was going to Egypt and he was coming from Syria. I saw him praying in the rain without a cloak."

Az-Zanji said, "I saw az-Zuhri using black dye." Malik said, "He used to use henna."

Al-Munkadir ibn Muhammad said, "I saw the mark of prostration on az-Zuhri's forehead. There was no mark on his nose."

Ibrahim ibn Sa'd reported from his father that the khalif Hisham settled a debt of 80,000 dirhams which Ibn Shihab owed. Ibrahim said, "I heard my father criticise Ibn Shihab for his debts and say to him, 'Hisham paid 80,000 dirhams for you and you know what the Messenger of Allah صلعم said about debts.' Ibn Shihab told my father, 'I rely on my property. By Allah, if I had this room and filled it with gold or silver to its roof, I would not think it a substitute for my property.'" Ibrahim said, "They were in the room."

Abu'z-Zinad said, "Az-Zuhri used to always tell Hisham to dismiss al-Walid ibn Yazid and criticise him, mentioning terrible matters which should not be said, even accusing him of paedophilia. He said to Hisham, 'You can only dismiss him.' Hisham could not do that because of the covenant he had made, but he was not offended by what az-Zuhri did, hoping that people would rally against him."

Abu'z- Zinad said, "One day I was with Hisham in the region of Fustat and I heard some of what az-Zuhri was saying about al-Walid, but I paid no attention. The attendant came and said, 'Al-Walid is at the door.' – 'Admit him,' he said. I brought him in and Hisham made room for him on his rug. I could see anger and evil in al-Walid's face. When al-Walid was appointed, he sent for me, 'Abdu'r-Rahman ibn al-Qasim, Ibn al-Munkadir, and Rabi'a. He sent for me alone at night. Supper was served and after some talk he asked me, 'Ibn Dhakwan, do you remember the day when I came to see Squinteye while you were with him and az-Zuhri was criticising me? Do you recall any of what he said on that day?' I replied, 'Amir al-Mu'minin, I remember the day you came and I saw the anger in your face.' He said, 'The servant whom you saw at Hisham's head conveyed all of that to me. I was standing at the door before I entered. He told me that you did not say anything concerning it.' I said, 'Yes, I did not say anything about it, Amir al-Mu'minin.' He said, 'I made a pledge with Allah Almighty that if he gave me power as I have today, I would kill az-Zuhri – but he has escaped me.'"

Az-Zuhri died in 124 AH some months before Hisham. Al-Walid I was keen to get his hands on him.

Muhammad ibn 'Umar said, "Az-Zuhri was born in 58 AH at the end of Mu'awiya's khalifate. It was the year in which 'A'isha, the wife of the Prophet صلعم died. Az-Zuhri went to his property at Thiluya Bashghab in 124 AH and stayed there. He became ill there and died. He left a will that he should be buried in the middle of the road. He died on the 17th Ramadan 124 AH at the age of 75."

Al-Husayn ibn al-Mutawakkil al-Asqalani said, "I saw the grave of az-Zuhri at Adami which is behind Shaghb and Bada. It is where the district of Palestine starts and the Hijaz ends. Az-Zuhri's estate was there. I saw that his grave was raised and white-washed. They said that az-Zuhri was reliable, and had a lot of *hadiths*, knowledge and transmission. He was a *faqih* with vast knowledge."

His brother, 'Abdullah ibn Muslim

His mother was a daughter of Uhban ibn Lu't. His children were Muhammad, Ibrahim and Umm Muhammad, whose mother was Umm Habib ibn Huwaytib.

The nephew of az-Zuhri said that his father was older than az-Zuhri and that his *kunya* was Abu Muhammad. He died before az-Zuhri. He met Ibn 'Umar and related from him and others. He was reliable, with few *hadiths*.

Muhammad ibn al-Munkadir ibn 'Abdullah

His mother was an *umm walad* and his *kunya* was Abu 'Abdullah. His children were 'Umar, Abdu'l-Malik, 'Abdullah, Yusuf, Ibrahim and Da'ud, by an *umm walad*.

Abu Ma'shar reported, "Al-Munkadir visited 'A'isha and said, 'I have a need, so help me.' She replied, 'I do not have anything. If I had 10,000 dirhams I would send them to you.' After he left her, 10,000 dirhams came to her from Khalid ibn Usayd. She remarked, 'I was being tested!' Then she sent for al-Munkadir and gave them to him. Thereupon he went to the market and bought a slave girl for 1,000 dirhams who bore him three children. They were the worshippers of Madina: Muhammad, Abu Bakr, and 'Umar, the sons of al-Munkadir."

Sufyan said, "Muhammad ibn al-Munkadir was worshipping when he was a lad, and they were a people of a house of worship. His mother used to tell him, 'Do not joke with the children.'"

He said, "He was asked, 'Which action is best?' He replied, 'Bringing happiness to the believer.' It was said, 'What remains which is pleasant?' He said, 'Being generous to brothers.'"

He said, "He prayed over a man called Baqara who had been a mischief-maker. He was asked, 'Do you pray over Baqara?' He said, 'I do not want Allah to see that in my heart I think that His mercy does not extend to Baqara,' or he said, 'to everyone'."

Ibn Abi Zinad said, "Muhammad ibn al-Munkadir, Safwan ibn Sulaym, Abu Hazim, Sulayman ibn Sulaym and Yazid ibn Khusayfa were people of worship and prayer. They used to meet after *'Asr* and after *'Isha'*. They related *hadiths* and they did not part until each of them had said something and made supplication. They were kind to one another. They used to attend the *'Ids* every year with Abu Sakhr al-Ayli, one of the devout worshippers. They met 'Umar ibn Dharr and he recounted stories to them and reminded them of the Next World. They continued like this until the *'Id* was over. They only met with him every *'Id*."

Ja'far ibn Sulayman reported that Muhammad ibn al-Munkadir used to place his cheek on the earth and then say to his mother, "O mother, put your foot on my cheek."

Ibn al-Mubarak said that Muhammad ibn al-Munkadir said, "''Umar spent the night in prayer and I spent the night at the feet of my mother – and I prefer my night to his night."

Sufyan said that Ibn al-Munkadir used to spend the night praying and he would say, "How many an eye is now awake in quest of my provision!"

He said, "He had a neighbour who was suffering and who used to raise his voice shouting in the night. So Muhammad raised his voice in praise. He was asked about that and replied, 'He is raising his voice with weeping and so I raise my voice with blessing.'"

Muhammad ibn Muhammad said, "Muhammad ibn al-Munkadir was asked, 'Can you make *hajj* when you have a debt?' He replied, '*Hajj* settles the debt.'"

Muhammad ibn al-Munkadir said, "I fight using supplication."

He said, "A Yemeni man entrusted him with a hundred dinars and went to the frontier. Muhammad asked him, 'If we need to, can we spend it until you return to us?' – 'Yes,' he replied. So he spent it. The man returned, wanting to go to Yemen and Muhammad did not have it. He asked him, 'When do you want to go?' He said, 'Tomorrow, Allah willing.' So Muhammad went to the mosque and spent the night there until dawn, praying to Allah for those dinars to come to him by whomever He wished and from wherever He wished. So someone brought them to him while he was in prostration – in a bag which he put in his sandal. He touched it with his hand and the bag contained a hundred dinars. He praised Allah and returned to his house. In the morning he gave them to their owner."

Muhammad ibn 'Umar said, "Our companions report that the one who put it there was 'Amir ibn 'Abdullah ibn az-Zubayr. He often used to do that."

Al-Hurr ibn Yazid al-Hadhdha' said, "In the case of Muhammad ibn al-Munkadir, Safwan ibn Sulaym was praying in the mosque in the middle of the night when someone came and placed fifty dinars in his sandal. He took it and praised Allah. Then Safwan sent to his house and said to his female client, Sallama, 'My brother Muhammad spent the night in distress. Take these dinars to him. Five, or four, of them will be enough for us.' She said, 'Now?' He said, 'Yes, you will find him praying at this moment, asking Allah, "Bring them to me from wherever You wish, however You wish and from whomever You wish."' She took 46, or 45, dinars to him. She stood listening to him saying, 'O Allah, bring them from wherever You wish, however You wish and from whomever You wish – now! O Allah!' He praised Allah for that."

'Abdu'r-Rahman ibn Abi'z-Zinad or another of his companions said, "Muhammad ibn al-Munkadir went on *hajj* every year and a number of his companions went on *hajj* with him. One day while he was in one of the houses of Makka he said to a slave of his, 'Go and buy such-and-such for us.' The boy replied, 'By Allah, we do not have anything, neither a little nor a lot, not one dirham or more!' He said, 'Go! Allah will bring it.' He asked, 'From where?' He said, 'Glory be to Allah.' Then he raised his voice in the *talbiya* and his companions who were with him repeated the *talbiya*. Ibrahim ibn Hisham was making *hajj* that year and heard their voices. He asked, 'Who are they?' He was told, 'Muhammad ibn al-Munakdir and his companions are making *hajj* and Muhammad is bearing their expense. He is paying for their transport and providing for them.' He said, 'Muhammad must be helped in what he is doing!' and he sent him 4,000 dirhams straight away. Muhammad gave them to his slave and told him, 'Bother you! Did I not tell you to buy for us what I told you and that Allah would bring this? Allah has brought it to us as you see, so go and buy what I told you!'"

Munkadir, the son of Muhammad ibn al-Munkadir, said, "We suffered a severe drought in Madina for some years. Muhammad said, 'By Allah, I was in the mosque after the middle of the night and there was not a cloud in the sky. At the front of the mosque I saw a man concealed in his cloak. I heard him making intense supplication. I heard him say, "I swear an oath to You, O Lord," and he repeated it. He continued to repeat his oath, "O Lord, this minute!" He said, 'By Allah, we immediately saw the clouds collecting and before I had not seen even a puff or anything in the sky. Then it rained and it poured. The sky contained such rain as I have never seen! Then I heard him say, "O Lord, no destruction or drowning in it! No affliction or obliteration in it!" When the Imam had said the *salam* for *Subh*, the man left concealing himself. I followed him to the feltmakers' alley where he entered a dwelling. In the morning, I inquired about him and they said, "This is Ziyad an-Najjar. This is a man who has no bed. He strives throughout the night in prayer and supplication, and he is one of the supplicants. He conceals every action he does."' Muhammad said, 'I remembered the words of the Messenger of Allahصلعم, "If the one with a hidden difficulty swears an oath to Allah, He will settle it."'"

Muhammad said, "I remember that after that I came across him and he disliked some of what I mentioned to him. He said, 'Conceal this, Abu 'Abdullah. Its repayment is with the one for whom we do it.'" Muhammad ibn al-Munkadir said, "I did not mention it after he forbade me. I said to myself, 'The supplication of a man like this is desired – and He knows that there are righteous people.'"

Malik ibn Anas said that he saw Muhammad ibn al-Munkadir in two red garments and two saffron garments which were not clean.

'Abdu'l-Malik ibn Qudama said, "I saw Muhammad ibn al-Munkadir praying with the buttons of his shirt undone."

Muhammad ibn 'Umar said, "Muhammad ibn al-Munkadir listened to Jabir ibn 'Abdullah, Umayma bint Ruqayqa, 'Urwa ibn az-Zubayr, 'Abdu'r-Rahman ibn Sa'id, Rabi'a ibn 'Abdullah ibn al-Hudayr, his uncle, al-Hasan al-Basri, and Sa'id ibn Jubayr."

He was reliable, a scrupulous worshipper, with few *hadiths* and mostly *isnads* from Jabir ibn 'Abdullah.

Muhammad ibn al-Munkadir died in Madina in either 130 or 131 AH.

'Umar ibn al-Munkadir

His mother was an *umm walad*, Umm Muhammad ibn al-Munkadir. 'Umar had no children. He was one of the striving men of worship.

Nafi' ibn 'Umar al-Jumahi reported that the mother of 'Umar ibn al-Munkadir said, "I would like to see you sleep." He said, "O mother, I face the night and it alarms me. *Subh* finds me without having fulfilled my need."

Nafi' ibn 'Umar said, "A man brought some money to Madina and said, 'Show me a man of Quraysh to whom I can offered this money.' They directed him to 'Umar ibn al-Munkadir. He gave it to him but he refused to accept it. He said, 'He refuses. Who besides him?' They said, 'We do not know anyone who resembles him except Abu Bakr ibn al-Munkadir.' So he offered it to him but he refused to accept it. He asked, 'Who after them?' – 'Muhammad ibn al-Munkadir,' they said. He went to him and he refused to accept it. The man said, 'O people of Madina! If you can all be like the children of al-Munkadir, then do so.'"

Muhammad ibn Layth said, "They mentioned something in the house of 'Umar ibn al-Munkadir and his mother said, 'It was like such-and-such.' 'Umar disagreed with her. When they left, they investigated 'Umar's statement and found that he had remembered it better than she had. He said, 'Mother, I want to you to put your foot on my cheek.' She asked, 'My son, why do you say that?' He continued to ask her to put her foot on his cheek."

'Abdullah ibn al-Mubarak said, "Abu Hazim gathered some of the reciters of the people of the mosque and they went to 'Umar ibn al-Munkadir. Abu Hazim spoke to him about easing the worship he had imposed on himself. He replied, 'I face the night and it alarms me. When I read the Qur'an, I recite it and one *ayat* follows another. The night ends and I still have not completed my need.'"

Nafi' ibn 'Umar said, "When the pain of 'Umar ibn al-Munkadir became intense, they invited Abu Hazim to see him. He was anxious and Abu Hazim asked him about that. He said, 'I fear that something will reach me from Allah from where I do not reckon, [referring to Qur'an 59:2].'" Nafi' said, "The *ayat* used to make him anxious and worried. He was a scrupulous worshipper."

Abu Bakr ibn al-Munkadir

His mother was an *umm walad* who was also the mother of Muhammad and 'Umar. His children were 'Abdullah and Ibrahim whose mother was 'Abda bint 'Abdullah.

Sa'id ibn 'Umar said, "A bedouin entered Madina and saw the situation of the Banu'l-Munkadir and their excellent position among people. He left Madina and a man met him and said, 'How did you find people? How did you find the people of Madina?' He replied, 'Well. If you are able to be like one of the family of al-Munkadir, then do so.'"

Muhammad ibn 'Umar said, "Abu Bakr was older than his brother Muhammad. He was reliable, with few *hadiths*."

Muhammad ibn al-Mundhir ibn az-Zubayr

His children were Sa'id, whose mother was Na'ila bint 'Abdullah; az-Zubayr and 'Atika, whose mother was al-Fari'a bint Muslim; Fulayh and Fulayha, whose mother was Fakhita bint 'Abdullah; and 'Ubayda, 'Umar, 'Ubaydullah, al-Mundhir, 'Amr and Umm 'Amr by an *umm walad*.

Abu'z-Zinad said, "Muhammad ibn al-Mundhir was one of the most forbearing and noble of people. When he passed along the road, fires were put out, out of respect for him. They said, 'This is Muhammad ibn al-Mundhir. Do not smoke him.' One day I saw him when the strap of his sandal broke. He removed the other one and left them without stopping for them."

A man of the family of Khalid ibn az-Zubayr exasperated him about something and he turned to him and said, "It is rare that the fools of a people are not abased."

Salih ibn Ibrahim ibn 'Abdu'r-Rahman

His mother was Umm Kulthum bint Sa'd. His children were Salim, Sa'd, Umm Kulthum, Umm 'Amr and 'Uthayma, whose mother was az-Za'um bint 'Ubaydullah; and 'Atika, whose mother was Umm Ishaq bint 'Umar.

He had few *hadiths* and died in Madina while Hisham was khalif and Ibrahim ibn Hisham was governor over Madina.

His brother, Sa'd ibn Ibrahim

Abu Ishaq. His mother was Umm Kulthum bint Sa'd ibn Abi Waqqas. His children were Ishaq and Amina, whose mother was Umm Kulthum bint Muhammad; Ibrahim and Sawda, whose mother was Amatu'r-Rahman; and Muhammad and Isma'il, by an *umm walad*. He was appointed qadi of Madina. He was reliable, with a lot of *hadith*. Sa'id ibn Banik said, "I saw Sa'd ibn Ibrahim giving judgement in the mosque."

Shu'ba reported that Sa'd ibn Ibrahim used to recite the entire Qur'an in twenty-four hours. He said that Sa'd used to fast all the time and recite the entire Qur'an every twenty-four hours.

Ibrahim ibn Sa'd said, "I remember my father had a number of turbans – I cannot remember how many – and he used to wear a turban and put a turban on me when I was young. I saw the children putting on turbans. I noticed that when people left *'Asr* and attended *Maghrib*, they removed the tunic and wore two garments."

They report that Sa'd ibn Ibrahim died in Madina in 127 AH at the age of 72.

'Abdu'l-Malik ibn Abi Bakr ibn 'Abdu'r-Rahman

His mother was Sara bint Hisham ibn al-Walid. His children were Rubayha – who married Suhayl ibn 'Abdu'l-'Aziz ibn Marwan – whose mother was Umm Hakam bint 'Umar. He was generous and wealthy. He is related from him and he died at the beginning of the khalifate of Hisham. He is reliable with *hadiths*.

He also had a brother, **al-Harith,** whose children were 'Abdullah, al-Mughira and Sara, whose mother was Kulthum bint Sa'id. He had another brother, **'Abdu'r-Rahman ibn Abi Bakr ibn 'Abdu'r-Rahman**, who had the same mother and is related from. There was also another brother, **'Umar,** whose mother was Qurayba bint 'Abdullah. His children were 'Isa, 'Abdullah and Zaynab, whose mother was Umm 'Asim bint Sulayman. He is related from.

'Abdu'r-Rahman ibn Aban ibn 'Uthman ibn 'Affan

His mother was Umm Sa'd bint 'Abdu'r-Rahman, whose mother was Umm Hasan bint az-Zubayr, whose mother was Asma' bint Abi Bakr. His children were Aban, 'Uthman and 'Atika, whose mother was Hantama bint Muhammad; and al-Walid, by an *umm walad*.

Musa ibn Muhammad said, "I did not see anyone combine the *deen*, authority and nobility more than 'Abdu'r-Rahman ibn Aban."

Muhammad ibn 'Umar said, "Muhammad and 'Abdullah – the sons of Abu Bakr, Bakr ibn Muhammad and other people of Madina related from him. He had few *hadiths*."

'Uthman said, "There is no hindering purchase for personal advantage. When the boundaries are set, there is no pre-emption."

Mus'ab ibn 'Uthman said, "'Abdu'r-Rahman ibn Aban used to buy for the People of the House and then commanded that they be clothed and oiled and then presented to him. He said, 'You are free for the sake of Allah. I am protecting myself against the agonies of death by you.' He died in his sleep in the mosque (i.e. after the prayer)."

Mus'ab said, "I heard a man of the people of knowledge say, 'The reason for the intensity of worship of 'Ali ibn 'Abdullah ibn 'Abbas was that he looked at 'Abdu'r-Rahman ibn Aban. He said, 'By Allah, I am more entitled to that than he is and closer to the Messenger of Allah صلعم!' So he devoted himself to worship."

Abu Bakr ibn 'Abdullah the younger

His son was an *umm walad*. Abu Bakr was his name. His children were 'Abdullah, 'Ubaydullah, Abu 'Uthman, Muhammad, Rabah, 'Abda, Layla and Umm Salama, whose mother was Umm Abiha bint 'Abdu'r-Rahman; Sa'id, whose mother was an *umm walad*; and Kathir, Aban, 'Umar, and 'Abdu'r-Rahman, by *umm walads*. He related from Sulayman ibn Abi Hathma. He had few *hadiths*.

'Abdu'l-Malik ibn 'Ubayd ibn Sa'id

His mother was Umm as-Saffah bint as-Saffah. Her children were al-Miswar and Da'ud, whose mother was Umm Hakim bint Da'ud. His *kunya* was Abu'l-Miswar.

Abu'l-Aswad Yatim 'Urwa

His name was Muhammad ibn 'Abdu'r-Rahman. His mother was *umm walad*. His children were 'Abdu'r-Rahman, Umm Kathir, Umm Hakim, Umm 'Abdullah and Umm az-Zubayr, whose mother was an *umm walad*. He died at the end of the Umayyads and is now without descendants. He was reliable, with few *hadiths*.

He related from Malik ibn Anas and others. Al-Aswad ibn Nawfal was one of the emigrants to Abyssinia and died there.

'Abdu'r-Rahman ibn al-Qasim ibn Muhammad

His mother was Qurayba bint 'Abdu'r-Rahman ibn Abi Bakr. His children were Isma'il and Asma', whose mother was Habbana bint 'Abdu'r-Rahman; and 'Abdullah who became qadi of Madina for al-Hasan ibn Zayd while al-Mansur was khalif, and whose mother was 'Atika bint Salih. His *kunya* was Abu Muhammad.

Aflah ibn Humayd said, "'Abdu'r-Rahman's ring was engraved with his name and his father's name."

Malik ibn Anas said that he saw 'Abdu'r-Rahman wearing a Harawi yellow shirt and a rose-coloured cloak.

'Abdu'r-Rahman ibn Abi'z-Zinad said, "When al-Walid II became khalif, he sent for my father and Abu'z-Zinad, and for 'Abdu'r-Rahman ibn al-Qasim, Muhammad ibn al-Munakdir, and Rab'a. They went to him in Syria. 'Abdu'r-Rahman fell ill and died at Faddayn in Syria while they were there. He was scrupulous, with a lot of *hadiths*.

Isma'il ibn 'Amr ibn Sa'id ibn al-'As

His mother was Umm Habib bint Hurayth. His children were 'Abdu'r-Rahman, 'Ubaydullah and Umm Isma'il, by an *umm walad*.

Isma'il's *kunya* was Abu Muhammad. He settled at al-A'was, eleven miles from Madina on the Iraqi road. He was a devout worshipper.

'Umar II said, "If I could do so, I would appoint al-Qasim ibn Muhammad or the man at al-A'was," that is, Isma'il ibn 'Amr.

Isma'il lived until the time of the Abbasids. It was said to him during the time when Da'ud came to Madina as governor of Makka and Madina, "Perhaps you should make yourself scarce." He said,

"No, by Allah, not for an instant." Da'ud intended to do something to him but was told, "There is no need for you to lay yourself open to the invocation of Isma'il against you." He left him alone, but he imprisoned Isma'il ibn Umayya and Ayyub ibn Musa in Madina. Ism'ail ibn 'Amr lived for only a short time after that.

Sulayman ibn Bilal, Abu Bakr ibn 'Abdullah ibn Abi Sabra and others related from him. He had few *hadiths*.

Ayyub ibn Musa ibn 'Amr

His mother was an *umm walad*. He had a son Muhammad, whose mother was Umm Habib bint Umayya. Ayyub was governor of Ta'if for one of the Umayyads. He was reliable and had *hadiths*.

'Abdullah ibn 'Ikrima ibn 'Abdu'r-Rahman

His *kunya* was Abu Muhammad and his mother was the daughter of 'Abdullah ibn Abi 'Amr. His children were 'Abdu'r-Rahman, Zaynab, Umm Hakim, Umm Salama and Fatima, whose mother was Umm 'Amr bint Abi Bakr; 'Ikrima, whose mother was Habiba bint Ibrahim; Ishaq, whose mother was Sara bint al-Muthanna; Abu Bakr, 'Umar, 'Uthman, Hisham, Umm Salama and Umm al-Qasim, whose mother was Mulayka bint Hijr; al-Mughira, whose mother was Umm 'Uthman bint Bistam; and 'Abdu'l-Malik and Khalid, whose mother was an *umm walad*. 'Abdullah had few *hadiths*.

His brother, al-Harith ibn 'Ikrima

His mother was the daughter of 'Abdullah ibn Abi 'Amr. His children were al-Mughira, whose mother was Salima bint Humayd; 'Abdullah and Umm Hakim, whose mother was Salama bint Muhammad; and another son whose mother was Umm Hakim bint Hujr. He had very few *hadiths*.

Abu Bakr ibn 'Ubaydullah ibn 'Abdullah ibn 'Umar ibn al-Khattab

His mother was 'A'isha bint 'Abdu'r-Rahman ibn Abi Bakr. His children were Muhammad, Khalid, Bilal, Ubayya and 'A'isha, whose mother was Umm Husayn bint Khalid. He related from Ibn 'Umar.

He died early on. He was the father of Khalid ibn Abi Bakr. Az-Zuhri related from him. He is reliable, with few *hadiths*.

Al-Qasim ibn 'Ubaydullah ibn 'Abdullah ibn 'Umar ibn al-Khattab

His mother was Umm 'Abdullah bint Muhammad. He died while Marwan ibn Muhammad was khalif. He had few *hadiths*.

'Umar ibn 'Abdullah ibn 'Abdullah ibn 'Umar ibn al-Khattab

His mother was Umm Salama bint al-Mukhtar. His children were 'Abdullah, 'Abdu'r-Rahman and 'Ubaydullah, by *umm walads*; and Asma', whose mother was an *umm walad*. He had few *hadiths*. Abu'z-Zinad related from him.

'Abdu'l-'Aziz ibn 'Abdullah ibn 'Umar ibn al-Khattab

His mother was Umm 'Abdullah bint 'Abdu'r-Rahman. His children were Muhammad, whose mother was Amatu'l-Hamid bint Salama; 'Umar, whose mother was Kayyisa bint 'Abdu'l-Hamid; 'Abdullah, who is al-'Abid, whose mother was Amatu'l-Hamid bint 'Abdullah; Ishaq, whose mother was al-Fari'a bint 'Abdu'r-Rahman; Amina, who first married Muhammad ibn 'Abdullah and then 'Abdullah ibn Muhammad, and whose mother was Umm Salama bint Ma'qil; and 'Umar, Abu Bakr and 'Abdu'l-Hamid, whose mother was an *umm walad*.

'Umar II appointed him over Madina, Kirman, and Yamana. Husayn ibn 'Ali rebelled while 'Umar II was governor of Madina and his brother, 'Abdullah ibn 'Abdu'l-'Aziz commanded that 'Umar II should not pray over him. He avoided him until he died.

'Abdullah ibn Waqid ibn 'Abdullah ibn 'Umar ibn al-Khattab

His mother was Amatullah bint 'Abdullah. His children were Waqid, Umm 'Uthman, Ruqayya, Sawda, and 'Atika, whose mother was Umm Jamil bint Abi Bakr. He related from Ibn 'Umar and Yahya ibn Sa'id, and Usama ibn Zayd related from him.

He died early on in 110 AH while Hisham was khalif.

Abu 'Ubayda ibn 'Ubaydullah ibn 'Abdullah ibn 'Umar ibn al-Khattab

His mother was Umm 'Abdullah bint al-Qasim. His children were Muhammad and al-Qasim, whose mother was Juwayriyya bint 'Ubaydullah.

Ja'far ibn Salim ibn 'Abdullah ibn 'Umar ibn al-Khattab

His mother was an *umm walad*. He related from his father and from al-Qasim ibn Muhammad. 'Abdullah ibn 'Umar related from him.

Abu Bakr ibn Salim ibn 'Abdullah

His mother was Umm al-Hakam bint Yazid. His children were Salim and Hushayma, whose mother was Burayha bint al-Mujabbir; Muhammad and Amatu'l-Hamid, whose mother was an *umm walad*; and 'Umar, whose mother was Sawda bint al-Mujabbir. He is related from.

Muhammad ibn Zayd ibn 'Abdullah ibn 'Umar ibn al-Khattab

His mother was Umm Hakim bint 'Ubaydullah. His children were Waqid, 'Umar, Abu Bakr, Zayd, 'Asim, Umm Hakim and Fatima, whose mother was an *umm walad*; 'Abdu'r-Rahman the elder, Bilal and 'Abdu'r-Rahman the younger, whose mother was Qurratu'l-'Ayn bint Huwayy; and Abu 'Ubayda, whose mother was an *umm walad*.

'Asim ibn 'Ubaydullah ibn 'Umar ibn al-Khattab

His mother was Umm Salama bint 'Abdullah. He lived to the time of the Abbasids and went to Abu'l-'Abbas 'Abdullah, the first Abbasid khalif. He had a lot of *hadith*, but is not used as evidence.

'Umar ibn Hafs ibn 'Asim ibn 'Umar ibn al-Khattab

His children were Abu Bakr, 'Ubaydullah, Zayd, 'Abdullah, 'Abdu'r-Rahman, Muhammad, 'Asim, Umm 'Asim, Umm Humayd, Umm 'Isa and Umm Miskin, whose mother was Fatima bint 'Umar ibn'Asim.

'Abdullah ibn 'Urwa ibn az-Zubayr

His mother was Fakhita bint al-Aswad. His children were 'Umar, Salih and 'A'isha, whose mother was Umm Hakim bint 'Abdullah; Salama, Salim, Musalim, Khadija and Safiyya, whose mother was Umm Salama bint Hamza. His *kunya* was Abu Bakr. Az-Zuhri related from him. He had few *hadiths*.

Sufyan ibn 'Uyayna said, "It was said to 'Abdullah ibn 'Urwa, 'You left Madina, the Abode of the *Hijra* and *Sunna*. If you were to return, you could meet people and people could meet you.' He asked, 'Who are the people? There are two kinds of people: someone who gloats over someone's loss, or someone who envies someone's blessing.'"

Yusuf ibn Ya'qub said, "I went with my father on an errand and he said to me, 'Do you have this shaykh? He is one of those remaining among Quraysh. You will find what you wish of *hadith* and noble opinion with him.' (He meant 'Abdullah ibn 'Urwa.) When we went to him, my father spoke to him for a long time. Then my father talked about the Umayyads and their behaviour and what people had experienced from them. He said, 'The hopes of the people of Quraysh were cut short.' 'Abdullah said, 'People will never have a sound position regarding Quraysh as long the Banu so-and-so are not appointed. When the Banu so-and-so are appointed, their ambitions will be ended.' Salam al-A'war, our companion, said to me, 'The Banu Hashim?' He indicated his affirmation by nodding."

Yahya ibn 'Urwa ibn az-Zubayr

His *kunya* was Abu 'Urwa. His mother was Umm Yahya bint al-Hakam. His children were 'Urwa, whose mother was Zaynab bint 'Ubayda; Marwan the elder, Muhammad the elder, az-Zubayr, Umm Yahya and Asma', whose mother was Umm Ibrahim bint Ibrahim; al-Hakam, Umm 'Abdullah and 'A'isha, whose mother was Umm

Ibrahim bint Ibrahim; and 'Abdu'l-Malik, Marwan and Muhammad, by an *umm walad*. Az-Zuhri related from him. He had few *hadiths*.

Muhammad ibn 'Urwa ibn az-Zubayr

His mother was Umm Yahya bint al-Hakam. He had a daughter, Umm Yahya, whose mother was Hafsa bint 'Abdu'r-Rahman.

'Uthman ibn 'Urwa ibn az-Zubayr

His mother was Umm Yahya bint al-Hakam. His children were 'Urwa, Abu Bakr, 'Abdu'r-Rahman, Yazid, Umm Yahya, Kulthum and Hafsa, whose mother was Qurayba bint 'Abdu'r-Rahman; Yahya and Hisham, by an *umm walad*; Khadija, Ubayya and Fatima, whose mother was Umm Habib bint 'Abdullah.

He had few *hadiths*. He died at the beginning of the khalifate of al-Mansur. He is related from.

Hisham ibn 'Urwa ibn az-Zubayr

His mother was an *umm walad*. His children were az-Zubayr, 'Urwa and Muhammad, whose mother was Fatima bint al-Mundhir. His *kunya* was Abu'-Mundhir.

Hisham said that his father told him, "I used to write and then erase it. I would give my family and wealth not to have erased it."

Muhammad ibn 'Umar said that he listened to Hisham, who married Fatima bint al-Mundhir. Hisham related from his father and from his wife, Fatima bint al-Mundhir. He related from Wahb ibn Kaysan. He was reliable and firm, with a lot of *hadith,* and he was an authority.

Shu'ba said, "Hisham did not listen to the *hadith* of his father about touching the penis," i.e. the *hadith* of Busra bint Safwan. Yahya said, "I asked Yahya about it and he said that he had reported it to him."

Hisham died in Baghdad and was buried in the Khayzuran cemetery in 146 AH.

'Ubaydullah ibn 'Urwa ibn az-Zubayr

His mother was Asma' bint Salama. His children were 'Urwa, 'Asim, Mus'ab and Hafsa, whose mother was the daughter of Riyah ibn Hafs. 'Ubaydullah was the youngest of 'Urwa's children. He related a dream from him but he did not hear any *hadith* from him. 'Ubaydullah lived to meet Muhammad ibn Umar al-Waqidi. I said to him, "Son, how old were you the day that 'Ubaydullah ibn 'Urwa died?" – "Nine," he replied.

'Umar ibn 'Abdullah ibn 'Urwa

His mother was Umm Hakim bint 'Abdullah. He had no children. He related from 'Urwa ibn az-Zubayr and al-Qasim ibn Muhammad. Ibn Jurayh related from him. He had few *hadiths*.

Yahya ibn 'Abbad ibn 'Abdullah ibn az-Zubayr

His mother was 'A'isha bint 'Abdu'r-Rahman. His children were Ya'qub, Ishaq, 'Abdu'r-Rahman and 'Abdu'l-Wahhab, whose mother was Asma' bint Thabit; 'Abdu'l-Malik, by an *umm walad*; 'A'isha and Sawfa, whose mother was Asma' bint 'Urwa, whose mother was Sawda bint 'Abdullah, whose mother was Safiya bint Abi 'Ubayd, whose mother was 'Atika bint Usayd, whose mother was Zaynab bint Abi 'Amra.

'Abdu'r-Rahman ibn Abi'z-Zinad said, "Yahya ibn 'Abbad had manliness. I did not see any youth more blessed than him."

'Abdullah ibn Abi Bakr and Muhammad ibn Ishaq related from him. He died early on at the age of 36. He was reliable, with a lot of *hadiths*.

Salama ibn Abi Salama ibn 'Abdu'r-Rahman ibn 'Awf

His mother was an *umm walad*. His children were Marwan, 'Umar, Muhammad and Umm Salama, whose mother was Umm 'Abbad bint Ibrahim; and Amatu'l-Wahid, whose mother was a Berber *umm walad*. Az-Zuhri related from him. He has few *hadiths*.

His brother, 'Umar ibn Abi Salama ibn 'Abdu'r-Rahman ibn 'Awf

His mother's name is not known. His children were Yahya, Ibrahim, Umm Muhammad and Tumadir, whose mother was Habbaba bint Muhammad.

Ya'qub ibn Ibrahim reported that 'Abdullah ibn 'Ali killed 'Umar ibn Abi Salama when they rebelled in Syria. 'Umar was with the sons of his sister among the Banu Umayya, and he was killed with them. Abu 'Awana and Hushaym related from him. He had a lot of *hadiths* but his *hadiths* are not used as evidence.

'Abdu'l-Majid ibn Sahl ibn 'Abdu'r-Rahman ibn 'Awf

His mother was an *umm walad*. His children were Suhayl, Sawra and Amatu'l-'Aziz, whose mother was Umm 'Amr bint 'Abdu'l-Zayd.

Al-Hasan ibn 'Uthman ibn 'Abdu'r-Rahman

His mother was Umm al-Hakam bint Sa'd ibn Abi Waqqas. His children were Jabir, Yahya and Sa'd, whose mother was Umm Yahya bint Yahya; Ibrahim and Umm al-Hakam, whose mother was an *umm walad*; and Fatima, whose mother was 'Atika bint Yazid.

'Abdu'r-Rahman ibn Humayd ibn 'Abdu'r-Rahman

His mother was an *umm walad*. His children were Humayd, Ibrahim, Humayd or Umm Humayd, whose mother was Amatu'r-Rahman bint Muhammad; and al-Qasim and Sa'id, who is Kura', whose mother was Umama bint al-Qasim.

He was reliable and had *hadiths*. He related from his father, Sa'id ibn al-Musayyab, Ibrahim ibn 'Abdu'r-Rahman and al-A'raj.

He died at the beginning of the khalifate of al-Mansur.

Ghurayr

His full name is 'Abdu'r-Rahman ibn al-Mughira. His mother was Humayda bint 'Abdullah. His children were Muhammad, Ibrahim the elder, Ya'qub, Humayd, Umm Hakim and al-Fari'a, whose mother was Hind bint Marwan; Sulayman and Ibrahim the younger, whose mother was Umm Kathir bint Muhammad; Yahya and ar-Raghum, whose mother was the daughter of Salih ibn Ibrahim; and 'Isa and Ghurayr, whose mother was 'Atika, the daughter of a Berber *umm walad*.

Abu Bakr ibn Hafs ibn 'Umar ibn Sa'd

His mother was Hunayda bint 'Umar. His children were 'Abdu'l-Malik, Muhammad and Hafsa, whose mother was Burayha bint Muhammad; and al-Muhabba and Umm Salama, whose mother was an *umm walad* called Su'da.

Al-Ash'ath ibn Ishaq ibn Sa'd ibn Abi Waqqas

His mother was Shajara bint Kulayb. His children were Hamza, Muhammad, Umm Isma'il, 'Ubayda and Umm Hisham, whose mother was Hafsa bint 'Amir.

Isma'il ibn Muhammad ibn Sa'd

His *kunya* was Abu Muhammad and his mother was an *umm walad*. His children were Abu Bakr, Umm Muhammad, Umm Kulthum and Umm al-Qasim, whose mother was Umm Sulayman bint 'Abdullah; and Hafsa, whose mother was Umm 'Amr bint 'Ubaydullah, whose mother was 'A'isha bint 'Abdu'r-Rahman. He has *hadiths* and is reliable. He died in 134 AH while as-Saffah was khalif.

Da'ud ibn 'Amir ibn Sa'd

His mother was Umm 'Ubaydullah. His children were 'Abdullah, whose mother was Umm Salama bint Ishaq; Ibrahim, who is Kardam the potter, Muhammad, Ishaq and Amatu'l-Hamid, who is Hammada, and their mother was Umm Hisham bint Maslama.

Qurayn ibn al-Muttalib ibn as-Sa'ib

His mother was Zubayba, an *umm walad*. His children were Muhammad, Ibrahim and Umm Ishaq, whose mother was Umm 'Abdullah bint 'Umar. Al-Muttalib circumcised Sa'id ibn al-Musayyab for his daughter. He is related from but had few *hadiths*.

Kathir ibn Kathir ibn al-Muttalib

His mother was 'A'isha bint 'Amr. Sufyan ibn 'Uyayna saw him and related from him. He was a poet. He also had a brother, Ja'far ibn Kathir, who had a son, 'Abdullah, by 'A'isha bint Hamza.

297

Their brother, Sa'id ibn Kathir ibn al-Muttalib

His mother was 'A'isha bint 'Amr. His children were 'Abdullah, who is Rabah, Isma'il, who is Salim, and Ibrahim, whose mother was Humayda bint 'Abdullah.

Ya'qub ibn Zayd ibn Talha

His mother was Khalida bint Mu'adh. His *kunya* was Abu 'Arafa. He was a story-teller. He had few *hadiths*. Malik ibn Anas reported from him. He died at the beginning of al-Mansur's khalifate.

Muhammad ibn 'Ali ibn 'Abdullah ibn al-'Abbas

His mother was al-'Aliya bint 'Ubaydullah. His children were 'Abdullah the younger, who is as-Saffah, the first Abbasid khalif, Da'ud, 'Ubaydullah, and Rayta, who died without issue, and their mother was Rayta bint 'Ubaydullah. He also had 'Abdullah the elder, who is al-Mansur who became khalif after his brother as-Saffah, and whose mother was an *umm walad*; Ibrahim, who was the Imam to whom the agents of the Abbasids called people, and whose mother was an *umm walad*; Yahya and al-'Aliyya, whose mother was Umm al-Hakam bint 'Abdullah; Musa, whose mother was an *umm walad*; al-'Abbas, whose mother was an *umm walad*; and Isma'il, Ya'qub, who is Abu'l-Asbat, and Lubaba who married Ja'far ibn Sulayman but had no children, by various *umm walads*.

Al-'Abbas ibn Muhammad mentioned that Muhammad ibn 'Ali died in Shara, Syria, while al-Walid II was khalif at the age of 60 in 125 AH. Abu Hashim 'Abdullah ibn Muhammad made him his executor and gave his books to him. Muhammad ibn 'Ali made a will in favour of Abu Hashim and Abu Hashim said to him, "This business is among your children." The Shi'ites used to go to Abu Hashim and afterwards they went to Muhammad ibn 'Ali.

Abu Hashim was a scholar who listened and read books. Muhammad ibn 'Ali listened also, and he asked Sa'id ibn Jubayr when to stop the *talbiya*.

Da'ud ibn 'Ali ibn 'Abdullah ibn al-'Abbas

His mother was an *umm walad*.

When as-Saffah was victorious, Da'ud was in Kufa and went up the *minbar* to address the people. He was surrounded and could not speak. So Da'ud ibn 'Ali jumped down in front of the *minbar* and spoke. He addressed them about their business and their progress and inspired the hopes of the people and promised them justice. They dispersed after his speech. As-Saffah appointed him over Makka and Madina. He went on *hajj* with the people in 132 AH, the first *hajj* made by the Abbasids. Then he went to Madina and remained there for some months. Then he died in 133 AH at the age of 52. He lived for eight months of Abbasid rule.

Muhammad ibn 'Abdu'r-Rahman and others related from Da'ud ibn 'Ali, and Da'ud related from his father.

'Isa ibn 'Ali ibn 'Abdullah ibn al-'Abbas

His mother was an *umm walad*, who is Umm Da'ud ibn 'Ali. He was one of the people of safety and well-being. He did not undertake any office for the people of his house until he died. He is related from. He died while al-Mahdi was khalif.

Husayn ibn 'Abdullah ibn 'Ubaydullah ibn al-'Abbas

His mother was Asma' bint 'Abdullah. He had a son called 'Abdullah and no other children. Al-Husyan died in 146 AH while Muhammad ibn Khalid was governor of Madina for al-Mansur. He prayed over Husayn. On the day he died he was 82. He related from his father and 'Ikrima. Muhammad ibn Ishaq, Ibn Jurayj, al-Hajjaj ibn Arta', Sharik ibn 'Abdullah, Sulayman ibn Bilal, 'Abdullah ibn al-Mubarak and Abu Bakr ibn Abi Sabra related from him. He had a lot of *hadiths* but I did not see them using his *hadith* for evidence.

Al-Mansur sent his son 'Abdullah ibn al-Husayn and he came to him from Madina and he married him to his aunt, Umm 'Isa bint 'Ali. He had no children. He died and Umm 'Isa inherited from him.

Al-'Abbas ibn 'Abdullah ibn Ma'bad ibn al-'Abbas

His mother was Umm Muhammad bint 'Ubaydullah. His children were Muhammad, whose mother was Umm Abiha bint Muhammad. Sufyan ibn 'Uyayna related from him.

Ibrahim ibn 'Abdullah ibn Ma'bad ibn al-'Abbas

His mother was an *umm walad*. His children were Muhammad, who lived in Hira, and Da'ud, and their mother was Maymuna bint al-'Abbas.

Muhammad ibn 'Umar ibn 'Ali ibn Abi Talib

His mother was Asma' bint 'Aqil. His children were 'Umar, 'Abdullah and 'Ubaydullah, whose mother was Khadija bint 'Ali; and Ja'far, whose mother was Umm Hashim bint Ja'far.

He is related from. He listened to his father and to 'Ali ibn Husayn. He had few *hadiths*, and lived up to the beginning of the khalifate of as-Saffah.

Muhammad ibn 'Amr ibn Husayn ibn 'Ali

His mother was Ramla bint 'Aqil. His children were Hasan and Ruqayya, whose mother was Humayda bint Muhammad, whose mother was Fatima the younger, daughter of 'Ali ibn Abi Talib; 'Umar, Muhammad, 'Abdullah and 'Ubaydullah, whose mother was Khadija bint 'Ali; Muhammad whose mother was Ramla bint Sa'id; Ja'far whose mother was an *umm walad*; and Da'ud, whose mother was an *umm walad*.

'Abdullah ibn Hasan ibn Hasan ibn 'Ali

His children were Muhammad – who was killed in Madina while al-Mansur was khalif, Ibrahim – who was killed in Bakhmara in Kufa while al-Mansur was khalif, Musa, Idris the elder, Harun, Fatima, Zaynab, Ruqayya, Kulthum and Umm Kulthum, whose mother was Hind bint Abi 'Ubayda; 'Isa, Idris the younger – the ruler of Andalusia and the Berbers, and Da'ud, whose mother was 'Atika bint 'Abdu'l-Malik; and Sulayman and Yahya, the master of the Daylami mountains, whose mother was Qurayba bint Rukayh.

His *kunya* was Abu Muhammad. Malik ibn Anas said, "I saw 'Abdullah ibn al-Hasan praying with his garment hanging down."

Hafs ibn 'Umar, the client of 'Abdullah ibn Hasan, said, "I saw 'Abdullah ibn Hasan doing *wudu'* and he wiped over his leather socks. I asked him, 'Do you wipe?' He said, 'Yes. 'Umar ibn al-

Khattab used to wipe – and whoever puts 'Umar between him and Allah is safe.'"

Muhammad ibn Umar said, "'Abdullah ibn Hasan was one of the worshippers. He had nobility, an imposing presence and a strong tongue. He lived up until the Abbasid reign. He went to as-Saffah in Anbar. He asked him about his sons, Muhammad and Ibrahim. He replied, 'They are in the desert. They prefer withdrawal.'" Muhammad ibn 'Umar reported that Hafs ibn 'Umar said, "'Abdullah ibn Hasan came to as-Saffah in Anbar and he honoured him, welcomed him, brought him near him, and did something which he did not do for anyone else.

"We used to talk with him at night. He spoke with him until the middle of the night. Then as-Saffah called for a basket of jewels which he opened and said, 'This, by Allah, Abu Muhammad, is what has come to me of the gems once owned by the Umayyads.' Then he divided it and gave him half, and as-Saffah sent the other half to his wife Umm Salama. He said, 'This is a deposit with you.' Then they talked for a time and as-Saffah became sleepy and his head nodded. 'Abdullah ibn Hasan recited these verses:

'Do you not see the fox in the evening
    building castles for the Banu Buqayla,
Hoping to live in them for as long as Nuh
    while Allah has commanded
        that they fall down every night?'

"Abu'l-'Abbas roused himself and understood and said, 'Abu Muhammad, you use such poetry with me! You have seen how I treat you and I have not stinted you anything.' He replied, 'Amir al-Mu'minin, it was a slip. By Allah, I did not mean any evil by it. They are simply verses which occurred to me and I recited them. If the Amir al-Mu'minin thinks he could overlook what I said, he should do so.' He said, 'I have done so.' Then he returned to Madina.

"When al-Mansur became khalif, he insisted on seeking out Muhammad and Ibrahim, the sons of 'Abdullah who had concealed themselves in the desert. Al-Mansur commanded Ziyad ibn 'Ubaydullah to seek them out. He failed to do so and was not serious in searching for them. So al-Mansur dismissed him and appointed Muhammad ibn Khalid over Madina and commanded him to search for them. He also avoided that and did not succeed. He knew their location, but sent horses in another direction to look for them.

"Al-Mansur heard about that and became angry with him. He dismissed him and appointed Riyah ibn 'Uthman al-Murri and ordered him to be diligent in searching for them and not to fail to find them."

'Abdu'r-Rahman ibn Abi'l-Mawali said, "Riyah ibn 'Uthman was serious about looking for them. He was very diligent in doing so, until they were afraid and began to move from place to place. Al-Mansur was infuriated by their concealment and wrote to Riyah ibn 'Uthman to arrest their father, 'Abdullah ibn Hasan, and his brothers, Hasan ibn Hasan, Da'ud ibn Hasan and Muhammad ibn 'Abdullah – their half-brother by Fatima bint Husayn, and their sons and others, and to tie them up and send them to him in ar-Rabadha. Al-Mansur was making *hajj* that year, so he wrote to him to take me with them and send me to him as well.

"I arrived after he had already begun the *hajj*. I was arrested and cast in irons and taken to join them in ar-Rabadha."

Muhammad ibn 'Umar said, "I saw 'Abdullah ibn Hasan and the people of his house brought out of Marwan's house after *'Asr* in irons and taken in bare litters with no carpet under them. I was a child approaching adolescence then and I remember what I saw."

'Abdu'r-Rahman ibn Abi'l-Mawali said, "Along with them he arrested about 400 people from Juhayna, Muzayna and other tribes. I saw them at ar-Rabada fettered in the sun."

He said, "I was imprisoned with 'Abdullah ibn Hasan and the people of his house. Al-Mansur came to ar-Rabadha after returning from the *hajj*. 'Abdullah asked al-Mansur to give him permission to come to see him but al-Mansur refused. He did not see him before he died. Then al-Mansur summoned me and I was brought to him. 'Isa ibn 'Ali was with him. When 'Isa saw me, he said, 'Yes, it is him, Amir al-Mu'minin. If you are severe with him, he will tell you where they are.' I was brought closer and greeted him. Al-Mansur said, 'The peace of Allah not on you! Where are the two profligate sons of the profligate, the two liars sons of the liar?' I said, 'Amir al-Mu'minin, will truthfulness help me with you?' He said, 'What is that?' I said, 'His wife is divorced' – and I made some oaths – 'if I know where they are!'

"He did not accept that. He said, 'The flogger!' The flogger was brought and I was made to stand and was given 400 lashes. I was left hanging there and then I was taken and returned to my companions in that condition. Then he sent for ad-Dibaj Muhammad ibn 'Abdullah, whose daughter was married to Ibrahim ibn 'Abdullah. When he was brought to him, he said, 'Tell me about the liars and what they have done. Where are they?' He said, 'By Allah, Amir al-Mu'minin, I have no knowledge of them.' He insisted, 'You will tell me.' He said, 'I have told you, by Allah, I am speaking the truth, I used to know them before today, but today, by Allah, I have no knowledge of them.'

"He said, 'Strip him!' He was stripped and given 100 lashes with an iron circle put round his neck. When his beating was finished, he was brought out and they put his shirt back on over the beating. He was brought to us and, by Allah, we could not remove the shirt because it was stuck to him with blood, until a sheep was milked on it. Then the shirt was removed and he was treated.

"Al-Mansur said, 'Take them to Iraq.' We were brought to Hashimiyya and imprisoned there. The first to die in prison was 'Abdullah ibn Hasan. The jailer came and said, 'The closest relative may come out and pray over him.' So his brother Hasan went out and prayed over him. Then he died after him, and Muhammad ibn 'Abdullah went out and prayed over him. Then Muhammad ibn 'Abdullah died and his head was sent to Khorasan with some Shi'ites. They took it around the districts of Khorasan and they began to swear by Allah: 'This is the head of Muhammad ibn 'Abdullah, son of Fatima the daughter of the Messenger of Allahصلعم,' making people think that this was the head of the Muhammad ibn 'Abdullah whom they claimed was described in a transmission which said he would rebel against al-Mansur."

'Abdu'r-Rahman ibn Abi'l-Mawali said, "'Ali ibn Hasan was in prison with us. He was the father of Husayn ibn 'Ali, the master of Fakhkh. He was one of the best of the people of his time in worship, devotion, and scrupulousness. He did not eat a single date from any of the land grants which as-Saffah and al-Mansur made. He did not do *wudu'* from their springs nor drink their water.

"He was married to his cousin, Zaynab bint 'Abdullah. He was a devout worshipper. It is said that in Madina there was no couple who engaged in worship more than them, meaning 'Ali ibn Hasan and his wife Zaynab. The jailer at al-Hashimiyya loved him, honoured him and was kind to him because of what he saw of his striving and worship. He brought him a pillow and said, 'Put your head on it.' He preferred to give it to his father Hasan. His father said to him. 'My son, your uncle, 'Abdullah ibn Hasan, is more entitled to it.' So he sent it to him. 'Abdullah ibn Hasan said, 'O brother, our wretched brother who is being tested on account of us and has been beaten is more entitled to it,' meaning Muhammad ibn 'Abdullah. So he sent it to him, saying, 'You are in a delicate condition, so this pillow should be under you head.' He accepted it and put it under his head."

Muhammad ibn 'Umar said, "'Abdullah ibn Hasan was 72 when he died. He died some months before his son, Muhammad ibn 'Abdullah, was killed. Muhammad ibn 'Abdullah was killed at the end of 145 AH in Ramadan. 'Abdullah ibn Hasan has *hadiths*."

Hasan ibn Hasan ibn Hasan ibn 'Ali ibn Abi Talib

His mother was Fatima bint al-Husayn. His children were 'Abdullah, who is Abu Ja'far and who died in prison, 'Ali, who is as-Sajjad (because of his worship) and who died in prison, and Hasan, and their mother was Fatima Umm Hibban bint 'Amir; 'Abbas who died in prison, whose mother was 'A'isha bint Talha; 'Ali the younger and Fatima, whose mother was Umm Habib bint 'Umar; and Umm Salama and Umm Kulthum by an *umm walad*.

Ibrahim ibn Hasan ibn Hasan ibn 'Ali ibn Abi Talib

His mother was Fatima bint Husayn. His children were Ishaq, Ya'qub, Isma'il, Umm Ishaq, who is Suhayqa, and Ruqayya, whose mother was Rubayha bint Muhammad; and Muhammad, 'Ali, Fatima and Hasana, by various *umm walads*. Ibrahim ibn Hasan died in prison.

Muhammad ibn 'Abdullah ibn 'Amr ibn 'Uthman ibn 'Affan

His mother was Fatima bint Husayn. He was called Muhammad ad-Dibaj (brocade) because of his beauty. His father, 'Abdullah ibn'Amr, had been called al-Mutrif because of his beauty.

His children were Khalid, 'Abdu'l-'Aziz, 'Ubaydullah, al-Qasim and 'Uthman, whose mother was Umm Kulthum bint Ibrahim, whose mother was Lubaba bint 'Abdullah.

Muhammad ibn 'Umar said, "Muhammad ibn 'Abdullah was the youngest of the children of Fatima bint Husayn. His brothers by his mother were kind to him and loved him and he was close to them and did not part from them."

Da'ud ibn 'Abdu'r-Rahman al-'Attar said, "I saw 'Abdullah ibn Hasan come over to his brother Muhammad ibn 'Abdullah. He found him asleep and leaned over him and kissed him. Then he left without awakening him."

Muhammad ibn 'Umar said, "Muhammad ibn 'Abdullah was one of those seized along with his brothers, the Banu Hasan ibn Hasan. They were brought to al-Mansur in ar-Rabadha and he beat him in front of them with 100 lashes and imprisoned him with them in Hashimiyya. He died in prison. He was a scholar with a lot of *hadiths*.

His brother Umayya ibn 'Abdullah ibn 'Amr

His mother was Umm 'Abdu'l-'Aziz bint 'Abdullah. He had a son, 'Uthman, whose mother was Habiba bint Ibrahim. He is related from. Umayya ibn 'Abdullah is the one whom Tayy met in the Battle of al-Muntahab and they defeated him.

Sa'id ibn Khalid ibn 'Amr ibn 'Uthman

His mother was Umm 'Uthman bint Sa'id, whose mother was Umayma bint Jarir. His children were 'Abdullah and Khalid, by an *umm walad*; Muhammad, by an *umm walad*; 'Abdu'l-Malik and al-Walid, by an *umm walad*; and Umm 'Abdu'l-Malik who married al-Walid II and bore him Sa'id, and Umm Salama who married Hisham ibn 'Abdu'l-Malik, and their mother was Umm 'Amr bint Marwan.

'Abdullah ibn Mu'awiya ibn 'Abdullah

His mother was Umm 'Awn bint 'Awn. He had a son Ja'far whose mother was Hannada bint ash-Sharqi.

He rebelled in Kufa when Marwan ibn Muhammad was khalif and Marwan sent an army against him. He concentrated his efforts on Isfahan and overcame it and its surrounding region. Many people joined him in 131 AH and then he was killed in Jayy. It is also said that he fled to Khorasan where Abu Muslim was agitating. He heard where he was and arrested him and kept him in prison until he died.

'Abdullah ibn Muhammad ibn 'Aqil ibn Abi Talib

His mother was Zaynab the younger bint 'Ali ibn Abi Talib, whose mother was an *umm walad*. His children were Muhammad, Hiram and Umm Hani', whose mother was Hamida bint Muslim; and Muslim and 'Aqil, whose mother was an *umm walad*.

His *kunya* was Abu Muhammad. He related from at-Tufayl, Rubayya' bint Mu'awwidh and Muhammad ibn al-Hanafiyya.

His *hadiths* are *munkar* and are not used as evidence. He had a lot of knowledge.

'Ubaydullah ibn 'Amr said, "'Abdullah ibn Muhammad came to Hisham ibn 'Abdu'l-Malik and he commanded about 4,000 dinars for him. I, Abu'l-Mulayh and another man called Muhammad ibn 'Utba of the people of Raqqa organised and collected the like of it for him.

"When we brought it to him, he said to us, 'What is this? If it is a gift I will accept it. If it is *sadaqa*, I have no need of it because the Messenger of Allah صلعم said "*Sadaqa* is not lawful for us, the People of the House.'" We said, 'It is a gift.' He accepted it."

Muhammad ibn 'Umar said, "'Abdullah ibn Muhammad ibn 'Aqil died in Madina before Muhammad ibn 'Abdullah rebelled. Muhammad ibn 'Abdullah rebelled in 145 AH.

Al-Qasim ibn al-'Abbas ibn Muhammad

His mother was an *umm walad*. His children were al-'Abbas, whose mother was Umm Salama bint Abi Sufyan; Kulthum, 'Uthayma, Sulayman and Umm al-Qasim, who is Qusayma, and their mother was an *umm walad*; and Yahya, Sadaqa, al-Fadl and 'Atika, whose mother was an *umm walad*.

Muhammad ibn 'Umar said that the *kunya* of al-Qasim ibn al-'Abbas was Abu'l-'Abbas. He was the grandfather of al-Qasim ibn al-Mu'tamir, one of the Banu Hamnan. He had few *hadiths*.

He died in Madina on one of the nights of the Haruriyya which took place in Madina in 130 AH.

'Abdu'r-Rahman ibn al-Harith ibn 'Abdullah

His mother was an *umm walad*. His children were 'Ayyash, 'Abdullah, al-Harith, al-Mughira, Fatima and Umm Salama, whose mother was Qariba bint Muhammad. He was reliable and had *hadiths*. Ziyad ibn 'Ubaydullah appointed him over Tabala and he became wealthy there. He later moved to a house in Madina which he called Tabala. Musa ibn Ja'far purchased it from his heirs. 'Abdu'r-Rahman died at the beginning of the khalifate of al-Mansur.

Al-Harith ibn 'Abdu'r-Rahman ibn al-Harith

His *kunya* was Abu 'Abdu'r-Rahman. He was the uncle of Muhammad ibn 'Abdu'r-Rahman. He died in Madina in 127 AH at the beginning of the khalifate of Marwan II at the age of 73. We do not know of anyone who related from him except for his nephew, Muhammad ibn 'Abdu'r-Rahman. He had few *hadiths*.

Ya'qub ibn 'Utba ibn al-Mughira ibn al-Akhnas

Abu'z-Zinad said, "There were ten men who formed a circle which became well-known, and one of them was Ya'qub ibn 'Utba. He was the most manly of them, and I did not ever hear a sound in his house."

Muhammad ibn 'Umar said, "These ten were the same age. They were *fuqaha'* and scholars. They included Ya'qub ibn 'Utba, 'Uthman ibn Muhammad ibn al-Akhnas, 'Abdullah, 'Abdu'r-Rahman and al-Harith, the sons of 'Ikrima ibn 'Abdu'r-Rahman, Sa'd ibn Ibrahim, as-Salt ibn Zubayd, Salih ibn Kaysan, 'Abdullah ibn Yazid and 'Abdullah ibn Yazid al-Hudhali."

He was reliable, with many *hadiths* and transmission and knowledge of *sira* and other things.

Abu Wajza as-Sa'di

He was Yazid ibn 'Ubayd, one of the Banu Sa'd ibn Bakr. He had few *hadiths* and was a poet and a scholar. He died in Madina in 130 AH.

'Imran ibn Abi Anas

They used to claim that they were from the Banu 'Amir ibn Lu'ayy, and the people used to say that they were their clients. After that they were ascribed to Yemen.

He died young in 127 AH while Hisham was khalif. He had *hadiths*.

'Abdullah ibn as-Sa'ib ibn Yazid

His grandfather was Sa'id ibn Thumama, the client of Banu 'Abd Shams in the *Jahiliya*. His *kunya* was Abu Muhammad. He died in 126 AH while al-Walid II was khalif. He was reliable, with few *hadiths*.

Makhlad ibn Khufaf ibn Ayma'

Khufaf and his father Ayma' were Companions of the Prophet صلعم. They used to camp at Ghayqa and came often to Madina. Makhlad related one *hadith*.

Yazid ibn 'Abdullah ibn Qusayt

His *kunya* was Abu 'Abdullah.

Muhammad ibn 'Umar said, "I reported from Yazid ibn 'Abdullah that Sa'id ibn al-Musayyab heard that he gave *fatwa*."

He died in Madina in 122 AH while Hisham was khalif. He was reliable with a lot of *hadiths*.

Jawtha ibn 'Ubayd ad-Dayli

His *kunya* was Abu 'Ubayd. Muhammad ibn 'Umar said that he heard from 'Umar ibn Talha that Jawtha ibn 'Ubayd died in Madina in 127 AH. He said, "I do not know that he related anything from any of the Companions of the Prophet صلعم." He had few *hadiths*.

Muhammad ibn 'Amr ibn Halhala ad-Dayli

He had an imposing appearance and clung to the mosque. Malik ibn Anas, Sulayman, ibn Bilal and 'Abdu'l-'Aziz ibn Muhammad ad-Darawardi related from him. He had *hadiths*.

Yazid ibn 'Abdullah ibn Usama

His *kunya* was Abu 'Abdullah. He was lame with a noticeable limp. He died in 139 AH in Madina. He was reliable, with a lot of *hadiths*.

Sharik ibn 'Abdullah ibn Abi Namir al-Laythi

His *kunya* was Abu 'Abdullah. He died after 140 AH, before the rebellion of Muhammad ibn 'Abdullah in Madina. He rebelled in 145 AH. He was reliable, with a lot *hadiths*.

'Ata' ibn Abi Marwan al-Aslami

His *kunya* was Abu Mus'ab. He was one of the Banu Malik ibn Afsa. He died at the beginning of the Abbasid khalifate. He had few *hadiths*. Ath-Thawri related from him.

Abu'l-Huwayrith

He is 'Abdu'r-Rahman ibn Mu'awiya al-Muradi, the ally of the Banu Nawfal. He died while Marwan II was *khalif*. He had *hadiths*.

Sa'id ibn 'Abdu'r-Rahman ibn Ruqaysh

Yazid ibn Ruqaysh was present at Badr. Sa'id listened to Anas ibn Malik and Malik ibn Anas related from him. He had few *hadiths*.

Muhammad ibn Abi Bakr ibn Muhammad

His mother was Fatima bint 'Umara ibn 'Amr. His children were 'Abdu'r-Rahman, 'Abdu'l-Malik, 'Abdu'l-Wahhab and Abu Bakr, whose mother was Amatu'l-Wahhab bint 'Abdullah; and Ibrahim, 'Umara, Umm 'Umar and Kabsha, whose mother was an *umm walad*.

'Abdu'r-Rahman ibn Abi'z-Zinad reported, "Abu Bakr ibn Muhammad ibn 'Amr and Ibn Hazm met me while I was standing at the door of Zayd ibn Thabit. He said to me, 'My son, (or 'Abdu'r-Rahman).' I said, 'Yes.' He said, 'May Allah bless you. How old are you?' I said, 'Seventeen.' He said, 'That is what is between me and Muhammad ibn Abi Bakr (his son).'"

His *kunya* was Abu 'Abdu'l-Malik.

Malik ibn Anas said, "Muhammad ibn Abi Bakr ibn Muhammad was qadi of Madina. Once he gave a judgement which was contrary to a *hadith* and when he returned to his house, his brother 'Abdullah ibn Abi Bakr, who was a righteous man said to him, 'My brother, you gave such-and-such a judgement.' Muhammad said to him, 'Yes, brother.' 'Abdullah said to him, 'My brother, where are you in relation to the *hadith* in giving judgement?' Muhammad said, 'Well, where is the action?' meaning the normative practice agreed on in Madina since they considered the practice on which there was agreement to be stronger than the single *hadith*."

Sa'id ibn Muslim said, "I saw Muhammad ibn Abi Bakr ibn Muhammad giving judgement in the mosque."

Muhammad ibn 'Umar said, "Muhammad ibn Abi Bakr died in 132 AH at the age of 72 at the beginning of the Abbasids. He was reliable, with *hadiths*."

'Abdullah ibn Abi Bakr ibn Muhammad ibn 'Amr ibn Hazm

His mother was Fatima bint 'Umara.

Muhammad ibn 'Umar said, "He died in Madina in 135 AH at the age of 70. He had no descendants."

Another said that he died before that, in 130 AH. Az-Zuhri related from 'Abdullah ibn Abi Bakr. The family of Hazm had a circle in the mosque. He was a scholar and reliable. He had a lot of *hadiths*.

Abu Tuwala

Muhammad ibn 'Umar said, "His name was 'Abdullah ibn 'Abdu'r-Rahman. His children were an-Nadr, whose mother was Munya bint Anas ibn Malik; 'Uqba, 'Abdu'l-Malik, Haritha, 'Abdu'r-Rahman, Ibrahim and Musa, whose mother was an *umm walad*; and 'Abdullah and 'Abdu'l-Wahid, whose mother was an *umm walad*."

Muhammad ibn 'Umar said, "When Abu Bakr ibn Muhammad became governor of Madina for 'Umar II, he appointed Abu Tuwala as qadi of Madina. He used to give judgement in the mosque."

Abu Tuwala related from Anas ibn Malik, and he died young at the end of the rule of the Umayyads and the beginning of the Abbasids. He was reliable with a lot of *hadiths*.

Sa'id ibn Sulayman ibn Zayd

His mother was Umm Humayd bint 'Abdullah. His children were Miskin, whose name was 'Abdul-Malik, Da'ud, 'Ubayda (a girl) and Sulama (a girl). He was *qadi* of Madina for Ibrahim ibn Hisham al-Makhzum. He died in the time of Marwan II. He had few *hadiths*.

Ibrahim ibn Yahya ibn Zayd

His mother was Bassama bint 'Umara. His children were Kharija, Muhammad and Idris, whose mother was Umm Salama bint an-Nu'man. Ibn Abi'z-Zinad said, "Ibrahim had two tresses. He was handsome and manly and lived until the Abbasid era."

Muhammad ibn 'Abdu'r-Rahman ibn 'Abdullah

His mother was Hind bint Zayd. His children were Ibrahim, 'Abdu'l-Malik and Amatu'l-Hamid, whose mother was an *umm walad*. 'Amra bint 'Abdu'r-Rahman was the aunt of the father of Muhammad ibn 'Abdu'r-Rahman. He was reliable and had *hadiths*. He died in 124 AH.

Abu'r-Rijal

His name was Muhammad ibn 'Abdu'r-Rahman. His mother was 'Amra bint 'Abdu'r-Rahman. His children were 'Abdullah and Haritha, whose mother was Humayda bint Sa'id; and Malik, Muhammad, 'Abdu'r-Rahman, 'A'isha and Abu Bakr, whose mother was Umm Ayyub bint Rifa'a.

His other *kunya* was Abu 'Abdu'r-Rahman. His *kunya* Abu'r-Rijal came from his son who had ten sons who became men (*rijal*). He did not name all of them for us. They also included Musa whose grandfather was Haritha ibn an-Nu'man, one of the people of Badr. He was reliable, with a lot of *hadiths*.

Ishaq ibn 'Abdullah ibn Abi Talha

His mother was Nubayta bint Rifa'a. He had a son Yahya, whose mother was Humayda bint Ubayd.

Muhammad ibn 'Umar said, "His *kunya* was Abu Yahya. He was better trained and firmer than his brother 'Abdullah. Malik ibn Anas did not advance anyone over him in *hadith*."

He and his brother 'Abdullah settled in the house of Abu Talha in Madina. Ishaq died in 132 AH. He was reliable, with a lot of *hadiths*.

'Abdullah ibn 'Abdullah ibn Abi Talha

His mother was an *umm walad*. His *kunya* was Abu Yahya.

He was younger than Ishaq and lived with him in the house of Abu Talha. He died in 134 AH in Madina. He had few *hadiths*.

'Umar ibn 'Abdullah ibn Abi Talha

His mother was Umm Kulthim bint 'Amr. His children were Hafs, whose mother was Umm al-Fadl bint 'Abdu'r-Rahman; and Umm 'Amr, whose mother is not named. He related from 'Umar ibn 'Abdullah ibn Abi Talha.

'Abaya ibn Rifa'a ibn Rafi' ibn Khadij

His mother was an *umm walad*. His children were Umm al-Fadl, Umm Yahya, who is Salama, al-Khansa', Tuladam and Asma', who is as-Sawda', and their mother was Umm Rafi' bint 'Ubaydullah; and ar-Rubayya', whose mother was an *umm walad*. His *kunya* was Abu Rifa'a.

Muhammad ibn Abi Umama ibn Sahl

His mother was Umm 'Abdullah bint 'Atik. His children were Sahl, 'Abda, Umm Sahl and Umm Rafi', whose mother was Ramla bint Muhammad; Nafi' and Maryam, by an *umm walad;* and Ibrahim by an *umm walad*.

Khubayb ibn 'Abdu'r-Rahman ibn 'Abdullah ibn Khubayb

His mother's name is not known. His son was called Bakkar, whose mother's name is not known. 'Ubaydullah ibn 'Umar, Malik ibn Anas and Shu'ba related from him. He died while Marwan II was khalif. He had few *hadiths*.

'Amr ibn Yahya ibn 'Umara

His mother was Umm an-Nu'man bint Abi Hanna. His children were Yahya and Maryam, whose mother was Hamida bint Muhammad; and Muhammad, whose mother was Qurayba bint Yusuf. He was reliable, with a lot of *hadiths*.

'Abdu'r-Rahman ibn 'Abdullah ibn 'Abdu'r-Rahman

His mother was Na'ila bint al-Harith. His children were Mu'adh, 'Umar, Umm al-Harith and Umm Humayd, whose mother was 'Abda bint Yazid; Miskin and Jabir, whose mother was an *umm walad*; and Aflah, al-Harith, Umm Jamil and 'Abda, whose mother was Khulayda bint Hasan. Some of them said that Umm Jamil was by an *umm walad*. Malik ibn Anas related from 'Abdu'r-Rahman.

Muhammad ibn 'Abdullah ibn 'Abdu'r-Rahman

His mother was Na'ila bint al-Harith. His children were Ya'qub, Isma'il, Ibrahim and Ishaq, whose mother was Humayda bint 'Abdullah. His *kunya* was Abu 'Abdu'r-Rahman. He was reliable, with few *hadiths*. Malik ibn Anas related from him.

Malik said, "The family of Abu Sa'sa'a had a circle between the Prophet's grave and the *minbar*. They included men of the people of knowledge, transmission and recognition. All of them gave *fatwa*."

Damra ibn Sa'id ibn Abi Hanna 'Amr

His mother was 'Affa bint Hibban. His children were Muhammad, Musa and Abu'l-Ghayth, whose name was Isma'il, and their mother was Amatu'llah bint Sa'd. Sa'id was killed in the Battle of al-Harra.

'Umara ibn Ghuzayya

His mother was Umm Isma'il bint Abi Hanna. His children were Sa'id and an-Nu'man, whose mother was Muwaysa bint an-Nu'man; and Kathira, whose mother was Umm al-Qasim bint Isma'il. He was reliable and had few *hadiths*.

Abu Jabir al-Bayadi

His name was Muhammad ibn 'Abdu'r-Rahman. His mother was Kabsha bint Farwa. He had a son Jabir, whose mother was Umm 'Amr bint Ka'b. Muhammad ibn 'Umar says that he died in 130 AH at the end of the Umayyad rule. He had few *hadiths*. I saw that they were cautious about his *hadiths*.

Ibrahim ibn 'Ubayd ibn Rifa'a

His mother was Sumayka bint Ka'b. His children were Rifa'a, Muhammad, Ishaq, Maryam, Sumayka and Rabi'a, whose mother was Umm Nu'man bint Muhammad.

Isma'il ibn 'Ubayd ibn Rifa'a

His mother was Sumayka bint La'b. Rafi'a ibn Malik was one of the twelve nobles. He was not present at Badr but his sons, Rifa'a and Khallad were.

Sa'id ibn 'Amr ibn Sulaym ibn 'Amr

His mother was Umm al-Banin bint Abi 'Ubada. He had few *hadiths*. Malik ibn Anas related from him. He died in Madina in 134 AH in the Abbasid era.

Marwan ibn Abi Sa'd ibn Aws

His *kunya* was Abu 'Abdu'l-Malik. He died in in 133 AH at the beginning of the rule of Abu'l-'Abbas.

Abu Layla

His name was 'Abdullah ibn Sahl ibn 'Abdu'r-Rahman. He is the one from whom Malik ibn Anas reported the *hadith* of Sahl ibn Hathma on *qasama*. 'Umar ibn al-Khattab appointed his grandfather 'Abdu'r-Rahman over Basra when 'Utba ibn Ghazwan died, and then he died forty days afterwards.

'Umara ibn 'Abdullah ibn Sayyad

His *kunya* was Abu Ayyub. He was reliable, with few *hadiths*.

Malik ibn Anas did not say that anyone was better than him. He related from him and 'Umara related from Sa'id ibn al-Musayyab.

They used to say, "We are the Banu Ashhab ibn an-Najjar. The Banu'n-Najjar made them retract from that when 49 men of them and one man from the Banu Sa'ida swore on the minbar that they were not part of them. So they were disassociated from them. They said. "We are the allies of the Banu Malik ibn an-Najjar, and that is how they are today. We do not know their true tribe."

'Abdullah ibn Sayyad is the one who was born circumcised and brought to the Prophet صلعم who said, "I have concealed something for you." He answered, "Smoke?" He said, "Baser. You do not exceed your worth." He is the one who was said to be the Dajjal because of the things he used to do. 'Abdullah ibn Sayyad became Muslim, went on *hajj*, raided with the Muslims and stayed in Madina. He died while Marwan II was khalif.

'Abdullah ibn Dinar

Abu 'Abdu'r-Rahman, the client of 'Abdullah ibn 'Umar ibn al-Khattab. He died in 127 AH. He was reliable, with a lot of *hadiths*.

'Abdullah ibn 'Umar

'Umar was the client of Umm al-Fadl. His *kunya* was Abu Muhammad. He died in 127 AH. He was reliable with few *hadiths*.

'Abdullah ibn 'Ali ibn Abi Rafi'

Abu Rafi' was the client of the Messenger of Allah صلعم. His grandmother was Salma, the client of the Prophet صلعم. 'Abdullah ibn 'Ali listened to his grandfather, Abu Rafi'. He had few *hadiths*, and was asked to give *fatwa*.

'Uthman ibn 'Ubaydullah ibn Rafi'

Rafi' was a slave of Abu Uhayha Sa'id ibn al-'As. He had two journeys with Quraysh in the *Jahiliyya*. Then he went to the Messenger of Allah صلعم who freed him. Muhammad ibn 'Ajlan related from 'Uthman ibn 'Ubaydullah and 'Uthman related from Ibn 'Umar, Rafi' ibn Khadij and Salama ibn al-Akwa'.

Muslim ibn Abi Muslim al-Khayyat

He related from Ibn 'Umar. He lived until he met Sufyan ibn 'Uyayna. He used to live in Madina at al-Hafra which is the quarter of the perfumers. He had few *hadiths*.

Hilal ibn Usama

He is Ibn Abi Maymuna. Malik ibn Anas related from him. He died at the end of Hisham's khalifate.

Bukayr ibn 'Abdullah ibn Al-Ashajj

The client of al-Miswar ibn Makhrama az-Zuhri. His *kunya* was Abu 'Abdullah. He died in Madina in 127 AH.

Muhammad ibn 'Umar said, "He was at the frontier a great deal. Few of the people of Madina related from him except his son Makhrama and ad-Dahhak ibn 'Uthman, who was his neighbour. He was reliable with a lot of *hadiths*."

Ya'qub ibn 'Abdullah ibn al-Ashajj

His *kunya* was Abu Yusuf. He was killed as a martyr at sea in 122 AH at the end of Hisham's khalifate. He was reliable and has *hadiths*.

Wahb ibn Kaysan

His *kunya* was Abu Nu'aym, the client of 'Abdullah ibn az-Zubayr ibn al-'Awwam. He died in 127 AH. I asked Muhammad ibn 'Umar about Wahb and he said, "He did not give *fatwa*. He was a reliable *muhaddith*. He used to pray and leave. He met a number of the Companions of the Messenger of Allah صلعم."

Wahb ibn Kaysan said, "I saw Sa'd ibn Abi Waqqas, Jabir ibn 'Abdullah, Abu Sa'id al-Khudri and Abu Hurayra wearing silk/wool."

Yazid ibn Ruman

Ruman was the client of the family of az-Zubayr. He died in 120 AH and related from Salih ibn Khawwat and others. He was a scholar with a lot of *hadiths*.

Isma'il ibn Abi Hakim

The client of the Banu 'Adi ibn Nawfal. No one acknowledges their claim to be clients of the family of az-Zubayr. He was a scribe of 'Umar ibn 'Abdu'l-'Aziz. He died in 130 AH. He had few *hadiths*.

Salim Abu'n-Nadir ibn Abi Umayya

Abu Umayya was the client of 'Umar ibn 'Abdullah at-Taymi. He died while Marwan II was khalif. He related from Malik ibn Abi 'Amr, Abu Murra, the client of Umm Hani', Busr ibn Sa'id, and Abu Salama ibn 'Abdu'r-Rahman. He was reliable, with a lot of *hadiths*.

'Abdu'r-Rahman ibn Mahran

Mahran was the client of the Banu Hashim. He has *hadiths*. Sa'id ibn Abi Sa'd al-Maqburi and Ibn Abi Dhi'b related from him.

Zayd ibn Aslam

Aslam was the client of 'Umar ibn al-Khattab. His *kunya* was Abu Usama.

Muhammad ibn 'Umar said, "I heard Malik ibn Anas say, 'Zayd ibn Aslam had a circle in the mosque of the Messenger of Allah صلعم and he related from Ibn 'Umar, his father, 'Ata' ibn Yassar, and 'Abdu'r-Rahman ibn Abi Sa'id al-Khudri. He had a lot of *hadiths*.'"

Malik ibn Anas reported that Zayd ibn Aslam was put in charge of the mines of the Banu Sulaym. There was a mine in which people were continually afflicted by the jinn. When Zayd was appointed over them, they complained about this to him, and he commanded that the *adhan* be called there very loudly. They did that, and then they ceased to be troubled, which remains the case today.

It is said that 'Abdullah ibn Wahb related that Malik ibn Anas said, "If someone came to Zayd ibn Aslam to ask him about something and he confused him, then he would tell him, 'Go away and learn how to ask. When you have learned that, then come and ask.'"

Muhammad ibn 'Umar said, "Zayd ibn Aslam died in Madina two years before Muhammad ibn 'Abdullah rebelled. He rebelled in 145 AH.

Khalid ibn Aslam

Aslam was the client of 'Umar ibn al-Khattab. He was related from. He was the strongest young man in Madina. His *kunya* was Abu Thawr. He was older than Zayd ibn Aslam.

Shayba ibn Nisah

Nisah was the client of Umm Salma bint Abi Umayya, the wife of the Messenger of Allah صلعم. He was a reciter. He died while Marwan II was khalif. He was reliable, with few *hadiths*.

Da'ud ibn al-Husayn

Al-Husayn was the client of 'Amr ibn 'Uthman ibn 'Affan. His *kunya* was Abu Sulayman. He related from 'Ikrima, 'Abdu'r-Rahman al-A'raj and Abu Sufyan, the client of Ibn Abi Ahmad. He was reliable and Malik ibn Anas related from him. He died in Madina in 135 AH at the age of 72.

Abu'z-Zinad

His name was 'Abdullah ibn Dhakwan, the client of Ramla bint Shayba. Ramla was married to 'Uthman ibn 'Affan. Abu'z-Zinad's actual *kunya* was Abu 'Abdu'r-Rahman, but he is usually referred to as Abu'z-Zinad.

'Abdu'r-Rahman ibn Abi'z-Zinad said that 'Umar II put Abu'z-Zinad in charge of the *kharaj* of Iraq, along with 'Abdu'l-Hamid ibn 'Abdu'r-Rahman, and so he went to Kufa. Hammad ibn Abi Sulayman was a close friend of Abu'z-Zinad. He used to go to him and converse with him. Abu'z-Zinad employed the nephew of Hammad ibn Abi Ishaq in some post in which he received 10,000 dirhams. Hammad went to him to thank him.

Malik ibn Anas said, "Abu'z-Zinad had a circle of his own in the mosque of the Messenger of Allah صلعم."

Muhammad ibn 'Umar reported from someone who saw 'Abdullah ibn Hasan and Sa'id ibn Hasan sitting beside Abu'z-Zinad in his circle.

I asked Muhammad ibn 'Umar who the seven were from whom Abu'z-Zinad related when he said, "The seven reported to me ..." He replied, "Sa'id ibn al-Musayyab, 'Urwa ibn az-Zubayr, Abu Bakr ibn 'Abdu'r-Rahman, al-Qasim ibn Muhammad, 'Ubaydullah ibn 'Abdullah, Kharija ibn Thabit and Sulayman ibn Yasar."

Muhammad ibn Umar said, "Abu'z-Zinad died suddenly in Madina on Friday night on the 17th Ramadan 130 AH at the age of 66. He was reliable, with a lot of *hadiths*. He was eloquent, with insight into Arabic, an intelligent scholar. He was in charge of the *kharaj* in Madina."

Rabi'a ar-Ra'y ibn Abi 'Abdu'r-Rahman

Abu 'Abdu'r-Rahman's name was Farukh. He was the client of the family of al-Munkadir at-Taymi. His *kunya* was Abu 'Uthman.

Isma'il ibn 'Abdullah heard Malik ibn Anas say, when wearing silk/wool was mentioned in his presence, "Rabi'a ibn Abi 'Abdu'r-Rahman used to wear a hat whose outside and inside were made of silk/wool. He did not see any harm in wearing silk/wool." He was asked, "Did he not make the lining silk/wool so that it did not show since other than silk/wool would be sufficient?" Malik said that by that he desired warmth and softness.

Malik ibn Anas said that Rabi'a said, "People are like children under the tutelage of their scholars, the tutelage of their fathers and of those who rule them."

Mutarrif said that Malik said, "We used to be thirty turbaned men in the circle of Rabi'a not counting those who were not turbaned. Rabi'a used to wear a turban."

He also heard Malik say, "The sweetness of *fiqh* has departed since Rabi'a ibn Abi 'Abdu'r-Rahman died."

Ibn Abi Sabr and 'Abdullah ibn Ja'far said, "When Rabi'a was ill, he sat in his house and a table was laid for his visitors which was always ready. Whenever people came to visit him, he said, 'They are afflicted! They are afflicted!' He continued like that until he was left. That was a pretence."

Sulayman ibn Bilal said, "I entered Rabi'a's house when he was intending to go on *hajj* and was preparing for that. I saw two mill-stones grinding sugar."

Muhammad ibn 'Umar said, "He had manliness and generosity as well as *fiqh* and knowledge. He had a circle in the mosque of the Messenger of Allah صلعم. For a time he and Abu'z-Zinad had a circle together. Then afterwards they separated and each sat in his own circle. Abu Ja'far Muhammad ibn 'Ali used to sit with Rabi'a in his circle and Ja'far ibn Muhammad continued to sit with Rabi'a.

"I asked, 'Why? Because the *wala'* of Rabi'a belonged to the al-Munkadir family?' He said, 'No, it was because of the brotherhood between Rabi'a and them.'"

Yahya ibn Sa'id said, "I did not see anyone with a stronger intellect than Rabi'a." Layth said, "He was the master of the people of Madina and their leader in *fatwa*."

Bakr ibn Mudar said, "Al-Walid I asked Rabi'a, 'Why did you abandon transmission?' He replied, 'Amir al-Mu'minin, time has passed and the people of contentment are few.'"

Muhammad ibn 'Umar said that he died in Madina in 136 AH at the end of as-Saffah's khalifate. He was reliable with a lot of *hadiths*. It seemed they were cautious about him because of his use of *ra'y*.

Safwan ibn Sulaym

The client of Hamid ibn 'Abdu'r-Rahman az-Zubri. His *kunya* was Abu 'Abdullah. He was reliable, with a lot of *hadiths*, a worshipper. He died in Madina in 136 AH.

Muhammad ibn Qays

The client of Mu'awiya ibn Abi Sufyan. He died in Madina during the civil war of al-Walid I. Abu Ma'shar Nujayh related from him. He was a scholar with a lot of *hadiths*.

Musa ibn Maysara

His *kunya* was Abu 'Urwa, the client of the Banu'd-Dayl. He is the maternal uncle of Thawr ibn Zayd ad-Dayli. Ad-Dahhak ibn 'Uthman related from him. He died at the end of Umayyad rule and he was reliable, with *hadiths*. Malik ibn Anas related from him.

'Abdullah ibn Zubayd

The client of 'Ali ibn Abi Talib, He was a brother of 'Ali ibn al-Husayn by the same mother. Their mother's name was Ghazzala. 'Abdullah related from 'Ali ibn al-Husayn, and Abu 'Alqama 'Abdullah ibn Muhammad related from him.

Thawr ibn Zubayd ad-Dayli

Their client. He is the cousin of Musa ibn Maysara. He related from 'Ikrima and from Abu'l-Ghayth and others. Malik ibn Anas and others related from him.

'Abdullah ibn Yazid ibn Hurmuz

The client of the Dawsites. His *kunya* was Abu Bakr. His father was in charge of the clients in the Battle of al-Harra.

Muhammad ibn 'Abdullah said, "Some people used to meet with 'Abdullah ibn Yazid in his house in the Banu Layth. They were al-Harith and 'Abdullah, the sons of 'Ikrima ibn 'Abdu'r-Rahman, Sa'd ibn Ibrahim, Salih ibn Kaysan, Rabi'a, Abu 'Ubayda ibn Muhammad and as-Salt ibn Zubayd, and they discussed *fiqh* and *hadith*. They only separated after eating."

'Abdullah ibn Yazid said, "I did not learn any knowledge on the day that I learned it except that it was for myself."

Malik ibn Anas said, "The people used to wear turbans, including 'Abdullah ibn Yazid ibn Hurmuz."

Malik ibn Anas said, "'Abdullah ibn Yazid was very deaf."

Mutarrif said, "I saw him and met him when I was young. He was one of the people of scrupulousness."

Salih ibn Kaysan

His *kunya* was Abu Muhammad.

'Abdullah ibn Ja'far said, "I visited Salih ibn Kaysan who was making a will. He said to me, 'I testify that my *wala'* belongs to a woman client of the family of Mu'ayqib ibn Abi Fatima ad-Dawsi.' Sa'id ibn 'Abdullah said to him, 'You must write it down.' He said, 'I will not have you as a witness. You are a doubter.' Sa'id used to be someone who would be in *wudu'* but was unsure of it."

Salih ibn Kaysan died in 140 AH before the rebellion of Muhammad ibn 'Abdullah in 145 AH. Salih related from 'Urwa, 'Ubaydullah ibn 'Abdullah, Abu Muhammad Nafi', the client of Abu Qatada, az-Zuhri and others. He was reliable, with a lot of *hadiths*.

Al-'Ala' ibn 'Abdu'r-Rahman ibn Ya'qub

The client of al-Haraqa of Juhayna. He lived until the beginning of the khalifate of al-Mansur. Malik ibn Anas said, "Al-'Ala' ibn 'Abdu'r-Rahman had a collection on paper and he reported what was in it. When a man came to him to write some of it and omit some of it, al-Ala' said, 'You either take it all or leave it all.'"

Muhammad ibn 'Umar said, "The paper of al-'Ala' was well-known in Madina. He was reliable, with a lot of *hadiths*. He died at the beginning of al-Mansur's khalifate."

Sulayman ibn Suhaym

His *kunya* was Abu Ayyub, the client of the Banu Ka'b of Khuza'a. He died at the beginning of al-Mansur's khalifate. He was reliable, with *hadiths*.

'Abdullah ibn Abi Lubayd

The client of the family of al-Akhnas ibn Shariq ath-Thaqafi, the allies of Zuhra. His *kunya* was Abu'l-Mughira. He spoke on *Qadar*. He was one of the devout isolated worshippers. He related from Sa'id ibn al-Musayyab and Abu Salama ibn 'Abdu'r-Rahman. He died at the beginning of the khalifate of al-Mansur. He had few *hadiths*.

Abu Hazim

His name was Salama ibn Dinar, the client of Banu Shaj'. He was lame. He was an ascetic worshipper. He used to tell stories after *Fajr* and after *'Asr* in the mosque of Madina. The khalif Sulayman came to Madina and people went to him. He sent for Abu Hazim. He came to him and was rude to him. He asked him, "Abu Hazim, what property do you have?" He replied, "I have two properties." He asked, "What are they?" He replied, "Trust in Allah and despair of having what other people possess."

Abi Hazim said, "I ask Allah in my prayer, even for salt."

Muhammad ibn 'Umar said, "The wife of Abu Hazim said, 'This hard winter has assailed us. We must have something to help us through it.' She mentioned clothes, food and wood. He said. 'All of that is necessary, but accept what is inevitable: death, then the resurrection, then standing before Allah and then the Garden and the Fire.'"

Muhammad ibn 'Umar said, "Abu Hazim had a donkey. He used to ride it to the mosque of the Messenger of Allah صلعم to attend the prayers. He died after 140 AH while al-Mansur was khalif. He was reliable, with a lot of *hadiths*."

'Abdu'r-Rahman ibn 'Ata'

The owner of ash-Shari'a, which is some land at Zuqaq Ruma near Madina. His *kunya* was Abu Muhammad. He was one of the clients of Quraysh. Ibn Abi Dhi'b, Hisham ibn Sa'd, Da'ud ibn Qays al-Farra', and Sulayman ibn Bilal related from him. He died in Madina in 143 AH while al-Mansur was khalif. He was reliable, with few *hadiths*.

Muhammad ibn Abi Harmala

The client of the Banu 'Amir ibn Lu'ayy. His *kunya* was Abu 'Abdullah. He was a scribe of Sulayman ibn Yasar when he was in charge of the market. He died at the beginning of the khalifate of al-Mansur. He had a lot of *hadiths*.

Harun ibn Abi 'A'isha

One of the clients of the people of Madina. Ibn Jurayh related from him.

✽✽✽✽✽

This generation also includes: **Sulayman ibn 'Ali ibn 'Abdullah ibn al-'Abbas**, whose mother was an *umm walad* and who died in Basra in 142 AH at the age of 59; **Yazid ibn Khusayfa ibn Yazid**, who was a devout worshipper, reliable, with a lot of *hadiths*; **Makhrama ibn Sulayman al-Walibi**, who was killed by the Kharijites at Qudayd in 130 AH and had few *hadiths*; **al-Walid ibn Sa'id ibn Sabdar al-Aslami**, Abu'l-'Abbas, who died in 130 AH and had few *hadiths*: **as-Salt ibn Zubayd ibn as-Salt**, who was appointed qadi of Madina; **Ayyub ibn Abi Umama ibn Sahl**, whose mother was Umm 'Abdullah bint 'Atik, and who had a son Yazid, whose mother was Hammara bint Muhammad; **al-Husayn ibn 'Abdullah ibn 'Amr**, Abu Muhammad, who had few *hadiths* and died in 126 AH; **Hakim ibn Hakim ibn 'Abbad**, who had few *hadiths* which are not used as evidence; his brother **'Uthman ibn Hakim**, who was reliable and from whom the Kufans related; **'Umar ibn Kathir ibn Aflah al-Ansari**, from whom Yahya ibn Sa'id al-Ansari related and who is reliable with *hadiths*; **'Abdu'r-Rahman ibn Kathir ibn Aflah**, who is related from; **Isma'il ibn Umayya ibn 'Amr**, whose mother was an *umm walad* and who died in 133 AH, a reliable man, with a lot of *hadiths*; **'Umar ibn 'Abdullah**, who is related from and is reliable, with few *hadiths*; **Ishaq ibn Abi Hakim**, who related from Ata' ibn Yasar and others and who had few *hadiths*; **Muhammad ibn Zayd ibn Talha**, whose mother was Khalifa bint Mu'adh and who had a son, 'Abdullah, whose mother was an *umm walad*; **'Umar ibn Salim ibn 'Abdullah ibn 'Umar ibn al-Khattab**, whose mother was Umm al-Hakam bint Yazid and who had a son Hafs, by an *umm walad;* **'Abdullah ibn Abi Sufyan**, the client of Ibn Abi Ahmad who died in Madina in 139 AH; **Sa'id ibn Khalid al-Qarizi**, one of the Banu Layth ibn Bakr, the allies of the Banu Zuhra, who died at end of the Umayyads; **Sudayq ibn Musa ibn 'Abdullah ibn az-Zubayr**, Abu Bakr, whose mother was Umm Ishaq bint Mujamma', and from whom Ibn Jurayj related; **al-Harith ibn al-Fudayl ibn al-Harith**, Abu 'Abdullah, whose mother was Zaynab bint 'Isa, and who had a son 'Abdullah, whose mother was Maryam bint 'Adi; **al-Qasim ibn 'Umayr**, Abu Rishdin, who had few *hadiths*; **Habib**, the client of 'Urwa ibn az-Zubayr, who died young at the end of the Umayyad period and had few *hadiths*; and **'Abdullah ibn 'Ubayda ibn Nushayt**, the brother of Musa ibn 'Ubayda, who was killed by the Kharijites at Qudayd in 130 AH.

Chapter Five
The Fifth Generation
of the *Tabi'un* of the People of Madina

Yahya ibn Sa'id ibn Qays

His *kunya* was Abu Sa'id and his mother was an *umm walad*. His children were 'Abdu'l-Hamid, 'Abdu'l-'Aziz, Amatu'l-Hamid – who married 'Ubaydullah ibn Muhammad ibn al-Mundhir, and Amatu'l-Hamid – who married a descendant of 'Umar ibn al-Khattab, and their mother was Umayma bint Sirma.

Sulayman ibn Bilal said, "Yahya ibn Sa'id went to North Africa … He had inherited something and also Rabi'a ibn Abi 'Abdu'r-Rahman asked to go with him when he commenced his post. He took the legacy, which was 500 dinars, with him to North Africa. People came to him to greet him. Rabi'a also came to him. When Rabi'a wanted to leave, he stopped him. When all the people had left, he ordered that the door be shut. Then he poured out the dinars in front of Rabi'a. He said, 'Abu 'Uthman, by Allah, there is no god but Him. I have not concealed a single dirham of it except for something which I spent on the road.' Then he gave 250 dinars to Rabi'a and kept 250 for himself."

Layth ibn Sa'd said, "A letter was brought to Yahya which was read out to him. He disliked its great length because he had no scribes. He began to criticise it until it was said to him, 'Let us read it out to you. Allow what you recognise and reject what you do not know.' He knew all of it."

Mu'awiya ibn Salih said that he saw engraved on the ring of Yahya ibn Sa'id, 'In the Name of Allah' or 'Praise be to Allah'.

Muhammad ibn 'Umar said, "When al-Walid I was appointed, he appointed Yusuf ibn Muhammad ath-Thaqafi over Madina and he appointed Sa'id ibn Ibrahim qadi of Madina. Then he dismissed him and made Yahya ibn Sa'id al-Ansari qadi."

Malik ibn Anas said, "When Yahya ibn Sa'id wanted to go to Iraq, I said to him, 'Write down a hundred *hadiths* of Ibn Shihab for me and bring them.' He wrote out a hundred of the *hadiths* of Ibn Shihab and brought them and gave them to me." I said to Malik, "Did he not read them to you nor you read them to him?" – "No," he said, "he had more *fiqh* than that."

Muhammad ibn 'Umar said, "Yahya ibn Sa'id came to al-Mansur in Kufa when he was at al-Hashimiyya and he appointed him qadi at al-Hashimiyya. He died in 143 AH. He was reliable and had *hadiths*. He was a trustworthy authority."

His brother, 'Abdu Rabbih Sa'id ibn Qays

His mother was an *umm walad*. She was Umm Yahya ibn Sa'id. His children were Umm Sa'id, who married Muhammad ibn As'ad; and Fatima, who married 'Abdu'l-Hamid ibn Yahya, and whose mother was an *umm walad*. He died in 139 AH. He was reliable, with a lot of *hadiths*, but less than his brother Yahya ibn Sa'id.

Their brother, Sa'd ibn Sa'id

His mother was an *umm walad*. His children were Sa'id, Qays, Muhammad and Umama, whose mother was Habiba bint Muhammad. He died in 141 AH. Abu Mu'awiya ad-Darir and 'Abdullah ibn Numayr related from him. He was reliable, with few *hadiths*, less than his brothers.

Ibrahim ibn 'Uqba ibn Abi Ayyash

The client of az-Zubayr ibn al-'Awwam. Az-Zubayr freed Abu 'Ayyash. He was older than his brother Musa ibn 'Uqba. He died before him. Sufyan ibn 'Uyayna met him and related from him.

Muhammad ibn 'Umar said, "Ibrahim, Musa and Muhammad, the sons of 'Uqba, had a circle in the mosque of the Messenger of Allah صلعم. All of them were *fuqaha'* and *hadith* scholars. Musa used to give *fatwa*. Ibrahim was reliable, with few *hadiths*."

Muhammad ibn 'Uqba

The client of az-Zubayr ibn al-'Awwam. His *kunya* was Abu Muhammad. He died before the rebellion of Muhammad ibn

'Abdullah. He was reliable, with few *hadiths*. He is related from, as are his brothers.

'Amr ibn Abi 'Amr

The client of al-Mutallib ibn 'Abdullah al-Makhzumi. His *kunya* was Abu 'Uthman. Abu 'Amr's name was Maysara. 'Amr died at the beginning of the khalifate of al-Mansur when Ziyad ibn 'Ubaydullah was in charge of Madina. Sulayman ibn Bilal related from 'Amr. He had *mursal hadiths*.

'Alqama ibn Abi 'Alqama

A client of 'A'isha, the wife of the Prophet صلعم. He died at the beginning of the khalifate of al-Mansur. Malik ibn Anas related from him and he had sound *hadiths*. 'Alqama has a book which he taught, on Arabic, grammar and poetry.

'Umar ibn 'Abdullah

The client of Ghufra bint Rabah, the sister of Bilal ibn Rabah. He sat with Sa'id ibn al-Musayyab, al-Qasim ibn Muhammad and others. He died after the rebellion of Muhammad ibn 'Abdullah. He was reliable with a lot of *hadiths*. He rarely gave an *isnad*. He mostly used *mursal hadiths*.

Usayd ibn Abi Usayd

The client of Abu Qatada al-Ansari. His *kunya* was Abu Ibrahim. He died at the beginning of the khalifate of al-Mansur. He had a lot of *hadiths*.

'Abbad ibn Abi Salih

The client of Juwayriyya, a Qaysi woman. He was older than his brother Suhayl. Suhayl related from him. He died while Marwan II was khalif. He had few *hadiths* and is considered weak.

His brother Suhayl ibn Abi Salih

Ibn Abi Dh'ib and other companions of his said, "Suhayl was once so angry with his brother 'Abbad that he began to talk to himself." Suhayl died while al-Mansur was khalif. He was reliable with a lot of *hadiths*, and both the people of Madina and the people of Iraq related from him.

Salih ibn Muhammad ibn Za'ida

Muhammad ibn 'Umar said, "I saw him when nothing was being heard from him." His *kunya* was Abu Waqid. He went on an expedition and died in Madina before the rebellion of Muhammad ibn 'Abdullah. He related from Sa'id ibn al-Musayyab, Abu Salama ibn'Abdu'r-Rahman and 'Umar ibn 'Abdu'l-'Aziz. He had *hadiths*, and he is weak.

Abu Ja'far al-Khatmi

His name was 'Umayr ibn Yazid of Aws. His mother was Umm al-Qasim bint 'Uqba. He had no children. Shu'ba, Hammad ibn Salama and Yahya ibn Sa'id al-Qattan related from him.

Muhammad ibn 'Abdu'r-Rahman ibn Labiba

Labiba is Umm Muhammad, a foreign woman. 'Abdu'r-Rahman was a client of Quraysh. He met Ibn 'Umar and related from him, and from 'Amir ibn Sa'd ibn Abi Waqqas. 'Abdu'l-Hamid ibn Ja'far and Usama ibn Zayd related from Muhammad ibn 'Abdu'r-Rahman. Muhammad ibn Umar saw him but did not relate anything from him. He had few *hadiths*.

'Abdu'r-Rahman ibn Harmala al-Aslami

His *kunya* was Harmala. He was one of the Banu Malik. He died during the rebellion of Muhammad ibn 'Abdullah.

'Abdu'r-Rahman ibn Muhammad

His *kunya* was Abu Muhammad. He was from al-Qara. He is related to al-Jawn ibn Khuzayma. He lived until the death of al-Mansur. He had few *hadiths*.

'Abdu'r-Rahman ibn Abi 'Awn ad-Dawsi

He was devoted to 'Abdullah ibn Hasan. Al-Mansur suspected

him of being aware of the plans of Muhammad ibn 'Abdullah. So he fled from him to Tard al-Qadum and concealed himself there with Muhammad ibn Ya'qub and died with him suddenly in 144 AH. He has *hadiths*.

Ishaq ibn 'Abdullah ibn Abi Farwa

His *kunya* was Abu Sulayman. Abu Farwa was the client of 'Uthman ibn 'Affan. He said that 'Ubayd al-Haffar brought a slave to Abu Farwa in his home and that 'Uthman freed him after that. Abu Farwa held the same opinion as the Kharijites, and he was killed with Ibn az-Zubayr and buried in the Masjid al-Haram. One of his children said that he was from the Baliy tribe. His name was al-Aswad ibn 'Umar. His son 'Abdullah ibn Abi Farwa was with Mus'ab ibn az-Zubayr in Iraq. Mus'ab trusted him and he became very wealthy with him. Ishaq ibn 'Abdullah had a circle in the mosque of the Messenger of Allahصلعم where his people sat with him – they were numerous in Madina. Ishaq was with Salih ibn 'Ali in Syria and the Syrians listened to him. Then he came to Madina and died there in 144 AH while al-Mansur was khalif. Ishaq had a lot of *hadiths*. He related *munkar hadiths* and his *hadiths* are not used as evidence.

His brother, 'Abdu'l-Hakim ibn 'Abdullah

Yahya ibn Sa'id al-Ansari related from him. He was firmer than his brother Ishaq. He was reliable with few *hadiths*. He used to give *fatwa* in Madina. He had a circle. His *kunya* was Abu 'Abdullah. He died in 156 AH at the end of the khalifate of al-Mansur. Muhammad ibn 'Umar listened to him, and a number of his brothers gave *fatwa* and transmitted. They included Salih ibn 'Abdullah, Abu'l-Hasan, Ibrahim and 'Abdu'l-Ghaffar, the sons of 'Abdullah.

Al-Muhajir ibn Yazid

The client of the family of Ibn Abi Dhi'b al-'Amiri. His *kunya* was Abu 'Abdullah.

Ibn Abi Dhi'b said, "I wrote with him to 'Ata' ibn Abi Rabah. He had few *hadiths*."

Al-Khattab ibn Salih ibn Dinar at-Tammar

A client of the family of Qatada ibn an-Nu'man al-Ansari. His *kunya* was Abu 'Umar. He was older than his brother Muhammad and more advanced. He died in 143 AH while al-Mansur was khalif.

Al-Muhajir ibn Mismar

The client of Sa'd ibn Abi Waqqas az-Zuhri. He died after the rebellion of Muhammad ibn 'Abdullah. It is said that was in 150 AH. He had sound *hadiths*.

His brother, Bukayr ibn Mismar

His *kunya* was Abu Muhammad. Muhammad ibn 'Umar met him and listened to him. He died in 153 AH. He had *hadiths*.

'Abdullah ibn Yazid ibn Fantas

His *kunya* was Abu Yazid. He died in 149 AH. Ibn Abi Dhi'b related from him. 'Abdullah related from Anas ibn Malik and Sa'id ibn al-Musayyab.

Muhammad ibn 'Ajlan

The client of Fatima bint al-Walid ibn 'Utba. His *kunya* was Abu 'Abdullah. He was a *faqih* and devout worshipper. He had a circle in the mosque. He used to give *fatwa*. Da'ud ibn Qays al-Farra' used to sit with him.

Muhammad ibn 'Umar said, "I heard 'Abdullah ibn Muhammad saying, 'My father was carried (in the womb) for more than three years.'"

Muhammad ibn 'Umar said, "I heard the women of the family of Jahhaf from the children of Zayd ibn al-Khattab say, 'No woman of us was pregnant for less than 30 months. Pregnancy was like that for us.' He wanted to make that the limit, but then a menstruation after three years – or more or less – disproved it. Then it was clear that the duration of pregnancy is not always the same." He said, "I heard Malik ibn Anas say, 'Pregnancy can be two years or more. I know of those whose pregnancy was more than that,' meaning himself."

Muhammad ibn 'Ajlan rebelled with Muhammad ibn 'Abdullah in Madina. When Muhammad ibn 'Abdullah was killed and Ja'far ibn Sulayman was appointed over Madina, he sent for Muhammad ibn 'Ajlan and he was brought before him. He rebuked him harshly. He said, "You rebelled with the liar." He commanded that his hand be cut off. Muhammad ibn 'Ajlan did not utter a word. He only mouthed something with his lips which could not be made out. It was thought that he was making supplication. Those of the *fuqaha'* and nobles of the people of Madina who were present with Ja'far ibn Sulayman stood up and said, "May Allah make the amir fortunate. Muhammad ibn 'Ajlan is the *faqih* of the people of Madina and its devout worshipper! The matter was confused, it seemed to him that he might have been the Mahdi who has been predicted." They continued to entreat him until he left him alone. Then Muhammad ibn 'Ajlan went back to his house without uttering a single word.

Muhammad ibn 'Umar said, "I saw him and listened to him. He died in 149 AH or 148 AH while al-Mansur was khalif. He was reliable, with a lot of *hadiths*."

Muhammad ibn Abi Maryam

The client of the Banu Sulaym and then of the Banu Nasira. He died after the rebellion of Muhammad ibn 'Abdullah in Madina.

His brother, 'Abdullah ibn Abi Maryam

He is Abu Yahya ibn 'Abdullah who was with Harun, the Amir al-Mu'minin. He died after Muhammad ibn 'Abdullah rebelled. He is related from.

Muslim ibn Abi Maryam

The client of one of the people of Madina. He is not the brother of Muhammad and 'Abdullah ibn Abi Maryam. Malik related from him. He was severe towards the *Qadariyya*. He was reliable, with few *hadiths*.

Muhammad ibn 'Abdu'r-Rahman ibn Abi Zinad said, "Muslim ibn Abi Maryam was severe against the *Qadariyya*, censuring them and what they said." He said, "He broke his foot and left it as it was without setting it. He was asked about that. He said, 'If He broke it, then who am I to mend it! I would be opposing Him in that case!'"

Al-Harith ibn 'Abdu'r-Rahman ibn Sa'd ad-Dawsi

He settled in al-A'was, about 11 miles from Madina on the road to Iraq. Muhammad ibn 'Umar said, "I met him and I saw him but did not listen to anything from him. He died a year after the rebellion of Muhammad ibn 'Abdullah. He had few *hadiths*. His brother, 'Abdullah ibn 'Abdu'r-Rahman ibn Sa'd ad-Dawsi, is also related from."

Yazid ibn Abi 'Ubayda

The client of Salama ibn al-Akwa' al-Aslami. He died in Madina two or three years after the rebellion of Muhammad ibn 'Abdullah. He was reliable, with many *hadiths*.

Muhammad ibn Abi Yahya

Abu Yahya was Sam'an, a client of 'Amr ibn 'Abbad. His *kunya* was Abu 'Abdullah. He is Abu Ibrahim ibn Muhammad. He died in Madina in 144 AH while al-Mansur was khalif. He was reliable with a lot of *hadiths*. Yahya ibn Sa'id al-Qattan related from him.

Isma'il ibn Rafi'

His *kunya* was Abu Rafi'. He is Ibn Abi 'Umaymir, a client of Muzayna. He died young in Madina. He had a lot of *hadiths* and was weak. He is the one who related the *hadith* on the Final Trumpet in full.

'Abdullah ibn Sa'id ibn Abi Hind

Abu Bakr, a client of Banu Shamkh of the Bani Fazara. He died in 146 AH or 147 AH while al-Mansur was khalif. He was reliable, with a lot of *hadiths*. Yahya ibn Sa'id al-Qattan related from him.

Sa'd ibn Ishaq ibn Ka'b

From Baliyy, an ally of the Ansar and then the Banu Salim. He died after 140 AH and before the rebellion of Muhammad ibn 'Abdullah in Madina. He was reliable in *hadiths*. Yahya ibn Sa'id al-Qattan related from him.

Salama ibn Wardan al-Junda'i

One of the Banu Kinana, their client. His *kunya* was Abu Ya'la. He saw several of the Companions of the Messenger of Allah صلعم. He had few *hadiths*. He was reliable and a *faqih*. He died at the end of the khalifate of al-Mansur.

Salama ibn Wardan said, "I saw Jabir ibn 'Abdullah, Anas ibn Malik, and 'Abdu'r-Rahman ibn al-Ashyam al-Aslami from among the Companions of the Messenger of Allah صلعم, and Malik ibn Aws, with white heads and beards."

'Isa ibn Hafs ibn 'Asim

His mother was Maymuna bint Sa'id. His children were Ubayya who married 'Ubaydullah ibn 'Urwa, Umm 'Amr and Umm Salama, whose mother was 'Abda bint 'Abdullah. He died in 157 AH in Madina at the age of 80. That was at the end of the khalifate of al-Mansur. He related from Nafi' and others. He had few *hadiths*. He was younger than his brother, 'Ubaydullah ibn 'Umar.

'Ubaydullah ibn 'Umar ibn Hafs

His mother was Fatima bint 'Umar. His children were Rabah, who is related from, Hafs and Bakkar, whose mother was Ubayya bint Abi Bakr; and Isma'il, whose mother was Fudayla bint Musa. His *kunya* was Abu 'Uthman.

When Muhammad ibn 'Abdullah rebelled against al-Mansur in Madina, 'Ubaydullah ibn 'Umar stayed on his estate and withdrew in it. He did not rebel with Muhammad. His brothers, 'Abdullah ibn 'Umar al-'Umari and Abu Bakr ibn 'Umar rebelled with him. Muhammad ibn 'Abdullah asked 'Abdullah ibn 'Umar, "Where is Abu 'Uthman?" He replied "On his estate. I and Abu Bakr ibn 'Umar are with you, so it is as if Abu 'Uthman were with us." Muhammad said, "Yes," and refrained from approaching him and all those who withdrew and did not rebel with him. He did not force anyone to rebel. When the business ended and Muhammad ibn 'Abdullah was killed and the people and their lands were safe, 'Ubaydullah ibn 'Umar entered Madina and remained there until he died in 147 AH, while al-Mansur was khalif. He was reliable, with a lot of *hadiths* which are used as evidence.

Abu Bakr ibn 'Umar ibn Hafs

His mother was Fatima bint 'Umar. He had no children. He was older than 'Ubaydullah. He rebelled with Muhammad ibn 'Abdullah, but was not killed. He died later.

'Abdullah ibn 'Umar ibn Hafs

His mother was Fatima bint 'Umar. His children were al-Qasim, Umm 'Umar and Umm 'Asim, whose mother was Hafsa bint Abi Bakr. 'Abdullah related from Nafi' a lot. 'Abdullah ibn 'Umar rebelled with Muhammad ibn 'Abdullah. He remained with him until he was killed. Then 'Abdullah concealed himself and was pursued and found and then al-Mansur commanded that he be imprisoned. He imprisoned him in a dungeon for two years and then he summoned him and said, "Did I not prefer you and honour you and yet you rebelled against me with the liar!" He replied, "Amir al-Mu'minin, we became involved in something whose true nature we did not recognise. If the Amir al-Mu'minin can pardon, forgive and preserve the descendants of 'Umar ibn al-Khattab, let him do so." So he let him go.

His *kunya* was Abu'l-Qasim. He abandoned it, saying, "I will not use the *kunya* of the Messenger of Allahﷺ," out of esteem for him. So he used the *kunya* Abu 'Abdu'r-Rahman. It was his *kunya* until he died. He died in Madina in 171 AH or 172 AH at the beginning of the khalifate of ar-Rashid. He had a lot of *hadiths* which are thought weak.

Abu Bakr ibn Muhammad ibn Zayd

His mother was an *umm walad* whose name was Sha'tha'. He had no children. He died after the rebellion of Muhammad ibn 'Abdullah in Madina, before 150 AH. He is related from him. He had a few *hadiths*.

'Umar ibn Muhammad ibn Zayd

His mother was Sha'tha'. He died a little after his brother Abu Bakr. He had no children. He is related from. He was reliable, with few *hadiths*. His brothers, 'Asim and Zayd are also related from.

Waqid ibn Muhammad ibn Zayd

His mother was Sha'tha'. His children were Ibrahim, 'Uthman, Zayd, Muhammad, 'Umar, 'Ubaydullah and Abu Bakr, whose mother was Ramla bint Musa. He is also related from.

'Abdu'r-Rahman ibn al-Mujabbir ibn 'Abdu'r-Rahman

His mother was 'A'isha, an *umm walad*. He listened to Salim ibn Muhammad, and Malik related from him.

Muhammad ibn 'Umar said, "I saw him and he died young and I did not listen to anything from him. His children were Muhammad, 'Umar, Zayd and Burayha, whose mother was Sawda bint Zayd ibn 'Abdullah ibn 'Umar ibn al-Khattab."

Abu Bakr ibn 'Umar ibn 'Abdu'r-Rahman

His mother was an *umm walad*. His children were 'Umar, 'Abdu'r-Rahman and Hafsa, whose mother was Umm Bilal bint Ma'bad.

Hashim ibn Hashim ibn 'Utba ibn Abi Waqqas

His mother was an *umm walad*. He had a son Hashim, whose mother was Umm 'Amr bint Sa'd. Hashim related from 'Amir ibn Sa'd and others. Abu Damra, 'Abdullah ibn Numayr and others related from him.

Muhammad ibn 'Abdullah ibn Hasan ibn Hasan ibn 'Ali

His mother was Hind bint Abi 'Ubayda ibn 'Abdullah. His children were 'Abdullah – who was killed in battle in the land of Qashmir by Hisham ibn 'Urwa, 'Ali – who studied in prison after being arrested in Egypt, Hasan – who was killed at Fakhkh Basra by Musa ibn 'Isa, Fatima – who married her cousin Hasan ibn Ibrahim, and Zaynab – who married Muhammad ibn Abi'l-'Abbas, the Amir al-Mu'minin. He went to her the night her father was in Madina and was with 'Isa ibn Musa and he died without consummating the marriage, and then she married 'Isa ibn 'Ali who divorced her, and then she married Muhammad ibn Ibrahim by whom she bore a girl who died young and then he divorced her, and then she married Ibrahim ibn Ibrahim. The mother of all these was Umm Salama bint Muhammad ibn Hasan. His children also included at-Tahir, whose mother was Fakhita bint Fulayh; and Ibrahim, whose mother was an *umm walad*.

His *kunya* was Abu 'Abdullah. He met Nafi', the client of 'Umar, and listened to him and others and related from them. He had a few *hadiths*. 'Abdullah ibn Ja'far and others related from him. He and his brother stayed in the desert and loved solitude. They did not visit the khalifs or the governors.

'Abdu'r-Rahman ibn Abi'l-Mawali said, "I heard 'Abdullah ibn Hasan say, 'I came to Hisham and he asked me, "Why is it that I do not see your sons Muhammad and Ibrahim coming to us?"' He replied, 'Amir al-Mu'minin, they love the desert and solitude. They do not stay away from the Amir al-Mu'minin out of anything they dislike.' So Hisham was silent."

When the Abbasids were victorious, they remained aloof and did not go to any of them. As-Saffah asked after them and their father, 'Abdullah ibn Hasan, told him the like of what he had said to Hisham. He left them alone.

When al-Mansur became khalif, he sought them out and they fled from him and isolated themselves. Their withdrawal and concealment increased. Al-Mansur appointed Ziyad ibn 'Ubaydallah al-Harithi over Makka and Madina and told him to seek them out. He ignored them and refrained from going out to look for them. Al-Mansur heard about this and dismissed him and appointed Muhammad ibn Khalid al-Qushayri and told him to seek them out in earnest. He did the like of what Ziyad had done and was not serious in searching for them. He heard that they were in one place and so he sent out riders to another place. In the meantime, their messengers brought them their news and what they needed. Al-Mansur heard about this and dismissed him and was angry with him.

Then he appointed Riyah ibn 'Uthman al-Murri over Madina and commanded him to seek them out and to be serious about them. So Riyah really searched for them, and did not tolerate them or ignore them. They were afraid and fled to the mountains. Riyah ibn 'Uthman was harsh towards their father and the people of their house. He wrote about this to al-Mansur who wrote back telling him to send them to him, so he sent them to him at ar-Rabadha. Then he sent them to Kufa and imprisoned them in al-Hashimiyya until they died in prison.

Muhammad ibn 'Abdullah heard about that and so he rebelled with those who were with him and some of Juhayna. Other bedouins joined him, as did many of the people of Madina, Quraysh and other tribes, and the bedouins and those who rallied to them. He established himself and rebelled against al-Mansur and claimed the khalifate. He took Madina and captured Riyah ibn 'Uthman and his son and nephew and imprisoned them in chains. He set aside a place in Madina for the clients of the Abbasids and imprisoned them in a house there.

Muhammad ibn 'Umar said, "Muhammad ibn 'Abdullah took Madina in the last two days of Jumada al-Akhira in 145 AH. We heard about this and we, who were young men, joined him. I was fifteen on that day. We reached him at Manayam Khashram, and people gathered round him to look at him and no one was held back from him. I approached until I saw him. I observed him while he was on a horse and he had a white burnous wrapped around him and a white turban. He was a dark-skinned man with pock-marks on his face. Then he went to Makka and it was taken for him. He sent his brother Ibrahim to Basra and he conquered it.

Al-Mansur heard about all this and it alarmed him and he prepared to fight him. He sent 'Isa ibn Musa against Muhammad ibn 'Abdullah in Madina. Al-Mansur's son, Muhammad, and a number of the generals of the people of Khorasan and their army went with him. 'Isa ibn Musa put Humayd ibn Qahtaba at-Ta'i in command of their vanguard, and equipped them with horses, mules, weapons and provisions, leaving nothing out. 'Isa ibn Musa also sent for Ibn Abi'l-Karram who was one of the companions of al-Mansur who inclined to the Abbasids. Al-Mansur trusted him. He and those with him met 'Isa ibn Musa and they proceeded until they overlooked Madina.

Muhammad ibn 'Abdullah and those with him came out and they fought a fierce battle for some days. A group of Juhayna called the Banu Shuja' stood fast with Muhammad ibn 'Abdullah until they were killed. Ibn Khudayr also went out with Muhammad ibn 'Abdullah. He was one of the descendants of Ibn az-Zubayr. When a lot of people had been killed for Muhammad ibn 'Abdullah and when he saw the gaps in his people and that the swords were decimating them, Ibn Khudayr asked Muhammad for permission to enter Madina. He gave it to him, not knowing what he intended. He went to Riyah ibn 'Uthman al-Murri and his son and killed them. Then he came back and told Muhammad. Then he advanced alone and fought so that he was killed immediately. Several men attacked Muhammad and pressed forward in the fight until Muhammad ibn 'Abdullah was killed. That was in the middle of Ramadan 145 AH. His head was taken to 'Isa ibn Musa and he called ibn Abi'l-Karram and showed it to him and he identified it for him, and 'Isa ibn Musa prostrated. He entered Madina and all the people were safe. When Muhammad ibn 'Abdullah rebelled, he lasted for two months and seventeen days until he was killed. On the day he was killed he was 53. 'Isa ibn Musa took charge of Madina. Then he went to Makka and went into *ihram* for *'umra*.

Ibrahim ibn 'Abdullah ibn Hasan

His mother was Hind ibn Abi 'Ubayda. His children were Hasan, whose mother was Umama bint 'Isma; and 'Ali and Ibrahim, by an *umm walad*.

When Muhammad ibn 'Abdullah was in control of Madina and Makka and Basra surrendered, Ibrahim ibn 'Abdullah entered it at the beginning of the day in Ramadan 145 AH and established himself there and the people of Basra supported him. 'Isa ibn Yunus, Mu'adh ibn Mu'adh, 'Abbad ibn al-'Awwam, Ishaq ibn Yusuf al-Azraq, Mu'awiya ibn Hushaym and a large group of the *fuqaha'* and people of knowledge rebelled with him. He remained in Basra during Ramadan and Shawwal.

When he heard that his brother Muhammad ibn 'Abdullah had been killed, Ibrahim ibn 'Abdullah prepared and set out against al-Mansur in Kufa. Al-Mansur wrote to 'Isa ibn Musa informing him of that and ordering him to meet him. Al-Mansur's messenger met him with his letter after he had assumed *ihram* for *'umra*. He abandoned that and headed for Ibrahim ibn 'Abdullah. Ibrahim advanced with a large group of people of unknown origin – more than the number of 'Isa's men. They met at Bakhamra, which is about 16 *farsakhs* [80 km] from Kufa, and fought a fierce battle. Humayd ibn Qahtaba, who was in charge of 'Isa's vanguard, and the people with him were defeated. 'Isa ibn Musa exhorted them to fight for Allah and the

Community, but they did not rally with him. They left him defeated and Humayd came to him defeated. 'Isa said to him, "Humayd, by Allah, return to obedience!" He replied, "There is no obedience in defeat." So he and all his people left until there was none of them left between 'Isa and the army of Ibrahim.

'Isa stood firm where he was and he remained with a hundred of his elite and entourage. It was said to him, "May Allah give you success, general – you should withdraw from this place until the people return to you." He rejected that advice and said, "I will remain here where I stand until either I am killed or Allah gives me victory. It will not be said that I was routed."

Ibrahim advanced with his army. He approached him and the dust of his army drew closer until 'Isa ibn Musa and those with him could see the army. At that point a horseman was seen approaching who wheeled round towards Ibrahim without deviating at all. It was Humayd ibn Qahtaba who had changed his breast-plate and had bound his head with a yellow band! His people turned back to follow him until all of those who had had been routed returned to join the fray.

There was a fierce battle and many were killed on both sides. Humayd ibn Qahtaba began to send heads to 'Isa ibn Musa until he was brought one head at which a large group shouted in an uproar, "The head of Ibrahim ibn 'Abdullah!" So 'Isa ibn Musa called Ibn Abi'l-Karram and showed it to him. He said, "That's not him."

They continued to fight on that day until a stray arrow struck the throat of Ibrahim ibn 'Abdullah and pierced it and he fell back. He said, "Help me down." He was lowered down from his mount, saying, "Allah's command is a fate decreed. We wanted one thing but Allah wanted another." He was brought down and he was a heavy man. His followers and friends gathered round him to protect him and fight to defend him. Humayd saw their group but did not know who it was. He told his companions, "Attack that group until you drive them back and find out why they have gathered." They attacked them and fought them fiercely until Ibrahim was left exposed. They reached him and cut off his head which they brought to 'Isa ibn Musa. He showed it to Ibn Abi'l-Karram and he said, "Yes, this is his head." So 'Isa dismounted and prostrated on the ground. He sent the head to al-Mansur.

Ibrahim was killed on Monday, the 25th Dhu'l-Qa'da 145 AH. On the day he was killed he was 48, and the period of the start of the rebellion until his death was five days short of three months.

Musa ibn 'Abdullah ibn Hasan ibn Hasan

His mother was Hind bint Abu 'Ubayd. His children were Muhammad, Ibrahim, 'Abdullah, Fatima, Zaynab, Ruqayya, Kulthum and Khadija, whose mother was Umm Salama bint Muhammad.

Idris the younger ibn 'Abdullah ibn Hasan

His mother was 'Atika bint 'Abdu'l-Malik ibn al-Harith.

When Muhammad ibn 'Abdullah was killed, Idris was young. When Husayn ibn 'Ali rebelled in Fakhkh, he rebelled with him. When Husayn was killed, Idris fled to Andalusia and the Berbers and remained there. He had a large number of children who eventually overcame that region. He left a daughter in Madina called Fatima who married Muhammad ibn Ibrahim ibn Muhammad and bore him a daughter whom he named Fatima after her mother's name, and then later on Muhammad ibn Ibrahim divorced her.

Yahya ibn 'Abdullah ibn Hasan

His mother was Qurayba bint Rukayh. He had a son Muhammad, whose mother was Khadija bint Ibrahim. Harun, the Amir al-Mu'minin carried out a search for Yahya and he hid from him in fear. He was caught in Daylam and many people came out to him. Harun sent al-Fadl ibn Yahya to him and granted him a safe conduct which he had requested. He went to him in safety and brought him to Harun who gave him permission to leave. He returned to Madina and died there. Yahya had rebelled with Husayn ibn 'Ali at Fakhkh but had slipped away that day.

'Ali ibn Hasan ibn Hasan

His mother was Fatima, who is Umm Hibba bint 'Amir. 'Ali used to be called as-Sajjad because of his worship, excellence, striving and scrupulousness. He had a son Husayn, who was the master of Fakhkh where he rebelled and summoned people to himself while Musa was khalif. That year al-'Abbas ibn Muhammad, Sulayman ibn Abi Ja'far, Musa ibn 'Isa and Muhammad ibn Sulayman went on *hajj*, and so they and their entourage and army joined those who were with him. They met him at Fakhkh and they fought him and he and those with him fought them. There were too many for them and his companions were defeated and killed. They sent his head to Musa al-Hadi, the Amir al-Mu'minin.

His children also included al-Hasan, Muhammad, 'Ubaydullah, Kulthum, Ruqayya, Fatima and Umm al-Hasan, whose mother was Zaynab bint 'Abdullah. Zaynab was also one of the devout worshippers. It used to be said, "In Madina there is no couple who worship more than 'Ali and his wife Zaynab bint 'Abdullah." When al-Mansur commanded that 'Abdullah ibn al-Hasan and his brothers and the people of his house be sent to him, this 'Ali was seized and sent with them and they were imprisoned in al-Hashimiyya in Kufa. 'Ali died in prison in 145 AH.

Hasan ibn Zayd ibn Hasan

His mother was an *umm walad*. His children were Muhammad, by whom he has his *kunya*, al-Qasim and Umm Kulthum – who married as-Saffah, the Amir al-Mu'minin and bore him two boys who died young, and their mother was Umm Salama bint Husayn. He also had 'Ali, Ibrahim, Zayd and 'Isa, whose mother was an *umm walad*; Isma'il and Ishaq al-A'war, by an *umm walad*; and 'Abdullah, whose mother was Rayyad bint Bistam. His *kunya* was Abu Muhammad. He had *hadiths* and he was reliable.

Al-Mansur appointed him over Madina for five years and then he criticised him, became angry with him, dismissed him and appropriated all his possessions and sold them and imprisoned him. After him, he appointed 'Abdu's-Samad ibn 'Ali. Muhammad al-Mahdi, who at that time was the heir apparent, wrote secretly to 'Abdu's-Samad, "Beware! Beware of Hasan ibn Zayd. Be kind to him and be generous to him." 'Abdu's-Samad did that while Hasan ibn Zayd remained in prison until al-Mansur died. Then al-Mahdi released him, brought him to him and returned everything to him which had been taken from him. They stayed together until al-Mahdi left for *hajj* in 168 AH with Hasan ibn Zayd. There was little water on the route and al-Mahdi feared that those with him would be thirsty. So he turned back from the journey and did not perform *hajj* that year. Hasan continued on to Makka, but then fell ill for some days and died at al-Hajir and was buried there in 168 AH.

'Abdullah ibn Muhammad ibn 'Umar

His mother was Khadija bint 'Ali ibn Husayn. He was called Dafin. He related from his father and others. He had few *hadiths*. He died at the end of the khalifate of al-Mansur. His brother, 'Ubaydullah ibn Muhammad, was also related from.

His brother, 'Umar ibn Mu'ammar

His mother was Khadija bint 'Ali ibn Husayn. He is also related from. His children were Ibrahim, Isma'il, Habiba and Musa by an *umm walad*; and Fatima, whose mother's name is not known.

Lut ibn Ishaq ibn al-Mughira

His mother was Umm Ishaq bint Sa'id. His *kunya* was Abu'l-Mughira. He was a worshipper and a scholar with few *hadiths*. He died while al-Mansur was khalif.

Muhammad ibn Lut ibn al-Mughira

His mother was an *umm walad*. He had a son 'Utba, whose mother was the daughter of 'Utba ibn 'Utba. His *kunya* was Abu'l-Mughira. He is related from. He died while al-Mansur was khalif. He had few *hadiths*.

Yazid ibn 'Abdu'l-Malik ibn al-Mughira

His children were 'Abdu'l-Wahid, whose mother's name is not known; and Khalid and Yahya, whose mother was an *umm walad*. His *kunya* was Abu Khalid. He is related from him and he was firm and steadfast, and has *hadiths*. He died in Madina in 167 AH.

Az-Zubayr ibn Sa'id ibn Sulayman

His mother was Humayda, who is Hammada ibn Ya'qub. His children were al-Qasim – by whom he had his *kunya*, Muhammad the elder and Ruqayya, whose mother was Umm al-Mughira bint Ishaq;

Ishaq, at-Tahir, Burayka, Umm al-Qasim, Fatima and Umm Sa'id, by an *umm walad*; al-Hasan, Sa'id, Muhammad the younger, Ibrahim, Suhayqa, Sukayna and Zaynab, whose mother was a daughter of Hasan ibn az-Zubayr; al-Fadl, Muhammad the middle, Kulthum the elder, Kulthum the younger and 'A'isha – all of whom were by an *umm walad*. He had few *hadiths*. He died while al-Mansur was khalif.

'Umar ibn Hamza ibn 'Abdullah ibn 'Umar ibn al-Khattab

His mother was Umm Hakim bint al-Mughira. He had a son Hamza, whose mother was Fatima bint Salim. Abu Usama and others related from him.

Mu'awiya ibn Ishaq ibn Talha

His mother was an *umm walad*. His children were Talha and Ishaq, whose mother was Umm Hamil bint Muyasarra; Umm Ishaq, by an *umm walad*; and Umm Yahya, by an *umm walad*. Ath-Thawri and Shu'ba related from Mu'awiya.

Muhammad ibn 'Imran ibn Ibrahim

His *kunya* was Abu Sulayman. His mother was Asma' bint Salama, whose mother was Hafsa bint 'Ubaydullah, whose mother was Asma' bint Zayd. He had a son 'Abdullah, by an *umm walad*. He was *qadi* of Madina for the Umayyads and then al-Mansur appointed him *qadi* of Madina. He was firm, awe-inspiring and majestic among men. He had few *hadiths*. He died in Madina in 144 AH. His people conveyed the news to al-Mansur who said, "Today Quraysh is levelled."

Talha ibn Yahya ibn Talha at-Taymi

His mother was Umm Aban or Umm Anas, the daughter of Abu Musa al-Ash'ari. His children were Yahya, Muhammad, Salih, Ishaq, 'Abdullah, 'Isa, Ya'qub, Isma'il, Nuh, Ibrahim, Yusuf, Da'ud, Sa'da, Umm 'Abdullah, 'A'isha and Umm Talha, by *umm walads*. He related from Talha ibn Yahya ath-Thawri and others.

His brother, Bilal ibn Yahya at-Taymi

His mother was an *umm walad*. His children were Yahya, Ishaq and 'Isa, whose mother was Rabi'a, an *umm walad*; and Talha, whose mother was Su'da bint Yahya. Al-Hazin al-Kinani praised Bilal and said:

"Bilal ibn Yahya was an unconcealed glory.
   All people have their finest, and crescent moons."

Their brother, Ishaq ibn Yahya ibn Talha

His mother was al-Hasna' bint Zabban. He had a son Muhammad whose mother's name is not known. Ishaq related from Mujahid, al-Musayyab and others. His brother, Talha ibn Yahya, was thought to be firmer in *hadith* than him. Ishaq's *kunya* was Abu Muhammad. He died in Madina while al-Mahdi was khalif, and was considered weak.

Rabi'a ibn 'Uthman

His mother was Umm Yahya bint al-Munkadir. His *kunya* was Abu 'Uthman. He was reliable, firm, with few *hadiths*. There was difficulty with him. He died in 154 AH in Madina while al-Mansur was khalif at the age of 77.

Musa ibn Muhammad ibn Ibrahim

His mother was Umm 'Isa bint 'Imran. His *kunya* was Abu Muhammad. He died in 151 AH while al-Mansur was khalif, at the age of 70. Ibn Abi Dhi'b related from him. He had a lot of *hadiths* and also has some unaccepted *hadiths*.

Ad-Dahhak ibn 'Uthman

His mother was Amina bint 'Abdullah. His children were 'Uthman and 'Abdu Rabb, whose mother was Maslama bint al-Mughira; and Muhammad, by an *umm walad*.

His *kunya* was Abu 'Uthman. He was reliable. Ath-Thawri, Ibn Abi Fudayk and others related from him. He died in Madina in 153 AH while al-Mansur was khalif. He was reliable with a lot of *hadiths*.

344

Usama ibn Zayd al-Laythi

A client of Layth. His *kunya* was Abu Zayd. He died in 153 AH at the age of about 70. He listened to al-Qasim ibn Muhammad and others. He had a lot of *hadiths* which were thought weak.

Al-Walid ibn Kathir

His *kunya* was Abu Muhammad, the client of the Banu Makhzum. He died in Kufa in 151 AH. Abu Usama and other Kufans related from him. He had knowledge of *sira* and of the expeditions of the Messenger of Allah صلعم. He had *hadiths*.

Jariya ibn Abi 'Imran

His *kunya* was Abu 'Imran. He had worth, worship and transmission of knowledge in the land. He died in Madina in 148 AH at the age of 74.

Muhammad ibn 'Umar said, "If Jariya had been told, 'The Rising will happen tomorrow,' he could not have striven any more." He said, "He is reliable in his *hadiths* which are few. We used to say to Malik concerning anything in which there was disagreement, 'Jariya related it.' He would reply, 'There is no one beyond Jariyya.'" He said, "I saw Malik enter the mosque and Jariya went to him and greeted him."

'Abdu'l-Hamid ibn Ja'far al-Hakami

It is said that he was one of the descendants of al-Fatiyun, who are the allies of Aws. His *kunya* was Abu'l-Fadl. He was reliable, with a lot of *hadith*. He died in Madina in 153 AH at the age of 70. Hushyam and others related from him. Yahya ibn Sa'id said, "Sufyan ath-Thawri used to attack 'Abdu'l-Hamid ibn Ja'far, but I do not know what the argument between the two was."

Muhammad ibn Ishaq ibn Yasar

The client of Qays ibn Makhrama. His *kunya* was Abu 'Abdullah. His grandfather was Yasar, one of the captives of 'Ayn at-Tamr. Muhammad ibn Ishaq was the first to collect the accounts of the expeditions of the Messenger of Allah صلعم and record them. He related from 'Asim ibn 'Umar, Yazid ibn Ruman, Muhammad ibn Ibrahim, and others. He related from Fatima bint al-Mundhir, the wife of Hisham ibn 'Urwa. Hisham heard of this and said, "He used to visit my wife!" as if he disliked that. He left Madina early on and only Ibrahim ibn Sa'd among them related from him.

Muhammad ibn Ishaq was with al-'Abbas ibn Muhammad at Jazira. He used to go to al-Mansur at Hira and write about the expeditions for him. The people of Kufa listened to him for that reason. The people of al-Jazira listened to him when he was with al-'Abbas ibn Muhammad. He went to Rayy and the people of Rayy listened to him. His transmitters from those lands are more numerous than those who related from him from among the people of Madina. He went to Baghdad and his son informed me that he died in Baghdad in 150 AH. He was buried in the Khayzaran graveyard. Another scholar said that he died in 151 AH. He had a lot of *hadiths*. Scholars wrote from him, although some of them consider him to be weak.

His brother, 'Umar ibn Ishaq

His *kunya* was Abu Hafs. Muhammad ibn 'Umar said, "I met him and wrote from him. He had *hadiths* and knowledge from Nafi' ibn Jubayr and others."

He had few *hadiths* and died in Madina in 154 AH as far as I know. He had a brother, Abu Bakr, who is related from.

Baradan ibn Abi'n-Nadr

He is Ibrahim ibn Salim, the client of 'Umar ibn 'Ubayd. His *kunya* was Abu Ishaq. He died in 153 AH at the age of 74. He related from Sa'id ibn al-Musayyab and others. He is reliable, with *hadiths*.

Da'ud ibn Qays al-Farra'

He is called ad-Dabbagh. His *kunya* was Abu Sulayman, the client of Quraysh. He died in Madina while al-Mansur was khalif. 'Abdullah ibn Maslama said, "I did not see two men in Madina better than Da'ud ibn Qays and al-Hajjaj ibn Safwan."

Khalid ibn al-Qasim said, "Hisham appointed Khalid ibn 'Abdu'l-Malik who used to insult 'Ali ibn Abi Talib on the minbar. One day I heard him on the minbar of the Messenger of Allah صلعم saying, 'By

346

Allah, the Messenger of Allahﷺappointed 'Ali knowing that he was such-and-such and such-and-such, but Fatima had spoken to him about him.'" Muhammad ibn 'Umar said, "Abu Qudayd reported that he saw Da'ud ibn Qays al-Farra' kneel and say, 'You are lying,' so that people could hear him."

Salih ibn Muhammad said, "I fell asleep while Khalid ibn 'Abdu'l-Malik was giving the *khutba*. I was alarmed by a dream in which the grave opened and a man came out of it saying, 'You have lied. You have lied.' When the *iqama* was given and we had prayed, I asked what the meaning of it was, and I was told that the one who had lied was Khalid ibn 'Abdu'-Malik."

Muhammad ibn 'Umar said, "Da'ud ibn Qays used to sit with Muhammad ibn 'Ajlan. When Muhammad ibn 'Ajlan died, Da'ud moved to another assembly. He was reliable, with sound *hadiths*.

Abu Hazra

His name was Ya'qub ibn Mujahid. His *kunya* was Abu Yusuf.

Muhammad ibn 'Umar said, "I think that he was the client of the Banu Makhzum. He was a storyteller. He died in Alexandria in 149 or 150 AH. He had few *hadiths*. Yahya al-Qattan related from him.

Musa ibn 'Ubayda ibn Nusayt ar-Rabadhi

His *kunya* was Abu 'Abdu'l-'Aziz. They that claim they are from Yemen – and people claim that they are clients. He died in Madina in 153 AH while al-Mansur was khalif. He was reliable, with many *hadiths*. He is not authoritative.

Mu'adh ibn Muhammad ibn 'Amr an-Najari

His *kunya* was Abu'l-Harith. He was the Imam of the mosque of the Messenger of Allahﷺin Ramadan for thirty years. He was a scholar. He died in Madina in 154 AH .

'Umar ibn Nafi'

The client of 'Abdullah ibn 'Umar ibn al-Khattab. He was reliable. Malik ibn Anas related from him. He had few *hadiths*, and they do not use him as proof. He died in Madina while al-Mansur was khalif. His brother, Abu Bakr, is also related from.

His brother, 'Abdullah ibn Nafi'

The client of 'Abdullah ibn 'Umar. His *kunya* was Abu Bakr. He died in 154 AH in Madina while al-Mansur was khalif. He has *hadiths*, but he is weak.

Yahya ibn 'Abdullah ibn Abi Qatada

One of Khazraj. His *kunya* was Abu 'Abdullah. His mother was an *umm walad*. He had a son Qatada, whose mother was Hudayda bint Nadla. He died in 162 AH.

'Abdullah ibn 'Amir al-Aslami

He is one of the Banu Malik ibn Afsa, of the brotherhood of Aslam. His *kunya* was Abu 'Amir. He was a reciter of the Qur'an. He used to lead the people of Madina in prayer in the month of Ramadan. He died in Madina in either 150, 151, or 152 AH. He had a lot of *hadiths*, but is thought weak.

Haram ibn 'Uthman al-Ansari

One of the Banu Salama. He died after the rebellion of Muhammad ibn 'Abdullah. It is said that it was 150 AH in Madina. He has a lot of *hadiths*, but is weak.

'Amr ibn 'Uthman ibn Hani'

The client of 'Uthman ibn 'Affan. Hani' is the one whom 'Ali ibn Abi Talib passed by while he was building a house in Madina. He asked, "Whose house is this?" – "Hani's," was the reply. 'Ali said "Also for Hani'!" Hani had gone blind. After the murder of 'Uthman, his son Hani' was ascribed to Hamdan. The Kufans related from 'Amr ibn 'Uthman ibn Hani'.

Muhammad ibn 'Abdu'r-Rahman ibn al-Mughira ibn al-Harith ibn Abi Dhi'b

His mother was Burayha bint 'Abdu'r-Rahman. The mother of Abu Dhi'b was Umm Habib bint al-As, and his maternal uncle was Sa'id ibn al-'As. Abu Dhi'b went to visit Caesar. 'Uthman ibn al-Huwayrith, who was called the Shaytan of Quraysh, took him to Caesar. Caesar imprisoned Abu Dhi'b until he died in prison.

Muhammad ibn 'Umar said, "Muhammad ibn 'Abdu'r-Rahman's *kunya* was Abu'l-Harith. He was born in 80 AH, the year of the Famine. He was the most scrupulous and best of people. They accused him of supporting the doctrine of *qadar*, but he was not a Qadarite. He denied their position and criticised it, but he was a generous man with whom anyone could sit without him driving him out or saying anything harsh to him. If someone was ill, he visited him. They used to suspect him of believing in *Qadar* for this reason and were doubtful about him. He used to pray all night long and made great efforts in his worship, so that it was said that if the Resurrection was going to take place the next day, he could not have increased his efforts."

His brother informed me: "He would fast every other day. Once there was an earthquake in Syria and a Syrian man came and he asked him about the earthquake. He began to tell him and he listened to him. When he had finished his account – and it was on a day on which he was not fasting – he said to him, 'Come and have lunch.' He replied, 'Leave it today.' He continued like that from that day until he died. He was in difficult circumstances and lived on bread and oil. He wore a hooded burnous and robe in both winter and summer. He was one of those who are unflinching in speaking the truth. He used to compose love sonnets when he was young and then later he sought *hadiths*. He said, 'If I had sought them when I was young, I would have met shaykhs with whom I was idle. I used to think light of that business until I grew older and more intelligent.' He used to memorise all his *hadiths*. He had no book of his own, nor anything to which he could refer, nor any *hadith* in writing to confirm anything."

He said, "I asked, Salama, his *umm walad*, 'Did he write?' She said, 'No, he did not have a single book.'"

He said, "The first day I and my brother Shamla came to him, we were turned back by the scribes. So my mother took us and smartened us up and gave me a notebook in which I had written some of the *hadiths* of Ibn Abi Dhi'b. I came and read it out to him, and both my reading and writing were poor. I stammered in it. He was exasperated and took the notebook and threw it aside, saying, 'Children who are not good at anything! Leave us!' So we got up. The following day the scribe turned us away. My mother said, 'Go to Ibn Abi Dhi'b.' My brother Shamla swore that he would not go to him, but I went to him. When he saw me, he said, 'Come, come! Go to so-and-so and take his book from him and then come.' He was patient with me until I had finished it all. I recognised that he desired Allah by it. Then my brother returned to him later. We both used to keep his company. He did not leave this world until I had directly heard from him everything that he related. It reached the point that when he was unsure about a *hadith*, he would turn to me and say, 'What do you say about such-and-such? How did I relate it to you?' and I would say, 'You related it to us in such-and-such a manner.' He would accept what I said."

Muhammad ibn 'Umar said, "I heard Ibn Abi Dhi'b when a man of Egypt asked him, 'Abu'l-Harith, do I say, "He related to me," in those *hadiths* which I read to you?' He replied, 'Whatever responsibility there is, is on my neck.'"

Muhammad ibn 'Umar said, "Ibn Abi Dhi'b used to go early to the prayer every *Jumu'a* and would pray until the Imams came out. I did not see him look at the position of the sun at all."

Muhammad ibn 'Umar said, "I saw Ibn Abi Dhi'b come to the house of his grandfathers which was between Safa and Marwa, and he collected its rent and took his share and divided the rest in shares between them."

Muhammad ibn 'Umar said, "Ibn Abi Dhi'b did not dye his white hair."

Muhammad ibn 'Umar said, "When Muhammad ibn 'Abdullah rebelled in Madina, Ibn Abi Dhi'b stayed in his house. He did not go out of it until Muhammad ibn 'Abdullah had been killed."

Muhammad ibn 'Umar said, "When a man normally sat with Ibn Abi Dhi'ib, and then did not come, he would ask the people in the assembly, 'What is happening with your companion?' If they said, 'We do not know,' he would ask, 'Where is his house?' If they said, 'We do not know,' he would become angry with them and say, 'What are you good for? A man sits with you and yet you do not know where to visit him if he is detained! If he had a need you would not be able to help him!' If they knew where his house was, he would say, 'Let us go to him in his house and ask after him and visit him.'"

Muhammad ibn 'Umar said, "I was sitting with Ibn Abi Dhi'b when an old man came to him and said, 'Do you remember, Abu'l-Harith, the day we raced at the Hammam and we ran under it and such-and-such happened?' He went on talking to him while Ibn Abi

Dhi'b remained silent, ignoring him. When he kept on about it, he said, 'Yes, I was a stupid child then.'"

Muhammad ibn 'Umar said, "Ziyad ibn 'Ubaydullah al-Harithi summoned Ibn Abi Dhi'b in order to appoint him to some office and he refused. Ziyad swore that he would appoint him. Ibn Abi Dhi'b swore that he would not do it. Ziyad said, 'Send his letter of appointment to him.' He said, 'I will not accept it.' He said, 'Send it to him whether he likes it or not and then drag him here by his foot!' Ziyad said to him, 'Son of a doer!' Ibn Abi Dhi'b said to him, 'By Allah, it is not out of the respect due to you that I have returned it to you a hundred times, but because I left it for Allah the Almighty.'

"Ziyad regretted what he had said and done to him, and said to those who were present, 'Someone like Ibn Abi Dhi'b should not have something like this done to him. His standing with the people of this land is great.' So Ziyad very much regretted what he had done to him. He said, 'We will go and placate him and release him from what I said to him.' They said, 'Do not do that. He will be contentious about it and you will not be safe from hearing what you dislike.'

"So he sent for his brother Talut and said, 'Here is 100 dinars – take them and give them to your brother and ask him to forgive me.' Talut said, 'I dare not do that. He will never forgive you!' He said, 'Take these dinars and give them to him.' He replied, 'If he knows they are from you, he will not accept them.' He said, 'Take them and spend them on something useful for him.' So he took them and bought a slavegirl for him with them. She was his *umm walad* and her name was Sallama. Ibn Abi Dhi'b did not know that. If he had known it, he would never have accepted her." He said, "Later, (when he had found out), he did not recall Ziyad's lie to him but that he wept and was grieved. He said, 'Were it not for fear of Allah, I would return her to him.'"

Muhammad ibn 'Umar said, "Al-Hasan ibn Zayd used to send Ibn Abi Dhi'b 15 dinars every month. When al-Mansur was angry with Hasan ibn Zayd, he dismissed him and appointed 'Abdu's-Samad ibn 'Ali over Madina. He commanded that Hasan ibn Zayd be jailed and confined. Al-Mahdi sent secretly to 'Abdu's-Samad to make things easier for al-Hasan ibn Zayd and not to confine him. So 'Abdu's-Samad sent for ten of the people of the mosque, including Ibn Abi Dhi'b, and said, 'Go to Hasan ibn Zayd and look at him and see how he is.' They went in, looked at him and came out. 'Abdu'r-Rahman ibn 'Abdi's-Samad called for them while al-Mahdi's messenger was with him, wanting him to hear what they said so that he would tell al-Mahdi. 'Abdu's-Samad said to them, 'How did you find the man in prison?' They said, 'We saw him in expansion – he is well and is comfortable.' Ibn Abi Dhi'b was silent and did not speak. He said, 'And what do you say?' He replied, 'They have lied to you and deceived you and misinformed you. The man is in a constricted place which is affecting him badly. I saw his constriction.' Then he rose to leave and 'Abdu's-Samad said to him. 'Come, what do you think?' He replied, 'My view is what I have just told you.'"

Muhammad ibn 'Umar said, "Ibn Abi Dhi'b visited 'Abdu's-Samad while he was the governor of Madina and spoke to him about something. 'Abdu's-Samad said to him, 'I think you are showing off.' Ibn Abi Dhi'b picked up a stick or something from the ground and said, 'By Allah, I think that anyone who shows off to people is more worthless than this.'"

Muhammad ibn 'Umar said, "Al-Mansur went on *hajj* and he summoned al-Hasan ibn Zayd and Ibn Abi Dhi'b. He wanted to provoke al-Hasan against Ibn Abi Dhi'b. Al-Mansur knew that al-Hasan's friend was not unaware of him. He asked Ibn Abi Dhi'b, 'We ask you by Allah, what do you know of al-Hasan ibn Zayd?' He replied, 'Since you adjure me, he invites us and consults with us, and we inform him of the truth – and then he leaves it and acts by his passion. If he wants something, he takes it. If he does not want it, he leaves it.' Al-Hasan said, 'I ask you by Allah, Amir al-Mu'minin, do not ask him about yourself.' Al-Mansur said to Ibn Abi Dhi'b, 'We ask you by Allah, what do you know of us? Do I not act by the truth? Do you think I am just?' Ibn Abi Dhi'b said, 'Since you have adjured me by Allah, I say: By Allah, no, I do not think you are just. You are a tyrant. You do injustice and abandon the people of good and excellence.'"

Muhammad ibn 'Umar said: "I was told by Muhammad ibn Ibrahim, Ibrahim ibn Yahya and 'Isa ibn 'Ali, 'We were with al-Mansur when Ibn Abi Dhi'b spoke those harsh words to him. We thought that al-Mansur would deal harshly with him. We began to gather up our garments and move back, out of fear of being splashed by his blood. Al-Mansur was upset and grieved. He told him, 'Get out.' So Allah provided Ibn Abi Dhi'b with safety from al-Mansur.

Ibn Abi Dhi'b went out to his *umm walad* Sallama who was with him. He said, 'Count the dinars which Hasan ibn Zayd brought you.' – 'Why?' she asked. He said, 'Al-Mansur asked me about him and I mentioned such-and-such about him while Hasan was present.' She said, 'Allah will replace it.' Hasan ibn Zayd went out and talked about what had happened with Ibn Abi'z-Zinad. He said, 'By Allah, his words did not offend me. I knew that he desired Allah by that, and that he did not desire this world. He did not please al-Mansur, but that was the truth in his view, and so he desired Allah by saying it.' When the new moon came, Hasan ibn Zayd increased it (the allowance he gave to Ibn Abi Dhi'b) by five dinars every month, making it ten. He continued to send it to him every month until he died. He said, 'I increased it because of his desire for Allah.'"

Muhammad ibn 'Umar said, "When Ja'far ibn Sulayman was governor over Madina the first time, he sent 1,000 dinars to Ibn Abi Dhi'b. Out of it he bought a Kurdish garment for ten dinars and wore it for years. Then his son wore it after him for thirty years. His circumstances were very poor. He was sent for and brought to them in Baghdad. They pressed him to accept something from them. They offered him 1,000 dinars but he would not accept it. They said, 'Take them and distribute them to whomever you see fit.' He took them and set out for Madina. While he was in Kufa, he fell ill and died. He was buried in Kufa at the age of 79. Ibn Abi Dhi'b gave *fatwa* in Madina. He was a reliable scholar, a scrupulous *faqih* and an excellent worshipper. He attacked the doctrine of *Qadar* – and the disagreement between him and Malik ibn Anas was not because of that."

Khalid ibn Ilyas

His mother was Umm Khalid bint Muhammad. He had a son Ilyas, whose mother was Umm Ghanim bint al-Yasa'.

Mus'ab ibn Thabit ibn 'Abdullah ibn az-Zubayr

His mother was an *umm walad*. His children were 'Abdullah, Abu Bakr, Mulayka and Ruqayya by an *umm walad*. His *kunya* was Abu 'Abdullah. He died in Madina in 157 AH.

Nafi' ibn Thabit ibn 'Abdullah ibn az-Zubayr

His mother was an *umm walad*. His children were 'Abdullah and

Amatu'l-Jabbar, whose mother was the daughter of 'Amir ibn Hamza. His *kunya* was Abu 'Abdullah. He died in 155 AH at the age of 72 while al-Mansur was khalif. He had few *hadiths*.

Khalid ibn Abi Bakr ibn 'Ubaydullah

His mother was Umm Husayn bint Khalid. His children were 'Abdullah, Isma'il and a daughter, whose mother was 'A'isha bint 'Umar. He died in 162 AH while al-Mahdi was khalif. He had a lot of *hadiths* and transmission.

Kathir ibn Zayd

His *kunya* was Abu Muhammad. He was the client of the Banu Sahm. He is called Ibn Safiyya, after his mother. He related from al-Muttalib ibn 'Abdullah al-Makhzumi and others. He died while al-Mansur was khalif. He had a lot of *hadiths*.

'Isa ibn Abi 'Isa al-Hannat

Abu 'Isa's name was Maysara. He was a client of Quraysh. 'Isa's *kunya* was Abu Muhammad. He used say, "I am an embalmer (*hannat*), a tailor and a baker. I did all of them." He came to Kufa on trade and met ash-Sha'bi and listened to him and related from him. He had a lot of *hadiths*, but is not used as evidence. He died while al-Mansur was khalif.

'Umar ibn Abi 'Atika

His *kunya* was Abu Hafs, a client of 'Abdullah ibn 'Umar. He was reliable in *hadiths*. He died in Madina in 155 AH while al-Mansur was khalif. He had a few *hadiths*.

Yahya ibn al-Mundhir ibn Khalid

His mother was Umm Aban bint Muhammad ibn Thabit. His children were 'Abdu'l-'Aziz, 'Abdullah and Umm Sa'id, whose mother was Sammaka bint Sulayman. He died in Madina in 152 AH while al-Mansur was khalif.

'Utba ibn Jabira ibn Mahmud

His mother was Umm Mahmud bint 'Abdu'r-Rahman. His children were ad-Dahhak and Muhammad, whose mother was Wahana bint Sirma. He died in 154 AH at the age of 70.

Yunus ibn Muhammad ibn Anas

His mother was Muslima bint Musafi'. His children were Muhammad, Yusuf, Da'ud, Musa, who is Sakhir, Harun who is Hajir, and Hammad, whose mother was Umm ar-Rabi' bint 'Uthaym. His *kunya* was Abu Muhammad. He died in 156 AH while al-Mansur was khalif at the age of 85.

'Umar ibn Suhban al-Aslami

Their client. His *kunya* was Abu Hafs, the uncle of Ibrahim ibn Muhammad. He died in 157 AH. 'Ubaydullah ibn Musa and others related from him. He had few *hadiths*.

Aflah ibn Sa'id al-Qubba'i

He settled in Qubba'. His *kunya* was Abu Muhammad. He was the client of Muzyana. He died in Madina in 156 AH while al-Mansur was khalif. He was reliable, with few *hadiths*.

Aflah ibn Humayd ibn Nafi'

A client of the family of Abu Ayyub al-Ansari. His *kunya* was Abu 'Abdu'r-Rahman. He is called Ibn Sufayra'. He listened to al-Qasim ibn Muhammad and his father and others. He died in 158 AH at the age of 80. He was reliable, with a lot of *hadiths*.

'Ubaydullah ibn 'Abdu'r-Rahman

The client of the family of Nawfal ibn 'Abd Manaf. His *kunya* was Abu Muhammad. He died in 154 AH at the age of 80. He had few *hadiths*.

'Uthman ibn 'Abdullah ibn Mawhab al-A'raj

The client of the family of al-Hakam ibn Abi'l-'As. His *kunya* was Abu 'Abdullah, He lived at Zuqaq al-Badin in Madina. He was firmer than 'Ubaydullah ibn 'Abdu'r-Rahman. He died in 160 AH while al-Mahdi was khalif. He had few *hadiths*.

Ya'qub ibn Muhammad

The client of the Banu Layth ibn Bakr. His *kunya* was Abu Yusuf. He died while al-Mansur was khalif and had few hadiths.

Abu'l-Ghusn

His name was Thabit ibn Qays, the client of the Banu Ghifar of Kinana. He died in 167 AH at the age of 105. He was early. He saw people and related from them. He was a shaykh with few *hadiths*.

Muhammad ibn 'Abdullah ibn Kathir al-Kindi

An ally of Quraysh. In Madina, he was appointed over the police and then made *qadi* and governor. He had transmission. He is related from.

Makhrama ibn Bukayr

His *kunya* was Abu'l-Miswar, the client of al-Miswar ibn Makhrama az-Zuhri. He was reliable, with a lot of *hadiths*. He died in Madina while al-Mahdi was khalif.

✳✳✳✳✳

This generation also includes **Qudama ibn Musa ibn 'Umar**, whose mother was Nufay'a bint 'Abdullah; **'Abdu'r-Rahman ibn 'Abdullah ibn Muhammad**, known as Ibn Abi 'Atiq, who is related from; **Unays ibn Abu Yahya**, Abu Yunus, who died in 145 or 146 AH and was reliable, with few *hadiths*; his brother, **'Abdullah ibn Abi Yahya**, who died in 152 AH and was reliable, with few *hadiths*; **Muhammad ibn 'Amr ibn 'Alqama al-Laythi**, Abu 'Abdullah, who died in Madina in 144 AH and had many *hadiths* but is thought weak; **Hafs ibn Abi Bakr ibn Hafs az-Zuhri**, who is related from; **Musa ibn Ishaq**, who is related from; **Muhammad ibn 'Abdullah ibn Abi Harra,** Abu 'Abdullah, the client of Aslam, who died in 157 or 158 AH; **'Abdullah ibn Abi 'Ubayda ibn Muhammad**, a scholar; **Musa ibn Abi 'Isa**, Abu Harun, who is related from; **'Asim ibn 'Umar ibn Hafs**, who was a poet and had *hadiths* but is thought weak; **Humayd ibn Ziyad al-Kharrat**, Abu Sakhr or Abu Sabh, from whom 'Abdullah ibn Wahb, Ibn Abi Fudayl and others related; **Musa ibn Ya'qub ibn 'Abdullah**, Abu Muhammad, whose mother was as-Sariyya bint Fadala, and who died at the end of the khalifate of al-Mansur; and **al-Mughira ibn 'Abdu'r-Rahman**, whose mother was Burayha bint 'Abdu'r-Rahman.

Chapter Six
The Sixth Generation
of the *Tabi'un* of the People of Madina

Malik ibn Anas

Muhammad ibn 'Umar reported that Malik ibn Anas said, "A pregnancy can last three years. Some people were carried for three years," meaning himself. More than one person related that.

Mutarrif ibn 'Abdullah al-Yasari said that Malik ibn Anas was tall, with a large bald head, and white hair and a beard which varied from very intense white to a reddish colour. His clothes were good Adeni ones. He disliked shaving the moustache and censured it and thought it was a form of self-mutilation.

Isma'il ibn 'Abdullah said, "The signet ring of Malik ibn Anas which he was wearing when he died had a bezel which was a black stone engraved with two lines: *'Allah is enough for me and the best of guardians.'* He used to wear it on his left hand. Sometimes I saw that his ring was often on his right hand. I do not doubt that he changed it from left to right when he did *wudu'* after going to the lavatory. Malik used to impose on himself what he did not oblige on others. He used to say, 'The scholar is not a scholar until he imposes on himself what he does not oblige as a judgement on other people so as to protect himself through actions which, if they were omitted, would not mean that any wrong had been committed.'"

Ma'n ibn 'Isa said, "I saw Malik wearing a ring on his left hand."

Muhammad ibn 'Umar said, "Malik did not dye his white hair."

Mutarrif ibn 'Abdullah al-Yasari said, "I asked Malik ibn Anas, 'What is engraved on your ring?' He replied, *'Allah is enough for me and the best of guardians.'* I asked, 'Why did you choose this particular engraving?' He said, 'I heard Allah Almighty say these words: *"'Allah is enough for us and the best of guardians.' So they returned with blessings and bounty from Allah and no evil touched them."*

(3:173-174)'" Mutarrif said, "I erased the engraving on my ring and engraved it with *'Allah is enough for me and the best of guardians'*."

Mutarrif ibn 'Abdullah al-Yasari said, "Malik ibn Anas reported to us, 'I used to come to Nafi', the client of Ibn 'Umar, for half of the day, or for as long as there was something to shade me from the sun. His house was at an-Naqi' at as-Surin. He was irritable. When he came out, I would leave him alone for a time as if I had not noticed him. Then I would turn to him and greet him and then leave him alone again until he entered the courtyard. Then I would say to him, "What did Ibn 'Umar say about such-and-such?" and he would answer me. Then I would withdraw from him.'"

Malik said, "I used to go to Ibn Hurmuz in the morning and did not leave his house until night. He was one of the *fuqaha'*."

Zayd ibn Da'ud, one of the best of our companions, said, "I dreamt that the grave opened and the Messenger of Allahصلعم was seated while some people were sitting apart. Someone shouted, 'Malik ibn Anas!' I saw Malik go to the Messenger of Allah who gave him something, saying, 'Divide this among the people.' So Malik took it out to divide it among the people. It was musk which he was giving them."

Mutarrif ibn 'Abdullah reported that one of his companions said, "I dreamt that a man was asking me what Malik said about such-and-such. I said, 'I do not know. But he was rarely asked about something without saying, "What Allah wills," before he gave his answer.' He said, 'If he said this about something more hidden than a hair, he would guide to what is correct.'"

Mutarrif said, "When Malik was going to enter his house, he would put his foot inside and say, *'What Allah wills. There is no power or strength except by Allah.'* It was remarked to him, 'When you want to enter your house, you say *"What Allah wills. There is no strength or power except by Allah."*' He said, 'I heard Allah say in his Book, *"Why, when you entered your garden, did you not say, 'As Allah wills, there is no strength but in Allah'?"* (18:39) My garden is my house.'"

Isma'il ibn 'Abdullah said, "Malik was asked about his *hadiths* and whether he had heard them directly. He said, 'I heard them from him when they were read to him. We do not consider reading to someone less than listening to him.'"

Mutarrif said that he heard Malik ibn Anas speak to some one who argued with him regarding reading to someone and who asserted that it is only allowed when it is transmitted orally. Malik strongly rejected that. Malik supported his argument by stating, "Do you think that if you read to a Qur'an reciter and were asked, 'Who read to you?' would you not say 'so-and- so' whether or not he had read to you a little or a lot? When you read to him, he gives you permission. That is with the Qur'an, and yet you do not want to allow it with the *hadith*! The Qur'an is greater than the *hadith*!"

Mutarrif said, "I kept the company of Malik ibn Anas for about twenty years and I did not see anyone to whom Malik read these books," meaning the *Muwatta'*.

Muhammad ibn 'Umar said, "I heard that Malik ibn Anas said, "It is extraordinary that the *muhaddith* wants to be spoken to directly, that is, when he already takes his *hadith* by reading ('*ard*) – how then can the *muhaddith* allow that? Is he not going to allow himself to be read to just as he reads to others?"

Muhammad ibn 'Umar said, "I asked Malik ibn Anas, 'Abdullah ibn'Umar al-'Umari, 'Abdu'r-Rahman ibn Abi'z-Zinad, 'Abdu'l-Halim ibn 'Abdullah ibn Abi Farwa and Abu Bakr ibn 'Abdullah ibn Abi Sabra about reading the *hadith* to the *muhaddith* or his *hadith* which he transmits, and they said that it is the same – and that is the knowledge of our land."

Mutarrif said, "A man said to Malik, 'I have heard 100,000 *hadiths*.' Malik said, '100,000 *hadiths*! You are a wood-gatherer collecting scraps at night.' He asked, 'What are scraps?' He replied, 'The wood which a man picks up at night. Sometimes he picks up a viper with it and it bites him.'"

Isma'il ibn 'Abdullah said, "Malik was asked about belief and whether it increases and decreases. He said. 'It increases. That is in the Book of Allah.' He was asked, 'Does it decrease, Abu 'Abdullah?' He said, 'I do not want to convey this.'"

Isma'il ibn 'Abdullah said, "Malik was asked what the *kunya* of his son Muhammad was. He said, 'Abu'l-Qasim,' as if he saw no harm in that."

Muhammad ibn 'Umar said, "When Muhammad ibn 'Abdullah rebelled in Madina, Malik stayed in his house and did not leave it until Muhammad had been killed."

Muhammad ibn 'Umar said that he heard Malik ibn Anas say, "When al-Mansur went on *hajj*, he summoned me, and I went to him and spoke to him. He asked me and I answered. He said, 'I have decided to command that copies be made of these books of yours which you have written (i.e. the *Muwatta'*), and then I will send a copy of them to every Muslim city and command people to learn what is in them, and not to exceed more than that with anything else and to leave other new knowledge. I think that the basis of knowledge is the transmission of the people of Madina and their knowledge.' I said, 'Amir al-Mu'minin, do not do this. The people already have their positions and they have heard *hadiths* and related transmissions. Each people have taken what came first to them, and they have based their *deen* on it in spite of the disagreement of some people and others. It would be harsh to turn them away from what they believe. Leave people with what they have and with what the people of each city have chosen for themselves.' Al-Mansur said, 'By my life, if you had obeyed me in that, I would have done it.'"

Muhammad ibn 'Umar said, "When Malik ibn Anas was summoned, consulted, listened to and his position accepted, some people hated and envied him and strove against him. When Ja'far ibn Sulayman was appointed over Madina, they tried to turn him against Malik and spoke against him a lot. They said, 'He does not think that the oaths of allegiance to you are worth anything. He relies on a *hadith* which is related from Thabit al-Ahnaf that a forced divorce is not binding.' Ja'far became angry and summoned Malik and presented what had been alleged to him about him as evidence against him. Then he stripped him, stretched him out and had him flogged. His arms were stretched until his shoulders were dislocated and he suffered dreadfully on account of it. By Allah, after that flogging, he continued to rise in people's esteem. It was as if that flogging was an adornment for him."

He said, "Malik used to attend the mosque and the prayers, the *Jumu'a*, the funerals, visit the sick, fulfil people's rights, and sit in the mosque. His companions consulted him. Then he stopped sitting in the mosque and he used to pray and then go to his home, and he stopped attending funerals. He used to go to the bereaved families and console them. Then he stopped all of that. He did not attend the prayers in the mosque nor the *Jumu'a,* and he did not go to anyone to

361

console them or to fulfil any right. People endured all of that from him. They desired what he had and they had great esteem for him until he died while he was like that. Once he was asked about this. He said, 'Not everyone can say what their excuse is.'"

He said, "Malik used to sit in his house, with couches and cushions placed to the right and left in the rest of the room for those of Quraysh, the Ansar and other people who came to him. His assembly was one of gravity and forbearance. Malik was an impressive man in whose assembly there was no wrangling, tumult, nor raising of voices. Strangers would ask him about *hadiths* and he would simply answer, *hadith* after *hadith*. Sometimes he gave permission to one of them to read to him. He had a scribe called Habib who copied his books and read to the group. No one who attended came near him or examined his books or asked about them, out of awe and respect for Malik. When Habib read and made a mistake, Malik would correct him, but that was rare."

Mutarrif ibn 'Abdullah said, "I did not see Malik ibn Anas being cupped except on a Wednesday or a Saturday. He did not accept the *hadiths* related on that."

Isma'il ibn 'Abdullah said, "Malik ibn Anas was ill for a few days (before he died) and one of his family was asked about what he said when he was dying. He said that he said the *shahada* and then he said, '*To Allah belongs the business before and afterwards.*' (30:4)"

He died in the morning of the 14th of Rabi' al-Awwal in 179 AH while Harun ar-Rashid was khalif. 'Abdullah ibn Muhammad, the governor of Madina at that time, prayed over him. He was known as 'Abdullah ibn Zaynab after his mother. He prayed over Malik where the funeral prayers are done and then Malik was buried in al-Baqi'. He was 85 on the day he died. Mus'ab ibn 'Abdullah az-Zubayri said, "I have the best recollection of Malik's death. He died in Safar 179 AH."

Ma'n ibn 'Isa said, "I saw a tent over the grave of Malik. Malik was reliable, trustworthy, scrupulous and an authoritative scholar."

Abu Uways

His name was 'Abdullah ibn 'Abdullah ibn Uways al-Asbahi, the nephew of Malik ibn Anas. Abu Uways related from az-Zuhri.

Hisham ibn Sa'd

His *kunya* was Abu 'Abbad, a client of the family of Abu Lahab ibn 'Abdu'l-Muttalib. He was a pro-Shi'ite for the family of Abu Talib. He owned biers. He died in Madina while al-Mahdi was khalif. He had a lot of *hadiths* but is thought weak.

Muhammad ibn Salih ibn Dinar at-Tammar

The client of 'A'isha bint Juz' ibn 'Amr, the mother of 'Amr ibn Qatada. His *kunya* was Abu 'Abdullah. He had an excellent intellect and met people and learned knowledge and the accounts about expeditions.

'Abdu'r-Rahman ibn Abi'z-Zinad said, "My father said to me, 'If you want the *Maghazi* in a sound form, then you must have the accounts of Muhammad ibn Salih ibn Dinar.' He was reliable, with a few *hadiths*."

He died in 168 AH at the age of about 80.

Muhammad ibn Hilal

He reported that his grandmother used to visit 'Uthman when he was under siege. Then she gave birth to Hilal and he missed her for a day. 'Uthman was told, "She has given birth to a son tonight." He sent her 50 dirhams and some cloth. He said, "This is your son's stipend and garment. When a year has passed we will raise it to 100 dirhams."

Az-Zubayr ibn 'Abdullah ibn Ruhayma

His *kunya* was Abu 'Abdullah, the client of 'Uthman ibn 'Affan by emancipation. Ruhayma's grandmother was Umm Abihi. He died at the beginning of the khalifate of al-Mahdi.

Muhammad ibn Khut

He was one of the devoted worshippers.

Muhammad ibn 'Umar said, "Muhammad ibn Khut had a circle in the mosque of the Messenger of Allah صلعم and those who sat in it were known for their worship and devotion. Whoever desired devotion would go and sit with them. They used to be called 'al-

Khutiyya', from his name. He had transmission as well as his practices.

Abu Mawdud

His name was 'Abdu'l-'Aziz ibn Abi Sufyan. He was also one of the people of practices and excellence. He was a *mutakallim* who used to admonish and remind. He grew old and died late.

Abu Mawdud said, "I saw that as-Sa'ib ibn Yazid had a white head and beard."

Salih ibn Hassan an-Nadri

One of the allies of al-Aws.

Muhammad ibn 'Umar said, "I met al-Mahdi [sic.] and he was manly and noble. The gathering was full when he related. He had singing girls which lowered his esteem with people. He used to relate from Muhammad ibn Ka'b al-Qurazi and others. He went to Kufa and the Kufans listened to him. He had few *hadiths*.

Husayn ibn 'Abdullah ibn Samira

His *kunya* was Abu 'Abdullah. He settled in Yanbu'.

'Abdullah ibn al-Hasan reported that his mother, Fatima bint Husayn, said, "The Messenger of Allah صلعم sent Zayd ibn Harith to Madina with some slaves, which included some captives, including Damira, the client of 'Ali. The Messenger of Allah صلعم commanded that they be sold. They were brothers. They came to him weeping and he asked, 'Why are you weeping?' They said, 'We will be split up between them.' He said, 'You will not be split up between them. Sell them all together.'"

Muhammad ibn 'Abdullah ibn Muslim

His mother was Umm Habib bint Habib. He is the one called 'the nephew of az-Zuhri'.

Muhammad ibn 'Umar said, "I asked ibn 'Abdullah, the nephew of az-Zuhri, 'Did did you hear this *hadith* from your uncle?' He replied, 'I was with him when Hisham the khalif commanded that he write down his *hadiths* for him. Scribes sat for him – to whom az-Zuhri dictated and they wrote. I attended this but sometimes I would have to go out to do something. My uncle would refrain from dictating until I had returned to my place.'"

Muhammad's *kunya* was Abu 'Abdullah. His slaves murdered him at the order of his son while he was at his property at Thulya in the region of Shaghbwabada. His son was a cunning fool who murdered him for his inheritance at the end of the khalifate of al-Mansur. Then his slaves in turn attacked and murdered him some years later. Muhammad was righteous and had a lot of *hadiths*.

'Abdullah ibn Ja'far ibn 'Abdu'r-Rahman

His *kunya* was Abu Ja'far. His mother was Burayha bint Muhammad. His children were Ja'far, al-Miswar and two daughters, and their mother was Kulthum bint Muhammad. 'Abdullah ibn Ja'far was one of the men of Madina. He had knowledge of the expeditions and of *fatwas*. It was hoped that he would be appointed *qadi* in Madina until he died childless. He was short, malformed and ugly.

Ibn Abi'z-Zinad said, "No *qadi* of Madina was dismissed or died but that it was said, ''Abdullah ibn Ja'far will be appointed next,' on account of his perfection, manliness, and knowledge – but he died without being appointed." 'Abdu'r-Rahman said, "I do not believe he was denied that for any reason except the fact that he rebelled with Muhammad ibn 'Abdullah."

Muhammad ibn 'Umar said, "I mentioned him one day to 'Abdullah ibn Muhammad ibn 'Imran and he said, 'You have mentioned someone who has complete manliness.'"

Muhammad ibn 'Umar said, "'Abdullah said to me, 'Once I was summoned with 'Abdullah ibn Muhammad ibn 'Imran the Qadi when he was a boy. I was included with him in that. I said, "I was summoned with this boy!" Then I said, "By Allah, I was summoned by his father when I was not a year old and then he forgot me."'"

'Abdullah ibn Ja'far was one of the men on whom Muhammad ibn 'Abdullah ibn Hasan relied, and he taught him his knowledge. When he entered Madina seeking to hide, he stayed in the house of 'Abdullah ibn Ja'far. 'Abdullah went and sat with the amirs and listened to their news and their discussion about Muhammad ibn 'Abdullah and where they were sending people to look for him. Then 'Abdullah went and informed Muhammad of all that. When Muhammad ibn 'Abdullah rebelled, 'Abdullah ibn Ja'far rebelled with him. When Muhammad ibn 'Abdullah was killed, he hid and remained in hiding until he asked for security and was given it. 'Abdullah ibn Ja'far said, "We did not rebel with Muhammad ibn 'Abdullah while having any doubts about what he was doing when he spoke to us – but we made a mistake. No one after him will fool me." He used to show regret for his having rebelled.

Muhammad ibn 'Umar said, "When the news of the death of my father, 'Umar ibn Waqid, came, I stayed in the house for three days and then I went out. I saw 'Abdullah ibn Ja'far on his mule at the wheat market. When he saw me, he stopped his mule and asked, 'What kept you from me?' I had previously asked for Jahdar, his slave. 'Did he come and you refused to see him or have you not told me that he was there?' he asked. 'What has kept you from me?' I replied, 'The death of my father.' He did not say a word to me until he had taken his mule back and then walked back from his house to console me. I said, 'May Allah preserve you! I did not want you to come to me on foot!' He said, 'I wanted to do that to fulfil what I owe you. Have you not heard the *hadith* of Umm Bakr bint al-Miswar?' – 'No,' I replied. He said, 'Umm Bakr bint al-Miswar reported to me that when al-Miswar was ill, Ibn 'Abbas came to visit in the middle of the day and al-Miswar said to him, "Abu 'Abbas, are there not other times to come?" Ibn 'Abbas replied, "The hour I love most is the one in which I settle what is owing when it is most difficult for me."'"

Muhammad ibn 'Umar said, "''Abdullah ibn Ja'far died in Madina in 170 AH, the year in which Harun ar-Rashid became khalif. On the day he died he was about 70. He had a lot of *hadiths* and was righteous."

Ibrahim ibn Sa'd ibn Ibrahim ibn 'Abdu'r-Rahman

His mother was Amatu'r-Rahman, one of the Banu 'Abd ibn Zam'a. His children were Sa'd and Muhammad, whose mother was an *umm walad*; Isma'il, by an *umm walad*; and Ya'qub, who was Abu Ishaq. He related from az-Zuhri, Salih ibn Kaysan and his father, and from al-Harith and 'Abdullah, the sons of 'Ikrima, and others. He was reliable, with a lot of *hadiths*. He settled in Baghdad with his son. He was put in charge of the treasury and related the *Maghazi* from Muhammad ibn Ishaq and other subjects. He was severe regarding *hadiths*, and died in Baghdad in 183 AH at the age of 75.

Muhammad ibn 'Abdullah ibn Muhammad

His mother was an *umm walad*. Ziyad ibn 'Ubaydullah al-Harith appointed him *qadi* of Madina. He died while Ziyad ibn 'Ubaydullah was governor.

His brother, Abu Bakr ibn 'Abdullah ibn Muhammad ibn Abi Sabra

His mother was an *umm walad*. He had a lot of knowledge, listening and transmission. He was appointed qadi of Makka for Ziyad ibn 'Ubaydullah. He gave *fatwa* in Madina. Then he wrote to him and he was summoned to Baghdad. He was appointed *qadi* for Musa ibn al-Mahdi who was the heir at that time. He died in Baghdad in 162 AH at the age of 60 while al-Mahdi was khalif. When Ibn Abi Sabra died, he sent for Abu Yusuf Ya'qub ibn Ibrahim to appoint him in his place. He remained *qadi* for Musa who was the heir and then left with him for Jurjan.

Muhammad ibn 'Umar reported that he heard Abu Bakr ibn Abi Sabra say, "Ibn Jurayh said to me, 'Write down the excellent *hadiths* which you have for me.' I wrote out a thousand *hadiths* for him and gave them to him. He did not read them to me, nor did I read them to him." Muhammad ibn 'Umar said, "Then I saw that Ibn Jurayh had inserted many of his *hadiths* into his book, saying, 'Abu Bakr ibn 'Abdullah (i.e. Ibn Abi Sabra) related to me ...'" He had a lot of *hadiths*, but is not authoritative.

Shu'ayb ibn Talha ibn 'Abdullah

His mother was an *umm walad*. His children were Salih, 'Isa, Ishaq, Muhammad, Ibrahim, Harun and Asma' by an *umm walad*; and 'Abda, whose mother was Hikma bint al-Mundhir. His *kunya* was Abu Muhammad. He died in 174 or 175 AH.

'Abdu'l-'Aziz ibn al-Muttalib

His mother was Umm al-Fadl bint Kulayb. He had a son called Suhayl. His *kunya* was Abu'l-Muttalib. He was *qadi* of Madina for al-Mansur. He had *hadiths* which he related.

367

Sa'id ibn 'Abdu'r-Rahman ibn Jamil

His mother was Umm Husayn bint Mu'adh of the Ansar of Banu Salim. He was appointed *qadi* in Baghdad in 'Askar al-Mahdi. He died in Baghdad.

'Abdu'r-Rahman ibn Muhammad ibn Abi Bakr

His mother was Amatu'l-Wahhab bint 'Abdullah, one of Aws. His children were Abu Bakr, 'Ubaydullah and Amatu'l-Wahhab, whose mother was 'A'isha bint Muhammad of an-Najjar; and 'A'isha, whose mother was an *umm walad*. His *kunya* was Abu Muhammad. He died while al-Mansur was khalif.

'Abdu'l-Malik ibn Muhammad ibn Abi Bakr

His *kunya* was Abu't-Tahir. His mother was Amatu'l-Wahhab bint 'Abdullah. His children were 'Abdullah and 'Abdu'r-Rahman, whose mother was Hind bint Thabit; and Amatu'l-Malik, whose mother's name is not known. He was a *qadi* for Harun ar-Rashid over 'Askar al-Mahdi. When he died Harun prayed over him, He was buried in the graveyard of al-'Abbasa. He had few *hadiths*.

Kharija ibn 'Abdullah ibn Sulayman

His mother was an *umm walad*. He had a son 'Abdullah whose mother was Umm 'Ubayda bint Sa'id. His *kunya* was Abu Zayd. He died in Madina in 165 AH in al-Mahdi's reign. He had few *hadiths*.

Haritha ibn Abi'l-Rijal

His name was Muhammad ibn 'Abdullah. His mother was Hamida bint Sa'd. He had a son 'Abdullah, whose mother was Munya bint Ayyub.

'Abdu'r-Rahman ibn 'Abdu'l-'Aziz ibn 'Abdullah

His mother was Mandus bint Hakim. His *kunya* was Abu Muhammad. He is the one who is called al-Hanifi. He went blind, and was a scholar of *Sira* and other subjects. He had a lot of *hadiths*. He died in 162 AH at the age of about 70.

Mujamma' ibn Ya'qub

His mother was Hasana bint Jariya. His children were 'Abdu'r-Rahman, whose mother was an *umm walad*; and Umm Ishaq, whose mother's name is not known. His *kunya* was Abu 'Abdullah. He died in Madina in 160 AH at the beginning of the khalifate of al-Mahdi. He was reliable, with few *hadiths*.

'Abdu'r-Rahman ibn Sulayman

His mother was Asma' bint Hanzala. His children were 'Umar, Kulthum and Qurayba, whose mother was an *umm walad*. He came to Kufa and stayed there and the Kufans related from him.

Muhammad ibn al-Fadl ibn 'Ubaydullah

His mother was 'Abda bint Rifa'a. His children were Sa'id and Maryam, whose mother was Hamamda bint Hurayr; and Tammah, whose mother was Umm Yahya bint Tammah. His *kunya* was Abu 'Abdullah. He died in Madina when al-Mansur was khalif.

'Abdullah ibn al-Hurayr ibn 'Abdu'r-Rahman

His mother was an *umm walad*. His children were al-Fadl, whose mother was Sahla bint Habis; and Sabr, 'Isa, al-Mundhir, 'Afra' and Umm Rafi', whose mother was Tamma bint Sahl.

Muhammad ibn Sahl ibn Abi Hathma

His mother was from Ashja'. He had a daughter Hammada, whose mother was Umm al-Hasan bint 'Umar. His *kunya* was Abu 'Abdullah. He died in 166 AH while al-Mahdi was khalif.

'Abdu'l-Majid ibn Abi 'Abs

His mother was an *umm walad*. His children were Ahmad and Maryam, whose mother was Sharifa bint al-Qasim. His *kunya* was Abu Muhammad. He died in 164 AH while al-Mahdi was khalif. He had few *hadiths*.

'Abdullah ibn al-Harith

His mother was Maryam bint 'Ali. His children were al-Harith and 'Isa, whose mother was Habbaba bint 'Isa. His *kunya* was Abu'l-Harith. He died in in 164 AH while al-Mahdi was khalif.

Sa'id ibn Muhammad

Muhammad ibn 'Umar said, "Sa'id ibn Muhammad was one of the people of the *deen*, scrupulousness, excellence, and intelligence. He had some marshland with a revenue of two dinars a year. He was thrifty with that and it was enough for him. He and his slavegirl would have lunch, and he would pick dates for her from his land and have the girl take them to his family. He was patient in his difficulty and did not complain about it at all, either a little or a lot. If something was sent to him, he would say, 'I am well-off.' He would become angry with whoever had sent it to him, and would be very annoyed. He used to come out to us and relate to us wearing his same two garments in winter and in summer – which we always saw were clean. He used to be invited to a wedding feast and would attend but not eat anything of it – but he would make supplication for its people. He would be asked, 'Why do you not eat this, Abu Muhammad?' He would reply, 'I do not want to accustom my stomach to good food, because then it will not be content with what I feed it. I do not want to make it greedy.'"

He said, "When 'Abdu'r-Rahman ibn Abi'z-Zinad was appointed over the *kharaj* of Madina, he sent 100 dinars to Sa'id ibn Muhammad. He said, 'By Allah, I will never accept them. They have nothing to do with me. Glory be to Allah! Is he not ashamed at this?' So Ibn Abi'z-Zinad appointed him to a post and sent him as an agent to Asad and Tayy. He said, 'I will not do it.' He continued to send messengers to him, until he went to him and said, 'I know that you want to do something for me. The best thing you can do for me is to dismiss me. I do not want this. By the praise of Allah, I have enough wealth so that I can do without it.' So he left him alone and dismissed him."

Ibn Abi Habiba

His name was Ibrahim ibn Isma'il. His *kunya* was Abu Isma'il, the client of 'Abdullah ibn Sa'd ibn Zayd al-Ashhali. He prayed and worshipped and fasted for sixty years and died in 165 AH while al-Mahdi was khalif, at the age of 82. He had few *hadiths*.

Yazid ibn 'Iyad al-Laythi

His *kunya* was Abu'l-Hakam. He moved to Basra and died there while al-Mahdi was khalif. He had few *hadiths* and is thought weak.

Usama ibn Zayd ibn Aslam

The client of 'Umar ibn al-Khattab. His *kunya* was Abu Zayd. He listened to al-Qasim ibn Muhammad, Salim ibn 'Abdullah, and Nafi', the client of Ibn 'Umar. He had many *hadiths*.

'Abdullah ibn Zayd ibn Aslam

The client of 'Umar ibn al-Khattab. He was the most reliable in *hadith* of the children of Aslam. He died in Madina at the beginning of al-Mahdi's khalifate.

'Abdu'r-Rahman ibn Zayd ibn Aslam

The client of 'Umar ibn al-Khattab. He died in Madina at the beginning of Harun ar-Rashid's khalifate. He had many *hadiths* and is very weak.

Da'ud ibn Khalid ibn Dinar

The client of the family of Hunayn, clients of the Banu 'Abbas. His *kunya* was Abu Sulayman.

Muhammad ibn Abi Yahya said, "Khalif ibn Dinar, the client of the family of Hunayn, the clients of the Abbasids. He had manliness." He said, "While I was with my father in the mosque, someone was shouting at the door of the house, 'May Allah have mercy on whoever helps Khalid ibn Dinar!' So some people went out to see him. While they were waiting for him to come out, a man of the house came out to them and said, 'May Allah reward you! Leave!' He was pouring with sweat. So the people went. After that he lived to have three sons: Da'ud, Shumayl and Yahya, and all of them took knowledge and transmitted from him. Khalid also had daughters. His line continued and they were merchants. When 'Abdu's-Samad ibn 'Ali arrived as governor of Madina, he sent for them because of their *wala'*, and offered them what was acceptable to him. They said, 'May Allah make the amir thrive! We are merchants and we have no need of being employed by the ruler, so spare us from that.' So he spared them and used to honour them."

'Abdu'l-'Aziz ibn 'Abdullah ibn Abi Salama al-Majishun

His *kunya* was Abu 'Abdullah, the client of the family of al-Hudayr at-Taymi. He died in Baghdad in 164 AH while al-Mahdi was khalif and al-Mahdi prayed over him and buried him in the Quraysh graveyard. He was reliable, with a lot of *hadiths*. The people of Baghdad related mostly from him from the people of Madina.

Yusuf ibn Ya'qub ibn Abi Salama

Yaqub is al-Majishun. His children and nephews were ascribed to that. Yusuf ibn al-Majishun said, "I was born in the reign of Sulayman and Sulayman allotted me a stipend soon after I was born. When 'Umar II was appointed, the *diwan* was presented and he came to my name and said, 'What do I know about the birth of this child? This is a child who is one of the people of shares.' So he reduced me to poverty."

Fulayh ibn Sulayman ibn Abi'l-Mughira ibn Hunayn

The client of the family of Zayd ibn al-Khattab. 'Ubayd ibn Hunayn was the one who related from Abu Hurayra, and who was the uncle of Abu Fulayh Sulayman ibn Abi'l-Mughira. Fulayh was called 'Abdu'l-Malik, but usually known by this nickname. Fulayh was a bodyguard for Hasan ibn Zayd when he was appointed governor of Madina for al-Mansur. There was a quarrel between them, and Hasan ibn Zayd used to criticise him and harass him.

'Abdu'r-Rahman ibn Abi'z-Zinad

Abu'z-Zinad's name was 'Abdullah ibn Dhakwan. Dhakwan was the client of Ramla bint Shayba. She was the wife of 'Uthman ibn 'Affan. 'Abdu'r-Rahman's *kunya* was Abu Muhammad. He was born in 100 AH while 'Umar II was khalif.

Muhammad ibn 'Umar reported that 'Abdu'r-Rahman said, "Muhammad ibn 'Abdu'l-Aziz az-Zuhri was devoted to Abu'z-Zinad. He was appointed *qadi* of Madina. There was a quarrel between 'Abdu'r-Rahman and 'Abdullah ibn Muhammad ibn Sam'an. 'Abdu'r-Rahman had heard some of what was said and so 'Abdullah said, 'Testify to him!' He took him to Muhammad ibn 'Abdu'l-'Aziz and he testified to what he had said, so he jailed him and gave him seventeen lashes."

Muhammad ibn 'Umar said, "'Abdu'r-Rahman was later put in charge of the *kharaj* of Madina and he used to help the people of good, scrupulousness and *hadith*. He was noble in his actions. He knew a lot of *hadith*. Once a man read to him and made a mistake in his reading. Those who were there laughed, while 'Abdu'r-Rahman remained silent. When the man stood up, he rebuked them for that. He said, 'Are you not ashamed of this!'"

He said, "A man read a *hadith* to him which he was writing and which he did not want everyone to hear. When the man got up, he turned to 'Abdu'r-Rahman and said, 'If I had told him to conceal it, he would have shouted it out, but I did not draw attention to it and so he does not know that I usually conceal it and will not think about it and so he will treat it like all the other *hadiths* which he has.'" 'Abdu'r-Rahman went to Baghdad and related to the people there. Then he fell ill and died there in 174 AH at the age of 73. He had a lot of *hadiths* which were weak.

Muhammad ibn 'Abdu'r-Rahman ibn Abi'z-Zinad

His *kunya* was Abu 'Abdullah. There were 17 years between him and his father – and 21 days between their deaths. They were buried in the graveyard at Bab at-Tin.

Muhammad ibn 'Umar reported that 'Abdu'r-Rahman said, "Abu Bakr ibn Muhammad ibn 'Amr ibn Hazm met me and asked, "Abdu'r-Rahman! Do you have any children?' – 'Yes,' I replied. 'How old are you?' he inquired. I replied, 'Seventeen.' He said, 'I had Muhammad when I was seventeen as well.'"

Muhammad ibn 'Umar said, "Muhammad ibn 'Abdu'r-Rahman met the men who related from his father – 'Alqama, Sharik ibn 'Abdullah ibn Abi Namir, and all the men who related to his father except Abu'z-Zinad. He used be asked to relate and would refuse, saying, 'Shall I relate when my father is alive?' His close friends were an exception, and he related *hadith* after *hadith* to them. He was dutiful to his father and esteemed and respected him." He said, "One day I saw him when he had a severe pain in his hip. He was sitting at the door, waiting for his father to give him permission before he left. His father's messenger came out and told him to go. So he left. I said to him, 'You should have just gone.' He said, 'Glory be to Allah – only when the limit of necessity is reached!' He said, 'However long I remain is as Allah wishes – I have no permission to go until he gives me permission.'" He said, "There were many qualities in Muhammad ibn 'Abdu'r-Rahman and none of them could be ignored: recitation of Qur'an, reading about the *Sunna*, Arabic, poetry, arithmetic, copying books in scrolls, and remembering rights."

Muhammad ibn 'Umar said, "I listened to our *qadi*, Muhammad ibn 'Imran at-Talhi, when he was brought a book to be read to him. He said, 'Read it to Muhammad ibn 'Abdu'r-Rahman.' It was said, 'No.' He said, 'Take it and read it to him, and then bring me to him.'" He said, "He was the most knowledgeable of people in the mathematics of the divisions and shares of inheritance, precision in *hadith* and their sciences."

Sulayman ibn Bilal said, "I have not seen anyone bold enough to go up to Zayd ibn Aslam and say to him, 'Did you hear it?' except Muhammad ibn 'Abdu'r-Rahman. I heard him say to Zayd ibn Aslam, 'Did you hear it, Abu Usama?'"

Muhammad ibn 'Umar said, "Muhammad ibn 'Abdu'r-Rahman was the most dutiful of people to his father. His father used to sit in his circle and once he was late in coming to it. His father said, 'O Muhammad.' He got up and stood upright. He commanded him to do something but he did not confirm it out of awe of him – until he asked someone who had understood what his father had said about it, and he informed him."

Muhammad ibn 'Umar said, "Muhammad ibn 'Abdu'r-Rahman was with his father 'Abdu'r-Rahman ibn Abi'z-Zinad in Bagdhad and he died 21 days after his father in 174 AH. He was 57 the day he died. They were buried together in the graveyard at Bab at-Tin. No one except Muhammad ibn 'Umar related from him."

Abu Mashar Najih

He was a *mukatib* of a woman of Makhzum and he paid what he owed and was freed. Then Umm Musa bint Mansur al-Himyariyya brought his *wala'*. He died in Baghdad in 170 AH and he had a lot of *hadiths*, but he was weak.

Isma'il ibn Ibrahim ibn 'Uqba

He was the nephew of Musa ibn 'Uqba. His *kunya* was Abu Ishaq. He met Nafi', the client of Ibn 'Umar and 'A'isha bint Sa'd ibn Abi Waqqas and related sound *hadiths* from them. He used to relate the *Maghazi* from his father Musa ibn 'Uqba. Muhammad ibn 'Umar and Isma'il ibn Abi Uways and others listened to him. He died in Madina at the beginning of the khalifate of al-Mahdi.

Muhammad ibn Muslim ibn Jammaz

The client of Banu Taym ibn Murra. His *kunya* was Abu 'Abdullah. He was a *faqih*, in his opinion, with insight into *hadiths*. But then he left that and turned to worship. He died in Madina in 177 AH while Harun was khalif.

Muhammad ibn 'Umar said, "When Muhammad ibn Muslim was dying, he only made a will about some matters. He said, 'I heard the people of the house complaining about a water-spout belonging to us which is in a house on their road. I met my father in this house while this water-spout was where it is. I want to move it to another place, but there is no proper place in this house in which to put it. I wanted to move it myself, but I am not strong enough to do it. I am afraid to pass it on to the daughters of my brother because they are weak and unprotected. Their father died young and they are weak, so I want them to speak to the people of that house about sparing me from having to deal with it, if they can do that tomorrow.

"'My neighbour Ishaq ibn Shu'ayb asked me to open up a window in my house in order to let the light into a dark room of his for him – and in return he was going to close up the skylight window, so that we were not exposed to view. I agreed and he brought the tools. Then I remembered that my nieces are still children and I am not sure that they will not be exposed – and so I refused to do it. Ask him to release me from saying yes and then no. There are three dirhams which have been sitting on the edge of a box of mine for more than thirty years. I used to deal in linen and I do not know whether they are mine, a deposit, or what is due to a creditor. Ask about them and then do whatever they tell you to do about them. The family of so-

and-so have left a bowl in pawn with me for two dinars. My family ate from it once, so ask its owner to absolve me. If he does not do so, then return the two dinars to him. As for the maintenance which I have left, which is about 70 dinars, a third of it is for my nieces as a legacy for them, and two-thirds are the shares of inheritance for my brother's sons.'"

Sahbal ibn Muhammad ibn Abi Yahya

Abu Yahya's name was Sam'an, the client of the Aslamis. The name of Sahbal was 'Abdullah. His *kunya* was Abu Muhammad. He was excellent, intelligent and good. He died in Madina in 162 AH while al-Mahdi was khalif. He had few *hadiths*, and is not known for that.

Sulayman ibn Bilal

His *kunya* was Abu Muhammad. He was the client of al-Qasim ibn Muhammad. He was a Berber, of handsome appearance and intelligent. He used to give *fatwa* in his land. He was put in charge of the *kharaj* of Madina. He died in Madina in 172 AH while Harun ar-Rashid was khalif. He was reliable, with a lot of *hadiths*.

Al-Mughira ibn 'Abdu'r-Rahman

His mother was an *umm walad*. He related from Abu'z-Zinad and others. He is the one who is called Qusayy, and is known as that.

Ubayy ibn 'Abbas ibn Sahl

His mother was Jamal bint Ja'da ibn Malik. His children were Sahl and Kulthum, whose mother was 'Atika bint 'Abdu'r-Rahman.

'Abdu'l-Muhaymin ibn 'Abbas

His mother was an *umm walad*. His children were 'Umar and Zabiyya, whose mother was Umayma bint 'Abdullah; 'Umar and Ubayya, whose mother was 'Abda bint 'Imran; and as-Sayyida, whose mother was Umm Amr bint Sahm.

Ayyub ibn an-Nu'man ibn 'Abdullah

His mother was Umm 'Uthman bint 'Amr. He had a son Thawab, whose mother was Sukayna bint Mutarrif.

Hisham ibn 'Abdullah

His mother was one of the Banu Murra. He was devoted to Hisham ibn 'Urwa. He was one of his close friends and listened to him a lot although he did not relate from him. He was a venerable man who studied matters thoroughly and commanded the correct and forbade the bad. When Harun, the Amir al-Mu'minin, went on *hajj*, Abu Bakr ibn 'Abdullah, his governor of Madina, went out that day to meet him and brought with him a number of the notables of the people of Madina, including Hisham ibn 'Abdullah. He met him at an-Naqara and greeted him. He asked him who was with him and he mentioned Hisham ibn 'Abdullah to him and praised him. He called him and he entered and greeted him and spoke to him and admonished him. So he appointed him *qadi* of Madina and allotted him 4,000 dinars. Hisham was generous in giving to his kin. His *kunya* was Abu'l-Walid.

✳✳✳✳✳

This generation also includes: **Ibrahim ibn al-Fadl ibn Salman**, the client of Hisham ibn Isma'il al-Makhzumi from whom Ibn Abi Nuhayh and others related; **Malik ibn Abi'r-Rihal** and **'Abdu'r-Rahman ibn Abi'r-Rijal**, the sons of Umm Ayyub bint Rifa'a; **Kathir ibn 'Abdullah**, who had few *hadiths* and was thought weak; **Shumayl ibn Dinar**, the client of the family of Hunayn, the client of the Abbasids, who is related from; **Yahya ibn Khalid**, a client of the family of Hunayn, a client of the Abbasids, who is related from; **Abu'l-Qasim ibn Abi'z-Zinad**, who is also related from and who went to Baghdad where they listened to him; **Muhammad ibn Muslim al-Jawsaq**, Abu 'Abdullah, a client of Makhzum who died in 160 AH; **Nafi' ibn Abi Nu'aym al-Qari'**, who related from Nafi, and recited to Shayba ibn Nisah and Abu Ja'far, the client of Ibn 'Ayyash; **Salama ibn Bukht**, the client of Banu Makhzum, who was reliable and related from 'Ikrima and others; **al-'Attaf ibn Khalid ibn 'Abdullah**, Abu Safwan, whose mother was Umm al-Miswar bint as-Salt, whose mother was the daughter of Zam'a bint al-Harith; **'Ali ibn Abi 'Ali ibn 'Utba**, whose mother was an *umm walad*, and from whom Muhammad ibn Isma'il, Muhammad ibn 'Umar and others related; **'Ubaydullah ibn 'Abdu'l-'Aziz**, whose mother was Mandus bint Hakim ibn 'Abbad, and who is related from; **Khalid ibn al-Qasim ibn 'Abdu'r-Rahman**, Abu Muhammad, who died in 163 AH at the age of 93 and had few *hadiths*; **'Uthman ibn ad-Dahhak**, from whom Muhammad ibn 'Umar al-Waqidi and others related; and his son, **ad-Dahhak ibn 'Uthman**, from whom Mus'ab ibn 'Abdullah az-Zubayri and others related.

Chapter Seven
The Seventh Generation
of the *Tabi'un* of the People of Madina

Ad-Darawardi

His name was 'Abdu'l-'Aziz ibn Muhammad. His *kunya* was Abu Muhammad. He was the client of the Bark ibn Wabara. His family originated from Daraward, a town in Khorasan, but he was born in Madina and grew up there. He listened to knowledge and *hadiths* in Madina. He remained there until his death in 187 AH. He had a lot of *hadiths* but made mistakes.

'Abdu'l-'Aziz ibn Abi Hazim

Abu Hazim's name was Salama ibn Dinar, the client of the Banu Ashja'. His *kunya* was Abu Tammam. He was born in 107 AH, and died suddenly in 184 AH in Madina on Friday in the mosque of the Prophetصلعم. In his house 4,000 dinars were found. He was buried. He had a lot of *hadiths*, but less than ad-Darawardi.

Abu 'Alqama al-Farwi

His name was 'Abdullah ibn Muhammad, a client of the family of 'Uthman ibn 'Affan. He met Nafi', Sa'id ibn Abi Sa'id al-Maqburi, and as-Salt ibn Zubayd and related from them. We met him in Madina in 189 AH and he died after that. He was reliable, with a few *hadiths*.

Ibrahim ibn Muhammad ibn Abi Yahya

The client of Aslam. His *kunya* was Abu Ishaq. He was ten years younger than his brother Sahbal. He died in Madina in 184 AH. He had a lot of *hadiths*, but his *hadiths* were left alone and not written down.

Hatim ibn Isma'il

His *kunya* was Abu Isma'il. Muhammad ibn 'Umar said, "He testified to me that he was the client of the Banu 'Abdu'l-Madan. He gave me a scroll of his father and said, 'Do not mention it until I am dead.' His origins lay with the people of Kufa, but he moved to Madina and settled there, dying there in 186 AH while Harun ar-Rashid was khalif. He was reliable and trustworthy, with a lot of *hadiths*."

Muhammad ibn 'Umar ibn Waqid

His *kunya* was Abu 'Abdullah al-Waqidi, the client of the Banu Sahm of Aslam. He moved from Madina to Baghdad and was appointed *qadi* for 'Abdullah ibn Harun, the Amir al-Mu'minin, in 'Askar al-Mahdi for four years. He knew the *Maghazi*, *Sira*, conquests, the differences of people concerning *hadith* and judgements, and their agreement on what they agreed. He explained all this in books which he produced, composed and related.

'Abdullah ibn 'Ubaydullah said that al-Waqidi told him, "When Harun ar-Rashid performed *hajj*, he came to Madina and told Yahya ibn Khalid, 'Find me a man who knows Madina and its sites, where Jibril used to descend to the Prophet صلعم, and in what manner he used to come to him, and the graves of the martyrs.' So Yahya ibn Khalid asked and everyone pointed him in my direction. So he sent for me and I came to him after *'Asr*. He said to me, 'O Shaykh, the Amir al-Mu'minin, may Allah exalt him, wants you to pray *'Isha'* in the mosque and then go with us to these sites and take us to them and to the places where Jibril, peace be upon him, used to descend.'

"So when I had prayed *'Isha'*, I remained there when the candles were put out. There were two men on donkeys there. Yahya asked, 'Where is the man?' – 'Here I am,' I said. I took him to the houses of the mosque and said, 'This is the place to which Jibril used to come.' They got off their donkeys and prayed two *rak'ats* and made supplication to Allah for a time. Then they mounted while I led the way. I did not fail to take them to any of the sites. There they prayed and made strenuous supplications, and this continued until we arrived back at the mosque when it was the time for *Fajr* and the *mu'adhdhin* gave the *adhan*. Then they went to their castle. Yahya ibn Khalid said to me, 'O shaykh, do not leave.' So I prayed *Subh* in the mosque.

"As he was in charge of the journey to Makka, Yahya ibn Khalid gave me permission to come after *Subh*. He had me sit near and said to me, 'The Amir al-Mu'minin, may Allah exalt him, is still weeping. He liked what you showed him and he has commanded 10,000 dirhams for you.' Then a striped garment was given to me. He said to me, 'O Shaykh, take it and may you be blessed in it. We are travelling today and you do not have to meet us wherever we are. We will come to rest in one place, Allah willing.'

"The Amir al-Mu'minin departed and I returned to my house with the money and we spent it on a debt we owed and I married off some children and we were comfortable. Then later on things became difficult for us and Umm 'Abdullah said to me, 'Abu 'Abdullah, why are you sitting here when the the wazir of the Amir al-Mu'minin knows you and has asked you to go wherever he is settled?'

"I left Madina for Iraq. When I reached Iraq I asked about the Amir al-Mu'minin and they told me that he was in Raqqa. I wanted to go back to Madina, but I realised my circumstances in Madina were not good. So I decided to go to Raqqa and went to the hire place. I found myself with a number of young men from the army who were making for Raqqa. When they saw me, they asked, 'Shaykh, where are you going?' I told them my news and that I was making for Raqqa. We enquired about hiring two camels, but they were too weak. They asked, 'Shaykh, can you travel by boat? It is easier for us than hiring camels.' I said to them, 'I do not know anything about this. It is up to you.'

"So we went to where the boats were and rented places on one. I have not seen anyone more dutiful, kinder or attentive to me than they were. They undertook to serve me and feed me as a child would do for a parent, until we reached the passport-control in Raqqa. The control was very difficult. They wrote down their number for their general and included me as one of them.

"After some days, permission for us arrived, and we crossed over with the people and I went to a place in an inn. I remained with them for some days and sought permission to visit Yahya ibn Khalid but he was difficult to approach. So I went to Abu'l-Bahtari who knew me. I met him and he said to me, 'Abu 'Abdullah, you have made a mistake and a fool of yourself, but I will not fail to mention you to him.'

I used to go to his door and then come back. My provisions were exhausted and I was ashamed before my companions and my garments were tattered. I despaired of Abu'l-Bakhtari. I did not tell my companions anything.

"Then I started back to Madina, sometimes by boat, sometimes on foot, until I reached Saylahin. While I was resting in its marketplace, a caravan from Baghdad arrived. I asked who they were and was told that they were from the people of the the the city of the Messenger صلعم and that their master was Bakkar az-Zubayri, whom the Amir al-Mu'minin had sent to act as *qadi* of Madina.

"Now az-Zubayri was one of the truest of people to me. I said to myself, 'I will wait until he stops and rests and then go to him.' I went to him after he had rested and finished his meal. I asked permission to enter and was given it. I entered and greeted him. He said to me, 'Abu 'Abdullah! What is your news since last I saw you?' I told him my news and all about Abu'l-Bakhtari. He said, 'Did you not know that Abu'l-Bakhtari does not want to mention you to anyone or even draw attention to your name? What do you think you should do?' I said, 'I think I will go to Madina.' He said, 'That is the wrong decision. You left Madina in the circumstances you know. The best course is to come with me, and I will mention your business to Yahya.'

"I rode with the people to Raqqa. When we had passed through the control, he said to me, 'Come with me,' – 'No,' I said, 'I will join my companions. I will come early to you so that we can go to Yahya ibn Khalid together, Allah willing.' I went to my companions and it was as if the sky had fallen in on them. They said to me, 'Abu 'Abdullah, what is your news? We were worried about you!' I told them my news and everyone thought that I should stay with az-Zubayri. They said, 'Here is your food and drink. Do not worry about it.' I went the next morning to the door of az-Zubayri and was told that he had already gone to Yahya ibn Khalid.

"So I went to the door of Yahya ibn Khalid and sat outside for a time. When my companion came out, he said to me, 'Abu 'Abdullah, I forgot to mention your business to him! Stay at the door and I will go back to him.' He went in and then the attendant came out and told me, 'Enter.' I went to him in a state of humiliation. It was in Ramadan when there were still three or four days left of it. When Yahya ibn Khalid saw me in that state, I saw concern in his face. He greeted me and brought me near. There were some people talking with him. He began to discuss one topic after another, but I refrained from joining in and so my presence began to draw attention to something other than what was being discussed. The people continued to give their answers as best as they could while I remained silent. When the assembly ended and the people left, I left too. The servant of Yahya ibn Khalid came out and met me by the screen. He said to me, 'The minister commands you to break the fast with him this evening.'

"When I went to my companions, I told them what had happened and said, 'I fear that he will be harsh with me. One of them said to me, 'Here are two loaves and a piece of cheese and here is my animal which you can ride, with my servant behind you. If the attendant gives you permission to enter, then enter and give what you have to the servant. If it is otherwise, then go to one of the mosques and eat what you have with you and drink the water of the mosque.'

"So I went to the door of Yahya ibn Khalid after the people had prayed *Maghrib*. When he saw me the attendant said, 'Shaykh, you are late. A messenger has gone to look for you more than once.' I gave what I had with me to the servant and told him to wait. I entered and everyone had already gone in. I greeted them and sat down. Water was brought and we did *wudu'*. I was the person nearest to him. We broke the fast and *'Isha'* came and he prayed with us. Then we took our seats. Yahya began to ask me questions to one side. The other people were giving answers which were different to the ones I had. When the night had passed, the people left and as I was leaving after some of them, the attendant came to me and said, 'The minister commands you to come to him tomorrow earlier than you came today.' He also gave me a bag. I did not know what was in it, but it filled me with relief.

"I went to where the servant was and left with him, accompanied by the attendant, until we reached my companions. I went to them and said, 'Look for a saddle for me.' I opened the bag and there were dinars in it. They said to me, 'How did he reply to you?' I said, 'The servant commanded me to come to him again earlier than the time I went yesterday evening.' I counted the dinars and there were 500. One of them said to me, 'I can buy your mount.' Another said, 'I will buy the saddle and bridle and what is necessary for it.' Another said, 'I will attend to your bath, dyeing your beard and perfume.' Another said, 'I will buy your garment. Consider what sort of garment you want.' I counted out 100 dinars. I gave them to the one in charge of their spending. My companions all swore that they would not cause me to lose a dinar or dirham. The next morning, each of them undertook what he had delegated himself to do. Before the time I prayed *Dhuhr* I was the noblest of people.

"I took what remained in the bag to az-Zubayri. When he saw me in this state, he was very happy. Then I told him the news, and he said to me, 'I am going to Madina.' I said, 'Yes, you know the state in which I left my family behind.' So I gave him 200 dinars to give to my family. Then I left him and went to my companions with everything that I had left in the bag. Then I prayed *'Asr* and prepared myself in the best manner, and then I presented myself at the door of Yahya ibn Khalid. When the attendant saw me, he came to me and admitted me. I went to Yahya and when he saw me in that state, I saw joy in his face. I took my seat and continued with the questions which he had been asking me and my answers – and my answers were different to the answers which other people had been giving him. I looked at the people and they scowled at me. Yahya began to ask me about this and that, and I answered his questions while the people were silent, and none of them said anything.

"When *Maghrib* came, Yahya stepped forward and we prayed, and then food was brought and we ate. Then he prayed *'Isha'* with us and we took our seats and continued the discussion. Yahya began to ask some of the other people as well, but then stopped. When it was time to leave, I left when the people left. Then a messenger caught up with me and said, 'The minister commands you to come to him every day at the same time as you came today.' He gave me a bag. I left with the messenger of the attendant until I reached my companions. I left a saddle with them. I gave the bag to my companions and they were very happy for me.

"On the following day, I told them, 'Prepare a house near you for me and buy me a slave girl, a slave who can cook, utensils and furniture.' By the time I had prayed *Dhuhr*, they had done all that for me. I asked them to break the fast with me and they only agreed to do so after great difficulty.

"I continued to go to Yahya every night, and whenever he saw me, his joy increased. He continued to give me 500 dinars every night until the day of the *'Id*. He said to me, "Abdullah, put on your finest

384

qadi garments tomorrow for the Amir al-Mu'minin and present your-self to him. He will ask me about you and I will tell him.'

"The following morning, on the day of the *'Id*, I went out in my best clothes with the people. The Amir al-Mu'minin went to the prayer place and began to look at me as I was still in the retinue. After he had left, I went to the door of Yahya ibn Khalid and we joined Yahya after the Amir al-Mu'minin had entered his house. He said to me, 'Abu 'Abdullah, enter with us.' I entered and the people also entered. He said to me, 'Abu 'Abdullah, the Amir al-Mu'minin asked about you. So I told him about our *hajj*, and that you were the man who showed him around that night, and he commanded 30,000 dirhams for you. I will pay it to you tomorrow, Allah willing.'

"Then the next morning I went to Yahya and said, 'May Allah give the minister success! When a need is presented, the minister can deal with it. May Allah exalt him for dealing with it!' He asked me, 'What is that?' I said, 'Permission to go home. I am yearning for my family and children.' He told me, 'Do not do it.' I kept at him until he gave me permission. He produced 30,000 dirhams for me and pre-pared a boat for me with all that was in it and commanded that fine things be purchased for me from Syria to take with me to Madina. He commanded his agent in Iraq to pay for my journey to Madina so that I was not obliged to pay a single dinar or dirham. I went to my com-panions, told them the news and begged them to accept from me what I gave them. They swore that they would not deprive me of a single dinar or dirham. By Allah, I have never seen the like of their good character – so how can I be blamed for my love for Yahya ibn Khalid?"

'Abdullah ibn 'Ubaydullah said, "I was sitting with al-Waqidi when Yahya ibn Khalid ibn Barmak was mentioned. Al-Waqidi asked for mercy on him and did so a lot. We said to him, 'Abu 'Abdullah, you ask for mercy on him a lot.' He replied, 'How could I not ask for mercy on a man whose fine state I will tell you about? There were less than ten days of the month of Sha'ban remaining and I had nei-ther flour, nor mush, nor any of the goods of this world in my house. I selected three of my brothers in my heart and said, "I will present my need to them." I went to my wife, Umm 'Abdullah, and she said, "What are you going to do, Abu 'Abdullah? This morning we have none of the goods of this world in the house: no food, nor mush, nor anything else, and this month (Ramadan) is coming." I told her, "I have selected three of my brothers to whom I will present my need." She asked, "Madinan or Iraqi?" I said, "Some are Madinan and some Iraqi." She said, "Tell me who they are." I said, "So-and-so." She said, "A man of lineage with wealth, but he expects favours. I do not think you should go to him. Name another." I told her another and she said, "A man of lineage with wealth, but he is a miser. I do not think you should go to him." I told her the third and she said, "A generous man of lineage, but he has nothing. You should not go to him."

"'Nonetheless I went to him and the door was opened. I asked permission to enter and he gave it to me. He greeted me and made me welcome and asked me, "What has brought you, Abu 'Abdullah?" I told him that the month was coming and that my circumstances were constricted. He paused for a moment and then he said, "Lift the cover of that cushion and take that bag and open it and empty it." There were a few dirhams in it. I took the bag and went to my house and called the man who usually did the shopping. I said, "Get ten *cafizs* of flour and a *cafiz* of rice and the same amount of sugar," until all our needs had been named.

"'While we were doing this, I heard a knock at the door and said, "See who it is." The slavegirl said, "It is so-and-so, son of so-and-so, son of 'Ali ibn al-Husayn ibn 'Ali ibn Abi Talib." I said "Admit him." I got up and greeted and welcomed him and said, "Descendant of the Messenger of Allah, what has brought you?" He said to me, "O uncle, the reason is that the month is coming and we have nothing." I told him, "Lift the cover of that cushion and take that bag and what is in it." He took the bag. Then I said to my companion, "You may go," and he went.

"'Umm 'Abdullah came in and asked me, "What did you do to help the lad?" I told her, "I gave him the bag and everything it contained." She said, "You have succeeded and done well!" Then I thought of a friend of mine near my house and I put on my shoes, went over to him and knocked on the door and was admitted. I entered and greeted him and he welcomed me. Then he asked me, "What has brought you, Abu 'Abdullah?" I told him that the month was coming and that my circumstances were constricted. He paused for a moment and then told me, "Lift the cover of that cushion and take that bag. Take half of what is in it and give me half." So I took the bag and took out 500 dirhams and gave him 500 dirhams.

"'I went back to my house and called the man in charge of buying my necessities and told him, "Get five *cafizs* of flour, and write down all the other things that I wanted before.' At that point there was a knock at the door and I told the servant, "See who it is." She went out and returned, saying, "It is a servant of someone noble." I told her, "Admit him." He had a note from Yahya ibn Khalid asking me to go to him immediately. I told the man, "Leave." I put on my clothes, mounted my animal, and went with my servant to the house of Yahya ibn Khalid, may Allah have mercy on him. I entered and he was sitting in the courtyard of his house. When he saw me and I greeted him, he welcomed me. He said, "Boy! A cushion!" I sat beside him and he said to me, "Abu 'Abdullah, do you know why I have called you?" – "No," I replied. He said, "I spent a sleepless night thinking about you and wondering what you have when this month is approaching." I said, "May Allah give the minister success! My story is long."

"'He told me, "However long the story is, we wish to hear it." I told him about Umm 'Abdullah and my three friends and what she had said about them. I told him about my request, and then the young man to whom I gave the bag, and then my second request. He called out, "Boy! An inkwell!" He wrote a note to the treasurer for a bag with 500 dinars. He told me, "Abu 'Abdullah, help yourself with this for the month." Then he wrote a note to his treasurer for a bag with 200 dinars. He said, "This is for Umm 'Abdullah, for her generosity and intelligence." Then he wrote another note for 200 dinars and he said, "This is for the Talibite." Then there was yet another note for a bag with 200 dinars in it and he said, "This is for the one who helped you." Then he said to me, "Go, Abu 'Abdullah, in the protection of Allah!"

"'I rode immediately to my friend who had given me the bag and gave him the 200 dinars and told him about Yahya. He almost died for joy. Then I went to the Talibite and gave him his bag and told him about Yahya. He made supplication and gave thanks. Then I went home and called Umm 'Abdullah and gave her the bag. She made supplication and asked Allah to reward him. So how can I be blamed for loving the Barmakis – and Yahya ibn Khalid in particular?'"

He died while he was *qadi*, in Dhu'l-Hijja 207 AH and Muhammad ibn Sama'a at-Tamimi prayed over him. He was *qadi* of

Baghdad on the western side at that time. Muhammad ibn 'Umar left a will naming 'Abdullah ibn Harun, the Amir al-Mu'minin, as executor. He accepted his instruction and settled his debts. Muhammad ibn 'Umar was 78 on the day he died. He was born at the beginning of 130 AH.

Husayn ibn Zayd ibn 'Ali

His *kunya* was Abu 'Abdullah. He went blind. His mother was an *umm walad*. His children were Mulayka, Maymuna – who married al-Mahdi, the Amir al-Mu'minin, and was widowed and then married 'Isa ibn Ja'far the elder, the son of al-Mansur – and 'Ulayya, and their mother was Kulthum as-Samma' bint 'Abdullah. He also had Yahya, Sukayna – who did not go out, Fatima – who married Muhammad ibn Ibrahim and bore him Hasan – Sulayman, Khadij, Zaynab and al-Hasan, and their mother was Khadija bint 'Umar. He also had 'Ali and Ja'far, whose mother was an *umm walad*. He had *hadiths*.

'Abdullah ibn Mus'ab ibn Thabit

His mother was an *umm walad*. His children were Abu Bakr, who was appointed over Madina for Harun, the Amir al-Mu'minin, and whose mother was 'Abda, who is Umm 'Abdullah bint Talha; Mus'ab, whose mother was Amatu'l-Jabbar bint Ibrahim, whose mother was Fakhita bint 'Abdu'r-Rahman; Muhammad the elder, Muhammad the younger, 'Ali and Ahmad, whose mother was Khadija bint Ibrahim, who is Qurayn bint 'Abdullah; and Umm Qurayn, whose mother was Sukayna bint al-Husayn ibn 'Ali. 'Abdullah's *kunya* was Abu Bakr. He died in Raqqa in Rabi' al-Awwal 184 AH at the age of 69, and he had a son born after he died who was named 'Abdullah, and whose mother was an *umm walad*. He had *hadiths*.

'Amir ibn Salih ibn 'Abdullah

His mother was Umm Habib bint Muhammad. He died in Baghdad while Harun was khalif. He was a poet with knowledge of the affairs of people. His *kunya* was Abu'l-Harith.

'Abdullah ibn 'Abdu'l-'Aziz ibn 'Abdullah

He is al-'Abid. His mother was Amatu'l-Hamid bint 'Abdullah. He was a devout worshipper and scholar. He died in Madina in 184 AH.

'Abdullah ibn Muhammad ibn 'Imran

His mother was an *umm walad*. He was appointed *qadi* of Madina for Harun, the Amir al-Mu'minin – and then he dismissed him and appointed him *qadi* of Makka. Then he dismissed him again and appointed him *qadi* of Madina. Then he dismissed him yet again and he remained with Harun. When he went to Rayy, he went with him. He died in Rayy in 189 AH. His *kunya* was Abu Muhammad. He had few *hadiths*.

Ibn Abi Thabit al-A'raj

His name was 'Abdu'l-'Aziz ibn 'Imran. His mother was Amatu'r-Rahman bint Hafs, whose mother was Amatu'l-Wahid bint A'idh. His children were Fatima and 'Ubayda the younger, whose mother was al-Fusayha, whose mother was as-Sa'ba bint 'Abdullah; Ibrahim and Umm Yahya, Amatu'r-Rahman, Umm Hafs, Umm al-Banin and Umm 'Amr, whose mother was an *umm walad*; and al-Barra and Umm Muhammad, whose mother was Hamida bint Muhammad.

Ibrahim ibn Ja'far ibn Mahmud

His mother was Kabla bint as-Sa'ib of the Banu Muharib. His children were Ya'qub, Isma'il and Umama, by various *umm walads*. His *kunya* was Abu Ishaq. He died in Shawwal in 191 AH.

Ma'n ibn 'Isa ibn Ma'n

His *kunya* was Abu Yahya, the client of al-Ashja', and he used to work with silk in Madina and sell it. He had slaves who were weavers, and he used to sell what they made and pay them. He died in Madina in Shawwal 198 AH. He was reliable, with a lot of *hadiths*, firm and trustworthy.

Muhammad ibn Isma'il ibn Muslim

His *kunya* was Abu Isma'il, the client of Banu'd-Dayl. He died in Madina in 198 AH. He related from Humayd al-Kharrat, Muhammad ibn Ishaq, 'Abdu'r-Rahman ibn Harmala, ad-Dahhak ibn 'Uthman, Rabi'a ibn 'Uthman and Yahya ibn 'Abdullah. He had a lot of *hadiths* but was not authoritative.

'Abdullah ibn Nafi' as-Sa'igh

His *kunya* was Abu Muhammad, the client of the Banu Makhzum. He clung to Malik ibn Anas with intense devotion. He never walked in front of him. He died in Madina in the month of Ramadan in 206 AH and he was less of an authority than Ma'n.

Abu Bakr al-A'sha

His name was 'Abdu'l-Hamid ibn 'Abdullah, who is Abu Uways ibn 'Abdullah, and his mother was the daughter of Malik ibn Anas. Abu Bakr was a master of Arabic, recitation and transmission from Nafi' ibn Abi Nu'aym, Sulayman ibn Bilal and others.

His brother, Isma'il ibn 'Abdullah

He is Abu Uways ibn 'Abdullah. His mother was the sister of Malik ibn Anas. His *kunya* was Abu 'Abdullah. He related from Malik ibn Anas, from his father, Kathir ibn 'Abdullah, Nafi' ibn Abi Nu'aym and the shaykhs of the people of Madina.

Mutarrif ibn 'Abdullah ibn Yasar al-Yasari

His *kunya* was Abu Mus'ab. Yasar was a *mukatib* of a man of Aslam and 'Abdullah ibn Abi Farwa paid off his *kitaba* for him, and so he was free and so he and his sons were with the family of 'Abdullah ibn Abi Farwa in their claims (as regards inheritance). Mutarrif was one of the followers of Malik ibn Anas. He was reliable. He was a little deaf. He died in Madina at the beginning of 210 AH.

'Atiq ibn Ya'qub

His *kunya* was Abu Bakr and his mother was Hafsa bint 'Umar ibn 'Atiq. His grandfather 'Umar and his father 'Atiq were both killed at the Battle of Qudayd. 'Atiq withdrew and settled in as-Suraqiyya and then he returned to Madina and remained there. He devoted himself to Malik ibn Anas and wrote his books from him: the *Muwatta'* and other selections. He used to cling to 'Abdullah ibn 'Abdu'l-'Aziz al-'Umari the Worshipper. He was one of the most excellent Muslims. He died in in 227 or 228 AH.

'Abdu'l-Jabbar ibn Sa'id ibn Sulayman

His mother was the daughter of 'Uthman ibn az-Zubayr and she was also the mother of all his brothers. He was appointed *qadi* of Madina for al-Ma'mun, the Amir al-Mu'minin. His father Sa'id ibn Sulayman had also been appointed *qadi* of Madina for al-Mahdi. He had some *hadiths* and he was listened to. He died in 229 AH in Madina.

Abu Ghaziya

His name was Muhammad ibn Musa an-Najjar. He was descended from Usama ibn Zayd on his mother's side. He had transmission, knowledge, and insight into *fatwa* and *fiqh*. He was appointed *qadi* of Madina while 'Ubaydullah ibn al-Hasan al-'Alawi was governor of Madina. That was while al-Ma'mun was khalif.

Abu Mus'ab

His name was Ahmad ibn Abi Bakr. He listened to Malik ibn Anas and related from him. He was one of the *fuqaha'* of the people of Madina. He was appointed over the police of Madina and the qadiship for 'Ubaydullah ibn al-Hasan after Abu Ghaziya.

Ya'qub ibn Muhammad ibn 'Isa

His *kunya* was Abu Yusuf. His father Muhammad ibn 'Isa was one of the important people of Madina and one of the people of manliness. He was handsome and noble. Ya'qub had a lot of knowledge and listening to *hadith*. He did not sit with Malik, but he met those after Malik from among the *fuqaha'* of Madina and their men and people of knowledge among them. He memorised *hadith*.

Muhammad ibn 'Ubaydullah ibn Muhammad

His *kunya* was Abu Thabit, the client of the family of 'Uthman ibn 'Affan. He was a merchant. He listened to Malik and other men of the people of Madina. He was excellent and good. He died in Muharram in 227 AH.

Ibrahim ibn Hamza ibn Muhammad

His mother was one of the family of Khalid ibn az-Zubayr, and his father's mother was an *umm walad*, and his grandfather's mother was an *umm walad*. His *kunya* was Abu Ishaq. Hamza and his son 'Umara were killed at the Battle of Qudayd. Ibrahim did not sit with Malik ibn Anas. He listened to 'Abdu'l-'Aziz ibn Muhammad ad-Darawardi, 'Abdu'l-'Aziz ibn Abi Hazim and other men of the people of Madina. He is reliable and truthful in *hadiths*. He came to ar-Rabadha often and resided there and traded there, but attended the *'Ids* in Madina.

'Abdu'l-Malik ibn 'Abdu'l-Aziz

His *kunya* was Abu Marwan. He was one of the companions of Malik ibn Anas. He had *fiqh* and transmission.

✻✳✻✳✻

This generation also includes: **Ibn at-Tawil**, or Muhammad ibn 'Abdu'r-Rahman, who had few *hadiths*; **Abu Damra**, or Anas ibn 'Iyad al-Layth, who was reliable, with a lot of *hadiths*; **Muhammad ibn Ma'n ibn Muhammad**, Abu Ma'n, who was reliable, with few *hadiths*; **Zakariyya ibn Manzur al-Qurazi**, Abu Yahya, who met Abu Hazim and 'Umar the client of Ghufra; and **Mus'ab ibn 'Abdullah ibn Mus'ab**, whose mother was Amatu'l-Jabbar bint Ibrahim.

✻✳✻✳✻

Thus ends the record of the seventh generation. It was the last generation of the *Tabi'un*.

✻✳✻✳✻

392

Glossary

Abbasids: the dynasty of khalifs who ruled from 132/750 to 656/1258 and had their capital in Baghdad. They based their claim to power on their descent from al-'Abbas, the uncle of the Prophet, may Allah bless him and grant him peace.

adhan: the call to prayer.

Amir al-Mu'minin: the Commander of the Believers, a title of respect given to the Khalif.

'Amwas: a major plague in Syria in 18/639 which killed many of the Companions.

Ansar: 'the Helpers', the people of Madina who welcomed and aided the Prophet صلعم and the *Muhajirun.*

al-'Aqiq: a valley about seven kilometres west of Madina.

'Arafa: a plain 15 miles to the east of Makka. One of the essential rites of the *hajj* is to stand on 'Arafa on the 9th of *Dhu'l-Hijja.*

ardabb or *irdabb:* a dry measure of about five and a half bushels.

'Asr: the mid-afternoon prayer.

ayat: a verse of the Qur'an.

Badr: a place near the coast, about 95 miles to the south of Madina, where, in 2 AH in the first battle fought by the newly established Muslim community, the 313 outnumbered Muslims led by the Messenger of Allah overwhelmingly defeated 1,000 Makkan idolaters.

Banu: lit. sons, a tribe or clan.

basmala: the words 'In the Name of Allah, the All Merciful, the All Compassionate'.

cafiz: Arabic *qafiz,* a dry measure equal to 12 *sa's.*

Battle of the Camel: one of the major confrontations in the first Civil War (*Fitna*) in which the forces of 'Ali defeated the forces of 'A'isha, Talha and az-Zubayr in a battle fought outside Basra in 36/656.

Dajjal: the false Messiah whose appearance marks the imminent end of the world.

Dayr al-Jamajim: a battle in Iraq in 82/701 which ended the rebellion of Ibn al-Ash'ath.

deen: the life-transaction, lit. the debt between two parties, in this usage between the Creator and created.

dhimma: obligation or contract, in particular a treaty of protection for non-Muslims living in Muslim territory.

dhimmi: a non-Muslim living under the protection of Muslim rule.

Dhuhr: the noon prayer.

Dhu'l-Hijja: the twelfth month of the Muslim calendar, the month of the *hajj.*

Dhu'l-Hulayfa: the *mıqat* of the people of Madina, now called Bayar 'Ali.

Dhu'l-Qa'da: the eleventh month of the Muslim calendar.

dinar: a gold coin 4.4 gm in weight.

dirham: a silver coin 3.08 gm in weight.

diwan: originally the register of soldiers and pensions under 'Umar. Subsequently it became a sort of governmental department – a *diwan* for the collection of taxes, a diwan for the writing of documents, and so administration in general. There were three main registers: one for those were were able to fight but needed weapons (*diwan al-muqatila*), one for stipends (*diwan al-'ata'*) and the muster roll (*diwan al-'ard*).

Duha: the voluntary mid-morning prayer.

Fajr: the dawn, or pre-dawn, prayer.

faqih (plural *fuqaha'*): a man learned in the knowledge of *fiqh* who by virtue of his knowledge can give a legal judgement.

farsakh: a measurement of length, about 3 miles/5 kilometres.

Fatiha: 'the Opener', the first *sura* of the Qur'an.

fatwa: an authoritative legal opinion or judgement given by a *mufti.*

fiqh: the science of the application of the *Shari'a.* A practitioner or expert in *fiqh* is called a *faqih.*

fitna: a word which means 'testing' or 'temptation', which refers to social and civil unrest, civil war, sedition or schism.

fuqaha': plural of *faqih.*

furqan: discrimination.

ghusl: the full ritual washing of the body.

hadd: Allah's boundary limits which define the lawful and unlawful. The *hadd* punishments are specific fixed penalties laid down by Allah for specified crimes.

hadith: reported speech of the Prophet.

hajj: the yearly pilgrimage to Makka.

hanut: an aromatic compound of camphor, reed perfume and red and white sandalwood, used for perfuming shrouds.

Haram: Sacred Precinct, a protected area in which certain behaviour is forbidden and other behaviour necessary. The area around the Ka'ba in Makka is a *Haram*, and the area around the Prophet's Mosque in Madina is a *Haram*. They are referred to together as *al-Haramayn*, 'the two *Harams*'.

Harra: A stony tract of black volcanic rock east of Madina, where a terrible battle took place in 63 AH (26th August 683 CE) between the forces of Yazid I and 'Abdullah ibn az-Zubayr which culminated in Madina being sacked and plundered.

Haruriyya: the first Kharijites or schismatics who separated themselves from 'Ali and based themselves at Harura', a town two miles from Kufa.

Hijaz: the region along the western seaboard of Arabia in which Makka, Madina, Jidda and Ta'if are situated.

Hijra: emigration in the way of Allah, especially designating the emigration of the Prophet صلعم from Makka to Madina.

hima: a place of pasturage and water prohibited to the general public. It was used for animals paid as *zakat* and mounts used for *jihad*.

hudud: plural of *hadd*.

'Id: a festival, either the festival at the end of Ramadan, or at the time of the *hajj*.

'Id al-Adha: the *'Id* held during the *hajj*.

'Id al-Fitr: the *'Id* held at the end of Ramadan.

'idda: a period after divorce or the death of her husband during which a woman must wait before re-marrying.

ifada: tawaf al-Ifada is the *tawaf* of the Ka'ba that the pilgrims must perform after coming from Mina to Makka on the 10th of Dhu'l-Hijja. It is one of the essential rites of *hajj*.

ihram: the ritual condition adopted by a person performing *hajj* or *'umra* which involves wearing certain garments and following certain rules of behaviour.

ijtihad: to struggle, to exercise personal judgement in legal matters based on the Qur'an and *Sunna*.

iqama: the call which announces that the obligatory prayer is about to begin.

irja': suspending or postponing judgement on whether or not someone is a believer.

'Isha': the night prayer.

isnad: the record of the names of the people who form the chain of human transmission by means of which a *hadith* is preserved.

istikhara: a prayer for Divine guidance performed by someone faced with a choice or decision.

Jahiliyya: the Time of Ignorance before the coming of Islam.

Jam': at Muzdalifa, a well-known place between 'Arafa and Mina, known as *al-Jam'* either because people gather there or because it is there that Adam rejoined Hawwa'.

jamra: lit. a small walled place, but in this usage a stone-built pillar. There are three *jamras* at Mina. One of the rites of *hajj* is to stone them.

Jamra al-'Aqaba: the largest of the three *jamras* at Mina. It is situated at the entrance of Mina from the direction of Makka.

al-Jazira: Mesopotamia, the name of a district covering north-eastern Syria and northern Iraq.

Jibril: or Jibra'il, the angel Gabriel who brought the revelation of the Qur'an to the Prophet Muhammad, may Allah bless him and grant him peace.

jihad: struggle, particularly fighting in the way of Allah to establish Islam.

jizya: a protection tax imposed on non-Muslims under the protection of Muslim rule.

jubbah: a long outer garement, open in front, with long sleeves.

Jumada: Jumada al-Ula and Jumada al-Akhira are the fifth and sixth months of the Muslim lunar calendar.

Jumu'a: the day of gathering, Friday, and particularly the *Jumu'a* prayer which is performed instead of *Dhuhr* by those who attend it.

Ka'ba: the cube-shaped building at the centre of the Haram in Makka, originally built by the Prophet Ibrahim. Also known as the House of Allah. It is towards the Ka'ba that Muslims face when praying.

kalam: 'theology' and dogmatics, the science of investigating and articulating religious belief. *Kalam* begins with the revealed tradition and uses rationalistic methods in order to understand and explain it and to resolve apparent contradictions.

katm: a plant used for dyeing hair.

khalifa: the khalif or caliph. The Arabic word from which khalif is derived is *khalifa*, while *khilafa* means the khalifate.

kharaj: land tax.

Kharijites: the earliest sect who separated themselves from the main body of the Muslims and declared war on all those who disagreed with them. They were of the opinion that a wrong action turns a Muslim into an unbeliever.

Khashabiyya: (from *khashaba*, a piece of wood), a disparaging term used for the followers of al-Mukhtar, because some of the clients following him were armed with wooden clubs rather than swords.

khatib: a speaker or orator; the one who delivers the *khutba*.

khuff: leather socks.

khul': a form of divorce in which a woman obtains a divorce by returning her dower, or by giving her ex-husband some other form of compensation.

khums: the fifth taken from the booty which is given to the ruler for him to distribute.

khutba: a speech, and in particular a standing speech given by the Imam before the *Jumu'a* prayer and after the two *'Id* prayers.

kitaba: a contract by which a slave acquires his freedom against a future payment, or payment by instalments, to his owner. Freedom is only granted once payment in full has been made.

kitabi: one of the People of the Book, a Christian or Jew.

kunya: a respectful but intimate way of addressing people as 'the father of so-and-so' or 'the mother of so-and-so'.

maghazi: battles, military expeditions, hence the historical accounts which record them.

Maghrib: the sunset prayer.

mahdi: 'the Divinely Guided', the descendant of the Prophet صلعم who will return at the end of time to establish justice.

mahmil: a camel litter, especially the one sent from Cairo with the covering for the Ka'ba at the time of the *hajj*.

Maqam: the Maqam Ibrahim is the place of the stone on which the Prophet Ibrahim stood while he and Isma'il were building the Ka'ba, which marks the place of the two *rak'at* prayer which is done immediately following *tawaf* of the Ka'ba.

maqsura: a box or compartment erected in the mosque for the ruler, as a means of protection, usually near the *mihrab*.

marzban: military governor of a Sasanian frontier district.

Masjid al-Haram: The Inviolable Mosque, the name of the mosque built around the Ka'ba in Makka.

mawla (plural *mawali*): client of an Arab tribe; a freed slave who remains part of the family. See *wala'*.

Mesopotamia: in Arabic, *al-Jazira,* the name of a district covering north-eastern Syria and northern Iraq.

Mihna: the Inquisition instituted by the Abbasid khalif, al-Ma'mun, which required all important people to publicly assert the erroneous belief that the Qur'an was created.

mihrab: the prayer niche, a recess in a mosque indicating the direction of *qibla.*

Mina: a valley five miles on the road to 'Arafa where the three *jamras* stand. It is part of the *hajj* to spend three or possibly four nights there.

minbar: the steps on which the Imam stands to deliver the *khutba.*

miqat (plural *mawaqit*): one of the designated places for entering into *ihram* for *'umra* or *hajj.*

mithqal: 'miskal', the weight of one dinar, the equivalent of 72 grains of barley (equals 4.4 grams). 10 dirhams weigh 7 *mithqals.*

mu'adhdhin: someone who calls the *adhan*, the call to prayer.

mudd: a measure of volume, approximately a double-handed scoop.

Mufassal: the *suras* of the Qur'an starting from *Surat Qaf* (50) to the end of the Qur'an.

mufti: a specialist in Islamic law who can issue a *fatwa.* His authority derives from his reputation as a scholar and the extent of his knowledge.

muhaddith: someone who transmits and studies *hadith.*

Muhajirun: Companions of the Messenger of Allah صلعم who accepted Islam in Makka and then made *hijra* to Madina prior to the Conquest of Makka in 8/630.

Muhammad ibn al-Hanafiyya: a son of 'Ali by a Hanafi woman. It was in his name that al-Mukhtar revolted in Kufa in 66/685.

Muharram: the first month of the Muslim year.

mukatib: a slave who has been given a *kitaba.*

munkar: 'denounced', a narration related by a weak reporter which goes against another authentic *hadith.*

Murji'ites: the opponents of the Kharijites. They held that it is faith and not actions which is important. There is also a political position held by the Murji'ites – called *irja'* – which suspends judgement on a person guilty of major sins.

mursal: a *hadith* which a man belonging to the generation after the Companions quotes directly from the Prophet صلعم without mentioning the Companion from whom he heard the *hadith.*

Musnad: a collection of *hadith* arranged in order according to the first authority named in each *hadith's isnad.*

mutakallim: Someone who studies the science of *kalam*, the science of investigating and articulating religious belief.

nabidh: a drink made by soaking grapes, raisins, dates, etc, in water without allowing them to ferment to the point of becoming intoxicating. If it does become intoxicating, it is still called *nabidh.*

Nafr: the day of either the 12th or 13th of Dhu'l-Hijja, when the pilgrims leave Mina after having completed all the ceremonies of *hajj* at 'Arafa, Muzdalifa and Mina.

Qadar: the Decree, used to designate the doctrine of the Qadariyya.

Qadariyya: an early sect who asserted that people have power (*qadar*) over their actions and hence free will in what they do. This was contrary to the Qur'anic view that there is no power except Allah.

qadhf: slanderous accusation; accusing a chaste person of fornication. Unless the accusation is supported by the testimony of four male witnesses, the penalty is eighty lashes.

qadi: a judge, qualified to judge all matters in accordance with the Shari'a and to dispense and enforce legal punishments.

qasama: an oath taken by fifty members of a tribe or locality to refute accusations of complicity in unclear cases of homicide.

qibla: the direction faced in the prayer which is towards the Ka'ba in Makka. The first *qibla* had been towards Jerusalem until it was changed, and so the early Muslims had prayed towards two *qiblas*.

qira: a measure of weight with various meanings, either a twelfth of a dirham, or a huge weight like that of Mount Uhud.

Quraysh: one of the great tribes of Arabia. The Prophet Muhammad صلعم belonged to this tribe, which had great powers spiritually and financially both before and after Islam came. Someone from this tribe is called a Qurayshi.

Rabi': Rabi' al-Awwal and Rabi' ath-Thani are the third and fourth months of the Muslim lunar calendar.

Rafidites: group of the Shi'a known for rejecting both Abu Bakr and 'Umar as well as 'Uthman.

Rajab: the seventh month of the Muslim calendar.

rajaz: 'trembling', a type of poetry with a particular metre which is easy on the ear and easily provokes emotions.

rak'at: a unit of the prayer consisting of a series of standings, bowing, prostrations and sittings.

Ramadan: the month of fasting, the ninth month in the Muslim calendar.

ra'y: opinion, a legal decision based on the use of common sense and personal opinion, utilised where there is no explicit guidance in the Qur'an and *Sunna* and where it is not possible to use *qiyas*.

ribat: the stronghold traditionally used by Muslims to prepare for their *jihad* against the enemies of Islam, situated on exposed points on the frontier.

Ridda: the defection of various Arab tribes away from Islam after the death of the Prophet صلعم which brought about the Ridda War.

ruku': bowing, particularly the bowing position in the prayer.

sa': a measure of volume equal to four *mudd*s, a *mudd* being a double-handed scoop.

sadaqa: giving in the way of Allah, a gift without any ulterior motive other than giving.

Safar: the second month in the Muslim calendar.

sahur: pre-dawn meal before a day of fasting.

salam: the greeting, *'As-salamu 'alaykum.'.* It terminates the prayer.

Sawad: lit. 'the Black', a fertile agricultural region of south-central Iraq which is 'black' with date-palms.

Sha'ban: the eighth month in the Muslim calendar.

Shari'a: The legal modality of a people based on the revelation of their Prophet. The final *Shari'a* is that of Islam.

shahada: bearing witness, particularly bearing witness that there is no god but Allah and Muhammad is the Messenger of Allah.

sharif: a descendant of the Prophet صلعم.

Shawwal: the tenth month of the Muslim calendar.

Shaytan: a devil, particularly Iblis.

Shi'a: lit. party or faction, specifically the party who claim that 'Ali should have succeeded the Prophet as the first khalif and that the leadership of the Muslims rightfully belongs to his descendants.

shirk: the unforgiveable wrong action of worshipping something or someone other than Allah or associating something or someone as a partner with Him.

Siffin: a ruined Roman town by the Euphrates in Syria where, in 37/657, a battle between the forces of 'Ali and Mu'awiya took place.

sira: 'conduct, behaviour, way of actions', hence a biography, particularly that of the Prophet Muhammad صلعم.

siwak: a toothstick.

Subh: the obligatory dawn prayer prayed before sunrise.

Sunna: lit. a form, the customary practice of a person or group of people. It has come to refer almost exclusively to the practice of the Messenger of Allah, may Allah bless him and grant him peace.

sura: a chapter of the Qur'an.

Tabi'un: 'the Followers', the second generation of the early Muslims who did not meet the Prophet Muhammad, may Allah bless him and grant him peace, but who learned the *deen* of Islam from his Companions.

tadbir: a contract given by a master to a slave whereby the slave will be freed after the master dies.

tafsir: commentary or explanation of the meanings of the *ayats* of the Noble Qur'an.

takbir: saying '*Allahu akbar*' or 'Allah is greater'.

takfir: to declare someone an unbeliever.

talbiya: saying '*Labbayk*' ('At Your service') during the *hajj*.

taqiya: concealment of one's views to escape persecution.

taqwa: awe or fear of Allah, which inspires a person to be on guard against wrong action and eager for actions which please Him.

tarawih: prayers performed at night during Ramadan.

Tarwiyya: 'drawing water', on the 8th Dhu'l-Hijja, the day before 'Arafa when the pilgrims gather water in preparation for the days of the *hajj* which lie ahead.

tashahhud: lit. to make *shahada*. In the context of the prayer, it is a formula which includes the *shahada* and is said in the final sitting position of each two *rak'at* cycle.

Tashriq: lit. 'drying meat in the sun', the days of the 10th, 11th, 12th and 13th of Dhu'l-Hijja when the pilgrims sacrifice their animals and stone the *jamras* at Mina.

tawaf: circling the Ka'ba, which is done in sets of seven circuits.

Tawaf al-Qudum: tawaf of arrival in Makka.

tayammum: purification for prayer with dust, earth or stone when water for *ghusl* or *wudu'* is unavailable or would be detrimental to health.

Uhud: a mountain just outside Madina where five years after the *Hijra*, the Muslims lost a battle against the Makkan idolaters. Many great Companions, and in particular Hamza, the uncle of the Prophet, were killed in this battle.

umm walad: lit. 'mother of a child', a slave-girl who has given birth to a child by her master and hence cannot be sold and becomes free when her master dies.

Umayyads: the first Muslim dynasty of khalifs who ruled in Damascus from 40/661 onwards until they were overthrown by the Abbasids in 132/750.

'umra: the lesser pilgrimage which can be performed at any time of the year.

'ushr: one tenth of the yield of land to be levied for public assistance.

wala': the tie of clientage established between a freed slave and the person who frees him, whereby the freed slave becomes integrated into the family of that person. See *mawla*.

waqf: perpetual endowment for a charitable use which makes the property inalienable.

witr: lit. odd, a single *rak'at*, prayed between *'Isha'* and *Fajr*, which makes the number of *sunna* prayers done in a day uneven.

wudu': ritual washing to be pure for the prayer.

Yarmuk: an important battle fought between the Muslims and the Byzantines in 13/636.

zakat: a wealth tax, one of the five pillars of Islam.

zakat al-fitr: the obligatory head tax paid by or on behalf of every Muslim at the end of Ramadan.

❊❊❊❊❊

Index

403

Battles